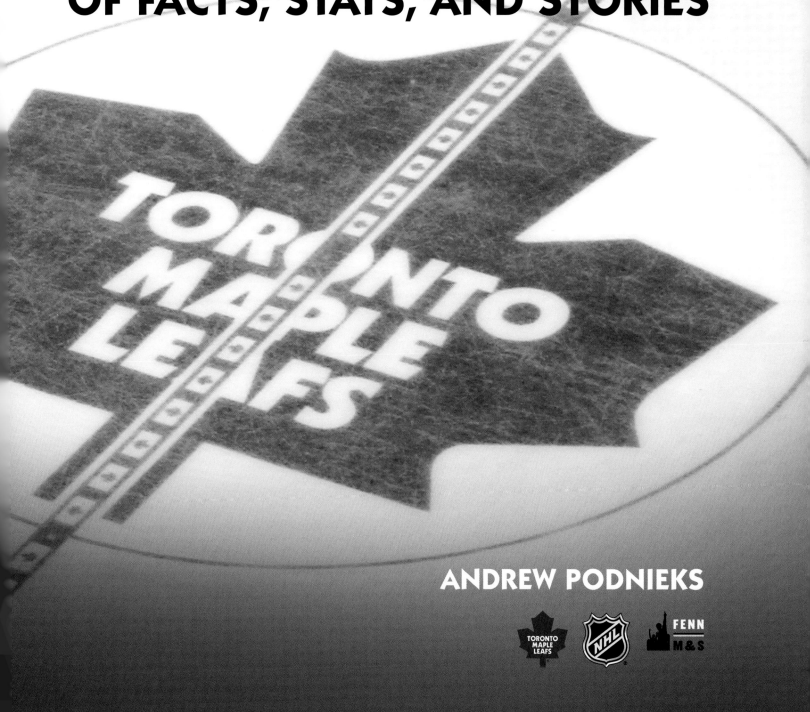

THE
TORONTO MAPLE LEAFS®
ULTIMATE BOOK
OF FACTS, STATS, AND STORIES

ANDREW PODNIEKS

Library and Archives Canada Cataloguing in Publication is available upon request
Published simultaneously in the United States of America by FENN/McClelland & Stewart,
a division of Random House LLC, a Penguin Random House Company, New York

Library of Congress Control Number is available upon request

ISBN: 9780771072222
ebook ISBN: 9780771072246

Edited by Gemma Wain and Elizabeth Kribs
Typeset in Fournier, Avenir and ITC Kabel, by M&S, Toronto
Printed and bound in the USA

FENN/McClelland & Stewart,
a division of Random House of Canada Limited,
a Penguin Random House Company
www.penguinrandomhouse.ca

1   2   3   4   5   19   18   17   16   15

FENN
M&S | Penguin
Random
House

CONTENTS

The ticket office at Maple Leaf Gardens

THE BIRTH OF THE TORONTO MAPLE LEAFS

The National Hockey League (NHL) was formed in 1917 as an alternative to the existing National Hockey Association (NHA). At the time, the NHA had been suspended, in large part to get rid of Eddie Livingstone, the unpopular owner of the Toronto Blue Shirts. The owners of the other four NHA clubs started the new league as a way to keep playing, and the Blue Shirts' players were assigned to a temporary Toronto franchise. When the NHA's suspension was made permanent, so was the NHL, and the Toronto Arena Hockey Club became an official member of the new league.

On December 13, 1919, just before the start of the 1919–20 season, the Arenas were bought by Charlie Querrie, Paul Ciceri, Frank Heffernan, Harry Sproule, Percy Hambly, and Hambly's brother Fred. Their first order of business was to change the team's nickname to the St. Pats in the hope of luring Toronto's large Irish population to the rink. The team continued to play out of the same downtown arena, on Mutual Street between Shuter and Dundas. Over time, the building came to be known as the Mutual Street Arena, but for many years it was simply called Arena Gardens (thus the name of the hockey club) or, even more affectionately, Andy's Igloo (in reference to the building's manager, Andy Taylor). The arena could seat about 8,000 people and its ice surface was Olympian by today's NHL standards— 230 feet by 90.

Arena Gardens was built in 1911–12 from designs by F.H. Herbert and the firm of Ross and MacFarlane. It was financed by a syndicate called Arena Gardens of Toronto, Limited. This group's president was Sir Henry Pellatt, whose famous house, Casa Loma, still sits atop a hill on Spadina Road. The arena cost $200,000 to build and was financed by a group of 15 businessmen: Aemilius Jarvis, Joseph Kilgour, R.A. Smith, Hume Blake, George W. Beardmore, Lawrence Solman, and George Horne of Toronto; and R. Reford, W.I. Gear, Colonel J. Carlson, R.S. Logan, Hartland MacDougall, E.A. Shepherd, A.G.B. Claxton, and G.A. Ross of Montreal.

The other great Toronto arena of this era was the Ravina Gardens (formerly the Ravina Rink) at 50 Rowland Avenue in Toronto's west end. Built in 1911, it was home to the Toronto Ravinas, a developmental farm club for the St. Pats where many future NHLers apprenticed in the manner that American Hockey League players do today. It was also frequently used by the Arenas and St. Pats for practices, and the New York Rangers even held their 1930–31 training camp there (it was torn down in 1962).

In 1927, Conn Smythe, who had been general manager of the New York Rangers the previous season (and was replaced by Lester Patrick before the team even played a game), convinced the St. Pats owners to sell the club to him. Smythe also convinced J.P. Bickell to retain his share of the ownership and to invest in the new club with associates Peter G. Campbell and Ed Bickle. On February 17, 1927, the team became the Maple Leafs (named after the maple leaf badges worn by Canadian soldiers) and won their first game 4–1 over the visiting New York Americans.

Conn Smythe watches training camp

As the club continued to draw ever-larger crowds, Smythe envisioned a grand new hockey palace in Toronto, unlike any other sports facility in the world. To this end, he formed Maple Leaf Gardens (MLG) Limited in 1930 to encourage investment in a new building. Financing for the $1.5 million project was made possible by Bickell, who used his influence with friend Sir John Aird, president of the Canadian Bank of Commerce, to secure the necessary loan (Bickell later became the Gardens' first president and then chairman of the board until his death in 1951). Smythe bought the choicest parcel of land—measuring 350 feet by 282 and bounded by Carlton, Church, and Wood Streets—from the T. Eaton Company, owners of the Eaton's department store chain.

The majestic Maple Leaf Gardens was designed by the pre-eminent Canadian architectural firm of the 20th century, Ross and Macdonald, who were renowned for creating some of Toronto's finest edifices: College Park, Union Station, and the Royal York Hotel. Ground was broken on June 1, 1931, and just 165 days later, on November 12, Maple Leaf Gardens hosted its first NHL game, which the Chicago Black Hawks won, 2–1.

During the construction, a daily average of 700 workers used a total of 13,500 cubic yards of concrete, 600 tons of reinforcing steel, 760 tons of structural steel, and 1.5 million bricks and tiles (the former provided by Conn Smythe's sand and gravel pits). The domed roof measured 207 feet by 225, and from street to ceiling it soared 150 feet high. No seat was farther than 65 feet from ice level, and capacity was an enormous 12,500.

When Maple Leaf Gardens opened, its amenities included a bowling alley, billiards room, and a full gymnasium. Smythe used to keep cats in the building to ensure that rodents stayed out, and he employed two full-time painters who touched up virtually every small crack or chip on a daily basis to maintain the building's pristine character.

Once the building had been completed, Smythe worked tirelessly to ensure it was the finest rink in the world. The Gardens was the first arena to have a four-faced time clock (installed in 1932); the first to use penalty clocks; the first to paint the ice surface so that fans could see the puck more clearly; the first to use a red/blue light, goal judge, and timer to determine last-second goals and announce the end of periods; the first to have separate penalty boxes (1962); the first to use Plexiglas (Herculite) instead of fencing above the boards (1947); the first to install an electronic system of measuring the on-ice time for each player (1947); the first to install escalators (1955); and the first to have a portable X-ray machine in the infirmary (1956).

By the 1990s, the NHL's landscape had changed dramatically. Expansion created a league of 30 teams by the year 2000, salaries soared, and the Internet enabled a growth in communication still far from fully realized today. In Toronto, the sports scene was also affected by the city's new team in the National Basketball Association, the Raptors, who were building a new arena at Bay Street and Lake Shore Boulevard, just two blocks from the Hockey Hall of Fame.

The Leafs sought to build their own arena, looking at sites ranging from the armoury at Moss Park to the Canadian National Exhibition grounds, but everything worked out perfectly when Raptors owner Allan Slaight agreed to sell the basketball team and the new arena, already under construction, to Leafs owner Steve Stavro on February 12, 1998. The Leafs redesigned much of the interior to accommodate the hockey club, and the long-standing MLG LTD. gave way to Maple Leaf Sports and Entertainment (MLSE).

Construction of Air Canada Centre had begun on March 12, 1997, from designs by Brisbin Brook Beynon Architects. The exterior featured a modern glass design incorporating the old Canada Post Delivery Building (circa 1939) that stood on the site.

The final game at Maple Leaf Gardens took place on February 13, 1999, with the Leafs playing Chicago, just as they had on the building's opening night some 68 years previous. For the ceremonial faceoff, former Leaf Red Horner—the oldest living Hall of Famer and a member of the inaugural 1931–32 Cup team—came to centre ice with Mush March, who had scored the first goal at MLG in 1931 as a member of the Black Hawks. In fact, March brought with him the very puck he had scored with, and used it for the closing ceremony, which featured a parade of dozens of Leafs alumni on the ice, from lesser-known names such as Moe Morris (who passed away just a short time later) to the ever-popular Borje Salming. The final tableau of the evening saw Horner holding high a flag bearing the motto MEMORIES AND DREAMS, a flag he would take with him to the opening of Air Canada Centre one week later.

That first game at the new arena featured the greatest rivalry in the sport—Toronto versus Montreal—and was won by the Leafs in dramatic fashion, with a Steve Thomas goal in overtime. The next afternoon, the Raptors played their first game at Air Canada Centre, and the night after that the first concert, by the Tragically Hip, took place.

A new era in hockey was born.

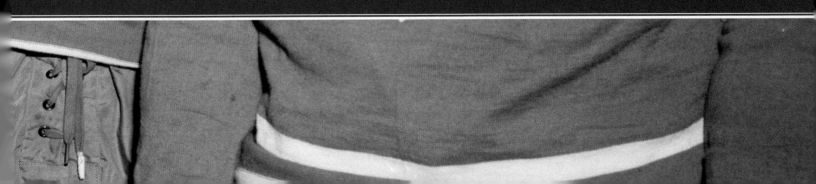

PART 1

THE HISTORY OF THE MAPLE LEAFS

THE MAPLE LEAF SWEATER

The Toronto Arenas joined the new NHL in 1917, wearing sweaters similar to the ones they used in their NHA incarnation as the Toronto Blue Shirts: simple blue sweaters with a large white *T* as the crest and white trim around the waist, cuff, and neck. Pants were also white.

The Toronto St. Pats' sweater, in keeping with the nickname, was primarily green, with a white neck, white bands at the elbows, and a band around the chest that incorporated the St. Pats name.

When the St. Pats became the Maple Leafs midway through the 1926–27 season, a makeshift sweater was employed for the rest of the schedule, using the same green-and-white sweater but with a maple leaf replacing ST. PATS on the chest. No pictures of this sweater are known to exist.

For the team's first season at Maple Leaf Gardens, 1931–32, the Leafs wore plain white sweaters with a maple leaf on the front, as documented in the famous photograph of opening night, November 12, 1931.

The Maple Leafs' first proper sweater was dark blue with several white stripes on the arms and legs, and a 48-point leaf on the chest with TORONTO MAPLE LEAFS inscribed therein. The design of the white road uniforms differed slightly from the blues during these early years (1928–34). They had three blue bands above and below the maple leaf, and the socks were also limited to three stripes. One small change was made to the blue home sweaters for the 1933–34 season: the three stripes on the chest, instead of being thin–thick–thin, were of equal width.

The uniform adopted in 1934 remained almost unchanged for more than 30 years. The socks still bore the three sets of three stripes (thin–thick–thin), but the arms now had two stripes that were matched by two other stripes along the waist of the sweater. The team name, which had sloped upward like a smile, now featured the word TORONTO sloping downward and MAPLE LEAFS straight across. Also, the leaf itself became veinous. By 1942, it had 35 points.

For the 1946–47 season, the now-familiar *C* and *A* appeared on the front of the captain's and alternate captains' sweaters for the first time. Also, in a short-lived

experiment in 1947–48, the lettering of TORONTO MAPLE LEAFS appeared in red. The team portraits are the only documented appearance of this variation. In 1960, the sweater was given six eyelets and a lace at the neck, a feature that lasted until 1973. In 1961, the Leafs began to put numbers on the arms of the sweaters so that players could be identified with greater ease from all angles of the Gardens and on television.

To celebrate Canada's Centennial, the Leafs significantly altered the sweater prior to the 1967 playoffs. The new leaf crest had 11 points, the lettering inside it was modified, and the stripes on the arms and waist were reduced to a single set of thin–thick–thin lines.

During the 1970–71 season, the NHL adopted the policy of the home team wearing white. The Leafs' sweater was again altered. The crest, while still featuring 11 points, changed design and the TORONTO lettering—like that of the words MAPLE LEAFS—now ran straight across rather than curving. The socks now had two thick stripes, the waist one thick band, and instead of stripes around the arms, a dark-blue stripe extended down from the neck to the wrist. Above the number on each arm there was now a miniature maple leaf. The Leafs were the last team to have player names stitched onto the sweater. When the league made it mandatory in 1977–78, Harold

Ballard even went so far as to have blue names on the blue sweater. But in 1978, names also appeared on the back of uniforms, both home and away.

Since the mid-1980s, patches have sometimes adorned the sweater. One was worn for the 1983–84 season to celebrate the city of Toronto's sesquicentennial; in memory of King Clancy, the 1986–87 uniform featured a shamrock topped with a crown on the arm; in 1990–91, to mark the

1. The 48-point maple leaf made its debut in the late 1920s, as evidenced by this sweater worn by Art Duncan

2. Charlie Conacher wore this sweater throughout his career with the Leafs, a version that included the 48-point maple leaf in addition to two bands of thin–thick–thin stripes at the waist and three similar bands on the sleeves

3. This King Clancy sweater is unique for its stripes. While this version of the crest was in use for many years, the thin–thick–thin bands at the waist and along the arms are unusual. The "thick" stripes are significantly wider than any other sweater during the Original Six years, and the stripes virtually cover the entire length of the arms

4. By 1942, the crest was subtly altered. Previously, the words *Toronto Maple Leafs* had sloped upwards like a smile. Now *Toronto* curved down and *Maple Leafs* appeared straight across. And the maple leaf itself was veinous, with a light white stitching in the blue crest

5. In a short-lived experiment in 1947–48, the Leafs used red lettering for their name inside the maple leaf, as seen here on Ted Kennedy

4.

5.

death of owner Harold E. Ballard, an HEB patch appeared; and in 2014–15 a patch to honour the late Pat Quinn was added to the Leafs' sweaters. To commemorate the NHL's 75th anniversary season in 1991–92, the Leafs employed two sweaters: one with a simple patch; the other (for games against Original Six opponents) a dark home sweater with a vintage crest.

A new Leaf uniform design was introduced in 1992 that blended the distant past with recent years. The socks reverted to the classic style that had existed for decades (three sets of thin–thick–thin stripes), while the crest from 1970 remained. The contrasting white arm-length band was discontinued, and the shoulder numbers appeared in between a miniature version of the old veined leaf and a set of two stripes farther down the arm.

In 1995–96, the sweater had a 65TH ANNIVERSARY MAPLE LEAF GARDENS patch sewn on the right-hand portion of the chest. That season, there was another sweater— worn for the game on the night of November 2, 1996,

only, to celebrate MLG's anniversary—which reverted to the classic Conn Smythe version.

For 1997–98, the sweater remained the same but the numbers changed style to match the lettering on the Leaf logo, while a mesh underarm was also incorporated after suggestions from players Tie Domi and Nick Kypreos. For the following season, to acknowledge the transition from Maple Leaf Gardens to Air Canada Centre, all players wore a special MEMORIES AND DREAMS patch above the right breast. And, for 10 games against Original Six teams (five home, five away), the Leafs played in a sweater featuring the old 35-point crest.

More tweaks came in the 2000–01 season. The Leafs added a silver outline to the lettering and replaced the maple leaf shoulder patches with a stylized TML in which all letters were superimposed on each other. They occasionally wore the Original Six sweater when playing against their greatest rivals, and on March 2, 2002, as part of the 75th anniversary of the Leafs, the team played to a

3–3 overtime tie with Buffalo wearing St. Pats sweaters with brown pants, gloves, and helmets.

Starting in 2007–08, the NHL mandated a change in uniform design that made sweaters and socks lighter, tighter, and more resistant to water (and sweat). The Leafs removed the shoulder patches and the stripes around the waist and eliminated the silver trim from around the numbers. Then, in 2010, the team restored several vintage elements. The two stripes around the waist were reintroduced, and the veinous version of the Leaf was again included on the shoulders. A band around the collar was brought back (white on dark sweaters, blue on the white sweaters) and eyelets and lacing once again added. The team also changed the typeface for the numbers and nameplates to add a more modern element. The current third sweater is a replica of the 1967–70 design, and the 2014 Winter Classic uniform was inspired by the sweater worn between 1927 and 1934.

6. The early 1960s sweater, as worn by Frank Mahovlich (left) and Red Kelly, sports the usual crest, but notice the stripes—only one at the waist and two at the elbows—and the blue at the shoulders, which almost reaches the top stripe at the elbow

7. The 1960s version of the sweater included six eyelets at the neck for a lace

8. In honour of Canada's centennial, Conn Smythe altered the sweater significantly for the 1967 playoffs. The new leaf crest was simplified to only 11 points, the lettering was modified, and the stripes on the waist and arms were trimmed to a single set of thin–thick–thin lines

9. Doug Gilmour wearing a version of the sweater, introduced in 1992, that blended old and new. The socks repeat the thin–thick–thin bands seen on Conacher's sweater, while this maple leaf crest was the one introduced in 1970. The numbers on the shoulders fit snugly between a miniature version of the Conacher-era maple leaf and a set of two stripes

10. Phil Kessel sports the current Leafs sweater, which combines modern elements with throwback features. The crest is from the 1970s, but the sleeves— with two narrow stripes and a vintage mini-crest at the shoulder—hearken back to earlier years. The socks too, with their three sets of thin–thick–thin, are reminiscent of the 1930s

GOALIE MASKS THROUGH THE YEARS

Johnny Bower wore this simple Plexiglas mask during practice but never in a game

Terry Sawchuk used an early-style mask that covered the face but did little to reduce the pain of a hard shot

The rounded mask of Doug Favell, one of the more acrobatic goalies of the 1970s, featured a large blue maple leaf

The lanky Wayne Thomas wore an elongated mask that had a Kabuki feel to it

Mike Palmateer, the "Popcorn Kid," wore a mask decorated with blue leafs in a diagonal pattern

Michel Larocque wore another blue-and-white-themed mask with his nickname—"Bunny"—down the middle

Peter Ing used a mask with a traditional blue maple leaf design

Curtis Joseph wore this mask only once—for the last game at Maple Leaf Gardens

The exciting design on this mask is based on the nickname of Eddie "the Eagle" Belfour

With a nod to the team's history, Jonathan Bernier's mask is decorated with a multi-point maple leaf

TORONTO VS. BOSTON

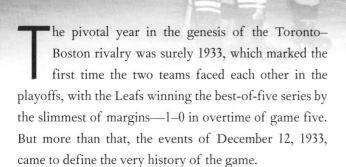

The pivotal year in the genesis of the Toronto–Boston rivalry was surely 1933, which marked the first time the two teams faced each other in the playoffs, with the Leafs winning the best-of-five series by the slimmest of margins—1–0 in overtime of game five. But more than that, the events of December 12, 1933, came to define the very history of the game.

On that night, top scoring Leafs forward Ace Bailey was taken off the ice after a hit from Eddie Shore, Boston's rough-and-tough, Hart Trophy–winning defenceman. Unfortunately, it marked the end of Bailey's playing career, but the incident would eventually lead to the creation of the NHL All-Star Game and the players' pension fund, each of which has had an important and positive impact on the game.

The Leafs won the first four playoff series between the teams before losing in 1939 and 1941, two years in which the Bruins went on to win the Cup. The Leafs then turned the tables, winning in 1948, 1949, and 1951 en route to Cup triumphs of their own.

The Bruins and the Leafs met again just after expansion, in the quarterfinals of the 1969 playoffs. Boston won that series, as well as two more in 1972 and 1974, and then the teams didn't meet again in the postseason until the spring of 2013. The rivalry has also intensified in recent years since the Leafs acquired Phil Kessel from the Bruins for three high draft choices (with which Boston selected Tyler Seguin, Jared Knight, and Dougie Hamilton), with each side claiming victory in the deal and each claim making every game between the teams extra special.

First NHL Game: December 3, 1924—Toronto 5, Boston 3

All-Time Regular-Season Record (GP–W–L–T–OTL–GF–GA): 653–266–281–98–8–1,940–1,933

All-Time Playoff Record (series): Toronto leads 8–6

Last Playoff Meeting: 2013 first round (Boston won 4–3)

Notable Names: Pat Burns (coach), Leo Boivin, Gerry Cheevers, Fern Flaman, Brian Leetch, Jacques Plante, Babe Pratt

Most Goals Scored with the Largest Margin:

Regular Season: January 8, 1944—Toronto 12, Boston 3

Playoffs: March 26, 1936—Toronto 8, Boston 3

TORONTO VS. CHICAGO

The Chicago–Toronto rivalry is in part based on firsts and lasts. For Toronto fans, the Hawks were the opposition for the first and last games at Maple Leaf Gardens, in 1931 and 1999 respectively. Similarly, the last game at the old Chicago Stadium, more colloquially referred to as the "Madhouse on Madison," was a playoff game on April 28, 1994, in which Félix Potvin shut out the Hawks, 1–0, and the Leafs eliminated Chicago in game six of a best-of-seven series. Hawks players may have scored the first and last goals at Maple Leaf Gardens, but Toronto's Mike Gartner has the distinction of having scored the last goal at the Stadium.

Although the Hawks won the first-ever playoff series between the two teams, in 1931, the Leafs came out on top the next year. Between 1940 and 1994, there were only five series between them, the Leafs winning all five. That 54-year unbeaten streak against one opponent in the play-offs is the longest in Toronto's history, broken only by a loss in the conference quarterfinals in 1995.

In the 1960s, an important aspect of the rivalry was the competition for bragging rights of having the best left winger. Frank Mahovlich patrolled the port side for the Leafs with his long, effortless stride and powerful presence, whereas Bobby Hull relied on his lethal slapshot to ensure his reputation as an all-star. The Big M and the Golden Jet battled it out for that left wing slot on end-of-year All-Star teams for the better part of a decade. Hull was on the First Team in 1959 and 1960, but Mahovlich took that spot the next year. In 1962, 1964, 1966, and 1968, Hull was the First Team's selection, while in 1963 it was Mahovlich. In each of these years, the player who wasn't on the First Team was on the Second Team (excepting 1968).

There was a 22-year stretch in which the teams didn't play each other in the Cup playoffs (1940–62), and, in fact, they have met in the Cup finals only twice. Chicago won in 1938, and the Leafs returned the favour in 1962. Their total of nine playoff meetings is the second-fewest among Original Six rivals. This is in large measure due to the teams seeming to have reversed fortunes at any given time. Often, when the Leafs have been in a

dominant period, the Hawks have consistently missed the playoffs, and vice versa. The realignment of the league prior to the 1998–99 season has also had an effect: with the Leafs in the Eastern Conference and Chicago in the Western, the only time the teams can now face each other in the postseason is in the Stanley Cup finals. The rivalry remains strong during the regular season, but the playoffs have proved to be less of a factor in recent times.

First NHL Game: November 17, 1926—Chicago 4, Toronto 1

All-Time Regular-Season Record: 641–285–259–96–1–1,928–1,822

All-Time Playoff Record (series): Toronto leads 6–3

Last Playoff Meeting: 1995 conference quarterfinals (Chicago won 4–3)

Notable Names: Max Bentley, Ed Belfour, Doug Gilmour, Harry Lumley, Pierre Pilote

Most Goals Scored with the Largest Margin:

Regular Season: March 8, 1947—Toronto 12, Chicago 4

Playoffs: April 12, 1986—Toronto 7, Chicago 2

TORONTO VS. DETROIT

As Toronto–Montreal is to Canada, so Toronto–Detroit is to North America. Indeed, while the intra-Canadian rivalry is intense for the symbolic, cultural aspect of English versus French, the Canada-versus-United States angle to the Leafs–Wings rivalry has been equally intense.

These two teams have met a remarkable 23 times in the playoffs, with the Leafs holding a slight edge. That the teams haven't played each other in the postseason for nearly two decades is both shocking and unfortunate, but expansion altered the landscape of a league that used to allow fans to see these two teams play 14 times a year—in the regular season alone. In 1998, when the league realigned, the Leafs moved from the Western Conference to the Eastern. As with Chicago, this meant the only way the Leafs and the Wings could meet in the playoffs would be if both teams made the Cup finals.

That wasn't always the case. Detroit joined the NHL in 1926 as the Cougars, a name they kept for four years,

before they became the Falcons. When Jim Norris took ownership of the team in 1932, he changed the name to the Red Wings based on the winged wheel of the Montreal Amateur Athletic Association, whose hockey club he had played for as a teen. He also believed the symbol would be a promotional advantage in a city that was the automotive hub of the United States.

Between 1934 and 1964, Toronto and Detroit met 19 times in the playoffs, more than any other two teams, and built a ferocious rivalry in the process. Perhaps the most famous incident occurred in the opening game of the 1950 playoffs in Detroit. Won easily by the Leafs, 5–0, the game (and series) took a turn at 8:46 of the third period. With the game well in hand for the Leafs, Detroit's Gordie Howe tried to check Toronto captain Ted Kennedy along the boards. Howe sustained an injury and didn't play again that season, but when the Wings won the Cup a week and a half later he came out onto the ice to celebrate, head bandaged.

First NHL Game: January 4, 1927—Toronto 2, Detroit 1

All-Time Regular-Season Record: 648–277–277–93–1–1,866–1,845

All-Time Playoff Record (series): Toronto leads 12–11

Last Playoff Meeting: 1993 conference quarterfinals (Toronto won 4–3)

Notable Names: Red Kelly, Frank Mahovlich, Norm Ullman, Larry Murphy, Borje Salming, Terry Sawchuk, Darryl Sittler

Most Goals Scored with the Largest Margin:

   Regular Season: January 2, 1971—Toronto 13, Detroit 0

   Playoffs: April 14, 1942—Toronto 9, Detroit 3

Between 1939 and 1949, the Leafs were the victors in seven out of eight meetings, winning the Stanley Cup five times. From 1950 to 1956, the Wings took all five series, winning the Cup four times.

The two teams reunited in the Eastern Conference in 2013 and were involved in a mutual celebration of sorts on January 1, 2014, when the Wings hosted the Leafs for the Winter Classic outdoor game at Michigan Stadium. A crowd of 105,491, which set a world record for attendance at a hockey game, watched as the Leafs won, 3–2, in a shootout.

The 105,491-strong crowd at the Winter Classic on January 1, 2014 set a world record for attendance at a hockey game

TORONTO VS. MONTREAL

There are few rivalries in sport that have the history, the enmity, the cultural significance, and the love-to-hate passion of Toronto and Montreal, Canada's English and French cultural and sporting capitals. Two of the founding franchises of the NHL, these teams have sustained their rivalry through myriad changes to the league's structure and through the hundreds of players who have passed down the importance of these games from one generation to the next.

The height of competitiveness was certainly achieved during the Original Six era, when teams played a 70-game schedule with 14 games against each opponent. The playoff rivalry between the Leafs and Habs has had its ups and downs, but there has been renewed hostility in recent years now that the two teams are in the same division again.

In the spring of 1918, Toronto beat Montreal in the first-ever NHL playoff series. Incredibly, over the next 26 years, they met only once more, in 1925. The 1940s saw the competition renewed as they faced each other three times over a four-year span. Then, in 1951, all five games of the Toronto–Montreal Cup finals went into overtime, with the Leafs winning four to claim the revered mug.

As plane travel and hockey's growing popularity allowed the NHL to expand throughout the United States, the league doubled in size from 6 to 12 teams in the summer of 1967. But before that happened, the 1967 Stanley Cup pitted the great Canadian rivals one last time—a final moment of glory in the Original Six era. Both teams won the Cup four times in the 1960s, but 1967 was particularly symbolic as it was Canada's Centennial year and Montreal was hosting the world's fair, Expo 67. The Leafs won in six games.

Once the league grew to 14 teams—and to 21 and then 30—the rivalry remained strong, but the teams played fewer games against each other. Then, in 1981, Toronto and Montreal started to play in different conferences. They met only three times a season, then two, and in the shortened 1994–95 season they didn't play each other at all.

However, when Ken Dryden was made president of the Leafs, it was one of his ambitions to rekindle the rivalry. By 1998, the two teams were back in the same division, meeting more and more frequently. The current format does mean, of course, that they can never meet in the Cup finals, but between 1918 and 1967 they had done so only five times anyway.

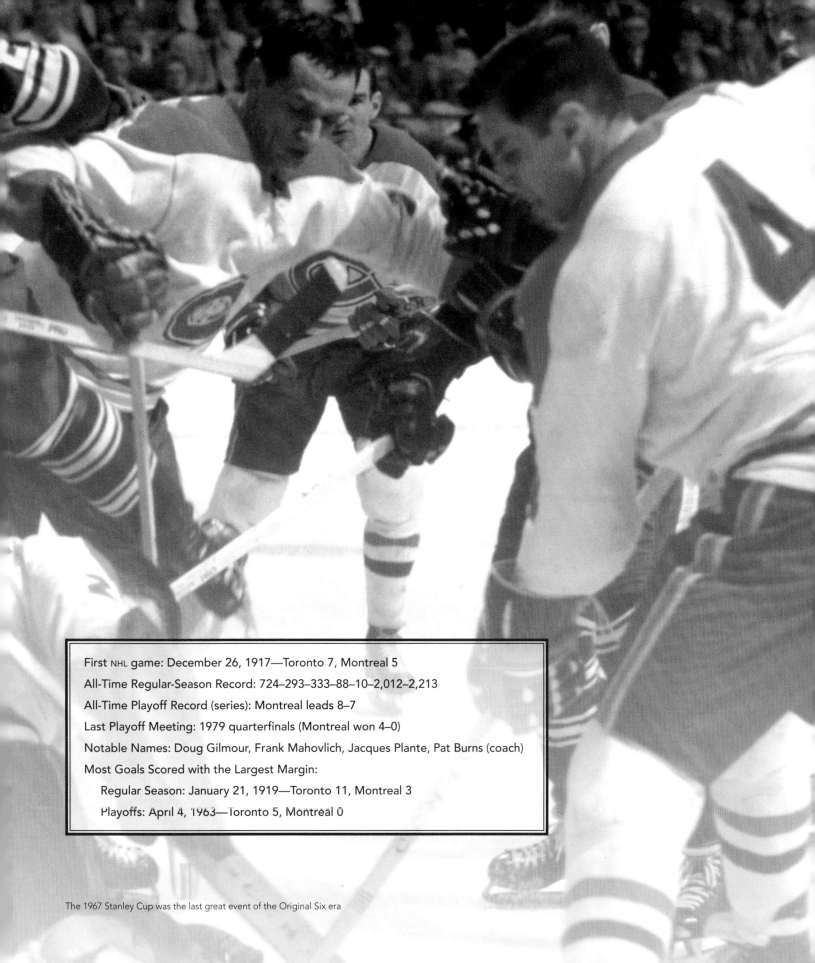

First NHL game: December 26, 1917—Toronto 7, Montreal 5

All-Time Regular-Season Record: 724–293–333–88–10–2,012–2,213

All-Time Playoff Record (series): Montreal leads 8–7

Last Playoff Meeting: 1979 quarterfinals (Montreal won 4–0)

Notable Names: Doug Gilmour, Frank Mahovlich, Jacques Plante, Pat Burns (coach)

Most Goals Scored with the Largest Margin:

   Regular Season: January 21, 1919—Toronto 11, Montreal 3

   Playoffs: April 4, 1963—Toronto 5, Montreal 0

The 1967 Stanley Cup was the last great event of the Original Six era

TORONTO VS. NEW YORK RANGERS

The Leafs have played the Rangers in the playoffs only eight times since the "Broadway Blueshirts" joined the NHL in 1926—the fewest meetings among all of Toronto's Original Six rivals—and the last time was more than four decades ago.

The reason is simple math. Since the Rangers joined the NHL in 1926, they have missed the playoffs 31 times. The Leafs, too, have missed the playoffs exactly 31 times since 1917. But in the almost 90 years the Rangers have been in the league, they and the Leafs have both missed the playoffs in the same year on only four occasions. As a result, there have been just 36 occasions when they have both been in the playoffs at the same time.

Oddly enough, the only three series the Leafs have won over New York were in 1932, 1942, and 1962, all years in which the Leafs won the Cup. And of the four Cup victories in the Rangers' long history, two have come at the expense of the Leafs—in 1933 and 1940. The first Leafs win was historic because it came in 1932, the first season the team played at Maple Leaf Gardens. It also marked the first time that a 3–0 sweep in the best-of-five

final series had been accomplished in three different cities. Game one was in New York, game two in Boston (as Madison Square Garden had been booked by the circus), and the last game was played in Toronto, at MLG.

The 1971 playoff series produced surely one of the oddest moments in Stanley Cup history. The Rangers won the opening game on home ice, 5–4, but in game two the Leafs stormed to a 2–0 lead. They were leading comfortably, 4–1, late in the game when a melee broke out involving everyone on the ice. At one point, the Rangers' Vic Hadfield grabbed the mask of goalie Jacques Plante and hurled it into the crowd. Needless to say, no New Yorker was going to toss the mask back to the Leafs' goalie and so, having no other face protection, Plante had to be replaced by Bernie Parent. The Leafs won that game and the next, but New York took the last three and advanced to the semifinals.

And that was that. Not since 1971 have the teams met in the playoffs, but on October 12, 2014, the teams met in New York for the 600th time in the regular season. The Leafs won, 6–3, their 274th victory in this 89-year-old series.

Leafs forward Bob Pulford rubs out Dean Prentice of the Rangers behind the goal

First NHL Game: November 20, 1926—Rangers 5, Toronto 1

All-Time Regular-Season Record: 599–280–216–95–8–1,894–1,726

All-Time Playoff Record (series): Rangers lead 5–3

Last Playoff Meeting: 1971 quarterfinals (Rangers won 4–2)

Notable Names: Glenn Anderson, Andy Bathgate, Johnny Bower, Dick Duff,
    Mike Gartner, Brian Leetch, Babe Pratt, Terry Sawchuk

Most Goals Scored with the Largest Margin:
    Regular Season: March 16, 1957—Toronto 14, Rangers 1
    Playoffs: April 7, 1962—Toronto 7, Rangers 1

GAMEDAY PROGRAMS

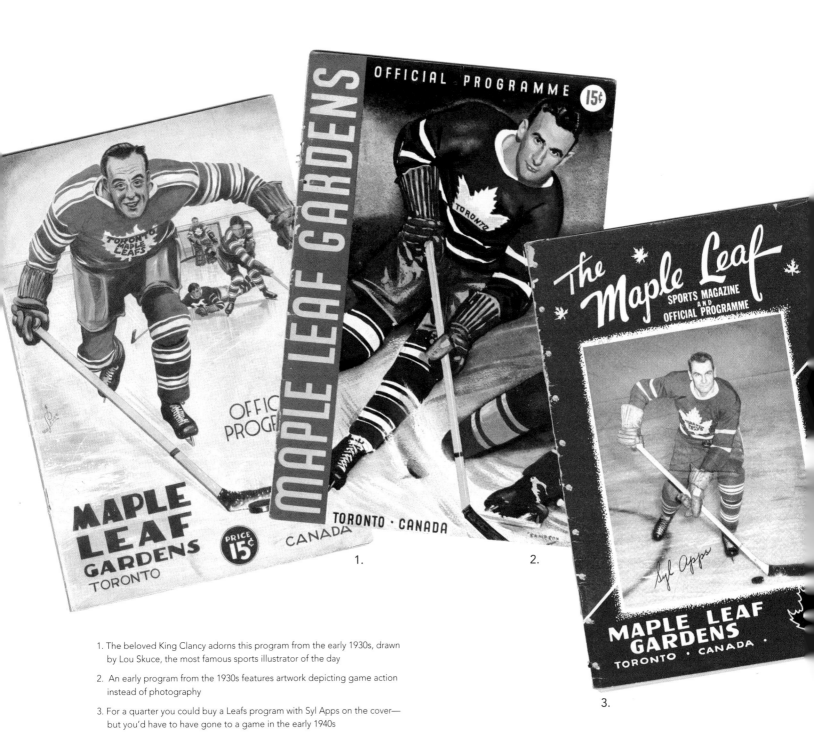

1. The beloved King Clancy adorns this program from the early 1930s, drawn by Lou Skuce, the most famous sports illustrator of the day

2. An early program from the 1930s features artwork depicting game action instead of photography

3. For a quarter you could buy a Leafs program with Syl Apps on the cover—but you'd have to have gone to a game in the early 1940s

4. The final season of the Original Six was 1966–67, and this program features Toronto and Montreal in the Stanley Cup finals

5. A program from the early 1970s featuring Darryl Sittler, who was named team captain in 1975

6. This cover from the 1990s blends old and new in a celebration of the team's history

7. One of the last programs from Maple Leaf Gardens featured a throwback image of Bobby Orr and Lanny McDonald from the mid-1970s

DECEMBER 19, 1917
TORONTO'S FIRST NHL GAME

"Wanderers beat the Toronto Blue Shirts 10 to 9 in the opening game of the National Hockey League series last night, but if there had been a few minutes more to go the result might easily have read the other way about, for Wanderers were fading toward the end, while the Blue Shirts, with youth in their favour, were smashing through the defence in a last effort to snatch victory out of defeat."

So began the *Toronto Star*'s account of the NHL's first game nearly 100 years ago. Incredible as it might seem, it remains, to this day, one of the league's highest-scoring games. The 1917–18 season started just before Christmas and featured the visiting Toronto Arenas—so new they were still called the Blue Shirts by the media—playing the Montreal Wanderers.

The Wanderers had been established in 1903 and were Stanley Cup champions five times between 1905 and 1910, in an era when teams won the Cup through league play or by challenging the champions from other leagues around the country. They joined the National Hockey Association in 1909 and continued into the NHL when the new league was formed in late fall 1917.

The Arenas, too, had their genesis in the NHA. The Toronto Blue Shirts had played in that league, but the other team owners despised the Blue Shirts' owner, Eddie Livingstone, and voted to start a new league without him. The team continued to play out of the Arena Gardens and was thus informally called the Toronto Arenas, even though its legal name at this point was, simply, the Toronto Hockey Club.

Before the game, the 700 fans in attendance were treated to a light show that ushered in a new era of professional hockey. The Wanderers had a 2–0 lead two minutes in, but Reg Noble and Harry Cameron tied the game within three minutes. The teams exchanged quick goals, but the Wanderers scored twice in the second half of the first period to take a 5–3 lead to the dressing room. Goalie Sammy Hebert was replaced by Art Brooks for the balance of the game for Toronto.

The score was 6–6 late in the second thanks to three goals by the visitors—namely Alf Skinner, Cy Denneny, and Noble—and only one by the Wanderers, but the locals scored three of their own in the dying moments to make it a 9–6 game after 40 minutes. The last of those was scored by Harry Hyland, his fifth goal of the game.

The Wanderers made it 10–6 early in the third on a goal from Dave Ritchie, but the Arenas rallied with three more goals. They fell just short of tying the game, and it ended 10–9 for the hosts. Reports were critical of Toronto's goaltending—"Sammy Hebert couldn't stop a flock of balloons"—and of captain Ken Randall, who was in the penalty box for four Wanderers goals. Indeed, there were 20 minor penalties and two majors called in the game, but witnesses were effusive in praise of Toronto's speed and their play with the puck in the offensive end.

While the Arenas later became the St. Pats and then the Maple Leafs, the Wanderers were just days away from becoming extinct. Their home rink, the Montreal Arena, burned to the ground on January 2, 1918, and the team withdrew from the league, never to return.

GAME SUMMARY

(assists not recorded for the 1917–18 season; penalties unknown)

Toronto 9, Montreal 10

1st Period	1. Wanderers, Ritchie 1:00
	2. Wanderers, McDonald 1:50
	3. Arenas, Noble 3:05
	4. Arenas, Cameron 5:15
	5. Wanderers, Hyland 6:05
	6. Arenas, Cameron 7:20
	7. Wanderers, Hyland 10:20
	8. Wanderers, Hyland 16:35
2nd Period	9. Arenas, Skinner 3:00
	10. Wanderers, Hyland 6:15
	11. Arenas, Denneny 9:00
	12. Arenas, Noble 14:45
	13. Wanderers, Bell 16:00
	14. Wanderers, Ross 17:30
	15. Wanderers, Hyland 19:30
3rd Period	16. Wanderers, Ritchie 4:30
	17. Arenas, Noble 7:15
	18. Arenas, Denneny 13:25
	19. Arenas, Noble 16:40

In Goal:

Wanderers—Lindsay

Toronto—Hebert (1st period), Brooks (2nd & 3rd periods)

Top: Jack Adams, a member of the Toronto Areans

Bottom: A program from Toronto's inaugural NHL season

FEBRUARY 17, 1927
FIRST GAME AS THE MAPLE LEAFS

The game started at 8:30 P.M. and finished at 10:21—a brisk 111 minutes. Earlier that day, William Hewitt, father of famous broadcaster Foster Hewitt and one of the great men of hockey's early days in his own right, had announced a historic name change to the world in his "Sporting Views and Reviews" column in the *Toronto Star*: "The Toronto Maple Leafs will make their bow to the public to-night in the game with New York Americans. They are the St. Pats no longer. The old name was discarded yesterday at a luncheon given to the players by the old and new owners of the club. The players showed their appreciation of Charlie Querrie by presenting him with a case of pipes. Charlie is going into retirement now, but they will have to tie him down on hockey nights."

Several hours after these words were published, the Maple Leafs—under new owner Conn Smythe—beat the visiting Americans, 4–1, and they did so with several storylines to whip fan interest from the get-go. The team's new coach, Alex Romeril, had been hired by Smythe, and Romeril's first decision was to move Hap Day from forward back to defence. Smythe had just signed his first player, centreman Carl Voss, who also played defence. Voss will forever be the answer to the trivia question, "Who was the first new member of the Maple Leafs?" The game was also notable for the team's new sweaters. Reporter Bob Hayes described the players this way: "They looked like a lot of galloping ghosts in white."

Billy Burch opened the scoring for the visitors early in the first period, but this was to be their only goal of the night. George "Paddy" Patterson is the answer to another trivia question thanks to his conversion of a great pass from Bill Brydge midway through the game to tie the score, 1–1. Ace Bailey scored an inspiring goal for the home side when he gave the Maple Leafs a 2–1 lead at 19:55 of the middle period. Bailey scored again in the third and Bert Corbeau got the final goal to salt away the win before an enthralled crowd at the Arena.

GAME SUMMARY

Toronto 4, NY Americans 1

1st Period	1. NY Americans, Burch (Conacher) 4:00
	Penalties: Day (TOR), Burch (NYA)
2nd Period	2. Toronto, Patterson (Brydge) 12:10
	3. Toronto, Bailey (Corbeau) 19:55
	Penalties: Day (TOR), Burch (NYA), Corbeau (TOR), Conacher (NYA) Brydge (TOR), Brydge (TOR)
3rd Period	4. Toronto, Bailey (unassisted) 16:00
	5. Toronto, Corbeau (unassisted) 16:10

In Goal:

NY Americans—Forbes

Toronto—Roach

Hap Day had a great career
with the Leafs, first as a player
and then as a coach

NOVEMBER 12, 1931
FIRST GAME AT MAPLE LEAF GARDENS

After this game, the sports pages of every Toronto newspaper ran a similar photograph: a view from the corner Blues of the pre-game ceremonies, which featured the 48th Highlanders. But it was perhaps the caption that appeared in the *Star* that said it best: "Brilliant colouring, splendid lighting, and plenty of seating accommodation is what met the expectant fan's eyes as they stepped into the palace to get their first view of the finest hockey arena on the North American continent." This is what Conn Smythe had envisioned when he built the Gardens, and on opening night he delivered. That Chicago won the game 2–1 was immaterial—the Leafs went on to win the Cup at the end of the season, and the first night at the Gardens assumed a place in Canada's cultural history.

The pre-game ceremonies were hosted by none other than Foster Hewitt, wearing a tuxedo and appearing in front of fans who knew his voice so well but his countenance not so much. Other participants and VIPs on the ice included: J.P. Bickell, president of the Gardens and a key financier in its construction; Hon. George Henry, the premier of Ontario; Ed Bickle and George Cottrelle, directors of Maple Leaf Gardens Ltd.; Toronto mayor W.J. Stewart; and NHL president Frank Calder. The band played "God Save the King," and then the mayor dropped

The famous image of the inaugural pre-game ceremonies at Maple Leaf Gardens, featuring the 48th Highlanders the puck for the ceremonial faceoff between Ace Bailey and Tommy Cook. Many of those watching were wearing their evening best.

As for the game, the record crowd of 13,542 got plenty of action from their Leafs—though few goals. The ice was in bad shape after the lengthy pre-game ceremonies, so it was destined to be a low-scoring game from the start. Charlie Gardiner was great in goal for the Hawks, and the players in front of him made the most of their few opportunities. Mush March made history as the first goal scorer at the Gardens, converting a nice pass from Tom Cook to open the scoring.

"In the second period, Charlie Conacher, accepting a pass from Joe Primeau, drilled a beautiful shot into the corner of the net" to tie the game, as Bert Perry described in *The Globe*. This came after a scary incident in which Conacher bore down on Gardiner and collided heavily with the Hawks goalie. Gardiner needed 15 minutes with the doctors before he had recovered to a suitable degree to continue, and he proved to be the game's star the rest of the way.

Early in the third, the Hawks got what was to be the winning goal when Vic Ripley snuck in through the Leafs defence and beat Lorne Chabot to make it 2–1. The Leafs did everything but tie the game the rest of the way. Clancy hit the post with one shot, and Conacher had a breakaway, only to shoot wide.

GAME SUMMARY

Toronto 1, Chicago 2

1st Period	1. Chicago, March (Cook) 2:30
	Penalties: Blair (TOR), Blair (TOR), Gottselig (CHI), Lowrey (CHI), Abel (CHI)
2nd Period	2. Toronto, Conacher (Primeau) 18:42
	Penalties: Jackson (TOR), Adams (CHI), Bailey (TOR), Clancy (TOR), Ripley (CHI), March (CHI), March (CHI), Wentworth (CHI)
3rd Period	3. Chicago, Ripley (unassisted) 2:35
	Primeau (TOR—major), Cook (CHI), Graham (CHI)

In Goal:

Chicago—Gardiner

Toronto—Chabot

APRIL 9, 1932
THE MAPLE LEAFS' FIRST STANLEY CUP WIN

Game. Set. Match. The Leafs won the Stanley Cup in their first season at Maple Leaf Gardens, and they did so by defeating the New York Rangers in three straight games of the best-of-five finals. It became known as the "tennis series" because of the scores of the games: 6–4, 6–2, 6–4. The victory put paid to rampant—and unfounded—speculation that Toronto would lose two games on purpose to ensure that the series went five games and so earn gate receipts from two more playoff matches.

"What a lacing the Leafs gave Colonel Hammond's Hussars in their emphatic answer to the murderous attack upon the integrity of professional hockey," wrote the legendary Lou Marsh (Hammond being the owner of the Rangers) in his review of the Cup-clinching game. He went

on to describe, with effusive praise, just how dominant the Leafs had been in these playoffs, noting, "No team you ever saw would have beaten those Leafs Saturday night."

This was a battle between a team of talented Leafs players and a Rangers team that depended largely on Frank Boucher. The Leafs had goals from five different players, while Boucher scored three times and assisted on the fourth Rangers tally.

Andy Blair, the lone multi-goal scorer for the Cup winners, scored the only two goals of the first to put the Leafs in control, but both came off fine plays by teammates—King Clancy for the first and Bob Gracie for the second. In both cases, Blair made no mistake with the great passes and "potted the pellet," in Marsh's unmistakable jargon.

Harvey Jackson made it 3–0 in the second before Boucher got one back for the Rangers, but a more serious moment captivated the fans late in the period. Charlie Conacher fired a hard shot that hit New York's goalie, John Ross Roach, in the solar plexus, and he fell to the ice in pain, unable to move for five minutes. Rally he did, though, and he managed to stop 44 of 50 shots on a busy night.

The Leafs scored three goals in the third to eliminate any possibility of a great rally from the visitors, and the two late goals from Boucher in the final two minutes made the score look closer than it actually was. At the game's end, the 14,366 fans in attendance were apoplectic with excitement. Their team had won the Cup for the first time in a decade and for the first time as the Toronto Maple Leafs.

GAME SUMMARY

Toronto 6, NY Rangers 4

1st Period	1. Toronto, Blair (Clancy) 5:39
	2. Toronto, Blair (Gracie) 6:11
	Penalties: Day (TOR), Heller (NYR), Jackson (TOR—minor, major), Blair (TOR), Dillon (NYR), Gainor (NYR), Seibert (NYR)
2nd Period	3. Toronto, Jackson (Primeau, Conacher) 10:57
	4. NY Rangers, Boucher (Heller) 15:24
	Penalties: Seibert (NYR), Seibert (NYR), Brennan (NYR)
3rd Period	5. Toronto, Finnigan (Day) 8:56
	6. Toronto, Bailey (Conacher, Day) 15:07
	7. NY Rangers, F. Cook (Boucher) 16:32
	8. Toronto, Gracie (Finnigan) 17:36
	9. NY Rangers, Boucher (F. Cook) 18:26
	10. NY Rangers, Boucher (unassisted) 19:26
	Penalties: Horner (TOR), Cotton (TOR), Keeling (NYR), Johnson (NYR), Finnigan (TOR), Finnigan (TOR), Keeling (NYR), Conacher (TOR)

In Goal:

NY Rangers—Roach

Toronto—Chabot

The Kid Line (l to r)—Charlie Conacher, Joe Primeau, and Busher Jackson

APRIL 18, 1942
THE LEAFS COMPLETE COMEBACK
FROM 3–0 DOWN TO WIN CUP

The night of the victory, all the talk concerned how Toronto teams seemed to like winning the Stanley Cup once a decade. Prior to this win in 1942, they had been champions in 1922 (as the St. Pats) and 1932. But this win was not about decades, and it wasn't about the 3–1 scoreline—it was about mounting the greatest comeback in the sport.

To this day, the 1942 Leafs are the only team to recover from a 3–0 game deficit in the Cup finals and win a championship. They did it through perseverance, great coaching, and, in the end, by playing a letter-perfect final game at Maple Leaf Gardens, where the previous week they had lost the first two games of the series by scores of 3–2 and 4–2, and then lost game three in Detroit by the even more one-sided count of 5–2.

The two teams came into game seven with the momentum wholly changed—Toronto had followed a 4–3 victory in Detroit in game four with two more dominant wins of 9–3 and 3–0. The first period of game seven remained scoreless, but only because of the great goaltending of Johnny Mowers in the Detroit cage. Syl Apps, Sweeney Schriner, and Pete Langelle all had sure goals taken away by Mowers, though the tide would turn in the final period.

In the second, the visiting Red Wings scored on an

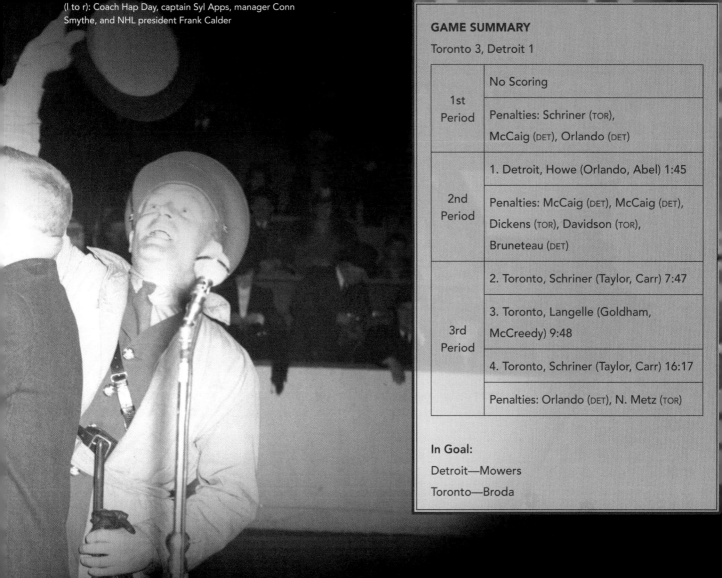

(l to r): Coach Hap Day, captain Syl Apps, manager Conn Smythe, and NHL president Frank Calder

odd-man rush, with Syd Howe doing the damage. The visitors played perfect defence and fought with every last ounce of energy to cling to that lead, but early in the third period Jimmy Orlando tripped Apps and was penalized. Orlando was so incensed he tossed his gloves and stick to the ice and clasped his head in his hands, like an Italian football player. The Red Wings killed off that penalty, but only barely. Before Orlando was able to get back into the play after serving his two minutes, Schriner had tied the game.

The momentum was all with Toronto after that. Langelle snapped the go-ahead goal from the slot soon after, a goal later dubbed "the shot heard 'round the

world," and Schriner added an insurance marker late in the game.

The official attendance was 16,218, the largest crowd for a hockey game in Canada at that time, but several hundred patrons were let in for a nominal fee after tremendous protest by ticketless fans at the turnstiles, making the actual number closer to 17,000. After the game was over, Conn Smythe and club president George Cottrelle came onto the ice with coach Hap Day and captain Syl Apps for the presentation of the Cup by NHL president Frank Calder. It was a night to remember, and the culmination of the greatest comeback ever accomplished in NHL history.

APRIL 21, 1951
BILL BARILKO'S CUP-WINNING GOAL

It is both wonderful and a shame that all these years later, fans know only of Bill Barilko's diving goal that gave the 1951 Maple Leafs the franchise's ninth championship. Wonderful, of course, because his heroics have become part of hockey's lore; a shame because there were so many incredible elements that preceded that goal at 2:53 of overtime.

Consider the strategizing of coach Joe Primeau. In an era when pulling a goalie for an extra skater was rarely done—and was very, very rarely successful—Primeau did just that in the last minute with his team trailing, 2–1. Indeed, he did it twice, the second time with only 39 seconds left in the game, a faceoff in the Montreal end, and the Leafs needing a goal. The first four games of the series had gone into overtime, but this seemed destined to finish in regulation, a Montreal victory a virtual surety.

The first pulling of Al Rollins came with 90 seconds remaining, and the Habs got possession of the puck, only to be thwarted by Harry Watson just as it seemed they'd score into the empty net and secure a 3–1 win. And Primeau wasn't done, pulling Rollins again in the final minute. He sent out six skaters as slowly as possible—Ted Kennedy, Sid Smith, Tod Sloan, Jimmy Thomson, Harry Watson, and Max Bentley. But just before the faceoff, Primeau called Thomson back and put out Gus Mortson instead.

Moments later, the action was frenetic. Kennedy won

Bill Barilko scores his Stanley Cup-winning overtime goal

the draw from Elmer Lach back to Bentley, who took a shot through traffic in front. The puck landed on Smith's stick, and he calmly found Sloan to the far side of the play. Sloan made no mistake, and in just seven seconds, the game was tied and headed to overtime.

It was Howie Meeker who started the winning play early in the extra period. He drove into the Montreal end, took the puck to the goal, got to his rebound, and fired a pass to Watson. "Big Harry" saw Barilko move in and got the puck to him. Barilko, who had been nailed to the bench earlier in the season, steered the puck past Gerry McNeil for the Cup-winning goal. It was the Leafs' fourth Cup in five years, and arguably their most impressive win.

For coach Primeau, it marked the first time a bench boss had won the Memorial Cup, Allan Cup, and Stanley Cup, a championship troika of the rarest sort. For captain Ted Kennedy, it was a game that started horribly and ended dreamily. Just a few seconds after the opening faceoff, he had fallen hard into the boards and lost consciousness. He was taken off on a stretcher, and the fans gasped at the thought that he was through for the night. Just a few minutes later, though, he was back in action, providing all the more inspiration for his teammates.

GAME SUMMARY

Toronto 3, Montreal 2

1st Period	No Scoring
	Penalties: Dawes (MTL) 0:27, Barilko (TOR) 16:04
2nd Period	1. Montreal, Richard (MacPherson) 8:56
	2. Toronto, Sloan (Kennedy) 12:00
3rd Period	3. Montreal, Meger (Harvey) 4:47
	4. Toronto, Sloan (Bentley, Smith) 19:28
	Penalties: Johnson (MTL) & Barilko (TOR), & Reay (MTL—misconduct) 10:36
Overtime	5. Toronto, Barilko (Meeker, Watson) 2:53

In Goal:

Montreal—McNeil

Toronto—Rollins

Barilko celebrates in the dressing room at Maple Leaf Gardens

MAY 2, 1967
THE LEAFS' CENTENNIAL CUP

It marked the end of an era—a time when the Original Six was giving way to a modern NHL in which expansion into the American West would transform hockey. But in Canada's Centennial year, there was one last hurrah for the giants of the game. The Leafs, so dominant in the first half of the 1960s, faced the Canadiens, who would go on to dominate the second half of the decade.

The teams had each won two games, at home and on the road, over the course of the first four, but Toronto took control of the series with a 4–1 win at the Forum three nights later. The Leafs, coached by Punch Imlach, were an ancient team, with several players in their late 30s or early 40s and on their last legs. The Habs, coached by Toe Blake, were a team in their prime.

The Leafs were led by goaltenders Terry Sawchuk and Johnny Bower, but Bower was injured and Sawchuk got the start in game six. Imlach, in a classy gesture, dressed Bower and had him on the end of the bench, but there was no way he was going to play. Imlach later

revealed as much: "I had Al Smith in uniform, parked in front of a television set in my room across the hall from the team dressing room. I dressed Bower because I wanted him and all my other veterans in uniform for our most gratifying Cup triumph."

Indeed, the veterans led the way, right to the end. No more symbolic—or significant—faceoff ever took place than the one in the final minute of the game, deep in the Leafs end. With netminder Gump Worsley on the bench for a sixth Montreal attacker, Imlach sent out five skaters who would all make it into the Hockey Hall of Fame: Allan Stanley, Tim Horton, Red Kelly, George Armstrong, and Bob Pulford. Stanley, a defenceman, took the faceoff and beat Jean Béliveau, getting the puck to Kelly, who forwarded it to "Army." The captain hit the empty net, and the Leafs won the game, 3–1. "We sure as hell ruined Canadiens plans to display the Cup at Expo 67!" Imlach rejoiced.

Jim Pappin got what turned out to be the game winner late in the second period on a lucky play. Trying to pass to

Pete Stemkowski in the crease, he hit the skate of Jacques Laperrière and the puck bounced in past a surprised Worsley. It wasn't pretty, but they all count.

After the game, governors and executives voted on who would win the Conn Smythe Trophy, but an announcement was held off until the next day because they felt it distracted from the victorious team. As a result, Dave Keon had to wait a day before being so honoured and receiving his $1,000 cheque. To this day, he is the lone Leaf to win the award, which was named after the great Leafs owner.

Punch Imlach in the dressing room after the game

GAME SUMMARY

Toronto 3, Montreal 1

1st Period	No Scoring
	Penalties: Conacher (TOR) 2:30, Backstrom (MTL) 5:16, Béliveau (MTL) 10:21, Conacher (TOR) 13:25, Ferguson (MTL) 18:50
2nd Period	1. Toronto, Ellis (Kelly, Stanley) 6:25
	2. Toronto, Pappin (Stemkowski, Pulford) 19:24
	Penalties: Harper (MTL) 3:05, Stemkowski (TOR) 7:14, Stanley (TOR) 13:23, Rousseau (MTL) 14:44
3rd Period	3. Montreal, Duff (Harris) 5:28
	4. Toronto, Armstrong (Pulford, Kelly) (en) 19:13
	Penalties: Pappin (TOR) 11:46

In Goal:

Montreal—Worsley

Toronto—Sawchuk

FEBRUARY 7, 1976
DARRYL SITTLER'S 10-POINT NIGHT

Darryl Sittler made a quick pass to right winger Lanny McDonald at centre ice. McDonald barrelled down the wing and ripped a low, hard shot past goalie Dave Reece, giving the Leafs a 1–0 lead over Boston on February 7, 1976, at 6:19 of the opening period. It was an innocuous start to what would become the single greatest game by an individual player in the NHL.

Less than a minute later, Sittler took a heavy hit in getting to the puck first. He chipped it to defenceman Ian Turnbull, who did almost exactly what McDonald had done but from the other side, skating down the left flank and blasting a shot over the glove of Reece. Jean Ratelle made it a one-goal game late in the period, and the Leafs skated to the dressing room holding a 2–1 lead.

Things became special in the second period, when the two teams combined for nine goals. Sittler made it 3–1 with his first of the night when he went hard to the net and converted a nice pass from Borje Salming, who had made a dash down the right side. Just 37 seconds later, on a power play, the two combined again, this time starting with a clean faceoff win back to Salming, who set up a blast from the point that beat the beleaguered Boston goalie. After a Bobby Schmautz goal for the Bruins, Sittler scored two quick ones to give him a second-period hat trick. The first was another long shot and the second was off a fine play by Jack Valiquette, who teed the puck up for Sittler at the top of the faceoff circle.

Johnny Bucyk made it 6–3, and then George Ferguson scored, with two teammates not named Sittler drawing the assists. It was the only goal of the night in which number 27 didn't have a hand. Sittler's finest assist came on the team's eighth goal, a cross-ice saucer pass—blue line to blue line—to McDonald, who fed Salming in front for a beautiful tip-in.

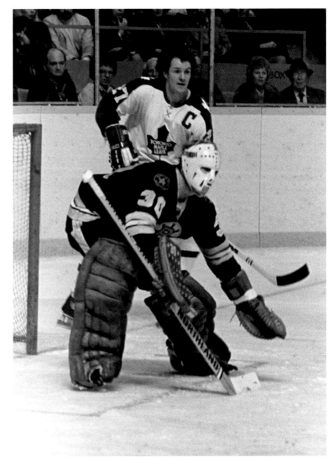

Sittler's 10-point night only seems more incredible with the passage of time— no other player in NHL history has ever had more than eight points in a game

In the second intermission, with the Leafs leading 8–4, the team's longtime and well-known publicist, Stan Obodiac, ran into the dressing room to tell Sittler he had seven points, only one behind the record set by Maurice Richard in 1944–45.

Sittler tied the Rocket in the first minute of the final period on another power play—his fourth goal, a thing of beauty. Salming fed him a pass at the Boston blue line while Sittler was in full flight. In a move reminiscent of many of Richard's goals, Sittler dashed around the defenceman on his off wing and snapped a quick shot past Reece to make it eight points and a share of one of the most coveted and difficult NHL records. But he wasn't done yet.

For his fifth goal, and ninth point, he took another simple pass outside the blue line, skated into Bruins territory with three opponents chasing him down, and let go a wrist shot that fooled the goalie. The record was all his, but the exclamation point would come with 3:25 left in the game.

Holding the puck behind the end red line to the side of the Boston goal, Sittler was looking for McDonald in front. He fed a quick pass to the slot, but the puck hit the skate of Brad Park and caromed into the net. Final score: 11–4. Six goals, four assists, 10 points in a single game, and a record surely never to be broken.

GAME SUMMARY

Toronto 11, Boston 4

1st Period	1. Toronto, McDonald (Sittler) 6:19
	2. Toronto, Turnbull (Sittler, Thompson) 7:01
	3. Boston, Ratelle (Schmautz) 16:54
	Penalties: Sims (BOS—minor; major) & Boutette (TOR—minor; major) 13:00
2nd Period	4. Toronto, Sittler (McDonald, Salming) 2:56
	5. Toronto, Salming (Sittler) (pp) 3:33
	6. Boston, Schmautz (Bucyk, Ratelle) 5:19
	7. Toronto, Sittler (unassisted) 8:12
	8. Toronto, Sittler (Valiquette, Ferguson) 10:27
	9. Boston, Bucyk (Ratelle, Schmantz) 11:06
	10. Toronto, Ferguson (Hammerstrom, Garland) 11:40
	11. Toronto, Salming (McDonald, Sittler) 13:57
	12. Boston, Ratelle (Schmautz, Bucyk) 14:35
	Penalties: Park (BOS) 3:29, Sheppard (BOS) 8:45, Ferguson (TOR) 16:27, Forbes (BOS) 19:44
3rd Period	13. Toronto, Sittler (Salming, Thompson) (pp) 0:44
	14. Toronto, Sittler (Thompson) 9:27
	15. Toronto, Sittler (McDonald) 16:35
	Penalties: Salming (TOR) 3:46, Edestrand (BOS) 9:50

In Goal:

Boston—Reece

Toronto—Thomas

FEBRUARY 13, 1999
THE LAST GAME AT MAPLE LEAF GARDENS

ell, this was it. From the first game at Maple Leaf Gardens on November 12, 1931, to the last, some 67 and a half years later, the time was nigh to move into a new arena—a modern facility that would be home to the Leafs in the 21st century as the Gardens had been to the team in the 20th.

Game time for the Saturday night finale on *Hockey Night in Canada* was set for 7 P.M., but by 5:30 the lobby was absolutely stuffed with fans and program sellers with thousands of souvenirs. Those souvenirs were purchased in bunches, and the atmosphere was electric during the warmup as the players took to the ice.

The game featured a historic pairing of players—captain Mats Sundin lined up for the Leafs and number 93 for the Chicago Blackhawks was none other than Doug Gilmour, so beloved by Leafs fans then and still now. He would have a goal and an assist this night. Fans were hoping for a reversal of opening night in 1931, when the visitors won, 2–1, but history repeated itself, though not without a fight.

Chicago had built a 3–0 lead by the early part of the second period, but goals from Steve Thomas and Kris King made it a 3–2 game after 40 minutes. In the third, though, the visitors skated away with the game and Reid Simpson

scored his second of the night. He would score just five goals and four assists all season, and two of those goals and one of those assists came on this special February 13.

Éric Dazé made it 5–2 at 5:19 to put the game pretty much out of reach. But it was the late Bob Probert (who also had two assists) who etched his name in the arena's history books alongside its first goal scorer, Mush March. Probert scored the last goal at Maple Leaf Gardens, making it 6–2 at 11:05.

After the game was over, the evening was only beginning. Players from both sides went to their dressing rooms while the ice was set up for the postgame ceremonies and then returned to their respective players' benches for a memorable event hosted by Ron MacLean. Dressed in top hat and tails, MacLean introduced dozens of former players: a few survivors from the 1930s, Hall of Famers from various decades, and a star-studded selection from more recent years.

The highlight of the evening came when 89-year-old Red Horner came out onto the ice waving a flag bearing the tag line MEMORIES AND DREAMS—a flag he would lift again at the opening of Air Canada Centre a week later—which was the Leafs' unifying theme as they shifted from old to new, from past to present and future.

Fans cheered and lingered, not wanting to leave, knowing that when they finally did so, it would be for the last time. It had been a great run at the world's most famous hockey rink, but it was time to move on.

GAME SUMMARY

Chicago 6, Toronto 2

1st Period	1. Chicago, Amonte (Gilmour) 4:18
	2. Chicago, Simpson (Probert, Laflamme) 6:41
	Penalties: Manson (CHI—major) & Domi (TOR—major) 8:31, K. King (TOR) 11:49, Moreau (CHI) 15:28
2nd Period	3. Chicago, Gilmour (Amonte, Dazé) 3:11
	4. Toronto, Thomas (Sullivan, Berard) 5:58
	5. Toronto, King (Warriner, Côté) 8:15
	Penalties: Korolev (TOR) 2:30, White (CHI) 4:52, Emerson (CHI) 5:23, D. King (TOR) 14:54, Manson (CHI) 16:39
3rd Period	6. Chicago, Simpson (Probert, Brown) 3:48
	7. Chicago, Dazé (Leroux, Manson) 5:19
	8. Chicago, Probert (Simpson) 11:05
	Penalties: Korolev (TOR) 7:36, Valk (TOR) 13:40, White (CHI) & Simpson (CHI) & Domi (TOR) 16:54

In Goal:

Chicago—Thibault

Toronto—Joseph

The last second of the final game at Maple Leaf Gardens, February 13, 1999

FEBRUARY 20, 1999
OPENING NIGHT AT AIR CANADA CENTRE

Since the closing of the Gardens one week earlier, the Leafs had been on the road, tying with New Jersey, 3–3, on Monday night and beating Buffalo in overtime on Wednesday thanks to a Sundin game-winner. They then drove back along the Queen Elizabeth Way to practise at their new home for a few days and prepare for another grand evening.

The opening of Air Canada Centre was electric in a different way to the final game at the Gardens. It wasn't all history and pomp and circumstance; it was more like 19,000 homeowners visiting their new house for the first time. "I was like everyone else out there," backup goalie Glenn Healy said. "I was just looking around."

The highlight of the opening ceremony was when the Leafs unveiled the new Stanley Cup banners, as well as the personalized banners for all retired and honoured numbers, each bearing a portrait of the player who wore the number. Then came the MEMORIES AND DREAMS flag—the symbolic changing of the arena guard, as it were—going up into the rafters in perpetuity. Vincent Damphousse, a former Leafs forward, and captain Mats Sundin took the opening faceoff, conducted by two young children. Then it was time for "O Canada," sung by John McDermott and the St. Mark's choir.

Ladislav Kohn, playing in place of the injured Freddy Modin, was the only lineup change from the previous

week's finale at the Gardens. Todd Warriner had the honour of scoring the first goal in the new building, although it was the Hockey Hall of Fame that kept the puck. Warriner actually fanned on his shot, but it made its way lazily through a maze of players and past goalie Jeff Hackett all the same.

Because of the ceremonies—and the completely new refrigeration system—the ice wasn't perfect, and this contributed to the game being low-scoring. Scott Thornton tied the game soon after Warriner's goal, but Sundin gave the Leafs a lead they held for nearly 25 minutes. A Vladimir Malakhov goal early in the third was all the Habs needed to send the game to extra time.

Steve Thomas's overtime winner was the result of good playmaking all around. He drove hard to the net, accepted a great pass from Kohn, and then calmly backhanded the winner past Jeff Hackett. "It's an incredible feeling to score the game-winning goal, especially in the first game in this building," Thomas, born in England but raised a Torontonian, exuded.

GAME SUMMARY

Toronto 3, Montreal 2

1st Period	1. Toronto, Warriner (Markov, King) 6:04
	2. Montreal, Thornton (Recchi, Stevenson) 15:42
	3. Toronto, Sundin (Thomas, Karpovtsev) 17:16
	Penalties: Johnson (TOR) 10:00, Recchi (MTL) 12:56
2nd Period	No Scoring
	Penalties: Corson (MTL) & Valk (TOR) 6:48, Recchi (MTL) 15:12, Côté (TOR) 15:34
3rd Period	4. Montreal, Malakhov (Recchi, Zholtok) 1:41 (pp)
	Penalties: Berezin (TOR—double minor) 1:14, Valk (TOR) 1:37, Corson (MTL—major) & Domi (TOR—major) 6:52, Brunet (MTL) 8:09, Rivet (MTL) 11:11, Koivu (MTL) 19:27
Overtime	5. Toronto, Thomas (Kohn, Sundin) 3:48

In Goal:

Montreal—Hackett

Toronto—Sawchuk

The Maple Leaf Gardens banner is raised to the rafters of Air Canada Centre during the opening ceremony

MAPLE LEAFS MILESTONES

First Goal at Maple Leaf Gardens

November 12, 1931, Mush March (Chicago), 2:30, 1st period

Last Goal at Maple Leaf Gardens

February 13, 1999, Bob Probert (Chicago), 11:05, 3rd period

First Goal at Air Canada Centre

February 20, 1999, Todd Warriner (Toronto), 6:04, 1st period

REGULAR SEASON

Games		
1st game	December 19, 1917	Montreal Wanderers 10, Toronto Arenas 9
100th game	January 25, 1922	Toronto St. Pats 3, Montreal Canadiens 1
1,000th game	January 9, 1943	Detroit Red Wings 4, Toronto 0
2,500th game	December 19, 1965	Toronto 3, Boston 1
5,000th game	December 8, 1997	Toronto 3, Dallas 0

Goals		
1st goal	December 19, 1917	Reg Noble
100th goal	February 23, 1918	Alf Skinner
1,000th goal	December 14, 1927	Bill Carson
5,000th goal	February 20, 1954	Ted Kennedy
10,000th goal	February 12, 1977	Darryl Sittler
15,000th goal	March 25, 1995	Dave Andreychuk

Wins		
1st win	December 22, 1917	Toronto Arenas 11, Ottawa Senators 4
100th win	March 9, 1925	Toronto St. Pats 3, Montreal Maroons 0
1,000th win	March 18, 1961	Toronto 6, Boston 2
2,500th win	October 6, 2007	Toronto 4, Montreal Canadiens 3 (OT)

Shutouts		
1st shutout	March 5, 1923	John Ross Roach
100th shutout	December 21, 1941	Turk Broda
200th shutout	December 25, 1958	Ed Chadwick
300th shutout	November 14, 1987	Ken Wregget

PLAYOFFS

Games

1st game	March 11, 1918	Toronto 7, Montreal Canadiens 3
100th game	March 24, 1942	NY Rangers 3, Toronto 0
250th game	April 4, 1964	Montreal Canadiens 4, Toronto 2
500th game	May 25, 2002	Toronto 1, Carolina 0

Goals

1st goal	March 11, 1918	Harry Meeking
100th goal	April 4, 1933	Ken Doraty
500th goal	April 9, 1959	Billy Harris
1,000th goal	April 8, 1990	Tom Fergus

Wins

1st win	March 11, 1918	Toronto 7, Montreal Canadiens 3
100th win	March 25, 1954	Toronto 3, Detroit 1
200th win	May 4, 1994	Toronto 5, San Jose 1
250th win	April 28, 2004	Toronto 4, Philadelphia 1

Shutouts

1st shutout	March 13, 1922	John Ross Roach
50th shutout	April 16, 2004	Ed Belfour

PART 2

THE LEAFS BY NAME AND NUMBER

LEAFS BY SWEATER NUMBER

1

Baz Bastien, Gordie Bell, Tim Bernhardt, Paul Bibeault, Johnny Bower, Turk Broda, Art Brooks, Lorne Chabot, Ed Chadwick, Gerry Cheevers, Bruce Dowie, Bruce Gamble, Benny Grant, George Hainsworth, Harry Holmes, Peter Ing, Joe Ironstone, Eddie Johnston, Mark LaForest, Michel Larocque, Bert Lindsay, Howie Lockhart, Harry Lumley, Cesare Maniago, Jean Marois, Gil Mayer, Frank McCool, Gerry McNamara, Gord McRae, Jacques Plante, Justin Pogge, Daren Puppa, Andrew Raycroft, Jeff Reese, Damian Rhodes, Curt Ridley, John Roach, Jim Rutherford, Rick St. Croix, Don Simmons, Al Smith, Gary Smith, Phil Stein, Vincent Tremblay, Dunc Wilson, Ross "Lefty" Wilson

2

Jack Arbour, Wade Belak, Carl Brewer, Garth Butcher, Harry Cameron, Bobby Copp, Bert Corbeau, Gerald Diduck, Jerome Dupont, Babe Dye, Dallas Eakins, Ted Fauss, Ray Gariepy, Bob Goldham, Larry Hillman, Red Horner, Greg Hotham, Trevor Johansen, Brian Leetch, Sylvain Lefebvre, Rick Ley, Joe Lundrigan, Darwin McCutcheon, Harry Mummery, Ric Nattress, Gary Nylund, Pierre Pilote, Babe Pratt, Beattie Ramsay, Marc Reaume, Luke Richardson, Luke Schenn, Art Smith, Wally Stanowski, Jim Thomson, Ian Turnbull, Rob Zettler

3

Al Arbour, Wade Belak, Jim Benning, Mickey Blake, Bill Brydge, Larry Carrière, Sylvain Côté, Hap Day, Dale DeGray, Art Duncan, Garnet Exelby, Daryl Evans, Fern Flaman, Jimmy Fowler,
Todd Gill, Ed Gorman, John Grisdale, Reg Hamilton, Pierre Hedin, Flash Hollett, Toots Holway, Syd Howe, Grant Jennings, Alex Levinsky, Bob Manno, Dave Manson, Brad Marsh, Matt Martin, Bucko McDonald, Jim Morrison, Gus Mortson, Ken Murray, Randy Murray, Bob Neely, Dion Phaneuf, Marcel Pronovost, Joel Quenneville, Ken Randall, Pat Ribble, Bob Rouse, Duane Rupp, Charlie Sands, Brad Selwood, Dave Shand, Normand Shay, Art Smith, Wally Stanowski, Red Stuart, Rob Zettler

4

Reid Bailey, Hugh Bolton, Cory Cross, Kevin Dahl, Bob Davidson, Hap Day, Art Duncan, Dave Dunn, Dave Ellett, Jeff Finger, Cody Franson, Greg Hotham, Trevor Johansen, Red Kelly, Steve Kraftcheck, Rick Lanz, Gary Leeman, Brad Maxwell, Bob McGill, Reg Noble, Mike Pelyk, Robert Picard, Babe Pratt, Tracy Pratt, Duane Rupp, Dave Shand, Darryl Shannon, D.J. Smith, Kurt Walker, Harry Watson

5

Jack Adams, Bill Barilko, Andy Blair, Garth Boesch, Bill Carson, King Clancy, Bob Davidson, Corb Dennenay, Reg Hamilton, Pep Kelly, Nick Metz, Moe Morris

6

Ace Bailey, George Carey, Charlie Conacher, Danny Cox, Babe Dye, Ron Ellis, Frank Heffernan, George Patterson, Alf Skinner, Carl Voss

7

Amos Arbour, Max Bentley, King Clancy, Terry Clancy, Danny Cox, Garnet Exelby, Kelly Fairchild, Jim Harrison, Jimmy Herbert, Tim Horton, Bingo Kampman, Derek King, Bert McCaffrey, Lanny McDonald, Jack McLean, Dave McLlwain, Harry Meeking, Sergio Momesso, Ken Murray, Frank Nighbor, Jason Podollan, Bud Poile, Joe Primeau, Mike Ridley, Gary Roberts, Doc Romnes, David Sacco, Rocky Saganiuk, Ganton Scott, Jack Shill, Billy Taylor, Greg Terrion, Gilles Thibaudeau, Bill Thoms, Ian White, Cully Wilson

8

Mike Allison, Tim Armstrong, Don Ashby, Ace Bailey, Ken Baumgartner, Aki-Petteri Berg, Gus Bodnar, Buzz Boll, Léo Bourgault, Murph Chamberlain, Carlo Colaiacovo, Rich Costello, Baldy Cotton, Jack Coughlin, Rusty Crawford, Tie Domi, Jim Dorey, Gerry Ehman, Ron Ellis, Alex Faulkner, Tim Gleason, Chris Govedaris, Todd Hawkins, Mel Hill, Shorty Horne, Greg Hotham, Pierre Jarry, Larry Keenan, Dmitri Khristich, Joe Klukay, Mike Komisarek, Les Kozak, Pete Langelle, Wilf Loughlin, John MacMillan, Norm Mann, Willie Marshall, Paul Masnick, Bob McGill, Sean McKenna, Richard Mulhern, Mike Neville, Reg Noble, Fred Perlini, Walt Poddubny, Rob Ramage, Larry Regan, Mickey Roach, Rocky Saganiuk, Brit Selby, Sid Smith, Jack Valiquette, Todd Warriner, Gary Yaremchuk

9

Jack Adams, Stewart Adams, Glenn Anderson, Lloyd Andrews, Nikolai Antropov, Colby Armstrong, Don Ashby, Andy Bathgate, Mark Bell, Dutch Cain, Lorne Carr, Lex Chisholm, Charlie Conacher, Russ Courtnall, Mike Craig, Dick Duff, Dick Gamble, Stewart Gavin, Alex Gray,

Dave Hannan, Niklas Hagman, Sammy Hebert, Josh Holden, Rolly Huard, Brent Imlach, Harvey Jackson, Calle Johansson, Pep Kelly, Ted Kennedy, Gerry Lowrey, Dan Maloney, Gerry Munro, Rod Smylie, Aleksander Suglobov, Norm Ullman

10

Glenn Anderson, John Anderson, Syl Apps, George Armstrong, Pete Bellefeuille, Bill Berg, Harry Cameron, Vincent Damphousse, Gerry Deniord, Babe Dye, George Ferguson, Ron Francis, Aaron Gavey, Stan Jackson, Butch Keeling, Ted Kennedy, Brad May, Harry Mummery, Nick Metz, Zdenek Nedved, Eric Pettinger, Joe Primeau, Marian Stastny, Alexander Steen, Garry Valk

11

Nik Antropov, Andy Blair, Fred Boimistruck, Bruce Boudreau, Baldy Cotton, Dave Creighton, Art Duncan, Philippe Dupuis, Ron Ellis, Alvin Fisher, Gerry Foley, Mike Gartner, Todd Gill, Gaston Gingras, Mark Greig, Lloyd Gross, Inge Hammarstrom, Red Horner, Johnny Ingoldsby, Harvey Jackson, Gerry James, Wes Jarvis, Olli Jokinen, Bill Knox, Larry Landon, Guy Larose, Gary Leeman, Al MacNeil, Jay McClement, Walt McKechnie, Howie Meeker, Don Metz, Rudy Migay, Bob Nevin, Owen Nolan, Murray Oliver, Cam Plante, Bud Poile, Dave Ritchie, Sweeney Schriner, Ganton Scott, Brit Selby, Fredrik Sjostrom, Tod Sloan, Rod Smylie, Bob Solinger, Chris Speyer, Steve Sullivan, Jiri Tlusty, Guy Trottier, Ron Wilson

12

Stewart Adams, Ace Bailey, Andy Blair, Serge Boisvert, Laurie Boschman, Bruce Boudreau, Wayne Carleton, Tim Connolly, Brandon Convery, Gord Drillon, Bill Ezinicki, Frank Finnigan, Tom Fitzgerald, Fern Flaman, Jim Harrison, Larry Hopkins,

Jeff Jackson, Paul Jacobs, Wes Jarvis, Roger Jenkins, Ross Johnstone, Ted Kennedy, Hec Kilrea, Kris King, Billy MacMillan, Gary McAdam, Cliff McBride, Dale McCourt, Larry Mickey, Mark Osborne, Rob Pearson, Walt Poddubny, Babe Pratt, Mason Raymond, Reg Reid, Stephane Robidas, Eddie Rodden, Ganton Scott, Doug Shedden, Art Smith, Lorne Stamler, Pete Stemkowski, Lee Stempniak, Ron Stewart, Steve Thomas, Errol Thompson, Dixon Ward

13

Joakim Lindstrom, Ken Linseman, Mats Sundin, Ken Yaremchuk

14

Dave Andreychuk, Pete Backor, Andy Barbe, Dusty Blair, George Boothman, Gord Brydson, Red Carr, Murph Chamberlain, Rob Cimetta, Bobby Copp, Baldy Cotton, Brian Cullen, Babe Dye, Miroslav Frycer, Bob Goldham, Bob Gracie, Slim Halderson, Herb Hamel, Ted Hampson, Darby Hendrickson, Jonas Hoglund, Buck Jones, Mike Kaszycki, Dave Keon, Craig Laughlin, Gerry Lowrey, Vic Lynn, Gus Marker, John McLellan, John McCreedy, Rudy Migay, Garry Monahan, Jim Morrison, Wilf Paiement, Al Pudas, Dave Reid, René Robert, Jesse Spring, Matt Stajan, Bill Thoms, Dave Tomlinson, Stan Weir, Ron Wilson

15

George Armstrong, Jim Benning, Pat Boutette, Wally Boyer, Bill Carson, Les Costello, Marty Dallman, Ken Doraty, Denis Dupéré, Mike Foligno, Lou Franceschetti, Dave Gagner, Benny Grant, Jack Hamilton, Billy Harris, Pat Hickey, Flash Hollett, Red Horner, Syd Howe, Mike Hudson, Peter Ihnacak, Art Jackson, Larry Jeffrey, Tomas Kaberle, Pep Kelly, Derek Laxdal, Claude Loiselle, Matt Lombardi, Paul Marshall,

Bob McGill, Howie Meeker, Don Metz, Nick Metz, Earl Miller, Dmitri Mironov, Joe Primeau, Paul Ranger, Gary Sabourin, Brit Selby, Tod Sloan, Brian Spencer, Bob Stephenson, Gaye Stewart, Bill Sutherland, Garry Unger, Mike Walton, Brian Wiseman, Ken Yaremchuk

16

Russ Adam, Syl Apps, Jamie Baker, Earl Balfour, Craig Berube, Lonny Bohonos, Léo Boivin, George Boothman, Nikolai Borschevsky, Léo Bourgault, Greg Britz, Arnie Brown, Ray Ceresino, Jack Church, Pete Conacher, Rich Costello, Russ Courtnall, Brian Cullen, Harold Darragh, Ernie Dickens, Tim Ecclestone, Bill Ezinicki, Paul Fenton, Benny Grant, Ray Hannigan, Bill Harris, Darby Hendrickson, Red Heron, Pat Hickey, Larry Hillman, Dan Hodgson, Tim Horton, Art Jackson, Gerry James, Wes Jarvis, Jimmy Jones, Mike Kaszycki, Rick Kehoe, Pep Kelly, Stanley Kemp, Gary Leeman, Alex Levinsky, Jamie Lundmark, Clarke MacArthur, Blair MacKasey, Fleming Mackell, Jim Mikol, Dickie Moore, Eric Nesterenko, Frank Nigro, Gerry O'Flaherty, Ed Olczyk, Bert Olmstead, Randy Osburn, George Parsons, Bud Poile, Bob Sabourin, Charlie Sands, Rod Seiling, Sid Smith, Wally Stanowski, Gaye Stewart, Bill Thoms, Darcy Tucker, Mike Walton, Bob Warner, Ken Yaremchuk

17

Stewart Adams, Murray Armstrong, Bob Bailey, Buzz Boll, Bruce Boudreau, Doug Brindley, Jerry Butler, Wendel Clark, Brian Conacher, Bob Davidson, Ab DeMarco, Dave Downie, Bruce Draper, Dick Duff, Denis Dupéré, Gerry Ehman, Paul Evans, Bill Ezinicki, Jack Forsey, Cal Gardner, Stewart Gavin, Bob Goldham, Benny Grant, Jack Hamilton, Gord Hannigan, Duke Harris, Bob Hassard, Red Heron, Paul Higgins, Bronco Horvath, Frank Howard, Art Jackson, Jim Jarvis, Bingo Kampman, Rick Kehoe, Joe Klukay, Tom Martin,

Don McKenney, Nick Metz, Jim Pappin, J.P. Parisé,
Eric Prentice, Fred Robertson, Duane Rupp, Charlie Sands,
Rod Seiling, Floyd Smith, Bill Stewart, Blaine Stoughton,
Harry Taylor, Rhys Thomson

18

Al Arbour, Norm Armstrong, Bob Bailey, Alain Bélanger,
Garth Boesch, Léo Boivin, Carl Brewer, Mike Brown, André
Champagne, Brian Conacher, Brian Cullen, Bob Davidson,
Kim Davis, Harold Druken, Paul Gagné, Paul Gardner,
Ernie Godden, Red Heron, Peter Ihnacak, Art Jackson,
Bill Juzda, Butch Keeling, Chad Kilger, Craig Laughlin,
Kevin Maguire, Kent Manderville, Bob Manno, Gus Marker,
Gary Marsh, Shep Mayer, Alyn McCauley, Jim McKenny,
Jack McLean, Don Metz, Windy O'Neill, Richard Panik,
Jim Pappin, George Parsons, Scott Pearson, Wayne Presley,
Wayne Primeau, David Reid, Fred Robertson, Ron Sedlbauer,
Jack Shill, Peter White, Jeremy Williams

19

Doug Baldwin, Bill Barilko, Léo Boivin, Hugh Bolton,
Bruce Boudreau, Turk Broda, Jack Church, Chuck Corrigan,
Barry Cullen, John Cullen, Bill Derlago, Kent Douglas, Jeff
Farkas, Tom Fergus, Bill Flett, Jack Hamilton, Paul Henderson,
Greg Hubick, Gerry James, Kenny Jonsson, Dmitri Khristich,
Joe Klukay, Joffrey Lupul, Norm Mann, Bucko McDonald,
Nick Metz, Fredrik Modin, Dominic Moore, Gus Mortson,
Eric Nesterenko, Mikael Renberg, Jack Shill, Ron Stewart,
Aleksander Suglobov, Billy Taylor, Don Webster, Johnny Wilson

20

Claire Alexander, George Armstrong, Don Ashby, Bob Bailey,
Ed Belfour, Mickey Blake, Hugh Bolton, David Booth,

Bill Burega, Larry Cahan, Ed Chadwick, Jack Church,
Frank Dunlap, Jeff Farkas, Hank Goldup, Reg Hamilton,
Christian Hanson, Bob Hassard, Tim Horton, Johnny Ingoldsby,
Ralph Intranuovo, Art Jackson, Mike Johnson, Terry Johnson,
Bingo Kampman, Mike Kaszycki, Ted Kennedy, Mark Kirton,
Jim Korn, Alexei Kudashov, Paul Lawless, Don Luce, Frank
Mathers, Gil Mayer, Kevin McClelland, John McCormack,
John McCreedy, Garry Monahan, Zdenek Nedved, Mike Pelyk,
Bob Pulford, Bobby Reynolds, Joe Sacco, Al Secord, Jack Shill,
Tod Sloan, Wally Stanowski, David Steckel, Rich Sutter,
Jim Thomson, Rick Vaive

21

Gary Aldcorn, Bob Bailey, Bill Barilko, Bobby Baun,
Gus Bodnar, Léo Boivin, Aaron Broten, Terry Clancy,
Mariusz Czerkawski, Bob Dawes, Gord Drillon, Mike Eastwood,
Frank Howard, Ron Hurst, Red Johnson, Pete Langelle,
Dan Lewicki, Parker MacDonald, Adam Mair, Norm Mann,
Jack Markle, Willie Marshall, Gil Mayer, Jamal Mayers,
Sean McKenna, Rudy Migay, Jim Morrison, Kirk Muller,
Mark Osborne, Mike Pelyk, John Pohl, Martin Prochazka,
Robert Reichel, Warren Rychel, Borje Salming, Darryl Sly,
Bob Solinger, Billy Taylor, Harry Taylor, James van Riemsdyk

22

Doug Acomb, Gary Aldcorn, Earl Balfour, Ken Baumgartner,
François Beauchemin, Jack Bionda, Chuck Blair, Mike Blaisdell,
Arnie Brown, Mike Bullard, Lex Chisholm, Brian Conacher,
Dave Creighton, Brian Cullen, Boyd Devereaux, Dave Fortier,
Jack Hamilton, Reg Hamilton, Gord Hannigan, Larry Hillman,
Ron Hurst, Larry Jeffrey, Danny Johnson, Forbes Kennedy,
Ken Klee, Igor Korolev, Fleming Mackell, Al MacNeil,
Frank Mahovlich, Brian Marchinko, Don Marshall, Gil Mayer,
Shep Mayer, Rudy Migay, Jim Morrison, George Parsons,
Scott Pearson, Michel Petit, Alexei Ponikarovsky,

Luke Richardson, Duane Rupp, Zach Sill, Tod Sloan, Sid Smith, Jerred Smithson, Brian Spencer, Cy Thomas, Errol Thompson, Ray Timgren, Rick Vaive, Glen Wesley, Tiger Williams

23

Bob Bailey, Earl Balfour, Hugh Bolton, Turk Broda, Jeff Brubaker, Randy Carlyle, Dave Creighton, Joe Crozier, Bob Dawes, Ernie Dickens, Harold Druken, Slava Duris, Dave Farrish, John Gibson, Todd Gill, Hank Goldup, Pat Graham, Gord Hannigan, Pat Hannigan, André Hinse, Dave Hutchison, Brett Lebda, Danny Lewicki, Billy MacMillan, Phil Maloney, Ryan O'Byrne, Alexei Ponikarovsky, Noel Price, Pat Quinn, Al Rollins, Phil Samis, Eddie Shack, Dale Smedsmo, Trevor Smith, Bob Solinger, Ken Strong, Petr Svoboda, Jeff Ware

24

Normand Aubin, Patrik Augusta, Earl Balfour, Gordie Bell, Drake Berehowsky, John Brenneman, Al Buchanan, Mike Byers, Gary Collins, Dan Daoust, Slava Duris, Aut Erickson, Jonas Frogren, Brian Glennie, Per Gustafsson, Peter Holland, Brent Imlach, Gary Jarrett, Ed Joyal, Bill Kendall, John-Michael Liles, John MacMillan, Al MacNeil, Darryl Maggs, Willie Marshall, Jack Martin, Bryan McCabe, Jim Morrison, Mike Nykoluk, Tom Pederson, Michel Petit, Joe Sacco, Terry Sawchuk, Don Simmons, Sid Smith, Ron Stewart, Scott Thornton, Randy Wood

25

Greg Andrusak, John Arundel, Earl Balfour, T.J. Brennan, Willie Brossart, Al Buchanan, Jack Caffery, Wayne Carleton, Bob Dawes, Paul DiPietro, Duke Edmundson, Scott Garland, Hal Gill, Bob Hassard, Jeff Jackson, Alexander Khavanov, Orland Kurtenbach, Tom Kurvers, Ed Litzenberger, Jyrki Lumme,

John MacMillan, Phil Maloney, Milan Marcetta, Terry Martin, Gil Mayer, Larry McIntyre, Jim McKenny, Eric Nesterenko, Joe Nieuwendyk, Ben Ondrus, George Parsons, Bud Poile, Marc Reaume, David Reid, Bill Root, Mike Santorelli, Rod Schutt, Jason Smith, Greg Smyth, Bob Solinger, Pete Stemkowski, Mike Stothers, Frank Sullivan, Bob Sykes, Steve Thomas, Darren Veitch, Leigh Verstraete, Ron Ward, Terry Yake, Gary Yaremchuk, Peter Zezel

26

Gary Aldcorn, Bobby Baun, Dave Burrows, Jack Capuano, Russ Courtnall, Chris Evans, Petter Granberg, Paul Healey, Jamie Heward, Bill Kitchen, Chris Kotsopoulos, Mike Krushelnyski, Rick Ley, Bob Liddington, Wally Maxwell, Bob McGill, Basil McRae, Gerry Meehan, Barry Melrose, Lyle Moffatt, Craig Muni, Randy Murray, Ben Ondrus, Nathan Perrott, Allan Stanley, Mike Stevens, Mike Van Ryn, Darren Veitch, Kurt Walker, Daniel Winnik, Craig Wolanin, Dmitri Yushkevich, Mike Zigomanis

27

Shayne Corson, Brian Cullen, Lucien DeBlois, Ken Girard, Miroslav Ihnacak, John Kordic, Frank Mahovlich, Bryan Marchment, Gerry Meehan, Gord Nelson, Mike Nykoluk, Michael Peca, Dave Semenko, Darryl Sittler

28

John Anderson, Bruce Boudreau, Carl Brewer, Randy Carlyle, Brian Curran, Tie Domi, Paul Evans, Dave Farrish, David Harlock, Benoît Hogue, Val James, Derek Laxdal, Kevin Maguire, Paul Marshall, Bill McCreary, Colton Orr, Mike Pelyk, Fred Perlini, Bill Root, Bob Rouse, Darryl Shannon, Greg Smyth, Leigh Verstraete, Blake Wesley, Rod Willard, Gary Yaremchuk

29

Drake Berehowsky, Jerry D'Amigo, Paul Evans, Martin Gerber, Todd Gill, Ken Hammond, Paul Higgins, Matt Lashoff, Joey MacDonald, Chris McRae, Craig Muni, Mike Palmateer, Fred Perlini, Karel Pilar, Justin Pogge, Felix Potvin, Darryl Shannon, Brad Smith, Bill Thoms, Vincent Tremblay

30

J-S Aubin, Tom Barrasso, Allan Bester, Sébastien Centomo, Scott Clemmensen, Don Edwards, Bruce Gamble, Paul Harrison, Ron Low, Bernie Parent, Terry Sawchuk, Ben Scrivens, Al Smith, Wayne Thomas, Vincent Tremblay, Rick Wamsley, Dunc Wilson, Ken Wregget

31

Allan Bester, Marcel Cousineau, Jiri Crha, Marv Edwards, Grant Fuhr, Pierre Hamel, Peter Ing, Curtis Joseph, Pavel Kubina, Murray McLachlan, Gord McRae, Bob Parent, Damian Rhodes, Al Smith, Ken Wregget

32

Greg Britz, Joe Colborne, Mike Eastwood, Alex Foster, Pierre Hamel, Benoît Hogue, Wes Jarvis, Nick Kypreos, Josh Leivo, Daniel Marois, Chris McRae, Craig Muni, Frank Nigro, Fred Perlini, Ken Strong, Mikael Tellqvist, Steve Thomas, Kris Versteeg, Gary Yaremchuk, Ron Zanussi

33

Bates Battaglia, Don Beaupre, Wade Belak, Jeff Brown, Luca Caputi, David Cooper, Tim Erixon, Doug Favell, Bob Halkidis, Benoît Hogue, Dave Hutchison, Al Iafrate, Craig Johnson, Matt Martin, Chris McAllister, Marc Moro, Craig Muni, Curt Ridley, Wayne Thomas, Bob Wren

34

Bryan Berard, Rob Cimetta, Rocky Dundas, Ted Fauss, Terry Johnson, Maxim Kondratiev, Derek Laxdal, Jamie Macoun, Craig Muni, Fred Perlini, Dave Reid, James Reimer, Bill Root, Jeff Serowik, Darryl Shannon, Leigh Verstraete, Ken Yaremchuk

35

Normand Aubin, Bruce Boudreau, Marty Dallman, Jean-Sébastien Giguère, Derek Laxdal, Marc Magnan, Jeff Reese, Curt Ridley, Corey Schwab, Vesa Toskala

36

Brendan Bell, Frank Bialowas, Len Esau, Carl Gunnarsson, Jamie Heward, Ken McRae, Mike Millar, Anton Stralman, Dmitri Yushkevich

37

Carter Ashton, Casey Baitley, Tim Brent, Darby Hendrickson, Trevor Kidd, Mark Kolesar, Don MacLean, Jason Podollan, Doug Shedden, Dave Tomlinson

38

David Harlock, Brad Leeb, Frazer McLaren, Jay Rosehill, Chris Snell, Yannick Tremblay

39

Kelly Chase, Matt Frattin, Simon Gamache, Travis Green, Mike Kennedy, Ladislav Kohn, Greg McKegg, John Mitchell, Alexei Ponikarovsky, Erik Westrum, Clarke Wilm, Ron Zanussi

40

Troy Bodie, Tie Domi, Kelly Fairchild, Ken McRae, Phil Oreskovic, Jussi Rynnas

41

Jason Allison, Paul Gagné, Nikolai Kulemin, Eric Lacroix, Matt Stajan, Shayne Toporowski

42

Kevyn Adams, Tyler Bozak, David Cooper, Tim Stapleton, Kyle Wellwood

43

Ken Belanger, Nathan Dempsey, Jay Harrison, Nazem Kadri

44

Brian Bradley, John Craighead, Anders Eriksson, Ryan Hollweg, Brayden Irwin, Staffan Kronwall, John McIntyre, Yanic Perreault, Morgan Rielly

45

Jonathan Bernier, Carlo Colaiacovo, Mark Fraser, Marcel Mueller, Zdenek Nedved, Viktor Stalberg

46

David Broll, Joey Crabb, Ben Ondrus, Roman Polak

47

Darryl Boyce, Leo Komarov

48

Ryan Hamilton, Jeremy Williams

49

Dmitri Yakushin

50

Darryl Boyce, Jonas Gustavsson, Stuart Percy

51

Jake Gardiner, Jeff Hamilton, Rickard Wallin

52

Robbie Earl, Sean Haggerty, Alexander Karpovtsev

53

Sam Carrick, Michael Kostka, John Pohl

54

Kris Newbury

55

Drake Berehowsky, Jason Blake, Korbinian Holzer, Ric Jackman, Danny Markov, Larry Murphy

56

Spencer Abbott, Andre Deveaux, Andy Wozniewski

57

Andrew MacWilliam

59

Keith Aulie, Jamie Devane, Jaime Sifers

63

Dave Bolland

67

Brandon Kozun, Robert Svehla

71

David Clarkson, Mike Foligno

72

Mathieu Schneider

73

Pavel Kubina

77

Pavel Kubina

80

Nik Antropov

81

Phil Kessel

84
Mikhail Grabovski

88
Eric Lindros

89
Alexander Mogilny

92
Jeff O'Neill

93
Doug Gilmour, Alexander Godynyuk

94
Sergei Berezin, Yanic Perreault

96
Phil Housley

99
Wilf Paiement

RETIRED NUMBERS

| October 17, 1992 | **5** | Bill Barilko |
| | **6** | Ace Bailey |

HONOURED NUMBERS

October 3, 1993	**9**	Ted Kennedy	February 8, 2003	**27**	Darryl Sittler
	10	Syl Apps	October 4, 2006	**4**	Hap Day
March 11, 1995	**1**	Johnny Bower		**4**	Red Kelly
	1	Turk Broda		**21**	Borje Salming
November 21, 1995	**7**	King Clancy	November 22, 2008	**17**	Wendel Clark
	7	Tim Horton	January 31, 2009	**93**	Doug Gilmour
February 28, 1998	**9**	Charlie Conacher	February 11, 2012	**13**	Mats Sundin
	10	George Armstrong			
October 3, 2001	**27**	Frank Mahovlich			

LEAFS BY BIRTHDATE

JANUARY

1 Murray Armstrong (1916), Doc Romnes (1907), Ken Yaremchuk (1964)

2 Jimmy Jones (1953), Robert Svehla (1969)

3 Drake Berehowsky (1972), Greg Britz (1961), Gord Brydson (1907), Cory Cross (1971), Matt Frattin (1988), Simon Gamache (1981), Moe Morris (1921), Rick St. Croix (1955), Mike Walton (1945), Todd Warriner (1974)

4 Earl Balfour (1933), David Broll (1993)

5 John Brenneman (1943), Vitezslav Duris (1954), Alvin Fisher (1893), Kevin Maguire (1963), Basil McRae (1961)

6 Slim Halderson (1900), Dickie Moore (1931), Leigh Verstraete (1962), Carl Voss (1907)

7 Babe Pratt (1916)

8 Garth Butcher (1963), Ron Ellis (1945), Marian Stastny (1953)

9 Bruce Boudreau (1955), Anders Eriksson (1975), Pep Kelly (1914), Dave McLlwain (1967), Scott Thornton (1971)

10 Frank Mahovlich (1938), Cliff McBride (1909), Don Metz (1916)

11 Dave Burrows (1949), Rob Ramage (1959), Dave Reid (1934)

12 Nikolai Borschevsky (1965), Daryl Evans (1961), Frank Heffernan (1892), Tim Horton (1930), Jack Shill (1913)

13 Paul Higgins (1962), Cesare Maniago (1939), Mike Palmateer (1954)

14 Peter Holland (1991), Greg Johnston (1965), Don MacLean (1977), Tom Pederson (1970)

15 Brett Lebda (1982), Aleksander Suglobov (1982)

16 Jamie Lundmark (1981)

17 Tim Bernhardt (1958), Léo Bourgault (1903), Jacques Plante (1929), Viktor Stalberg (1986)

18 Syl Apps Sr. (1915), Alain Bélanger (1956), Mike Blaisdell (1960), Josh Holden (1978), Jaime Sifers (1983), Jesse Spring (1901)

19 Sylvain Côté (1966), Gord Hannigan (1929), Harvey Jackson (1911), Mike Komisarek (1982), Pat Quinn (1943)

20 Inge Hammarstrom (1948), Maxim Kondratiev (1983)

21 Brian Bradley (1965), Dmitri Yakushin (1978)

22 John Mitchell (1985), Ken Murray (1948)

23 Mark Kolesar (1973), Leo Komarov (1987)

24 Jeff Farkas (1978), Gus Mortson (1925)

25 Troy Bodie (1985), Corb Dennenay (1894), Aut Erickson (1938), Fern Flaman (1927), Mark Greig (1970)

26 Amos Arbour (1895), Harold Druken (1979), Vic Lynn (1925), Dale McCourt (1957), Frank Nighbor (1893), Phil Oreskovic (1987), Alf Skinner (1896)

27 Carlo Colaiacovo (1983), Alexander Godynyuk (1970), Dave Manson (1967)

28 Arnie Brown (1942), Paul Henderson (1943)

29 Mike Foligno (1959), Tim Gleason (1983), Billy Harris (1952), Joe Primeau (1906)

30 Larry Carrière (1952), Joe Colborne (1990), Rocky Dundas (1967), Alexander Khavanov (1972)

31 Mikhail Grabovski (1984), Jack McLean (1923)

FEBRUARY

1 Dutch Cain (1902), Bob Stephenson (1954), Billy Stuart (1900)

2 Chris Govedaris (1970), Alex Levinsky (1910)

3 Mark Kirton (1958), Norm Shay (1899), Tiger Williams (1954)

4 Sam Carrick (1992), Brandon Convery (1974), Joe Sacco (1969), Gary Smith (1944), Jerred Smithson (1979), Lee Stempniak (1983)

5 Larry Hillman (1937)

6 Harry Cameron (1890), Kent Douglas (1936), Paul Gagné (1962), Mike Hudson (1967)

7 Joey MacDonald (1980), Richard Panik (1991), Marc Reaume (1934)

8 Jack Marks (1882), Kirk Muller (1966), Trevor Smith (1985)

9 Bert Corbeau (1894), Chris Speyer (1902)

10 Bob Davidson (1912), Bud Poile (1924)

11 Sean Haggerty (1976), Paul Harrison (1955), Derek King (1967), Frank Nigro (1960), Eddie Shack (1937)

12 Owen Nolan (1972), Michel Petit (1964)

13 Gaston Gingras (1959), Mats Sundin (1971)

14 Murph Chamberlain (1915), Val James (1957), Calle Johansson (1967), Gerry Lowrey (1906), Walt Poddubny (1960)

15 Rob Cimetta (1970), Marty Dallman (1963), Mel Hill (1914), Adam Mair (1979)

16 Les Costello (1928), Korbinian Holzer (1988), Lanny McDonald (1953), Nick Metz (1914)

17 Marc Magnan (1962), Al Pudas (1899), Reg Reid (1899), Jim Rutherford (1949)

18 Nik Antropov (1980), Dick Duff (1936), Kris King (1966), Alexander Mogilny (1969), Jason Podollan (1976), Goldie Prodger (1892)

19 Joe Crozier (1929), Jerry D'Amigo (1991), Pierre Hedin (1978), Gary Leeman (1964), Kris Newbury (1982), Bob Parent (1958)

20 Jamie Devane (1991)

21 Charlie Cotch (1900), Jerome Dupont (1962), Derek Laxdal (1966)

22 Aaron Gavey (1974), Eddie Gerard (1890), Mike Stothers (1962)

23 Andre Deveaux (1984), Jeff O'Neill (1976), Jim Thomson (1927)

24 Jeff Brubaker (1958), Tim Erixon (1991), Paul E. Evans (1955)

25 King Clancy (1903), Duke Harris (1942)

27 Andy Blair (1908), Jerry Butler (1951), Dallas Eakins (1967), Mike Kaszycki (1956)

28 Eric Lindros (1973), Wilf Loughlin (1896), Jack McDonald (1887)

29 Dan Daoust (1960)

MARCH

1 Max Bentley (1920), Pat Boutette (1952), Ron Francis (1963), Richard Mulhern (1955), Allan Stanley (1926), Alexander Steen (1984)

2 Tomas Kaberle (1978), Stan Kemp (1924), Jay McClement (1983)

3 Steve Kraftcheck (1929), Brian Leetch (1968), Norm Mann (1913), Zdenek Nedved (1975), Colton Orr (1982), Martin Prochazka (1972), Stéphane Robidas (1977), Al Secord (1958)

4 Ladislav Kohn (1975), Gilles Thibaudeau (1963)

5 Bryan Berard (1977), Paul Gardner (1956), Bob Halkidis (1966), Pat Hannigan (1936), Bill Thoms (1910)

6 Buzz Boll (1911), Joe Matte (1893), Daniel Winnik (1985)

7 Gary Aldcorn (1935), Jack Arbour (1898), Greg Hotham (1956), Billy MacMillan (1943), Sean McKenna (1962)

8 Don Ashby (1955), Brandon Kozun (1990), Larry Murphy (1961), Tracy Pratt (1943), Rob Zettler (1968)

9 Phil Housley (1964), Paul Jacobs (1894), Gary Marsh (1946), Morgan Rielly (1994)

10 Tim Brent (1984), Mike Bullard (1961), Christian Hanson (1986)

11 Ken Baumgartner (1966), Sprague Cleghorn (1890), Dave Downie (1909), Bill Ezinicki (1924)

12 Bronco Horvath (1930), Bingo Kampman (1914), Danny Lewicki (1931), Cam Plante (1964)

13 Gordie Bell (1925), Bill Burega (1932), Ernie Godden (1961), Blaine Stoughton (1953)

15 Stu Gavin (1960), James Reimer (1988), David Steckel (1982), Darcy Tucker (1975), Peter White (1969)

16 David Harlock (1971), Jiri Tlusty (1988)

17 Larry Hopkins (1954), Bob Sabourin (1933), Stan Weir (1952)

18 Craig Johnson (1972), Matt Lombardi (1982), Bob Nevin (1938), Brad Selwood (1948), Jack Valiquette (1954)

19 Tyler Bozak (1986), Lyle Moffat (1948)

20 Paul Healey (1975)

21 Al Iafrate (1966), Howie Lockhart (1895)

22 Dave Keon (1940), John Kordic (1965), Eddie Rodden (1901), Dunc Wilson (1948)

23 Don Marshall (1932), Johnny McCreedy (1911), Wayne Presley (1965), Daren Puppa (1965), Ganton Scott (1903)

24 Brayden Irwin (1987), Jeff Reese (1966)

25 Bill Barilko (1927), Andrew MacWilliam (1990), Ken Wregget (1964)

26 Allan Bester (1964), Sébastien Centomo (1971), Bob Hassard (1929), Trevor Kidd (1972), Michael Peca (1974), Luke Richardson (1969)

27 Brit Selby (1945)

28 Mike Allison (1961), John Anderson (1957), Lou Franceschetti (1958), Harry Taylor (1926)

29 Art Brooks (1887), Frank Mathers (1924), Duane Rupp (1938)

30 Dave Ellett (1964), Jamie Heward (1971), Pierre Jarry (1949), Trevor Johansen (1957)

31 Tom Barrasso (1965), Brendan Bell (1983), David Clarkson (1984), Sammy Hebert (1893), Brad Marsh (1958), Bob Pulford (1936)

APRIL

1 Carter Ashton (1991), Lex Chisholm (1915), Bill Kendall (1910), Guy Trottier (1941)

2 Terry Clancy (1943)

3 Joey Crabb (1983), Bernie Parent (1945), Darryl Sly (1939), T.J. Brennan (1989)

4 Yanic Perreault (1971)

5 Doug Favell (1945)

6 Gerald Diduck (1965), Jimmy Fowler (1915), Hal Gill (1975), Clarke MacArthur (1985), Darryl Maggs (1949)

7 Eric Brewer (1979), Ross Johnstone (1926), Alexander Karpovtsev (1970)

9 Kelly Fairchild (1973), Alexei Ponikarovsky (1980), Rickard Wallin (1980)

10 Dion Phaneuf (1985)

12 Kent Manderville (1971), Bert McCaffrey (1893), Gord McRae (1948), Fred Perlini (1962)

13 Paul Bibeault (1919), Jiri Crha (1950), Mariusz Czerkawski (1972), Flash Hollett (1912), Mike Kennedy (1972), Brad Smith (1958)

14 Paul Masnick (1931)

15 Hugh Bolton (1929), Ryan Hamilton (1985), Harry Holmes (1889), Pavel Kubina (1977), Bill McCreary Jr. (1960)

16 Boyd Devereaux (1978), Bunny Larocque (1952)

17 Borje Salming (1951)

19 Randy Carlyle (1956), André Hinse (1945), Darwin McCutheon (1962)

21 Ed Belfour (1965)

22 Justin Pogge (1986), Peter Zezel (1965)

23 Ryan Hollweg (1983), Ken McRae (1968), Dale Smedsmo (1951), Greg Smyth (1966)

24 Ray Ceresino (1929), Philippe Dupuis (1985), Jeff Jackson (1955), Ken Klee (1971), Darren Veitch (1960)

25 Glenn Smith (1895)

26 Pat Ribble (1954)

27 Mike Krushelnyski (1960), Bob McGill (1962)

28 Peter Ing (1969), Mike Millar (1965), Roman Polak (1986), Wally Stanowski (1919)

29 Pete Backor (1919), Jim Benning (1963), Reg Hamilton (1914), Curtis Joseph (1967), John McIntyre (1969), Doug Shedden (1961)

30 Spencer Abbott (1988), Jeff Brown (1966), Marcel Cousineau (1973), Fleming Mackell (1929), Matt Martin (1971), Don McKenney (1934)

MAY

1 Bryan Marchment (1969), Rod Willard (1960)

2 Dave Hutchison (1952), Greg Terrion (1960)

3 Peter Ihnacak (1957), Billy Taylor (1919)

4 Larry Landon (1958), Andrew Raycroft (1980), James van Riemsdyk (1989)

5 Russ Adam (1961), Grant Jennings (1965), Mikael Renberg (1972)

6 Garry Edmundson (1932), Fredrik Sjostrom (1983), Harry Watson (1923)

7 Tim Connolly (1981), Mickey Roach (1895)

8 Ed Chadwick (1933), Eddie Joyal (1940), Dave Tomlinson (1969)

9 Ken Strong (1963)

10 Ab DeMarco, Sr. (1916), Gordie Nelson (1947)

12 Tim Armstrong (1967), Bob Goldham (1922), Warren Rychel (1967), Chris Snell (1971)

13 Babe Dye (1898), D.J. Smith (1977), Kris Versteeg (1986)

14 Ken Belanger (1974), Rick Vaive (1959), Mike Van Ryn (1979)

15 Doug Acomb (1949), Turk Broda (1914), Pat Hickey (1953), Jack Markle (1907), Dave Reid (1964)

16 Scott Garland (1952), Jean-Sébastien Giguère (1977), Floyd Smith (1935), Kyle Wellwood (1983)

17 Al Buchanan (1927)

18 Ron Hurst (1931), Stuart Percy (1993)

19 Jeff Ware (1977)

20 Lonny Bohonos (1973), Vesa Toskala (1977)

21 Alex Faulkner (1936)

22 Chuck Corrigan (1916), George Patterson (1906), Jussi Rynnas (1987)

23 Gary Roberts (1966), Charlie Sands (1911)

24 Jack Church (1915), Bruce Gamble (1938), Zach Sill (1988)

25 Pat Graham (1961), Ric Nattress (1962), Robert Picard (1957), Rick Wamsley (1959), Andy Wozniewski (1980)

26 Josh Leivo (1993)

28 Reid Bailey (1956), Red Horner (1909), Damian Rhodes (1969), Errol Thompson (1950), Ron Wilson (1955)

29 Jason Allison (1975), Bob Bailey (1931), Willie Brossart (1949), Claude Loiselle (1963), Alyn McCauley (1977)

30 Wes Jarvis (1958)

JUNE

1 Serge Boisvert (1959)

2 Russ Courtnall (1965), Robbie Earl (1985), John Gibson (1959), Jack Hamilton (1925)

3 Len Esau (1968)

4 François Beauchemin (1980), Laurie Boschman (1960), Nick Kypreos (1966), Wayne Primeau (1976), Ian White (1984)

5 Dave Bolland (1986), Cully Wilson (1892)

6 Mike Craig (1971), Per Gustafsson (1970)

8 Doug Brindley (1949), Herb Hamel (1904), Bryan McCabe (1975)

10 Kurt Walker (1954)

11 Keith Aulie (1989), Hec Kilrea (1907), Jim Mikol (1938)

12 Mathieu Schneider (1969)

14 Jack Adams (1895), Hap Day (1901), Parker MacDonald (1933), Johnny Wilson (1929)

15 Marcel Pronovost (1930)

16 Clare Alexander (1945), Barry Cullen (1935), Tom Fergus (1962), Chris McAllister (1975), Frank Sullivan (1929)

17 Dave Fortier (1951), Greg McKegg (1992)

18 Bob Rouse (1964)

19 Walt McKechnie (1947)

20 Petr Svodoba (1980)

21 Jack Coughlin (1892), Lucien DeBlois (1957), Denis Dupéré (1948), Alex Gray (1899), Johnny Ingoldsby (1924), Ron Low (1950), Darryl Shannon (1968)

23 Ken Doraty (1906), Reg Noble (1896), Félix Potvin (1971), John Ross Roach (1900)

24 Mike Brown (1985), Dave Creighton (1930), Drew McIntyre (1983)

25 Ernie Dickens (1921), Doug Gilmour (1963), Ben Ondrus (1982), Robert Reichel (1971)

26 George Hainsworth (1895)

27 Rich Costello (1963), Shorty Horne (1904)

28 Joe Ironstone (1898), Ric Jackman (1978), George Parsons (1914), Gaye Stewart (1923)

29 John Pohl (1979)

30 Jack Caffery (1934), Ted Fauss (1961)

JULY

1 Mike Eastwood (1967)

2 Lorne Carr (1910), Paul Lawless (1964)

3 Ace Bailey (1903), Wade Belak (1976), Don Webster (1924)

4 Art Duncan (1891), Jake Forbes (1897), Jake Gardiner (1990), Kevin McClelland (1962)

6 George Armstrong (1930), Steve Sullivan (1974)

7 Darryl Boyce (1984), Jack Capuano (1966)

8 Brad Maxwell (1957), Mike Ridley (1963)

9 Frank Finnigan (1900), Jim Harrison (1947), Red Kelly (1927), Mike Mitchell (1893)

10 Mark LaForest (1962), Marcel Mueller (1988), Blake Wesley (1959)

11 Danny Markov (1976), Sid Smith (1925), Ron Stewart (1932)

12 Dave Semenko (1957)

13 Larry McIntyre (1949), Brian Wiseman (1971)

14 Nathan Dempsey (1974), Benny Grant (1908), Ray Hannigan (1927), Nikolai Kulemin (1986), Bobby Reynolds (1967)

15 Rick Kehoe (1951), Eric Lacroix (1971), Ed Litzenberger (1932), Barry Melrose (1956), Steve Thomas (1963)

16 Jyrki Lumme (1966), Jay Rosehill (1985)

17 Marc Moro (1977)

19 J-S Aubin (1977), Craig Muni (1962), Ryan O'Byrne (1984), Tim Stapleton (1982)

21 Bill Flett (1943), Alexei Kudashov (1971)

23 Chuck Blair (1928), Scott Clemmensen (1977), Dmitri Khristich (1969), Bert Lindsay (1881)

25 Gord Spence (1897)

26 Normand Aubin (1960), Erik Westrum (1979)

27 Andy Barbe (1923), Bill Johnson (1928), Craig Wolanin (1967)

28 Aki-Petteri Berg (1977), Jim Korn (1957)

29 Pete Conacher (1932), Billy Harris (1935)

31 David Sacco (1970)

AUGUST

1 Dave Farrish (1956), Gus Marker (1905), Anton Stralman (1986)

2 Léo Boivin (1932), John Cullen (1964), Todd Hawkins (1966), Brian Marchinko (1948), John McCormack (1925)

3 Dominic Moore (1980), Rob Pearson (1971)

4 Wayne Carleton (1946), Gerry Deniord (1902)

5 Mark Bell (1980), Cy Thomas (1926)

6 John McLellan (1928), Shayne Toporowski (1975)

7 Jonathan Bernier (1988)

8 Cody Franson (1987)

9 Larry Regan (1930), Lorne Stamler (1951), Rhys Thomson (1918)

10 Frank Dunlap (1924), Butch Keeling (1905)

11 Ken Linseman (1958), Dave Shand (1956)

13 Shayne Corson (1966), Mark Osborne (1961)

15 Marv Edwards (1935), Gary Yaremchuk (1961)

16 Garnet Exelby (1981), Ed Olczyk (1966)

17 Jim Dorey (1947), Buck Jones (1918), Jamie Macoun (1961)

18 Forbes Kennedy (1935)

19 Dave Dunn (1948)

22 George Ferguson (1952), Ken Hammond (1963), Eric Prentice (1926)

23 John Grisdale (1948), Glenn Healy (1962)

24 Gus Bodnar (1925), Wally Maxwell (1933), Gil Mayer (1930), Randy Murray (1945)

25 Bill Derlago (1958), Harry Mummery (1889), Pete Stemkowski (1943)

26 Alex Foster (1984), Chris McRae (1965)

27 Petter Granberg (1992), Stanton Jackson (1898), Brad Leeb (1979)

28 Andy Bathgate (1932), Tom Fitzgerald (1968), Jonas Frogren (1980), Darby Hendrickson (1972)

29 Baz Bastien (1919), Brian Glennie (1946), Dan Hodgson (1965), Jonas Hoglund (1972)

31 Jamie Baker (1966), Brian Conacher (1941), Guy Larose (1967), Gerry O'Flaherty (1950), Ron Zanussi (1956)

SEPTEMBER

1 Dale DeGray (1963)

2 Jason Blake (1973)

3 Martin Gerber (1974), Gary Jarrett (1942), Gerry Meehan (1946), Brian Spencer (1949)

4 Ray Gariepy (1928), Jeff Hamilton (1977), Sergio Momesso (1965), Bert Olmstead (1926)

6 Rolly Huard (1902), Igor Korolev (1970), Bill Root (1959)

7 Orland Kurtenbach (1936), Paul Marshall (1960)

8 Paul DiPietro (1970)

9 Bob Baun (1936)

10 Staffan Kronwall (1982), Joe Nieuwendyk (1966), Jim Pappin (1939)

11 Mike Byers (1946), Shep Mayer (1923)

12 Joe Lundrigan (1948), Earl Miller (1905), Paul Ranger (1984), Ron Ward (1944)

13 Harold Darragh (1902), Don Simmons (1931), Phil Stein (1913)

14 Chris Evans (1946), Tom Kurvers (1962), Craig Laughlin (1957)

15 Bob Liddington (1948), Joel Quenneville (1958)

16 Stewart Adams (1904), Pierre Hamel (1952), Rick Lanz (1961), Bob Wren (1974)

18 Jack Bionda (1933), Darryl Sittler (1950)

19 Don Beaupre (1961), Rick DiPietro (1981), Milan Marcetta (1936), Mikael Tellqvist (1979)

22 Gerry Foley (1932), Gerry McNamara (1934)

23 Joffrey Lupul (1983), Dixon Ward (1968)

24 Tim Ecclestone (1947), Toots Holway (1902), Dan Maloney (1950), Curt Ridley (1951)

25 Frank Bialowas (1969), George Boothman (1916), Ed Gorman (1892)

26 Bob Sykes (1951)

27 Wally Boyer (1937), Miroslav Frycer (1959), Al MacNeil (1935)

28 Don Edwards (1955), Grant Fuhr (1962), Syd Howe (1911), Windy O'Neill (1923), Rod Smylie (1895)

29 Dave Andreychuk (1963), Mark Fraser (1986), Matt Lashoff (1986), Mike Pelyk (1947), Ray Timgren (1928)

OCTOBER

1 Danny Johnson (1944), Larry Keenan (1940)

2 Glenn Anderson (1960), Bruce Draper (1940), Bill Kitchen (1960), Don Luce (1948), Glen Wesley (1968)

3 Mike Johnson (1974), Phil Kessel (1987), Michel Larocque (1976), Daniel Marois (1968)

5 Lorne Chabot (1900)

6 Kenny Jonsson (1974), Phil Maloney (1927), Bill Stewart (1957)

7 Garth Boesch (1920)

8 Kevyn Adams (1974), Fredrik Modin (1974)

9 Al Rollins (1926), Wayne Thomas (1947)

11 Jim Morrison (1931), Mike Neville (1904)

12 Danny Cox (1903), Larry Jeffrey (1940), Randy Wood (1963)

13 Rod Schutt (1956)

14 Sylvain Lefebvre (1967)

15 Jack Howard (1911), Rocky Saganiuk (1957), Lefty Wilson (1919)

16 Stew Adams (1904), Tom Martin (1947), Wilf Paiement (1955)

17 Norm Armstrong (1938)

19 Pete Bellefeuille (1901)

20 Murray McLachlan (1948), Garry Monahan (1946)

21 Bill Berg (1967), Carl Brewer (1938), Larry Mickey (1943), Vince Tremblay (1959)

22 Bill Brydge (1898), Gerry James (1934), Fred Robertson (1911), Ron Sedlbauer (1954), Terry Yake (1968)

23 Gord Drillon (1913)

24 Jamal Mayers (1974), Clarke Wilm (1976)

25 Kelly Chase (1967), Wendel Clark (1966), John MacMillan (1935), Terry Martin (1955)

27 Casey Bailey (1991), Frank McCool (1918)

28 Benoît Hogue (1966), Les Kozak (1940), Gary Nylund (1963)

29 Mike Gartner (1959), Hank Goldup (1918), Bill Juzda (1920)

30 Cal Gardner (1924)

31 Mickey Blake (1912), Kim Davis (1957), Jimmy Herbert (1897), Bob Manno (1956), Bucko McDonald (1914), Eric Nesterenko (1933)

NOVEMBER

1 Al Arbour (1932), Tie Domi (1969)

2 Doug Baldwin (1922), David Cooper (1973), Rick Ley (1948), Jason Smith (1973), Ted Stackhouse (1894)

3 Gerry Ehman (1932), Jay Harrison (1982)

4 Lloyd Andrews (1900), John Arundel (1927), Pete Langelle (1917), Howie Meeker (1924), Harry Meeking (1894), Corey Schwab (1970)

5 Sergei Berezin (1971), Baldy Cotton (1902), Brian Curran (1963)

6 Joe Klukay (1922)

7 Rusty Crawford (1885), Jack Forsey (1914)

8 Johnny Bower (1924), Bob Gracie (1910)

9 Todd Gill (1965), Bob Neely (1953)

10 Al Smith (1945), Bill Sutherland (1934)

11 Brian Cullen (1933), Harry Lumley (1926)

12 Greg Hubick (1951)

13 Patrik Augusta (1969)

14 Greg Andrusak (1969), Aaron Broten (1960), Murray Oliver (1937), Rod Seiling (1944)

15 Bobby Copp (1918), Yannick Tremblay (1975)

16 Dick Gamble (1928), Brent Imlach (1946)

18 Roger Jenkins (1911), Rudy Migay (1928)

19 Miroslav Ihnacak (1962), Dmitri Yushkevich (1971)

23 Colby Armstrong (1982), John Craighead (1971), Paul Knox (1933)

24 David Booth (1984), Eddie Johnston (1935)

25 Bill Carson (1900), John-Michael Liles (1980)

26 Dave Hannan (1961), Randy Osburn (1952)

27 Chad Kilger (1976), Chris Kotsopoulos (1958), Garry Valk (1967)

28 Terry Johnson (1958), Gerry Munro (1897)

29 Bobby Dawes (1924), Brad May (1971), Art Smith (1906)

30 Sweeney Schriner (1911), Tod Sloan (1927)

DECEMBER

1 Willie Marshall (1931), Jim McKenny (1946), Paddy Nolan (1897)

2 Rich Sutter (1963)

4 Gary Sabourin (1943)

5 Niklas Hagman (1979), Olli Jokinen (1978), Joakim Lindstrom (1983)

7 Gerry Cheevers (1940), James Jarvis (1907), Garry Unger (1947)

8 Kenny Girard (1936), Nathan Perrott (1976)

9 Bruce Dowie (1962), Noel Price (1935)

11 Dave Gagner (1964), Ted Hampson (1936), Ralph Intranuovo (1973), Mike Nykoluk (1934), Jean-Paul Parisé (1941), Pierre Pilote (1931)

12 Ted Kennedy (1925), Beattie Ramsay (1895)

13 Bates Battaglia (1975), Blair MacKasey (1955), Bob Warner (1950)

14 Eric Pettinger (1904), Ken Randall (1888), Mike Santorelli (1985)

15 Art Jackson (1915)

17 Craig Berube (1965), Vincent Damphousse (1967)

18 Jeff Finger (1979)

19 Scott Pearson (1969)

20 Charlie Conacher (1909), Travis Green (1970)

22 Paul Fenton (1959), Ian Turnbull (1953)

23 Karel Pilar (1977), Bob Solinger (1925)

25 Larry Cahan (1933), Dmitri Mironov (1965)

26 Norm Ullman (1935)

28 Phil Samis (1927), Terry Sawchuk (1929)

30 Kevin Dahl (1968), Mike Stevens (1965), Jim Thomson (1965)

31 Red Heron (1917), Gary McAdam (1955), René Robert (1948)

LEAFS BY BIRTHPLACE

BY COUNTRY		
Canada	756	
United States	83	K. Adams, Bailey, Barrasso, Battaglia, Berard, J. Blake, Brennan, Britz, Broten, M. Brown, Brubaker, Capuano, Clemmensen, Connolly, R. Costello, Crabb, D'Amigo, Eakins, Earl, Ellett, Erixon, Fairchild, Farkas, Fauss, Fenton, Fergus, Finger, Fitzgerald, Foley, Foster, Gardiner, Gill, Gleason, Haggerty, Jeff Hamilton, Hanson, Hendrickson, Hollweg, Housley, Iafrate, V. James, Jenkins, C. Johnson, Kessel, Klee, Komisarek, Korn, Kurvers, Lashoff, Lebda, Leetch, Levinsky, Liles, M. Martin, McCreary, Mummery, O'Flaherty, Olczyk, Pederson, Pohl, T. Pratt, Presley, Reynolds, Rhodes, M. Roach, Romnes, D. Sacco, J. Sacco, Schneider, Serowik, Sifers, Smedsmo, Spring, Stapleton, Steckel, Stempniak, van Riemsdyk, Voss, Walker, Westrum, Wolanin, Wood, Wozniewski
Sweden	22	Eriksson, Frogren, Granberg, Gunnarsson, Gustafsson, Gustavsson, Hammarstrom, Hedin, Hoglund, C. Johansson, Jonsson, S. Kronwall, Lindstrom, Modin, Renberg, Salming, Sjostrom, Stalberg, Stralman, Sundin, Tellqvist, Wallin
Czechoslovakia/ Czech Republic	19	Augusta, Crha, Duris, Frycer, M. Ihnacak, P. Ihnacak, Kaberle, Kohn, Kubina, Lanz, Nedved, Panik, Pilar, Prochazka, Polak, Reichel, Stastny, Svoboda, Tlusty
Soviet Union/ Russia	19	Antropov, Berezin, Borschevsky, Godynyuk, Karpovtsev, Khavanov, Komarov, Kondratiev, Korolev, Kudashov, Kulemin, Markov, Mironov, Mogilny, Ponikarovsky, Schriner, Suglobov, Yakushin, Yushkevich
Finland	7	Berg, Hagman, Jokinen, Lumme, Pudas, Rynnas, Toskala
Great Britain	4	Mann, Pettinger, Robertson, S. Thomas
Germany	3	Grabovski, Holzer, Mueller
Scotland	2	C. Blair, Gray
Bahamas	1	Deveaux
Northern Ireland	1	O. Nolan
Norway	1	B. Johnson
Poland	1	Czerkawski
Slovakia	1	Svehla
Switzerland	1	Gerber
Wales	1	C. Thomas
Ukraine	1	Khristich

Ontario	455	
Quebec	70	J-S Aubin, N. Aubin, Beauchemin, A. Bélanger, Bellefeuille, Bernier, Bibeault, Boisvert, Carey, Carrière, Centomo, Chabot, Chamberlain, Cleghorn, Côté, Cousineau, Damphousse, Daoust, DeBlois, Dupéré, Dupuis, Finnigan, Gamache, Giguère, Gingras, Gorman, P. Hamel, Hinse, Hogue, Jacobs, Jarry, E. Johnston, R. Johnstone, Keon, Krushelnyski, Lacroix, Larocque, Larose, Lefebvre, Lombardi, MacKell, D. Marois, J. Marois, D. Marshall, J. McDonald, McKenna, G. McRae, Momesso, D. Moore, Morrison, Bernie Parent, Perreault, Petit, Picard, Pilote, J. Plante, Potvin, Pronovost, Reaume, Ritchie, Robert, Robidas, Sloan, Thibaudeau, V. Tremblay, Y. Tremblay, Trottier, Turnbull, P. White, Zettler
Saskatchewan	68	Aldcorn, C. Armstrong, M. Armstrong, Aulie, Baun, Belak, Bentley, Blaisdell, Boesch, Boll, Boschman, Bower, Bozak, Brossart, Butcher, L. Carr, Chase, Church, Clark, Corrigan, Dahl, Dawes, Dundas, Dunn, Ehman, Esau, Exelby, Flaman, Forsey, Garland, Hampson, Hassard, Heward, Hubick, G. James, Jennings, Kirton, Kozak, Kurtenbach, Litzenberger, Lynn, Manson, Marchinko, Marker, Masnick, McAllister, L. McIntyre, Melrose, D. Metz, N. Metz, Miller, Nelson, Olmstead, Ramsay, Rollins, Rupp, Schenn, Schwab, Snell, Solinger, Stephenson, Sutherland, Toporowski, Veitch, Watson, J. Williams, T. Williams, Wilm
Alberta	62	S. Adams, Benning, Berube, Boothman, Colborne, Cross, Dempsey, Diduck, Edmundson, Erickson, Flett, Frattin, Fuhr, Greig, Jim Harrison, Healey, Hodgson, Holden, T. Johnson, Joyal, Kordic, Leeb, Liddington, Lundmark, Lupul, MacArthur, J. MacMillan, MacWilliams, Magnan, Manderville, Marcetta, McCool, McCormack, L. McDonald, McGill, Mickey, Moffat, Mulhern, Ondrus, Phaneuf, Pogge, Raymond, Rosehill, Saganiuk, Samis, Scrivens, Shand, J. Smith, R. Stewart, R. Sutter, Tucker, Ullman, Unger, Valk, Versteeg, Verstraete, D. Ward, Weir, B. Wesley, G. Wesley, G. Yaremchuk, K. Yaremchuk
Manitoba	58	Arundel, Ashton, Baldwin, Bathgate, Baumgartner, E. Belfour, G. Bell, Bialowas, A. Blair, Bodie, Bohonos, Boyer, Broda, Buchanan, Burega, A. Carr, Crozier, Davis, Derlago, Dickens, Ezinicki, C. Gardner, Halderson, Hill, D. Johnson, Juzda, Kendall, Kidd, Kolesar, Langelle, Laxdal, Loughlin, Low, Mathers, B. Maxwell, McCreedy, McLaren, McLean, Nesterenko, C. Orr, C. Plante, W. Pratt, Reimer, C. Ridley, M. Ridley, Sawchuk, Semenko, Stamler, Stanowski, Steen, Stemkowski, Stoughton, B. Taylor, H. Taylor, J. Thomson, I. White, C. Wilson, Wregget
British Columbia	20	G. Anderson, Andrusak, Ashby, E. Brewer, Courtnall, Craighead, Franson, T. Green, M. Kennedy, Maggs, Maniago, Nylund, O'Byrne, Podollan, Rielly, Rouse, Smithson, Spencer, Tomlinson, Yake
Nova Scotia	8	Hollett, S. Jackson, J. MacDonald, P. MacDonald, MacLean, MacNeil, Sill, Stackhouse
New Brunswick	6	Copp, Drillon, D. Gamble, Higgins, F. Kennedy, Stuart
Prince Edward Island	4	Boyce, B. MacMillan, P. Nolan, Thompson
Newfoundland	3	Druken, Faulkner, Lundrigan

LEAFS ACQUIRE KING CLANCY FROM OTTAWA

OCTOBER 11, 1930

Never before or since has a player of King Clancy's calibre been acquired with money made at the racetrack. But Leafs owner Conn Smythe was a horseman through and through, and when he placed a large wager on a filly named Rare Jewel, he knew what he was doing. The bet paid out, and that money gave Smythe the freedom to contact the financially struggling Ottawa Senators, ready to bargain. The deal was made for $35,000—at that point the largest sum ever paid for a player—and the Leafs got a personality who would remain associated with the team for six decades. Smythe included Art Smith and Eric Pettinger in the deal, but both played only one middling season in the nation's capital. It was the cash Ottawa needed more than the players.

Clancy was an all-star in every sense of the word. Small but ridiculously feisty, he was a skilled defenceman who stood up for his teammates. Though he got himself pummelled more often than not, he earned the love of his colleagues along the way. A proud Irishman, he was as good on the ice with a joke as he was with a hit.

The Senators finished in last place in 1930–31 and the team suspended operations at season's end, the Smythe money not nearly enough to staunch the flow out the door. Clancy, meanwhile, partnered with Hap Day on the Toronto blue line, providing the team with all-star defending every game.

Clancy proved so popular that on March 17, 1934 (St. Patrick's Day), he became the first Leafs player to be given a special night of honour at Maple Leaf Gardens. And it was one to remember. Decked out in green finery, he was paraded out to centre ice in a large sleigh. After gifts and celebrations, he kept his green sweater on for the game, only to have the Rangers complain, forcing him to return to the Blue and White.

After nearly seven seasons with the Leafs, Clancy retired in 1937, but by this time he had helped the Leafs to win the Stanley Cup in 1932 and advance to the finals on two other occasions. He later became an NHL referee and in 1953 assumed head coaching duties for the Leafs, eventually taking up the role of assistant general manager. Clancy was inducted into the Hockey Hall of Fame in 1958 and was involved with the team until his death on November 8, 1986.

The Leafs donated the King Clancy Trophy to the NHL, awarded annually since 1988 to "the player who best exemplifies leadership qualities on and off the ice and has made a noteworthy contribution to his community." Later, the Leafs honoured his—and Tim Horton's—number 7, and their banners hang from the rafters of Air Canada Centre forevermore.

Clancy sits on a float during King Clancy Night at Maple Leaf Gardens, March, 17, 1934

SWEENEY SCHRINER WORTH THE PRICE

MAY 18, 1939

The 1930s were both cruel and kind to the Leafs under coach Dick Irvin. The team won the Stanley Cup in 1932—a tremendous feat, of course—but they also lost five of the six Cup finals they went to during that decade. Conn Smythe knew something had to be done, and Red Dutton, the general manager of the New York Americans, was also in the mood to try to cure his team of lethargy. And so Smythe and Dutton made a blockbuster deal that reverberated throughout the league: Buzz Boll, Busher Jackson, Doc Romnes, Jim Fowler, and Murray Armstrong to the New York Americans for Sweeney Schriner.

The deal was a shocker for many reasons. Schriner had been awarded the Calder Trophy four years earlier, and that early admiration proved well earned. He won the scoring championship the next two years—narrowly missing out on a third in a row—and was clearly one of the best players in the league, playing for one of the worst teams.

Busher Jackson was a deity in Toronto, a longtime member of the famous Kid Line, and a top scorer in his own right. But his production had slipped and he had fallen into Smythe's black books as a result of his colourful nights out. In truth, the core of the deal was Jackson for Schriner, but Dutton also regarded Armstrong highly and thought of him as a lure. Nonetheless, it was the Leafs who scored big with this one. Schriner was with the Leafs for six productive years, helping the team to the three Cup finals—two of which they won, in 1942 and 1945.

Indeed, Schriner was a central figure in the 1942 finals, when the Leafs rallied from being down three games to none. The Detroit Red Wings had a 1–0 lead in the ultimate game, but Schriner scored his first to tie the game and then added an insurance goal in a 3–1 victory. He was inducted into the Hockey Hall of Fame in 1962.

Dutton's acquisitions played well, but on a team destined for underachieving. Finances were always a worry, and by 1942 the Americans had folded, leaving the NHL with six clubs for the next 25 years.

Armstrong's greater glory came after he retired. He coached at the University of Denver, where he pioneered the practice of recruiting Canadians—today a common strategy at all Division I colleges in the NCAA. He coached Denver for 21 years and won five national championships.

Sweeney Schriner (left) and Frank McCool in the dressing room on April 6, 1945, after the 1–0 win over Detroit in game one of the Stanley Cup finals

LEAFS ACQUIRE A LEGEND

SEPTEMBER 10, 1943

Sometimes circumstances other than a player's skill or a team's need result in a player changing teams, and such was the case with Ted Kennedy, a one-time prospect of the Montreal Canadiens who never got to play a game with the Habs but who became a legend with their archrivals, the Maple Leafs.

A teenaged Kennedy had been playing junior hockey in Montreal but returned home to Port Colborne, Ontario, because he was homesick. The great Nels Stewart, by this time a coach in Kennedy's hometown, offered to take the youngster under his wing and suggested to the Leafs that they acquire him. The difficulty lay in the fact that owner and GM Conn Smythe was overseas and had instructed his friend and assistant, Frank Selke, not to make any trades without consulting him first. But time was of the essence, and the deal was too good to pass up, so Selke traded Frank Eddolls to the Canadiens for Kennedy.

Eddolls had been a top prospect at one point, but his stock had dropped after he suffered a knee injury that put his career in jeopardy. The Habs were convinced he would recover, and they felt encumbered by Kennedy's recalcitrance to return to Montreal, so the deal was made.

Eddolls's portfolio looks awfully thin. He had an unimpressive year with Montreal in 1944–45 and spent much of the next two years in the minors. The Habs traded him to the Rangers, where he played for parts of five seasons, but he didn't distinguish himself. Ted Kennedy, by contrast, became one of the greatest Leafs of all time, a Hall of Famer, a captain and Cup champion—a hero remembered to this very day for his leadership and accomplishments. He averaged a point a game as a rookie and displayed a tenacity that inspired those around him.

In the 1945 playoffs, he and linemates Bob Davidson and Mel Hill shut down the potent Maurice Richard line, eliminating Montreal in six games en route to a dramatic Cup win over Detroit in the finals. Two years later, Kennedy scored the Cup-winning goal.

In the fall of 1948, Kennedy was named captain upon the retirement of another legend, Syl Apps. The Leafs won the Cup again in 1949 and in 1951, and during their four Cup victories in the 1940s it was Kennedy who was the team's leading playoff scorer each year. In 1954–55, Kennedy was awarded the Hart Trophy in his last full season. He retired that summer, but a year and a half later—with the Leafs off to a poor start—Smythe coaxed him back onto the ice for the last half of the season.

In all, "Teeder" played 696 regular-season games with the Leafs, won the Cup five times, and was inducted into the Hockey Hall of Fame in 1966. His number 9 was honoured by the Leafs in 1993, and he remains one of the cornerstones of the franchise's glorious history.

BENTLEY THE BEST IN BLOCKBUSTER

NOVEMBER 2, 1947

Syl Apps, ever the team player, informed Leafs GM Conn Smythe before the start of the 1947–48 season that the upcoming year would be his last. The classy captain had done it all with the team, but he wanted to tackle new challenges—and he wanted to go out on top so that fans would remember him for his great skills, not for playing past his prime.

Smythe had long admired the skill of Max Bentley, the slick Chicago centre, and Bentley was playing on a team that had finished last in the regular-season standings the previous year with a dismal record of 19–37–4. When the Hawks got off to another dreadful start in the 1947–48 season, Smythe saw an opportunity.

Bentley played on a famous line with his brother Doug and Bill Mosienko. Dubbed the Pony Line because they were all small and fast, they led the Chicago offence. Indeed, Max had won the Art Ross Trophy the past two years, and all three had finished among the top 10 leading scorers the previous year.

In the end, Smythe acquired Max and Cy Thomas for a quintet of front-line Leafs: Gus Bodnar, Bud Poile, Gaye Stewart, Bob Goldham, and Ernie Dickens. It was a dramatic gamble for the Hawks to give up their best player, but they needed to do something. For Smythe, volume was an acceptable sacrifice to get the best player in the deal.

The trade helped the Leafs improve, but it damaged the Hawks to the same degree. Toronto cruised to an impressive first-place finish in the regular season before going on to a second straight Stanley Cup win. The Hawks finished in last place again and missed the playoffs. This was a period that saw Chicago appear in the postseason only once in a dozen years, finishing dead last in the league nine times. They'd acquired five new forwards, but it was defence that was their undoing.

Many of the players the Hawks acquired were soon traded in other multiplayer deals. Bodnar, who remained with Chicago for seven seasons, was the longest survivor, while Poile was traded a year and a half later in a five-player deal with Detroit; Stewart and Goldham were also sent to the Red Wings in a huge nine-player swap in the summer of 1950; Dickens retired as a Hawk after four years.

Bentley wasn't Syl Apps, but he was a star centre who stayed with the Leafs for the better part of six seasons, helping the team to three Stanley Cups. He was both a scorer and passer, a dual skill much admired by Smythe, and his speed and stickhandling were intimidating as he drove into the opposition end. Smythe's foresight and Chicago's desperation produced a lopsided deal that had ramifications for both teams for several years.

(l to r): Cy Thomas, Max Bentley, and Joe Klukay

Kelly hugs the Stanley Cup in 1963

RED KELLY COMES TO THE LEAFS AS A CENTREMAN

FEBRUARY 10, 1960

An unassuming man rather than a polished superstar, Red Kelly was one of the greatest players in NHL history and the only man to star during two dynasties with different teams—and in different positions.

Kelly was an all-star defenceman with the Red Wings during the first half of the 1950s. These were Detroit's greatest years, when they won the Stanley Cup four times in a six-year stretch—1950, 1952, 1954, and 1955. Kelly was the inaugural recipient of the Norris Trophy in 1954–55, and was given the Lady Byng Trophy for gentlemanly play three times during these championship seasons. In every year between 1949 and 1957, he was named to either the First or Second All-Star Team, the only defenceman to be honoured with such consistency. Kelly was a superb skater who could rush the puck out of his own end, but he was also defensively responsible and clever with his body.

But as the 1950s advanced, it was clear that Montreal was the team to beat and the Red Wings' fortunes faded. Worse for Kelly, he and general manager Jack Adams didn't see eye to eye during the toughest days of his career. Finally, on February 5, 1960, Adams traded Kelly and Billy McNeill to the Rangers for Bill Gadsby and Eddie Shack.

Both Red Wings players refused to go, and Kelly announced his retirement. NHL president Clarence Campbell had no choice but to nullify the deal, much to the disappointment of Adams. However, a week and a half later, the GM struck another deal: Kelly was sent to Toronto for Marc Reaume.

Leafs coach Punch Imlach immediately moved Kelly from defence to centre, a curious move given that older players often make the opposite move, to where speed and skating aren't as important as positional play. But Imlach knew Kelly's assets were still his speed and skating, and Kelly responded with seven sensational seasons and four Stanley Cup victories.

Kelly played on a line with Frank Mahovlich, centring the Big M during his most productive seasons. Kelly also won a fourth Byng Trophy in 1960–61. A year later, he was making history of another sort, acting as an elected member of Parliament while playing full time in the NHL. He travelled weekly between Toronto and Ottawa in order to act in both capacities, and in the spring of 1962, while a sitting MP, he won the Stanley Cup with the Leafs for the first time.

Reaume, a fifth defenceman with the Leafs, had a far less successful tenure with the Red Wings. He played only half a season before finding himself in the American Hockey League, playing only a few games in the NHL after expansion. This was, in every sense, one of the most one-sided trades in NHL history.

Kelly retired in 1967 and turned to coaching with the expansion Los Angeles Kings. In 1969, he became only the fourth player to have the waiting period waived for his induction into the Hockey Hall of Fame. Of those players who have never played for Montreal, he remains the only NHLer to win the Stanley Cup eight times.

MULTI-PLAYER SWAP KEYS A CUP WIN

FEBRUARY 22, 1964

Some trades are the result of months of talks and can be seen coming; others are bolts that come from nowhere. The Leafs had won the Cup in 1962 and again in 1963, the latter arguably their most impressive victory of the postwar era. They finished atop the regular-season standings with 35 wins and 82 points, and they lost only two of 10 playoff games during their championship run.

The 1963–64 team was performing at a comparable level, but Montreal and Chicago were doing even better. Late in the season, Leafs coach Punch Imlach was unsatisfied, so he made a huge, successful, and controversial trade with the New York Rangers. Rising stars Dick Duff, Rod Seiling, and Bob Nevin, along with Arnie Brown and Bill Collins, were sent to the Blueshirts in exchange for two established stars: Andy Bathgate and Don McKenney. It was a deal that would help the Leafs in the immediate future and New York in the long term. Bathgate, after all, had won the Hart Trophy in 1958–59 and had been selected to the end-of-year All-Star Team four times.

By season's end, the Rangers were still out of the playoffs, finishing fifth and winning only 22 games of 70. The Leafs finished with 78 points, only four fewer than the previous year, but they were in third place rather than first. Nevertheless, they went on to win the Cup, in large measure because of the contributions of Bathgate and McKenney. Some players, however, quietly noted that this time they needed two seven-game series to clinch the win.

Though he made an important contribution to the 1964 Cup-winning campaign, Bathgate was a star player coming to a team that played not as individuals but as a group. The Leafs had no superstar, only a team that played with incredible cohesion. Bathgate had trouble adapting, despite his many skills, and the fit was less than perfect.

The Leafs failed to win the Cup in either 1965 or 1966, and Bathgate was traded again, to Detroit, in another multiplayer deal. He and Billy Harris went to the Red Wings, and Marcel Pronovost and Larry Jeffrey came to the Leafs. McKenney, too, lasted only one more season before he was claimed by Detroit in the waiver draft.

Duff, meanwhile, ended up in Montreal after half a season with New York and was a star for the Canadiens, leading the team to the Cup four times. Nevin soon became captain of the Rangers and stayed with the team for seven seasons. Although they never won the Cup during this era, they did become a top NHL team after expansion, while the Leafs fell out of contention.

Seiling was a stud on the New York blue line for 10 years, while Brown formed a defensive partnership with Harry Howell, who won the Norris Trophy in 1967, making him the last player not named Orr to do so for the next eight seasons.

Nevin (left) and Duff celebrate following the 2–1 win over Chicago in game six of the 1962 Stanley Cup final

THE END OF THE MAHOVLICH ERA

MARCH 3, 1968

Like any superstar player, Frank Mahovlich was always front and centre. When the team won, he got most of the credit; when the team lost, he shouldered much of the blame.

For Mahovlich, that team was the 1960s Maple Leafs. The Big M was so good that Chicago offered a million dollars for his services in 1962. He was a brilliant left winger, but the smooth-skating stride that looked good in victory looked lazy in defeat.

Perhaps the 1960–61 season said it all, both pro and con. By the 56-game mark, Mahovlich had 48 goals and looked certain to become only the second player after Maurice Richard to join the half-century club. But each game down the stretch saw him go goalless, and he ended the season still at 48. A great number, to be sure, but a disappointment given his incredible season.

Mahovlich was frequently at odds with coach and GM Punch Imlach. Their stormy relationship lasted nearly a decade, neither man dealing with the other's personality particularly well. Imlach liked to motivate through threats and tough talk; Mahovlich withdrew when such motivation came his way.

By the midway point of the 1967–68 season, it was clear the Leafs were not going to make the playoffs, a first during the Imlach era. Their run of four Cup wins in six seasons was a distant memory after expansion, and Mahovlich took leave of the team early in 1967–68.

On March 3, 1968, Imlach made a sensational trade. He sent Mahovlich, Pete Stemkowski, Garry Unger, and the rights to Carl Brewer to Detroit for Norm Ullman, Paul Henderson, Floyd Smith, and Doug Barrie. The Big M was no longer number 27 on the Leafs' port side. Instead, the team had a great veteran in Ullman, a promising youngster in Henderson, and two other players who never managed to leave much of a mark on the team.

Mahovlich still had many miles left in his skates. He played with the Wings on a line with Gordie Howe and Alex Delvecchio, scoring 49 goals in 1968–69 (narrowly missing out on that elusive half-century for a second time). After Detroit traded him to Montreal, he won the Cup twice more before moving to the World Hockey Association.

Stemkowski had several more serviceable years in the league, while Unger became the NHL's Iron Man, playing in 914 consecutive games. Brewer, who had also been at odds with Imlach, retired, was reinstated as an amateur, and then joined the Red Wings in 1969.

The Leafs got their money's worth in Ullman, though. He played on a line with youngsters Henderson and Ron Ellis, forming a highly productive trio for several years. That success didn't translate to team wins in the playoffs, however, and Ullman, aging and looking for ice time, left for the World Hockey Association in 1975.

Henderson had his best year in 1971–72, when he had 38 goals for the Leafs. This great season earned him an invitation, along with Ellis, to Team Canada's training camp for the 1972 Summit Series. The rest, as they say, is history.

FLETCHER'S MAMMOTH REBUILD STARTS WITH FUHR

SEPTEMBER 19, 1991

When the new president and general manager of the Leafs was introduced at a press conference on June 4, 1991, few could have foreseen the rapidity with which Cliff Fletcher took a struggling team and made it a Stanley Cup contender.

Owner Harold Ballard had passed away on April 11, 1990, and interim boss Donald Crump made it his first priority to find a new man to head up the club's hockey operations. With no experience in such matters, he called around the league to enquire as to who the best man might be, and the name Cliff Fletcher was repeated to him many times over.

Fletcher had made the Atlanta/Calgary Flames into a Cup contender and then, in 1989, a Cup winner. Taking the logical first step, he determined that the team needed a star goalie first and foremost—a masked marvel who could give the Leafs a chance at victory every time he donned the pads.

For the 1990–91 season, the team had used Jeff Reese and Peter Ing, a tandem that finished second-worst in goals-against average. But Fletcher knew he could deal with Edmonton general manager Glen Sather. The Oilers had goalie Grant Fuhr, who was suspended indefinitely. In February 1991, he was reinstated, but the Oilers already had Bill Ranford as their number-one goaltender.

During training camp in 1991— the Leafs having finished 20th out of 21 teams the previous season—Fletcher acquired Grant Fuhr, Glenn Anderson, and Craig Berube for Vincent Damphousse, Peter Ing, Scott Thornton,

Luke Richardson, and future considerations. It was a huge deal that had an immediate effect on the team's on-ice performance, as well as giving Fletcher credibility in the eyes of the millions of Leafs fans from coast to coast.

The Leafs were giving up two key ingredients on their team—Damphousse, their top scorer, and Richardson, a hard-hitting, stay-at-home defenceman—but they got two sensational players in return.

Grant Fuhr was the finest goalie of the 1980s. Wayne Gretzky often said that the Oilers won all of those Cups because of Fuhr, who backstopped the team to five championships in eight years and who was often left alone as the last line of defence while the high-scoring forwards did their thing at the other end of the ice. Acrobatic, with the right temperament for a goalie—calm, unfazed, relaxed—he brought the Leafs up to 14th in GAA in his first year. More importantly, he gave Fletcher time to work on more trades. As luck would have it, rookie Félix Potvin would emerge a year and a half later, making Fuhr himself available as part of another blockbuster deal.

Anderson was a winner, plain and simple. One of the top-scoring forwards of the 1980s, he was a clutch performer in the playoffs and he more than compensated for the loss of Damphousse. Like Fuhr, he brought a winning aura with him and was a significant addition to the team, both symbolically (coming from the great Oilers) and through his play on the ice.

Fuhr in the net for the Leafs

BIGGEST DEAL EVER LANDS LEAFS DOUGIE

JANUARY 2, 1992

Cliff Fletcher had made his mark with the deal to land Grant Fuhr, but that was only stage one of a massive rebuild that culminated midway through the 1991–92 season in a huge trade with his old team, the Calgary Flames.

One of the key players from Calgary's 1989 Cup win was diminutive centre Doug Gilmour, but over the next two years he became dissatisfied with his contractual situation and asked for a trade. Fletcher knew the team's GM—it was none other than Doug Risebrough, the former player whom Fletcher had tutored while in Calgary. The two men talked about needs and troubles. The Leafs may have had Fuhr in goal, but their inability to score was only too evident. Risebrough needed to get value for a player who could leave at the end of the season and who had left the team the previous day.

The talk turned to other players and other needs, and by the time all was said and done, the men had agreed to the largest deal in NHL history. Ten players swapped teams, five going each way. The Leafs acquired Doug Gilmour, Jamie Macoun, Ric Nattress, Kent Manderville, and Rick Wamsley; they gave up Gary Leeman, Alexander Godynyuk, Jeff Reese, Michel Petit, and Craig Berube.

It is almost impossible to view this trade as anything but a swindle. Gilmour became the face of the Leafs for the next several years. He set records for most assists

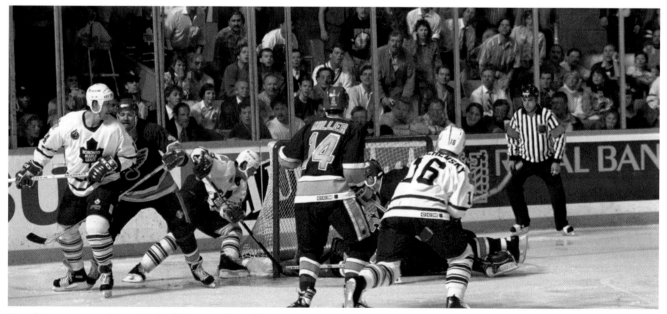

One of the most memorable goals in Leafs history was Doug Gilmour's overtime winner against Curtis Joseph and the St. Louis Blues

and points in a season, led the team to two appearances in the Campbell Conference finals, and was the epitome of determination, hustle, and skill. His competitive fire was unmatched.

Macoun and Nattress had formed a defensive tandem that was the foundation of Calgary's Cup win, and they were transported to the Leafs blue line to play the same roles (although Macoun had a longer-lasting impact). Manderville and Wamsley were important pieces of the larger puzzle. None of the Flames' acquisitions had any impact on their new team.

Still, the Leafs were a work in progress. Although Gilmour was brilliant from the moment he arrived, the team missed the playoffs, albeit narrowly, in 1991–92. That summer, Fletcher hired Pat Burns as bench boss. The gruff former cop was a no-nonsense, defensive-minded coach who brought order to Toronto's play.

The 1992–93 season was one of the most important in the modern history of the franchise. In addition to Félix Potvin in goal, and the Calgary defence pairing, the team had Gilmour to lead the attack. Then Fletcher added Dave Andreychuk from Buffalo, a big, awkward player who scored dozens of goals from in close.

Gilmour had 95 assists and 127 points that year, both records, and the Leafs finished with 99 points. "Dougie" was runner-up to Mario Lemieux for the Hart Trophy, but the Leafs made a great run in the playoffs, knocking out Detroit in overtime of game seven at the Joe Louis Arena en route to the Campbell Conference finals. Their Cup campaign ended in game seven, on home ice, against Wayne Gretzky's hat-trick performance for Los Angeles.

Gilmour was made captain when Fletcher traded Wendel Clark to Quebec for Mats Sundin, and then was traded himself in 1997 once Sundin had taken over as the team's dominant player—as he would remain for more than a dozen years. In all, Gilmour had 452 points in 393 regular-season games with the Leafs and set a record for career playoff points with 77 in 52 games.

LEAFS GET SUNDIN . . .
BUT THE PRICE IS STEEP

JUNE 28, 1994

Some hockey players, no matter how talented, are just never embraced by a city's fans; others, no matter the talent, become instant heroes and focal points. Wendel Clark might not have been the biggest or most talented player in the 1985 NHL Entry Draft, but he was the first—and remains the only—first-overall selection in Leafs history, and he became an immediate hero.

Clark was a left winger who could do it all. His wrist shot was as good as any in the league. His ability to hit cleanly with full force was intimidating, and he was only too happy to back up his actions to fight in the name of creating a mood for a game, to defend a teammate, or simply offer a symbolic refusal to lie down and give up. These were his trademarks.

The Leafs had the number-one pick because of a dismal 1984–85 season, but Clark gave fans hope, gave them something to cheer about, gave them reason once again to "be-Leaf." As an 18-year-old rookie, he scored 34 goals and was a contender for the Calder Trophy. The next year, he reached 37 goals, but his style of play in a league that was starting to be dominated by larger players took its toll, notably on his back. Over the next three seasons, he missed significant time, playing only 81 games in that span.

Clark was soon named team captain and regained his strength, fought more judiciously, and focused more on scoring. Once Cliff Fletcher brought in Grant Fuhr, Doug Gilmour, and coach Pat Burns, Clark had plenty of support, responding with a career year in 1993–94, when he had 46 goals and 76 points.

Ever the brilliant strategist, Fletcher recognized that Clark might never have as good a year again, meaning his value would never be as great on the trade market. He also knew the team was close to the Cup finals, and at the 1994 draft, he went for broke, making a deal that was symbolically significant, and one he felt would help the Leafs. The Toronto GM traded captain Clark, Sylvain Lefebvre, Landon Wilson, and a first-round draft choice in 1994 (Jeff Kealty) to the Quebec Nordiques for Mats Sundin, Garth Butcher, Todd Warriner, and a first round pick in 1994 (Nolan Baumgartner).

The only non-Canadian captain in team history, Mats Sundin had his number 13 honoured by the team soon after he retired

Obviously, the core of the deal was Clark for Sundin. Mats was 23 years old to Clark's 28, had been the first-overall draft choice in 1989, and was a large, towering centreman who could take the punishment of the modern game. Sundin had scored 103 points in one season but had found himself in coach Pierre Pagé's doghouse. After talking to Swedish compatriot Borje Salming, Sundin realized how special it was to play in Toronto and welcomed the trade.

Sundin's arrival marked the transition from the Wendel-and-Dougie era to the Mats era. Gilmour was traded midway through the 1996–97 season, at which point number 13 became the first non-Canadian captain in Leafs history. And as Gilmour was vital to Pat Burns's success, so Sundin was to Pat Quinn when he became bench boss in 1998.

Sundin did not disappoint, and though it was difficult to accept that Clark had been traded, it was understandable why. Sundin led the team in scoring for 12 of the 13 years he was with the Leafs, and, as with Gilmour, Toronto twice appeared in the Eastern Conference finals, in 1999 and 2002. He was a point-a-game player with incredible consistency, and by the time he signed with Vancouver in 2008, he was the Leafs' all-time leader in both goals (420) and points (987).

NOTABLE DEBUTS

THE MOST SUCCESSFUL LEAF DEBUTS

(Maple Leafs who registered at least a point in their first NHL game)

PLAYER	NHL DEBUT	STATS	PLAYER	NHL DEBUT	STATS
Gaye Stewart	October 31, 1942	2 goals, 1 assist	Jack Church	December 10, 1938	1 assist
Gus Bodnar	October 30, 1943	2 goals, 1 assist*	Bud Poile	October 31, 1942	1 assist
Jack McLean	November 12, 1942	1 goal, 2 assists	Ted Kennedy	March 7, 1943	1 assist
Joe Matte	January 17, 1920	2 goals	Moe Morris	October 30, 1943	1 assist
Shep Mayer	October 31, 1942	2 goals	Frank Dunlap	November 6, 1943	1 assist
Jiri Tlusty	October 25, 2007	2 goals	Harry Taylor	November 17, 1946	1 assist
George Boothman	October 23, 1942	1 goal, 1 assist	Johnny McCormack	January 31, 1948	1 assist
Wally Boyer	December 11, 1965	1 goal, 1 assist	Léo Boivin	March 8, 1952	1 assist
Brad Selwood	October 11, 1970	1 goal, 1 assist	Ron Hurst	November 13, 1955	1 assist
Ron Wilson	March 4, 1978	1 goal, 1 assist	Bill Burega	January 14, 1956	1 assist
Charlie Sands	March 18, 1933	2 assists	Ted Hampson	October 10, 1959	1 assist
Lanny McDonald	October 10, 1973	2 assists	Rod Seiling	March 2, 1963	1 assist
Andy Blair	November 15, 1928	1 goal	Wayne Carleton	January 1, 1966	1 assist
Charlie Conacher	November 14, 1929	1 goal	Ken Murray	April 5, 1970	1 assist
Rolly Huard	December 13, 1930	1 goal	Rick Kehoe	January 1, 1972	1 assist
Bob Gracie	March 3, 1931	1 goal	Laurie Boschman	October 10, 1979	1 assist
Don Metz	November 19, 1939	1 goal	Greg Hotham	October 10, 1979	1 assist
Red Carr	October 30, 1943	1 goal	Bob McGill	October 6, 1981	1 assist
Don Webster	November 11, 1943	1 goal	Ernie Godden	November 28, 1981	1 assist
Garth Boesch	October 16, 1946	1 goal	Fred Perlini	December 30, 1981	1 assist
Gary Aldcorn	October 11, 1956	1 goal	Peter Ihnacak	October 6, 1982	1 assist
Les Kozak	January 13, 1962	1 goal	Dan Hodgson	October 16, 1985	1 assist
Red Armstrong	December 15, 1962	1 goal	Vincent Damphousse	October 9, 1986	1 assist
Claire Alexander	November 30, 1974	1 goal	Marty Dallman	March 9, 1988	1 assist
Mark Kirton	October 10, 1979	1 goal	Kent Manderville	March 4, 1992	1 assist
Miroslav Ihnacak	January 10, 1986	1 goal	Kelly Fairchild	March 20, 1996	1 assist
Daryl Evans	January 31, 1987	1 goal	Mike Johnson	March 16, 1997	1 assist
Daniel Marois	October 6, 1988	1 goal	Danny Markov	February 2, 1998	1 assist
David Sacco	March 4, 1994	1 goal	Nikolai Antropov	October 13, 1999	1 assist
Adam Mair	November 29, 1999	1 goal	Pierre Hedin	January 13, 2004	1 assist
Matt Stajan	April 5, 2003	1 goal	Ian White	March 26, 2006	1 assist
Jeremy Williams	April 18, 2006	1 goal	Tyler Bozak	October 13, 2009	1 assist
Nikolai Kulemin	October 9, 2008	1 goal	Viktor Stalberg	October 1, 2009	1 assist
Murph Chamberlain	November 4, 1937	1 assist	Ryan Hamilton	March 23, 2012	1 assist
			Stuart Percy	October 8, 2014	1 assist
			Brandon Kozun	October 8, 2014	1 assist
			Andrew MacWilliam	March 11, 2015	1 assist

* Scored his first goal after just 15 seconds, an NHL record

ALL GOALIES WHO MADE THEIR NHL DEBUTS WITH THE LEAFS

NAME AND OPPONENT	DATE	MIN	GA	DECISION
Mike Mitchell vs. Ottawa	December 23, 1919	60	3	L
Howie Lockhart vs. Montreal	January 10, 1920	51	9	ND
Vernon Forbes vs. Ottawa	February 28, 1920	60	1	L
John Ross Roach vs. Hamilton	December 24, 1921	60	4	L
Benny Grant vs. NY Americans	January 10, 1929	44	2	L
Turk Broda vs. Detroit	November 5, 1936	60	3	L
Phil Stein vs. Detroit*	January 18, 1940	70	2	T
Jean Marois vs. Chicago	December 18, 1943	60	4	W
Frank McCool vs. NY Rangers	October 28, 1944	60	1	T
Baz Bastien vs. Boston	October 27, 1945	60	1	T
Gordie Bell vs. Detroit	November 8, 1945	60	3	L
Gil Mayer vs. Detroit	December 1, 1949	60	2	L
Al Rollins vs. Boston	December 24, 1949	40	4	ND
Ed Chadwick vs. Montreal	February 8, 1956	60	1	T
Cesare Maniago vs. Detroit	February 25, 1961	60	1	W
Gerry McNamara vs. Montreal	February 15, 1961	60	3	L
Gerry Cheevers vs. Chicago	December 2, 1961	60	4	W
Gary Smith vs. NY Rangers	February 19, 1966	60	3	L
Al Smith vs. Detroit	February 20, 1966	5	0	ND
Murray McLachlan vs. Buffalo	November 18, 1970	12	1	ND
Gord McRae vs. NY Islanders	January 31, 1973	60	3	W
Pierre Hamel vs. California	November 15, 1974	60	3	W
Mike Palmateer vs. Detroit	October 28, 1976	60	1	W
Vincent Tremblay vs. Quebec	January 5, 1980	12	2	ND
Jiri Crha vs. Hartford	February 16, 1980	30	1	W
Bob Parent vs. Montreal	March 6, 1982	60	6	L
Ken Wregget vs. Hartford	December 8, 1983	60	6	W
Allan Bester vs. St. Louis	January 8, 1984	23	0	ND
Bruce Dowie vs. Montreal	March 17, 1984	12	0	ND
Jeff Reese vs. Winnipeg	January 10, 1988	60	4	L
Peter Ing vs. NY Islanders	November 16, 1989	57	6	L
Damian Rhodes vs. Detroit	March 22, 1991	60	1	W
Félix Potvin vs. Chicago	November 14, 1991	60	3	L
Marcel Cousineau vs. Buffalo	November 21, 1996	16	0	ND
Mikael Tellqvist vs. Montreal	January 18, 2003	15	1	W
Justin Pogge vs. Atlanta	December 22, 2008	60	2	W
Jonas Gustavsson vs. Washington	October 3, 2009	38	3	L
James Reimer vs. Atlanta	December 20, 2010	14	0	ND
Jussi Rynnas vs. Carolina	March 27, 2012	39	0	ND
Ben Scrivens vs. Columbus	November 3, 2011	60	1	W

* Only NHL game

LEAFS IN THE HOCKEY HALL OF FAME

(List is alphabetical; first year indicates year of induction; years in brackets indicate service as a Leaf unless otherwise noted)

PLAYERS

1959	Jack Adams (1917–19 Arenas; 1922–26 St. Pats)	**1972**	Harry Holmes (1917–19 Arenas)
2008	Glenn Anderson (1991–94)	**1965**	Red Horner (1928–40)
1961	Syl Apps (1936–43, 1945–48)	**1977**	Tim Horton (1949–70)
1996	Al Arbour (inducted as a builder; played with Leafs 1961–64, 1965–66)	**1965**	Syd Howe (1931–32)
		1958	Dick Irvin Sr. (inducted as a player; coached Leafs 1930–40)
1975	George Armstrong (1949–71)		
1978	Ace Bailey (1926–34)	**1971**	Harvey Jackson (1929–39)
1978	Andy Bathgate (1963–65)	**1969**	Red Kelly (1960–67)
2011	Ed Belfour (2002–06)	**1966**	Ted Kennedy (1942–57)
1966	Max Bentley (1947–53)	**1986**	Dave Keon (1960–75)
1986	Léo Boivin (1951–54)	**2004**	Brian Leetch (2003–04)
1976	Johnny Bower (1958–70)	**1980**	Harry Lumley (1952–56)
1967	Turk Broda (1936–43, 1945–52)	**1981**	Frank Mahovlich (1956–68)
1962	Harry Cameron (1919–23 St. Pats)	**1992**	Frank Mathers (1948–50; 1951–52)
1985	Gerry Cheevers (1961–62)	**1992**	Lanny McDonald (1973–79)
1958	King Clancy (1930–37)	**1974**	Dickie Moore (1964–65)
1958	Sprague Cleghorn (1920–21 St. Pats)	**2004**	Larry Murphy (1995–97)
1961	Charlie Conacher (1929–38)	**2011**	Joe Nieuwendyk (2003–04)
1962	Rusty Crawford (1917–19 Arenas)	**1947**	Frank Nighbor (1929–30)
1961	Hap Day (1924–37)	**1962**	Reg Noble (1917–19 Arenas; 1919–25 St. Pats)
1975	Gord Drillon (1936–42)	**1985**	Bert Olmstead (1958–62)
2006	Dick Duff (1954–64)	**1984**	Bernie Parent (1970–72)
1970	Babe Dye (1919–26 St. Pats; 1930–31)	**1975**	Pierre Pilote (1968–69)
1990	Fern Flaman (1950–54)	**1978**	Jacques Plante (1970–73)
2007	Ron Francis (2003–04)	**1990**	Bud Poile (1942–47)
2003	Grant Fuhr (1991–93)	**1966**	Babe Pratt (1942–46)
2001	Mike Gartner (1993–96)	**1963**	Joe Primeau (1927–36)
1945	Eddie Gerard (1921–22 St. Pats)	**1978**	Marcel Pronovost (1965–70)
2011	Doug Gilmour (1991–97; 2003)	**1991**	Bob Pulford (1956–70)
1961	George Hainsworth (1933–37)	**1996**	Borje Salming (1973–89)

1971	Terry Sawchuk (1964–67)	2012	Mats Sundin (1994–2008)
1962	Sweeney Schriner (1939–43; 1944–46)	1982	Norm Ullman (1968–75)
1989	Darryl Sittler (1970–82)	1973	Carl Voss (1926–27 St. Pats; 1928–29)
1981	Allan Stanley (1958–68)	1994	Harry Watson (1946–55)

BUILDERS

1977	Harold Ballard (1961–91)	1947	William A. Hewitt
1978	J.P. Bickell (1927–51)	1984	Punch Imlach (1958–69, 1979–81)
2014	Pat Burns (1992–96)	2002	Roger Nielson (1977–79)
2004	Cliff Fletcher (1991–97)	1960	Frank J. Selke (1927–46)
2007	Jim Gregory (1969–79)	1958	Conn Smythe (1927–61)
1965	Foster Hewitt (1923–81)		

The Hockey Hall of Fame in downtown Toronto

TROPHY WINNERS

JACK ADAMS AWARD

1992–93   Pat Burns

LADY BYNG MEMORIAL TROPHY

1931–32   Joe Primeau

1937–38   Gord Drillon

1941–42   Syl Apps

1951–52   Sid Smith

1954–55   Sid Smith

1960–61   Red Kelly

1961–62   Dave Keon

1962–63   Dave Keon

2002–03   Alexander Mogilny

CALDER MEMORIAL TROPHY

1936–37   Syl Apps

1942–43   Gaye Stewart

1943–44   Gus Bodnar

1944–45   Frank McCool

1946–47   Howie Meeker

1957–58   Frank Mahovlich

1960–61   Dave Keon

1962–63   Kent Douglas

1965–66   Brit Selby

KING CLANCY TROPHY

1999–2000 Curtis Joseph

CONN SMYTHE TROPHY

1966–67   Dave Keon

HART MEMORIAL TROPHY

1943–44   Babe Pratt

1954–55   Ted Kennedy

BILL MASTERTON TROPHY

2007–08   Jason Blake

ART ROSS TROPHY

1922–23   Babe Dye (St. Pats)

1924–25   Babe Dye (St. Pats)

1928–29   Ace Bailey

1931–32   Harvey Jackson

1933–34   Charlie Conacher

1934–35   Charlie Conacher

1937–38   Gord Drillon

FRANK J. SELKE TROPHY

1992–93   Doug Gilmour

VEZINA TROPHY

1940–41   Turk Broda

1947–48   Turk Broda

1950–51   Al Rollins

1953–54   Harry Lumley

1960–61   Johnny Bower

1964–65   Johnny Bower & Terry Sawchuk

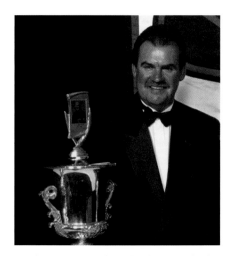

Coach Pat Burns won the Jack Adams Award with the Leafs in 1992–93

TORONTO MAPLE LEAFS TROPHIES

J.P. BICKELL MEMORIAL CUP

"Presented by Maple Leaf Gardens Limited in respectful memory of J.P. Bickell, esq., and in appreciation of his invaluable services as president from the year of its inauguration in 1931 until 1932, chairman of the board for 11 succeeding years and a director until his decease in 1951. To be awarded to a player of the Maple Leaf hockey team at such times and for such merit as may be designated and determined by the Board of Directors." Awarded at the discretion of the Board of Directors to a Leaf for a tremendous feat, one season of spectacular play, or remarkable service over a number of years.

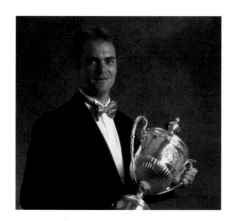

Curtis Joseph with the Bickell Cup in 1999

1953	Ted Kennedy	1965	Johnny Bower
1954	Harry Lumley	1966	Allan Stanley
1955	Ted Kennedy	1967	Terry Sawchuk
1956	Tod Sloan	1969	Tim Horton
1959	George Armstrong & Bob Pulford	1971	Bob Baun
1960	Johnny Bower	1972	King Clancy
1961	Red Kelly	1979	Mike Palmateer
1962	Dave Keon	1993	Doug Gilmour
1963	Dave Keon	1995	Bob Davidson
1964	Johnny Bower	1999	Mats Sundin & Curtis Joseph
		2003	Pat Quinn

MOLSON CUP

1974	Borje Salming	1989	Gary Leeman	2004	Ed Belfour
1975	Darryl Sittler	1990	Gary Leeman	2005	Mats Sundin
1976	Darryl Sittler	1991	Peter Ing	2006	Mats Sundin
1977	Borje Salming	1992	Grant Fuhr	2007	Mats Sundin
1978	Borje Salming	1993	Doug Gilmour	2008	Vesa Toskala
1979	Darryl Sittler	1994	Doug Gilmour	2009	Vesa Toskala
1980	Borje Salming	1995	Mats Sundin	2010	Phil Kessel
1981	Darryl Sittler & Wilf Paiement	1996	Félix Potvin	2011	Phil Kessel
1982	Michel Larocque	1997	Félix Potvin	2012	Phil Kessel
1983	Rick Vaive	1998	Félix Potvin	2013	James Reimer
1984	Rick Vaive	1999	Curtis Joseph	2014	Jonathan Bernier
1985	Bill Derlago	2000	Curtis Joseph		
1986	Ken Wregget	2001	Curtis Joseph		
1987	Rick Vaive	2002	Mats Sundin		
1988	Ken Wregget	2003	Ed Belfour		

PART 3

THE LEAFS AND THE ALL-STAR GAME

THE BIRTH OF THE ALL-STAR GAME

The night of December 13, 1933, changed the course of hockey forever. In a Maple Leafs–Bruins game in Boston, star defenceman Eddie Shore hit Ace Bailey, and the league's top scorer was knocked unconscious. It marked the end of Bailey's playing career.

Toronto's Red Horner—the "bad man of hockey," as he had been labelled across the league—responded, and Shore, too, was knocked unconscious.

Both players regained consciousness a few minutes later, after being helped to their respective dressing rooms. Indeed, Shore was well enough to visit Bailey to apologize. Bailey graciously said, "It's all part of the game."

On February 14, 1934, the Leafs held an all-star game in Ace's honour at Maple Leaf Gardens. The Leafs were pitted against a team made up of the best players from around the league, with the proceeds going to Ace and his young family.

Prior to the game, the all-stars skated onto the ice in their club sweaters and had a group photo taken. Each individual was then presented with a special all-star sweater by NHL president Frank Calder, Lester Patrick, Leafs officials, and the now-retired Ace Bailey. When goalie Charlie Gardiner came out to receive his number 1, the fans knew that Shore, who wore number 2, would be next. An ominous silence filled the air as Shore skated to centre ice, but when Bailey extended his hand to him, the crowd went wild. His sporting gesture made clear that Bailey had forgiven his former opponent.

The ceremonies reached another historic moment when Leafs owner Conn Smythe handed Ace his number 6 sweater and announced: "Allow me to present this sweater that you have worn so long and nobly for the Maple Leafs. No other player will ever use this number on the Maple Leaf hockey team."

This was the first time in hockey that a number had been retired for a player. It was also the first time an "all-star game" had been played in the NHL. Another similar event took place three years later for the deceased Howie Morenz, and two years after that for the late Babe Siebert.

In 1947, when the league and players established a pension fund for retired players, it was decided that the all-star format used for the Ace Bailey game would be used for an annual event to benefit the pension fund. Thus the NHL All-Star Game was born, and for the next two decades it featured the Stanley Cup champions against the best of the rest of the league—just as it had that night at Maple Leaf Gardens.

Ace Bailey (left) and Boston's Eddie Shore shake hands

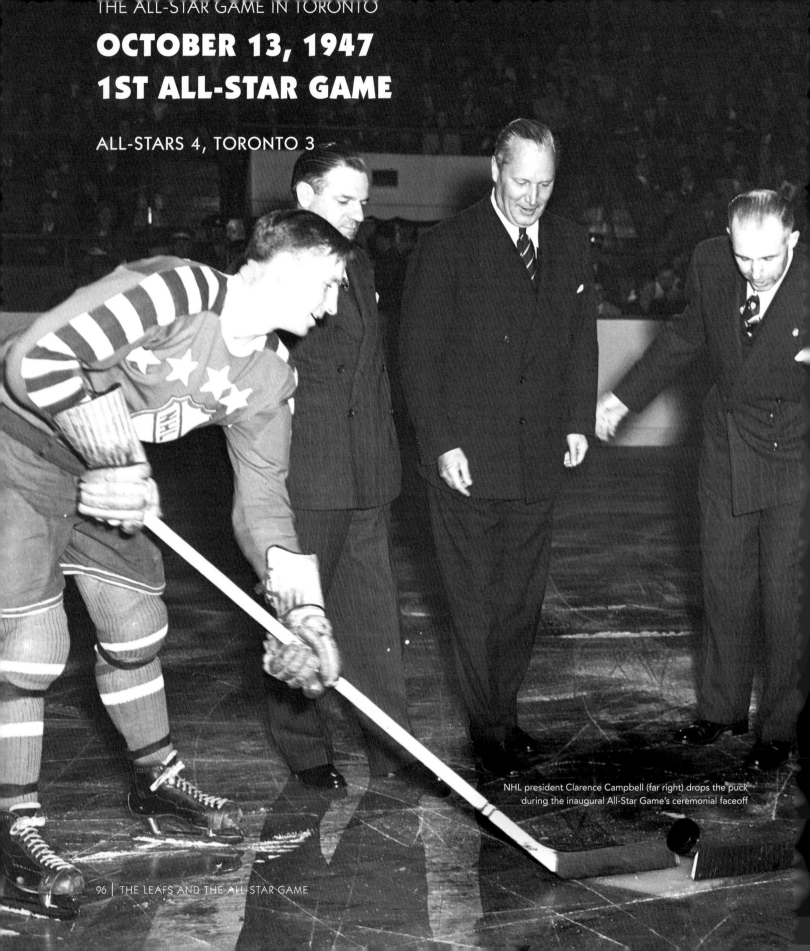

OCTOBER 13, 1947
1ST ALL-STAR GAME

ALL-STARS 4, TORONTO 3

NHL president Clarence Campbell (far right) drops the puck during the inaugural All-Star Game's ceremonial faceoff

At the meeting of the NHL's board of governors in the spring of 1947, the motion to hold a game of some sort, with the profits possibly going to a players' pension fund, was approved, but the matter was far from fully resolved.

Both Toronto and Chicago put themselves forward to host the game for the 1947–48 season, and it was suggested that two such games be played. The board opted for a single event, and since the Leafs had proposed that theirs be played prior to the start of the season, on October 13— as opposed to the Black Hawks, who had proposed December 10—Toronto was given the go-ahead. Chicago was immediately awarded the following year's event.

As with the game played in honour of Ace Bailey, the first NHL All-Star Game pitted the Stanley Cup champions against a team comprising the best players from the rest of the league. The "best" were those voted to the First and Second All-Star Teams, and five extras: one additional player from each of Detroit and Chicago, and three additional players from the New York Rangers.

It was decided that the coach of the inaugural All-Star team was to be Dick Irvin. Player expenses would be footed by each individual's club, while uniforms and officiating were placed under the aegis of the league. Proceeds were to be split, with one-third going to local Toronto charities and the rest to a new resource called the Players Emergency (Benevolent and Disability) Fund.

This new fund extended beyond the game. All players agreed to contribute $900 a season (a lofty sum at a time when most salaries were about $5,000), and the owners would put in 25 cents from the sale of every playoff-game ticket. Players could start collecting a pension at age 45 to the tune of $8 (per year of service) each month. In other words, a player who was in the NHL for 10 years would receive a pension of $80 per month for the rest of his life.

The Leafs went all out to make the first All-Star Game a memorable one. The top people in the game were invited to the Thanksgiving Day football game at Varsity Stadium between the Toronto Argonauts and Hamilton Tigers, followed by a glitzy meal at the Royal York Hotel to precede the hockey game.

The All-Star team was made up of players who were very familiar with one another. The two defence pairings were partners in league play too—Ken Reardon and Butch Bouchard from Montreal, Jack Stewart and Bill Quackenbush from Detroit.

Forwards included Boston's complete Kraut Line of Milt Schmidt, Woody Dumart, and Bobby Bauer; the Pony Line from Chicago (Bill Mosienko and brothers Max and Doug Bentley); and Rangers teammates Edgar Laprade, Tony Leswick, and Grant Warwick. Maurice Richard and Ted Lindsay were the only odd ones out, albeit world-class ones.

By playing teammates as much as he was able, coach Irvin managed to rein in the enmity that players on rival teams felt for each other. Richard, however, was in a class by himself in this respect. When asked afterwards about playing alongside Lindsay, the "Rocket" gruffly replied: "I didn't talk to him. We didn't even say hello. He tried talking to me, but I just ignored him. I don't like him, not even for an All-Star Game."

The game itself was fiercely contested—the proud Cup-winning Leafs were determined to prove their worth, and the All-Stars were equally set on taking down the champs. In the end, the familiarity of the hosts gave way to a stunning comeback by their guests. Harry Watson scored the only goal of the first period for the Leafs, and the teams had two each in the second. But in the third, two quick goals from Richard and Doug Bentley gave the All-Stars a 4–3 win before a capacity crowd of 14,169.

"We were so determined to win that game, you could almost hear the fellows grinding their teeth as they walked to the ice," said All-Star Ken Reardon. "I never saw a group so fired up in all my hockey career."

OCTOBER 10, 1949
3RD ALL-STAR GAME

ALL-STARS 3, TORONTO 1

A view of the action in front of Leafs goalie Turk Broda

Although the Leafs won the Stanley Cup in 1948, the second All-Star Game was played in Chicago as a consolation of sorts for not being chosen to host the inaugural edition. Thanks to the Leafs winning the Cup for the third time in a row—becoming the first franchise to do so in NHL history—the Gardens was back as host for the third "glitter game," as sportswriters of the day liked to call it.

Toronto had won the Cup this year in exactly the same manner as they had the year previous, by eliminating Boston in the semifinals and then sweeping aside the Red Wings in four definitive games. With this win, the All-Star Game started its 20-year tradition of being held in the city of the Cup champions.

The many festivities on game day were again luxurious. There was a luncheon at the Royal York Hotel, during which Montreal Canadiens general manager Dick Irvin acquired Knobby Warwick from Boston for cash. After their repast, everyone headed up to Varsity Stadium for the annual Thanksgiving Day football game between the Argos and the Hamilton Wildcats.

Tommy Ivan, whose Detroit team had succumbed to the Leafs in the Cup finals, was coach of the All-Stars. As usual, he took the 12 players voted to the end-of-year First and Second All-Star Teams, as well as some additions.

This year, the extras were Paul Ronty of the Bruins, two Black Hawks (Bill Mosienko and Bob Goldham), and four Rangers: Pat Egan, Buddy O'Connor, Tony Leswick, and Edgar Laprade. Ivan did the sensible thing by keeping Detroit's remarkable Production Line (Gordie Howe, Ted Lindsay, and Sid Abel) together; he did the same with the Pony Line of Doug Bentley, Bill Mosienko, and Roy Conacher.

Just as in 1947, the Leafs didn't have a single man on either All-Star Team despite winning the Cup. Harry Watson, Cal Gardner, and Howie Meeker made up the first line; the second consisted of Max Bentley, Joe Klukay, and Ray Timgren. The third forward combination featured Ted Kennedy, Sid Smith, and Fleming Mackell.

For the third year in a row, the Leafs lost, but coach Hap Day was quick to point out that it was far better to lose the All-Star Game as Cup champions than to win after having been eliminated in the previous year's playoffs.

Bill Barilko opened the scoring for the Leafs late in the first, only to see the lead vanish three minutes later on a shorthanded goal by former Leaf defenceman Goldham. Paul Ronty got the only goal of the second, and Doug Bentley finished the scoring early in the third. Nearly $18,000 was raised for the pension fund on the night, thanks to a massive crowd of 13,541.

OCTOBER 9, 1951
5TH ALL-STAR GAME

FIRST ALL-STARS 2, SECOND ALL-STARS 2

Tod Sloan and Ken Mosdell

The league made a significant alteration for the 1951 All-Star Game, as a glitch in the game's formatting had led to an awkward and one-sided blowout the previous year. In 1950, the Red Wings had not only been Cup winners, they had placed five players on either the First or Second All-Star Team. These five played for Detroit in the All-Star Game, thus depleting the All-Stars' lineup.

The result was a 7–1 thrashing by Detroit, so the following year the NHL decided to make the game a matchup between two All-Star teams: one (First) featured players from the U.S.–based teams, while the other (Second) was primarily a Toronto–Montreal team, augmented by three players from American teams: goalie Charlie Rayner (Rangers), defenceman Leo Reise (Detroit), and forward Sid Abel (also Detroit). It was arguably the best All-Star Game to date, ending in a thrilling tie. Naysayers, though, complained that there was no winner and suggested that a 10-minute overtime be played.

The buildup to the game had been marked by both sadness and controversy. In the case of the former, the Leafs' hero from the 1951 playoffs, Bill Barilko, perished in a plane crash in northern Ontario in August. It was Barilko's overtime goal in game five at home that had given the Leafs the Cup in what, to this day, is the only final series in which every game went into overtime. Just weeks after he scored that goal, his plane crashed on the way home from a fishing trip. The plane and his body remained undiscovered for 11 years.

As for the controversy, the Second Team coach, Dick Irvin, added his Montreal goalie, Gerry McNeil, to the team instead of Al Rollins, the Leafs goalie who had just won the Vezina Trophy as well as the Cup, and who had finished runner-up in voting for the Calder Trophy. "I know he is much better than Rollins," Irvin said, almost as if trying to incite Toronto fans, "and besides, I want the best players on my team. I don't consider Mr. Rollins a very good goaler."

As usual, there was a luncheon at the Royal York Hotel on the afternoon of the game. The game itself featured two important rule changes. First, the goal crease grew in size by one foot out from the goal and six inches from each post, making it a four-by-eight-foot area. More important, the icing rule was changed. Previously, the goalie was allowed to touch the puck to create an icing call, but now a defending skater had to go back to touch the puck. The intention was obvious—the league wanted to make a "race for the puck" part of the icing play, with the possibility that an offensive skater might get to the puck first to negate the call.

In the first period, veteran Gordie Howe scored the opening goal for the First Team on a power play, with Floyd Curry in the penalty box. Teams exchanged goals in the second, Tod Sloan tying the score early, on another man advantage, before Johnny Peirson gave the First Team a 2–1 lead late in the period. In the third, Ken Mosdell tied the score at 9:25, and that's how the game ended.

Second All-Star Team goalie Gerry McNeil fails to make a save

OCTOBER 6, 1962
16TH ALL-STAR GAME

TORONTO 4, ALL-STARS 1

George Armstrong (left) shakes hands with
Gordie Howe prior to the game

By this time, the NHL All-Star Game had established itself in the hearts and minds of hockey fans, and it was an important start to the season in many respects. But as its reputation soared, so did the intrigue surrounding it. To wit, coach Punch Imlach and his use of the game as a negotiating tool with his players in 1962.

One league rule for the All-Star Game stated that players must be under contract in order to play. But a week and a half before the 1962 game, only two Leafs had signed on the proverbial dotted line: captain George Armstrong and defenceman Kent Douglas. The majority of the players were hoping to garner tidy pay increases in light of their Cup win, which had included a four-game sweep of the Habs in the finals, but Imlach was playing hardball. In the end, everyone signed in time to play in the All-Star Game, and only one earned the kind of pay hike they had all hoped for.

The night before the game, the league held a magnificent banquet at the Royal York Hotel, attended by more than 200 owners, executives, and the top brass from the six NHL teams. Several of them retired to one particular suite, Room 11-268, where talk turned to Frank Mahovlich, the Leafs' star left winger, who had yet to sign a contract. Chicago owner James Norris asked Harold Ballard, a member of Toronto's seven-man management committee, what it would take to pry the Big M from the Leafs, to which Ballard roared with hyperbole, "A million dollars!" Norris promptly gave Ballard $1,000 in cash as a deposit and promised to bring a cheque for the balance the next day. The Hawks immediately went public with the news, which ran in the morning papers and tossed the World Series from the front page.

The next day, Stafford Smythe, son of Conn and another member of the Leafs committee, made it clear that Mahovlich was not going anywhere. Indeed, as Smythe told Norris this news, Mahovlich was in another office at the Gardens signing a new, four-year contract worth a then-staggering $110,000. That night, the Big M scored a goal in his team's impressive win over the All-Stars.

The Leafs had three players voted onto the Second All-Star Team—Mahovlich, Dave Keon, and Carl Brewer—all of whom played for Toronto in the game. The All-Stars were evenly split across the other five teams—the Canadiens had five players, Chicago four, and Boston, Detroit, and New York three each.

All-Stars coach Rudy Pilous of the Black Hawks made history by playing three goalies, each for one period. Although the decision was popular with fans, it didn't help his side win. The teams swapped early goals and then the Leafs scored three in the second half of the period to take a 4–1 lead to the dressing room. The fiercely contested second and third periods were entertaining for the large gathering of 14,236 fans, but no more goals were counted and the Leafs started the new season as the old had ended—with a win.

For the first time, a presentation took place after the game for the most valuable player. Inaugural honours went to Eddie Shack of the Leafs. "Eddie the Entertainer" quipped of his special prize: "Just like everybody else—a jewellery case with no jewellery!"

OCTOBER 5, 1963
17TH ALL-STAR GAME

TORONTO 3, ALL-STARS 3

Red Kelly moves in alone on
All-Star goalie Glenn Hall

All the talk the previous year had been about Frank Mahovlich because of the famous million-dollar offer made by Jim Norris of Chicago for the Leafs' superstar left winger. The Big M was the centre of attention once again in 1963, this time because he was so dominant in the game itself.

The game was back in Toronto because the Leafs had won the Cup again, this time in even more convincing fashion. They had needed only 10 playoff games in total, beating both Montreal and Detroit in five games apiece. The All-Star coach, Detroit's Sid Abel, had his work cut out for him heading into the game. Three Leafs—Mahovlich, Tim Horton, and the ageless Johnny Bower—had been named to the two All-Star Teams, and as they were playing for Toronto, they had to be replaced. On top of this, star forward Stan Mikita of the Black Hawks refused to play because he was trying to increase his previous year's salary of $14,000 to a whopping $24,000 for the upcoming season. No contract, no play, although the matter would be resolved before the start of the regular season.

Abel's choices to the team included three of his own Red Wings (Marcel Pronovost, Norm Ullman, and Alex Delvecchio); two Rangers (Harry Howell and Camille Henry); three Canadiens (Jean Béliveau, Bernie Geoffrion, and Claude Provost); and two Bruins (Johnny Bucyk and Dean Prentice). Tom Johnson was another addition to the team, and his was the miracle story of the year. He had suffered a serious eye injury at the end of the previous season. After his 15 seasons and six Stanley Cups with Montreal, the Habs released him, believing his career was over. But Johnson made an impressive recovery over the summer and was signed by the Bruins, for whom he had two fruitful seasons before retiring.

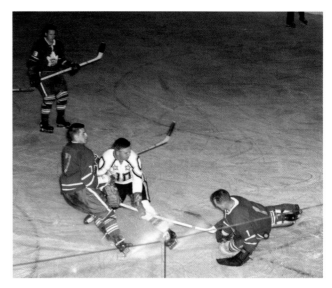

Alex Delvecchio beats Johnny Bower's pokecheck, but the puck doesn't go in the net.

During the 1963 All-Star Game, Gordie Howe was promoting the first of what was to become many autobiographies: *Hockey . . . Here's Howe!* The cover featured Howe with two of his young sons, Marty and Mark (incredibly, the three would play in the NHL together some 16 years later). Howe was already a legend. At the start of the 1963–64 season, he had 539 career goals, only five behind the all-time leader, Maurice Richard.

Mahovlich was named MVP of the game thanks to his two goals and one assist. Playing on a line with Red Kelly and Ed Litzenberger, he opened the scoring at 2:22 of the first and gave the Leafs a 2–1 lead later in the period, after Henri Richard had tied the score. Bobby Hull tied the game, 2–2, before the first intermission, and after a scoreless middle period, the teams exchanged goals in the third to make it 3–3. The crowd of 14,034 helped raise $42,534 for the players' pension fund.

OCTOBER 10, 1964
18TH ALL-STAR GAME

ALL-STARS 3, TORONTO 2

(l to r): Gordie Howe, Jean Béliveau, Bobby Hull, and goalie Terry Sawchuk

For the second time in their history, the Leafs had won the Stanley Cup three times in succession. This time was extra-special because it marked only the second time the winning team had been taken to seven games in both the semifinals and finals (the first was Detroit in 1950). Game six of the finals against Detroit was perhaps the most memorable. Defenceman Bobby Baun blocked a shot in the third period and was later carried off on a stretcher. He returned to score the winning goal in overtime, only discovering after the game that he had a cracked ankle. Two nights later, the Leafs won game seven on home ice, 4–0, to become champions for the 12th time in franchise history.

One Leafs player from this most recent troika of victories who wasn't in the All-Star Game lineup was Red Kelly. Injured? Nope. Contract dispute? Nope. Member of Parliament? Yep. Kelly was a sitting MP while he was playing, and at the time of the game, he was halfway around the world, in Tokyo, representing the Canadian government on an official site visit ahead of the 1964 Summer Olympics.

The traditional pre–game day banquet was another roaring success, attended by more than 200 executives. NHL president Clarence Campbell announced that the pension fund now contained in excess of $3.5 million. He also had the pleasure of introducing two new league trophies. The first, dedicated to Leafs owner Conn Smythe, would be awarded to the most valuable player of the Cup playoffs every spring. The second, named after Lester Patrick, was an annual award for those who had made a significant contribution to hockey in the United States.

The banquet also acted as the NHL awards dinner.

Frank Boucher presented the Lady Byng Trophy to Boston's Kenny Wharram; Syl Apps handed over the Calder Trophy to Canadiens defenceman Jacques Laperrière; Jim Norris gave his father's eponymous trophy to a Hawks blueliner, Pierre Pilote; Bill Durnan awarded the Vezina Trophy, which he had won six times, to Montreal's Charlie Hodge; Bobby Hull gave longtime teammate Stan Mikita the Art Ross Trophy; and Gordie Howe presented the Hart Trophy to respected adversary Jean Béliveau.

As coach of the Cup runner-up Red Wings, Sid Abel was All-Star coach for a third time. He faced an uphill battle after four players withdrew their services because of injury—Ken Wharram, Henri Richard, Bill Gadsby, and Camille Henry. But Gordie Howe was back on the All-Star Team for a record 16th time. Indeed, he had played in every All-Star Game except two—the first, in 1947, and again in 1956 because of injury. He recorded an assist in the game, increasing his record for points in All-Star Game history to 12. Terry Sawchuk, meanwhile, set a goaltender record by appearing in his 10th All-Star Game.

It was a muted game by previous standards. A scoreless first period was followed by a second with three goals—two to the visitors—and the All-Stars took a 3–1 lead early in the third, before a late Leafs goal brought the score closer. There were two interesting aspects, however. The first was a penalty to goalie Hodge, the first such punishment in All-Star history. The second was that coach Abel did away with the tradition of creating forward lines with players from the same team. The result was a first line of Howe, Béliveau, and Hull, one of the finest threesomes ever to skate together.

JANUARY 16, 1968
21ST ALL-STAR GAME

TORONTO 4, ALL-STARS 3

The Leafs' Bob Pulford is stymied by Terry Sawchuk
on a clear chance in front of goal

The 21st NHL All-Star Game was nothing if not eventful. Played at Maple Leaf Gardens because Toronto had won the Cup the previous year, this was to be the final time the champions were made the hosts automatically. It was also the year that the game was moved from the preseason to midseason (as a result, there was no game in the calendar year 1966), when it would no longer compete for fan interest in the U.S. with the World Series. This was all the more important because in 1967–68 the league had doubled in size—the Original Six was now the Expansion Twelve—but Toronto and Montreal were still the only teams representing Canada.

The new alignment of the NHL placed the six long-standing teams in the East Division and the six newcomers in the West, ensuring one old and one new team would play in the Cup finals. It was decided that future All-Star Games would be played in alternating cities, irrespective of who won the Cup.

The 1968 game was to produce one of the oddest pieces of All-Star trivia: Who is the only player to appear in an NHL All-Star Game who never played in the NHL during the year of the game? The answer: Toronto goalie Al Smith. The tandem of Bruce Gamble and Johnny Bower was supposed to have played, but Bower was struggling with a sore elbow, so coach Punch Imlach called up

Smith, only to send him back to the Tulsa Oilers for the rest of the year after the game.

This game was attended by a record 15,753 fans, all of whom got to see Bobby Orr play in his first All-Star Game. His evening ended a bit early when a clean but hard hit from Pete Stemkowski broke Orr's collarbone. (Orr missed the next 10 Bruins games.) Teams exchanged goals in the first and early in the second, but Stemkowski scored the go-ahead goal late in the period, and Ron Ellis made it a 4–2 game early in the third. Norm Ullman closed out the scoring.

Who could have known then that Maple Leaf Gardens would never host another All-Star Game—and that the city of Toronto wouldn't host the event again for another 32 years?

Toronto's Wayne Carleton is surrounded by greatness as Gordie Howe checks him while Bobby Orr and Bobby Baun watch the loose puck

n retrospect, it's incomprehensible to think that 32 years had passed since Toronto last hosted the All-Star Game. In the interim, NHL president Clarence Campbell had been succeeded by John Ziegler, and then Ziegler by commissioner Gary Bettman. The 12-team league was now 30, and two rounds of playoffs had become four.

The Cup champs versus the best of the rest gave way to various incarnations of All-Star matchups. Initially, it was East Division against West, then Wales Conference versus Campbell, even later Eastern versus Western Conference, and then North America versus the World. This latest format had come about for two reasons. First, fans wanted to see some variety in a game that had perhaps become stale. Second, in the 1980s and early 1990s, the NHL had become a much more international league, and by 2000 nearly a third of all players were from Europe. It was hoped that the new format would fuel a rivalry to hail a new era of NHL excellence from around the world.

Fortunately for the Maple Leafs, they were front and centre in this movement. Their captain and star centre was the towering, much-respected Mats Sundin—who, needless to say, played for the World. He was one of only three Swedes on the team (along with defenceman Nicklas Lidstrom and goalie Tommy Salo) in an international era dominated by the Czechs, who had 10 players on the roster. There were two other Leafs playing in the game—defenceman Dmitri Yushkevich, also with the World, and goalie Curtis Joseph for the North Americans.

Acquiring the showcase 50th All-Star Game can be traced to the efforts of Cliff Fletcher and later Ken Dryden. Fletcher had made it a priority to get the game almost from the moment he was hired in 1991. When Dryden was made team president in 1997, he took over the task and was rewarded with the game in 2000.

Never before had an All-Star Game involved so many elements. It was no longer a one-night event; it was a week. Canada's major junior leagues held their Top Prospects Game on the Wednesday, Team Orr beating Team Cherry, 6–3, while the Canadian and American women's national teams played on Friday before a tremendous crowd, Canada winning, 6–0.

Then a group of amateurs took to Nathan Phillips Square to set a world record for the longest continuous hockey game (72 hours). And on Saturday morning, an open practice drew a sold-out crowd of more than 19,000, impressing even the most jaded of players. The skills competition and FANtasy events, too, were spectacular successes—and all of these took place prior to the actual All-Star Game.

The two coaches were decided on January 4, 2000, based on the best winning percentage at that point in the regular season. Happily, Pat Quinn was named coach of the North Americans. He had last been behind the bench in 1981, and the 19-year gap was a coaching record. He was also the first Leafs coach to be appointed as All-Star bench boss since Punch Imlach in the 1968 game.

If all of this wasn't enough, the pre-game ceremonies featured the formal leaguewide retirement of Wayne Gretzky's number 99. The Great One's reception, as expected, was deafening.

As for the game, the World scored early on a Pavol Demitra goal at 3:12 and cruised to victory by scoring the only four goals of the final period. But the 9–4 score was only a part of the festivities. The greater story was the All-Star Game coming back to the hockey capital of the world, and doing so with a success unimaginable in any other city.

Coach Pat Quinn guides the North American All-Stars at Air Canada Centre

ALL-STAR LEAFS BY NUMBERS

ALL-STAR GAME STATISTICS, YEAR BY YEAR

February 16, 1934, Maple Leaf Gardens
Ace Bailey Benefit Game
Toronto 7, All-Stars 3

		G	A	P	PIM
11	Busher Jackson	2	1	3	0
5	Andy Blair	1	2	3	0
15	Ken Doraty	1	1	2	0
12	Hec Kilrea	1	1	2	0
8	Baldy Cotton	1	0	1	0
4	Hap Day	1	0	1	0
10	Joe Primeau	0	1	1	0
14	Bill Thoms	0	1	1	0
17	Buzz Boll	0	0	0	0
7	King Clancy	0	0	0	0
9	Charlie Conacher	0	0	0	0
2	Red Horner	0	0	0	0
3	Alex Levinsky	0	0	0	0
16	Charlie Sands	0	0	0	0

		MIN	GA	W–L–T	GAA
1	George Hainsworth	60	3	W	3.00

Coach: DICK IRVIN

November 3, 1937, Forum, Montreal
Howie Morenz Memorial Game
All-Stars 6, Montreal 5

		G	A	P	PIM
8	Charlie Conacher	1	1	2	0
5	Red Horner	0	0	0	2
9	Busher Jackson	0	0	0	0

October 29, 1939, Forum, Montreal
Babe Siebert Memorial Game
All-Stars 5, Montreal 2

		G	A	P	PIM
10	Syl Apps	1	3	4	0
12	Gord Drillon	0	0	0	0

October 13, 1947, Maple Leaf Gardens
All-Stars 4, Toronto 3

		G	A	P	PIM
4	Harry Watson	1	2	3	0
10	Syl Apps	1	1	2	0
12	Bill Ezinicki	1	1	2	4
19	Gus Mortson	0	1	1	4
14	Vic Lynn	0	0	0	2
21	Bill Barilko	0	0	0	0
2	Bob Goldham	0	0	0	0
9	Ted Kennedy	0	0	0	0
17	Joe Klukay	0	0	0	0
22	Fleming Mackell	0	0	0	0
15	Howie Meeker	0	0	0	0
5	Don Metz	0	0	0	0
7	Bud Poile	0	0	0	0
3	Wally Stanowski	0	0	0	0
16	Gaye Stewart	0	0	0	0
20	Jim Thomson	0	0	0	0

		MIN	GA	W–L–T	GAA
1	Turk Broda	60	4	L	4.00

Coach: HAP DAY

November 3, 1948, Chicago Stadium, Chicago
All-Stars 3, Toronto 1

		G	A	P	PIM
7	Max Bentley	1	0	1	0
15	Les Costello	0	1	1	0
3	Gus Mortson	0	0	0	5
12	Bill Ezinicki	0	0	0	2
18	Bill Juzda	0	0	0	2
19	Bill Barilko	0	0	0	0
5	Garth Boesch	0	0	0	0
17	Cal Gardner	0	0	0	0
9	Ted Kennedy	0	0	0	0
8	Joe Klukay	0	0	0	0
14	Vic Lynn	0	0	0	0
16	Fleming Mackell	0	0	0	0
20	Frank Mathers	0	0	0	0
11	Howie Meeker	0	0	0	0
2	Jim Thomson	0	0	0	0
4	Harry Watson	0	0	0	0

		MIN	GA	W–L–T	GAA
1	Turk Broda	60	3	L	3.00

Coach: HAP DAY

October 10, 1949, Maple Leaf Gardens
All-Stars 3, Toronto 1

		G	A	P	PIM
19	Bill Barilko	1	0	1	0
17	Cal Gardner	0	1	1	0
4	Harry Watson	0	1	1	0
2	Jim Thomson	0	0	0	4
5	Garth Boesch	0	0	0	2
11	Howie Meeker	0	0	0	2
24	Sid Smith	0	0	0	2
7	Max Bentley	0	0	0	0
23	Bob Dawes	0	0	0	0
18	Bill Juzda	0	0	0	0
9	Ted Kennedy	0	0	0	0

		G	A	P	PIM
8	Joe Klukay	0	0	0	0
14	Vic Lynn	0	0	0	0
16	Fleming Mackell	0	0	0	0
22	Ray Timgren	0	0	0	0

		MIN	GA	W–L–T	GAA
1	Turk Broda	60	3	L	3.00

Coach: HAP DAY

October 8, 1950, Olympia, Detroit
Detroit 7, All-Stars 1

		G	A	P	PIM
24	Sid Smith	1	0	1	0
12	Ted Kennedy	0	0	0	0
3	Gus Mortson	0	0	0	0
4	Jim Thomson	0	0	0	0

		MIN	GA	W–L–T	GAA
1	Turk Broda	29	4	ND	8.28

October 9, 1951, Maple Leaf Gardens
First All-Stars 2, Second All-Stars 2

The All-Star format changed for the 1951 game. The First All-Stars, supplemented by players from the four American clubs, played the Second All-Stars, with added players from the two Canadian clubs.

		G	A	P	PIM
15	Tod Sloan	1	1	2	2
7	Max Bentley	0	1	1	0
3	Gus Mortson	0	1	1	0
4	Harry Watson	0	1	1	0
8	Ted Kennedy	0	0	0	0
24	Sid Smith	0	0	0	0
2	Jim Thomson	0	0	0	0

Coach: JOE PRIMEAU*

* Although all Leafs played for the Second All-Stars, Primeau coached the First All-Stars.

October 5, 1952, Olympia, Detroit
First All-Stars 1, Second All-Stars 1

		G	A	P	PIM
2	Jim Thomson	0	0	0	6
12	Fern Flaman	0	0	0	0
3	Gus Mortson*	0	0	0	0
16	Tod Sloan	0	0	0	0
24	Sid Smith	0	0	0	0
4	Harry Watson	0	0	0	0

* All Leafs played for the Second All-Stars except Mortson, who played with the First All-Stars.

October 3, 1953, Forum, Montreal
All-Stars 3, Montreal 1

For the 1953 game, the NHL reverted to its previous format: the Stanley Cup champions versus the rest of the league.

		G	A	P	PIM
8	Sid Smith	0	0	0	2
2	Jim Thomson	0	0	0	0
24	Harry Watson	0	0	0	0

October 2, 1954, Olympia, Detroit
All-Stars 2, Detroit 2

		G	A	P	PIM
12	Ted Kennedy	0	1	1	0
18	Tim Horton	0	0	0	2
8	Sid Smith	0	0	0	0

		MIN	GA	W–L–T	GAA
1	Harry Lumley	31	2	ND	3.87

Coach: KING CLANCY

October 2, 1955, Olympia, Detroit
Detroit 3, All-Stars 1

		G	A	P	PIM
8	Sid Smith	0	1	1	0
10	Jim Morrison	0	0	0	2
17	Ron Stewart	0	0	0	2

		MIN	GA	W–L–T	GAA
9	Harry Lumley	33	2	L	3.64

October 9, 1956, Forum, Montreal
Montreal 1, All-Stars 1

		G	A	P	PIM
10	George Armstrong	0	0	0	0
5	Hugh Bolton	0	0	0	0
6	Dick Duff	0	0	0	0
3	Jim Morrison	0	0	0	0
12	Tod Sloan	0	0	0	0

October 5, 1957, Forum, Montreal
All-Stars 5, Montreal 3

		G	A	P	PIM
16	Rudy Migay	0	1	1	2
3	Jim Morrison	0	1	1	0
17	George Armstrong	0	0	0	0
8	Dick Duff	0	0	0	0

October 4, 1958, Forum, Montreal
Montreal 6, All-Stars 3

		G	A	P	PIM
15	Billy Harris	0	1	1	0
16	Dick Duff	0	0	0	2

October 3, 1959, Forum, Montreal
Montreal 6, All-Stars 1

		G	A	P	PIM
24	George Armstrong	0	0	0	0
5	Carl Brewer	0	0	0	0
15	Frank Mahovlich	0	0	0	0
16	Bert Olmstead	0	0	0	0

Coach: PUNCH IMLACH

October 1, 1960, Forum, Montreal
All-Stars 2, Montreal 1

		G	A	P	PIM
19	Frank Mahovlich	1	0	1	0
4	Red Kelly	0	1	1	0
2	Bob Armstrong	0	0	0	0
20	Bob Pulford	0	0	0	0
18	Allan Stanley	0	0	0	0

Coach: PUNCH IMLACH

October 7, 1961, Chicago Stadium, Chicago
All-Stars 3, Chicago 1

		G	A	P	PIM
8	Frank Mahovlich	0	0	0	6
18	Tim Horton	0	0	0	0

		MIN	GA	W–L–T	GAA
1	Johnny Bower	30	1	W	2.00

October 6, 1962, Maple Leaf Gardens
Toronto 4, All-Stars 1

		G	A	P	PIM
23	Eddie Shack	1	0	1	4
9	Dick Duff	1	0	1	0
27	Frank Mahovlich	1	0	1	0
20	Bob Pulford	1	0	1	0
10	George Armstrong	0	1	1	0

19	Kent Douglas	0	1	1	0
14	Dave Keon	0	1	1	0
26	Allan Stanley	0	1	1	0
12	Ron Stewart	0	1	1	0
2	Carl Brewer	0	0	0	4
21	Bob Baun	0	0	0	2
4	Red Kelly	0	0	0	2
11	Bob Nevin	0	0	0	2
15	Billy Harris	0	0	0	0
22	Larry Hillman	0	0	0	0
7	Tim Horton	0	0	0	0
25	Ed Litzenberger	0	0	0	0
24	John MacMillan	0	0	0	0

		MIN	GA	W–L–T	GAA
1	Johnny Bower	60	1	W	1.00

Coach: PUNCH IMLACH

October 5, 1963, Maple Leaf Gardens
Toronto 3, All-Stars 3

		G	A	P	PIM
27	Frank Mahovlich	2	1	3	0
25	Ed Litzenberger	1	1	2	0
21	Bob Baun	0	1	1	2
10	George Armstrong	0	1	1	0
4	Red Kelly	0	1	1	0
14	Dave Keon	0	1	1	0
7	Tim Horton	0	0	0	4
26	Allan Stanley	0	0	0	4
9	Dick Duff	0	0	0	2
19	Kent Douglas	0	0	0	0
15	Billy Harris	0	0	0	0
22	Larry Hillman	0	0	0	0
8	John MacMillan	0	0	0	0
11	Bob Nevin	0	0	0	0
20	Bob Pulford	0	0	0	0
23	Eddie Shack	0	0	0	0
12	Ron Stewart	0	0	0	0

		MIN	GA	W–L–T	GAA
1	Johnny Bower	40	2	ND	3.00
24	Don Simmons	20	1	T	3.00

Coach: PUNCH IMLACH

October 10, 1964, Maple Leaf Gardens
All-Stars 3, Toronto 2

		G	A	P	PIM
19	Kent Douglas	1	0	1	4
18	Jim Pappin	1	0	1	0
9	Andy Bathgate	0	1	1	2
18	Gerry Ehman	0	1	1	0
27	Frank Mahovlich	0	1	1	0
21	Bob Baun	0	0	0	4
12	Ron Stewart	0	0	0	2
10	George Armstrong	0	0	0	0
2	Carl Brewer	0	0	0	0
11	Ron Ellis	0	0	0	0
15	Billy Harris	0	0	0	0
22	Larry Hillman	0	0	0	0
7	Tim Horton	0	0	0	0
14	Dave Keon	0	0	0	0
17	Don McKenney	0	0	0	0
20	Bob Pulford	0	0	0	0
23	Eddie Shack	0	0	0	0

		MIN	GA	W–L–T	GAA
1	Johnny Bower	30	0	ND	0.00
23	Terry Sawchuk	31	3	L	5.81

Coach: PUNCH IMLACH

October 20, 1965, Forum, Montreal
All-Stars 5, Montreal 2

		G	A	P	PIM
2	Bob Baun	0	1	1	0
11	Ron Ellis	0	0	0	2
22	Frank Mahovlich	0	0	0	0

January 18, 1967, Forum, Montreal*
Montreal 3, All-Stars 0

		G	A	P	PIM
14	Dave Keon	0	0	0	0
22	Frank Mahovlich	0	0	0	0
2	Allan Stanley	0	0	0	0

* For the first time since the Ace Bailey benefit game, the All-Star Game was played at midseason. Thus, there was no game during the 1966 calendar year.

January 16, 1968, Maple Leaf Gardens
Toronto 4, All-Stars 3

		G	A	P	PIM
12	Pete Stemkowski	1	1	2	2
25	Wayne Carleton	0	2	2	0
2	Larry Hillman	0	2	2	0
27	Frank Mahovlich	0	2	2	0
8	Ron Ellis	1	0	1	0
11	Murray Oliver	1	0	1	0
26	Allan Stanley	1	0	1	0
4	Duane Rupp	0	1	1	0
16	Mike Walton	0	0	0	2
10	George Armstrong	0	0	0	0
22	Brian Conacher	0	0	0	0
7	Tim Horton	0	0	0	0
14	Dave Keon	0	0	0	0
18	Jim Pappin	0	0	0	0
3	Marcel Pronovost	0	0	0	0
20	Bob Pulford	0	0	0	0

		MIN	GA	W–L–T	GAA
30	Bruce Gamble	40	2	W	3.00
1	Al Smith	20	1	ND	3.00

Coach: PUNCH IMLACH

January 21, 1969, Forum, Montreal
East 3, West 3

Starting with the 1968–69 season, the game matched All-Stars from the East Division against All-Stars from the West.

		G	A	P	PIM
14	Norm Ullman	0	1	1	0
7	Tim Horton	0	0	0	4

January 20, 1970, The Arena, St. Louis
East 4, West 4

		G	A	P	PIM
12	Ron Ellis	0	0	0	0
14	Dave Keon	0	0	0	0

January 19, 1971, Boston Garden, Boston
West 2, East 1

		G	A	P	PIM
14	Dave Keon	0	0	0	0

January 25, 1972, Metropolitan Sports Center, Bloomington, Minnesota
East 3, West 2

		G	A	P	PIM
17	Paul Henderson	0	0	0	0

January 30, 1973, Madison Square Garden, New York
East 5, West 4

		G	A	P	PIM
21	Paul Henderson	1	0	1	0
14	Dave Keon	0	0	0	0

January 29, 1974, Chicago Stadium, Chicago
West 6, East 4

		G	A	P	PIM
9	Norm Ullman	0	2	2	0
18	Jim McKenny	0	0	0	0

January 21, 1975, Forum, Montreal
Wales 7, Campbell 1

		G	A	P	PIM
27	Darryl Sittler	1	1	2	0

Janaury 20, 1976, Spectrum, Phladelphia
Wales 7, Campbell 5

		G	A	P	PIM
21	Borje Salming	0	0	0	0

		MIN	GA	W–L–T	GAA
1	Wayne Thomas	31	4	ND	7.74

January 25, 1977, Pacific Coliseum, Vancouver
Wales 4, Campbell 3

		G	A	P	PIM
9	Lanny McDonald	2	0	2	0
21	Borje Salming	0	0	0	2
2	Ian Turnbull	0	0	0	0

January 24, 1978, Memorial Auditorium, Buffalo
Wales 3, Campbell 2 (OT)

		G	A	P	PIM
27	Darryl Sittler	1	0	1	0
21	Borje Salming	0	1	1	2
9	Lanny McDonald	0	0	0	2

Challenge Cup 1979, Madison Square Garden
All-Stars vs. Soviet Union National Team

February 8	All-Stars 4, Soviet Union 2
February 10	Soviet Union 5, All-Stars 4
February 11	Soviet Union 6, All-Stars 0

		GP	G	A	P	PIM
27	Darryl Sittler	3	0	1	1	0
21	Borje Salming	3	0	0	0	2
7	Lanny McDonald	3	0	0	0	2

February 5, 1980, Joe Louis Arena, Detroit
Wales 6, Campbell 3

		G	A	P	PIM
27	Darryl Sittler	0	1	1	0
24	Dave Burrows	0	0	0	0

February 10, 1981, Forum, Los Angeles
Campbell 4, Wales 1

		G	A	P	PIM
4	Robert Picard	0	0	0	0

February 9, 1982, Capital Centre, Washington
Wales 4, Campbell 2

		G	A	P	PIM
22	Rick Vaive	1	0	1	0
2	Bob Manno	0	0	0	0

February 8, 1983, Nassau Veterans Memorial Coliseum,
Uniondale (Long Island), New York
Campbell 9, Wales 3

		G	A	P	PIM
22	Rick Vaive	1	0	1	0

January 31, 1984, Brendan Byrne Arena, East Rutherford,
New Jersey
Wales 7, Campbell 6

		G	A	P	PIM
22	Rick Vaive	0	3	3	0

February 12, 1985, Olympic Saddledome, Calgary
Wales 6, Campbell 4

		G	A	P	PIM
14	Miroslav Frycer	1	0	1	0

February 4, 1986, Hartford Civic Center, Hartford
Wales 4, Campbell 3 (OT)

		G	A	P	PIM
15	Wendel Clark	0	0	0	0

Rendezvous '87, Le Colisée, Quebec
All-Stars vs. Soviet Union National Team

| February 11 | All-Stars 4, Soviet Union 3 |
| February 13 | Soviet Union 5, All-Stars 3 |

No Leafs selected to team

February 9, 1988, The Arena, St. Louis
Wales 6, Campbell 5

		G	A	P	PIM
33	Al Iafrate	0	0	0	0

February 7, 1989, Northlands Coliseum, Edmonton
Campbell 9, Wales 5

		G	A	P	PIM
10	Gary Leeman	1	1	2	0

January 21, 1990, Civic Arena, Pittsburgh
Wales 12, Campbell 7

		G	A	P	PIM
33	Al Iafrate	0	0	0	2

January 19, 1991, Chicago Stadium, Chicago
Campbell 11, Wales 5

		G	A	P	PIM
10	Vincent Damphousse	4	0	4	0

January 18, 1992, Spectrum, Philadelphia
Campbell 10, Wales 6

		G	A	P	PIM
4	Dave Ellett	0	1	1	0

February 6, 1993, Forum, Montreal
Wales 16, Campbell 6

		G	A	P	PIM
93	Doug Gilmour	1	0	1	0

January 22, 1994, Madison Square Garden, New York
East 9, West 8

		G	A	P	PIM
14	Dave Andreychuk	1	1	2	0
93	Doug Gilmour	0	1	1	0

		MIN	GA	W–L–T	GAA
29	Félix Potvin	20	3	ND	9.00

January 21, 1995, San Jose Arena, San Jose

No Game

January 20, 1996, FleetCenter, Boston
East 5, West 4

		G	A	P	PIM
13	Mats Sundin	0	1	1	0
11	Mike Gartner	0	0	0	0
55	Larry Murphy	0	0	0	0

		MIN	GA	W–L–T	GAA
29	Félix Potvin	20	1	ND	3.00

January 18, 1997, San Jose Arena, San Jose
East 11, West 7

		G	A	P	PIM
13	Mats Sundin	0	1	1	0

January 18, 1998, GM Place, Vancouver
North America 8, World 7

		G	A	P	PIM
13	Mats Sundin	0	1	1	0

January 24, 1999, Ice Palace, Tampa
North America 8, World 6

		G	A	P	PIM
13	Mats Sundin	1	3	4	0

February 6, 2000, Air Canada Centre, Toronto
World 9, North America 4

		G	A	P	PIM
13	Mats Sundin	0	0	0	0
36	Dmitri Yushkevich	1	1	2	0

		MIN	GA	W–L–T	GAA
31	Curtis Joseph	20	3	ND	9.00

February 1, 2001, Pepsi Center, Denver
North America 14, World 12

		G	A	P	PIM
13	Mats Sundin	2	2	4	0

February 2, 2002, Staples Center, Los Angeles
World 8, North America 5

		G	A	P	PIM
15	Tomas Kaberle	0	1	1	0
13	Mats Sundin	0	2	2	0

Coach: PAT QUINN

February 2, 2003, Office Depot Center, Sunrise, Florida
Western 6, Eastern 5 (OT)

No Leafs selected to team

February 8, 2004, Xcel Energy Center, St. Paul, Minnesota
Eastern 6, Western 4

		G	A	P	PIM
7	Gary Roberts	0	1	1	0
13	Mats Sundin	0	2	2	0

Coach: PAT QUINN

2005

No Game

2006

No Game—NHL at the Olympics

January 24, 2007, American Airlines Center, Dallas
Western 12, Eastern 9

		G	A	P	PIM
15	Tomas Kaberle	0	0	0	0

January 27, 2008, Philips Arena, Atlanta
Eastern 8, Western 7

		G	A	P	PIM
15	Tomas Kaberle	0	0	0	0

January 25, 2009, Bell Centre, Montreal
Eastern 12, Western 11 (OT)

		G	A	P	PIM
15	Tomas Kaberle	0	2	2	0

2010

No Game—NHL at the Olympics

January 30, 2011, RBC Center, Raleigh, North Carolina
Team Lidstrom 11, Team Staal 10

		G	A	P	PIM
18	Phil Kessel	0	0	0	0

January 29, 2012, Scotiabank Place, Ottawa
Team Chara 12, Team Alfredsson 9

		G	A	P	PIM
81	Phil Kessel	1	2	3	0
19	Joffrey Lupul	2	0	2	0
3	Dion Phaneuf	0	0	0	0

2013

No Game

2014

No Game—NHL at the Olympics

January 25, 2015, Nationwide Arena, Columbus
Team Toews 17, Team Foligno 12

		G	A	P	PIM
81	Phil Kessel	0	0	0	0

ALL-STAR GAME STATISTICS

ALL-STAR COACHES

	G	W	L	T
Punch Imlach	6	3	2	1
Hap Day	3	0	3	0
Pat Quinn	2	1	1	0
Dick Irvin	1	1	0	0
King Clancy	1	0	0	1
Joe Primeau	1	0	0	1

ALL-STAR GOALIES (ranked by GAA)

		G	MIN	GA	W–L–T	GAA
1	Johnny Bower	4	159:43	4	2–0–0	1.50
1	Al Smith	1	20:00	1	0–0–0	3.00
24	Don Simmons	1	20:00	1	0–0–1	3.00
30	Bruce Gamble	1	40:00	2	1–0–0	3.00
1	George Hainsworth	1	60:00	3	1–0–0	3.00
9, 1	Harry Lumley	2	63:09	4	0–1–0	3.75
1	Turk Broda	4	208:48	14	0–3–0	4.02
23	Terry Sawchuk	1	30:17	3	0–1–0	5.81
29	Félix Potvin	2	40:00	4	0–0–0	6.00
1	Wayne Thomas	1	30:26	4	0–0–0	7.74
31	Curtis Joseph	1	20:00	3	0–0–0	9.00

ALL-TIME ALL-STAR PLAYER REGISTER

		GP	G	A	P	PIM
14	Dave Andreychuk	1	1	1	2	0
10	Syl Apps	2	2	4	6	0
2	Bob Armstrong	1	0	0	0	0
24, 17, 10	George Armstrong	7	0	2	2	0
19, 21	Bill Barilko	3	1	0	1	0
9	Andy Bathgate	1	0	1	1	2
2, 21	Bobby Baun	4	0	2	2	8
7	Max Bentley	3	1	1	2	0
5	Andy Blair	1	1	2	3	0
5	Garth Boesch	2	0	0	0	2
17	Buzz Boll	1	0	0	0	0
5	Hugh Bolton	1	0	0	0	0
2, 5	Carl Brewer	3	0	0	0	4
24	Dave Burrows	1	0	0	0	0
25	Wayne Carleton	1	0	2	2	0
7	King Clancy	1	0	0	0	0
15	Wendel Clark	1	0	0	0	0
22	Brian Conacher	1	0	0	0	0
8, 9	Charlie Conacher	2	1	1	2	0
15	Les Costello	1	0	1	1	0
8	Baldy Cotton	1	1	0	1	0
10	Vincent Damphousse	1	4	0	4	0
23	Bob Dawes	1	0	0	0	0
4	Hap Day	1	1	0	1	0
15	Ken Doraty	1	1	1	2	0
19	Kent Douglas	3	1	1	2	4
12	Gord Drillon	1	0	0	0	0
9, 16, 8, 6	Dick Duff	5	1	0	1	4
8	Gerry Ehman	1	0	1	1	0
4	Dave Ellett	1	0	1	1	0
12, 8, 11	Ron Ellis	4	1	0	1	2
12	Bill Ezinicki	2	1	1	2	6
12	Fern Flaman	1	0	0	0	0
14	Miroslav Frycer	1	1	0	1	0
17	Cal Gardner	2	0	1	1	0
11	Mike Gartner	1	0	0	0	0
93	Doug Gilmour	2	1	1	2	0
2	Bob Goldham	1	0	0	0	0
15	Billy Harris	4	0	1	1	0
21, 17	Paul Henderson	2	1	0	1	0
2, 22	Larry Hillman	4	0	2	2	0
5, 2	Red Horner	2	0	0	0	2
7, 18	Tim Horton	7	0	0	0	10

#	Name	GP	G	A	Pts	PIM
33	Al Iafrate	2	0	0	0	2
9, 11	Busher Jackson	2	2	1	3	0
18	Bill Juzda	2	0	0	0	2
15	Tomas Kaberle	3	0	3	3	0
4	Red Kelly	3	0	2	2	2
8, 12, 9	Ted Kennedy	6	0	1	1	0
14	Dave Keon	8	0	2	2	0
18, 81	Phil Kessel	2	1	2	3	0
12	Hec Kilrea	1	1	1	2	0
8, 17	Joe Klukay	3	0	0	0	0
10	Gary Leeman	1	1	1	2	0
3	Alex Levinsky	1	0	0	0	0
25	Ed Litzenberger	2	1	1	2	0
19	Joffrey Lupul	1	2	0	2	0
14	Vic Lynn	3	0	0	0	2
16, 22	Fleming Mackell	3	0	0	0	0
8, 24	John MacMillan	2	0	0	0	0
22, 27, 8, 19, 15	Frank Mahovlich	9	4	4	8	6
2	Bob Manno	1	0	0	0	0
20	Frank Mathers	1	0	0	0	0
9	Lanny McDonald	2	2	0	2	2
17	Don McKenney	1	0	0	0	0
18	Jim McKenny	1	0	0	0	0
11, 15	Howie Meeker	3	0	0	0	2
5	Don Metz	1	0	0	0	0
16	Rudy Migay	1	0	1	1	2
3, 10	Jim Morrison	3	0	1	1	2
3, 19	Gus Mortson	5	0	2	2	9
55	Larry Murphy	1	0	0	0	0
11	Bob Nevin	2	0	0	0	2
11	Murray Oliver	1	1	0	1	0
16	Bert Olmstead	1	0	0	0	0
18	Jim Pappin	2	1	0	1	0
3	Dion Phaneuf	1	0	0	0	0
4	Robert Picard	1	0	0	0	0
7	Bud Poile	1	0	0	0	0
10	Joe Primeau	1	0	1	1	0
3	Marcel Pronovost	1	0	0	0	0
20	Bob Pulford	5	1	0	1	0
7	Gary Roberts	1	0	1	1	0
4	Duane Rupp	1	0	1	1	0
21	Borje Salming	3	0	1	1	4
16	Charlie Sands	1	0	0	0	0
23	Eddie Shack	3	1	0	1	4
27	Darryl Sittler	3	2	2	4	0
12, 16, 15	Tod Sloan	3	1	1	2	2
8, 24	Sid Smith	7	1	1	2	4
2, 26, 18	Allan Stanley	5	1	1	2	4
3	Wally Stanowski	1	0	0	0	0
12	Pete Stemkowski	1	1	1	2	2
16	Gaye Stewart	1	0	0	0	0
12, 17	Ron Stewart	4	0	1	1	4
13	Mats Sundin	8	3	12	15	0
14	Bill Thoms	1	0	1	1	0
4, 2, 20	Jim Thomson	7	0	0	0	10
22	Ray Timgren	1	0	0	0	0
2	Ian Turnbull	1	0	0	0	0
9, 14	Norm Ullman	2	0	3	3	0
22	Rick Vaive	3	2	3	5	0
16	Mike Walton	1	0	0	0	2
24, 4	Harry Watson	6	1	4	5	0
36	Dmitri Yushkevich	1	1	1	2	0

LEAFS ALL-STAR GAME RECORDS

MOST VALUABLE PLAYER
(began in 1962)

1962	Eddie Shack
1963	Frank Mahovlich
1968	Bruce Gamble
1991	Vincent Damphousse

MOST GAMES PLAYED

9	Frank Mahovlich
8	Dave Keon
	Mats Sundin
7	George Armstrong
	Tim Horton
	Sid Smith
	Jim Thomson
6	Ted Kennedy
	Harry Watson

MOST GOALS

4	Vincent Damphousse
	Frank Mahovlich

MOST ASSISTS

12	Mats Sundin

MOST POINTS

15	Mats Sundin
8	Frank Mahovlich

MOST PENALTY MINUTES

10	Tim Horton
	Jim Thomson
9	Gus Mortson

The Leafs' Vincent Damphousse (#10) was named MVP of the 1991 All-Star Game after a record-tying, four-goal performance

END-OF-YEAR ALL-STAR TEAM SELECTIONS

1930–31 King Clancy, defence (First Team)

1931–32 Harvey Jackson, left wing (First Team)

King Clancy, defence (Second Team)

Charlie Conacher, right wing (Second Team)

Dick Irvin, coach (Second Team)

1932–33 King Clancy, defence (Second Team)

Charlie Conacher, right wing (Second Team)

Harvey Jackson, left wing (Second Team)

Dick Irvin, coach (Second Team)

1933–34 King Clancy, defence (First Team)

Charlie Conacher, right wing (First Team)

Harvey Jackson, left wing (First Team)

Joe Primeau, centre (Second Team)

Dick Irvin, coach (Second Team)

1934–35 Charlie Conacher, right wing (First Team)

Harvey Jackson, left wing (First Team)

Dick Irvin, coach (Second Team)

1935–36 Charlie Conacher, right wing (First Team)

Bill Thoms, centre (Second Team)

1936–37 Harvey Jackson, left wing (First Team)

1937–38 Gord Drillon, right wing (First Team)

Syl Apps, centre (Second Team)

1938–39 Syl Apps, centre (First Team)

Gord Drillon, right wing (First Team)

1939–40 None

1940–41 Turk Broda, goal (First Team)

Wally Stanowski, defence (First Team)

Sweeney Schriner, left wing (First Team)

Syl Apps, centre (Second Team)

1941–42 Syl Apps, centre (First Team)

Turk Broda, goal (Second Team)

Bucko McDonald, defence (Second Team)

Gord Drillon, right wing (Second Team)

1942–43 Lorne Carr, right wing (First Team)

Syl Apps, centre (Second Team)

1943–44 Babe Pratt, defence (First Team)

Lorne Carr, right wing (First Team)

Paul Bibeault, goal (Second Team)

Hap Day, coach (Second Team)

1944–45 Babe Pratt, defence (Second Team)

1945–46 Gaye Stewart, left wing (First Team)

1946–47 None

1947–48 Turk Broda, goal (First Team)

1948–49 None

1949–50 Gus Mortson, defence (First Team)

Ted Kennedy, centre (Second Team)

1950–51 Jim Thomson, defence (Second Team)

Ted Kennedy, centre (Second Team)

Sid Smith, left wing (Second Team)

1951–52 Jim Thomson, defence (Second Team)

Sid Smith, left wing (Second Team)

1952–53 None

1953–54 Harry Lumley, goal (First Team)

Tim Horton, defence (Second Team)

Ted Kennedy, centre (Second Team)

1954–55 Harry Lumley, goal (First Team)

Sid Smith, left wing (First Team)

1955–56 Tod Sloan, centre (Second Team)

1956–59 None

1959–60 Allan Stanley, defence (Second Team)

1960–61 Johnny Bower, goal (First Team)

Frank Mahovlich, left wing (First Team)

Allan Stanley, defence (Second Team)

1961–62 Carl Brewer, defence (Second Team)

Dave Keon, centre (Second Team)

Frank Mahovlich, left wing (Second Team)

1962–63 Carl Brewer, defence (First Team)

Frank Mahovlich, left wing (First Team)

Tim Horton, defence (Second Team)

1963–64 Tim Horton, defence (First Team)

Frank Mahovlich, left wing (Second Team)

1964–65 Carl Brewer, defence (Second Team)

Frank Mahovlich, left wing (Second Team)

1965–66	Allan Stanley, defence (Second Team)
	Frank Mahovlich, left wing (Second Team)
1966–67	Tim Horton, defence (Second Team)
1967–68	Tim Horton, defence (First Team)
1968–69	Tim Horton, defence (First Team)
1969–70	None
1970–71	Jacques Plante, goal (Second Team)
	Dave Keon, centre (Second Team)
1971–74	None
1974–75	Borje Salming, defence (Second Team)
1975–76	Borje Salming, defence (Second Team)

1976–77	Borje Salming, defence (First Team)
	Lanny McDonald, right wing (Second Team)
1977–78	Borje Salming, defence (Second Team)
	Darryl Sittler, centre (Second Team)
1978–79	Borje Salming, defence (Second Team)
1979–80	Borje Salming, defence (Second Team)
1980–97	None
2001–02	Mats Sundin, centre (Second Team)
2003–04	Bryan McCabe, defence (Second Team)
2005–15	None

MOST END-OF-YEAR ALL-STAR TEAM SELECTIONS

6　Tim Horton (3 First Team, 3 Second Team)

　　Frank Mahovlich (2 First Team, 4 Second Team)

　　Borje Salming (1 First Team, 5 Second Team)

5　Harvey Jackson (4 First Team, 1 Second Team)

　　Charlie Conacher (3 First Team, 2 Second Team)

　　Syl Apps (2 First Team, 3 Second Team)

4　King Clancy (2 First Team, 2 Second Team)

　　Dick Irvin, coach (4 Second Team)

3　Turk Broda (2 First Team, 1 Second Team)

　　Gord Drillon (2 First Team, 1 Second Team)

　　Johnny Bower (1 First Team, 2 Second Team)

　　Sid Smith (1 First Team, 2 Second Team)

　　Ted Kennedy (3 Second Team)

　　Allan Stanley (3 Second Team)

Borje Salming was selected for the end-of-year All-Star Teams no less than six times

PART 4

THE LEAFS AND
THE STANLEY CUP

1918: TORONTO ARENAS WIN THE CUP

The first year of the NHL was a mishmash of past, present, and future. Coming out of the shadow of the National Hockey Association, the NHL had a rough start when one of the league's four teams—the Montreal Wanderers—withdrew because its arena had burned to the ground. On January 2, 1918, the ammonia plant at the Westmount Arena, which was used to create artificial ice, exploded. By the time firefighters were able to douse the blaze, the building was lost. As a result, the NHL had to continue with only three teams—Toronto Arenas, Montreal Canadiens, and Ottawa Senators.

This first NHL season was divided into two halves. The first consisted of 14 games and the second eight, after which the winner of the first half played the winner of the second half for the league championship. The Canadiens, with a 10–4 record, claimed the former while the Arenas, 5–3, claimed the latter. These two teams then played a two-game, total-goals series.

In the first game, in Toronto, the Arenas got three goals from Harry Meeking and won easily, 7–3, putting them in the driver's seat. The second game, two nights later in Montreal, saw the home side win, but only by a single goal. The 4–3 score gave Toronto the series win by an aggregate of 10–7.

At this point, however, the Stanley Cup was still up for grabs. The Arenas had to play the Pacific Coast Hockey Association (PCHA) champion, the Vancouver Millionaires, who had defeated the Seattle Metropolitans 3–2 in their league's series. The best-of-five, cross-country finals was unique in that, while their league championships had the same format, the NHL and PCHA used different sets of rules, and both were in play for this 1918 Cup finals. Games one, three, and five were played under NHL rules, which called for six players a side, no forward passing, no kicking the puck, allowed a substitution for a penalized player, and featured minor penalties set at three minutes.

PCHA rules called for seven players a side, forward passing and kicking the puck permitted only between the blue lines, and no substitute for the first penalized player. A second penalty to a team did not begin until the first was served.

Because of the huge distance between cities, it was decided that Toronto would host all the games—and, indeed, the series went the distance. Toronto won the opener 5–3 after jumping into an early 3–0 lead, but Vancouver came right back to tie the series with a 6–4 win three nights later in what was a nasty game by all accounts.

As in game one, the Arenas skated to an early 3–0 lead in game three and won more convincingly, 6–3, to take a crucial lead in the series, but the Millionaires responded with an even more convincing 8–1 shellacking to force a decisive fifth game. The pattern was clear by now that the rules of play were critical to success, Toronto having won both games played under eastern rules, and Vancouver both of those under western regulations.

Game five, of course, was played six skaters a side, and the Arenas took full advantage of a game they had played all year—barely. The first two periods were penalty-filled but scoreless. Alf Skinner got the opening goal for the home side a minute into the third, but the great Cyclone Taylor tied the game several minutes later. Corb Denneny put Toronto ahead again near the 11-minute mark, and that turned out to be the decisive goal. Toronto's first year in the NHL had given the team its first Stanley Cup.

NHL FINALS				
March 11 (at Toronto)	Toronto	7	Montreal	3
March 13 (at Montreal)	Toronto	3	Montreal	4
STANLEY CUP FINALS				
March 20 (at Toronto)	Toronto	5	Vancouver	3
March 23 (at Toronto)	Vancouver	6	Toronto	4
March 26 (at Toronto)	Toronto	6	Vancouver	3
March 28 (at Toronto)	Vancouver	8	Toronto	1
March 30 (at Toronto)	Toronto	2	Vancouver	1

1922: ST. PATS PICK UP WHERE ARENAS LEFT OFF

Things had gotten simpler in some respects and more complex in others since the last time Toronto competed for the Stanley Cup. The simple part was that the NHL was now a four-team league again—the Hamilton Tigers joining Toronto, Montreal, and Ottawa—and each team played a single, 24-game schedule over the year. The top two still played a two-game, total-goals series, but this time the winner had to wait to see which team it would play for the Cup, because hockey in the west had expanded at a greater rate than in the east.

In 1922, the winner in the east was Toronto, after they handed Ottawa a 5–4 loss in the opening game and then held the Senators to a 0–0 tie in the return game. The western representative in the Cup finals was decided by a playdown between the Pacific Coast Hockey Association champion and the Western Canada Hockey League (WCHL) champ. The WCHL was the new kid on the block and had done wonders recruiting top players from across the country. This year, the Millionaires prevailed over the Regina Capitals, 5–2, in another two-game, total-goals series. So, as in 1918, it was Toronto and Vancouver playing in a best-of-five, with all games played at the Arena Gardens. Again, eastern rules were used for the odd-numbered games and western rules for games two and four, and again the series went the limit.

Oddly, and mirror opposite to 1918, the first four games were won by the team less familiar with the rules. Jack Adams starred for the victorious Vancouver in the series opener. He

NHL FINALS

March 11 (at Toronto)	Toronto	5	Ottawa	4
March 13 (at Ottawa)	Toronto	0	Ottawa	0

STANLEY CUP FINALS

March 17 (at Toronto)	Vancouver	4	Toronto	3
March 21 (at Toronto)	Toronto	2	Vancouver	1
March 23 (at Toronto)	Vancouver	3	Toronto	0
March 25 (at Toronto)	Toronto	6	Vancouver	0
March 28 (at Toronto)	Toronto	5	Vancouver	1

scored two goals in the first period, but Babe Dye's second of the evening in the middle period tied the game 3–3. Late in the final period, though, Adams completed his hat trick to give the Millionaires a stunning 4–3 win.

Adams got his fourth goal of the series early in game two, and it held up for much of the game. It took a goal from Corb Denneny early in the third period to tie the score, and then Dye notched the winner in overtime to tie the series for the St. Pats.

Hugh Lehman recorded the shutout in game three for Vancouver, a rough-and-tumble 60 minutes in which the Millionaires scored a goal in each period. Not to be outdone, the Arenas came right back with a 6–0 whitewash thanks to goaltending from John Ross Roach and two goals each from Dye and Lloyd Andrews.

Interestingly, when the Arenas lost Harry Cameron to injury for this game, Vancouver allowed Toronto to use Eddie Gerard of the Ottawa Senators as a substitute. But Gerard was so impressive that the Millionaires refused to permit him to play in the decisive game, so Gerard has the distinction of playing only one game with the St. Pats, and winning the Cup in the process.

That victory came as the result of the tremendous play of Babe Dye. He scored four of his team's five goals in the 5–1 game, giving him nine for the series, still an NHL record for most goals in a five-game series.

1932: A FIRST FOR THE GARDENS AND MAPLE LEAFS

I t was the dawn of a new era in Toronto when Maple Leaf Gardens opened its doors on November 12, 1931. Foster Hewitt took his perch in the new gondola, as he called it, and NHL hockey was never to be the same again.

There were now eight teams in the league, after the demise of Ottawa and Philadelphia over the summer, and they were divided into two divisions. The Canadian Division included the Leafs, Montreal Canadiens, Montreal Maroons, and New York Americans. The American Division featured Boston, Detroit, Chicago, and the New York Rangers. Teams played a 48-game schedule.

The Leafs had made only three changes of note from the previous season, but all were significant. First, they hired Dick Irvin as coach, replacing Art Duncan. Irvin had become available after Chicago fired him. They also

acquired Frank Finnigan, who had played in Ottawa but, like all Senators players, was looking for a new home after the franchise took a year off from operating. And they bought Harry Darragh from the Bruins in a cash deal.

But the stars of the team were the three young forwards known affectionately as the Kid Line—Charlie Conacher, Joe Primeau, and Harvey Jackson. All three finished among the top four leading scorers: Busher Jackson was atop the leaderboard, with 53 points; Gentleman Joe was next, with 50; and Conacher was fourth, with 48 (the Canadiens' Howie Morenz was third, with 49 points).

The playoff format in 1932 was, to the 21st-century fan, counter-intuitive. The first round featured the first-place teams in each division playing a best-of-five; those in second place played a two-game, total-goals series; and

the third-place teams met in another two-game, total-goals series. The winners of the two latter series then played each other under the same format, and that winner played the first-place winner for the Stanley Cup (the NHL had assumed total control of the coveted trophy in 1926, eliminating other leagues and challenges from Cup competition).

The problem with this format was that, right off the bat, one of the best two teams in the league was eliminated, and the possibility of a third-place team in the finals was very real. So when the Rangers (first in the American Division) beat the Habs (first in the Canadian Division) in four games, the lesser teams now had a better chance of winning than if one of them had had to play the Blueshirts or Canadiens.

The second-place Leafs played their Chicago counterparts in the first round. Toronto lost the opening game 1–0, but rallied for an impressive 6–1 in game two to advance to the next round. They then played the Maroons (third-place winners over Detroit), and, after a 1–1 tie in the opening game, pulled out a 3–2 victory in the second game. Bob Gracie was the hero, scoring late in the first overtime period to ensure the victory.

That put the Leafs and Rangers in a best-of-five for the Cup. In the first game at Madison Square Garden (MSG), the teams exchanged goals in the first period, but the Kid Line took over in the middle period, scoring four times to take Toronto to a 5–1 lead. The Leafs cruised to a 6–4 victory.

Game two, two nights later, was played in Boston because MSG was booked by the circus, a frequent problem for the Rangers over the years. The away game didn't help, and the Leafs prevailed, 6–2. Toronto had trailed 2–0 early in the middle period but tied the game by the intermission and pulled away with four unanswered goals in the third, two coming from diminutive defenceman King Clancy.

The final game, played at Maple Leaf Gardens, saw the home side jump into an early 3–0 lead and skate to a 6–4 win, claiming the Cup in their first year at their new home. These finals quickly became known as the "tennis series" because of the scores—6–4, 6–2, 6–4—and the Leafs won the championship for the first time in a decade.

QUARTERFINALS				
March 27 (at Chicago)	Chicago	1	Toronto	0
March 29 (at Toronto)	Toronto	6	Chicago	1

SEMIFINALS				
March 31 (at Montreal)	Toronto	1	Montreal Maroons	1
April 2 (at Toronto)	Toronto	3	Montreal Maroons	2

FINALS				
April 5 (at New York)	Toronto	6	NY Rangers	4
April 7 (at Boston)	Toronto	6	NY Rangers	2
April 9 (at Toronto)	Toronto	6	NY Rangers	4

1942: A LONG WAIT OVER THANKS TO A HISTORIC COMEBACK

The Leafs had made several changes to their roster before the start of the 1941–42 season. First, they acquired veteran Lorne Carr from the New York Americans. They then signed three rookies: Bob Goldham, Ernie Dickens, and Johnny McCreedy. It might not have seemed like much at the start of the year, but by the end, it proved critical to success.

Although the league was now seven teams strong and compressed into a single division, the playoff format was still the same. The top two teams played a best-of-seven, while the teams in third and fourth place and in fifth and sixth played two-game, total-goals series. The two winners then played against each other in another two-game, total-goals series, with the victor going to the Cup finals. The 48-game schedule eliminated only one team from the playoffs.

The Rangers and Leafs finished first and second in the league; their series needed six games to decide a winner. The Leafs won the first two games, 3–1 and 4–2, but Sugar Jim Henry blanked the Blue and White, 3–0, to make the series closer. Both teams won once more each

setting up a sixth game at the Gardens, and the series was capped by one of the most dramatic finishes ever when Nick Metz scored the winning goal to break a 2–2 tie with only six seconds left in regulation time and overtime a seeming certainty.

Toronto had five days off before starting the finals against Detroit, but the Leafs couldn't stop the hot Don Grosso, who had two goals and an assist in the Red Wing's 3–2 opening win. Grosso scored two more in game two, and the visitors skated to a solid 4–2 victory heading back to Detroit, with a chance to clinch the series on home ice. All looked to be on track when they shut down the Leafs and skated to a 5–2 win, their biggest yet.

After the game, Conn Smythe and coach Hap Day tried to figure out what had gone wrong. There was no margin of error left, so they tried to shake up the team to get a reaction. Day benched star veterans Gord Drillon

and Bucko McDonald and inserted Don Metz and Hank Goldup into the lineup.

Toronto fell behind 2–0 in the second period of game four, but two late goals tied the score. After falling behind again early in the third, they rallied with two goals to win, 4–3. The Leafs were still alive—and heading home. Again, Day tinkered, benching Hank Goldup in favour of Gaye Stewart, who had been called up from the minors. Don Metz scored a hat trick as the Leafs waltzed to a 9–3 win, and Day looked more and more a brilliant coach.

Game six was all Leafs. Turk Broda was sensational in goal, and Don Metz, rookie Bob Goldham, and Billy Taylor were the scorers in the 3–0 win. A final 3–1 win on home ice before a record crowd of 16,218 gave the Leafs the victory. It was a historic win for Toronto, coming back as they had from the brink of defeat. For the Red Wings, it was a devastating loss.

SEMIFINALS

March 21 (at Toronto)	Toronto	3	NY Rangers	1
March 22 (at New York)	Toronto	4	NY Rangers	2
March 24 (at New York)	NY Rangers	3	Toronto	0
March 28 (at Toronto)	Toronto	2	NY Rangers	1
March 29 (at New York)	NY Rangers	3	Toronto	1
March 31 (at Toronto)	Toronto	3	NY Rangers	2

FINALS

April 4 (at Toronto)	Detroit	3	Toronto	2
April 7 (at Toronto)	Detroit	4	Toronto	2
April 9 (at Detroit)	Detroit	5	Toronto	2
April 12 (at Detroit)	Toronto	4	Detroit	3
April 14 (at Toronto)	Toronto	9	Detroit	3
April 16 (at Detroit)	Toronto	3	Detroit	0
April 18 (at Toronto)	Toronto	3	Detroit	1

The New York Rangers congratulate Toronto players as the Leafs advance to the Stanley Cup finals

1945: A WARTIME CUP

The "Original Six," as the league was later dubbed, was born in 1942 with the folding of the Brooklyn Americans, leaving the NHL with six teams that would forge the game's identity for the next quarter-century. But almost as soon as the golden era of the game began, it was decimated by players leaving to fulfill their wartime duties. For the 1944–45 season, no team was harder hit than the Leafs—notably in goal, as Turk Broda was in the RCAF and so was unavailable.

Nevertheless, Toronto managed to finish third in the standings with a decent, though unspectacular, 24–22–4 record in the 50-game schedule. The team's 52 points, however, put them far behind the Canadiens, who were in first place with a 38–8–4 record and 80 points, and Detroit in second, with a 31–14–5 record and 67 points.

The playoff format called for the first- and third-place teams to meet in a best-of-seven and the second- and fourth-place teams to meet in another series. When the Leafs and Habs began their series at the Forum, any and all expected Montreal to win handily. The only hope the Leafs had was the fact that, during the regular season, their record against their archrivals had been 5–4–1.

Toronto made their intentions clear in game one, when Frank "Ulcers" McCool shut out the home side and Ted Kennedy notched the only goal in a 1–0 win. Two nights later, the Leafs sent panic through the streets of Montreal by winning, 3–2. The Habs recovered to win two of the next three, including a 10–3 pasting, but Toronto did the unthinkable and took game six, 3–2, eliminating the heavy favourites.

The Leafs had scored 45 fewer goals during the regular season, allowed 40 more, and finished 28 points behind the Habs in the standings, but it was the Canadiens whose summer started early while Toronto headed to the Cup finals.

The Red Wings, meanwhile, beat Boston in seven to advance, and in the finals history nearly repeated itself. Just as the Leafs fell behind 3–0 in 1942 only to tie the series and then win it, so the Wings managed three years later to match those results for the first six games. McCool was simply sensational in the first three games, posting shutouts as the Leafs got just enough scoring to win by scores of 1–0, 2–0, and 1–0. Sweeney Schriner, Kennedy, Moe Morris, and Gus Bodnar had gotten the necessary goals to give the Leafs a huge lead in the series, with the seemingly inevitable Cup celebrations slated for after game four on April 14, 1945, at the Gardens.

Although the Wings finally scored on McCool in the opening period, they were trailing 3–2 after 40 minutes, and the defensive-minded Leafs still seemed poised to win. Three Detroit goals put Toronto's dream to rest, and the teams headed to the train station for game five in Detroit. Both goalies were razor sharp in that game, but Harry Lumley was that little bit better and the Wings got the only two goals of the game, both of which came in the third period.

Lumley was sensational again in game six, and a scoreless game went to overtime before Ed Bruneteau scored at 14:16 in the fourth period to force a deciding game. The Red Wings looked to be doing to the Leafs what the Leafs had done to the Wings three years earlier. But the Leafs recovered in the nick of time, scoring early in the first and later in the third to win, 2–1. It was the city's fifth Stanley Cup, and the start of the team's greatest years.

SEMIFINALS

March 20 (at Montreal)	Toronto	1	Montreal	0
March 22 (at Montreal)	Toronto	3	Montreal	2
March 24 (at Toronto)	Montreal	4	Toronto	1
March 27 (at Toronto)	Toronto	4	Montreal	3
March 29 (at Montreal)	Montreal	10	Toronto	3
March 31 (at Toronto)	Toronto	3	Montreal	2

FINALS

April 6 (at Detroit)	Toronto	1	Detroit	0
April 8 (at Detroit)	Toronto	2	Detroit	0
April 12 (at Toronto)	Toronto	1	Detroit	0
April 14 (at Toronto)	Detroit	5	Toronto	3
April 19 (at Detroit)	Detroit	2	Toronto	0
April 21 (at Toronto)	Detroit	1	Toronto	0
April 22 (at Detroit)	Toronto	2	Detroit	1

Montreal goalie Bill Durnan handles the puck during game three of the semifinals

1947: A GREAT RECOVERY

From 1945 to 1947, the Leafs became the first team to win the Cup, miss the playoffs, and win the Cup again in successive years. The regular-season schedule was now 60 games long, and each team played every other 12 times. Toronto put together an excellent season in which they finished in second place with 72 points, six fewer than Montreal. The Leafs led the league in goals scored with 209, and with Turk Broda in net they were second in goals against.

The Canadiens handled Boston in five games in one of the semifinals, and the Leafs played Detroit in the other. There was one major hurdle for the Blue and White, but it was dealt with effectively by Conn Smythe. The Leafs took the first game, 3–2, with a gutsy performance. Pete Horeck tied the score late in the third period for the Wings, but rookie Howie Meeker gave the Leafs a win with a goal at 3:05 of overtime. Meeker, who had set a record earlier in the season that still stands today— five goals by a rookie in a single game—was the best player on the ice, playing on a line with Ted Kennedy and Vic Lynn.

The problem occurred in game two, when the Red Wings waltzed to a 9–1 win. After the game, Smythe chastised his team, wondering not why they had lost game two but how they had managed to win game one at all. This reverse psychology of sorts worked, and the Leafs came right back to dominate game three in Detroit. Syl Apps scored twice in the third to salt a 4–1 win, but a near riot broke out near the end of the game involving

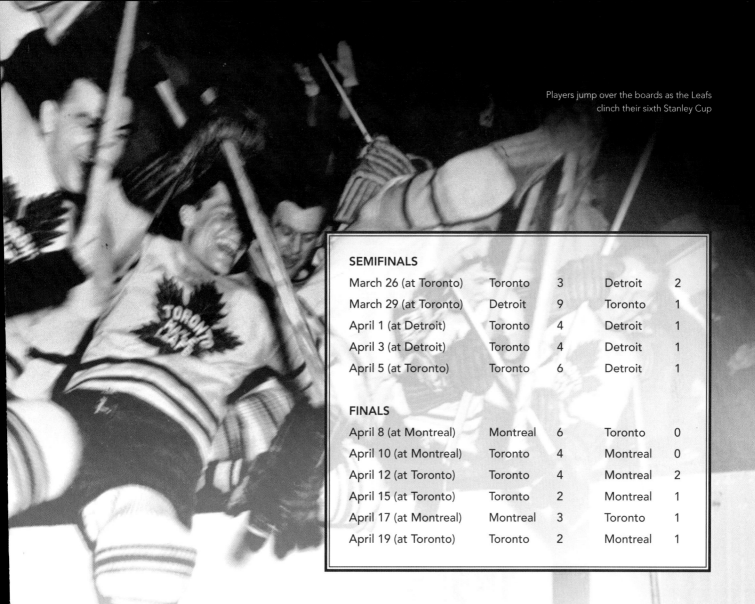

SEMIFINALS				
March 26 (at Toronto)	Toronto	3	Detroit	2
March 29 (at Toronto)	Detroit	9	Toronto	1
April 1 (at Detroit)	Toronto	4	Detroit	1
April 3 (at Detroit)	Toronto	4	Detroit	1
April 5 (at Toronto)	Toronto	6	Detroit	1
FINALS				
April 8 (at Montreal)	Montreal	6	Toronto	0
April 10 (at Montreal)	Toronto	4	Montreal	0
April 12 (at Toronto)	Toronto	4	Montreal	2
April 15 (at Toronto)	Toronto	2	Montreal	1
April 17 (at Montreal)	Montreal	3	Toronto	1
April 19 (at Toronto)	Toronto	2	Montreal	1

another rookie, Gordie Howe, teammate Ted Lindsay, and several Leafs players.

Toronto outclassed the Wings the rest of the way, winning the last two games by a cumulative score of 10–2. Broda was almost unbeatable in goal, and the league's best offence could not be stopped by Detroit's defence.

The win set up the first all-Canadian finals since 1935, and it was not one for the faint of heart. Montreal was already without the injured Ken Mosdell and Ken Reardon, and in the second period, Nick Metz was lost to the Leafs for the rest of the year after separating his shoulder while checking Maurice Richard. The Habs won the opener by a one-sided score of 6–0, but that result merely ignited the Leafs, who responded with a 4–0 win. And more than that,

they got under the skin of Richard, the great Montreal scorer. Toronto won the next game as well, 4–2.

Richard was back for game four, but he was a muted version of his usual self, and the Leafs easily held him off the score sheet. Nonetheless, it wasn't until late in the first period of overtime that the Leafs eked out a win. Apps brought the puck out from behind the goal and lifted a backhand over Bill Durnan.

With his team trailing three games to one, Richard was back to his old ways, scoring twice in a 3–1 win, but the Leafs won the Cup with a 2–1 victory on home ice, in front of 14,546 ecstatic fans. It was their second title in three years, but they were only just getting started.

1948: A JOYFUL REPEAT

Conn Smythe was a genius in every aspect of his life. A superb businessman with an excellent hockey mind, he was successful for all the right reasons. This was no more evident than early in the 1947–48 season.

Over the summer, Smythe hadn't made a single significant personnel change to his Cup-winning team, and the new season began as the old had finished. Chicago, meanwhile, was looking at another in a long line of dreadful results, and general manager Bill Tobin felt he had to do something to get the team going again. Smythe was a willing partner.

When the dust had settled, it was called the biggest trade in the nearly two decades since Smythe had bought King Clancy from Ottawa for the astronomical sum of $35,000. On November 2, 1947, Smythe sent Gaye Stewart, Bob Goldham, Bud Poile, Gus Bodnar, and Ernie Dickens to the Hawks for Max Bentley and Cy Thomas. All five Leafs were solid players, and in an era when teams could dress only 15 skaters (and one goalie), Smythe's deal amounted to trading one-third of his lineup for Max Bentley (Thomas was thrown in).

But Smythe knew he could replace those players with others from the farm team's roster, and, more important, he knew that the side that got the best player always won the trade. In this case, the best player was Max Bentley.

The Leafs finished in first place in the standings with a record of 32–15–13—their 77 points were five more than second-place Detroit earned. The Hawks failed to make the playoffs, finishing dead last for the second straight year.

Although a mismatch on paper, the semifinal series against Boston was trickier than Leafs fans would have hoped for. The Bruins led the first game 4–2 early in the third, but Syl Apps and Jim Thomson tied the game with quick goals midway through, and Nick Metz scored the winner late in the first period of overtime.

In game two the Bruins led again, 3–2 in the second, but the Leafs turned up the power thanks to a hat trick from Ted Kennedy, and won, 5–3. The next game, in Boston, ended badly for both teams. The Leafs won easily, 5–1, but fans were irate. Fortunately, a near riot was avoided, and the next game was much tamer, the Bruins avoiding elimination on home ice with a 3–2 win. Kennedy broke a 2–2 tie in the third period of game five to give the Leafs the series and another Cup finals date with the Red Wings.

This Detroit–Toronto series was not competitive. The Leafs were at the very top of their game and won in four straight. Broda allowed just seven goals, and Kennedy led the way with a playoff tally of 8 goals and 14 points . The Leafs had won the Cup for the third time in four years.

Max Bentley scores his second during game two of the Stanley Cup finals

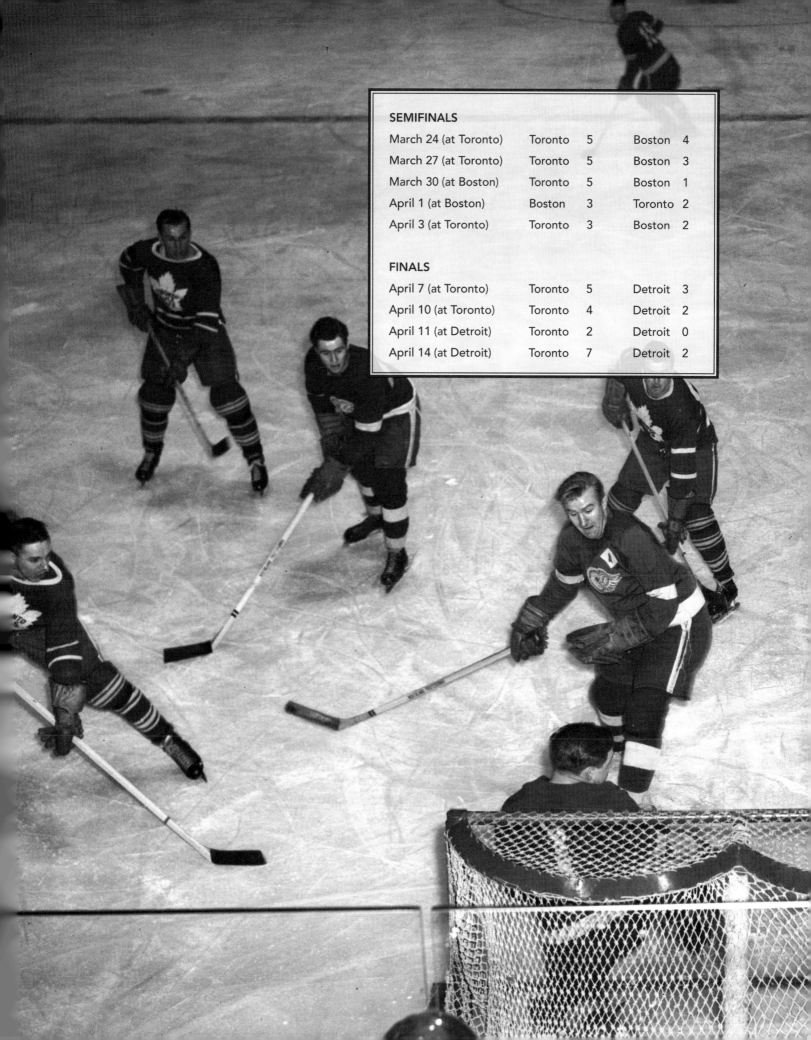

SEMIFINALS				
March 24 (at Toronto)	Toronto	5	Boston	4
March 27 (at Toronto)	Toronto	5	Boston	3
March 30 (at Boston)	Toronto	5	Boston	1
April 1 (at Boston)	Boston	3	Toronto	2
April 3 (at Toronto)	Toronto	3	Boston	2

FINALS				
April 7 (at Toronto)	Toronto	5	Detroit	3
April 10 (at Toronto)	Toronto	4	Detroit	2
April 11 (at Detroit)	Toronto	2	Detroit	0
April 14 (at Detroit)	Toronto	7	Detroit	2

1949: A HISTORIC DYNASTY

When the Leafs won the Stanley Cup in 1949, they became the first NHL team to win three in a row. But this year, they were as surprising a victor as they had been impressive the previous year. In the 1948–49 regular season, they finished with a disappointing 22–25–13 record, good enough for just 57 points and fourth place, well behind Detroit (75 points), Boston (66), and Montreal (65).

The off-season was as active this year as the 1948 summer had been docile. Syl Apps and Nick Metz both retired, leaving large holes in the roster, but Conn Smythe acquired Bill Juzda, a hard-hitting defenceman, and welcomed several others: Tod Sloan, Ray Timgren, Les Costello, Frank Mathers, and Ray Ceresino.

The Leafs played Boston in the semifinals, with the Bruins claiming home-ice advantage. Yet it was Toronto who jumped out of the gate, winning both games on the

road in impressive fashion. Although Broda got the shut-out in game one, he was seldom tested. The Leafs scored once in every period. Harry Watson with the first two and Max Bentley the third. In game two, Watson was again the hero. The Leafs were trailing 2–1 after two periods, but the big forward scored twice in the final period to turn defeat into victory. The winning goal came with only 1:19 left in regulation and forced Boston to pull goalie Frank Brimsek in the dying seconds to try to tie the game.

Back at the Gardens, it was the visitors who again prevailed, Boston winning in overtime on a goal from Woody Dumart. This was the only moment of success for the B's, however, as the Leafs won the next two games to advance to the Stanley Cup finals—and another date with Detroit.

Once again, though, such was the superiority of the Leafs that the Red Wings failed to win a single game. In every game, Toronto scored three goals, and in each

greatest money goalie of the Original Six era, did the rest, allowing only five goals.

The Leafs recorded victories of 3–2 and 3–1 in Detroit before heading home. It was game three at the Gardens that Detroit came closest to winning. Black Jack Stewart gave the Wings an early 1–0 lead, and they had a two-man advantage in the second period, which might have put the game out of reach with a goal or two. Instead,

the Leafs' penalty killers stood tall, and seconds after Bill Ezinicki came out of the penalty box, he scored to tie the game. Less than two minutes later, Toronto went ahead on a Ted Kennedy goal, and increased their lead to 3–1 before the end of the period.

They earned another 3–1 win in the ultimate game, claiming their third Cup in as many years and their fourth in five seasons.

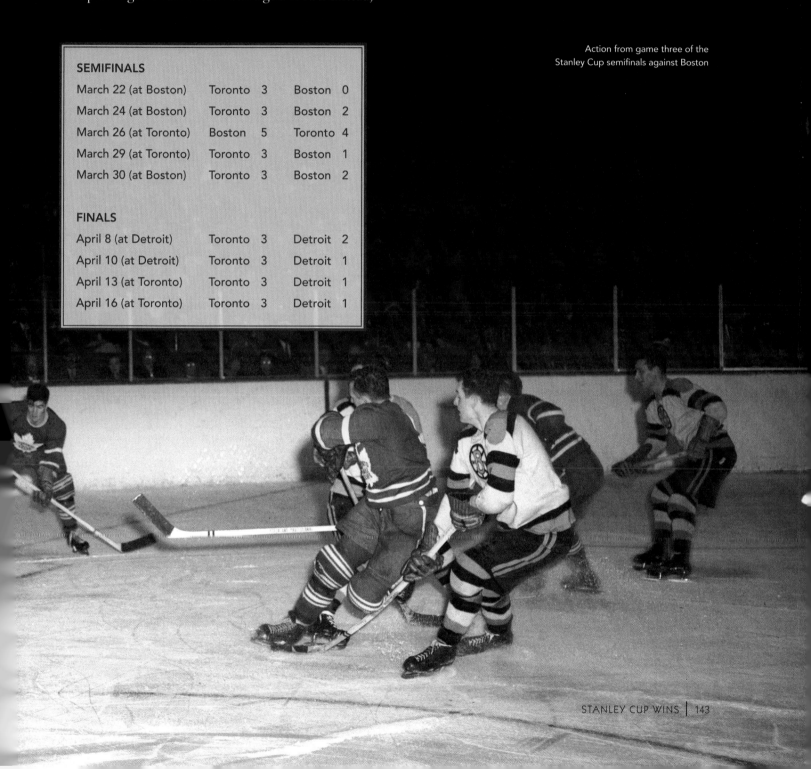

Action from game three of the
Stanley Cup semifinals against Boston

SEMIFINALS

March 22 (at Boston)	Toronto	3	Boston	0
March 24 (at Boston)	Toronto	3	Boston	2
March 26 (at Toronto)	Boston	5	Toronto	4
March 29 (at Toronto)	Toronto	3	Boston	1
March 30 (at Boston)	Toronto	3	Boston	2

FINALS

April 8 (at Detroit)	Toronto	3	Detroit	2
April 10 (at Detroit)	Toronto	3	Detroit	1
April 13 (at Toronto)	Toronto	3	Detroit	1
April 16 (at Toronto)	Toronto	3	Detroit	1

1951: FIFTH VICTORY IN SEVEN YEARS

The biggest change for the Leafs between 1949–50 and 1950–51 was behind the bench. Joe Primeau, the much-beloved member of the Kid Line in his playing days, was the new coach, and he had several new faces to incorporate into his lineup. As Turk Broda eased into the twilight of his career, Primeau decided to give both Broda and Al Rollins equal billing in the crease. Garth Boesch had retired to his farm, but Hugh Bolton had come in as a replacement. Dan Lewicki was another new arrival on the team.

The Leafs got off to a great start in the 70-game season, going unbeaten in 11 games at one point. By Christmas, it was clear that they and the Red Wings were the best of the bunch, and by season's end this hypothesis had been proved beyond a doubt. Both teams recorded 11 shut-outs, far and away the most in the league. They were the only teams to score more than 178 goals—Detroit had 236 and the Leafs 212; and they were first and second in goals against—Toronto with 138, Detroit right behind with 139.

More important, Detroit finished in first place with a 44–13–13 record for 101 points, and the Leafs were second with a 41–16–13 record and 95 points. But in the playoffs, the third-place Canadiens beat Detroit in six games to advance to the finals, and in the other series, Toronto faced Boston.

The Leafs started off in much the same manner as Detroit, losing game one on home ice, 2–0. The second-highest-scoring team in the league couldn't put a single puck past Jack Gelineau, and Lorne Ferguson and Woody Dumart scored the only goals the visitors needed.

Game two has an asterisk beside it. In old-world Toronto, when Sundays were reserved for rest and church, this Saturday-night game between the Leafs and Bruins started . . . but never finished. Tied one-all after two periods, neither side could score in the third, so overtime was played. That first extra period failed to yield a goal, but by this time it was 11:45 P.M. The game had to be abandoned because curfew laws forbade sporting activities on a Sunday. If needed, the game would have been played in its entirety at the end of the series.

Nonetheless, the Leafs left Toronto without a win, but when they got to Boston Garden, they regained their regular-season form. The amazing Broda shut out the Bruins, and after a scoreless opening period, the Leafs skated to a 3–0 win. They won the next two games as convincingly—3–1 and 4–1—and a series that had looked to be up for grabs was now firmly in Toronto's grasp. A 6–0 hammering in the decisive game took the Leafs to the finals to face the Habs.

Never before and never since has a finals produced such a close series, one in which every game went to overtime. The margin of victory—or defeat—was razor-thin for both teams every night, but the Leafs managed to come out on top the requisite four times.

Sid Smith was the hero in game one, at 5:51 of overtime, and Rocket Richard gave the Habs a win in game two at 2:55 of the fourth period. But after that, it was all Leafs. Ted Kennedy, Harry Watson, and, most famously, Bill Barilko provided the heroics in extra time. This win marked the pinnacle of the Leafs dynasty, and the end of it as well. It would be another 11 years before they held the Cup again.

Leafs captain Ted Kennedy addresses the crowd at Maple Leaf Gardens

SEMIFINALS

March 28 (at Toronto)	Boston	2	Toronto	0
March 31 (at Toronto)	Toronto	1	Boston	1
April 1 (at Boston)	Toronto	3	Boston	0
April 3 (at Boston)	Toronto	3	Boston	1
April 7 (at Toronto)	Toronto	4	Boston	1
April 8 (at Boston)	Toronto	6	Boston	0

FINALS

April 11 (at Toronto)	Toronto	3	Montreal	2
April 14 (at Toronto)	Montreal	3	Toronto	2
April 17 (at Montreal)	Toronto	2	Montreal	1
April 19 (at Montreal)	Toronto	3	Montreal	2
April 21 (at Toronto)	Toronto	3	Montreal	2

1962: A LONG WAIT OVER

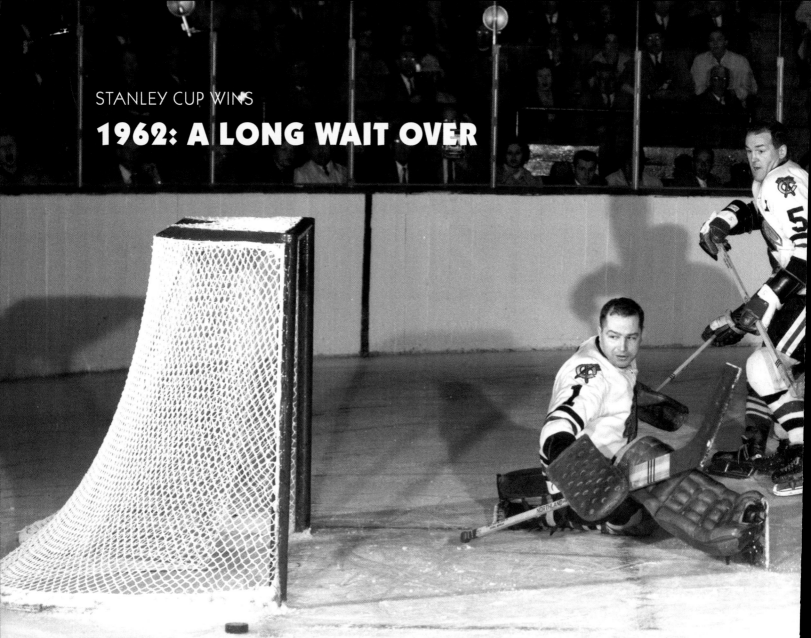

By the time the 1961–62 season had started, there were as many reasons to think the Leafs wouldn't win the Cup as to believe they would. It had been more than a decade since their last victory, but since Punch Imlach had taken over as coach during the 1958–59 season, there was renewed hope within the club.

Imlach took the Leafs to a shocking playoff appearance in 1959, thanks to one of the greatest stretch runs in league history, but the team lost to the Habs in both the 1959 and 1960 playoffs—understandable given Montreal's dominance during these years. In 1961, Detroit won the semifinal matchup in five fairly routine games, but at this time Toronto had a lineup that was as good as any in the league.

The ageless and legendary Johnny Bower was at the height of his powers in goal. Frank Mahovlich was among the top three or four players in the league. And the team was full of future Hall of Famers entering their prime: Tim Horton, Dave Keon, Red Kelly, and George Armstrong, to name but a few.

The Leafs had an excellent regular season in 1961–62, finishing in second place—well behind Montreal, but well ahead of Chicago. They were second in goals scored (232 to Montreal's 259), and second in fewest goals allowed (180 to Montreal's 166).

But those dominant Habs fell by the wayside in six games to Chicago, the Cup holders, in the first round of the

SEMIFINALS				
March 27 (at Toronto)	Toronto	4	NY Rangers	2
March 29 (at Toronto)	Toronto	2	NY Rangers	1
April 1 (at New York)	NY Rangers	5	Toronto	4
April 3 (at New York)	NY Rangers	4	Toronto	2
April 5 (at Toronto)	Toronto	3	NY Rangers	2
April 7 (at Toronto)	Toronto	7	NY Rangers	1
FINALS				
April 10 (at Toronto)	Toronto	4	Chicago	1
April 12 (at Toronto)	Toronto	3	Chicago	2
April 15 (at Chicago)	Chicago	3	Toronto	0
April 17 (at Chicago)	Chicago	4	Toronto	1
April 19 (at Toronto)	Toronto	8	Chicago	4
April 22 (at Chicago)	Toronto	2	Chicago	1

playoffs, while the Leafs faced the Rangers in the other semifinal series. Toronto started strongly at home, winning the games by scores of 4–2 and 2–1. This marked their 15th and 16th consecutive home wins against the Rangers.

The Rangers returned the favour at Madison Square Garden, winning both games to even the series. Game five, back in Toronto, was a true test for the Leafs. They led 2–0 midway through the game, only to have the Rangers tie the score and force overtime. The fourth period settled nothing, but in the second OT, centreman Red Kelly knocked in a rebound at 4:23.

Game six was also played in Toronto, and the Leafs made it 17 in a row, winning easily, 7–1, and advancing to the Cup finals to face the Black Hawks. This series went the same way as the semifinals, as the home team won the first four games. Goaltending was a central feature. In game one, Toronto won, 4–1, but that tally could have been much higher but for the play of "Mr. Goalie,"

Glenn Hall. In game two, the Leafs led 1–0 for 45 minutes, but the Gardens fans became desolate when Stan Mikita tied the game midway through the third period. Just a minute later, though, Mahovlich restored the lead, and the Leafs went on to win, 3–2.

Hall got the easy shutout in a 3–0 win in game three, but in the first period, Bower pulled a groin muscle while making a save on a Bobby Hull shot. He tried to play through the pain, but at 14:40 had to pull himself, forcing Don Simmons to mind the cage. Simmons gave up a goal almost immediately, and the Hawks coasted to a 4–1 win.

The news was bad for the Leafs: Bower would not play again in the series. Simmons, however, rose to the occasion. In the pivotal game five, he was excellent, and his mates sent eight shots past a beleaguered Hall in a stunning 8–4 win. Three nights later, in Chicago, the Leafs erased a 1–0 deficit early in the third to win, 2–1, and claim their first Stanley Cup in 11 years.

1963: A DOMINANT REPEAT

I t was the height of the Original Six era, and the top four teams were separated by only five points, one of the tightest finishes in NHL history. On top were the Leafs, a team that had made only two significant roster changes over the summer: Bert Olmstead had retired, and the Leafs signed rookie Kent Douglas, who at season's end was given the Calder Trophy. The team had a 35–23–12 record and 82 points—one better than Chicago, three ahead of Montreal, and five up on Detroit. Bringing up the rear were the Rangers, with 56 points, and the Bruins, with only 45.

The Leafs, too, were at their dominant best, taking down the Habs in a five-game semifinal. Bob Pulford scored early in the opening game, and the team never looked back, building a 3–0 lead and limiting Montreal's scoring chances. This 3–1 win in game one at the Gardens led to a 3–2 win two nights later, again at home. Although Jean Béliveau

made it 1–0 early, captain George Armstrong tied the game just 47 seconds later. Dave Keon broke a 2–2 tie late in the second with the game-winner, and Johnny Bower outperformed Jacques Plante in the battle of the goaltenders.

Game three, the first to be played in Montreal, was the turning point. Bower was sensational, shutting out the Habs' attack in a 2–0 win, stopping all 32 shots along the way. Toronto now held a commanding 3–0 series lead, and Montreal's 3–1 win in game four merely allowed them to save face on home ice. The Leafs came back to the Gardens and thrashed their rivals, 5–0, with Bower again recording a clean sheet. He had allowed only six goals in the series.

In the other semifinal, Detroit lost the first two games to Chicago, then stormed back to win the next four to gain the other spot in the Cup finals. The Leafs had home-ice advantage once more, and again used it to the good.

SEMIFINALS

March 26 (at Toronto)	Toronto	3	Montreal	1
March 28 (at Toronto)	Toronto	3	Montreal	2
March 30 (at Montreal)	Toronto	2	Montreal	0
April 2 (at Montreal)	Montreal	3	Toronto	1
April 4 (at Toronto)	Toronto	5	Montreal	0

FINALS

April 9 (at Toronto)	Toronto	4	Detroit	2
April 11 (at Toronto)	Toronto	4	Detroit	2
April 14 (at Detroit)	Detroit	3	Toronto	2
April 16 (at Detroit)	Toronto	4	Detroit	2
April 18 (at Toronto)	Toronto	3	Detroit	1

1964: ANOTHER THREE-PEAT FOR THE MAPLE LEAFS

As with the regular season of 1962–63, this next season was closely contested between four teams as the Rangers and Bruins were badly in arrears and out of the playoffs. The order differed from the previous year, and the ensuing Toronto–Montreal series resulted in the Habs gaining home ice.

The Leafs finished third with a more middling record of 33–25–12. They started off with pretty much the same lineup as the previous playoffs, but coach Punch Imlach was unimpressed and felt he needed to shake things up. On February 22, 1964, he closed a multiplayer deal with the Rangers, trading Dick Duff, Bob Nevin, Arnie Brown, Bill Collins, and Rod Seiling to the Blueshirts for Andy Bathgate and Don McKenney. Some say the deal worked—the Leafs won the Cup, after all—but others argue that if the deal hadn't been made, the team could have won even more Cups in the 1960s than it did. The debate continues.

Montreal scored the only goal of the first period of the first playoff game, the result of mass confusion. The game set a record as referee Frank Udvari whistled 31 penalties. Indeed, there were so many players in the box in the first period that the timekeeper failed to let Dave Keon out at the correct time, and the Habs scored during this extended power play. However, falling behind 2–0 only inspired the Leafs.

Imlach called Frank Mahovlich's performance in game two his best in three years. The Big M scored once and added a key assist in the first period, sending the Leafs to a 2–1 road victory. Game three was a lost opportunity for Toronto. Bob Pulford's two goals had them in front by one after two periods, but two late goals gave the Habs a win despite being badly outplayed. Henri Richard scored the winner with just 25 seconds left in the third.

There were another 30 penalties in game four, and it was another brilliant night from Mahovlich, who had a hand in all Leafs scoring in the 5–3 win (two goals, three assists). Toronto scored four times on the power play, and Montreal goalie Charlie Hodge was overrun by the Leafs' offence. The teams then won each succeeding home game—Montreal 4–2, and the Leafs 3–0—setting the stage for game seven in Montreal.

Rare are the times a player scores all three of his team's goals. Rarer still does this happen in the playoffs, and never before had this happened in a game seven. But on this night, Dave Keon stole all the thunder. He scored two goals midway through the opening period, and after Ralph Backstrom made it 2–1 in the third, Keon added his hat-trick goal into the empty net at 19:49 to give the Leafs a place in a third straight Cup finals.

SEMIFINALS				
March 26 (at Montreal)	Montreal	2	Toronto	0
March 28 (at Montreal)	Toronto	2	Montreal	1
March 31 (at Toronto)	Montreal	3	Toronto	2
April 2 (at Toronto)	Toronto	5	Montreal	3
April 4 (at Montreal)	Montreal	4	Toronto	2
April 7 (at Toronto)	Toronto	3	Montreal	0
April 9 (at Montreal)	Toronto	3	Montreal	1
FINALS				
April 11 (at Toronto)	Toronto	3	Detroit	2
April 14 (at Toronto)	Detroit	4	Toronto	3
April 16 (at Detroit)	Detroit	4	Toronto	3
April 18 (at Detroit)	Toronto	4	Detroit	2
April 21 (at Toronto)	Detroit	2	Toronto	1
April 23 (at Toronto)	Toronto	4	Detroit	3
April 25 (at Toronto)	Toronto	4	Detroit	0

The Stanley Cup parade heads toward City Hall in downtown Toronto

It took Detroit seven games to get by Chicago this year, but it was to be another Red Wings–Maple Leafs matchup, and this was the most dramatic in a long history of playoff battles between the teams. In a 2–2 game to open the series, with overtime looking certain, Bob Pulford outskated Gordie Howe to a loose puck and beat Sawchuk with a shot with only two seconds left in regulation.

In game two, the Leafs tied the game in the final minute, only to lose on a Larry Jeffrey goal in overtime. Game three? More of the same. Alex Delvecchio scored at 19:43 to break a 3–3 tie and give Detroit another late win.

Games four and five were more traditional wins— one apiece—sending the series back to Detroit, where the Wings had the chance to take the Cup. But in overtime, Bobby Baun scored on a point shot that fooled Sawchuk. Baun had broken a bone in his leg blocking a shot in the third and had been carried off on a stretcher, and his OT heroics became a famous moment in Stanley Cup history.

In game seven, back at the Gardens, it was all Johnny Bower. Bathgate's early goal gave the Leafs the lead, and with the 4–0 victory, the Leafs had won the Cup for the third successive time.

1967: THE LAST GREAT DAY OF THE ORIGINAL SIX

The Leafs failed to win a fourth straight Cup in 1965, having been eliminated by Montreal in six games. In 1966, they were disposed of in four straight—again by the Habs, who went on to win the Cup in both years and were looking dynastic themselves. This was the backdrop for the historic 1966–67 season, the last in which the NHL would feature only six teams. In the summer of 1967, the league doubled in size.

But the class of the 1966–67 regular season was Chicago. The Hawks finished with a stunning record of 41–17–12, good for 94 points, some 17 ahead of Montreal. The Habs finished only two up on the Leafs and five up on the surging Rangers, setting up a semifinal round featuring Chicago and Toronto in one series and the Habs and Rangers in the other.

The Leafs had experienced incredible highs and lows. From mid-January through to the second week of February, the team lost 10 games in a row, and soon afterward coach Punch Imlach took a medical leave of absence because of stress. The effervescent King Clancy took over, the team relaxed, and in the 10 games Imlach sat out, the Leafs won seven and tied one.

When Punch returned, the Leafs were ready for a playoff battle. They had an ancient lineup, dubbed the Over-the-Hill Gang by sportswriters. The highly favoured Hawks won the first playoff game on home ice, 5–2, but in game two the Leafs claimed home-ice advantage with an impressive 3–1 victory. The teams split the next two games in Toronto as well, the Leafs winning the first, 3–1, before losing the next, 4–3.

The pivotal fifth game in Chicago was all Toronto. Imlach, who had used three goalies in almost equal measure all season—ancient warriors Terry Sawchuk and Johnny Bower and newcomer Bruce Gamble—pulled Bower after the first period with the score tied 2–2. Sawchuk played shutout hockey the rest of the way, and the Leafs got the only two goals of the final period for the win. Back home, they did the same thing, scoring twice in the third to break a 1–1 tie. This time, Sawchuk played the full 60 minutes.

The Habs swept the Rangers to set up an all-Canadian final in the nation's Centennial year. The series revolved around goaltending, with the Leafs' veteran duo going up against the Habs' youngster, Rogie Vachon. The Habs chased Sawchuk in the opener, swamping the Leafs and winning easily, 6–2. In game two, though, Bower was the difference, and the Leafs skated to a 3–0 victory.

Again, the two teams split wins in Toronto. Game three was a gem, going to double overtime before Bob Pulford won the game for the Leafs. Vachon faced 62 shots and Bower 54 shots—a true goalies' duel. In the warm-up before game four, Bower was injured and couldn't play, and Sawchuk was not sharp in a 6–2 loss.

That set the stage for a crucial game five. Playing on the road, the Leafs again rose to the occasion. Sawchuk had to play again, but atoned for his last outing. Meanwhile Vachon gave his first weak performance at the worst

Dave Keon flies by J.C. Tremblay of Montreal

possible time for the Habs. With their 4–1 victory, the Leafs went home with a chance at the Cup.

Veteran Gump Worsley started in goal for Montreal. A scoreless first period was followed by two Toronto goals in the second, first from Ron Ellis and then, with only 36 seconds left, Jim Pappin. When Dick Duff made it a 2–1 game early in the third, fans were on pins and needles for the conclusion. The Habs sent out six skaters in the final minute with a faceoff deep in the Toronto end, but the Leafs won the draw and captain George Armstrong scored into the empty net to ice a 3–1 win and a Centennial-year Cup to remember.

SEMIFINALS

April 6 (at Chicago)	Chicago	5	Toronto	2
April 9 (at Chicago)	Toronto	3	Chicago	1
April 11 (at Toronto)	Toronto	3	Chicago	1
April 13 (at Toronto)	Chicago	4	Toronto	3
April 15 (at Chicago)	Toronto	4	Chicago	2
April 18 (at Toronto)	Toronto	3	Chicago	1

FINALS

April 20 (at Montreal)	Montreal	6	Toronto	2
April 22 (at Montreal)	Toronto	3	Montreal	0
April 25 (at Toronto)	Toronto	3	Montreal	2
April 27 (at Montreal)	Montreal	6	Toronto	2
April 29 (at Montreal)	Toronto	4	Montreal	1
May 2 (at Toronto)	Toronto	3	Montreal	1

ALL-TIME PLAYOFF REGISTER

Stats for each skater read:

YEAR	GP	G	A	P	PIM

Stats for each goaltender read:

YEAR	GP	W-L	MIN	GA	SO	GAA

JACK ADAMS

1918	2	2	0	2	3
1925	2	1	0	1	7
Totals	4	3	0	3	10

KEVYN ADAMS

1999	7	0	2	2	14
2000	12	1	0	1	7
Totals	19	1	2	3	21

CLAIRE ALEXANDER

1975	7	0	0	0	0
1976	9	2	4	6	4
Totals	16	2	4	4	4

MIKE ALLISON

1987	13	3	5	8	15

GLENN ANDERSON

1993	21	7	11	18	31

JOHN ANDERSON

1978	2	0	0	0	0
1979	6	0	2	2	0
1980	3	1	1	2	0
1981	2	0	0	0	0
1983	4	2	4	6	0
Totals	17	3	7	10	0

LLOYD ANDREWS

1922	7	2	0	2	5

DAVE ANDREYCHUK

1993	21	12	7	19	35
1994	18	5	5	10	16
1995	7	3	2	5	25
Totals	46	20	14	34	76

GREG ANDRUSAK

2000	3	0	0	0	2

NIKOLAI ANTROPOV

2000	3	0	0	0	4
2001	9	2	1	3	12
2003	3	0	0	0	0
2004	13	0	2	2	18
Totals	28	2	3	5	34

SYL APPS

1937	2	0	1	1	0
1938	7	1	4	5	0
1939	10	2	6	8	2
1940	10	5	2	7	2
1941	7	3	2	5	2
1942	13	5	9	14	2
1947	11	5	1	6	0
1948	9	4	4	8	0
Totals	69	25	29	54	8

AL ARBOUR

1962	8	0	0	0	6
1964	1	0	0	0	0
1965	1	0	0	0	2
Totals	9	0	0	0	8

GEORGE ARMSTRONG

1952	4	0	0	0	2
1954	5	1	0	1	2
1955	4	1	0	1	4
1956	5	4	2	6	0
1959	12	0	4	4	10
1960	10	1	4	5	4
1961	5	1	1	2	0
1962	12	7	5	12	2
1963	10	3	6	9	4
1964	14	5	8	13	10
1965	6	1	0	1	4
1966	4	0	1	1	4
1967	9	2	1	3	6
1969	4	0	0	0	0
1971	6	0	2	2	0
Totals	110	26	34	60	52

MURRAY ARMSTRONG

1938	3	0	0	0	0

DON ASHBY

1977	9	1	0	1	4

NORMAND AUBIN

1983	1	0	0	0	0

ACE BAILEY

1929	4	1	2	3	4
1931	2	1	1	2	0
1932	7	1	0	1	4
1933	8	0	1	1	4
Totals	21	3	4	7	12

BOB BAILEY

1954	5	0	2	2	4
1955	1	0	0	0	0
Totals	6	0	2	2	4

REID BAILEY

1983	2	0	0	0	2

EARL BALFOUR

1952	1	0	0	0	0
1956	3	0	1	1	2
Totals	4	0	1	1	2

BILL BARILKO

1947	11	0	3	3	18
1948	9	1	0	1	17
1949	9	0	1	1	20
1950	7	1	1	2	18
1951	11	3	2	5	31
Totals	47	5	7	12	104

ANDY BATHGATE

1964	14	5	4	9	25
1965	6	1	0	1	6
Totals	20	6	4	10	31

KEN BAUMGARTNER

1993	7	1	0	1	0
1994	10	0	0	0	18
Totals	17	1	0	1	18

BOB BAUN

1959	12	0	0	0	24
1960	10	1	0	1	17
1961	3	0	0	0	8
1962	12	0	3	3	19
1963	10	0	3	3	6
1964	14	2	3	5	42
1965	6	0	1	1	14
1966	4	0	1	1	8
1967	10	0	0	0	4
1971	6	0	1	1	19
1972	5	0	0	0	4
Totals	92	3	12	15	165

DON BEAUPRE

1996	2	0–0	20	2	0	6.00

WADE BELAK

2002	16	1	0	1	18
2003	2	0	0	0	4
2004	4	0	0	0	14
Totals	22	1	0	1	36

ED BELFOUR

2003	7	3–4	532	24	0	2.71
2004*	13	6–7	774	27	3	2.09
Totals	20	9–11	1,306	51	3	2.34

*8 PIM

JIM BENNING

1983	4	1	1	2	2

MAX BENTLEY

1948	9	4	7	11	0
1949	9	4	3	7	2
1950	7	3	3	6	0
1951	11	2	11	13	4
1952	4	1	0	1	2
Totals	40	14	24	38	8

BRYAN BERARD

1999	17	1	8	9	8

SERGEI BEREZIN

1999	17	6	6	12	4
2000	12	4	4	8	0
2001	11	2	5	7	2
Totals	40	12	15	27	6

AKI-PETTERI BERG

2001	11	0	2	2	4
2002	20	0	1	1	37
2003	7	1	1	2	2
2004	10	0	0	0	2
Totals	48	1	4	5	45

BILL BERG

1993	21	1	1	2	18
1994	18	1	2	3	10
1995	7	0	1	1	4
Totals	46	2	4	6	32

ALLAN BESTER

1987	1	0–0	39	1	0	1.54
1988	5	2–3	253	21	0	4.98
1990	4	0–3	196	14	0	4.29
Totals	10	2–6	488	36	0	4.43

PAUL BIBEAULT

1944	5	1–4	300	23	0	4.60

ANDY BLAIR

1929	4	3	0	3	2
1931	2	1	0	1	0
1932	7	2	2	4	6
1933	9	0	2	2	4
1934	5	0	2	2	16
1935	2	0	0	0	2
1936	9	0	0	0	2
Totals	38	6	6	12	32

MIKE BLAISDELL

1988	6	1	2	3	10

Gus Bodnar (left) and Frank McCool

GUS BODNAR

1944	5	0	0	0	0
1945	13	3	1	4	4
1947	1	0	0	0	0
Totals	19	3	1	4	4

GARTH BOESCH

1947	11	0	2	2	6
1948	8	2	1	3	2
1949	9	0	2	2	6
1950	6	0	0	0	4
Totals	34	2	5	7	18

LONNY BOHONOS

1999	9	3	6	9	2

LÉO BOIVIN

1954	5	0	0	0	2

BUZZ BOLL

1933	1	0	0	0	0
1934	5	0	0	0	9
1935	5	0	0	0	0
1936	9	7	3	10	2
1937	2	0	0	0	0
1938	7	0	0	0	2
Totals	29	7	3	10	13

HUGH BOLTON

1952	3	0	0	0	4
1954	5	0	1	1	4
1955	4	0	3	3	6
1956	5	0	1	1	0
Totals	17	0	5	5	14

GEORGE BOOTHMAN

1944	5	2	1	3	2

NIKOLAI BORSCHEVSKY

1993	16	2	7	9	0
1994	15	2	2	4	4
Totals	31	4	9	13	4

LAURIE BOSCHMAN

1980	3	1	1	2	18
1981	3	0	0	0	7
Totals	6	1	1	2	25

BRUCE BOUDREAU

1977	3	0	0	0	0
1981	2	1	0	1	0
1983	4	1	0	1	4
Totals	9	2	0	2	4

PAT BOUTETTE

1976	10	1	4	5	16
1977	9	0	4	4	17
1978	13	3	3	6	40
1979	6	2	2	4	22
Totals	38	6	13	19	95

JOHNNY BOWER

1959	12	5–7	749	39	0	3.12
1960	10	4–6	645	31	0	2.88
1961	3	0–3	180	9	0	3.00
1962	10	5–4	579	22	0	2.28
1963*	10	8–2	600	16	2	1.60
1964	14	8–6	850	30	2	2.12
1965	5	2–3	317	13	0	2.46
1966	2	0–2	120	8	0	4.00
1967	4	2–0	155	5	1	1.94
1969	4	0–2	154	11	0	4.29
Totals	74	34–35	4,349	184	5	2.58

*One assist

WALLY BOYER

1966	4	0	1	1	0

TYLER BOZAK

2013	5	1	1	2	4

CARL BREWER

1959	12	0	6	6	40
1960	10	2	3	5	16
1961	5	0	0	0	4
1962	8	0	2	2	22
1963	10	0	1	1	12
1964	12	0	1	1	30
1965	6	1	2	3	12
Totals	63	3	15	18	136

TURK BRODA

1937	2	0–2	134	5	0	2.24
1938	7	3–4	453	13	1	1.72
1939	10	5–5	617	20	2	1.94
1940	10	6–4	658	19	1	1.46
1941	7	3–4	438	15	0	2.05
1942	13	8–5	780	31	1	2.38
1943	6	2–4	441	20	0	2.72
1947	11	8–3	681	27	1	2.38
1948	9	8–1	558	20	1	2.15
1949	9	8–1	575	15	1	1.57
1950	7	3–4	450	10	3	1.33
1951	8	5–1*	493	9	2	1.10
1952	2	0–2	120	7	0	3.50
Totals	101	59–40	6,398	211	13	1.97

*One tie

WILLIE BROSSART

1974	1	0	0	0	0

DAVE BURROWS

1979	6	0	1	1	7
1980	3	0	1	1	2
Totals	9	0	2	2	9

GARTH BUTCHER

1995	7	0	0	0	8

JERRY BUTLER

1978	13	1	1	2	18
1979	6	0	0	0	4
Totals	19	1	1	2	22

LARRY CAHAN

1955	4	0	0	0	0

HARRY CAMERON

1918	7	3	2	5	0
1921	2	0	0	0	2
1922	7	0	1	1	27
Totals	16	3	3	6	29

RANDY CARLYLE

1977	9	0	1	1	20
1978	7	0	1	1	8
Totals	16	0	2	2	28

LORNE CARR

1942	13	3	2	5	6
1943	6	1	2	3	0
1944	5	0	1	1	0
1945	13	2	2	4	5
Totals	37	6	7	13	11

LARRY CARRIÈRE

1980	2	0	0	0	0

LORNE CHABOT

1929	4	2–2	243	5	0	1.23
1931	2	0–2	140	4	0	1.71
1932	7	5–1*	438	15	0	2.05
1933	9	4–5	688	18	2	1.57
Totals	22	11–10	1,509	42	2	1.57

*One tie

MURPH CHAMBERLAIN

1938	5	0	0	0	2
1939	10	2	5	7	4
1940	3	0	0	0	0
Totals	18	2	5	7	6

LEX CHISHOLM

1941	3	1	0	1	0

JACK CHURCH

1939	1	0	0	0	0
1940	10	1	1	2	6
1941	5	0	0	0	8
Totals	16	1	1	2	14

KING CLANCY

1931	2	1	0	1	0
1932	7	2	1	3	14
1933	9	0	3	3	14
1934	3	0	0	0	8
1935	7	1	0	1	8
1936	9	2	2	4	10
Totals	37	6	6	12	54

WENDEL CLARK

1986	10	5	1	6	47
1987	13	6	5	11	38
1990	5	1	1	2	19
1993	21	10	10	20	51
1994	18	9	7	16	24
1996	6	2	2	4	2
2000	6	1	1	2	4
Totals	79	34	27	61	185

SPRAGUE CLEGHORN

1921	2	0	0	0	0

JOE COLBORNE

Year	GP	G	A	Pts	PIM
2013	2	0	0	0	0

GARY COLLINS

Year	GP	G	A	Pts	PIM
1959	2	0	0	0	0

BRIAN CONACHER

Year	GP	G	A	Pts	PIM
1967	12	3	2	5	21

CHARLIE CONACHER

Year	GP	G	A	Pts	PIM
1931	2	0	1	1	0
1932	7	6	2	8	6
1933	9	1	1	2	10
1934	5	3	2	5	0
1935	7	1	4	5	6
1936	9	3	2	5	12
1937	2	0	0	0	5
Totals	41	14	12	26	39

BRANDON CONVERY

Year	GP	G	A	Pts	PIM
1996	5	0	0	0	2

BERT CORBEAU

Year	GP	G	A	Pts	PIM
1925	2	0	0	0	10

SHAYNE CORSON

Year	GP	G	A	Pts	PIM
2001	11	1	1	2	14
2002	19	1	6	7	33
2003	2	0	0	0	2
Totals	32	2	7	9	49

LES COSTELLO

Year	GP	G	A	Pts	PIM
1948	5	2	2	4	2
1950	1	0	0	0	0
Totals	6	2	2	4	2

SYLVAIN CÔTÉ

Year	GP	G	A	Pts	PIM
1999	17	2	1	3	10

BALDY COTTON

Year	GP	G	A	Pts	PIM
1929	4	0	0	0	2
1931	2	0	0	0	2
1932	7	2	2	4	8
1933	9	0	3	3	6
1934	5	0	2	2	0
1935	7	0	0	0	17
Totals	34	2	7	9	35

RUSS COURTNALL

Year	GP	G	A	Pts	PIM
1986	10	3	6	9	8
1987	13	3	4	7	11
1988	6	2	1	3	0
Totals	29	8	11	19	19

DAN COX

Year	GP	G	A	Pts	PIM
1929	4	0	1	1	4

MIKE CRAIG

Year	GP	G	A	Pts	PIM
1995	2	0	1	1	2
1996	6	0	0	0	18
Totals	8	0	1	1	20

RUSTY CRAWFORD

Year	GP	G	A	Pts	PIM
1918	2	2	1	3	0

DAVE CREIGHTON

Year	GP	G	A	Pts	PIM
1959	5	0	1	1	0

JIRI CRHA

Year	GP	W–L	MIN	GA	SO	GAA
1980	2	0–2	121	10	0	4.96
1981	3	0–2	65	11	0	10.15
Totals	5	0–4	186	21	0	6.77

CORY CROSS

Year	GP	G	A	Pts	PIM
2000	12	0	2	2	2
2001	11	2	1	3	10
2002	12	0	0	0	8
Totals	35	2	3	5	20

BARRY CULLEN

Year	GP	G	A	Pts	PIM
1959	2	0	0	0	0

BRIAN CULLEN

Year	GP	G	A	Pts	PIM
1955	4	1	0	1	0
1956	5	1	0	1	2
1959	10	1	0	1	0
Totals	19	3	0	3	2

JOHN CULLEN

Year	GP	G	A	Pts	PIM
1993	12	2	3	5	0
1994	3	0	0	0	0
Totals	15	2	3	5	0

BRIAN CURRAN

Year	GP	G	A	Pts	PIM
1988	6	0	0	0	41
1990	5	0	1	1	19
Totals	11	0	1	1	60

VINCENT DAMPHOUSSE

Year	GP	G	A	Pts	PIM
1987	12	1	5	6	8
1988	6	0	1	1	10
1990	5	0	2	2	2
Totals	23	1	8	9	20

DAN DAOUST

Year	GP	G	A	Pts	PIM
1986	10	2	2	4	19
1987	13	5	2	7	42
1988	4	0	0	0	2
1990	5	0	1	1	20
Totals	32	7	5	12	83

HAROLD DARRAGH

Year	GP	G	A	Pts	PIM
1932	7	0	1	1	2

BOB DAVIDSON

Year	GP	G	A	Pts	PIM
1936	9	1	3	4	2
1937	2	0	0	0	5
1938	7	0	2	2	10
1939	10	1	1	2	6
1940	10	0	3	3	16
1941	7	0	2	2	7
1942	13	1	2	3	20
1943	6	1	2	3	7
1944	5	0	0	0	4
1945	13	1	2	3	2
Totals	82	5	17	22	79

BOB DAWES

Year	GP	G	A	Pts	PIM
1949	9	0	0	0	2

HAP DAY

Year	GP	G	A	Pts	PIM
1925	2	0	0	0	0
1929	4	1	0	1	4
1931	2	0	3	3	7
1932	7	3	3	6	6
1933	9	0	1	1	21
1934	5	0	0	0	6
1935	7	0	0	0	4
1936	9	0	0	0	8
1937	2	0	0	0	0
Totals	47	4	7	11	56

DALE DeGRAY

Year	GP	G	A	Pts	PIM
1988	5	0	1	1	16

NATHAN DEMPSEY

Year	GP	G	A	Pts	PIM
2002	6	0	2	2	0

CORB DENNENAY

Year	GP	G	A	Pts	PIM
1918	7	3	2	5	3
1921	2	0	0	0	0
1922	7	4	2	6	2
Totals	16	7	4	11	5

BILL DERLAGO

Year	GP	G	A	Pts	PIM
1980	3	0	0	0	4
1981	3	1	0	1	2
1983	4	3	0	3	2
Totals	10	4	0	4	8

ERNIE DICKENS

Year	GP	G	A	Pts	PIM
1942	13	0	0	0	4

GERALD DIDUCK

Year	GP	G	A	Pts	PIM
2000	10	0	1	1	14

PAUL DiPIETRO

Year	GP	G	A	Pts	PIM
1995	7	1	1	2	0

TIE DOMI

Year	GP	G	A	Pts	PIM
1995	7	1	0	1	0
1996	6	0	2	2	4
1999	14	0	2	2	24
2000	12	0	1	1	20
2001	8	0	1	1	20
2002	19	1	3	4	61
2003	7	1	0	1	13
2004	13	2	2	4	41
Totals	86	5	11	16	183

KEN DORATY

Year	GP	G	A	Pts	PIM
1933	9	5	0	5	4
1934	5	2	2	4	0
1935	1	0	0	0	0
Totals	15	7	2	9	4

JIM DOREY

Year	GP	G	A	Pts	PIM
1969	4	0	1	1	21
1971	6	0	1	1	19
Totals	10	0	2	2	40

KENT DOUGLAS

Year	GP	G	A	Pts	PIM
1963	10	1	1	2	2
1965	5	0	1	1	19
1966	4	0	1	1	12
Totals	19	1	3	4	33

GORD DRILLON

Year	GP	G	A	Pts	PIM
1937	2	0	0	0	0
1938	7	7	1	8	2
1939	10	7	6	13	4
1940	10	3	1	4	0
1941	7	3	2	5	2
1942	9	2	3	5	2
Totals	45	22	13	35	10

DICK DUFF

Year	GP	G	A	Pts	PIM
1956	5	1	4	5	2
1959	12	4	3	7	8
1960	10	2	4	6	6
1961	5	0	1	1	2
1962	12	3	10	13	20
1963	10	4	1	5	2
Totals	54	14	23	37	40

ART DUNCAN

Year	GP	G	A	Pts	PIM
1929	4	0	0	0	4
1931	1	0	0	0	0
Totals	5	0	0	0	4

DAVE DUNN

Year	GP	G	A	Pts	PIM
1975	7	1	1	2	24
1976	3	0	0	0	17
Totals	10	1	1	2	41

DENIS DUPÉRÉ

Year	GP	G	A	Pts	PIM
1971	6	0	0	0	0
1972	5	0	0	0	0
1974	3	0	0	0	0
Totals	14	0	0	0	0

VITEZSLAV DURIS
1981 3 0 1 1 2

BABE DYE
1921 2 0 0 0 9
1922 7 11 2 13 5
1925 2 0 0 0 0
Totals 11 11 2 13 14

DALLAS EAKINS
1999 1 0 0 0 0

MIKE EASTWOOD
1993 10 1 2 3 8
1994 18 3 2 5 12
Totals 28 4 4 8 20

TIM ECCLESTONE
1974 4 0 1 1 0

GARRY EDMUNDSON
1960 9 0 1 1 4

GERRY EHMAN
1959 12 6 7 13 8
1960 9 0 0 0 0
1964 9 1 0 1 4
Totals 30 7 7 14 12

DAVE ELLETT
1993 21 4 8 12 8
1994 18 3 15 18 31
1995 7 0 2 2 0
1996 6 0 0 0 4
Totals 52 7 25 32 43

RON ELLIS
1965 6 3 0 3 2
1966 4 0 0 0 2
1967 12 2 1 3 4
1969 4 2 1 3 2
1971 6 1 1 2 2
1972 5 1 1 2 4
1974 4 2 1 3 0
1975 7 3 0 3 2
1978 13 3 2 5 0
1979 6 1 1 2 2
1980 3 0 0 0 0
Totals 70 18 8 26 20

AUT ERICKSON
1967 1 0 0 0 2

ANDERS ERIKSSON
2002 10 0 0 0 0

DARYL EVANS
1987 1 0 0 0 0

PAUL EVANS
1977 2 0 0 0 0

BILL EZINICKI
1947 11 0 2 2 30
1948 9 3 1 4 6
1949 9 1 4 5 20
1950 5 0 0 0 13
Totals 34 4 7 11 69

JEFF FARKAS
2000 3 1 0 1 0
2002 2 0 0 0 0
Totals 5 1 0 1 0

DAVE FARRISH
1980 3 0 0 0 10
1981 1 0 0 0 0
Totals 4 0 0 0 10

DOUG FAVELL
1974 3 0–3 182 10 0 3.30

TOM FERGUS
1986 10 5 7 12 6
1987 2 0 1 1 2
1988 6 2 3 5 2
1990 5 2 1 3 4
Totals 23 9 12 21 14

GEORGE FERGUSON
1974 3 0 1 1 2
1975 7 1 0 1 7
1976 10 2 4 6 2
1977 9 0 3 3 7
1978 13 5 1 6 7
Totals 42 8 9 17 25

FRANK FINNIGAN
1932 7 2 3 5 8
1935 7 1 2 3 2
1936 9 0 3 3 0
1937 2 0 0 0 0
Totals 25 3 8 11 10

TOM FITZGERALD
2003 7 0 1 1 4
2004 10 0 0 0 6
Totals 17 0 1 1 10

FERNIE FLAMAN
1951 9 1 0 1 8
1952 4 0 2 2 18
1954 2 0 0 0 0
Totals 15 1 2 3 26

BILL FLETT
1975 5 0 0 0 2

MIKE FOLIGNO
1993 18 2 6 8 42

JAKE FORBES
1921 2 0–2 120 7 0 3.50

JACK FORSEY
1943 3 0 1 1 0

JIM FOWLER
1937 2 0 0 0 0
1938 7 0 2 2 0
1939 9 0 1 1 2
Totals 18 0 3 3 2

LOU FRANCESCHETTI
1990 5 0 1 1 26

RON FRANCIS
2004 12 0 4 4 2

CODY FRANSON
2013 7 3 3 6 0

MARK FRASER
2013 4 0 1 1 7

MATT FRATTIN
2013 6 0 2 2 0

MIROSLAV FRYCER
1983 4 2 5 7 0
1986 10 1 3 4 10
1988 3 0 0 0 6
Totals 17 3 8 11 16

DAVE GAGNER
1996 6 0 2 2 6

BRUCE GAMBLE
1969 3 0–2 86 13 0 9.07

JAKE GARDINER
2013 6 1 4 5 0

CAL GARDNER
1949 9 2 5 7 0
1950 7 1 0 1 4
1951 11 1 1 2 4
1952 3 0 0 0 2
Totals 30 4 6 10 10

PAUL GARDNER
1979 6 0 1 1 4

SCOTT GARLAND
1976 7 1 2 3 35

MIKE GARTNER
1994 18 5 6 11 14
1995 5 2 2 4 2
1996 6 4 1 5 4
Totals 29 11 9 20 20

STEWART GAVIN
1983 4 0 0 0 0

EDDIE GERARD
1922 1 0 0 0 0

TODD GILL
1986 1 0 0 0 0
1987 13 2 2 4 42
1988 6 1 3 4 20
1990 5 0 3 3 16
1993 21 1 10 11 26
1994 18 1 5 6 37
1995 7 0 3 3 6
1996 6 0 0 0 24
Totals 77 5 26 31 171

DOUG GILMOUR
1993 21 10 25 35 30
1994 18 6 22 28 42
1995 7 0 6 6 6
1996 6 1 7 8 12
Totals 52 17 60 77 90

Doug Gilmour and Wayne Gretzky shake hands after the 1993 playoffs, one of the most memorable series ever played at Maple Leafs Gardens

GASTON GINGRAS

1983	3	1	2	3	2

BRIAN GLENNIE

1971	3	0	0	0	0
1972	5	0	0	0	25
1974	3	0	0	0	10
1976	6	0	1	1	15
1977	2	0	0	0	0
1978	13	0	0	0	16
Totals	32	0	1	1	66

BOB GOLDHAM

1942	13	2	2	4	31

HANK GOLDUP

1940	10	5	1	6	4
1941	7	0	0	0	0
1942	9	0	0	0	2
Totals	26	5	1	6	6

CHRIS GOVEDARIS

1994	2	0	0	0	0

MIKHAIL GRABOVSKI

2013	7	0	2	2	2

BOB GRACIE

1931	2	0	0	0	0
1932	7	3	1	4	0
1933	9	0	1	1	0
Totals	18	3	2	5	0

TRAVIS GREEN

2002	20	3	6	9	34
2003	4	2	1	3	4
Totals	24	5	7	12	38

CARL GUNNARSSON

2013	7	0	1	1	0

GEORGE HAINSWORTH

1934	5	2–3	302	11	0	2.19
1935	7	3–4	460	12	2	1.57
1936	9	3–6	541	27	0	2.99
Totals	21	8–13	1,303	50	2	2.30

JACK HAMILTON

1943	6	1	1	2	0
1944	5	1	0	1	0
Totals	11	2	1	3	0

REG HAMILTON

1937	2	0	1	1	2
1938	7	0	1	1	2
1939	10	0	2	2	4
1940	10	0	0	0	0
1941	7	1	2	3	13
1943	6	1	1	2	9
1944	5	1	0	1	8
1945	13	0	0	0	6
Totals	60	3	7	10	44

RYAN HAMILTON

2013	2	0	1	1	0

INGE HAMMARSTROM

1974	4	1	0	1	0
1975	7	1	3	4	4
1977	2	0	0	0	0
Totals	13	2	3	5	4

DAVE HANNAN

1990	3	1	0	1	4

GORD HANNIGAN

1954	5	2	0	2	4
1956	4	0	0	0	4
Totals	9	2	0	2	8

BILLY HARRIS

1956	5	1	0	1	4
1959	12	3	4	7	16
1960	9	0	3	3	4
1961	5	1	0	1	0
1962	12	2	1	3	2
1963	10	0	1	1	0
1964	9	1	1	2	4
Totals	62	8	10	18	30

BILLY HARRIS

1983	4	0	1	1	2

JIM HARRISON

1971	6	0	1	1	33
1972	5	1	0	1	10
Totals	11	1	1	2	43

PAUL HARRISON

1979	2	0–1	91	7	0	4.62
1981	1	0–0	40	1	0	1.50
Totals	3	0–1	131	8	0	3.66

GLENN HEALY

1999	1	0–0	20	0	0	0.00

PAUL HEALEY

2002	18	0	1	1	2
2003	4	0	1	1	2
Totals	22	0	2	2	4

PAUL HENDERSON

1969	4	0	1	1	0
1971	6	5	1	6	4
1972	5	1	2	3	6
1974	4	0	2	2	2
Totals	19	6	6	12	12

DARBY HENDRICKSON

1994	2	0	0	0	0

RED HERON

1939	2	0	0	0	4
1940	9	2	0	2	2
1941	7	0	2	2	0
Totals	18	2	2	4	6

PAT HICKEY

1980	3	0	0	0	2
1981	2	0	0	0	0
Totals	5	0	0	0	2

PAUL HIGGINS

1983	1	0	0	0	0

MEL HILL

1943	6	3	0	3	0
1945	13	2	3	5	6
Totals	19	5	3	8	6

LARRY HILLMAN

1961	5	0	0	0	0
1964	11	0	0	0	2
1966	4	1	1	2	6
1967	12	1	2	3	0
Totals	32	2	3	5	8

JONAS HOGLUND

2000	12	2	4	6	2
2001	10	0	0	0	4
2002	20	4	6	10	2
2003	7	0	1	1	0
Totals	49	6	11	17	8

BENOÎT HOGUE

1995	7	0	0	0	6

FLASH HOLLETT

1935	7	0	0	0	6

HARRY HOLMES

1918*	7	4–3	420	26	0	3.71

*First game in the NHL

TOOTS HOLWAY

1925	2	0	0	0	0

GEORGE HORNE

1929	4	0	0	0	4

RED HORNER

1929	4	1	0	1	2
1931	2	0	0	0	4
1932	7	2	2	4	20
1933	9	1	0	1	10
1934	5	1	0	1	6
1935	7	0	1	1	4
1936	9	1	2	3	22
1937	2	0	0	0	7
1938	7	0	1	1	14
1939	10	1	2	3	26
1940	9	0	2	2	55
Totals	71	7	10	17	170

TIM HORTON

1950	1	0	0	0	2
1954	5	1	1	2	4
1956	2	0	0	0	4
1959	12	0	3	3	16
1960	10	0	1	1	6
1961	5	0	0	0	0
1962	12	3	13	16	16
1963	10	1	3	4	10
1964	14	0	4	4	20
1965	6	0	2	2	13
1966	4	1	0	1	12
1967	12	3	5	8	25
1969	4	0	0	0	7
Totals	97	9	32	41	135

PHIL HOUSLEY

2003	3	0	0	0	0

RON HURST

1956	3	0	2	2	4

DAVE HUTCHISON

1979	6	0	3	3	23

AL IAFRATE

1986	10	0	3	3	4
1987	13	1	3	4	11
1988	6	3	4	7	6
Totals	29	4	10	14	21

MIROSLAV IHNACAK

1987	1	0	0	0	0

PETER IHNACAK

1986	10	2	3	5	12
1987	13	2	4	6	9
1988	5	0	3	3	4
Totals	28	4	10	14	25

ART JACKSON

1935	7	0	0	0	2
1936	8	0	3	3	2
1937	2	0	0	0	0
1945	8	0	0	0	0
Totals	25	0	3	3	4

BUSHER JACKSON

1931	2	0	0	0	2
1932	7	5	2	7	13
1933	9	3	1	4	2
1934	5	1	0	1	8
1935	7	3	2	5	2
1936	9	3	2	5	4
1937	2	1	0	1	2
1938	6	1	0	1	8
1939	7	0	1	1	2
Totals	54	17	8	25	43

GERRY JAMES
1956	5	1	0	1	8
1960	10	0	0	0	0
Totals	15	1	0	1	8

PIERRE JARRY
1972	5	0	1	1	0

WES JARVIS
1987	2	0	0	0	2

LARRY JEFFREY
1967	6	0	1	1	4

GRANT JENNINGS
1995	4	0	0	0	0

TREVOR JOHANSEN
1978	13	0	3	3	21

CALLE JOHANSSON
2004	4	0	0	0	2

MIKE JOHNSON
1999	17	3	2	5	4

TERRY JOHNSON
1987	2	0	0	0	0
1988	3	0	0	0	10
Totals	5	0	0	0	10

EDDIE JOHNSTON
1974	1	0–1	60	6	0	6.00

ROSS JOHNSTONE
1944	3	0	0	0	0

BUCK JONES
1943	6	0	0	0	8

JIMMY JONES
1978	13	1	5	6	7
1979	6	0	0	0	4
Totals	19	1	5	6	11

KENNY JONSSON
1995	4	0	0	0	0

CURTIS JOSEPH
1999	17	9–8–0	1,011	41	1	2.43
2000	12	6–6–0	729	25	1	2.06
2001*	11	7–4–0	685	24	3	2.10
2002*	20	10–10–0	1,253	48	3	2.30
Totals	60	32–28–0	3,678	138	8	2.25

*4 PIM

BILL JUZDA
1949	9	0	2	2	8
1950	7	0	0	0	16
1951	11	0	0	0	7
1952	3	0	0	0	2
Totals	30	0	2	2	33

TOMAS KABERLE
1999	14	0	3	3	2
2000	12	1	4	5	0
2001	11	1	3	4	0
2002	20	2	8	10	16
2003	7	2	1	3	0
2004	13	0	3	3	6
Totals	77	6	22	28	24

NAZEM KADRI
2013	7	1	3	4	10

BINGO KAMPMAN
1938	7	0	1	1	6
1939	10	1	1	2	20
1940	10	0	0	0	0
1941	7	0	0	0	0
1942	13	0	2	2	12
Totals	47	1	4	5	38

ALEXANDER KARPOVTSEV
2000	11	0	3	3	4

MIKE KASZYCKI
1980	2	0	0	0	2

RICK KEHOE
1972	2	0	0	0	2

RED KELLY
1960	10	3	8	11	2
1961	2	1	0	1	0
1962	12	4	6	10	0
1963	10	2	6	8	6
1964	14	4	9	13	4
1965	6	3	2	5	2
1966	4	0	2	2	0
1967	12	0	5	5	2
Totals	70	17	38	55	16

PEP KELLY
1935	7	2	0	2	4
1936	9	2	3	5	4
1938	7	2	2	4	2
1939	10	1	0	1	0
1940	6	0	1	1	0
Totals	39	7	6	13	10

FORBES KENNEDY
1969	1	0	0	0	38

TED KENNEDY
1944	5	1	1	2	4
1945	13	7	2	9	2
1947	11	4	5	9	4
1948	9	8	6	14	0
1949	9	2	6	8	2
1950	7	1	2	3	8
1951	11	4	5	9	6
1952	4	0	0	0	4
1954	5	1	1	2	2
1955	4	1	3	4	0
Totals	78	29	31	60	32

DAVE KEON
1961	5	1	1	2	0
1962	12	5	3	8	0
1963	10	7	5	12	0
1964	14	7	2	9	2
1965	6	2	2	4	2
1966	4	0	2	2	0
1967	12	3	5	8	0
1969	4	1	3	4	2
1971	6	3	2	5	0
1972	5	2	3	5	0
1974	4	1	2	3	0
1975	7	0	5	5	0
Totals	89	32	35	67	6

PHIL KESSEL
2013	7	4	2	6	2

DMITRI KHRISTICH
2000	12	1	2	3	0

TREVOR KIDD
2004	1	0–0	33	1	0	1.82

CHAD KILGER
2004	13	2	1	3	0

HEC KILREA
1934	5	2	0	2	2
1935	6	0	0	0	4
Totals	11	2	0	2	6

DEREK KING
1999	16	1	3	4	4

KRIS KING
1999	17	1	1	2	25
2000	1	0	0	0	2
Totals	18	1	1	2	27

Dave Keon takes a drink from the Stanley Cup as Harold Ballard (left) looks on, April 18, 1963

KEN KLEE

Year	GP	G	A	Pts	PIM
2004	11	0	0	0	6

JOE KLUKAY

Year	GP	G	A	Pts	PIM
1943	1	0	0	0	0
1947	11	1	0	1	0
1948	9	1	1	2	2
1949	9	2	3	5	4
1950	7	3	0	3	4
1951	11	4	3	7	0
1952	4	1	1	2	0
1955	4	0	0	0	4
Totals	56	12	8	20	14

LADISLAV KOHN

Year	GP	G	A	Pts	PIM
1999	2	0	0	0	5

MARK KOLESAR

Year	GP	G	A	Pts	PIM
1996	3	1	0	1	2

LEO KOMAROV

Year	GP	G	A	Pts	PIM
2013	7	0	0	0	17

JOHN KORDIC

Year	GP	G	A	Pts	PIM
1990	5	0	1	1	33

JIM KORN

Year	GP	G	A	Pts	PIM
1983	3	0	0	0	26

IGOR KOROLEV

Year	GP	G	A	Pts	PIM
1999	1	0	0	0	0
2000	12	0	4	4	6
2001	11	0	0	0	0
Totals	24	0	4	4	6

MICHAEL KOSTKA

Year	GP	G	A	Pts	PIM
2013	1	0	0	0	0

CHRIS KOTSOPOULOS

Year	GP	G	A	Pts	PIM
1986	10	1	0	1	14
1987	7	0	0	0	14
Totals	17	1	0	1	28

MIKE KRUSHELNYSKI

Year	GP	G	A	Pts	PIM
1993	16	3	7	10	8
1994	6	0	0	0	0
Totals	22	3	7	10	8

NIKOLAI KULEMIN

Year	GP	G	A	Pts	PIM
2013	7	0	1	1	0

ORLAND KURTENBACH

Year	GP	G	A	Pts	PIM
1966	4	0	0	0	20

TOM KURVERS

Year	GP	G	A	Pts	PIM
1990	5	0	3	3	4

NICK KYPREOS

Year	GP	G	A	Pts	PIM
1996	5	0	0	0	4

ÉRIC LACROIX

Year	GP	G	A	Pts	PIM
1994	2	0	0	0	0

PETE LANGELLE

Year	GP	G	A	Pts	PIM
1939	11	1	2	3	2
1940	10	0	3	3	0
1941	7	1	1	2	0
1942	13	3	3	6	2
Totals	41	5	9	14	4

RICK LANZ

Year	GP	G	A	Pts	PIM
1987	13	1	3	4	27
1988	1	0	0	0	2
Totals	14	1	3	4	29

MICHEL LAROCQUE

Year	GP	W-L	MIN	GA	SO	GAA
1981	2	0–1	75	8	0	6.40

GARY LEEMAN

Year	GP	G	A	Pts	PIM
1983	2	0	0	0	2
1986	10	2	10	12	2
1987	5	0	1	1	14
1988	2	2	0	2	2
1990	5	3	3	6	16
Totals	24	7	14	21	36

BRIAN LEETCH

Year	GP	G	A	Pts	PIM
2004	13	0	8	8	6

SYLVAIN LEFEBVRE

Year	GP	G	A	Pts	PIM
1993	21	3	3	6	20
1994	18	0	3	3	16
Totals	39	3	6	9	36

ALEX LEVINSKY

Year	GP	G	A	Pts	PIM
1931	2	0	0	0	0
1932	7	0	0	0	6
1933	9	1	0	1	14
1934	5	0	0	0	6
Totals	23	1	0	1	26

DANNY LEWICKI

Year	GP	G	A	Pts	PIM
1951	9	0	0	0	0

RICK LEY

Year	GP	G	A	Pts	PIM
1969	3	0	0	0	9
1971	6	0	2	2	4
1972	5	0	0	0	7
Totals	14	0	2	2	20

JOHN-MICHAEL LILES

Year	GP	G	A	Pts	PIM
2013	4	0	0	0	2

ED LITZENBERGER

Year	GP	G	A	Pts	PIM
1962	10	0	2	2	4
1963	9	1	2	3	6
1964	1	0	0	0	10
Totals	20	1	4	5	20

HARRY LUMLEY

Year	GP	W-L	MIN	GA	SO	GAA
1954	5	1–4	322	15	0	2.80
1955	4	0–4	240	14	0	3.50
1956	5	1–4	305	14	1	2.75
Totals	14	2–12	867	43	1	2.98

JYRKKI LUMME

Year	GP	G	A	Pts	PIM
2002	14	0	0	0	4
2003	7	0	2	2	4

JOFFREY LUPUL

Year	GP	G	A	Pts	PIM
2013	7	3	1	4	4

VIC LYNN

Year	GP	G	A	Pts	PIM
1947	11	4	1	5	16
1948	9	2	5	7	20
1949	8	0	1	1	2
1950	7	0	2	2	2
Totals	35	6	9	15	40

CLARKE MacARTHUR

Year	GP	G	A	Pts	PIM
2013	5	2	1	3	2

PARKER MacDONALD

Year	GP	G	A	Pts	PIM
1955	4	0	0	0	4

FLEMING MacKELL

Year	GP	G	A	Pts	PIM
1949	9	2	4	6	4
1950	7	1	1	2	11
1951	11	2	3	5	9
Totals	27	5	8	13	24

DON MacLEAN

Year	GP	G	A	Pts	PIM
2002	3	0	0	0	0

BILLY MacMILLAN

Year	GP	G	A	Pts	PIM
1971	6	0	3	3	2
1972	5	0	0	0	0
Totals	11	0	3	3	2

JOHN MacMILLAN

Year	GP	G	A	Pts	PIM
1961	4	0	0	0	0
1962	3	0	0	0	0
1963	1	0	0	0	0
Totals	8	0	0	0	0

JAMIE MACOUN

Year	GP	G	A	Pts	PIM
1993	21	0	6	6	36
1994	18	1	1	2	12
1995	7	1	2	3	8
1996	6	0	2	2	8
Totals	52	2	11	13	64

KEVIN MAGUIRE

Year	GP	G	A	Pts	PIM
1987	1	0	0	0	0

FRANK MAHOVLICH

Year	GP	G	A	Pts	PIM
1959	12	6	5	11	18
1960	10	3	1	4	27
1961	5	1	1	2	6
1962	12	6	6	12	29
1963	9	0	2	2	8
1964	14	4	11	15	20
1965	6	0	3	3	9
1966	4	1	0	1	10
1967	12	3	7	10	8
Totals	84	24	36	60	135

ADAM MAIR

Year	GP	G	A	Pts	PIM
1999	5	1	0	1	14
2000	5	0	0	0	8
Totals	10	1	0	1	22

DAN MALONEY

Year	GP	G	A	Pts	PIM
1978	13	1	3	4	17
1979	6	3	3	6	2
1981	3	0	0	0	4
Totals	22	4	6	10	23

KENT MANDERVILLE

Year	GP	G	A	Pts	PIM
1993	18	1	0	1	8
1994	12	1	0	1	4
1995	7	0	0	0	6
Totals	37	2	0	2	18

CESARE MANIAGO

Year	GP	W-L	MIN	GA	SO	GAA
1961	2	1–1	145	6	0	2.48

NORM MANN

Year	GP	G	A	Pts	PIM
1936	1	0	0	0	0

DAVE MANSON

Year	GP	G	A	Pts	PIM
2001	2	0	0	0	2

MILAN MARCETTA

Year	GP	G	A	Pts	PIM
1967	3	0	0	0	0

BRYAN MARCHMENT

Year	GP	G	A	Pts	PIM
2004	13	0	0	0	8

GUS MARKER

Year	GP	G	A	Pts	PIM
1939	10	2	2	4	0
1940	10	1	3	4	23
1941	7	0	0	0	5
Totals	27	3	5	8	28

DANIIL MARKOV

Year	GP	G	A	Pts	PIM
1999	17	0	6	6	18
2000	12	0	3	3	10
2001	11	1	1	2	12
Totals	40	1	10	11	40

DANIEL MAROIS

Year	GP	G	A	Pts	PIM
1988	3	1	0	1	0
1990	5	2	2	4	12
Totals	8	3	2	5	12

BRAD MARSH

1990	5	1	0	1	2

DON MARSHALL

1972	1	0	0	0	0

TERRY MARTIN

1980	3	2	0	2	7
1981	3	0	0	0	0
1983	4	0	0	0	9
Totals	10	2	0	2	16

BRAD MAXWELL

1986	3	0	1	1	12

CHRIS McALLISTER

1999	6	0	1	1	4

BRYAN McCABE

2001	11	2	3	5	16
2002	20	5	5	10	30
2003	7	0	3	3	10
2004	13	3	5	8	14
Totals	51	10	16	26	70

ALYN McCAULEY

2000	5	0	0	0	6
2001	10	0	0	0	2
2002	20	5	10	15	4
Totals	35	5	10	15	12

JAY McCLEMENT

2013	7	0	0	0	0

FRANK McCOOL

1945	13	8–5	808	30	4	2.23

JOHN McCORMACK

1950	6	1	0	1	0

JOHN McCREEDY

1942	13	4	3	7	6
1945	8	0	0	0	0
Totals	21	4	3	7	6

BUCKO McDONALD

1939	10	0	0	0	4
1940	10	0	0	0	0
1941	7	2	0	2	2
1942	13	0	1	1	2
1943	6	1	0	1	4
Totals	46	3	1	4	12

LANNY McDONALD

1975	7	0	0	0	2
1976	10	4	4	8	4
1977	9	10	7	17	6
1978	13	3	4	7	10
1979	6	3	2	5	0
Totals	45	20	17	37	22

BOB McGILL

1986	9	0	0	0	35
1987	3	0	0	0	0
Totals	12	0	0	0	35

JOHN McINTYRE

1990	2	0	0	0	2

WALT McKECHNIE

1979	6	4	3	7	9

SEAN McKENNA

1988	2	0	0	0	0

DON McKENNEY

1964	12	4	8	12	0
1965	6	0	0	0	0
Totals	18	4	8	12	0

JIM McKENNY

1971	6	2	1	3	2
1972	5	3	0	3	2
1974	4	0	2	2	0
1975	7	0	1	1	2
1976	6	2	3	5	2
1977	9	0	2	2	2
Totals	37	7	9	16	10

FRAZER McLAREN

2013	1	0	0	0	2

JACK McLEAN

1943	6	2	2	4	2
1944	3	0	0	0	6
1945	4	0	0	0	0
Totals	13	2	2	4	8

DAVE McLLWAIN

1993	4	0	0	0	0

GORD McRAE

1975	7	2–5	442	21	0	2.85
1976	1	0–0	13	1	0	4.62
Totals	8	2–5	455	22	0	2.90

KEN McRAE

1994	6	0	0	0	4

HOWIE MEEKER

1947	11	3	3	6	6
1948	9	2	4	6	15
1950	7	0	1	1	4
1951	11	1	1	2	14
1952	4	0	0	0	11
Totals	42	6	9	15	50

HARRY MEEKING

1918	7	4	2	6	0

BARRY MELROSE

1981	3	0	1	1	15
1983	4	0	1	1	23
Totals	7	0	2	2	38

DON METZ

1940	2	0	0	0	0
1941	5	1	1	2	2
1942	13	4	3	7	0
1945	11	0	1	1	4
1947	11	2	3	5	4
1948	2	0	0	0	0
1949	3	0	0	0	0
Totals	47	7	8	15	10

NICK METZ

1935	6	1	1	2	0
1937	2	0	0	0	0
1938	7	0	2	2	0
1939	10	3	3	6	6
1940	9	1	3	4	9
1941	7	3	4	7	0
1942	13	4	4	8	12
1945	7	1	1	2	2
1947	6	4	2	6	0
1948	9	2	0	2	2
Totals	76	19	20	39	31

LARRY MICKEY

1969	3	0	0	0	5

RUDY MIGAY

1954	5	1	0	1	4
1955	3	0	0	0	10
1956	5	0	0	0	6
1959	2	0	0	0	0
Totals	15	1	0	1	20

EARL MILLER

1932	7	0	0	0	0

DMITRI MIRONOV

1993	14	1	2	3	2
1994	18	6	9	15	6
1995	6	2	1	3	2
Totals	38	9	12	21	10

FREDRIK MODIN

1999	8	0	0	0	6

ALEXANDER MOGILNY

2002	20	8	3	11	8
2003	6	5	2	7	4
2004	13	2	4	6	8
Totals	39	15	9	24	20

GARRY MONAHAN

1971	6	2	0	2	2
1972	5	0	0	0	0
1974	4	0	1	1	7
Totals	15	2	1	3	9

DICKIE MOORE

1965	5	1	1	2	6

MOE MORRIS

1944	5	1	2	3	2
1945	13	3	0	3	14
Totals	18	4	2	6	16

JIM MORRISON

1952	2	0	0	0	0
1954	5	0	0	0	4
1955	4	0	1	1	4
1956	5	0	0	0	4
Totals	16	0	1	1	12

GUS MORTSON

1947	11	1	3	4	22
1948	5	1	2	3	2
1949	9	2	1	3	8
1950	7	0	0	0	18
1951	11	0	1	1	4
1952	4	0	0	0	8
Totals	47	4	7	11	62

RICHARD MULHERN

1980	1	0	0	0	0

KIRK MULLER

1996	6	3	2	5	0

HARRY MUMMERY

1918	7	1	4	5	0

LARRY MURPHY

1996	6	0	2	2	4

BOB NEELY

1974	4	1	3	4	0
1975	3	0	0	0	2
1976	10	3	1	4	7
1977	9	1	3	4	6
Totals	26	5	7	12	15

ERIC NESTERENKO

1954	5	0	1	1	9
1955	4	0	1	1	6
Totals	9	0	2	2	15

MIKE NEVILLE

1925	2	0	0	0	0

BOB NEVIN

1961	5	1	0	1	2
1962	12	2	4	6	6
1963	10	3	0	3	2
Totals	27	6	4	10	10

JOE NIEUWENDYK

2004	9	6	0	6	4

FRANK NIGRO

1983	3	0	0	0	2

REG NOBLE

1918	7	3	2	5	3
1921	2	0	0	0	0
1922	7	0	2	2	20
Totals	16	3	4	7	23

OWEN NOLAN

2003	7	0	2	2	2

GARY NYLUND

1986	10	0	2	2	25

RYAN O'BYRNE

2013	6	0	0	0	4

Reg Noble of the Toronto St. Pats

ED OLCZYK

1988	6	5	4	9	2
1990	5	1	2	3	14
Totals	11	6	6	12	16

MURRAY OLIVER

1969	4	1	2	3	0

BERT OLMSTEAD

1959	12	4	2	6	13
1960	10	3	4	7	0
1961	3	1	2	3	10
1962	4	0	1	1	0
Totals	29	8	9	17	23

WINDY O'NEILL

1944	4	0	0	0	6

COLTON ORR

2013	7	0	0	0	18

MARK OSBORNE

1987	9	1	3	4	6
1988	6	1	3	4	16
1990	5	2	3	5	12
1993	19	1	1	2	16
1994	18	4	2	6	52
Totals	57	9	12	21	102

WILF PAIEMENT

1980	3	0	2	2	17
1981	3	0	0	0	2
Totals	6	0	2	2	19

MIKE PALMATEER

1977	6	3–3	360	16	0	2.67
1978	13	6–7	795	32	2	2.42
1979	5	2–3	298	17	0	3.42
1980	1	0–1	60	7	0	7.00
1983	4	1–3	252	17	0	4.05
Totals	29	12–17	1,765	89	2	2.99

JIM PAPPIN

1964	11	0	0	0	0
1967	12	7	8	15	12
Totals	23	7	8	15	12

BERNIE PARENT

1971	4	2–2	235	9	0	2.30
1972	4	1–3	243	13	0	3.21
Totals	8	3–5	478	22	0	2.76

GEORGE PARSONS

1938	7	3	2	5	11

ROB PEARSON

1993	14	2	2	4	31
1994	14	1	0	1	32
Totals	28	3	2	5	63

SCOTT PEARSON

1990	2	2	0	2	10

MIKE PELYK

1969	4	0	0	0	8
1971	6	0	0	0	10
1972	5	0	0	0	8
1974	4	0	0	0	4
1977	9	0	2	2	4
1978	12	0	1	1	7
Totals	40	0	3	3	41

YANIC PERREAULT

1999	17	3	6	9	6
2000	1	0	1	1	0
2001	11	2	3	5	4
Totals	29	5	10	15	10

ERIC PETTINGER

1929	4	1	0	1	8

DION PHANEUF

2013	7	1	2	3	6

KAREL PILAR

2002	11	0	4	4	12
2004	1	1	0	1	0
Totals	12	1	4	5	12

PIERRE PILOTE

1969	4	0	1	1	4

JACQUES PLANTE

1971	3	0–2	134	7	0	3.13
1972	1	0–1	60	5	0	5.00
Totals	4	0–3	194	12	0	3.71

WALT PODDUBNY

1983	4	3	1	4	0
1986	9	4	1	5	4
Totals	13	7	2	9	4

BUD POILE

1943	6	2	4	6	4
1947	7	2	0	2	2
Totals	13	4	4	8	6

ALEXEI PONIKAROVSKY

2002	10	0	0	0	4
2004	13	1	3	4	8
Totals	23	1	3	4	12

FÉLIX POTVIN

1993	21	11–10	1,308	62	1	2.84
1994	18	9–9	1,124	46	3	2.46
1995	7	3–4	424	20	1	2.83
1996	6	2–4	350	19	0	3.26
Totals	52	25–27	3,206	147	5	2.75

TRACY PRATT

1977	4	0	0	0	0

BABE PRATT

1943	6	1	2	3	8
1944	5	0	3	3	4
1945	13	2	4	6	8
Totals	24	3	9	12	20

WAYNE PRESLEY

1996	5	0	0	0	2

NOEL PRICE

1959	5	0	0	0	2

JOE PRIMEAU

1931	2	0	0	0	0
1932	7	0	6	6	2
1933	8	0	1	1	4
1934	5	2	4	6	6
1935	7	0	3	3	0
1936	9	3	4	7	0
Totals	38	5	18	23	12

MARCEL PRONOVOST

1966	4	0	0	0	6
1967	12	1	0	1	8
Totals	16	1	0	1	14

BOB PULFORD

1959	12	4	4	8	8
1960	10	4	1	5	10
1961	5	0	0	0	8
1962	12	7	1	8	24
1963	10	2	5	7	14
1964	14	5	3	8	20
1965	6	1	1	2	16
1966	4	1	1	2	12
1967	12	1	10	11	12
1969	4	0	0	0	2
Totals	89	25	26	51	126

DAREN PUPPA

1993	1	0–0	20	1	0	3.00

JOEL QUENNEVILLE

1979	6	0	1	1	4

PAT QUINN

1969	4	0	0	0	13

ROB RAMAGE

1990	5	1	2	3	20

KEN RANDALL

1918	7	2	1	3	0
1921	2	0	0	0	6
1922	5	2	0	2	13
Totals	14	4	1	5	19

MARC REAUME

1955	4	0	0	0	2
1956	5	0	2	2	6
1959	10	0	0	0	0
Totals	19	0	2	2	8

JEFF REESE

1990	2	1–1	108	6	0	3.33

LARRY REGAN

1959	8	1	1	2	2
1960	10	3	3	6	0
1961	4	0	0	0	0
Totals	22	4	4	8	2

ROBERT REICHEL

2002	18	0	3	3	4
2003	7	2	1	3	0
2004	12	0	2	2	8
Totals	37	2	6	8	12

DAVE REID

1990	3	0	0	0	0

REG REID

1925	2	0	0	0	0

JAMES REIMER

2013	7	3–4	438	21	0	2.88

MIKAEL RENBERG

2002	3	0	0	0	2
2003	7	1	0	1	8
2004	2	0	0	0	4
Totals	12	1	0	1	14

DAMIAN RHODES

1994	1	0–0	1	1	0	0.00

LUKE RICHARDSON

1988	2	0	0	0	0
1990	5	0	0	0	22
Totals	7	0	0	0	22

MIKE RIDLEY

1995	7	3	1	4	2

JOHN ROSS ROACH

1922	7	4–2–1	425	13	2	1.84
1925	2	0–2–0	120	5	0	2.50
Totals	9	4–4–1	545	18	2	1.98

RENÉ ROBERT

1981	3	0	2	2	2

GARY ROBERTS

2001	11	2	9	11	0
2002	19	7	12	19	56
2003	7	1	1	2	8
2004	13	4	4	8	10
Totals	50	14	26	40	74

FRED ROBERTSON

1932	7	0	0	0	0

AL ROLLINS

1951	4	3–1	211	6	0	1.71
1952	2	0–2	120	6	0	3.00
Totals	6	3–3	331	12	0	2.18

DOC ROMNES

1939	10	1	4	5	0

BILL ROOT

1986	7	0	2	2	13
1987	13	1	0	1	12
Totals	20	1	2	3	25

BOB ROUSE

1993	21	3	8	11	29
1994	18	0	3	3	29
Totals	39	3	11	14	58

WARREN RYCHEL

1995	3	0	0	0	0

ROCKY SAGANIUK

1979	3	1	0	1	5
1980	3	0	0	0	10
Totals	6	1	0	1	15

RICK ST. CROIX

1983	1	0–0	1	1	0	60.00

BORJE SALMING

1974	4	0	1	1	4
1975	7	0	4	4	6
1976	10	3	4	7	9
1977	9	3	6	9	6
1978	6	2	2	4	6
1979	6	0	1	1	8
1980	3	1	1	2	2
1981	3	0	2	2	4
1983	4	1	4	5	10
1986	10	1	6	7	14
1987	13	0	3	3	14
1988	6	1	3	4	8
Totals	81	12	37	49	91

PHIL SAMIS

1948	5	0	1	1	2

Bob Pulford scores the overtime, game-winning goal in game three of the 1967 Stanley Cup finals

CHARLIE SANDS
1933	9	2	2	4	2
1934	4	1	0	1	0
Totals	13	3	2	5	2

TERRY SAWCHUK
1965	1	0–1	60	3	0	3.00
1966	2	0–2	120	6	0	3.00
1967	10	6–4	568	25	0	2.64
Totals	13	6–7	748	34	0	2.73

MATHIEU SCHNEIDER
1996	6	0	4	4	8

SWEENEY SCHRINER
1940	10	1	3	4	4
1941	7	2	1	3	4
1942	13	6	3	9	10
1943	4	2	2	4	0
1945	13	3	1	4	4
Totals	47	14	10	24	22

COREY SCHWAB
2002	1	0–0	12	0	0	0.00

AL SECORD
1988	6	1	0	1	16

RON SEDLBAUER
1981	2	0	1	1	2

ROD SEILING
1975	7	0	0	0	0
1976	10	0	1	1	6
Totals	17	0	1	1	6

BRIT SELBY
1966	4	0	0	0	0
1969	4	0	0	0	4
Totals	8	0	0	0	4

BRAD SELWOOD
1972	5	0	0	0	4

EDDIE SHACK
1961	4	0	0	0	2
1962	9	0	0	0	18
1963	10	2	1	3	11
1964	13	0	1	1	25
1965	5	1	0	1	8
1966	4	2	1	3	33
1967	8	0	0	0	8
1974	4	1	0	1	2
Totals	57	6	3	9	107

DAVE SHAND
1981	3	0	0	0	0
1983	4	1	0	1	13
Totals	7	1	0	1	13

JACK SHILL
1934	1	0	0	0	0
1936	9	0	3	3	8
1937	2	0	0	0	0
Totals	12	0	3	3	8

DON SIMMONS
1962	3	2–0	165	8	0	2.91

DARRYL SITTLER
1971	6	2	1	3	31
1972	3	0	0	0	2
1974	4	2	1	3	6
1975	7	2	1	3	15
1976	10	5	7	12	19
1977	9	5	16	21	4
1978	13	3	8	11	12
1979	6	5	4	9	17
1980	3	1	2	3	10
1981	3	0	0	0	4
Totals	64	25	40	65	120

ALF SKINNER
1918	5	8	1	9	0

TOD SLOAN
1951	11	4	5	9	18
1952	4	0	0	0	10
1954	5	1	1	2	24
1955	4	0	0	0	2
1956	2	0	0	0	5
Totals	26	5	6	11	59

ART SMITH
1929	4	1	1	2	8

BRAD SMITH
1986	6	2	1	3	20
1987	11	1	1	2	24
Totals	17	3	2	5	44

FLOYD SMITH
1969	4	0	0	0	0

SID SMITH
1948	2	0	0	0	0
1949	6	5	2	7	0
1950	7	0	3	3	2
1951	11	7	3	10	0
1952	4	0	0	0	0
1954	5	1	1	2	0
1955	4	3	1	4	0
1956	5	1	0	1	0
Totals	44	17	10	27	2

ROD SMYLIE
1921	2	0	0	0	0
1922	6	1	2	3	2
1925	2	0	0	0	0
Totals	10	1	2	3	2

BRIAN SPENCER
1971	6	0	1	1	17

TED STACKHOUSE
1922	5	0	0	0	0

MATT STAJAN
2004	3	0	0	0	2

ALLAN STANLEY
1959	12	0	3	3	2
1960	10	2	3	5	2
1961	5	0	3	3	0
1962	12	0	3	3	6
1963	10	1	6	7	8
1964	14	1	6	7	20
1965	6	0	1	1	12
1966	1	0	0	0	0
1967	12	0	2	2	10
Totals	82	4	27	31	60

WALLY STANOWSKI
1940	10	1	0	1	2
1941	7	0	3	3	2
1942	13	2	8	10	2
1945	13	0	1	1	5
1947	8	0	0	0	0
1948	9	0	2	2	2
Totals	60	3	14	17	13

MARIAN STASTNY
1986	3	0	0	0	0

PETE STEMKOWSKI
1965	6	0	3	3	7
1966	4	0	0	0	26
1967	12	5	7	12	20
Totals	22	5	10	15	53

GAYE STEWART
1942	3	0	0	0	0
1943	4	0	2	2	4
1947	11	2	5	7	8
Totals	18	2	7	9	12

RON STEWART
1954	5	0	1	1	10
1955	4	0	0	0	2
1956	5	1	1	2	2
1959	12	3	3	6	6
1960	10	0	2	2	2
1961	5	1	0	1	2
1962	11	1	6	7	4
1963	10	4	0	4	2
1964	14	0	4	4	24
1965	6	0	1	1	2
Totals	82	10	18	28	56

BLAINE STOUGHTON
1975	7	4	2	6	2

RED STUART
1921	2	0	0	0	0
1922	7	1	0	1	6
Totals	9	1	0	1	6

STEVE SULLIVAN
1999	13	3	3	6	14

MATS SUNDIN
1995	7	5	4	9	4
1996	6	3	1	4	4
1999	17	8	8	16	16
2000	12	3	5	8	10
2001	11	6	7	13	14
2002	8	2	5	7	4
2003	7	1	3	4	6
2004	9	4	5	9	8
Totals	77	32	38	70	66

RICH SUTTER
1995	4	0	0	0	2

ROBERT SVEHLA
2003	7	0	3	3	2

BILLY TAYLOR
1940	2	1	0	1	0
1941	7	0	3	3	5
1942	13	2	8	10	4
1943	6	2	2	4	0
Totals	28	5	13	18	9

HARRY TAYLOR
1949	1	0	0	0	0

GREG TERRION
1983	4	1	2	3	2
1986	10	0	3	3	17
1987	13	0	2	2	14
1988	5	0	2	2	4
Totals	32	1	9	10	37

STEVE THOMAS
1986	10	6	8	14	9
1987	13	2	3	5	13
1999	17	6	3	9	12
2000	12	6	3	9	10
2001	11	6	3	9	4
Totals	63	26	20	46	48

WAYNE THOMAS
1976	10	5–5	587	34	1	3.48
1977	4	1–2	202	12	0	3.56
Totals	14	6–7	789	46	1	3.50

ERROL THOMPSON
1974	2	0	1	1	0
1975	6	0	0	0	9
1976	10	3	3	6	0
1977	9	2	0	2	0
Totals	27	5	4	9	9

BILL THOMS

Year	GP	G	A	Pts	PIM
1933	9	1	1	2	4
1934	5	0	2	2	0
1935	7	2	0	2	0
1936	9	3	5	8	0
1937	2	0	0	0	0
1938	7	0	1	1	0
Totals	39	6	9	15	4

JIM THOMSON

Year	GP	G	A	Pts	PIM
1947	11	0	1	1	22
1948	9	1	1	2	9
1949	9	1	5	6	10
1950	7	0	2	2	7
1951	11	0	1	1	34
1952	4	0	0	0	25
1954	3	0	0	0	2
1955	4	0	0	0	16
1956	5	0	3	3	10
Totals	63	2	13	15	135

RAY TIMGREN

Year	GP	G	A	Pts	PIM
1949	9	3	3	6	2
1950	6	0	4	4	2
1951	11	0	1	1	2
1952	4	0	1	1	0
Totals	30	3	9	12	6

GUY TROTTIER

Year	GP	G	A	Pts	PIM
1971	5	0	0	0	0
1972	4	1	0	1	16
Totals	9	1	0	1	16

DARCY TUCKER

Year	GP	G	A	Pts	PIM
2000	12	4	2	6	15
2001	11	0	2	2	6
2002	17	4	4	8	38
2003	6	0	3	3	6
2004	12	2	0	2	14
Totals	58	10	11	21	79

IAN TURNBULL

Year	GP	G	A	Pts	PIM
1974	4	0	0	0	8
1975	7	0	2	2	4
1976	10	2	9	11	29
1977	9	4	4	8	10
1978	13	6	10	16	10
1979	6	0	4	4	27
1980	3	0	3	3	2
1981	3	1	0	1	4
Totals	55	13	32	45	94

NORM ULLMAN

Year	GP	G	A	Pts	PIM
1969	4	1	0	1	0
1971	6	0	2	2	2
1972	5	1	3	4	2
1974	4	1	1	2	0
1975	7	0	0	0	2
Totals	26	3	6	9	6

RICK VAIVE

Year	GP	G	A	Pts	PIM
1980	3	1	0	1	11
1981	3	1	0	1	4
1983	4	2	5	7	6
1986	9	6	2	8	9
1987	13	4	2	6	23
Totals	32	14	9	23	53

JACK VALIQUETTE

Year	GP	G	A	Pts	PIM
1976	10	2	3	5	2
1978	13	1	3	4	2
Totals	23	3	6	9	4

GARRY VALK

Year	GP	G	A	Pts	PIM
1999	17	3	4	7	22
2000	12	1	2	3	14
2001	5	1	0	1	2
2002	11	1	0	1	4
Totals	45	6	6	12	42

JAMES VAN RIEMSDYK

Year	GP	G	A	Pts	PIM
2013	7	2	5	7	4

KURT WALKER

Year	GP	G	A	Pts	PIM
1976	6	0	0	0	24
1978	10	0	0	0	10
Totals	16	0	0	0	34

MIKE WALTON

Year	GP	G	A	Pts	PIM
1967	12	4	3	7	2
1969	4	0	0	0	4
Totals	16	4	3	7	6

BOB WARNER

Year	GP	G	A	Pts	PIM
1976	2	0	0	0	0
1977	2	0	0	0	0
Totals	4	0	0	0	0

TODD WARRINER

Year	GP	G	A	Pts	PIM
1996	6	1	1	2	2
1999	9	0	0	0	2
Totals	15	1	1	2	4

HARRY WATSON

Year	GP	G	A	Pts	PIM
1947	11	3	2	5	6
1948	9	5	2	7	9
1949	9	4	2	6	2
1950	7	0	0	0	2
1951	5	1	2	3	4
1952	4	1	0	1	2
1954	5	0	1	1	2
Totals	50	14	9	23	27

DON WEBSTER

Year	GP	G	A	Pts	PIM
1944	5	0	0	0	12

STAN WEIR

Year	GP	G	A	Pts	PIM
1976	9	1	3	4	0
1977	7	2	1	3	0
1978	13	3	1	4	0
Totals	29	6	5	11	0

GLEN WESLEY

Year	GP	G	A	Pts	PIM
2003	5	0	1	1	2

TIGER WILLIAMS

Year	GP	G	A	Pts	PIM
1975	7	1	3	4	25
1976	10	0	0	0	75
1977	9	3	6	9	29
1978	12	1	2	3	63
1979	6	0	0	0	48
Totals	44	5	11	16	240

CLARKE WILM

Year	GP	G	A	Pts	PIM
2004	5	0	1	1	2

JOHNNY WILSON

Year	GP	G	A	Pts	PIM
1960	10	1	2	3	2

RON WILSON

Year	GP	G	A	Pts	PIM
1979	3	0	1	1	0
1980	3	1	2	3	2
Totals	6	1	3	4	2

RANDY WOOD

Year	GP	G	A	Pts	PIM
1995	7	2	0	2	6

KEN WREGGET

Year	GP	W-L	Min	GA	SO	GAA
1986	10	6–4	607	32	1	3.16
1987*	13	7–6	761	29	1	2.29
1988	2	0–1	108	11	0	6.11
Totals	25	13–11	1,476	72	2	2.93

*One assist

BOB WREN

Year	GP	G	A	Pts	PIM
2002	1	0	0	0	0

KEN YAREMCHUK

Year	GP	G	A	Pts	PIM
1987	6	0	0	0	0
1988	6	0	2	2	10
Totals	12	0	2	2	10

DMITRY YUSHKEVICH

Year	GP	G	A	Pts	PIM
1996	4	0	0	0	0
1999	17	1	5	6	22
2000	12	1	1	2	4
2001	11	0	4	4	12
Totals	44	2	10	12	38

RON ZANUSSI

Year	GP	G	A	Pts	PIM
1981	3	0	0	0	0

ROB ZETTLER

Year	GP	G	A	Pts	PIM
1996	2	0	0	0	0

PETER ZEZEL

Year	GP	G	A	Pts	PIM
1993	20	2	1	3	6
1994	18	2	4	6	8
Totals	38	4	5	9	14

Darcy Tucker

ALL-TIME PLAYOFF SCORES

All shutouts are listed in square brackets; overtime goalscorers are listed in parentheses.

1918

NHL Finals	March 11 (at Toronto)	Toronto 7	Montreal 3
	March 13 (at Montreal)	Toronto 3	Montreal 4
	Toronto won two-game, total-goals series, 10–7		
Stanley Cup Finals	March 20 (at Toronto)	Toronto 5	Vancouver 3
	March 23 (at Toronto)	Vancouver 6	Toronto 4
	March 26 (at Toronto)	Toronto 6	Vancouver 3
	March 28 (at Toronto)	Vancouver 8	Toronto 1
	March 30 (at Toronto)	Toronto 2	Vancouver 1
	Toronto won Stanley Cup best-of-five, 3–2		

1919 & 1920   Did Not Qualify

1921

NHL Finals	March 10 (at Ottawa)	Ottawa 5	Toronto 0 [Benedict]
	March 15 (at Toronto)	Ottawa 2	Toronto 0 [Benedict]
	Ottawa won two-game, total-goals series, 7–0		

1922

NHL Finals	March 11 (at Toronto)	Toronto 5	Ottawa 4
	March 13 (at Ottawa)	Toronto 0	Ottawa 0 [Roach (T)/ Benedict (O)]
	Toronto won two-game, total-goals series, 5–4		
Stanley Cup Finals	March 17 (at Toronto)	Vancouver 4	Toronto 3
	March 21 (at Toronto)	Toronto 2	Vancouver 1 (Dye 4:50 OT)
	March 23 (at Toronto)	Vancouver 3	Toronto 0 [Lehman]
	March 25 (at Toronto)	Toronto 6	Vancouver 0 [Roach]
	March 28 (at Toronto)	Toronto 5	Vancouver 1
	Toronto won Stanley Cup best-of-five, 3–2		

1923 & 1924   Did Not Qualify

1925

NHL Semifinals	March 11 (at Montreal)	Montreal 3	Toronto 2
	March 13 (at Toronto)	Montreal 2	Toronto 0 [Vézina]
	Montreal won two-game, total-goals series, 5–2		

1926, 1927, 1928   Did Not Qualify

1929

Quarterfinals	March 19 (at Detroit)	Toronto 3	Detroit Cougars 1
	March 21 (at Toronto)	Toronto 4	Detroit Cougars 1
	Toronto won two-game, total-goals series, 7–2		
Semifinals	March 24 (at New York)	NY Rangers 1	Toronto 0 [Roach]
	March 26 (at Toronto)	NY Rangers 2	Toronto 1 (F. Boucher 2:03 OT)
	NY Rangers won best-of-three, 2–0		

1930

Did Not Qualify

1931

Quarterfinals	March 24 (at Toronto)	Toronto 2	Chicago 2
	March 26 (at Chicago)	Chicago 2	Toronto 1 (S. Adams 19:20 OT)
	Chicago won two-game, total-goals series, 4–3		

1932

Quarterfinals	March 27 (at Chicago)	Chicago 1	Toronto 0 [Gardiner]
	March 29 (at Toronto)	Toronto 6	Chicago 1
	Toronto won two-game, total-goals series, 6–2		
Semifinals	March 31 (at Montreal)	Toronto 1	Montreal Maroons 1
	April 2 (at Toronto)	Toronto 3	Montreal Maroons 2 (Gracie 17:59 OT)
	Toronto won two-game, total-goals series, 4–3		
Finals	April 5 (at New York)	Toronto 6	NY Rangers 4
	April 7 (at Boston)	Toronto 6	NY Rangers 2
	April 9 (at Toronto)	Toronto 6	NY Rangers 4
	Toronto won Stanley Cup best-of-five, 3–0		

1933

Semifinals	March 25 (at Boston)	Boston 2	Toronto 1 (Barry 14:14 OT)
	March 28 (at Boston)	Toronto 1	Boston 0 [Chabot] (H. Jackson 15:03 OT)
	March 30 (at Toronto)	Boston 2	Toronto 1 (Shore 4:23 OT)
	April 1 (at Toronto)	Toronto 5	Boston 3
	April 3 (at Toronto)	Toronto 1	Boston 0 [Chabot] (Doraty 104:46 OT)
	Toronto won best-of-five, 3–2		
Finals	April 4 (at New York)	NY Rangers 5	Toronto 1
	April 8 (at Toronto)	NY Rangers 3	Toronto 1
	April 11 (at Toronto)	Toronto 3	NY Rangers 2
	April 13 (at Toronto)	NY Rangers 1	Toronto 0 [Aitkenhead] (Bill Cook 7:33 OT)
	NY Rangers won Stanley Cup best-of-five, 3–1		

1934

Semifinals	March 22 (at Toronto)	Detroit 2	Toronto 1 (H. Lewis 1:33 OT)
	March 24 (at Toronto)	Detroit 6	Toronto 3
	March 26 (at Detroit)	Toronto 3	Detroit 1
	March 28 (at Detroit)	Toronto 5	Detroit 1
	March 30 (at Detroit)	Detroit 1	Toronto 0 [Cude]
	Detroit won best-of-five, 3–2		

1935

Semifinals	March 23 (at Boston)	Boston 1	Toronto 0 [Thompson] (Clapper 33:26 OT)
	March 26 (at Boston)	Toronto 2	Boston 0 [Hainsworth]
	March 28 (at Toronto)	Toronto 3	Boston 0 [Hainsworth]
	March 30 (at Toronto)	Toronto 2	Boston 1 (P. Kelly 1:36 OT)
	Toronto won best-of-five, 3–1		
Finals	April 4 (at Toronto)	Maroons 3	Toronto 2 (D. Trottier 5:28 OT)
	April 6 (at Toronto)	Maroons 3	Toronto 1
	April 9 (at Montreal)	Maroons 4	Toronto 1
	Maroons won Stanley Cup best-of-five, 3–0		

1936

Quarterfinals	March 24 (at Boston)	Boston 3	Toronto 0 [Thompson]
	March 26 (at Toronto)	Toronto 8	Boston 3
	Toronto won two-game, total-goals series, 8–6		
Semifinals	March 28 (at Toronto)	Toronto 3	NY Americans 1
	March 31 (at New York)	NY Americans 1	Toronto 0 [Worters]
	April 2 (at Toronto)	Toronto 3	Americans 1
	Toronto won best-of-three, 2–1		
Finals	April 5 (at Detroit)	Detroit 3	Toronto 1
	April 7 (at Detroit)	Detroit 9	Toronto 4
	April 9 (at Toronto)	Toronto 4	Detroit 3 (Boll 0:31 OT)
	April 11 (at Toronto)	Detroit 3	Toronto 2
	Detroit won Stanley Cup best-of-five, 3–1		

1937

Quarterfinals	March 23 (at Toronto)	NY Rangers 3	Toronto 0 [Kerr]
	March 25 (at New York)	NY Rangers 2	Toronto 1 (Pratt 13:05 OT)
	NY Rangers won best-of-three, 2–0		
Semifinals	March 24 (at Toronto)	Toronto 1	Boston 0 [Broda] (Parsons 21:32 OT)
	March 26 (at Toronto)	Toronto 2	Boston 1
	March 29 (at Boston)	Toronto 3	Boston 2 (Drillon 10:04 OT)
	Toronto won best-of-five, 3–0		

Finals	April 5 (at Toronto)*	Chicago 3	Toronto 1
	April 7 (at Toronto)	Toronto 5	Chicago 1
	April 10 (at Chicago)	Chicago 2	Toronto 1
	April 12 (at Chicago)	Chicago 4	Toronto 1
	Chicago won Stanley Cup best-of-five, 3–1		
	*Hawks goalie Alfie Moore pulled out of a local Toronto tavern to play goal for Chicago		

1939

Quarterfinals	March 21 (at Toronto)	Toronto 4	NY Americans 0 [Broda]
	March 23 (at New York)	Toronto 2	NY Americans 0 [Broda]
	Toronto won best-of-three, 2–0		
Semifinals	March 28 (at Toronto)	Toronto 4	Detroit 1
	March 30 (at Detroit)	Detroit 3	Toronto 1
	April 1 (at Toronto)	Toronto 5	Detroit 4 (Drillon 5:42 OT)
	Toronto won best-of-three, 2–1		
Finals	April 6 (at Boston)	Boston 2	Toronto 1
	April 9 (at Boston)	Toronto 3	Boston 2 (Romnes 10:38 OT)
	April 11 (at Toronto)	Boston 3	Toronto 1
	April 13 (at Toronto)	Boston 2	Toronto 0 [Brimsek]
	April 16 (at Boston)	Boston 3	Toronto 1
	Boston won Stanley Cup best-of-seven, 4–1		

1940

Quarterfinals	March 19 (at Toronto)	Toronto 3	Chicago 2 (Apps 6:35 OT)
	March 21 (at Chicago)	Toronto 2	Chicago 1
	Toronto won best-of-three, 2–0		
Semifinals	March 26 (at Toronto)	Toronto 2	Detroit 1
	March 28 (at Detroit)	Toronto 3	Detroit 1
	Toronto won best-of-three, 2–0		
Finals	April 2 (at New York)	NY Rangers 2	Toronto 1 (Pike 15:30 OT)
	April 3 (at New York)	NY Rangers 6	Toronto 2
	April 6 (at Toronto)	Toronto 2	NY Rangers 1
	April 9 (at Toronto)	Toronto 3	NY Rangers 0 [Broda]
	April 11 (at Toronto)*	NY Rangers 2	Toronto 1 (Patrick 31:43 OT)
	April 13 (at Toronto)	NY Rangers 3	Toronto 2 (B. Hextall 2:07 OT)
	NY Rangers won Stanley Cup best-of-seven, 4–2		
	*Game could not be played at Madison Square Garden as it was previously booked for the circus		

1941

Semifinals	March 20 (at Boston)	Boston 3	Toronto 0 [Brimsek]
	March 22 (at Boston)	Toronto 5	Boston 3
	March 25 (at Toronto)	Toronto 7	Boston 2
	March 27 (at Toronto)	Boston 2	Toronto 1
	March 29 (at Boston)	Toronto 2	Boston 1 (Langelle 17:31 OT)
	April 1 (at Toronto)	Boston 2	Toronto 1
	April 3 (at Boston)	Boston 2	Toronto 1
	Boston won best-of-seven, 4–3		

1942

Semifinals	March 21 (at Toronto)	Toronto 3	NY Rangers 1
	March 22 (at New York)	Toronto 4	NY Rangers 2
	March 24 (at New York)	NY Rangers 3	Toronto 0 [Henry]
	March 28 (at Toronto)	Toronto 2	NY Rangers 1
	March 29 (at New York)	NY Rangers 3	Toronto 1
	March 31 (at Toronto)	Toronto 3	NY Rangers 2
	Toronto won best-of-seven, 4–2		
Finals	April 4 (at Toronto)	Detroit 3	Toronto 2
	April 7 (at Toronto)	Detroit 4	Toronto 2
	April 9 (at Detroit)	Detroit 5	Toronto 2
	April 12 (at Detroit)	Toronto 4	Detroit 3
	April 14 (at Toronto)	Toronto 9	Detroit 3
	April 16 (at Detroit)	Toronto 3	Detroit 0 [Broda]
	April 18 (at Toronto)	Toronto 3	Detroit 1
	Toronto won Stanley Cup best-of-seven, 4–3		

1943

Semifinals	March 21 (at Detroit)	Detroit 4	Toronto 2
	March 23 (at Detroit)	Toronto 3	Detroit 2 (McLean 70:18 OT)
	March 25 (at Toronto)	Detroit 4	Toronto 2
	March 27 (at Toronto)	Toronto 6	Detroit 3
	March 28 (at Detroit)	Detroit 4	Toronto 2
	March 30 (at Toronto)	Detroit 3	Toronto 2 (A. Brown 9:21 OT)
	Detroit won best-of-seven, 4–2		

1944

Semifinals	March 21 (at Montreal)	Toronto 3	Montreal 1
	March 23 (at Montreal)	Montreal 5	Toronto 1
	March 25 (at Toronto)	Montreal 2	Toronto 1
	March 28 (at Toronto)	Montreal 4	Toronto 1
	March 30 (at Montreal)	Montreal 11	Toronto 0 [Durnan]
	Montreal won best-of-seven, 4–1		

1945

	March 20 (at Montreal)	Toronto 1	Montreal 0 [McCool]
	March 22 (at Montreal)	Toronto 3	Montreal 2
	March 24 (at Toronto)	Montreal 4	Toronto 1
Semifinals	March 27 (at Toronto)	Toronto 4	Montreal 3 (Bodnar 12:36 OT)
	March 29 (at Montreal)	Montreal 10	Toronto 3
	March 31 (at Toronto)	Toronto 3	Montreal 2
	Toronto won best-of-seven, 4–2		
	April 6 (at Detroit)	Toronto 1	Detroit 0 [McCool]
	April 8 (at Detroit)	Toronto 2	Detroit 0 [McCool]
	April 12 (at Toronto)	Toronto 1	Detroit 0 [McCool]
	April 14 (at Toronto)	Detroit 5	Toronto 3
Finals	April 19 (at Detroit)	Detroit 2	Toronto 0 [Lumley]
	April 21 (at Toronto)	Detroit 1	Toronto 0 [Lumley] (E. Bruneteau 14:16 OT)
	April 22 (at Detroit)	Toronto 2	Detroit 1
	Toronto won Stanley Cup best-of-seven, 4–3		

1946

Did Not Qualify

1947

	March 26 (at Toronto)	Toronto 3	Detroit 2 (Meeker 3:05 OT)
	March 29 (at Toronto)	Detroit 9	Toronto 1
Semifinals	April 1 (at Detroit)	Toronto 4	Detroit 1
	April 3 (at Detroit)	Toronto 4	Detroit 1
	April 5 (at Toronto)	Toronto 6	Detroit 1
	Toronto won best-of-seven, 4–1		
	April 8 (at Montreal)	Montreal 6	Toronto 0 [Durnan]
	April 10 (at Montreal)	Toronto 4	Montreal 0 [Broda]
	April 12 (at Toronto)	Toronto 4	Montreal 2
Finals	April 15 (at Toronto)	Toronto 2	Montreal 1 (Apps 16:36 OT)
	April 17 (at Montreal)	Montreal 3	Toronto 1
	April 19 (at Toronto)	Toronto 2	Montreal 1
	Toronto won Stanley Cup best-of-seven, 4–2		

1948

	March 24 (at Toronto)	Toronto 5	Boston 4 (N. Metz 17:03 OT)
	March 27 (at Toronto)	Toronto 5	Boston 3
Semifinals	March 30 (at Boston)	Toronto 5	Boston 1
	April 1 (at Boston)	Boston 3	Toronto 2
	April 3 (at Toronto)	Toronto 3	Boston 2
	Toronto won best-of-seven, 4–1		

Finals	April 7 (at Toronto)	Toronto 5	Detroit 3
	April 10 (at Toronto)	Toronto 4	Detroit 2
	April 11 (at Detroit)	Toronto 2	Detroit 0 [Broda]
	April 14 (at Detroit)	Toronto 7	Detroit 2
	Toronto won Stanley Cup best-of-seven, 4–0		

1949

Semifinals	March 22 (at Boston)	Toronto 3	Boston 0 [Broda]
	March 24 (at Boston)	Toronto 3	Boston 2
	March 26 (at Toronto)	Boston 5	Toronto 4 (Dumart 16:14 OT)
	March 29 (at Toronto)	Toronto 3	Boston 1
	March 30 (at Boston)	Toronto 3	Boston 2
	Toronto won best-of-seven, 4–1		
Finals	April 8 (at Detroit)	Toronto 3	Detroit 2 (Klukay 17:31 OT)
	April 10 (at Detroit)	Toronto 3	Detroit 1
	April 13 (at Toronto)	Toronto 3	Detroit 1
	April 16 (at Toronto)	Toronto 3	Detroit 1
	Toronto won Stanley Cup best-of-seven, 4–0		

1950

Semifinals	March 28 (at Detroit)	Toronto 5	Detroit 0 [Broda]
	March 30 (at Detroit)	Detroit 3	Toronto 1
	April 1 (at Toronto)	Toronto 2	Detroit 0 [Broda]
	April 4 (at Toronto)	Detroit 2	Toronto 1 (Reise 20:38 OT)
	April 6 (at Detroit)	Toronto 2	Detroit 0 [Broda]
	April 8 (at Toronto)	Detroit 4	Toronto 0 [Lumley]
	April 9 (at Detroit)	Detroit 1	Toronto 0 [Lumley] (Reise 8:39 OT)
	Detroit won best-of-seven, 4–3		

1951

Semifinals	March 28 (at Toronto)	Boston 2	Toronto 0 [Gelineau]
	March 31 (at Toronto)	Toronto 1	Boston 1 (20:00 OT)*
	April 1 (at Boston)	Toronto 3	Boston 0 [Broda]
	April 3 (at Boston)	Toronto 3	Boston 1
	April 7 (at Toronto)	Toronto 4	Boston 1
	April 8 (at Boston)	Toronto 6	Boston 0 [Broda]
	Toronto won best-of-seven 4–1		
	*Game halted after one period of overtime due to Toronto curfew bylaw		

Finals	April 11 (at Toronto)	Toronto 3	Montreal 2 (S. Smith 5:51 OT)
	April 14 (at Toronto)	Montreal 3	Toronto 2 (M. Richard 2:55 OT)
	April 17 (at Montreal)	Toronto 2	Montreal 1 (Kennedy 4:47 OT)
	April 19 (at Montreal)	Toronto 3	Montreal 2 (H. Watson 5:15 OT)
	April 21 (at Toronto)	Toronto 3	Montreal 2 (Barilko 2:53 OT)
	Toronto won Stanley Cup best-of-seven, 4–1		

1952

Semifinals	March 25 (at Detroit)	Detroit 3	Toronto 0 [Sawchuk]
	March 27 (at Detroit)	Detroit 1	Toronto 0 [Sawchuk]
	March 29 (at Toronto)	Detroit 6	Toronto 2
	April 1 (at Toronto)	Detroit 3	Toronto 1
	Detroit won best-of-seven, 4–0		

1953

Did Not Qualify

1954

Semifinals	March 23 (at Detroit)	Detroit 5	Toronto 0 [Sawchuk]
	March 25 (at Detroit)	Toronto 3	Detroit 1
	March 27 (at Toronto)	Detroit 3	Toronto 1
	March 30 (at Toronto)	Detroit 2	Toronto 1
	April 1 (at Detroit)	Detroit 4	Toronto 3 (Lindsay 21:01 OT)
	Detroit won best-of-seven, 4–1		

1955

Semifinals	March 22 (at Detroit)	Detroit 7	Toronto 4
	March 24 (at Detroit)	Detroit 2	Toronto 1
	March 26 (at Toronto)	Detroit 2	Toronto 1
	March 29 (at Toronto)	Detroit 3	Toronto 0 [Sawchuk]
	Detroit won best-of-seven, 4–0		

1956

Semifinals	March 20 (at Detroit)	Detroit 3	Toronto 2
	March 22 (at Detroit)	Detroit 3	Toronto 1
	March 24 (at Toronto)	Detroit 5	Toronto 4 (Lindsay 4:22 OT)
	March 27 (at Toronto)	Toronto 2	Detroit 0 [Lumley]
	March 29 (at Detroit)	Detroit 3	Toronto 1
	Detroit won best-of-seven, 4–1		

1957 & 58

Did Not Qualify

1959

Semifinals	March 24 (at Boston)	Boston 5	Toronto 1
	March 26 (at Boston)	Boston 4	Toronto 2
	March 28 (at Toronto)	Toronto 3	Boston 2 (Ehman 5:02 OT)
	March 31 (at Toronto)	Toronto 3	Boston 2 (F. Mahovlich 11:21 OT)
	April 2 (at Boston)	Toronto 4	Boston 1
	April 4 (at Toronto)	Boston 5	Toronto 4
	April 7 (at Boston)	Toronto 3	Boston 2
	Toronto won best-of-seven, 4–3		
Finals	April 9 (at Montreal)	Montreal 5	Toronto 3
	April 11 (at Montreal)	Montreal 3	Toronto 1
	April 14 (at Toronto)	Toronto 3	Montreal 2 (Duff 10:06 OT)
	April 16 (at Toronto)	Montreal 3	Toronto 2
	April 18 (at Montreal)	Montreal 5	Toronto 3
	Montreal won Stanley Cup best-of-seven, 4–1		

1960

Semifinals	March 23 (at Toronto)	Detroit 2	Toronto 1
	March 26 (at Toronto)	Toronto 4	Detroit 2
	March 27 (at Detroit)	Toronto 5	Detroit 4 (F. Mahovlich 43:00 OT)
	March 29 (at Detroit)	Detroit 2	Toronto 1 (Melnyk 1:54 OT)
	April 2 (at Toronto)	Toronto 5	Detroit 4
	April 3 (at Detroit)	Toronto 4	Detroit 2
	Toronto won best-of-seven, 4–2		
Finals	April 7 (at Montreal)	Montreal 4	Toronto 2
	April 9 (at Montreal)	Montreal 2	Toronto 1
	April 12 (at Toronto)	Montreal 5	Toronto 2
	April 14 (at Toronto)	Montreal 4	Toronto 0 [Plante]
	Montreal won Stanley Cup best-of-seven, 4–0		

1961

Semifinals	March 22 (at Toronto)	Toronto 3	Detroit 2 (Armstrong 24:51 OT)
	March 25 (at Toronto)	Detroit 4	Toronto 2
	March 26 (at Detroit)	Detroit 2	Toronto 0 [Sawchuk]
	March 28 (at Detroit)	Detroit 4	Toronto 1
	April 1 (at Toronto)	Detroit 3	Toronto 2
	Detroit won best-of-seven, 4–1		

1962

Semifinals			
	March 27 (at Toronto)	Toronto 4	NY Rangers 2
	March 29 (at Toronto)	Toronto 2	NY Rangers 1
	April 1 (at New York)	NY Rangers 5	Toronto 4
	April 3 (at New York)	NY Rangers 4	Toronto 2
	April 5 (at Toronto)	Toronto 3	NY Rangers 2 (Kelly 24:23 OT)
	April 7 (at Toronto)	Toronto 7	NY Rangers 1
	Toronto won best-of-seven, 4–2		

Finals			
	April 10 (at Toronto)	Toronto 4	Chicago 1
	April 12 (at Toronto)	Toronto 3	Chicago 2
	April 15 (at Chicago)	Chicago 3	Toronto 0 [Hall]
	April 17 (at Chicago)	Chicago 4	Toronto 1
	April 19 (at Toronto)	Toronto 8	Chicago 4
	April 22 (at Chicago)	Toronto 2	Chicago 1
	Toronto won Stanley Cup best-of-seven, 4–2		

1963

Semifinals			
	March 26 (at Toronto)	Toronto 3	Montreal 1
	March 28 (at Toronto)	Toronto 3	Montreal 2
	March 30 (at Montreal)	Toronto 2	Montreal 0 [Bower]
	April 2 (at Montreal)	Montreal 3	Toronto 1
	April 4 (at Toronto)	Toronto 5	Montreal 0 [Bower]
	Toronto won best-of-seven, 4–1		

Finals			
	April 9 (at Toronto)	Toronto 4	Detroit 2
	April 11 (at Toronto)	Toronto 4	Detroit 2
	April 14 (at Detroit)	Detroit 3	Toronto 2
	April 16 (at Detroit)	Toronto 4	Detroit 2
	April 18 (at Toronto)	Toronto 3	Detroit 1
	Toronto won Stanley Cup best-of-seven, 4–1		

1964

Semifinals			
	March 26 (at Montreal)	Montreal 2	Toronto 0 [Hodge]
	March 28 (at Montreal)	Toronto 2	Montreal 1
	March 31 (at Toronto)	Montreal 3	Toronto 2
	April 2 (at Toronto)	Toronto 5	Montreal 3
	April 4 (at Montreal)	Montreal 4	Toronto 2
	April 7 (at Toronto)	Toronto 3	Montreal 0 [Bower]
	April 9 (at Montreal)	Toronto 3	Montreal 1
	Toronto won best-of-seven, 4–3		

Finals	April 11 (at Toronto)	Toronto 3	Detroit 2
	April 14 (at Toronto)	Detroit 4	Toronto 3 (Jeffrey 7:52 OT)
	April 16 (at Detroit)	Detroit 4	Toronto 3
	April 18 (at Detroit)	Toronto 4	Detroit 2
	April 21 (at Toronto)	Detroit 2	Toronto 1
	April 23 (at Toronto)	Toronto 4	Detroit 3 (Baun 1:43 OT)
	April 25 (at Toronto)	Toronto 4	Detroit 0 [Bower]
	Toronto won Stanley Cup best-of-seven, 4–3		

1965

Semifinals	April 1 (at Montreal)	Montreal 3	Toronto 2
	April 3 (at Montreal)	Montreal 3	Toronto 1
	April 6 (at Toronto)	Toronto 3	Montreal 2 (Keon 4:17 OT)
	April 8 (at Toronto)	Toronto 4	Montreal 2
	April 10 (at Montreal)	Montreal 3	Toronto 1
	April 13 (at Toronto)	Montreal 4	Toronto 3 (C. Provost 16:33 OT)
	Montreal won best-of-seven, 4–2		

1966

Semifinals	April 7 (at Montreal)	Montreal 4	Toronto 3
	April 9 (at Montreal)	Montreal 2	Toronto 0 [Worsley]
	April 12 (at Toronto)	Montreal 5	Toronto 2
	April 14 (at Toronto)	Montreal 4	Toronto 1
	Montreal won best-of-seven, 4–0		

1967

Semifinals	April 6 (at Chicago)	Chicago 5	Toronto 2
	April 9 (at Chicago)	Toronto 3	Chicago 1
	April 11 (at Toronto)	Toronto 3	Chicago 1
	April 13 (at Toronto)	Chicago 4	Toronto 3
	April 15 (at Chicago)	Toronto 4	Chicago 2
	April 18 (at Toronto)	Toronto 3	Chicago 1
	Toronto won best-of-seven, 4–2		
Finals	April 20 (at Montreal)	Montreal 6	Toronto 2
	April 22 (at Montreal)	Toronto 3	Montreal 0 [Bower]
	April 25 (at Toronto)	Toronto 3	Montreal 2 (Pulford 28:26 OT)
	April 27 (at Toronto)	Montreal 6	Toronto 2
	April 29 (at Montreal)	Toronto 4	Montreal 1
	May 2 (at Toronto)	Toronto 3	Montreal 1
	Toronto won Stanley Cup best-of-seven, 4–2		

1968

Did Not Qualify

1969

Quarterfinals	April 2 (at Boston)	Boston 10	Toronto 0 [Cheevers]
	April 3 (at Boston)	Boston 7	Toronto 0 [Cheevers]
	April 5 (at Toronto)	Boston 4	Toronto 3
	April 6 (at Toronto)	Boston 3	Toronto 2
	Boston won best-of-seven, 4–0		

1970

Did Not Qualify

1971

Quarterfinals	April 7 (at New York)	NY Rangers 5	Toronto 4
	April 8 (at New York)	Toronto 4	NY Rangers 1
	April 10 (at Toronto)	Toronto 3	NY Rangers 1
	April 11 (at Toronto)	NY Rangers 4	Toronto 2
	April 13 (at New York)	NY Rangers 3	Toronto 1
	April 15 (at Toronto)	NY Rangers 2	Toronto 1 (Nevin 9:07 OT)
	NY Rangers won best-of-seven, 4–2		

1972

Quarterfinals	April 5 (at Boston)	Boston 5	Toronto 0 [Cheevers]
	April 6 (at Boston)	Toronto 4	Boston 3 (Harrison 2:58 OT)
	April 8 (at Toronto)	Boston 2	Toronto 0 [Cheevers]
	April 9 (at Toronto)	Boston 5	Toronto 4
	April 11 (at Boston)	Boston 3	Toronto 2
	Boston won best-of-seven, 4–1		

1973

Did Not Qualify

1974

Quarterfinals	April 10 (at Boston)	Boston 1	Toronto 0 [Gilbert]
	April 11 (at Toronto)	Boston 6	Toronto 3
	April 13 (at Toronto)	Boston 6	Toronto 3
	April 14 (at Toronto)	Boston 4	Toronto 3 (Hodge 1:27 OT)
	Boston won best-of-seven, 4–0		

1975

Preliminary Round	April 8 (at Los Angeles)	Los Angeles 3	Toronto 2 (Murphy 8:53 OT)
	April 10 (at Toronto)	Toronto 3	Los Angeles 2 (Stoughton 10:19 OT)
	April 11 (at Los Angeles)	Toronto 2	Los Angeles 1
	Toronto won best-of-three, 2–1		
Quarterfinals	April 13 (at Philadelphia)	Philadelphia 6	Toronto 3
	April 15 (at Philadelphia)	Philadelphia 3	Toronto 0 [Parent]
	April 17 (at Toronto)	Philadelphia 2	Toronto 0 [Parent]
	April 19 (at Toronto)	Philadelphia 4	Toronto 3 (Dupont 1:45 OT)
	Philadelphia won best-of-seven, 4–0		

1976

Preliminary Round	April 6 (at Toronto)	Toronto 4	Pittsburgh 1
	April 8 (at Pittsburgh)	Pittsburgh 2	Toronto 0 [Plasse]
	April 9 (at Toronto)	Toronto 4	Pittsburgh 0 [Thomas]
	Toronto won best-of-three, 2–1		
Quarterfinals	April 12 (at Philadelphia)	Philadelphia 4	Toronto 1
	April 13 (at Philadelphia)	Philadelphia 3	Toronto 1
	April 15 (at Toronto)	Toronto 5	Philadelphia 4
	April 17 (at Toronto)	Toronto 4	Philadelphia 3
	April 20 (at Philadelphia)	Philadelphia 7	Toronto 1
	April 22 (at Toronto)	Toronto 8	Philadelphia 5
	April 25 (at Philadelphia)	Philadelphia 7	Toronto 3
	Philadelphia won best-of-seven, 4–3		

1977

Preliminary Round	April 5 (at Pittsburgh)	Toronto 4	Pittsburgh 2
	April 7 (at Toronto)	Pittsburgh 6	Toronto 4
	April 9 (at Pittsburgh)	Toronto 5	Pittsburgh 2
	Toronto won best-of-three, 2–1		
Quarterfinals	April 11 (at Philadelphia)	Toronto 3	Philadelphia 2
	April 13 (at Philadelphia)	Toronto 4	Philadelphia 1
	April 15 (at Toronto)	Philadelphia 4	Toronto 3 (MacLeish 2:55 OT)
	April 17 (at Toronto)	Philadelphia 6	Toronto 5 (Leach 19:10 OT)
	April 19 (at Philadelphia)	Philadelphia 2	Toronto 0 [Stephenson]
	April 21 (at Toronto)	Philadelphia 4	Toronto 3
	Philadelphia won best-of-seven, 4–2		

1978

Preliminary Round	April 11 (at Toronto)	Toronto 7	Los Angeles 3
	April 13 (at Los Angeles)	Toronto 4	Los Angeles 0 [Palmateer]
	Toronto won best-of-three, 2–0		
Quarterfinals	April 17 (at New York)	NY Islanders 4	Toronto 1
	April 19 (at New York)	NY Islanders 3	Toronto 2 (Bossy 2:50 OT)
	April 21 (at Toronto)	Toronto 2	NY Islanders 0 [Palmateer]
	April 23 (at Toronto)	Toronto 3	NY Islanders 1
	April 25 (at New York)	NY Islanders 2	Toronto 1 (Nystrom 8:02 OT)
	April 27 (at Toronto)	Toronto 5	NY Islanders 2
	April 29 (at New York)	Toronto 2	NY Islanders 1 (McDonald 4:13 OT)
	Toronto won best-of-seven, 4–3		

Semifinals	May 2 (at Montreal)	Montreal 5	Toronto 3
	May 4 (at Montreal)	Montreal 3	Toronto 2
	May 6 (at Toronto)	Montreal 6	Toronto 1
	May 9 (at Toronto)	Montreal 2	Toronto 0 [K. Dryden]
	Montreal won best-of-seven, 4–0		

1979

Preliminary Round	April 10 (at Atlanta)	Toronto 2	Atlanta 1
	April 12 (at Toronto)	Toronto 7	Atlanta 4
	Toronto won best-of-three, 2–0		

Quarterfinals	April 16 (at Montreal)	Montreal 5	Toronto 2
	April 18 (at Montreal)	Montreal 5	Toronto 1
	April 21 (at Toronto)	Montreal 4	Toronto 3 (Connor 25:25 OT)
	April 22 (at Toronto)	Montreal 5	Toronto 4 (Robinson 4:14 OT)
	Montreal won best-of-seven, 4–0		

1980

Preliminary Round	April 8 (at Minnesota)	Minnesota 6	Toronto 3
	April 9 (at Minnesota)	Minnesota 7	Toronto 2
	April 11 (at Toronto)	Minnesota 4	Toronto 3 (Al MacAdam 0:32 OT)
	Minnesota won best-of-five, 3–0		

1981

Preliminary Round	April 8 (at New York)	NY Islanders 9	Toronto 2
	April 9 (at New York)	NY Islanders 5	Toronto 1
	April 11 (at Toronto)	NY Islanders 6	Toronto 1
	NY Islanders won best-of-five, 3–0		

1982
Did Not Qualify

1983

Preliminary Round	April 6 (at Minnesota)	Minnesota 5	Toronto 4
	April 7 (at Minnesota)	Minnesota 5	Toronto 4 (B. Smith 5:03 OT)
	April 9 (at Toronto)	Toronto 6	Minnesota 3
	April 10 (at Toronto)	Minnesota 5	Toronto 4 (Ciccarelli 8:05 OT)
	Minnesota won best-of-five, 3–1		

1984 & 1985
Did Not Qualify

1986

Division Semifinals	April 9 (at Chicago)	Toronto 5	Chicago 3
	April 10 (at Chicago)	Toronto 6	Chicago 4
	April 12 (at Toronto)	Toronto 7	Chicago 2
	Toronto won best-of-five, 3–0		

	April 18 (at St. Louis)	St. Louis 6	Toronto 1
	April 20 (at St. Louis)	Toronto 3	St. Louis 0 [Wregget]
	April 22 (at Toronto)	Toronto 5	St. Louis 2
Division Finals	April 24 (at Toronto)	St. Louis 7	Toronto 4
	April 26 (at St. Louis)	St. Louis 4	Toronto 3 (Reeds 7:11 OT)
	April 28 (at Toronto)	Toronto 5	St. Louis 3
	April 30 (at St. Louis)	St. Louis 2	Toronto 1
	St. Louis won best-of-seven, 4–3		

1987

	April 8 (at St. Louis)	St. Louis 3	Toronto 1
	April 9 (at St. Louis)	Toronto 3	St. Louis 2 (Lanz 10:17 OT)
	April 11 (at Toronto)	St. Louis 5	Toronto 3
Division Semifinals	April 12 (at Toronto)	Toronto 2	St. Louis 1
	April 14 (at St. Louis)	Toronto 2	St. Louis 1
	April 16 (at Toronto)	Toronto 4	St. Louis 0 [Wregget]
	Toronto won best-of-seven, 4–2		

	April 21 (at Detroit)	Toronto 4	Detroit 2
	April 23 (at Detroit)	Toronto 7	Detroit 2
	April 25 (at Toronto)	Detroit 4	Toronto 2
Division Finals	April 27 (at Toronto)	Toronto 3	Detroit 2 (Allison 9:31 OT)
	April 29 (at Detroit)	Detroit 3	Toronto 0 [Hanlon]
	May 1 (at Toronto)	Detroit 4	Toronto 2
	May 3 (at Detroit)	Detroit 3	Toronto 0 [Hanlon]
	Detroit won best-of-seven, 4–3		

1988

	April 6 (at Detroit)	Toronto 6	Detroit 2
	April 7 (at Detroit)	Detroit 6	Toronto 2
	April 9 (at Toronto)	Detroit 6	Toronto 3
Division Semifinals	April 10 (at Toronto)	Detroit 8	Toronto 0 [Hanlon]
	April 12 (at Detroit)	Toronto 6	Detroit 5 (Olczyk 0:34 OT)
	April 14 (at Toronto)	Detroit 5	Toronto 3
	Detroit won best-of-seven, 4–2		

1989
Did Not Qualify

1990

	April 4 (at St. Louis)	St. Louis 4	Toronto 2
	April 6 (at St. Louis)	St. Louis 4	Toronto 2
Division Semifinals	April 8 (at Toronto)	St. Louis 6	Toronto 5 (Momesso 6:04 OT)
	April 10 (at Toronto)	Toronto 4	St. Louis 2
	April 12 (at St. Louis)	St. Louis 4	Toronto 3
	St. Louis won best-of-seven, 4–1		

1991 & 1992

Did Not Qualify

1993

Conference Quarterfinals	April 19 (at Detroit)	Detroit 6	Toronto 3
	April 21 (at Detroit)	Detroit 6	Toronto 2
	April 23 (at Toronto)	Toronto 4	Detroit 2
	April 25 (at Toronto)	Toronto 3	Detroit 2
	April 27 (at Detroit)	Toronto 5	Detroit 4 (Foligno 2:05 OT)
	April 29 (at Toronto)	Detroit 7	Toronto 3
	May 1 (at Detroit)	Toronto 4	Detroit 3 (Borschevsky 2:35 OT)
	Toronto won best-of-seven, 4–3		
Conference Semifinals	May 3 (at Toronto)	Toronto 2	St. Louis 1 (Gilmour 23:16 OT)
	May 5 (at Toronto)	St. Louis 2	Toronto 1 (J. Brown 23:03 OT)
	May 7 (at St. Louis)	St. Louis 4	Toronto 3
	May 9 (at St. Louis)	Toronto 4	St. Louis 1
	May 11 (at Toronto)	Toronto 5	St. Louis 1
	May 13 (at St. Louis)	St. Louis 2	Toronto 1
	May 15 (at Toronto)	Toronto 6	St. Louis 0 [Potvin]
	Toronto won best-of-seven, 4–3		
Conference Finals	May 17 (at Toronto)	Toronto 4	Los Angeles 1
	May 19 (at Toronto)	Los Angeles 3	Toronto 2
	May 21 (at Los Angeles)	Los Angeles 4	Toronto 2
	May 23 (at Los Angeles)	Toronto 4	Los Angeles 2
	May 25 (at Toronto)	Toronto 3	Los Angeles 2 (G. Anderson 19:20 OT)
	May 27 (at Los Angeles)	Los Angeles 5	Toronto 4 (Gretzky 1:41 OT)
	May 29 (at Toronto)	Los Angeles 5	Toronto 4
	Los Angeles won best-of-seven, 4–3		

1994

Conference Quarterfinals	April 18 (at Toronto)	Toronto 5	Chicago 1
	April 20 (at Toronto)	Toronto 1	Chicago 0 [Potvin] (Gill 2:15 OT)
	April 23 (at Chicago)	Chicago 5	Toronto 4
	April 24 (at Chicago)	Chicago 4	Toronto 3 (Roenick 1:23 OT)
	April 26 (at Toronto)	Toronto 1	Chicago 0 [Potvin]
	April 28 (at Chicago)	Toronto 1	Chicago 0 [Potvin]
	Toronto won best-of-seven, 4–2		

Conference Semifinals	May 2 (at Toronto)	San Jose 3	Toronto 2
	May 4 (at Toronto)	Toronto 5	San Jose 1
	May 6 (at San Jose)	San Jose 5	Toronto 2
	May 8 (at San Jose)	Toronto 8	San Jose 3
	May 10 (at San Jose)	San Jose 5	Toronto 2
	May 12 (at Toronto)	Toronto 3	San Jose 2 (Gartner 8:53 OT)
	May 14 (at Toronto)	Toronto 4	San Jose 2
	Toronto won best-of-seven, 4–3		
Conference Finals	May 16 (at Toronto)	Toronto 3	Vancouver 2 (Zezel 16:55 OT)
	May 18 (at Toronto)	Vancouver 4	Toronto 3
	May 20 (at Vancouver)	Vancouver 4	Toronto 0 [McLean]
	May 22 (at Vancouver)	Vancouver 2	Toronto 0 [McLean]
	May 24 (at Vancouver)	Vancouver 4	Toronto 3 (G. Adams 20:14 OT)
	Vancouver won best-of-seven, 4–1		

1995

Conference Quarterfinals	May 7 (at Chicago)	Toronto 5	Chicago 3
	May 9 (at Chicago)	Toronto 3	Chicago 0 [Potvin]
	May 11 (at Toronto)	Chicago 3	Toronto 2
	May 13 (at Toronto)	Chicago 3	Toronto 1
	May 15 (at Chicago)	Chicago 4	Toronto 2
	May 17 (at Toronto)	Toronto 5	Chicago 4 (Wood 10:00 OT)
	May 19 (at Chicago)	Chicago 5	Toronto 2
	Chicago won best-of-seven, 4–3		

1996

Conference Quarterfinals	April 16 (at Toronto)	St. Louis 3	Toronto 1
	April 18 (at Toronto)	Toronto 5	St. Louis 4 (Sundin 4:02 OT)
	April 21 (at St. Louis)	St. Louis 3	Toronto 2 (G. Anderson 1:24 OT)
	April 23 (at St. Louis)	St. Louis 5	Toronto 1
	April 25 (at Toronto)	Toronto 5	St. Louis 4 (Gartner 7:31 OT)
	April 27 (at St. Louis)	St. Louis 2	Toronto 1
	St. Louis won best-of-seven, 4–2		

1997 & 1998   Did Not Qualify

1999

Conference Quarterfinals	April 22 (at Toronto)	Philadelphia 3	Toronto 0 [Vanbiesbrouck]
	April 24 (at Toronto)	Toronto 2	Philadelphia 1
	April 26 (at Philadelphia)	Toronto 2	Philadelphia 1
	April 28 (at Philadelphia)	Philadelphia 5	Toronto 2
	April 30 (at Toronto)	Toronto 2	Philadelphia 1
	May 2 (at Philadelphia)	Toronto 1	Philadelphia 0 [Joseph]
	Toronto won best-of-seven, 4–2		

Conference Semifinals	May 7 (at Toronto)	Pittsburgh 2	Toronto 0 [Barrasso]
	May 9 (at Toronto)	Toronto 4	Pittsburgh 2
	May 11 (at Pittsburgh)	Pittsburgh 4	Toronto 3
	May 13 (at Pittsburgh)	Toronto 3	Pittsburgh 2
	May 15 (at Toronto)	Toronto 4	Pittsburgh 1
	May 17 (at Pittsburgh)	Toronto 4	Pittsburgh 3
	Toronto won best-of-seven, 4–2		
Conference Finals	May 23 (at Toronto)	Buffalo 5	Toronto 4
	May 25 (at Toronto)	Toronto 6	Buffalo 3
	May 27 (at Buffalo)	Buffalo 4	Toronto 2
	May 29 (at Buffalo)	Buffalo 5	Toronto 2
	May 31 (at Toronto)	Buffalo 4	Toronto 2
	Buffalo won best-of-seven, 4–1		

2000

Conference Quarterfinals	April 12 (at Toronto)	Toronto 2	Ottawa 0 [Joseph]
	April 15 (at Toronto)	Toronto 5	Ottawa 1
	April 17 (at Ottawa)	Ottawa 4	Toronto 3
	April 19 (at Ottawa)	Ottawa 2	Toronto 1
	April 22 (at Toronto)	Toronto 2	Ottawa 1
	April 24 (at Ottawa)	Toronto 4	Ottawa 2
	Toronto won best-of-seven, 4–2		
Conference Semifinals	April 27 (at Toronto)	Toronto 2	New Jersey 1
	April 29 (at Toronto)	New Jersey 1	Toronto 0 [Brodeur]
	May 1 (at New Jersey)	New Jersey 5	Toronto 1
	May 3 (at New Jersey)	Toronto 3	New Jersey 2
	May 6 (at Toronto)	New Jersey 4	Toronto 3
	May 8 (at New Jersey)	New Jersey 3	Toronto 0 [Brodeur]
	New Jersey won best-of seven, 4–2		

2001

Conference Quarterfinals	April 13 (at Ottawa)	Toronto 1	Ottawa 0 [Joseph] (Sundin 10:49 OT)
	April 14 (at Ottawa)	Toronto 3	Ottawa 0 [Joseph]
	April 16 (at Toronto)	Toronto 3	Ottawa 2 (Cross 2:16 OT)
	April 18 (at Toronto)	Toronto 3	Ottawa 1
	Toronto won best-of-seven, 4–0		

	April 26 (at New Jersey)	Toronto 2	New Jersey 0
	April 28 (at New Jersey)	New Jersey 6	Toronto 5 (McKay 5:31 OT)
	May 1 (at Toronto)	New Jersey 3	Toronto 2 (Rafalski 7:00 OT)
Conference	May 3 (at Toronto)	Toronto 3	New Jersey 1
Semifinals	May 5 (at New Jersey)	Toronto 3	New Jersey 2
	May 7 (at Toronto)	New Jersey 4	Toronto 2
	May 9 (at New Jersey)	New Jersey 5	Toronto 1
	New Jersey won best-of-seven, 4–3		

2002

	April 18 (at Toronto)	Toronto 3	NY Islanders 1
	April 20 (at Toronto)	Toronto 2	NY Islanders 0 [Joseph]
	April 23 (at New York)	NY Islanders 6	Toronto 1
Conference	April 24 (at New York)	NY Islanders 4	Toronto 3
Quarterfinals	April 26 (at Toronto)	Toronto 6	NY Islanders 3
	April 28 (at New York)	NY Islanders 5	Toronto 3
	April 30 (at Toronto)	Toronto 4	NY Islanders 2
	Toronto won best-of-seven, 4–3		

	May 2 (at Toronto)	Ottawa 5	Toronto 0 [Lalime]
	May 4 (at Toronto)	Toronto 3	Ottawa 2 (Roberts 44:30 OT)
	May 6 (at Ottawa)	Ottawa 3	Toronto 2
Conference	May 8 (at Ottawa)	Toronto 2	Ottawa 1
Semifinals	May 10 (at Toronto)	Ottawa 4	Toronto 2
	May 12 (at Ottawa)	Toronto 4	Ottawa 3
	May 14 (at Toronto)	Toronto 3	Ottawa 0 [Joseph]
	Toronto won best-of-seven, 4–3		

	May 16 (at Carolina)	Toronto 2	Carolina 1
	May 19 (at Carolina)	Carolina 2	Toronto 1 (Wallin 13:42 OT)
	May 21 (at Toronto)	Carolina 2	Toronto 1 (O'Neill 6:01 OT)
Conference	May 23 (at Toronto)	Carolina 3	Toronto 0 [Irbe]
Finals	May 25 (at Carolina)	Toronto 1	Carolina 0 [Joseph]
	May 28 (at Toronto)	Carolina 2	Toronto 1 (Gélinas 8:05 OT)
	Carolina won best-of-seven, 4–2		

2003

	April 9 (at Philadelphia)	Toronto 5	Philadelphia 3
	April 11 (at Philadelphia)	Philadelphia 4	Toronto 1
	April 14 (at Toronto)	Toronto 4	Philadelphia 3 (Kaberle 27:20 OT)
Conference	April 16 (at Toronto)	Philadelphia 3	Toronto 2 (Recchi 53:54 OT)
Quarterfinals	April 19 (at Philadelphia)	Philadelphia 4	Toronto 1
	April 21 (at Toronto)	Toronto 2	Philadelphia 1 (Green 30:51 OT)
	April 22 (at Philadelphia)	Philadelphia 6	Toronto 1
	Philadelphia won best-of-seven, 4–3		

2004

	April 8 (at Toronto)	Ottawa 4	Toronto 2
	April 10 (at Toronto)	Toronto 2	Ottawa 0 [Belfour]
	April 12 (at Ottawa)	Toronto 2	Ottawa 0 [Belfour]
Conference	April 14 (at Ottawa)	Ottawa 4	Toronto 1
Quarterfinals	April 16 (at Toronto)	Toronto 2	Ottawa 0 [Belfour]
	April 18 (at Ottawa)	Ottawa 2	Toronto 1 (Fisher 21:47 OT)
	April 20 (at Toronto)	Toronto 4	Ottawa 1
	Toronto won best-of-seven, 4–3		
	April 22 (at Philadelphia)	Philadelphia 3	Toronto 1
	April 25 (at Philadelphia)	Philadelphia 2	Toronto 1
Conference	April 28 (at Toronto)	Toronto 4	Philadelphia 1
Semifinals	April 30 (at Toronto)	Toronto 3	Philadelphia 1
	May 2 (at Philadelphia)	Philadelphia 7	Toronto 2
	May 4 (at Toronto)	Philadelphia 3	Toronto 2 (Roenick 7:39 OT)
	Philadelphia won best-of-seven, 4–2		

2005

No Season

2006–12

Did Not Qualify

2013

	May 1 (at Boston)	Boston 4	Toronto 1
	May 4 (at Boston)	Toronto 4	Boston 2
	May 6 (at Toronto)	Boston 5	Toronto 2
Conference	May 8 (at Toronto)	Boston 4	Toronto 3 (Krejci 13:06 OT)
Quarterfinals	May 10 (at Boston)	Toronto 2	Boston 1
	May 12 (at Toronto)	Toronto 2	Boston 1
	May 13 (at Boston)	Boston 5	Toronto 4 (Bergeron 6:05 OT)
	Boston won best-of-seven, 4–3		

2014 & 2015

Did Not Qualify

PART 5

ALL-TIME LEAFS SCORES AND STATS

ALL-TIME REGULAR-SEASON SCORES

All shutouts are noted with the goalie's name enclosed in square brackets—"[Broda]" means Turk Broda registered a shutout that game; scoring information, including all empty-net (EN) and overtime (OT) goals, is recorded in parentheses.

1917–18
First Half

DECEMBER
19 Toronto 9 at Wanderers 10*
22 Ottawa 4 at Toronto 11
26 Montreal 5 at Toronto 7
29 Toronto 2 at Montreal 9
* Art Brooks replaced Sammy Hebert in Toronto goal at the start of the second period.

JANUARY
2   Toronto 6 at Ottawa 5
5   Wanderers 0 at Toronto 1*
9   Montreal 4 at Toronto 6
14 Toronto 6 at Ottawa 9
16 Ottawa 4 at Toronto 5**
19 Toronto 1 at Montreal 5
26 Toronto 3 at Ottawa 6
28 Montreal 1 at Toronto 5 (all goals in 1st)***
* The only "game" of its kind in the NHL. The Wanderers' building had burned down three days earlier, but team owner Sammy Lichtenhein elected to cut his losses and not send his team to Toronto for the Saturday game at the Arena. The Arenas, about to lose gate receipts, took a legal precaution by "playing" the game anyway. Thus, at 8:30 P.M., Harry Holmes took his place in goal (his first game as an Arena), Harry Cameron and Ken Randall lined up on defence, and Alf Skinner, Corb Dennenay, and Harry Meeking played forward. Referee Lou Marsh dropped the puck and Dennenay skated in and scored. The team left the ice, winning 1–0 by default.
** Game played without any substitutions.
*** Joe Hall and Alf Skinner were fined $15 and arrested for stick-swinging.

FEBRUARY
2   Toronto 2 at Montreal 11
4   Ottawa 2 at Toronto 8*

Second Half

9   Toronto 7 at Montreal 3
11 Ottawa 1 at Toronto 3
13 Toronto 6 at Ottawa 1
18 Montreal 9 at Toronto 0 [Vézina]
20 Toronto 4 at Montreal 5 (McDonald 4:50 OT)
23 Ottawa 3 at Toronto 9**
* Ken Randall was fined $5 for using bad language.
** Randall had been temporarily suspended by NHL president Frank Calder. However, he was told he would be allowed to play if he paid referee Lou Marsh the $35 in unpaid fines he owed. Randall paid $32 in bills and $3 in pennies, but when someone knocked the coins from Marsh's hand onto the ice, the start of the game was delayed some minutes until all the coins could be collected.

MARCH
2   Montreal 3 at Toronto 5
6   Toronto 3 at Ottawa 9

1918–19
First Half

DECEMBER
23 Montreal 4 at Toronto 3
26 Toronto 2 at Ottawa 5
28 Toronto 3 at Montreal 6
31 Ottawa 2 at Toronto 4

JANUARY
7   Montreal 7 at Toronto 6
9   Toronto 2 at Ottawa 4
11 Toronto 3 at Montreal 13
14 Ottawa 2 at Toronto 5*
21 Montreal 3 at Toronto 11
23 Toronto 2 at Ottawa 3**

Second Half

28 Ottawa 2 at Toronto 1 (Cameron 16:00 OT)
* Cy Dennenay and Ken Randall were given match penalties and fined $15 for fighting; Randall was fined an additional $10 for bad language.
** Rusty Crawford was given a major penalty at 6:00 of the first; Toronto was forced to play one man short the rest of the game.

FEBRUARY
1   Toronto 0 at Montreal 10 [Vézina]
4   Montreal 3 at Toronto 6
6   Toronto 1 at Ottawa 3
11 Montreal 4 at Toronto 6
15 Toronto 2 at Montreal 8
18 Ottawa 4 at Toronto 3 (Broadbent 2:30 OT)
20 Toronto 3 at Ottawa 9

1919–20
December 13, 1919: The Arenas changed their name to the St. Patricks (although they were tentatively called the "Tecumsehs").

First Half

DECEMBER
23 Toronto 0 at Ottawa 3 [Benedict]
27 Bulldogs 4 at Toronto 7
31 Montreal 1 at Toronto 5

JANUARY

3	Ottawa 3 at Toronto 4*
7	Toronto 5 at Bulldogs 7
10	Toronto 7 at Montreal 14**
14	Montreal 4 at Toronto 3
17	Bulldogs 3 at Toronto 8
21	Toronto 2 at Montreal 3
24	Ottawa 3 at Toronto 5***
28	Toronto 0 at Ottawa 7 [Benedict]
31	Toronto 6 at Bulldogs 10 (Malone scored 7 goals)

* Referee Steve Vair injured his shoulder at 18:00 of the first; the teams went to the dressing room and the extra two minutes was added to the second period.
** First game played at Mount Royal Arena.
*** Clint Benedict, the Ottawa goalie, was given a minor penalty.

Second Half

FEBRUARY

4	Montreal 6 at Toronto 5
7	Toronto 4 at Ottawa 3*
11	Bulldogs 2 at Toronto 7
16	Toronto 4 at Bulldogs 3
18	Toronto 8 at Montreal 2
21	Ottawa 5 at Toronto 3
25	Toronto 8 at Bulldogs 2
28	Ottawa 1 at Toronto 0 [Benedict]

* At the end of the first period, the Toronto players were promised a bonus of $25 if they won the game; they did, and were paid the next day.

MARCH

3	Toronto 4 at Ottawa 7
6	Bulldogs 2 at Toronto 11*
10	Toronto 2 at Bulldogs 7
13	Montreal 4 at Toronto 11

* Toronto goalie Howie Lockhart played in goal for Quebec, as regular Bulldogs goalie Frank Brophy was injured and could not make the trip.

1920–21

First Half

DECEMBER

22	Toronto 3 at Ottawa 6
25	Montreal 4 at Toronto 5
29	Ottawa 8 at Toronto 1

JANUARY

3	Toronto 5 at Hamilton 4
8	Hamilton 3 at Toronto 2 (Couture 5:00 OT)
12	Toronto 4 at Hamilton 2
15	Ottawa 5 at Toronto 2
17	Toronto 5 at Montreal 9
19	Montreal 2 at Toronto 7
22	Toronto 5 at Ottawa 4 (Dennenay 15:30 OT)

Second Half

26	Hamilton 3 at Toronto 10
29	Toronto 2 at Montreal 4

FEBRUARY

2	Toronto 3 at Ottawa 4*
5	Montreal 6 at Toronto 10
9	Toronto 5 at Montreal 3**
12	Toronto 6 at Hamilton 4
16	Ottawa 3 at Toronto 4***
19	Hamilton 4 at Toronto 5
23	Toronto 4 at Hamilton 7
26	Ottawa 2 at Toronto 4
28	Toronto 0 at Montreal 4 [Vézina]

* There were two delays during the game caused by power failures; a row of candles around the rink was set up to augment the lighting.
** Reg Noble was fined $50 for arguing with referee Cooper Smeaton.
*** The game was delayed three minutes from the end when Jake Forbes, in net for Toronto, suffered a bad cut that had to be stitched.

MARCH

2	Toronto 3 at Ottawa 2
5	Hamilton 3 at Toronto 4 (Cameron 3:00 OT)*
7	Montreal 4 at Toronto 6

* Randall was fined $25 for stick-swinging.

1921–22

DECEMBER

17	Montreal 2 at Toronto 5
21	Toronto 5 at Ottawa 4*
24	Hamilton 4 at Toronto 2
28	Toronto 4 at Hamilton 3
31	Toronto 3 at Montreal 5

* Governor General Viscount Byng and Lady Byng were in attendance.

JANUARY

4	Ottawa 2 at Toronto 3 (Stuart won game in final minute)
7	Hamilton 2 at Toronto 5
11	Toronto 2 at Ottawa 7
14	Ottawa 5 at Toronto 2*
18	Toronto 4 at Hamilton 9
21	Toronto 5 at Montreal 3**
25	Montreal 1 at Toronto 3
28	Ottawa 2 at Toronto 1

* At 9:20 of the third, with Toronto trailing 3–2, Babe Dye was given a minor penalty he felt was unwarranted. He began to shove referee Percy Le Sueur and was given a five-minute major; he then used bad language and was given five more. Noble and Randall got minors when play resumed, and with Toronto playing with only two skaters, Ottawa scored two goals. Dye's penalties meant the St. Pats played one man down the rest of the game.
** Dye scored a goal in the second, but after play had resumed for a full two minutes, referee Cooper Smeaton disallowed the goal on advice from the goal judge, who, reversing his initial decision, said the puck had not crossed the goal line.

FEBRUARY

1   Toronto 5 at Hamilton 4

4   Montreal 1 at Toronto 3

8   Toronto 4 at Montreal 6

11 Toronto 4 at Ottawa 4

15 Hamilton 4 at Toronto 6

18 Toronto 4 at Montreal 6

22 Toronto 3 at Hamilton 4

25 Ottawa 5 at Toronto 7

MARCH

1   Toronto 3 at Ottawa 2

4   Hamilton 4 at Toronto 8*

7   Montreal 8 at Toronto 7

* Montreal's owners offered all Hamilton players $25 if they beat Toronto. The St. Pats won and Montreal missed the playoffs.

1922–23

DECEMBER

16 Montreal 2 at Toronto 7

20 Toronto 2 at Ottawa 7*

23 Hamilton 4 at Toronto 9

27 Toronto 6 at Hamilton 9

30 Toronto 2 at Montreal 8

* The game was delayed 75 minutes because trains from Toronto were late in arriving; players had to dress on the train.

JANUARY

3   Ottawa 2 at Toronto 3 (Dye 5:15 OT)*

6   Toronto 1 at Ottawa 2**

10 Toronto 7 at Hamilton 6 (Dye 0:40 OT)

13 Montreal 2 at Toronto 2

17 Hamilton 5 at Toronto 2

20 Toronto 1 at Montreal 3

24 Toronto 2 at Ottawa 1 (Noble 1:09 OT)

27 Montreal 2 at Toronto 4

31 Toronto 1 at Ottawa 2 (all goals in 1st)

* In a pre-game ceremony, the St. Pats presented the Senators' Eddie Gerard with a tie pin to acknowledge their appreciation for his contribution to their Cup-winning 1922 playoff campaign, during which he played one game for Toronto.

** Both teams played 38 minutes without making a single change.

FEBRUARY

3   Hamilton 5 at Toronto 6

7   Toronto 4 at Hamilton 2

10 Toronto 3 at Montreal 5*

14 Ottawa 4 at Toronto 6

17 Toronto 3 at Hamilton 2

21 Toronto 1 at Ottawa 6

24 Montreal 3 at Toronto 4*

28 Toronto 0 at Montreal 3 [Vézina]

* The game was delayed three times when overhead light bulbs burst because of leaks in the roof and their glass had to be cleaned from the ice.

MARCH

3   Hamilton 3 at Toronto 4

5   Ottawa 0 at Toronto 2 [Roach] (both goals in 3rd)

1923–24

DECEMBER

15 Montreal 1 at Toronto 2

19 Toronto 2 at Ottawa 5

22 Hamilton 2 at Toronto 5

26 Toronto 2 at Hamilton 1*

29 Toronto 0 at Montreal 3 [Vézina]

* Fans pelted the ice with eggs when referee Jerry Laflamme disallowed a Hamilton goal by Mickey Roach in the last minute of play.

JANUARY

2   Ottawa 4 at Toronto 3

5   Toronto 3 at Ottawa 7

9   Toronto 3 at Hamilton 5

12 Montreal 3 at Toronto 5

16 Hamilton 1 at Toronto 3

19 Toronto 2 at Montreal 0 [Roach] (both goals in 2nd)

23 Ottawa 5 at Toronto 1

26 Montreal 1 at Toronto 2

30 Toronto 2 at Ottawa 7*

* With eight minutes left in the game, referee Art Ross gave Toronto three major, or match, penalties, leaving them to play five skaters versus two for the rest of the game. Toronto formally protested the outcome, but St. Pats coach Charlie Querrie was fined $200 for arguing with Ross.

FEBRUARY

2   Hamilton 4 at Toronto 2

6   Toronto 4 at Hamilton 6

9   Toronto 3 at Montreal 5

13 Ottawa 2 at Toronto 4

16 Toronto 2 at Ottawa 1

20 Toronto 1 at Hamilton 3

23 Hamilton 1 at Toronto 2*

27 Toronto 1 at Montreal 6

* Game was delayed 10 minutes to allow fans to enter.

MARCH

1   Montreal 4 at Toronto 1

5   Ottawa 8 at Toronto 4

1924–25

NOVEMBER

29 Toronto 1 at Montreal 7*

* First game played at the Forum.

DECEMBER

3	Boston 3 at Toronto 5*
5	Hamilton 10 at Toronto 3
10	Toronto 6 at Ottawa 3
13	Maroons 3 at Toronto 1
17	Montreal 5 at Toronto 2
22	Toronto 10 at Boston 1
25	Toronto 1 at Hamilton 8
27	Ottawa 4 at Toronto 3**
31	Toronto 2 at Maroons 1

* Reg Noble, trying to buy time during a Boston power play, threw the puck into the crowd. The puck was retrieved and he was given a two-minute penalty.

** Ottawa goalie Alec Connell was penalized. King Clancy took his place in net, and during the ensuing power play, the Senators scored a goal shorthanded.

JANUARY

3	Montreal 3 at Toronto 1
5	Toronto 3 at Boston 2
10	Hamilton 1 at Toronto 3
14	Ottawa 2 at Toronto 3
17	Toronto 1 at Maroons 2
21	Toronto 4 at Montreal 2
24	Boston 3 at Toronto 4
28	Toronto 0 at Hamilton 4 [Forbes]
31	Toronto 2 at Ottawa 1 (all goals in 3rd)

FEBRUARY

4	Maroons 2 at Toronto 3
7	Montreal 4 at Toronto 5
10	Toronto 5 at Boston 1*
14	Hamilton 1 at Toronto 3
18	Ottawa 2 at Toronto 4
21	Toronto 2 at Maroons 1
25	Toronto 3 at Montreal 1
28	Boston 1 at Toronto 5

* Babe Dye was awarded a goal after Boston goalie Doc Stewart threw his stick.

MARCH

4	Toronto 2 at Hamilton 3
7	Toronto 0 at Ottawa 3 [Connell]
9	Maroons 0 at Toronto 3 [Roach]

1925–26

NOVEMBER

28	Boston 3 at Toronto 2

DECEMBER

1	Toronto 2 at Maroons 4
5	Americans 3 at Toronto 5
9	Toronto 3 at Pirates 6
12	Montreal 0 at Toronto 4 [Roach]
19	Pirates 1 at Toronto 1

23	Toronto 2 at Ottawa 4
26	Maroons 2 at Toronto 0 [Benedict]
29	Toronto 0 at Boston 3 [Stewart]
30	Toronto 1 at Americans 2 (Green 8:00 OT)

JANUARY

1	Ottawa 0 at Toronto 3 [Roach]
5	Toronto 4 at Montreal 5
9	Boston 2 at Toronto 3
12	Toronto 2 at Maroons 5
15	Americans 3 at Toronto 4
21	Toronto 4 at Pirates 5
23	Montreal 2 at Toronto 6
26	Toronto 3 at Montreal 6
29	Pirates 2 at Toronto 3

FEBRUARY

2	Toronto 2 at Boston 3 (all goals in 1st)
3	Toronto 1 at Americans 1 (both goals in 2nd)
6	Ottawa 1 at Toronto 4
9	Maroons 5 at Toronto 3
11	Toronto 1 at Ottawa 2
13	Boston 7 at Toronto 4
16	Toronto 3 at Americans 2
18	Toronto 2 at Maroons 5
20	Pirates 1 at Toronto 3
22	Toronto 1 at Boston 2 (Hitchman 2:25 OT)
27	Maroons 4 at Toronto 3*

* Game was delayed with four minutes left when Babe Dye refused to give the referee the puck; the referee left the ice and did not return for some time. Toronto's Bert Corbeau was suspended for one game after a brawl with Babe Siebert.

MARCH

4	Toronto 2 at Pirates 7
6	Americans 2 at Toronto 4
11	Montreal 3 at Toronto 5
13	Ottawa 1 at Toronto 1
16	Toronto 1 at Montreal 6
17	Toronto 0 at Ottawa 4 [Connell]

1926–27

NOVEMBER

17	Toronto 1 at Chicago 4
20	Rangers 5 at Toronto 1
25	Ottawa 2 at Toronto 2
30	Pirates 0 at Toronto 6 [Roach]

DECEMBER

2	Toronto 0 at Montreal 2 [Hainsworth]
4	Americans 1 at Toronto 0 [Forbes]
9	Chicago 2 at Toronto 5

11   Toronto 1 at Ottawa 2

14   Toronto 0 at Maroons 3 [Benedict]

18   Montreal 2 at Toronto 0 [Hainsworth]

20   Toronto 0 at Americans 2 [Forbes]

21   Toronto 5 at Boston 3

25   Toronto 2 at Pirates 3

30   Boston 1 at Toronto 4*

* Art Ross of Boston protested Toronto's use of Al Pudas, believing Pudas to be ineligible.

JANUARY

1   Maroons 3 at Toronto 0 [Benedict] (all goals in 3rd)

4   Toronto 2 at Cougars 1

8   Americans 1 at Toronto 3

11   Toronto 1 at Ottawa 4

13   Toronto 1 at Rangers 1

15   Cougars 1 at Toronto 1

19   Toronto 3 at Chicago 4 (Fraser 2:30 OT)*

22   Toronto 0 at Montreal 4 [Hainsworth] (all goals in 1st)

27   Maroons 5 at Toronto 3

29   Chicago 1 at Toronto 6

* Babe Dye was fined $15 for bad language.

FEBRUARY

1   Toronto 0 at Boston 1 [Stewart]

3   Toronto 0 at Americans 0 [Roach (T)/Forbes (A)]

5   Boston 0 at Toronto 1 [Roach]

8   Toronto 0 at Maroons 3 [Benedict]

10   Rangers 3 at Toronto 2

12   Ottawa 1 at Toronto 0 [Connell]

16   Toronto 1 at Cougars 5

17   Americans 1 at Toronto 4*

19   Maroons 2 at Toronto 1 (Munro 12:40 OT)

22   Toronto 3 at Rangers 2 (Bailey 8:47 OT)

24   Montreal 3 at Toronto 2

26   Toronto 1 at Pirates 1

* First game played as the Maple Leafs.

MARCH

1   Pirates 1 at Toronto 4

5   Cougars 2 at Toronto 4

10   Toronto 2 at Montreal 4

12   Toronto 1 at Maroons 0 [Roach]*

19   Ottawa 2 at Toronto 0 [Connell] (both goals in 3rd)

21   Toronto 4 at Americans 1

24   Toronto 0 at Ottawa 4 [Connell]

26   Montreal 1 at Toronto 2

* Ace Bailey's goal was awarded when Maroons goalie Clint Benedict threw his stick.

1927–28

NOVEMBER

15   Rangers 4 at Toronto 2*

19   Chicago 2 at Toronto 4

22   Toronto 0 at Boston 1 [Winkler]

24   Toronto 2 at Americans 1

26   Toronto 2 at Pirates 1 (Bailey 0:44 OT)

* W.D. Ross, lieutenant governor of Ontario, faced off the opening puck.

DECEMBER

3   Maroons 2 at Toronto 1 (all goals in 1st)*

6   Toronto 0 at Ottawa 0 [Roach (T)/Connell (O)]

8   Toronto 1 at Montreal 2 (Joliat 3:47 OT)

10   Ottawa 0 at Toronto 0 [Connell (O)/Roach (T)]

14   Toronto 4 at Chicago 2

17   Cougars 1 at Toronto 0 (Copper 9:00 OT) [Holmes]

20   Americans 2 at Toronto 5

22   Pirates 3 at Toronto 2 (McKinnon 0:35 OT)

24   Toronto 1 at Ottawa 1

29   Boston 1 at Toronto 2 (all goals in 3rd)

* Hap Day was fined $25 after refusing to leave the ice when given a penalty for charging the goalie.

JANUARY

2   Toronto 4 at Chicago 1

5   Toronto 1 at Maroons 2

7   Montreal 9 at Toronto 1*

10   Toronto 1 at Americans 2 (all goals in 3rd)

12   Toronto 2 at Cougars 1

14   Rangers 1 at Toronto 6

17   Toronto 2 at Rangers 1

21   Ottawa 1 at Toronto 2

26   Toronto 0 at Maroons 1 [Benedict]

28   Chicago 1 at Toronto 4

31   Toronto 0 at Ottawa 4 [Connell]

* Bill Carson was awarded the Leafs' only goal, in the third, when Montreal player Gardiner threw his stick.

FEBRUARY

2   Toronto 4 at Montreal 3

4   Cougars 0 at Toronto 2 [Roach]

7   Montreal 2 at Toronto 1 (all goals in 2nd)

11   Americans 2 at Toronto 2

14   Pirates 4 at Toronto 2

16   Toronto 3 at Americans 2

18   Toronto 1 at Maroons 2

21   Toronto 0 at Montreal 0 [Roach (T)/Hainsworth (M)]

23   Maroons 2 at Toronto 2

28   Toronto 0 at Rangers 1 [Chabot]

MARCH

1   Toronto 2 at Pirates 4

3   Boston 0 at Toronto 0 [Winkler (B)/Ironstone (T)]

6   Toronto 1 at Cougars 3

8   Americans 2 at Toronto 4

13   Ottawa 1 at Toronto 1

17   Montreal 3 at Toronto 5*

20   Toronto 6 at Boston 2**

24   Maroons 8 at Toronto 4

* "Parents' Night" at Arena Gardens.

** Sailor Herbert was presented with a gold watch by Boston sportswriters.

1928-29

NOVEMBER

15   Chicago 0 at Toronto 2 [Chabot] (both goals in 2nd)

17   Montreal 2 at Toronto 4

20   Toronto 1 at Ottawa 4*

22   Toronto 0 at Americans 3 [Walsh]

24   Maroons 1 at Toronto 4

27   Toronto 0 at Maroons 4 [Benedict]

* King Clancy scored Ottawa's first goal while Toronto had four men in the penalty box and only goaltender Lorne Chabot and Andy Blair on the ice.

DECEMBER

1   Americans 0 at Toronto 3 [Chabot]

4   Toronto 3 at Montreal 1

8   Ottawa 2 at Toronto 1 (Boucher 6:30 OT)

11   Toronto 2 at Rangers 3

15   Boston 0 at Toronto 2 [Chabot]

20   Toronto 3 at Maroons 6

22   Pirates 3 at Toronto 2

25   Maroons 1 at Toronto 4

27   Toronto 2 at Pirates 0 [Chabot]

29   Cougars 3 at Toronto 4

JANUARY

1   Rangers 3 at Toronto 2

3   Toronto 2 at Chicago 0 [Chabot]

5   Ottawa 1 at Toronto 3

8   Toronto 2 at Boston 5

10   Toronto 0 at Americans 2 [Worters]*

12   Americans 1 at Toronto 0 [Worters] (Connors 6:00 OT)

17   Montreal 1 at Toronto 1 (both goals in 2nd)

20   Toronto 1 at Cougars 2

22   Toronto 0 at Rangers 1 [Roach]

24   Toronto 1 at Montreal 1

26   Chicago 0 at Toronto 2 [Chabot]

29   Toronto 2 at Ottawa 4 (Finnigan 7:40/Grosvenor 9:00 OT)**

31   Boston 3 at Toronto 1

* Benny Grant replaced Lorne Chabot 16 minutes into the first period after Chabot was cut badly over eye.

** Both goals scored with three Leafs in the penalty box.

FEBRUARY

2   Toronto 3 at Boston 0 [Chabot]

3   Toronto 3 at Americans 1

5   Toronto 0 at Pirates 0 [Chabot (T)/Miller (P)]

9   Pirates 1 at Toronto 2

14   Rangers 1 at Toronto 3

16   Maroons 0 at Toronto 3 [Chabot] (all goals in 3rd)

17   Toronto 0 at Cougars 2 [Dolson]

23   Montreal 1 at Toronto 2

28   Toronto 4 at Maroons 0 [Chabot]

MARCH

2   Ottawa 1 at Toronto 1 (both goals in 3rd)

7   Toronto 1 at Chicago 1*

9   Cougars 0 at Toronto 3 [Chabot]

12   Toronto 1 at Montreal 2 (all goals in 2nd)**

14   Americans 0 at Toronto 5 [Chabot/Grant]***

16   Toronto 0 at Ottawa 2 [Connell]

* Played at Fort Erie, Ontario.

** Benny Grant replaced Lorne Chabot to start the second.

*** Grant replaced Chabot in the second.

1929-30

NOVEMBER

14   Chicago 2 at Toronto 2*

16   Boston 6 at Toronto 5

19   Toronto 5 at Pirates 10

21   Toronto 2 at Montreal 3 (Leduc 7:23 OT)

23   Ottawa 6 at Toronto 2

26   Toronto 4 at Rangers 3

30   Falcons 0 at Toronto 1 [Chabot]

* W.D. Ross, lieutenant governor of Ontario, faced off the opening puck. A moment of silence was observed for Shorty Horne, who had drowned during the summer.

DECEMBER

3   Americans 0 at Toronto 6 [Chabot]

5   Toronto 2 at Ottawa 9*

7   Montreal 1 at Toronto 0 [Hainsworth]

10   Toronto 0 at Americans 1 [Worters]

14   Rangers 6 at Toronto 7 (Cotton [T] 1:30/Cotton [T] 2:50/Boucher [R] 3:20 OT)

15   Toronto 3 at Falcons 5

17   Toronto 1 at Maroons 3

21   Pirates 1 at Toronto 2 (Duncan 3:00 OT)

25   Toronto 2 at Boston 6

29   Toronto 4 at Chicago 3

* Red Horner and Charlie Conacher were fined $25 for leaving the bench during a fight.

JANUARY

1   Maroons 3 at Toronto 5

4   Montreal 3 at Toronto 4*

7   Toronto 1 at Americans 1 (both goals in 2nd)

9   Ottawa 0 at Toronto 4 [Chabot]

14   Toronto 1 at Maroons 1

16   Toronto 1 at Ottawa 2

18   Americans 1 at Toronto 4

25 Falcons 2 at Toronto 1

30 Maroons 3 at Toronto 0 [Walsh]

* Prior to the game of December 14, 1929, vs. Rangers, Leaf fan Ivan Mickailoff had offered a watch to the Leaf who scored the winning goal that night. Before the start of this game, he presented Baldy Cotton with the timepiece.

FEBRUARY

1   Chicago 0 at Toronto 6 [Chabot]

4   Toronto 1 at Montreal 3

6   Montreal 3 at Toronto 3 (Larochelle [M] tied game at 19:31)

9   Toronto 3 at Americans 2

11 Toronto 5 at Boston 6 (Conacher [T] 2:18/Clapper [B] 7:06/Shore [B] 8:20 OT)

15 Boston 5 at Toronto 3

18 Toronto 5 at Rangers 1

20 Toronto 4 at Pirates 0 [Chabot] (all goals in 3rd)

22 Ottawa 1 at Toronto 0 [Connell]

25 Toronto 0 at Ottawa 2 [Connell] (Finnigan 0:20/Finnigan 2:30 OT)

27 Toronto 2 at Montreal 6

MARCH

1   Rangers 3 at Toronto 3

4   Americans 1 at Toronto 1

8   Maroons 3 at Toronto 2

9   Toronto 2 at Falcons 1

11 Pirates 2 at Toronto 3

15 Toronto 3 at Maroons 0 [Chabot]

18 Toronto 1 at Chicago 4

1930–31

NOVEMBER

13 Americans 0 at Toronto 0 [Worters (A)/Chabot (T)]

15 Quakers 0 at Toronto 4 [Chabot]

18 Toronto 3 at Maroons 0 [Chabot]*

20 Toronto 0 at Americans 0 [Grant (T)/Worters (A)]

22 Ottawa 0 at Toronto 2 [Chabot]

25 Toronto 1 at Quakers 2

29 Falcons 2 at Toronto 4

* Ace Bailey was awarded Toronto's second goal when Maroons defenceman Lionel Conacher threw his stick to stop a shot.

DECEMBER

2   Toronto 2 at Boston 3

6   Rangers 2 at Toronto 4

9   Toronto 1 at Montreal 2

13 Boston 7 at Toronto 3

18 Maroons 2 at Toronto 1

20 Chicago 1 at Toronto 3

23 Toronto 4 at Maroons 4

25 Toronto 1 at Falcons 10

28 Toronto 3 at Chicago 2

JANUARY

1   Americans 0 at Toronto 2 [Chabot] (both goals in 3rd)

3   Montreal 1 at Toronto 2*

6   Toronto 2 at Ottawa 2

8   Maroons 0 at Toronto 1 [Chabot]

10 Toronto 1 at Montreal 6

15 Toronto 1 at Rangers 1

17 Montreal 1 at Toronto 3

22 Toronto 4 at Maroons 2

24 Ottawa 2 at Toronto 5

27 Toronto 2 at Americans 3

29 Toronto 3 at Ottawa 2

31 Quakers 2 at Toronto 3

* A fan threw a chair at referee Odie Cleghorn.

FEBRUARY

1   Toronto 0 at Falcons 2 [Dolson]

3   Toronto 1 at Montreal 2

7   Americans 0 at Toronto 2 [Chabot]

14 Falcons 1 at Toronto 1

19 Ottawa 2 at Toronto 1

21 Boston 2 at Toronto 4

24 Toronto 1 at Americans 1

26 Toronto 1 at Rangers 4

28 Montreal 5 at Toronto 5 (Morenz [M] 4:00/Gagnon [M] 5:05/Blair [T] 7:30/Conacher [T] 8:10 OT)

MARCH

3   Toronto 5 at Quakers 1

5   Maroons 6 at Toronto 5

7   Rangers 2 at Toronto 5

10 Toronto 3 at Boston 3*

15 Toronto 2 at Chicago 1

19 Chicago 2 at Toronto 8

21 Toronto 9 at Ottawa 6

* Boston scored in the overtime period right off a faceoff in front of the goal, but King Clancy protested to the referee that he was offside when the puck was dropped. The referee believed Clancy and nullified the goal. The Leafs won the next draw and kept the score tied.

1931–32

The beginning of the Maple Leaf Gardens era.

NOVEMBER

12 Chicago 2 at Toronto 1*

14 Montreal 1 at Toronto 1

18 Toronto 1 at Chicago 1

21 Rangers 5 at Toronto 3

26 Toronto 2 at Montreal 3

28 Boston 5 at Toronto 6 (Blair 1:45 OT)

* First regular-season game at Maple Leaf Gardens. The puck was dropped by Mayor W.J. Stewart between Tommy Cook of the Hawks and the Leafs' Ace Bailey. Mush March of Chicago scored at 2:30 of the first period; Charlie Conacher of Toronto at 18:42 of the second; Vic Ripley of Chicago at 2:35 of the third.

DECEMBER

1   Americans 2 at Toronto 2

3   Toronto 2 at Maroons 8

5   Maroons 0 at Toronto 4 [Chabot]

8   Toronto 4 at Rangers 2

12 Falcons 1 at Toronto 3

15 Toronto 2 at Americans 2

19 Maroons 2 at Toronto 4

20 Toronto 0 at Chicago 1 [Gardiner] (March 9:10 OT)

22 Americans 3 at Toronto 9

24 Toronto 2 at Montreal 1 (H. Jackson 9:55 OT)*

26 Montreal 2 at Toronto 0 [Hainsworth] (Morenz 2:15/Lepine 2:55 OT)

29 Toronto 5 at Americans 0 [Chabot]**

31 Maroons 1 at Toronto 3

* Baldy Cotton challenged referee Cooper Smeaton after receiving a penalty late in the third.
** Lorne Chabot was badly cut and the game was delayed while he was attended to.

JANUARY

3   Toronto 2 at Falcons 3 (Sorrell 3:05 OT)

5   Toronto 3 at Boston 3

10 Toronto 0 at Rangers 2 [Roach]

12 Falcons 4 at Toronto 7

14 Toronto 6 at Maroons 4

17 Toronto 0 at Americans 4 [Worters]

19 Americans 3 at Toronto 11

21 Toronto 1 at Montreal 3 (Joliat 19:48—EN)*

23 Montreal 0 at Toronto 2 [Chabot]

30 Rangers 3 at Toronto 6 (Finnigan 0:25/H. Jackson 2:10/Clancy 3:15 OT)

* This game is the earliest known instance in the NHL of a team surrendering a goal after pulling a goalie in the dying seconds for an extra attacker.

FEBRUARY

3   Toronto 0 at Chicago 7 [Gardiner]

6   Boston 0 at Toronto 6 [Chabot]

7   Toronto 1 at Falcons 3

13 Maroons 0 at Toronto 6 [Grant]

16 Toronto 0 at Boston 3 [Thompson]

18 Rangers 3 at Toronto 5*

20 Toronto 0 at Maroons 3 [Walsh]

23 Toronto 4 at Americans 4

25 Falcons 5 at Toronto 3

27 Chicago 2 at Toronto 4

* Toward the end of the game, Dick Irvin pulled a clever trick. According to the rules of the day, any player who stepped on the ice while his team was at full strength received an automatic major penalty. Three majors meant an automatic one-game suspension. On his bench were Charlie Conacher and Red Horner, both injured and both with two majors to their credit that season. Irvin told them both to get on the ice during play, and both received majors and one-game suspensions. As they weren't in condition to play anyway, the punishment only served to give them a clean slate in terms of cumulative penalties when they were healthy.

MARCH

1   Americans 1 at Toronto 3

5   Montreal 1 at Toronto 1

10 Toronto 1 at Maroons 3

12 Boston 3 at Toronto 5 (Horner 8:50/Conacher 9:42 OT)

15 Toronto 2 at Boston 6*

17 Toronto 6 at Rangers 3

19 Chicago 3 at Toronto 11**

20 Toronto 3 at Falcons 2

22 Toronto 2 at Montreal 4

* One of the more unique games in the history of the NHL. Shortly after the opening faceoff, Leaf goalie Lorne Chabot was assessed a minor penalty (two minutes), which he had to serve himself. During the ensuing Bruin power play, three Leaf defencemen took turns playing in goal. Each allowed a goal. Marty Barry scored on Red Horner, adding a second goal just seconds later against Alex Levinsky. George Owen then scored on King Clancy.
** Chicago goalie Charlie Gardiner was hurt by a shot at 18:12 of the first period. There was an early intermission, but he couldn't continue and was replaced by Wilf Cude. Late in the second, Cude was knocked unconscious by a shot and was carried off. After a delay, he was able to continue.

1932–33

NOVEMBER

10 Boston 1 at Toronto 1*

12 Rangers 2 at Toronto 4

17 Toronto 1 at Chicago 3

20 Toronto 0 at Rangers 7 [Aitkenhead]**

24 Montreal 0 at Toronto 2 [Chabot] (both goals in 2nd)

26 Maroons 2 at Toronto 3

27 Toronto 2 at Falcons 1

* H.A. Bruce, lieutenant governor of Ontario, dropped the puck, and the 1932 Stanley Cup banner was raised to the rafters.
** New York mayor Joseph V. McKee dropped the puck.

DECEMBER

3   Ottawa 1 at Toronto 4

8   Toronto 0 at Maroons 1 [Walsh]

10 Americans 2 at Toronto 2
    (McVeigh [A] 1:54/Bailey [T] 2:56 OT)*

13 Toronto 1 at Boston 5**

15 Ottawa 1 at Toronto 4

17 Falcons 0 at Toronto 3 [Chabot]

20 Toronto 2 at Montreal 1

22 Toronto 0 at Americans 1 [Worters]

24 Chicago 2 at Toronto 1***

27 Toronto 4 at Chicago 3

29 Maroons 0 at Toronto 1 [Chabot]

* Both overtime goals scored on the power play.
** Boston manager Art Ross was fined $50 for hitting Toronto defenceman King Clancy.
*** Young Canada Night.

JANUARY

1   Toronto 2 at Detroit 2

3   Toronto 2 at Rangers 4

5   Toronto 2 at Maroons 2

7   Falcons 6 at Toronto 1*

10 Rangers 2 at Toronto 3

14 Toronto 5 at Ottawa 3 (Bailey 3:20/Cotton 5:00 [PP] OT)

17   Toronto 1 at Americans 3

19   Boston 0 at Toronto 3 [Chabot]

24   Toronto 4 at Ottawa 2

26   Toronto 2 at Boston 4

28   Montreal 2 at Toronto 4

31   Americans 1 at Toronto 7
* The first nationwide broadcast of a Leafs game by Foster Hewitt on CBC radio.

FEBRUARY

4   Chicago 2 at Toronto 2

7   Toronto 0 at Montreal 2 [Hainsworth]

11   Rangers 1 at Toronto 2

14   Toronto 2 at Boston 7

16   Toronto 5 at Rangers 2

18   Falcons 1 at Toronto 4

23   Toronto 3 at Ottawa 0 [Chabot]

25   Americans 1 at Toronto 5

28   Montreal 2 at Toronto 1

MARCH

2   Toronto 3 at Montreal 4

4   Maroons 2 at Toronto 4

5   Toronto 2 at Chicago 1

7   Toronto 2 at Maroons 7*

11   Boston 6 at Toronto 2

16   Toronto 0 at Falcons 1 [Roach]

18   Ottawa 2 at Toronto 6

21   Toronto 3 at Americans 4

23   Chicago 2 at Toronto 2 (McFadden [C] tied game at 19:59)
* Before the game, a fan sent a live black rabbit to the Leafs dressing room with instructions
  to put it in Baldy Cotton's locker. After the loss, Cotton had it removed for good.

1933–34

NOVEMBER

9   Boston 1 at Toronto 6*

11   Rangers 3 at Toronto 4

18   Ottawa 1 at Toronto 4**

21   Toronto 1 at Rangers 1

25   Montreal 1 at Toronto 0 [Chabot]

28   Americans 3 at Toronto 7

30   Toronto 1 at Maroons 0 [Hainsworth]
* H.A. Bruce, lieutenant governor of Ontario, dropped the puck.
** Ottawa formally protested, claiming that the goal creases painted on the ice were too
   small and that Toronto scored twice inside what should have been the crease.

DECEMBER

2   Maroons 3 at Toronto 8

3   Toronto 3 at Detroit 0 [Hainsworth]

5   Toronto 9 at Americans 1

7   Toronto 1 at Ottawa 4

9   Chicago 0 at Toronto 1 [Hainsworth]

12   Toronto 4 at Boston 1*

14   Toronto 0 at Montreal 2 [Chabot]

16   Montreal 1 at Toronto 3

23   Maroons 2 at Toronto 8**

26   Toronto 2 at Boston 2

28   Toronto 2 at Rangers 2

30   Detroit 1 at Toronto 8
* The game in which Ace Bailey's career was ended.
** Young Canada Night.

JANUARY

1   Toronto 2 at Chicago 1

4   Toronto 1 at Montreal 4

6   Ottawa 3 at Toronto 7

11   Toronto 1 at Americans 1

13   Americans 2 at Toronto 2

16   Toronto 7 at Ottawa 4 (Doraty 1:35/Doraty 2:20/Doraty 9:05 OT)

18   Boston 2 at Toronto 6*

20   Chicago 2 at Toronto 2

21   Toronto 2 at Detroit 4 (Lewis 4:17/Lewis 9:55 OT)

23   Maroons 4 at Toronto 8

25   Toronto 0 at Maroons 6 [Kerr]

27   Detroit 2 at Toronto 2

28   Toronto 0 at Chicago 2 [Gardner]
* As a result of the Bailey incident, all Bruins wore helmets for this game as a precaution.

FEBRUARY

1   Toronto 5 at Rangers 5

3   Ottawa 4 at Toronto 8

4   Toronto 1 at Detroit 2

8   Toronto 3 at Americans 3

10   Montreal 2 at Toronto 4

17   Boston 4 at Toronto 6

20   Toronto 2 at Montreal 3 (Joliat 6:27 OT)

24   Rangers 3 at Toronto 8

27   Toronto 2 at Maroons 1 (Thoms 8:06 OT)

MARCH

3   Detroit 4 at Toronto 6

6   Toronto 2 at Boston 7*

8   Toronto 1 at Ottawa 3

10   Americans 5 at Toronto 8

15   Chicago 2 at Toronto 1

17   Rangers 2 at Toronto 3**

18   Toronto 2 at Chicago 3
* Ace Bailey dropped the first puck.
** King Clancy Night.

1934–35

NOVEMBER

8   Boston 3 at Toronto 5

10   Montreal 1 at Toronto 2 (Doraty [T] tied game at 19:50; H. Jackson 5:37 OT)

15   Toronto 1 at Americans 0 [Hainsworth]

17   Maroons 1 at Toronto 2

18   Toronto 5 at Chicago 0 [Hainsworth]

20   Toronto 5 at Eagles 2

24   Detroit 2 at Toronto 3

DECEMBER

1   Eagles 3 at Toronto 4

2   Toronto 0 at Detroit 3 [N. Smith]

4   Toronto 1 at Boston 0 [Hainsworth]

8   Rangers 5 at Toronto 2

11   Toronto 8 at Rangers 4

13   Toronto 4 at Maroons 2 (Conacher 5:09/Boll 7:53 OT)

15   Americans 3 at Toronto 4

20   Toronto 1 at Eagles 1

22   Chicago 0 at Toronto 1 [Hainsworth]*

25   Toronto 6 at Montreal 2

27   Toronto 4 at Americans 3 (Kelly 2:44 OT)

29   Maroons 4 at Toronto 2

* Young Canada Night.

JANUARY

1   Detroit 1 at Toronto 0 [Roach]

5   Montreal 1 at Toronto 3 (all goals in 3rd)

8   Toronto 1 at Boston 3

10   Toronto 5 at Americans 5

12   Chicago 1 at Toronto 5

13   Toronto 2 at Detroit 0 [Hainsworth]

15   Toronto 3 at Chicago 2*

17   Toronto 3 at Montreal 4

19   Eagles 2 at Toronto 6

20   Toronto 1 at Chicago 2

22   Toronto 2 at Eagles 1

26   Detroit 0 at Toronto 0 [Roach (D)/Hainsworth (T)]

29   Toronto 5 at Rangers 7

31   Rangers 3 at Toronto 2

* Originally scheduled for February 26.

FEBRUARY

2   Americans 2 at Toronto 1

7   Boston 4 at Toronto 4 (Barry [B] tied game at 19:25)

9   Maroons 2 at Toronto 4

12   Toronto 5 at Boston 6 (Kelly [T] 5:05/Kaminsky [B] 8:11/Clapper [B] 8:23 OT)

14   Toronto 0 at Rangers 3 [Kerr]

16   Rangers 1 at Toronto 5

19   Toronto 3 at Maroons 1

23   Chicago 1 at Toronto 4

24   Toronto 2 at Detroit 4

MARCH

2   Americans 0 at Toronto 6 [Hainsworth]

5   Toronto 10 at Montreal 3

9   Boston 7 at Toronto 4

12   Toronto 1 at Maroons 0 [Hainsworth]

16   Montreal 3 at Toronto 5

19   Eagles 3 at Toronto 5

1935–36

NOVEMBER

9   Americans 5 at Toronto 5 (N. Metz [T] 0:37/Schriner [A] 7:42 OT)*

14   Toronto 1 at Rangers 0 [Hainsworth]

16   Rangers 2 at Toronto 3

19   Toronto 7 at Montreal 2

21   Toronto 3 at Chicago 4

23   Maroons 5 at Toronto 2

24   Toronto 1 at Detroit 2**

26   Toronto 2 at Boston 1

30   Montreal 3 at Toronto 8

* Puck dropped by R.S. McLaughlin to start the season.

** Detroit's Scotty Bowman was given a penalty, but Syd Howe went to the penalty box. After the penalty had elapsed, the Leafs complained that the wrong Wing had sat out. Howe was then given a minor himself for sitting out Bowman's penalty.

DECEMBER

7   Chicago 1 at Toronto 2 (H. Jackson 2:12 OT)

10   Toronto 2 at Americans 4

14   Detroit 4 at Toronto 2 (Lewis 4:01/Bruneteau 7:27 OT)

17   Toronto 1 at Maroons 0 [Hainsworth]

19   Boston 0 at Toronto 0 [Thompson (B)/Hainsworth (T)]

21   Americans 3 at Toronto 5*

26   Toronto 2 at Montreal 0 [Hainsworth] **

28   Rangers 3 at Toronto 9

* Young Canada Night.

** Game was held up for 20 minutes after fans littered the ice with coins, bottles, and papers to show their displeasure with a penalty call to a Hab.

JANUARY

2   Toronto 2 at Maroons 5*

4   Maroons 1 at Toronto 1 (both goals in 3rd)

11   Montreal 7 at Toronto 3

14   Toronto 1 at Boston 4

16   Toronto 0 at Rangers 1 [Kerr]

18   Boston 2 at Toronto 5**

19   Toronto 0 at Detroit 4 [N. Smith]

21   Montreal at Toronto***

23   Toronto 2 at Americans 3 (Jerwa 3:00 OT)

25   Detroit 1 at Toronto 6

30   Toronto 0 at Montreal 3 [Cude]

* Included a bench-clearing brawl that lasted 20 minutes and comprised 11 fights.

** Dr. Allan R. Dafoe, the man who delivered the Dionne quintuplets, was in attendance.

*** Postponed to February 20 due to the death of King George V.

FEBRUARY

1   Chicago 2 at Toronto 3 (N. Metz 8:29 OT)

2   Toronto 0 at Chicago 2 [Karakas] (both goals in 3rd)

4   Toronto 3 at Boston 0 [Hainsworth]

6   Toronto 3 at Americans 4*

8   Americans 0 at Toronto 3**

13   Toronto 1 at Maroons 2

15   Detroit 2 at Toronto 3 (Thoms 8:15 OT)

20   Montreal 1 at Toronto 2

22   Maroons 0 at Toronto 1 [Hainsworth]

23   Toronto 1 at Chicago 5

25   Rangers 2 at Toronto 2

29   Chicago 2 at Toronto 4

* Red Horner suffered a bad concussion after a crosscheck from Red Dutton.

** After calling a penalty shot against the Americans for a Dutton foul, referee Mike Rodden was accidentally knocked unconscious. Rodden recovered to finish the first, but was replaced by Ag Smith for the balance of the game.

MARCH

3   Toronto 0 at Rangers 0 [Hainsworth (T)/Kerr (R)]

7   Montreal 1 at Toronto 8

10   Toronto 2 at Americans 3

12   Toronto 6 at Montreal 3*

14   Maroons 1 at Toronto 0 [Chabot]

15   Toronto 2 at Detroit 1 (Conacher 7:30 OT)

17   Toronto 1 at Maroons 2

19   Boston 2 at Toronto 2**

21   Americans 1 at Toronto 4

* Conn Smythe and Dick Irvin were involved in a penalty-box melee.

** Charlie Conacher set an NHL record with 13 shots on goal.

1936–37

NOVEMBER

5   Detroit 3 at Toronto 1*

7   Americans 3 at Toronto 2

14   Chicago 2 at Toronto 6**

15   Toronto 1 at Chicago 1

21   Boston 4 at Toronto 3

22   Toronto 2 at Detroit 4

24   Toronto 1 at Rangers 5

26   Toronto 4 at Montreal 2***

28   Montreal 2 at Toronto 4

* H.A. Bruce, lieutenant governor of Ontario, dropped the puck.

** The Hawks complained that the blue lines weren't painted up the boards.

*** Early in the third, Earl Seibert got a penalty. Irate Montreal fans threw bottles onto the ice, then stormed over the boards and surrounded the referee.

DECEMBER

1   Toronto 2 at Maroons 1

5   Maroons 3 at Toronto 1

12   Rangers 5 at Toronto 3 (Dillon 1:15/Patrick 7:28 OT)

17   Toronto 5 at Americans 1

19   Americans 1 at Toronto 3*

22   Toronto 4 at Boston 2

26   Boston 2 at Toronto 1

31   Toronto 1 at Maroons 3 (Ward 4:46/Gracie 6:07 OT)

* Young Canada Night.

JANUARY

2   Maroons 0 at Toronto 0 [Connell (M)/Broda (T)]

3   Toronto 2 at Detroit 4

7   Toronto 1 at Montreal 4

9   Montreal 1 at Toronto 2

10   Toronto 1 at Chicago 2*

16   Chicago 2 at Toronto 3 (N. Metz 2:09 OT)

19   Toronto 6 at Boston 2

21   Toronto 3 at Americans 6

23   Rangers 0 at Toronto 4 [Broda]

24   Toronto 2 at Rangers 4

26   Montreal 3 at Toronto 1

30   Maroons 4 at Toronto 7

* Syl Apps was given a penalty by referee Bill Stewart for kicking the puck. Conn Smythe officially protested the call and, two days later, President Frank Calder clarified the rule, siding with Smythe and Apps.

FEBRUARY

2   Toronto 1 at Maroons 3

4   Toronto 2 at Americans 1

6   Americans 0 at Toronto 5 [Broda]

9   Rangers 5 at Toronto 1

13   Boston 3 at Toronto 0 [Thompson]

14   Toronto 3 at Detroit 3

18   Detroit 1 at Toronto 3

20   Americans 3 at Toronto 4

21   Toronto 1 at Americans 3

23   Toronto 1 at Rangers 2

25   Toronto 3 at Montreal 1

27   Maroons 2 at Toronto 3

MARCH

6   Montreal 1 at Toronto 3 (Jackson 2:05/Fowler 5:40 OT)

7   Toronto 2 at Chicago 2*

11   Toronto 2 at Maroons 3

13   Chicago 2 at Toronto 3

16   Toronto 1 at Boston 1

18   Toronto 2 at Montreal 1

20   Detroit 2 at Toronto 3

* "Presentation Night" at the Gardens. Syl Apps received a travelling bag and golf clubs; Toe Blake and Babe Siebert each received travelling bags.

1937–38

NOVEMBER

4   Detroit 2 at Toronto 2 (Barry [D] tied game at 19:46)*

6   Americans 3 at Toronto 6**

13 Chicago 3 at Toronto 7

14 Toronto 3 at Chicago 3

18 Toronto 6 at Montreal 6 (H. Jackson [T] tied game at 19:54)

20 Boston 3 at Toronto 2

21 Toronto 5 at Detroit 0 [Broda]

23 Toronto 1 at Maroons 2

25 Toronto 3 at Rangers 1

27 Maroons 0 at Toronto 4 [Broda]

* Gordon Conant, attorney general of Ontario, dropped the puck.

** Hap Day, now with the Americans, was given a floral horseshoe prior to the game.

DECEMBER

4 Montreal 3 at Toronto 3

11 Rangers 6 at Toronto 3

14 Toronto 1 at Boston 3

16 Toronto 4 at Montreal 2

18 Americans 2 at Toronto 3

25 Detroit 1 at Toronto 1 (both goals in 2nd)*

26 Toronto 3 at Detroit 1

28 Toronto 3 at Americans 0 [Broda]

* Young Canada Night.

JANUARY

1 Montreal 4 at Toronto 6

4 Toronto 3 at Boston 6

6 Toronto 3 at Maroons 6

8 Rangers 2 at Toronto 3*

13 Maroons 2 at Toronto 3

15 Chicago 4 at Toronto 4

16 Toronto 7 at Chicago 2

20 Toronto 1 at Americans 1 (both goals in 2nd)

22 Boston 9 at Toronto 1

29 Detroit 1 at Toronto 4

* Moncton's mayor presented a gold watch to native son Gord Drillon during the pre-game ceremonies.

FEBRUARY

1 Toronto 1 at Montreal 6

3 Montreal 0 at Toronto 3 [Broda]

5 Boston 1 at Toronto 3

6 Toronto 1 at Rangers 2*

10 Maroons 0 at Toronto 3 [Broda] (Apps 1:01/Parsons 2:06/Kelly 3:33 OT)**

12 Chicago 2 at Toronto 1

13 Toronto 1 at Chicago 1

17 Toronto 2 at Maroons 1

19 Americans 4 at Toronto 0 [Robertson]

20 Toronto 3 at Americans 2

22 Toronto 0 at Boston 2 [Thompson]

26 Rangers 4 at Toronto 2

* In the first, Conn Smythe thought an offside call had been missed and came storming onto the ice to protest to referee Billy Boyd, who then wrestled him to the ice.

** Newmarket Night: Bill Thoms, Pep Kelly, Herbie Cain (Maroons), and Don Wilson (Habs) all received gifts from Newmarket's mayor, S.J. Boyd.

MARCH

1 Toronto 5 at Maroons 3

5 Maroons 0 at Toronto 2 [Broda] (both goals in 1st)*

6 Toronto 6 at Montreal 3

8 Toronto 3 at Rangers 4

12 Montreal 3 at Toronto 3**

17 Toronto 7 at Detroit 2

19 Americans 5 at Toronto 8***

20 Toronto 2 at Americans 4

* Toronto Night: The Danforth Businessmen's Association honoured locals Jim Fowler and Bob Davidson of the Leafs.

** Swansea Night: Honours for George Parsons. Aurèle Joliat was also given a lifelong achievement award by the *Globe and Mail* on behalf of Toronto. It was his last game in the city.

*** Busher Jackson and Reg Hamilton were given silver chests by the West Toronto Businessmen's Association. Red Horner also received gifts from friends.

1938–39

NOVEMBER

3 Boston 3 at Toronto 2*

5 Chicago 2 at Toronto 0 [Karakas] (both goals in 2nd)

10 Toronto 2 at Montreal 0 [Broda]

12 Montreal 1 at Toronto 4

15 Toronto 1 at Boston 1

17 Toronto 1 at Americans 0 [Broda]

19 Americans 2 at Toronto 1 (Schriner 3:52 OT)

20 Toronto 1 at Chicago 1

24 Toronto 2 at Rangers 6

26 Detroit 0 at Toronto 5 [Broda]

* Albert Matthews, lieutenant governor of Ontario, dropped the puck.

DECEMBER

3 Montreal 3 at Toronto 1

4 Toronto 0 at Detroit 1 [Thompson]

10 Chicago 1 at Toronto 4

15 Toronto 4 at Chicago 4

17 Rangers 3 at Toronto 2

24 Detroit 0 at Toronto 2 [Broda]*

26 Toronto 2 at Rangers 0 [Broda]

27 Toronto 2 at Boston 8

31 Americans 3 at Toronto 2

* Young Canada Night.

JANUARY

1 Toronto 1 at Americans 5

3 Montreal 2 at Toronto 2

7 Boston 0 at Toronto 2 [Broda]

8 Toronto 0 at Chicago 1 [Karakas]

12 Toronto 9 at Montreal 4

14 Chicago 1 at Toronto 3*

15 Toronto 0 at Detroit 1 [Thompson]

17 Toronto 1 at Boston 2

21 Americans 2 at Toronto 7

24 Toronto 1 at Americans 4

28 Detroit 0 at Toronto 6 [Broda]

29 Toronto 2 at Detroit 2

* Chicago's Bill Thoms received presents from Newmarket and Aurora friends during the first intermission.

FEBRUARY

2 Boston 2 at Toronto 1

4 Rangers 4 at Toronto 2

5 Toronto 5 at Rangers 5*

7 Toronto 0 at Boston 2 [Brimsek]

11 Montreal 3 at Toronto 3

12 Toronto 4 at Montreal 3**

18 Rangers 1 at Toronto 2

19 Toronto 4 at Chicago 3 (Marker 4:35 OT)

25 Boston 0 at Toronto 1 [Broda]***

26 Toronto 1 at Detroit 5

28 Toronto 1 at Americans 1

* Rangers' Clint Smith was awarded a goal in the third after a thrown stick.
** Montreal's Herb Cain was awarded a goal when Gord Drillon threw his stick.
*** Presentations were made to Dit Clapper, Jack Portland, and Johnny Crawford of Boston, and Noel MacDonald, who was voted outstanding female athlete of 1938.

MARCH

2 Toronto 1 at Montreal 3

4 Chicago 1 at Toronto 1*

11 Detroit 1 at Toronto 5**

14 Americans 3 at Toronto 7

18 Rangers 1 at Toronto 2

19 Toronto 2 at Rangers 6

* Referee Mickey Ion and Chicago's Baldy Northcott were each presented with a silver telephone set from Brantford sports fans.
** Charlie Conacher Night was celebrated during first intermission.

1939–40

NOVEMBER

4 Boston 0 at Toronto 5 [Broda]

11 Rangers 1 at Toronto 1

12 Toronto 1 at Rangers 0 [Broda]

18 Detroit 0 at Toronto 3 [Broda]

19 Toronto 7 at Detroit 1

25 Americans 3 at Toronto 4

26 Toronto 1 at Americans 2 (Wiseman 1:08 OT)

28 Toronto 2 at Boston 6

DECEMBER

2 Chicago 3 at Toronto 3

3 Toronto 3 at Chicago 1 (Schriner 3:10/Goldup 8:09 OT)

7 Toronto 1 at Montreal 4

9 Montreal 0 at Toronto 3 [Broda]

14 Boston 1 at Toronto 1

16 Americans 1 at Toronto 5

17 Toronto 4 at Americans 1

19 Toronto 2 at Boston 3 (Dumart [B] 2:28/Bauer [B] 8:07/McDonald [T] 9:36 OT)

21 Toronto 1 at Chicago 3

23 Detroit 1 at Toronto 5*

25 Toronto 1 at Rangers 4

28 Toronto 6 at Montreal 4

30 Chicago 2 at Toronto 4

31 Toronto 3 at Detroit 2

* Young Canada Night.

JANUARY

4 Toronto 1 at Chicago 2

6 Montreal 1 at Toronto 3 (all goals in 3rd)

9 Toronto 3 at Americans 2

11 Boston 5 at Toronto 2

13 Rangers 4 at Toronto 1

18 Detroit 2 at Toronto 2

20 Americans 1 at Toronto 5

21 Toronto 2 at Detroit 3

23 Toronto 1 at Boston 4

25 Toronto 0 at Rangers 3 [Kerr]

27 Montreal 1 at Toronto 3

FEBRUARY

3 Chicago 3 at Toronto 2

8 Toronto 1 at Rangers 2

10 Rangers 4 at Toronto 4 (Goldup [T] 0:09/MacDonald [R] 1:17 OT)

17 Montreal 1 at Toronto 3

18 Toronto 2 at Montreal 1

20 Toronto 0 at Boston 5 [Brimsek]

22 Toronto 2 at Detroit 1

24 Boston 1 at Toronto 3

29 Detroit 1 at Toronto 3

MARCH

2 Rangers 1 at Toronto 1

9 Chicago 2 at Toronto 5

10 Toronto 1 at Chicago 2

14 Toronto 8 at Montreal 4

16 Americans 6 at Toronto 8

17 Toronto 2 at Americans 5

1940–41

NOVEMBER

2 Rangers 4 at Toronto 1

9 Detroit 0 at Toronto 3 [Broda]

14 Toronto 6 at Montreal 2

16 Montreal 2 at Toronto 4

17 Toronto 4 at Boston 1

21 Toronto 2 at Americans 1 (Apps 1:16 OT)

23 Chicago 1 at Toronto 0 [Goodman]

24 Toronto 4 at Chicago 2

26 Toronto 4 at Rangers 2

30 Americans 1 at Toronto 6

DECEMBER

1 Toronto 3 at Detroit 1

7 Boston 2 at Toronto 3

12 Montreal 3 at Toronto 4

14 Chicago 1 at Toronto 2 (all goals in 3rd)

15 Toronto 4 at Chicago 1

17 Toronto 2 at Boston 5

21 Americans 2 at Toronto 2*

22 Toronto 1 at Americans 2

25 Toronto 2 at Detroit 3

28 Rangers 2 at Toronto 3

29 Toronto 2 at Rangers 3
* Young Canada Night.

JANUARY

4 Detroit 3 at Toronto 1

7 Toronto 4 at Montreal 3 (D. Metz 5:23 OT)

9 Rangers 2 at Toronto 3 (Apps 9:57 OT)*

11 Americans 0 at Toronto 9 [Broda]

18 Boston 1 at Toronto 0 [Brimsek]

19 Toronto 3 at Americans 3

23 Toronto 3 at Montreal 2

25 Montreal 2 at Toronto 2

26 Toronto 2 at Detroit 0 [Broda]

30 Detroit 1 at Toronto 2
* Originally scheduled for March 13.

FEBRUARY

1 Chicago 1 at Toronto 3

2 Toronto 1 at Chicago 4

8 Boston 3 at Toronto 2

15 Rangers 3 at Toronto 4

16 Toronto 4 at Rangers 1

18 Toronto 2 at Boston 2

20 Montreal 1 at Toronto 2

22 Detroit 2 at Toronto 6

23 Toronto 0 at Detroit 3 [Mowers]

25 Toronto 4 at Americans 4

MARCH

1 Boston 0 at Toronto 0 [Brimsek (B)/Broda (T)]

6 Toronto 3 at Montreal 4

8 Americans 1 at Toronto 6

9 Toronto 5 at Rangers 8

11 Toronto 2 at Boston 3

15 Chicago 1 at Toronto 7

16 Toronto 3 at Chicago 0 [Broda]

1941—42

NOVEMBER

1 Rangers 4 at Toronto 3

8 Boston 0 at Toronto 2 [Broda] (both goals in 2nd)

13 Montreal 2 at Toronto 4

15 Detroit 1 at Toronto 2

18 Toronto 8 at Rangers 6

20 Toronto 4 at Detroit 3 (Goldup [T] 0:47/Carr [T] 3:18/Abel [D] 9:19 OT)

22 Chicago 0 at Toronto 3 [Broda]

23 Toronto 2 at Chicago 3

29 Brooklyn 2 at Toronto 8

30 Toronto 5 at Brooklyn 1

DECEMBER

2 Toronto 1 at Boston 3 (Wiseman 6:47/Hamill 7:21 OT)

6 Montreal 1 at Toronto 3

11 Toronto 1 at Montreal 2 (Heffernan 6:50 OT)

13 Rangers 1 at Toronto 2

14 Toronto 4 at Detroit 0 [Broda]

20 Chicago 2 at Toronto 0 [LoPresti]*

21 Toronto 3 at Chicago 0 [Broda]

25 Boston 0 at Toronto 2 [Broda] (both goals in 3rd)

27 Detroit 3 at Toronto 5

28 Toronto 1 at Brooklyn 2

30 Toronto 1 at Boston 4
* Young Canada Night.

JANUARY

1 Toronto 3 at Rangers 3

3 Brooklyn 2 at Toronto 4

10 Detroit 6 at Toronto 4

15 Toronto 3 at Montreal 2 (N. Metz 0:31 OT)

17 Chicago 4 at Toronto 2

24 Brooklyn 2 at Toronto 3

25 Toronto 4 at Chicago 6

27 Toronto 0 at Boston 0 [Broda (T)/Brimsek (B)]

29 Montreal 3 at Toronto 7

31 Boston 3 at Toronto 2 (Schmidt 2:54 OT)

FEBRUARY

1 Toronto 2 at Rangers 7

5 Toronto 3 at Detroit 3

7 Rangers 4 at Toronto 6

8 Toronto 4 at Brooklyn 3

12 Toronto 6 at Montreal 4

14   Detroit 2 at Toronto 4

21   Brooklyn 3 at Toronto 4

22   Toronto 0 at Detroit 3 [Mowers]

28   Chicago 2 at Toronto 8

MARCH

1   Toronto 4 at Chicago 3

3   Toronto 3 at Boston 5

5   Montreal 5 at Toronto 2

7   Rangers 2 at Toronto 4

8   Toronto 0 at Rangers 2 [Henry]

14   Boston 4 at Toronto 6

15   Toronto 3 at Brooklyn 6

19   Toronto 3 at Montreal 7

1942–43

OCTOBER

31   Rangers 2 at Toronto 7*

* Private Alex Chisholm, decorated for his service at Dieppe, dropped the puck.

NOVEMBER

7   Detroit 2 at Toronto 5

12   Boston 1 at Toronto 3

14   Chicago 4 at Toronto 3

15   Toronto 4 at Chicago 5

19   Toronto 7 at Rangers 3

21   Montreal 0 at Toronto 8 [Broda]

22   Toronto 6 at Boston 7

26   Toronto 1 at Detroit 2

28   Rangers 6 at Toronto 8

29   Toronto 2 at Chicago 3

DECEMBER

3   Toronto 2 at Montreal 4

5   Montreal 1 at Toronto 9

6   Toronto 2 at Detroit 2

10   Chicago 2 at Toronto 7

12   Detroit 4 at Toronto 5

13   Toronto 2 at Chicago 5

17   Toronto 8 at Montreal 1

19   Boston 3 at Toronto 3

20   Toronto 8 at Rangers 2

22   Toronto 4 at Boston 4

26   Boston 2 at Toronto 7

27   Toronto 1 at Rangers 3

JANUARY

2   Montreal 3 at Toronto 6

3   Toronto 4 at Montreal 4

9   Detroit 4 at Toronto 0 [Mowers] (all goals in 3rd)

10   Toronto 4 at Boston 5

16   Montreal 4 at Toronto 8

17   Toronto 0 at Montreal 2 [Bibeault]

21   Rangers 4 at Toronto 7

23   Chicago 3 at Toronto 5

30   Boston 5 at Toronto 3

31   Toronto 3 at Chicago 3

FEBRUARY

4   Detroit 3 at Toronto 2

6   Rangers 2 at Toronto 3

7   Toronto 3 at Detroit 5

9   Toronto 1 at Boston 3

13   Chicago 2 at Toronto 3

14   Toronto 4 at Rangers 4

20   Boston 2 at Toronto 4

21   Toronto 0 at Chicago 5 [Gardiner]

27   Chicago 4 at Toronto 1

28   Toronto 4 at Montreal 2

MARCH

2   Rangers 4 at Toronto 0 [Beveridge]

6   Montreal 2 at Toronto 2

7   Toronto 5 at Rangers 5

9   Toronto 5 at Boston 5

11   Toronto 1 at Detroit 2

13   Detroit 1 at Toronto 3

14   Toronto 5 at Detroit 3

1943–44

OCTOBER

30   Rangers 2 at Toronto 5

31   Toronto 4 at Chicago 1

NOVEMBER

4   Toronto 5 at Detroit 5 (Carr [T] tied game at 19:42)

6   Boston 5 at Toronto 2

7   Toronto 7 at Rangers 4

11   Detroit 2 at Toronto 2

13   Chicago 4 at Toronto 1

18   Toronto 2 at Montreal 5

20   Montreal 7 at Toronto 2

21   Toronto 5 at Rangers 2

23   Toronto 5 at Boston 8

27   Boston 4 at Toronto 7

28   Toronto 4 at Detroit 6

DECEMBER

2   Detroit 5 at Toronto 6

4   Rangers 4 at Toronto 11

11   Montreal 2 at Toronto 4

12   Toronto 2 at Chicago 3

16   Detroit 4 at Toronto 1

18   Chicago 4 at Toronto 8

19   Toronto 5 at Chicago 2

21   Toronto 5 at Boston 8

25   Rangers 5 at Toronto 3

31   Toronto 4 at Rangers 0 [Bibeault]

JANUARY

1   Toronto 5 at Boston 2

4   Toronto 3 at Montreal 6

7   Chicago 1 at Toronto 6

8   Boston 3 at Toronto 12

11   Montreal 0 at Toronto 5 [Bibeault]

15   Detroit 6 at Toronto 4

16   Toronto 1 at Detroit 4

18   Toronto 7 at Boston 2

22   Rangers 5 at Toronto 1*

23   Toronto 3 at Chicago 5

27   Toronto 2 at Montreal 2

29   Chicago 4 at Toronto 3

* Young Canada Night.

FEBRUARY

5   Detroit 1 at Toronto 3

6   Toronto 2 at Detroit 3

12   Montreal 3 at Toronto 2

13   Toronto 6 at Rangers 3

19   Boston 4 at Toronto 10

20   Toronto 0 at Chicago 0 [Bibeault (T)/Karakas (C)]

24   Toronto 1 at Montreal 3

26   Chicago 3 at Toronto 2

29   Toronto 7 at Boston 3

MARCH

4   Montreal 5 at Toronto 2

5   Toronto 3 at Montreal 8

9   Toronto 8 at Rangers 0 [Bibeault]

11   Rangers 0 at Toronto 5 [Bibeault]

12   Toronto 1 at Detroit 4

18   Boston 2 at Toronto 10*

* Boston was forced to use Toronto's spare goalie, Benny Grant. Babe Pratt received $100 from E.W. Bickle as "most popular Leaf" on the night.

1944–45

OCTOBER

28   Rangers 1 at Toronto 2*

29   Toronto 11 at Chicago 5

* Puck was dropped by J.G. Parker, chairman of the Toronto National War Finance Committee.

NOVEMBER

2   Toronto 4 at Montreal 1

4   Boston 2 at Toronto 7

9   Toronto 6 at Rangers 3

11   Montreal 1 at Toronto 3

12   Toronto 2 at Detroit 4

15   Detroit 8 at Toronto 4

18   Chicago 4 at Toronto 5

19   Toronto 4 at Chicago 3

23   Toronto 1 at Boston 5

25   Montreal 0 at Toronto 2 [McCool] (both goals in 3rd)

26   Toronto 1 at Montreal 4

DECEMBER

2   Rangers 3 at Toronto 4

3   Toronto 4 at Boston 5

9   Boston 5 at Toronto 3

14   Toronto 2 at Montreal 2*

16   Detroit 1 at Toronto 1

23   Detroit 5 at Toronto 4**

25   Toronto 4 at Detroit 6

27   Toronto 8 at Rangers 2

30   Chicago 0 at Toronto 4 [McCool]

* Special lights were placed over the goals in the Forum to provide extra lighting for the benefit of the goalies. With two minutes left to go and the score tied, the lights went out. The Leafs refused to play until they were turned back on, which they eventually were.

** Young Canada Night.

JANUARY

4   Montreal 2 at Toronto 4

6   Detroit 5 at Toronto 2

9   Rangers 5 at Toronto 4

11   Toronto 4 at Montreal 7

13   Boston 1 at Toronto 2

14   Toronto 0 at Detroit 3 [Lumley]

16   Toronto 3 at Boston 5

20   Chicago 4 at Toronto 8*

21   Toronto 0 at Chicago 4 [Karakas]

27   Rangers 0 at Toronto 3 [McCool]

28   Toronto 7 at Rangers 0 [McCool]

* Conn Smythe was in attendance for the first time since 1942, an absence due to the war and subsequent injuries.

FEBRUARY

3   Boston 4 at Toronto 2

4   Toronto 4 at Chicago 3

6   Toronto 5 at Boston 1

10   Chicago 2 at Toronto 1

11   Toronto 1 at Chicago 2

17   Montreal 4 at Toronto 3

18   Toronto 1 at Detroit 6

24 Rangers 4 at Toronto 4

25 Toronto 2 at Montreal 5

27 Chicago 3 at Toronto 3

MARCH

3 Montreal 2 at Toronto 3

4 Toronto 6 at Rangers 3

6 Toronto 5 at Boston 2

10 Boston 2 at Toronto 9

11 Toronto 3 at Detroit 2

17 Detroit 4 at Toronto 3

18 Toronto 5 at Rangers 6 (Warwick won game at 19:59)

1945–46

OCTOBER

27 Boston 1 at Toronto 1*

* Puck dropped by six Victoria Cross holders: Corporal Fred Topham, Private Smoky Smith, Major Fred Tilson, Lieutenant Colonel Paul Triquet, Lieutenant Colonel D.V. Currie, and Major J.J. Mahony.

NOVEMBER

1 Toronto 2 at Montreal 4

3 Rangers 4 at Toronto 1

4 Toronto 4 at Chicago 7

7 Boston 4 at Toronto 3

8 Toronto 2 at Detroit 3

10 Chicago 2 at Toronto 3*

11 Toronto 3 at Chicago 5

14 Montreal 6 at Toronto 1

17 Detroit 6 at Toronto 5

18 Toronto 3 at Rangers 1

24 Rangers 3 at Toronto 4

25 Toronto 3 at Boston 5

* Babe Pratt received a silver spoon for being a star of the game, but gave the spoon to his defence partner, the young Jim Thomson.

DECEMBER

1 Chicago 8 at Toronto 2

2 Toronto 5 at Chicago 3

8 Montreal 1 at Toronto 0 [Durnan]

9 Toronto 1 at Rangers 2

13 Toronto 4 at Montreal 3

15 Detroit 1 at Toronto 3

16 Toronto 3 at Boston 3

22 Rangers 5 at Toronto 5*

23 Toronto 4 at Rangers 3

25 Toronto 3 at Detroit 6

26 Montreal 4 at Toronto 2

29 Boston 4 at Toronto 3

* Young Canada Night.

JANUARY

1 Toronto 1 at Chicago 3

5 Chicago 3 at Toronto 0 [Karakas]

10 Toronto 5 at Montreal 4

12 Detroit 3 at Toronto 9

19 Rangers 1 at Toronto 3

20 Toronto 3 at Detroit 1

23 Toronto 1 at Boston 7

26 Chicago 5 at Toronto 6

FEBRUARY

2 Boston 5 at Toronto 3

3 Toronto 6 at Rangers 6

6 Toronto 3 at Boston 3

9 Detroit 1 at Toronto 4

10 Toronto 2 at Detroit 2

16 Montreal 4 at Toronto 2 (Blake 19:32—EN)

23 Boston 2 at Toronto 7

24 Toronto 2 at Montreal 6

27 Rangers 6 at Toronto 4 (Laprade 19:40—EN)

MARCH

2 Chicago 4 at Toronto 9

3 Toronto 5 at Rangers 2

6 Toronto 5 at Chicago 2

9 Montreal 2 at Toronto 1

10 Toronto 3 at Boston 7

14 Toronto 2 at Montreal 2

16 Detroit 3 at Toronto 7

17 Toronto 11 at Detroit 7

1946–47

OCTOBER

16 Toronto 3 at Detroit 3 (Abel [D] tied game at 19:49 with goalie out)*

19 Detroit 3 at Toronto 6**

23 Toronto 3 at Boston 3 (Stewart [T] tied game at 19:43 with goalie out)

26 Chicago 1 at Toronto 2

30 Toronto 5 at Chicago 2

31 Toronto at Montreal***

* Gordie Howe scored his first NHL goal; Bob Goldham won a $50 savings bond for scoring the first Leafs goal of the season

** Nick Metz was acting captain. Toronto mayor Robert Saunders faced off the opening puck.

*** Postponed to November 1 because of "transportation uncertainties."

NOVEMBER

1 Toronto 1 at Montreal 1

2 Boston 5 at Toronto 0 [Brimsek]*

9 Rangers 2 at Toronto 4

10 Toronto 4 at Chicago 2

16 Montreal 0 at Toronto 3 [Broda]

17 Toronto 5 at Rangers 4

20 Toronto 1 at Boston 4 (all goals in 3rd)

23 Detroit 4 at Toronto 2

24 Toronto 5 at Detroit 0 [Broda]

27 Toronto 2 at Chicago 5

30 Chicago 0 at Toronto 11 [Broda]

* Milt Schmidt was awarded a goal when Turk Broda threw his stick.

DECEMBER

4 Toronto 2 at Boston 2

7 Boston 1 at Toronto 5

8 Toronto 5 at Detroit 4

11 Montreal 3 at Toronto 2

14 Rangers 2 at Toronto 3

15 Toronto 4 at Chicago 3

19 Detroit 1 at Toronto 3*

21 Chicago 1 at Toronto 3

22 Toronto 3 at Rangers 1

25 Toronto 2 at Detroit 1

26 Toronto 1 at Montreal 4

28 Boston 3 at Toronto 4

* Young Canada Night.

JANUARY

1 Detroit 1 at Toronto 2

2 Toronto 5 at Rangers 4

4 Rangers 2 at Toronto 0 [Rayner]

8 Chicago 4 at Toronto 10

11 Boston 3 at Toronto 4

12 Toronto 2 at Rangers 3

15 Montreal 1 at Toronto 2

16 Toronto 1 at Montreal 1

18 Detroit 4 at Toronto 7

19 Toronto 2 at Boston 3

25 Rangers 1 at Toronto 0 [Rayner]

26 Toronto 6 at Chicago 6

30 Toronto 0 at Montreal 2 [Durnan]

FEBRUARY

1 Chicago 5 at Toronto 4

6 Toronto 2 at Montreal 8

8 Boston 2 at Toronto 5

15 Montreal 4 at Toronto 4

16 Toronto 2 at Rangers 6

19 Toronto 3 at Chicago 5

22 Rangers 0 at Toronto 2 [Broda] (both goals in 1st)

23 Toronto 2 at Montreal 2 (Reardon [M] tied game at 19:53 with goalie out)

26 Montreal 1 at Toronto 0 [Durnan]

27 Toronto 3 at Detroit 3

MARCH

1 Detroit 5 at Toronto 4

5 Toronto 4 at Boston 5

8 Chicago 4 at Toronto 12

9 Toronto 4 at Rangers 2

15 Boston 5 at Toronto 5*

16 Toronto 3 at Boston 5

19 Montreal 4 at Toronto 5

22 Rangers 3 at Toronto 5

23 Toronto 5 at Detroit 3

* Dit Clapper Night: Baldy Cotton, E.W. Bickle, Weston Adams, and Art Ross presented him with a silver cocktail service.

1947–48

OCTOBER

18 Detroit 2 at Toronto 2*

19 Toronto 0 at Detroit 2 [Lumley]

22 Rangers 1 at Toronto 3

25 Chicago 1 at Toronto 5

29 Montreal 1 at Toronto 3

* Field Marshal Viscount Alexander of Tunis, governor general of Canada, dropped the puck.

NOVEMBER

1 Boston 1 at Toronto 1 (Henderson [B] tied game at 19:52 with goalie out)

2 Toronto 4 at Rangers 7

6 Toronto 0 at Montreal 3 [Durnan]

8 Rangers 2 at Toronto 7

9 Toronto 6 at Detroit 0 [Broda]*

12 Chicago 5 at Toronto 4

15 Detroit 3 at Toronto 5

16 Toronto 5 at Chicago 4

19 Toronto 2 at Boston 7

22 Boston 3 at Toronto 4

27 Toronto 0 at Montreal 2 [Durnan]

29 Montreal 1 at Toronto 3

30 Toronto 0 at Boston 0 [Broda (T)/Brimsek (B)]

* McGratton replaced Lumley in the Detroit goal at 12:00 of the third period.

DECEMBER

3 Toronto 4 at Rangers 1

6 Chicago 5 at Toronto 12

7 Toronto 3 at Chicago 2

10 Toronto 2 at Detroit 2

13 Rangers 4 at Toronto 1

14 Toronto 1 at Boston 1

20 Detroit 4 at Toronto 4

21 Toronto 3 at Chicago 1

25 Toronto 3 at Montreal 0 [Broda] (all goals in 2nd)

27 Boston 1 at Toronto 2

28 Toronto 1 at Rangers 1

JANUARY

1	Montreal 1 at Toronto 2
3	Rangers 5 at Toronto 5
10	Chicago 4 at Toronto 6
11	Toronto 2 at Detroit 2
15	Toronto 4 at Montreal 8
17	Boston 1 at Toronto 4
18	Toronto 2 at Rangers 2
21	Toronto 1 at Boston 2
24	Chicago 1 at Toronto 2
25	Toronto 4 at Chicago 4
28	Montreal 3 at Toronto 3
31	Detroit 2 at Toronto 3

FEBRUARY

1	Toronto 0 at Detroit 3 [Lumley]
4	Toronto 4 at Boston 2
7	Rangers 0 at Toronto 3 [Broda]
14	Montreal 2 at Toronto 4
15	Toronto 4 at Rangers 4 (Watson [T] tied game at 19:45 with goalie out)
19	Toronto 1 at Montreal 3
21	Detroit 2 at Toronto 3
22	Toronto 3 at Chicago 2
25	Boston 2 at Toronto 4
28	Chicago 3 at Toronto 4

MARCH

2	Toronto 0 at Rangers 1 [Henry]
3	Montreal 3 at Toronto 2
6	Rangers 1 at Toronto 2
7	Toronto 1 at Boston 3
11	Toronto 1 at Montreal 3
13	Boston 2 at Toronto 5
14	Toronto 3 at Chicago 0 [Broda]
20	Detroit 3 at Toronto 5
21	Toronto 5 at Detroit 2

1948–49

OCTOBER

16	Boston 4 at Toronto 1*
21	Toronto 0 at Montreal 5 [Durnan]
23	Chicago 1 at Toronto 6
24	Toronto 1 at Detroit 2
27	Montreal 2 at Toronto 3
30	Detroit 1 at Toronto 2
31	Toronto 1 at Chicago 2 (D. Bentley won game at 19:49)**

* Brigadier General H.D. Crerar dropped the puck. Turk Broda was presented with the Vézina Trophy by Clarence Campbell.
** The ice was so bad that referee Butch Keeling had teams switch ends midway through the third period.

NOVEMBER

6	Rangers 3 at Toronto 3
13	Chicago 6 at Toronto 3
14	Toronto 4 at Rangers 4
17	Toronto 1 at Boston 2
20	Boston 2 at Toronto 2
21	Toronto 3 at Chicago 3
24	Montreal 3 at Toronto 3
25	Toronto 2 at Montreal 0 [Broda] (both goals in 3rd)
27	Rangers 0 at Toronto 3 [Broda]
28	Toronto 2 at Boston 6

DECEMBER

1	Toronto 3 at Detroit 5
4	Chicago 6 at Toronto 4
5	Toronto 2 at Chicago 0 [Broda] (both goals in 2nd)
8	Detroit 4 at Toronto 3
11	Boston 2 at Toronto 3
12	Toronto 4 at Boston 3
15	Toronto 1 at Rangers 3
18	Rangers 3 at Toronto 3*
19	Toronto 1 at Detroit 5
25	Detroit 1 at Toronto 2
30	Toronto 2 at Montreal 3

* Young Canada Night.

JANUARY

1	Montreal 3 at Toronto 5*
2	Toronto 2 at Rangers 4
5	Boston 0 at Toronto 4 [Broda]
8	Chicago 3 at Toronto 3
9	Toronto 2 at Detroit 2
15	Rangers 1 at Toronto 2
16	Toronto 0 at Rangers 4 [Rayner]
19	Montreal 4 at Toronto 1
22	Detroit 2 at Toronto 2
23	Toronto 1 at Detroit 2
26	Toronto 3 at Boston 1
29	Chicago 4 at Toronto 4
30	Toronto 2 at Chicago 4

* Gardner and Reardon were fined $250 and $200 respectively, and suspended for one game against each other for a stick-swinging incident.

FEBRUARY

3	Toronto 4 at Montreal 1
5	Rangers 1 at Toronto 1 (both goals in 3rd)
6	Toronto 4 at Boston 2
9	Montreal 2 at Toronto 2
12	Detroit 1 at Toronto 3
13	Toronto 3 at Rangers 0 [Broda]
17	Toronto 0 at Montreal 3 [Durnan]

19   Boston 2 at Toronto 5

20   Toronto 4 at Chicago 3*

26   Chicago 2 at Toronto 2**

* Red Hamill was fined $250 and suspended one game for a stick-swinging incident.

** A North Bay delegation honoured native son Bill Tobin of Chicago during the first intermission.

MARCH

2   Montreal 2 at Toronto 0 [Durnan]

5   Rangers 1 at Toronto 7

6   Toronto 4 at Rangers 3

9   Toronto 0 at Detroit 5 [Lumley]

12   Boston 2 at Toronto 1

13   Toronto 3 at Chicago 1

17   Toronto 1 at Montreal 3

19   Detroit 5 at Toronto 2

20   Toronto 2 at Boston 7

1949–50

OCTOBER

15   Chicago 4 at Toronto 4

16   Toronto 5 at Detroit 1

19   Montreal 3 at Toronto 1

22   Rangers 2 at Toronto 2

27   Toronto 2 at Montreal 0 [Broda]

29   Boston 1 at Toronto 8

30   Toronto 4 at Rangers 2

NOVEMBER

2   Rangers 3 at Toronto 3

5   Detroit 4 at Toronto 3

6   Toronto 4 at Chicago 2

10   Toronto 2 at Montreal 4

12   Chicago 0 at Toronto 4 [Broda]

13   Toronto 2 at Boston 4

16   Montreal 0 at Toronto 1 [Broda]

19   Detroit 5 at Toronto 2

20   Toronto 2 at Detroit 5

23   Toronto 1 at Boston 3 (Peirson 18:54—EN)

24   Toronto 3 at Montreal 5

26   Boston 3 at Toronto 3

27   Toronto 3 at Chicago 6

DECEMBER

1   Detroit 2 at Toronto 0 [Lumley] (both goals in 1st)*

3   Rangers 0 at Toronto 2 (both goals in 3rd)

4   Toronto 2 at Detroit 1

8   Toronto 4 at Chicago 1

10   Boston 1 at Toronto 2

11   Toronto 0 at Boston 2 [Gelineau]

14   Montreal 2 at Toronto 2

15   Toronto 1 at Montreal 4

17   Chicago 7 at Toronto 1

18   Toronto 2 at Rangers 0 [Broda]

21   Toronto 1 at Detroit 7

24   Boston 8 at Toronto 4 (Rollins replaces Broda at start of 2nd)

25   Toronto 1 at Rangers 3

28   Montreal 1 at Toronto 1

31   Detroit 5 at Toronto 1

* Turk Broda was benched because Conn Smythe said he was too fat—Gil Mayer played in goal. Broda returned two days later for the shutout.

JANUARY

1   Toronto 0 at Detroit 5 [Lumley]

4   Chicago 4 at Toronto 4

7   Chicago 2 at Toronto 5

11   Toronto 2 at Rangers 1

14   Boston 3 at Toronto 4

18   Montreal 1 at Toronto 0 [Durnan]

19   Toronto 4 at Montreal 2

21   Rangers 1 at Toronto 2

22   Toronto 1 at Detroit 0 [Broda]

25   Rangers 1 at Toronto 5

28   Chicago 1 at Toronto 9

29   Toronto 4 at Chicago 0 [Broda]

FEBRUARY

1   Toronto 0 at Chicago 3 [Brimsek]

4   Detroit 3 at Toronto 3

5   Toronto 2 at Boston 1

8   Toronto 3 at Boston 1*

11   Montreal 0 at Toronto 2 [Broda]

12   Toronto 1 at Chicago 1

16   Montreal 3 at Toronto 3

18   Detroit 2 at Toronto 3

19   Toronto 1 at Rangers 2**

22   Boston 1 at Toronto 3

25   Rangers 2 at Toronto 4

* The second of two consecutive road games played in the same city.

** With the Leafs pressing and their goalie, Turk Broda, on the bench, the Rangers goalie took a shot, just missing the empty net.

MARCH

1   Toronto 2 at Boston 5

4   Detroit 2 at Toronto 3

5   Toronto 2 at Rangers 5

9   Toronto 1 at Montreal 1

11   Rangers 0 at Toronto 4 [Broda]

12   Toronto 2 at Boston 2

15   Toronto 0 at Chicago 4 [Brimsek]

18   Chicago 1 at Toronto 2

19   Toronto 0 at Detroit 5 [Lumley]

22 Montreal 2 at Toronto 1

25 Boston 0 at Toronto 8 [Rollins]

26 Toronto 3 at Rangers 5

1950–51

OCTOBER

14 Chicago 2 at Toronto 1*

15 Toronto 4 at Detroit 4

18 Toronto 2 at Boston 0 [Broda] (both goals in 3rd)

21 Rangers 0 at Toronto 5 [Broda]

22 Toronto 5 at Chicago 3

25 Detroit 0 at Toronto 1 [Broda]

28 Boston 2 at Toronto 4

29 Toronto 3 at Chicago 3
* Brigadier General John Rockingham dropped the puck.

NOVEMBER

1   Montreal 3 at Toronto 5

2   Toronto 2 at Montreal 1

4   Rangers 2 at Toronto 2 (all goals in 2nd)

8   Toronto 5 at Rangers 3

11 Detroit 3 at Toronto 1

12 Toronto 7 at Boston 0 [Broda]

16 Toronto 2 at Montreal 5

18 Rangers 4 at Toronto 5

19 Toronto 1 at Boston 3

22 Chicago 2 at Toronto 5

23 Toronto 2 at Detroit 1

25 Montreal 1 at Toronto 4

26 Toronto 3 at Rangers 2

30 Toronto 0 at Montreal 0 [Rollins (T)/McNeil (M)]

DECEMBER

2   Chicago 0 at Toronto 0 [Rollins (T)/Broda (T)/Lumley (M)]*

3   Toronto 3 at Chicago 3

6   Montreal 1 at Toronto 3

9   Boston 1 at Toronto 8

10 Toronto 2 at Detroit 3

13 Detroit 4 at Toronto 3

14 Toronto 7 at Chicago 1

16 Chicago 3 at Toronto 2

17 Toronto 4 at Boston 2

20 Montreal 1 at Toronto 6

23 Boston 2 at Toronto 2**

27 Toronto 1 at Rangers 3

30 Detroit 3 at Toronto 1

31 Toronto 4 at Detroit 2 (McCormack 19:58—EN)
* Turk Broda replaced Al Rollins at 6:50 of the second period. They shared the shutout.
** Young Canada Night.

JANUARY

6   Rangers 4 at Toronto 2

9   Toronto 3 at Detroit 3

13 Chicago 3 at Toronto 3

14 Toronto 1 at Rangers 2

18 Toronto 5 at Montreal 2

20 Boston 1 at Toronto 2

21 Toronto 0 at Detroit 0 [Rollins (T)/Sawchuk (D)]

24 Montreal 3 at Toronto 4

27 Rangers 1 at Toronto 2

28 Toronto 4 at Chicago 3

FEBRUARY

1   Toronto 3 at Montreal 1

3   Chicago 3 at Toronto 6

4   Toronto 3 at Boston 3

7   Montreal 1 at Toronto 3

10 Detroit 2 at Toronto 1

11 Toronto 5 at Chicago 3 (Sloan 19:22—EN)

15 Toronto 2 at Montreal 2

17 Rangers 0 at Toronto 2 [Rollins]

18 Toronto 5 at Rangers 2

21 Detroit 2 at Toronto 2

24 Boston 2 at Toronto 6

MARCH

1   Toronto 1 at Montreal 3

3   Chicago 0 at Toronto 3 [Broda]

5   Toronto 1 at Detroit 3

7   Detroit 3 at Toronto 0 [Sawchuk]*

10 Boston 3 at Toronto 5

11 Toronto 1 at Boston 3

14 Toronto 3 at Rangers 1 (Thomson 18:52—EN)

15 Toronto 5 at Chicago 3

17 Rangers 1 at Toronto 3

18 Toronto 4 at Rangers 1

21 Montreal 0 at Toronto 2 [Rollins]

24 Boston 1 at Toronto 4

25 Toronto 1 at Boston 0 [Rollins]
* Game was delayed when both starting goalies—Terry Sawchuk of Detroit and Turk Broda of Toronto—were injured in the warmup. Sawchuk played and got a shutout; Broda was replaced by Rollins.

1951–52

OCTOBER

13 Chicago 3 at Toronto 1*

14 Toronto 3 at Detroit 2

17 Boston 2 at Toronto 4 (Gardner 19:40—EN)

20 Rangers 3 at Toronto 2

21 Toronto 1 at Chicago 1

27   Detroit 2 at Toronto 1

29   Toronto 2 at Detroit 2

31   Montreal 0 at Toronto 1 [Rollins]
* Princess Elizabeth and Prince Philip were in attendance.

NOVEMBER

1   Toronto 4 at Montreal 2

3   Rangers 2 at Toronto 1

7   Chicago 0 at Toronto 1 [Rollins]

8   Toronto 3 at Chicago 1

10   Detroit 3 at Toronto 3

11   Toronto 1 at Boston 1

14   Toronto 2 at Rangers 2 (Ronty [R] tied game at 19:18 with goalie out)

17   Boston 1 at Toronto 1 (Schmidt [B] tied game at 19:35 with goalie out)

18   Toronto 0 at Chicago 1 [Lumley]

21   Chicago 1 at Toronto 5

24   Montreal 2 at Toronto 4

25   Toronto 4 at Boston 1

29   Toronto 1 at Montreal 5

DECEMBER

1   Rangers 2 at Toronto 8

2   Toronto 2 at Detroit 1

5   Detroit 2 at Toronto 2

8   Chicago 1 at Toronto 3 (Watson 19:44—EN)

9   Toronto 2 at Rangers 7

13   Toronto 1 at Detroit 3

15   Rangers 1 at Toronto 4

16   Toronto 3 at Chicago 4

20   Toronto 1 at Montreal 4

22   Boston 2 at Toronto 3*

23   Toronto 2 at Boston 4

26   Montreal 3 at Toronto 2

29   Boston 0 at Toronto 4 [Rollins]

30   Toronto 2 at Rangers 2
* Turk Broda Night and Young Canada Night at the Gardens.

JANUARY

3   Toronto 1 at Montreal 3

5   Chicago 1 at Toronto 2

9   Toronto 2 at Rangers 1

12   Detroit 3 at Toronto 5

13   Toronto 1 at Detroit 2

15   Toronto 1 at Boston 0 [Rollins]

17   Toronto 2 at Montreal 2

19   Boston 2 at Toronto 6

20   Toronto 3 at Chicago 1

23   Montreal 4 at Toronto 2

24   Toronto 2 at Detroit 2

26   Rangers 3 at Toronto 3

27   Toronto 3 at Boston 0 [Rollins]

FEBRUARY

2   Boston 1 at Toronto 1

3   Toronto 1 at Chicago 3*

6   Rangers at Toronto**

9   Montreal 2 at Toronto 3

10   Toronto 4 at Rangers 3

13   Detroit 3 at Toronto 1 (Howe 19:18—EN)

14   Toronto 1 at Montreal 3

16   Chicago 2 at Toronto 2

19   Rangers 3 at Toronto 3***

21   Toronto 1 at Chicago 5

23   Detroit 3 at Toronto 1 (Abel 19:55—EN)

27   Toronto 3 at Rangers 1
* Afternoon game.
** Postponed to February 19 due to the death of King George VI.
*** Toronto's Gus Mortson was fined $100 for attempting to kick Hy Buller.

MARCH

1   Boston 1 at Toronto 1

2   Toronto 2 at Boston 2

5   Montreal 2 at Toronto 6

8   Detroit 3 at Toronto 6

9   Toronto 1 at Detroit 6

13   Toronto 1 at Montreal 3

15   Rangers 2 at Toronto 5

16   Toronto 4 at Rangers 2

19   Montreal 3 at Toronto 0 [McNeil]

22   Chicago 3 at Toronto 2

23   Toronto 2 at Boston 4*
* Al Rollins replaced Turk Broda at 10:00 of the second period.

1952–53

OCTOBER

11   Chicago 6 at Toronto 2*

12   Toronto 4 at Detroit 4 (Kennedy [T] scores at 19:15 to tie the game)

16   Toronto 1 at Boston 2

18   Rangers 3 at Toronto 4

19   Toronto 3 at Chicago 2

22   Detroit 4 at Toronto 5

25   Boston 4 at Toronto 0 [Henry]

29   Montreal 5 at Toronto 7 (Kennedy 19:30—EN)
* Conn Smythe dropped the puck to open the season.

NOVEMBER

1   Boston 2 at Toronto 3*

2   Toronto 4 at Detroit 2

5   Rangers 1 at Toronto 4

6   Toronto 1 at Montreal 3

8   Detroit 3 at Toronto 3

11   Toronto 0 at Boston 4 [Henry] (all goals in 1st)

13   Toronto 3 at Montreal 1 (all goals in 2nd)

15   Chicago 3 at Toronto 1

16   Toronto 6 at Rangers 3

19   Boston 2 at Toronto 1

22   Montreal 2 at Toronto 2

23   Toronto 5 at Boston 6

26   Toronto 2 at Rangers 4

27   Toronto 3 at Chicago 3 (Smith [T] scored at 18:52 with goalie out)

29   Detroit 3 at Toronto 1

30   Toronto 1 at Detroit 4

* First Leafs telecast on CBC television.

DECEMBER

4   Toronto 2 at Montreal 1*

6   Rangers 2 at Toronto 2

7   Toronto 2 at Chicago 0 [Lumley] (both goals in 2nd)

10   Montreal 2 at Toronto 1

13   Detroit 3 at Toronto 1

14   Toronto 2 at Rangers 2

18   Toronto 1 at Detroit 1

20   Chicago 1 at Toronto 4

21   Toronto 2 at Chicago 4

24   Montreal 0 at Toronto 2 [Lumley] (both goals in 3rd)

27   Boston 0 at Toronto 3 [Lumley]

31   Toronto 3 at Rangers 3

* A moment of silence was observed for the passing of James Norris, Sr.

JANUARY

1   Toronto 1 at Boston 5

3   Chicago 1 at Toronto 1 (both goals in 1st)

10   Boston 1 at Toronto 3

11   Toronto 2 at Detroit 5

14   Chicago 0 at Toronto 3 [Lumley] (all goals in 3rd)

17   Rangers 0 at Toronto 1 [Lumley]

18   Toronto 1 at Boston 2

21   Montreal 1 at Toronto 0 [McNeil]

22   Toronto 1 at Montreal 4

24   Detroit 0 at Toronto 2 [Lumley]

25   Toronto 4 at Chicago 3

29   Toronto 2 at Boston 2

31   Rangers 0 at Toronto 4 [Lumley]

FEBRUARY

1   Toronto 1 at Detroit 5

5   Toronto 0 at Montreal 2 [McNeil] (both goals in 3rd)

7   Chicago 4 at Toronto 2

8   Toronto 2 at Chicago 4 (McFadden 19:20—EN)

14   Montreal 2 at Toronto 2

15   Toronto 2 at Rangers 1

18   Detroit 0 at Toronto 2 [Lumley] (Flaman 19:55—EN)

21   Boston 2 at Toronto 2

25   Montreal 2 at Toronto 1

26   Toronto 1 at Montreal 4

28   Rangers 0 at Toronto 3 [Lumley]

MARCH

1   Toronto 2 at Rangers 4 (Kullman 19:49—EN)

5   Toronto 1 at Chicago 3

7   Detroit 3 at Toronto 0 [Sawchuk]

8   Toronto 1 at Detroit 3

14   Boston 3 at Toronto 1 (Dumart 19:25—EN)

15   Toronto 1 at Rangers 1

18   Chicago 3 at Toronto 4

19   Toronto 4 at Montreal 1

21   Rangers 0 at Toronto 5 [Lumley]

22   Toronto 3 at Boston 1

1953–54

OCTOBER

10   Chicago 2 at Toronto 6*

11   Toronto 0 at Detroit 4 [Gatherum]

15   Toronto 4 at Boston 1

17   Rangers 1 at Toronto 1

18   Toronto 2 at Chicago 1

21   Detroit 1 at Toronto 1

24   Boston 3 at Toronto 2**

25   Toronto 0 at Detroit 2 [Sawchuk]

29   Toronto 1 at Montreal 3

31   Rangers 1 at Toronto 4

* Ted Kennedy was presented with the Bickell Cup in a pre-game ceremony.

** In a pre-game ceremony, Gardens associate Henry Roxborough presented Ted Kennedy with an award to acknowledge scoring his 20th goal of the season in a previous game. Kennedy then scored after just eight seconds, tying an NHL record.

NOVEMBER

1   Toronto 2 at Rangers 2 (Kennedy [T] tied game at 18:26 with goalie out)

4   Chicago 1 at Toronto 3

7   Detroit 2 at Toronto 2

8   Toronto 2 at Chicago 1

11   Montreal 1 at Toronto 4

14   Boston 0 at Toronto 2 [Lumley] (Horton 19:19—EN)

15   Toronto 1 at Boston 1

19   Toronto 0 at Montreal 1 [McNeil]

21   Rangers 0 at Toronto 1 [Lumley]

22   Toronto 5 at Chicago 1

26   Toronto 0 at Detroit 2 [Sawchuk]

28   Montreal 1 at Toronto 3

29   Toronto 1 at Boston 2

DECEMBER

3   Toronto 1 at Montreal 5

5   Detroit 0 at Toronto 3 [Lumley]

6   Toronto 3 at Rangers 3 (W. Hergesheimer [R] tied game at 19:32 with goalie out)

9   Montreal 0 at Toronto 3 [Lumley]*

12   Chicago 0 at Toronto 2 [Lumley]

13   Toronto 2 at Rangers 1

17   Toronto 2 at Boston 3

19   Rangers 2 at Toronto 3**

20   Toronto 1 at Chicago 4

26   Detroit 2 at Toronto 4

30   Montreal 2 at Toronto 2

* Dubbed the "War of 1812." At 18:12 of the third, a bench-clearing brawl erupted, and when it was over, referee Frank Udvari handed out 18 misconducts (nine per side) and two majors (one each), leaving each team with only a goalie and three skaters (there were no subs left on the benches) to play out the final 1:48.

** Young Canada Night.

JANUARY

2   Chicago 0 at Toronto 4 [Lumley]

3   Toronto 0 at Detroit 0 [Lumley (T)/Sawchuk (D)]

7   Toronto 3 at Montreal 7

9   Boston 2 at Toronto 3

10   Toronto 1 at Rangers 4

13   Chicago 1 at Toronto 2

16   Rangers 0 at Toronto 4 [Lumley]

17   Toronto 3 at Chicago 1 (all goals in 3rd)

23   Detroit 1 at Toronto 4

24   Toronto 0 at Detroit 2 [Sawchuk]

27   Montreal 2 at Toronto 0 [McNeil]

30   Boston 2 at Toronto 4 (Migay 19:59—EN)

31   Toronto 0 at Boston 2 [Henry]

FEBRUARY

4   Toronto 4 at Montreal 2 (Smith 19:42—EN)

6   Chicago 0 at Toronto 6 [Lumley]

7   Toronto 1 at Chicago 2

10   Boston 3 at Toronto 2

11   Toronto 3 at Boston 1

13   Montreal 2 at Toronto 2

14   Toronto 3 at Rangers 3

17   Detroit 0 at Toronto 0 [Sawchuk (D)/Lumley (T)]

20   Boston 2 at Toronto 3

21   Toronto 1 at Rangers 6

25   Toronto 0 at Montreal 0 [Lumley (T)/Plante (M)]

27   Chicago 2 at Toronto 4

28   Toronto 1 at Chicago 2

MARCH

3   Rangers 3 at Toronto 3

4   Toronto 3 at Detroit 3

6   Detroit 3 at Toronto 1 (all goals in 1st)

7   Toronto 4 at Rangers 0 [Lumley]

11   Toronto 3 at Montreal 0 [Lumley]

13   Boston 2 at Toronto 1

14   Toronto 0 at Boston 3 [Henry] (all goals in 2nd)

17   Montreal 1 at Toronto 3 (Migay 19:22—EN)

20   Rangers 5 at Toronto 2

21   Toronto 1 at Detroit 6

1954–55

OCTOBER

7   Toronto 1 at Detroit 2

9   Chicago 3 at Toronto 3*

16   Rangers 4 at Toronto 2 (Prentice 19:00—EN)

17   Toronto 1 at Boston 1 (McKenney [B] tied game at 18:43 with goalie out)

21   Toronto 3 at Montreal 1

23   Boston 3 at Toronto 3

27   Montreal 3 at Toronto 1

30   Rangers 1 at Toronto 3

* Gus Ryder and Marilyn Bell were honoured at the opening ceremony.

NOVEMBER

3   Detroit 1 at Toronto 1

6   Chicago 2 at Toronto 5

7   Toronto 2 at Chicago 1

10   Toronto 2 at Rangers 1

11   Toronto 1 at Detroit 0 [Lumley]

13   Detroit 0 at Toronto 1 [Lumley]

14   Toronto 3 at Boston 1

17   Montreal 2 at Toronto 5

18   Toronto 4 at Montreal 5 (Béliveau won game at 19:46—PP)*

20   Boston 1 at Toronto 0 [Henderson]

21   Toronto 2 at Rangers 2

25   Toronto 0 at Detroit 2 [Sawchuk]

27   Rangers 1 at Toronto 3

28   Toronto 1 at Chicago 1

* Leafs played the last two periods under protest because Charlie Hodge dressed for Montreal even though his name was not on the roster.

DECEMBER

1   Boston 0 at Toronto 6 [Lumley]

4   Detroit 0 at Toronto 1 [Lumley]

5   Toronto 4 at Boston 2

8   Montreal 1 at Toronto 3

9   Toronto 0 at Montreal 2 [Hodge]

11   Chicago 2 at Toronto 1

12   Toronto 1 at Rangers 1

15   Toronto 8 at Chicago 3*

18   Rangers 1 at Toronto 3

19   Toronto 3 at Rangers 3 (Lewicki [R] tied game at 19:54)

25   Detroit 3 at Toronto 2

26 Toronto 1 at Detroit 1

29 Montreal 1 at Toronto 1

30 Toronto 1 at Detroit 4
* Played at St. Louis.

JANUARY

1   Chicago 2 at Toronto 2

2   Toronto 2 at Chicago 3*

5   Boston 2 at Toronto 1

8   Rangers 0 at Toronto 5 [Lumley]

9   Toronto 1 at Boston 1

12 Toronto 0 at Rangers 0 [Lumley (T)/Worsley (R)]

15 Boston 2 at Toronto 4

16 Toronto 4 at Chicago 2

19 Chicago 3 at Toronto 3

20 Toronto 2 at Montreal 6

22 Detroit 1 at Toronto 3

23 Toronto 0 at Detroit 4 [Sawchuk]

26 Montreal 1 at Toronto 1

29 Rangers 3 at Toronto 1

30 Toronto 0 at Boston 3 [Henderson]
* Played at St. Louis.

FEBRUARY

3   Toronto 2 at Montreal 3

5   Chicago 2 at Toronto 2*

6   Toronto 4 at Chicago 2

9   Montreal 1 at Toronto 3**

12 Detroit 2 at Toronto 1

13 Toronto 3 at Boston 3 (Cullen [T] tied game at 18:23 with goalie out)

19 Boston 1 at Toronto 1

20 Toronto 1 at Chicago 4

23 Toronto 3 at Rangers 1 (Thomson 19:23—EN)

24 Toronto 1 at Montreal 1

26 Detroit 1 at Toronto 1
* A power failure late in the game ruined TV coverage, the public-address system, and the penalty clocks.
** Lumley was penalized for using an oversized stick—it was too long and its blade was too high.

MARCH

2   Montreal 3 at Toronto 2

5   Boston 2 at Toronto 2

6   Toronto 1 at Boston 3

10 Toronto 0 at Montreal 0 [Lumley (T)/Plante (M)]*

12 Rangers 2 at Toronto 1

13 Toronto 1 at Detroit 6

19 Chicago 0 at Toronto 5 [Lumley]

20 Toronto 2 at Rangers 3
* A Zamboni ice resurfacer was used for the first time ever in a Canadian NHL game.

1955–56

OCTOBER

6   Toronto 0 at Montreal 2 [Plante]

8   Detroit 2 at Toronto 4

9   Toronto 1 at Chicago 3

12 Toronto 0 at Boston 2 [Sawchuk]

15 Boston 2 at Toronto 2

16 Toronto 0 at Detroit 6 [Hall]*

19 Toronto 2 at Rangers 6

22 Rangers 2 at Toronto 3

26 Montreal 1 at Toronto 2

29 Chicago 0 at Toronto 2 [Lumley]
* Toronto's Jim Thomson threw Ted Lindsay's stick into the crowd during a last-minute fight. Lindsay responded in kind; both were given misconducts.

NOVEMBER

2   Detroit 1 at Toronto 3

3   Toronto 3 at Montreal 3 (Stewart [T] tied game at 19:52 with goalie out)

5   Rangers 3 at Toronto 0 [Worsley]

6   Toronto 1 at Detroit 4

11 Toronto 0 at Chicago 2 [Rollins]

12 Boston 3 at Toronto 2

13 Toronto 1 at Rangers 4

16 Montreal 3 at Toronto 2

19 Boston 2 at Toronto 3

20 Toronto 1 at Boston 1

24 Toronto 2 at Chicago 3

26 Chicago 4 at Toronto 7

27 Toronto 2 at Detroit 1 (all goals in 1st)

30 Detroit 3 at Toronto 3

DECEMBER

3   Montreal 3 at Toronto 1

4   Toronto 0 at Boston 5 [Sawchuk]

7   Toronto 1 at Rangers 3 (Bathgate 19:12—EN)

8   Toronto 1 at Montreal 3

10 Rangers 1 at Toronto 6

11 Toronto 3 at Chicago 3

15 Toronto 0 at Detroit 4 [Hall]

17 Boston 1 at Toronto 5

18 Toronto 1 at Rangers 4

24 Chicago 2 at Toronto 5

25 Toronto 1 at Detroit 1

28 Montreal 0 at Toronto 2 [Lumley]

29 Toronto 2 at Montreal 5

31 Detroit 2 at Toronto 2

JANUARY

4   Chicago 2 at Toronto 4 (Stewart 19:11—EN)

7   Boston 2 at Toronto 6

14   Rangers 6 at Toronto 5

15   Toronto 4 at Boston 1

18   Montreal 3 at Toronto 2

19   Toronto 1 at Montreal 3

21   Detroit 2 at Toronto 4

22   Toronto 1 at Detroit 4*

25   Chicago 1 at Toronto 3

28   Rangers 3 at Toronto 1 (Hebenton 19:18—EN)

29   Toronto 1 at Boston 3

* When Harry Lumley was injured at 6:59 of the third, Detroit trainer Lefty Wilson played goal for the Leafs, shutting out his own team for the final 13:01 of the game.

FEBRUARY

1   Toronto 2 at Rangers 5

4   Chicago 4 at Toronto 2

5   Toronto 2 at Chicago 3

8   Montreal 1 at Toronto 1

9   Toronto 1 at Boston 1 (both goals in 1st)

11   Rangers 0 at Toronto 5 [Chadwick]

12   Toronto 1 at Chicago 1

15   Boston 0 at Toronto 1 [Chadwick]

16   Toronto 1 at Montreal 8

18   Detroit 6 at Toronto 1

22   Toronto 4 at Rangers 2 (Hannigan 19:58—EN)

24   Toronto 2 at Chicago 1

25   Boston 3 at Toronto 1 (Stasiuk 19:56—EN)

29   Montreal 1 at Toronto 4

MARCH

3   Detroit 2 at Toronto 2

4   Toronto 2 at Boston 2

8   Toronto 3 at Montreal 4

10   Rangers 2 at Toronto 5

11   Toronto 2 at Rangers 4

17   Chicago 1 at Toronto 1

18   Toronto 2 at Detroit 0 [Lumley]

1956–57

OCTOBER

11   Toronto 4 at Boston 4

13   Detroit 4 at Toronto 1 (Kelly 19:35—EN)*

14   Toronto 1 at Chicago 0 [Chadwick]

18   Toronto 3 at Detroit 3

20   Boston 2 at Toronto 2

25   Toronto 3 at Montreal 2

27   Chicago 2 at Toronto 5

28   Toronto 1 at Rangers 1

31   Rangers 2 at Toronto 7

* The pre-game ceremony involved many Leafs from the 1932 Cup-winning team.

NOVEMBER

3   Detroit 2 at Toronto 1*

7   Montreal 4 at Toronto 3

8   Toronto 2 at Chicago 5

10   Chicago 1 at Toronto 4

15   Toronto 2 at Detroit 4

17   Chicago 6 at Toronto 3

18   Toronto 3 at Boston 4

21   Toronto 3 at Rangers 3

22   Toronto 2 at Detroit 2 (Barry Cullen [T] tied game at 18:45 with goalie out)

24   Boston 3 at Toronto 2

25   Toronto 1 at Boston 3 (Mohns 19:32—EN)

29   Toronto 2 at Montreal 4

* After pulling the goalie, Toronto tied the game, but referee Frank Udvari disallowed the goal as he didn't see the red light come on.

DECEMBER

1   Detroit 0 at Toronto 4 [Chadwick]

2   Toronto 2 at Rangers 4 (Bathgate 19:04—EN)

5   Montreal 3 at Toronto 1

8   Rangers 0 at Toronto 0 [Worsley (R)/Chadwick (T)]

9   Toronto 2 at Chicago 1

13   Toronto 2 at Montreal 6

15   Rangers 1 at Toronto 2

16   Toronto 2 at Boston 4

20   Toronto 2 at Montreal 4

22   Boston 3 at Toronto 2

23   Toronto 3 at Rangers 1 (Migay 19:24—EN)

26   Montreal 0 at Toronto 1 [Chadwick]

29   Chicago 3 at Toronto 6

30   Toronto 0 at Chicago 2 [Rollins] (Skov 19:57—EN)

JANUARY

2   Detroit 2 at Toronto 0 [Hall]

5   Boston 2 at Toronto 3

6   Toronto 1 at Detroit 2

9   Toronto 4 at Rangers 3

10   Toronto 1 at Montreal 2 (Marshall won game at 19:54)*

12   Chicago 3 at Toronto 4

13   Toronto 1 at Chicago 1

16   Montreal 3 at Toronto 2

19   Boston 1 at Toronto 4

20   Toronto 3 at Boston 2

23   Rangers 4 at Toronto 4

26   Detroit 4 at Toronto 1

27   Toronto 1 at Detroit 3

* Dick Duff tied the game for Toronto at 18:37 with the goalie out and Maurice Richard in the penalty box; Richard stormed after referee Frank Udvari and drew a 10-minute misconduct.

FEBRUARY

2   Chicago 3 at Toronto 3

3   Toronto 3 at Chicago 6 (Skov 18:30—EN)

6   Montreal 1 at Toronto 1

9   Rangers 4 at Toronto 4

10   Toronto 1 at Boston 5

13   Boston 2 at Toronto 2

14   Toronto 2 at Montreal 1

16   Detroit 3 at Toronto 1

17   Toronto 2 at Rangers 3

23   Boston 5 at Toronto 2

24   Toronto 2 at Detroit 1

MARCH

2   Chicago 4 at Toronto 3

3   Toronto 0 at Chicago 0 [Chadwick (T)/Rollins (C)]

6   Montreal 1 at Toronto 3

9   Rangers 2 at Toronto 1

10   Toronto 3 at Boston 3 (Stasiuk [B] tied game at 19:25 with goalie out)

14   Toronto 4 at Montreal 8

16   Rangers 1 at Toronto 14

17   Toronto 5 at Rangers 3 (Armstrong 19:40—EN)

20   Montreal 2 at Toronto 1

23   Detroit 5 at Toronto 3 (Lindsay 19:50—EN)

24   Toronto 1 at Detroit 4

1957–58

OCTOBER

8   Toronto 0 at Chicago 1 [Hall]

12   Detroit 5 at Toronto 3

17   Toronto 3 at Montreal 9

19   Boston 0 at Toronto 7 [Chadwick]

20   Toronto 1 at Detroit 3

23   Toronto 0 at Rangers 3 [Worsley]

26   Rangers 0 at Toronto 3 [Chadwick]

30   Montreal 6 at Toronto 2

31   Toronto 3 at Montreal 1

NOVEMBER

2   Chicago 3 at Toronto 3

6   Rangers 4 at Toronto 2 (Bathgate 19:55—EN)

7   Toronto 5 at Boston 3

9   Detroit 3 at Toronto 3

10   Toronto 1 at Chicago 3

13   Montreal 4 at Toronto 2

16   Boston 4 at Toronto 2

17   Toronto 2 at Boston 2

20   Chicago 1 at Toronto 2

23   Detroit 2 at Toronto 1

24   Toronto 5 at Rangers 1

28   Toronto 3 at Detroit 3 (Duff (T) tied game at 19:15 with goalie out)

30   Boston 2 at Toronto 3

DECEMBER

1   Toronto 7 at Chicago 2

4   Montreal 0 at Toronto 0 [Plante (M)/Chadwick (T)]

5   Toronto 3 at Montreal 4 (Moore won game at 19:40)

7   Rangers 3 at Toronto 3

8   Toronto 2 at Rangers 1

14   Chicago 1 at Toronto 4

15   Toronto 3 at Boston 1 (Pulford 19:54—EN)

19   Toronto 2 at Detroit 3

21   Boston 3 at Toronto 3*

22   Toronto 2 at Rangers 5

25   Montreal 4 at Toronto 5

28   Rangers 1 at Toronto 6

29   Toronto 1 at Chicago 2

* Young Canada Night.

JANUARY

2   Toronto 2 at Montreal 5

4   Chicago 4 at Toronto 2 (Lindsay 19:49—EN)

5   Toronto 2 at Detroit 3

8   Toronto 5 at Rangers 5 (Henry [R] tied game at 19:35 with goalie out)

11   Boston 2 at Toronto 2

12   Toronto 5 at Boston 3

16   Toronto 2 at Montreal 5

18   Detroit 1 at Toronto 2

19   Toronto 3 at Chicago 5

22   Montreal 2 at Toronto 0 [Plante]

25   Rangers 1 at Toronto 7

26   Toronto 3 at Boston 3 (Labine [B] tied game at 19:59 with goalie out)

29   Chicago 4 at Toronto 1

FEBRUARY

1   Detroit 2 at Toronto 9

2   Toronto 1 at Detroit 3

8   Boston 7 at Toronto 3

9   Toronto 2 at Boston 0 [Chadwick]

12   Montreal 5 at Toronto 2

15   Detroit 6 at Toronto 3

16   Toronto 1 at Detroit 4

22   Chicago 1 at Toronto 3 (Mahovlich 10:40—EN)

23   Toronto 2 at Rangers 4 (Bathgate 19:31—EN)

27   Toronto 1 at Montreal 4

MARCH

1   Rangers 5 at Toronto 4

2   Toronto 6 at Chicago 5

5   Chicago 2 at Toronto 5

8   Boston 3 at Toronto 3

9   Toronto 0 at Boston 7 [Simmons]

12   Montreal 5 at Toronto 3

15   Detroit 3 at Toronto 1

16   Toronto 2 at Chicago 3

18   Toronto 2 at Detroit 4

20   Toronto 4 at Montreal 7

22   Rangers 7 at Toronto 0 [Worsley]

23   Toronto 2 at Rangers 3

1958–59

OCTOBER

11   Chicago 3 at Toronto 1*

12   Toronto 2 at Chicago 5

16   Toronto 3 at Montreal 4

18   Boston 2 at Toronto 3

19   Toronto 1 at Detroit 3

25   Detroit 0 at Toronto 3 [Bower]

26   Toronto 2 at Rangers 3

29   Montreal 5 at Toronto 0 [Plante]

* Hap Day dropped the first puck.

NOVEMBER

1   Rangers 3 at Toronto 4

2   Toronto 0 at Boston 2 [Simmons]

8   Boston 3 at Toronto 5

9   Toronto 2 at Detroit 0 [Chadwick]

12   Montreal 4 at Toronto 1

15   Detroit 4 at Toronto 1

16   Toronto 4 at Boston 4*

19   Toronto 4 at Rangers 7

22   Rangers 2 at Toronto 2

23   Toronto 3 at Chicago 3

26   Detroit 5 at Toronto 2

27   Toronto 2 at Detroit 3 (all goals in 3rd)

29   Chicago 2 at Toronto 1

30   Toronto 2 at Boston 1

* Leafs coach Punch Imlach threatened players with a $200 fine each if they didn't get at
  least one road point against both Boston and New York.

DECEMBER

4   Toronto 2 at Montreal 2

6   Boston 1 at Toronto 4

7   Toronto 2 at Rangers 0 [Bower]

10   Toronto 2 at Chicago 2

13   Rangers 4 at Toronto 4 (Duff [T] tied game at 18:38 with goalie out)

14   Toronto 3 at Boston 6 (McKenney 19:15—EN)

18   Toronto 1 at Montreal 4

20   Boston 2 at Toronto 2

21   Toronto 1 at Rangers 5

25   Toronto 2 at Detroit 0 [Chadwick]

27   Chicago 2 at Toronto 2 (all goals in 1st)

28   Toronto 3 at Chicago 4

31   Montreal 0 at Toronto 2 [Chadwick]

JANUARY

3   Chicago 2 at Toronto 1

4   Toronto 4 at Rangers 2 (Armstrong 19:26—EN)

7   Detroit 1 at Toronto 3 (Duff 19:45—EN)

8   Toronto 0 at Montreal 3 [Plante]

10   Boston 1 at Toronto 4

11   Toronto 6 at Detroit 6

14   Rangers 3 at Toronto 2

17   Detroit 1 at Toronto 2

18   Toronto 3 at Boston 4

21   Montreal 1 at Toronto 3

24   Boston 3 at Toronto 1

25   Toronto 4 at Chicago 1

31   Rangers 5 at Toronto 2

FEBRUARY

1   Toronto 4 at Boston 6 (Gendron 18:56—EN)

5   Toronto 6 at Montreal 3 [Pronovost (M) replaced Plante at start of 3rd]

7   Detroit 1 at Toronto 4

8   Toronto 2 at Chicago 7

11   Montreal 5 at Toronto 2

14   Chicago 1 at Toronto 5

15   Toronto 2 at Detroit 4

21   Rangers 1 at Toronto 1

22   Toronto 1 at Chicago 5

25   Montreal 2 at Toronto 3

28   Detroit 4 at Toronto 2 (Kelly 19:21—EN)

MARCH

1   Toronto 1 at Rangers 1

4   Chicago 2 at Toronto 5

5   Toronto 1 at Montreal 2

7   Boston 1 at Toronto 4

8   Toronto 3 at Boston 4

11   Montreal 6 at Toronto 2

14   Rangers 0 at Toronto 5 [Bower]

15   Toronto 6 at Rangers 5

19   Toronto 6 at Montreal 3 [Cyr (M) replaced Pronovost
     at start of 3rd]

21   Chicago 1 at Toronto 5

22   Toronto 6 at Detroit 4

1959–60

OCTOBER

10   Chicago 3 at Toronto 6*

11   Toronto 3 at Chicago 1

15   Toronto 2 at Montreal 4

17   Boston 0 at Toronto 3 [Bower]

18   Toronto 0 at Detroit 3 [Sawchuk]

21   Toronto 3 at Rangers 2

24   Rangers 1 at Toronto 1

28   Montreal 1 at Toronto 1

31   Boston 3 at Toronto 4

* Puck dropped by Prime Minister John Diefenbaker.

NOVEMBER

1   Toronto 3 at Boston 6

4   Rangers 1 at Toronto 4

7   Detroit 2 at Toronto 2

10   Toronto 3 at Chicago 1 (Stewart 19:12—EN)

12   Toronto 0 at Montreal 3 [Plante]

14   Chicago 3 at Toronto 3

15   Toronto 2 at Rangers 2

18   Detroit 2 at Toronto 3

21   Montreal 4 at Toronto 1 (Marshall 19:15—EN)

22   Toronto 2 at Boston 1

26   Toronto 4 at Chicago 3

28   Boston 2 at Toronto 2

29   Toronto 4 at Detroit 1

DECEMBER

2   Montreal 0 at Toronto 1 [Bower]

5   Rangers 3 at Toronto 6

6   Toronto 0 at Rangers 6 [Paille]

10   Toronto 3 at Boston 6

12   Chicago 4 at Toronto 2 (Sloan 19:09—EN)

13   Toronto 2 at Detroit 4

17   Toronto 2 at Montreal 8

19   Detroit 2 at Toronto 4

20   Toronto 4 at Chicago 7

26   Rangers 0 at Toronto 4 [Bower]

27   Toronto 6 at Rangers 3

30   Montreal 3 at Toronto 2 (Pulford [T] scored at 19:48 with goalie out)

31   Toronto 4 at Detroit 2

JANUARY

2   Chicago 4 at Toronto 2

3   Toronto 4 at Chicago 0 [Bower]

6   Detroit 1 at Toronto 3

9   Boston 3 at Toronto 2

10   Toronto 0 at Boston 4 [Simmons]

14   Toronto 1 at Montreal 3

16   Rangers 1 at Toronto 3 (Pulford 19:47—EN)

17   Toronto 3 at Detroit 4

23   Boston 3 at Toronto 3

24   Toronto 2 at Boston 6

27   Chicago 1 at Toronto 2

30   Rangers 2 at Toronto 3

31   Toronto 3 at Chicago 3

FEBRUARY

3   Toronto 4 at Rangers 2

4   Toronto 2 at Montreal 4

6   Detroit 4 at Toronto 6 (Stewart 19:27—EN)

7   Toronto 0 at Boston 3 [Lumley]

10   Montreal 4 at Toronto 2 (Provost 19:50—EN)

13   Detroit 1 at Toronto 7 (Leafs scored all seven in the 3rd)

14   Toronto 3 at Detroit 1

17   Boston 1 at Toronto 3

20   Chicago 1 at Toronto 3

21   Toronto 5 at Chicago 7

24   Montreal 1 at Toronto 3

27   Detroit 4 at Toronto 3

28   Toronto 5 at Rangers 3*

* Pay TV was provided to 1,000 homes in Etobicoke for $1 on a trial basis for all remaining Sunday games.

MARCH

3   Toronto 1 at Montreal 5

5   Boston 2 at Toronto 5

6   Toronto 3 at Boston 1 (Kelly 19:43—EN)

9   Montreal 9 at Toronto 4

12   Rangers 4 at Toronto 1

13   Toronto 2 at Rangers 2

17   Toronto 6 at Montreal 2

19   Chicago 0 at Toronto 1 [Bower]

20   Toronto 3 at Detroit 2 (Wilson won game at 18:32)

1960–61

OCTOBER

6   Toronto 0 at Montreal 5 [Plante]

8   Rangers 5 at Toronto 2*

9   Toronto 3 at Detroit 3

12   Toronto 0 at Chicago 3 [Hall]

15   Boston 1 at Toronto 1

16   Toronto 7 at Rangers 2

19   Montreal 1 at Toronto 3

22   Detroit 2 at Toronto 1

23   Toronto 3 at Detroit 1

29   Chicago 4 at Toronto 8

30   Toronto 3 at Rangers 1

* Keiller MacKay, lieutenant governor of Ontario, dropped the first puck.

NOVEMBER

2   Boston 2 at Toronto 2

3   Toronto 1 at Montreal 3

5   Rangers 3 at Toronto 7

9   Toronto 0 at Chicago 2 [Hall]

12   Chicago 1 at Toronto 7*

13   Toronto 4 at Boston 2 (Mahovlich 19:44—EN)

16   Detroit 3 at Toronto 3

19   Montreal 3 at Toronto 6

20   Toronto 3 at Boston 2

24   Toronto 1 at Chicago 2

26   Detroit 3 at Toronto 3 (Pronovost [D] tied game at 19:35 with goalie out)

27   Toronto 0 at Detroit 2 [Sawchuk]**

* Game marked Maple Leaf Gardens' 29th anniversary; Lou Marsh and Charlie Conacher dropped the first puck.

** Gordie Howe of Detroit became the first NHL player to reach 1,000 points.

DECEMBER

1   Toronto 3 at Montreal 6*

3   Rangers 2 at Toronto 5

4   Toronto 5 at Boston 2

7   Montreal 6 at Toronto 2

10   Chicago 2 at Toronto 5

11   Toronto 6 at Chicago 1

15   Toronto 4 at Montreal 2

17   Boston 3 at Toronto 3

18   Toronto 3 at Rangers 2

24   Detroit 4 at Toronto 4

25   Toronto 4 at Boston 1

28   Montreal 4 at Toronto 1

31   Rangers 1 at Toronto 2

* Leafs coach Punch Imlach was fined $200 for public criticism of the referee.

JANUARY

1   Toronto 4 at Rangers 1 (all goals in 3rd)

4   Detroit 4 at Toronto 6

5   Toronto 4 at Detroit 1

7   Boston 1 at Toronto 4

8   Toronto 1 at Chicago 5

12   Toronto 2 at Montreal 6

14   Chicago 1 at Toronto 4

15   Toronto 6 at Boston 4

18   Rangers 4 at Toronto 4 (Kelly [T] tied game at 19:35 with goalie out)

21   Boston 3 at Toronto 1

25   Montreal 3 at Toronto 5 (Kelly 19:45—EN)

26   Toronto 4 at Boston 5

28   Chicago 1 at Toronto 2

29   Toronto 4 at Rangers 1

FEBRUARY

2   Toronto 5 at Detroit 0 [Bower]

4   Detroit 2 at Toronto 4

5   Toronto 1 at Chicago 1

8   Rangers 3 at Toronto 5

11   Boston 3 at Toronto 6

12   Toronto 4 at Detroit 2 (Keon 18:46—EN)

15   Montreal 3 at Toronto 1 (Marshall 18:55—EN)

18   Chicago 2 at Toronto 5

19   Toronto 2 at Rangers 4

23   Toronto 4 at Montreal 2*

25   Detroit 1 at Toronto 3

26   Toronto 2 at Detroit 2

* King Clancy was coach.

MARCH

1   Montreal 1 at Toronto 3

4   Rangers 4 at Toronto 5

5   Toronto 1 at Chicago 3

11   Chicago 2 at Toronto 2

12   Toronto 5 at Boston 0 [Bower]

16   Toronto 2 at Montreal 5

18   Boston 2 at Toronto 6

19   Toronto 2 at Rangers 2

1961–62

OCTOBER

12   Toronto 4 at Detroit 2 (Duff 19:51—EN)

14   Boston 2 at Toronto 3*

15   Toronto 1 at Rangers 2

21   Chicago 1 at Toronto 1

22   Toronto 9 at Boston 1

28   Rangers 1 at Toronto 5

29   Toronto 2 at Rangers 4

* Puck dropped by Prime Minister Louis St. Laurent.

NOVEMBER

1   Montreal 2 at Toronto 3

4   Chicago 1 at Toronto 2

5   Toronto 3 at Detroit 2

7   Toronto 0 at Chicago 6 [Hall]

9   Toronto 2 at Montreal 5

11   Detroit 1 at Toronto 5

12   Toronto 3 at Boston 4

15   Montreal 2 at Toronto 3

18   Detroit 1 at Toronto 6

19   Toronto 3 at Rangers 5 (Ingarfield 19:10—EN)

23   Toronto 5 at Chicago 2

25   Rangers 0 at Toronto 6 [Bower]

26   Toronto 4 at Boston 1 (Stewart 19:48—EN)

29   Montreal 2 at Toronto 2

30   Toronto 1 at Montreal 1

DECEMBER

2   Chicago 4 at Toronto 6

3   Toronto 1 at Detroit 3 (Ullman 19:48—EN)

7   Toronto 1 at Montreal 4

9   Boston 2 at Toronto 9

10   Toronto 3 at Rangers 2

16   Rangers 2 at Toronto 4

17   Toronto 4 at Boston 1 (Keon 19:50—EN)

23   Boston 7 at Toronto 4

25   Toronto 3 at Chicago 3

27   Chicago 0 at Toronto 0 [Hall (C)/Bower (T)]

30   Detroit 4 at Toronto 6

31   Toronto 2 at Detroit 4

JANUARY

3   Montreal 1 at Toronto 3

6   Chicago 3 at Toronto 6

7   Toronto 4 at Rangers 3

10   Boston 5 at Toronto 7

11   Toronto 2 at Montreal 4

13   Detroit 3 at Toronto 4

14   Toronto 2 at Chicago 2

17   Rangers 2 at Toronto 4

20   Boston 5 at Toronto 4

21   Toronto 5 at Boston 1

24   Toronto 1 at Chicago 2

27   Detroit 2 at Toronto 4

28   Toronto 2 at Detroit 2

FEBRUARY

1   Toronto 2 at Montreal 5

3   Rangers 1 at Toronto 4

4   Toronto 1 at Chicago 2

7   Boston 2 at Toronto 2

10   Montreal 4 at Toronto 2

11   Toronto 0 at Detroit 5 [Bassen]

17   Rangers 3 at Toronto 5

18   Toronto 2 at Rangers 6

21   Montreal 4 at Toronto 2

24   Boston 2 at Toronto 7

25   Toronto 8 at Detroit 2

28   Chicago 2 at Toronto 4

MARCH

3   Rangers 1 at Toronto 3 (Kelly 19:37—EN)

4   Toronto 5 at Boston 1

8   Toronto 1 at Montreal 1

10   Detroit 0 at Toronto 2 [Simmons]

11   Toronto 3 at Chicago 2

14   Montreal 2 at Toronto 5

17   Chicago 3 at Toronto 1

18   Toronto 2 at Rangers 2

22   Toronto 1 at Montreal 4

24   Detroit 2 at Toronto 2

25   Toronto 4 at Boston 5

1962–63

OCTOBER

10   Toronto 3 at Chicago 1

13   Boston 2 at Toronto 2

14   Toronto 3 at Rangers 5

18   Toronto 2 at Montreal 4

20   Chicago 1 at Toronto 3 (Armstrong 19:57—EN)

21   Toronto 6 at Boston 4 (Mahovlich 19:17—EN)

27   Rangers 5 at Toronto 1

28   Toronto 0 at Detroit 2 [Sawchuk] (Howe 19:27—EN)

31   Montreal 4 at Toronto 3

NOVEMBER

1   Toronto 3 at Montreal 1

3   Detroit 7 at Toronto 3

7   Toronto 5 at Rangers 1

10   Rangers 3 at Toronto 5

11   Toronto 5 at Chicago 3

14   Montreal 2 at Toronto 4

17   Detroit 2 at Toronto 3

18   Toronto 1 at Rangers 3

22   Toronto 0 at Chicago 1 [Hall]

24   Rangers 1 at Toronto 4

25   Toronto 2 at Boston 5

29   Toronto 4 at Montreal 4

DECEMBER

1   Boston 2 at Toronto 8

2   Toronto 3 at Detroit 1 (Pulford 19:54—EN)

5   Montreal 1 at Toronto 2

8   Chicago 1 at Toronto 1 (both goals in 2nd)

9   Toronto 3 at Detroit 4

15   Boston 2 at Toronto 8

16   Toronto 6 at Chicago 2

20   Toronto 4 at Montreal 4

22   Rangers 2 at Toronto 4 (Keon 19:46—EN)

23   Toronto 5 at Boston 4

25   Toronto 1 at Detroit 2

26   Detroit 4 at Toronto 5

29   Chicago 1 at Toronto 1

JANUARY

1   Toronto 0 at Boston 3 [Johnston]

2   Toronto 2 at Rangers 3

5   Boston 2 at Toronto 4

6   Toronto 5 at Chicago 1

9   Chicago 3 at Toronto 1

12   Detroit 1 at Toronto 2

13   Toronto 2 at Boston 2

17   Toronto 4 at Montreal 6

19   Chicago 4 at Toronto 1

20   Toronto 2 at Detroit 2

23   Montreal 1 at Toronto 5

24   Toronto 6 at Boston 3

26   Boston 5 at Toronto 2 (Boivin 18:33—EN)

27   Toronto 4 at Rangers 2

31   Toronto 6 at Montreal 3

FEBRUARY

2   Rangers 2 at Toronto 2

3   Toronto 1 at Chicago 3

9   Montreal 3 at Toronto 3 (H. Richard tied game at 19:02 with goalie out)

10   Toronto 1 at Detroit 2

13   Detroit 2 at Toronto 6

16   Rangers 2 at Toronto 4

17   Toronto 1 at Rangers 4

20   Montreal 1 at Toronto 2 (all goals in 2nd)

23   Boston 4 at Toronto 2

27   Chicago 3 at Toronto 6

MARCH

2   Rangers 3 at Toronto 4

3   Toronto 6 at Boston 3

6   Boston 0 at Toronto 4 [Bower]

9   Detroit 3 at Toronto 5

10   Toronto 1 at Chicago 1 (both goals in 3rd)

14   Toronto 3 at Montreal 3

16   Chicago 0 at Toronto 3 [Simmons]

17   Toronto 2 at Rangers 1

20   Montreal 3 at Toronto 3 (Keon tied game at 19:52 with goalie out)

23   Detroit 2 at Toronto 1

24   Toronto 2 at Detroit 3

1963–64

OCTOBER

12   Boston 1 at Toronto 5

13   Toronto 2 at Chicago 4

16   Toronto 4 at Montreal 2

19   Detroit 1 at Toronto 2

20   Toronto 2 at Detroit 3

26   Rangers 4 at Toronto 6

27   Toronto 0 at Boston 2 [Johnston]

30   Montreal 3 at Toronto 6

NOVEMBER

2   Chicago 2 at Toronto 0 [Hall]

7   Toronto 4 at Boston 3

9   Chicago 3 at Toronto 3

13   Toronto 2 at Montreal 2

14   Toronto 5 at Rangers 4

16   Rangers 4 at Toronto 5

17   Toronto 0 at Chicago 6 [Hall]

20   Montreal 3 at Toronto 1

23   Boston 1 at Toronto 4

24   Toronto 3 at Rangers 3

28   Toronto 0 at Chicago 2 [Hall]

30   Detroit 1 at Toronto 1

DECEMBER

1   Toronto 4 at Detroit 1

4   Montreal 0 at Toronto 3 [Simmons]

7   Chicago 0 at Toronto 3 [Simmons]

8   Toronto 5 at Detroit 3

11   Detroit 3 at Toronto 1

14   Rangers 3 at Toronto 5

15   Toronto 4 at Boston 4

18   Toronto 3 at Montreal 7

21   Detroit 0 at Toronto 2 [Bower]

22   Toronto 1 at Rangers 1

25   Toronto 5 at Boston 1

28   Boston 0 at Toronto 2 [Bower]

29   Toronto 0 at Chicago 2 [Hall]

31   Toronto 5 at Detroit 4

JANUARY

4   Chicago 0 at Toronto 3 [Bower]*

5   Toronto 2 at Rangers 3

8   Montreal 1 at Toronto 6

11   Boston 1 at Toronto 3

12   Toronto 3 at Boston 6 (Boivin 19:41—EN)

15   Rangers 5 at Toronto 4

18   Boston 11 at Toronto 0 [Johnston]

19   Toronto 2 at Chicago 0 [Simmons]

22   Montreal 3 at Toronto 0 [Hodge]

25   Rangers 1 at Toronto 1

26   Toronto 0 at Boston 2 [Johnston]

29   Toronto 1 at Montreal 2

* Chicago's Howie Young was suspended five games for using bad language.

FEBRUARY

1   Boston 1 at Toronto 5

2   Toronto 2 at Detroit 2

5   Montreal 2 at Toronto 0 [Hodge]

8   Chicago 3 at Toronto 3 (Keon [T] tied game at 19:12 with goalie out)

9   Toronto 1 at Chicago 2

12   Toronto 0 at Montreal 4 [Hodge]

15   Chicago 0 at Toronto 4 [Bower]

16   Toronto 2 at Rangers 4 (Ingarfield 19:32—EN)

19   Detroit 1 at Toronto 1

22   Rangers 2 at Toronto 5

23   Toronto 4 at Rangers 3 (Keon won game at 19:32)

26   Toronto 0 at Montreal 1 [Hodge]

29   Chicago 1 at Toronto 4

MARCH

1   Toronto 3 at Boston 5

3   Toronto 2 at Detroit 3

4   Boston 4 at Toronto 4 (Kelly [T] tied game at 19:39 with goalie out)

7   Detroit 2 at Toronto 4

8   Toronto 3 at Chicago 4

11   Montreal 0 at Toronto 1 [Bower]

14   Rangers 3 at Toronto 7

15   Toronto 3 at Rangers 1

18   Toronto 2 at Montreal 2

21   Detroit 3 at Toronto 5

22   Toronto 4 at Detroit 1

1964–65

OCTOBER

15   Toronto 5 at Detroit 3

17   Boston 2 at Toronto 7

18   Toronto 3 at Rangers 3

22   Toronto 2 at Boston 2

24   Rangers 1 at Toronto 1

27   Toronto 3 at Chicago 2

28   Montreal 5 at Toronto 2

31   Chicago 1 at Toronto 5

NOVEMBER

1   Toronto 2 at Detroit 4

5   Toronto 2 at Montreal 2

7   Rangers 1 at Toronto 0 [Plante]

11   Detroit 1 at Toronto 3 (Pulford 19:51—EN)

14   Boston 3 at Toronto 1

15   Toronto 2 at Chicago 4

18   Montreal 1 at Toronto 3

21   Chicago 0 at Toronto 1 [Sawchuk]

22   Toronto 3 at Boston 1

25   Toronto 3 at Rangers 6

26   Toronto 4 at Chicago 2

28   Rangers 4 at Toronto 1

29   Toronto 1 at Detroit 1

DECEMBER

3   Toronto 2 at Montreal 4

5   Detroit 2 at Toronto 10

9   Montreal 3 at Toronto 2

12   Boston 3 at Toronto 6

13   Toronto 3 at Rangers 3 (Ellis [T] tied game at 19:59 with goalie out)

17   Toronto 2 at Montreal 2

19   Rangers 3 at Toronto 6

20   Toronto 1 at Detroit 3

25   Toronto 3 at Chicago 3

26   Chicago 5 at Toronto 3

30   Montreal 4 at Toronto 3

JANUARY

1   Toronto 0 at Boston 3 [Johnston]

2   Detroit 1 at Toronto 3

3   Toronto 3 at Rangers 3

6   Toronto 3 at Chicago 1

9   Boston 1 at Toronto 2

10   Toronto 6 at Rangers 0 [Bower]

13   Chicago 0 at Toronto 0 [DeJordy (C)/Bower (T)]

14   Toronto 5 at Montreal 3

16   Detroit 4 at Toronto 2

17   Toronto 3 at Boston 1

20   Montreal 2 at Toronto 1

23   Rangers 1 at Toronto 1

24   Toronto 1 at Detroit 4

30   Boston 1 at Toronto 6

31   Toronto 4 at Boston 2

FEBRUARY

4   Toronto 5 at Montreal 2

6   Chicago 6 at Toronto 3

7   Toronto 2 at Chicago 1

10   Montreal 2 at Toronto 6

13   Detroit 1 at Toronto 2

14   Toronto 2 at Boston 2

20   Chicago 3 at Toronto 4

21   Toronto 2 at Detroit 3

24   Boston 3 at Toronto 1

27   Rangers 4 at Toronto 3

28   Toronto 2 at Rangers 6

MARCH

4   Toronto 2 at Montreal 2

6   Chicago 1 at Toronto 4

7   Toronto 3 at Boston 3

10   Detroit 4 at Toronto 2

13   Boston 2 at Toronto 0 [Norris]

14   Toronto 3 at Chicago 5

18   Toronto 1 at Montreal 4

20   Rangers 1 at Toronto 4

21   Toronto 10 at Rangers 1

24   Montreal 2 at Toronto 3

27   Detroit 4 at Toronto 1

28   Toronto 4 at Detroit 0 [Bower] (Keon 19:57—EN)

1965–66

OCTOBER

23   Chicago 4 at Toronto 0 [Hall]

24   Toronto 0 at Detroit 3 [Crozier]

27   Toronto 2 at Boston 1

30   Detroit 3 at Toronto 4

NOVEMBER

3   Toronto 2 at Rangers 2

4   Toronto 1 at Montreal 5

6   Rangers 4 at Toronto 2

7   Toronto 0 at Chicago 9 [Hall]

10   Montreal 3 at Toronto 3

13   Rangers 2 at Toronto 5

14   Toronto 0 at Boston 2 [Parent]

18   Toronto 3 at Montreal 1 (Pulford 19:34—EN)

20   Chicago 1 at Toronto 3

21   Toronto 7 at Chicago 3

24   Montreal 2 at Toronto 1

27   Boston 2 at Toronto 1

28   Toronto 4 at Rangers 2 (Pulford 19:20—EN)

DECEMBER

1   Toronto 2 at Rangers 2

4   Detroit 5 at Toronto 3 (Henderson 19:58—EN)

5   Toronto 1 at Detroit 5

11   Boston 3 at Toronto 8

12   Toronto 1 at Rangers 1

15   Detroit 3 at Toronto 5

16   Toronto 3 at Montreal 2

18   Rangers 4 at Toronto 8

19   Toronto 3 at Boston 1

25   Chicago 3 at Toronto 5

26   Toronto 1 at Chicago 1

29   Montreal 2 at Toronto 3

JANUARY

1   Boston 3 at Toronto 6

2   Toronto 0 at Detroit 4 [Crozier]

8   Detroit 3 at Toronto 1

9   Toronto 3 at Chicago 5 (Nesterenko 19:48—EN)

13   Toronto 6 at Montreal 0 [Bower]

15   Boston 1 at Toronto 6

16   Toronto 0 at Detroit 4 [Crozier]

19   Rangers 2 at Toronto 6

22   Chicago 0 at Toronto 4 [Bower]

23   Toronto 1 at Boston 2

29   Boston 3 at Toronto 6

30   Toronto 4 at Rangers 8

FEBRUARY

3   Toronto 4 at Montreal 5

5   Chicago 2 at Toronto 5

6   Toronto 2 at Chicago 3

9   Rangers 0 at Toronto 3 [Sawchuk]

12   Detroit 3 at Toronto 3 (Henderson (D) tied game at 19:59 with goalie out)

13   Toronto 4 at Boston 4

16   Montreal 1 at Toronto 3

19   Rangers 3 at Toronto 1

20   Toronto 1 at Detroit 4

23   Toronto 3 at Chicago 2

26   Boston 2 at Toronto 3

27   Toronto 2 at Rangers 2

MARCH

2   Montreal 3 at Toronto 3

3   Toronto 4 at Montreal 0 [Gamble]

5   Chicago 0 at Toronto 5 [Gamble]

6   Toronto 5 at Boston 3

9   Detroit 0 at Toronto 1 [Gamble]

12   Boston 0 at Toronto 6 [Gamble]

13   Toronto 1 at Chicago 5

16   Montreal 7 at Toronto 2

19   Chicago 2 at Toronto 4*

20   Toronto 1 at Detroit 6

24   Toronto 2 at Montreal 0 [Bower]

26   Detroit 1 at Toronto 3

27   Toronto 5 at Rangers 1

30   Montreal 3 at Toronto 1

31   Toronto 1 at Boston 3**

* Toronto's Kent Douglas was suspended for two games for swinging at linesman John D'Amico.

** Johnny Bower and Terry Sawchuk alternated in goal several times during this game.

APRIL

2   Rangers 3 at Toronto 3*

3   Toronto 3 at Detroit 3**

* Terry Sawchuk and Bruce Gamble alternated many times in goal during this game.

** Leafs used three goalies: Johnny Bower (first), Terry Sawchuk (second), Bruce Gamble (third). Bower was alleged to have had the flu after the first, thus allowing a third goalie to dress. He was later well enough to coach the third period while Punch Imlach watched the end of the game from the stands.

1966–67

OCTOBER

22   Rangers 4 at Toronto 4*

23   Toronto 0 at Rangers 1 [Giacomin]

26   Detroit 2 at Toronto 3

29   Boston 3 at Toronto 3

* John P. Robarts, premier of Ontario, dropped the first puck.

NOVEMBER

2 Montreal 2 at Toronto 2

3 Toronto 2 at Detroit 2

5 Rangers 1 at Toronto 3 (Conacher 19:58—EN)

6 Toronto 3 at Rangers 3

9 Toronto 3 at Montreal 2

10 Toronto 0 at Boston 4 [Cheevers]

12 Toronto 3 at Detroit 3

13 Toronto 1 at Chicago 6

19 Montreal 1 at Toronto 5

20 Toronto 2 at Chicago 2

23 Chicago 3 at Toronto 6*

26 Boston 2 at Toronto 4

27 Toronto 0 at Rangers 5 [Giacomin]

30 Montreal 2 at Toronto 3

* Glenn Hall replaced Denis DeJordy in Chicago goal for a penalty shot only.

DECEMBER

3 Detroit 2 at Toronto 5

4 Toronto 8 at Boston 3

7 Toronto 3 at Montreal 6

10 Chicago 3 at Toronto 5

11 Toronto 1 at Detroit 4 (Howe 19:48—EN)

14 Boston 1 at Toronto 2

17 Rangers 3 at Toronto 1

18 Toronto 1 at Chicago 3

21 Toronto 2 at Montreal 6

24 Boston 0 at Toronto 3 [Bower]

25 Toronto 4 at Boston 2

31 Chicago 5 at Toronto 1

JANUARY

1 Toronto 2 at Rangers 1

4 Rangers 1 at Toronto 1

7 Boston 2 at Toronto 5

8 Toronto 1 at Detroit 3

11 Toronto 2 at Montreal 1

14 Detroit 2 at Toronto 5

15 Toronto 0 at Chicago 4 [DeJordy]

19 Toronto 2 at Detroit 6

21 Detroit 5 at Toronto 4

22 Toronto 1 at Boston 3 (Westfall 19:40—EN)

25 Montreal 3 at Toronto 1

28 Chicago 5 at Toronto 2

29 Toronto 1 at Chicago 5

FEBRUARY

1 Toronto 1 at Montreal 7

5 Toronto 1 at Rangers 4

8 Detroit 5 at Toronto 2

11 Chicago 4 at Toronto 4

12 Toronto 2 at Boston 1

15 Rangers 0 at Toronto 6 [Bower]

18 Boston 3 at Toronto 5*

22 Montreal 2 at Toronto 5

23 Toronto 4 at Detroit 2

25 Detroit 0 at Toronto 4 [Sawchuk]

26 Toronto 4 at Rangers 2

* King Clancy took over as coach temporarily from this game until March 12.

MARCH

1 Toronto 1 at Montreal 1 (Pappin [T] tied game at 19:11 with goalie out)

4 Chicago 0 at Toronto 3 [Sawchuk]*

5 Toronto 2 at Chicago 5

8 Montreal 4 at Toronto 6

11 Rangers 2 at Toronto 2

12 Toronto 0 at Chicago 5 [Hall]**

15 Detroit 4 at Toronto 2

18 Chicago 5 at Toronto 9

19 Toronto 6 at Detroit 5***

22 Montreal 5 at Toronto 3

23 Toronto 5 at Boston 3

25 Boston 3 at Toronto 4

26 Toronto 0 at Rangers 4 [Giacomin]

29 Toronto 3 at Montreal 5

* Terry Sawchuk's 100th career shutout.
** Afternoon game. Punch Imlach returned as coach.
*** Afternoon game.

APRIL

1 Rangers 1 at Toronto 5

2 Toronto 5 at Boston 2

1967–68

During this season, Punch Imlach fined each player $100 for every home loss to an expansion team.

OCTOBER

14 Chicago 1 at Toronto 5*

15 Toronto 5 at Chicago 3 (Mahovlich 19:05—EN)

18 Detroit 3 at Toronto 2

19 Toronto 0 at Montreal 1 [Worsley]

21 Rangers 5 at Toronto 3

25 Los Angeles 2 at Toronto 4

28 Oakland 2 at Toronto 5

29 Toronto 2 at Rangers 3

* Robert Stanfield, leader of the official Opposition in Parliament, was present at the opening ceremony.

NOVEMBER

1 Montreal 0 at Toronto 5 [Bower]

2 Toronto 9 at Detroit 3

4 Rangers 2 at Toronto 4

5 Toronto 2 at Boston 2

8   Toronto 6 at Oakland 1

9   Toronto 1 at Los Angeles 4 (Joyal 18:32—EN)

11 Toronto 1 at North Stars 2

15 Boston 2 at Toronto 4

18 Chicago 2 at Toronto 2

19 Toronto 2 at Boston 6

22 North Stars 0 at Toronto 3 [Gamble]

25 Detroit 2 at Toronto 3

29 Montreal 1 at Toronto 2

30 Toronto 3 at Detroit 3

DECEMBER

2   Oakland 0 at Toronto 3 [Bower]

6   Toronto 1 at North Stars 1

9   Boston 3 at Toronto 3 (Armstrong [T] tied game at 19:57 with goalie out)

10 Toronto 1 at St. Louis 2

13 Pittsburgh 2 at Toronto 1

16 Rangers 2 at Toronto 4

17 Toronto 0 at Chicago 2 [DeJordy] (Mohns 19:12—EN)

20 Toronto 0 at Montreal 5 [Worsley]

23 Detroit 3 at Toronto 5

25 Toronto 3 at Detroit 1

27 Montreal 2 at Toronto 2

30 St. Louis 1 at Toronto 8

31 Toronto 0 at Rangers 4 [Giacomin]

JANUARY

3   Toronto 1 at Montreal 1

6   Boston 3 at Toronto 3

7   Toronto 2 at Rangers 6

10 Detroit 1 at Toronto 2

12 Toronto 3 at Pittsburgh 4

13 Pittsburgh 0 at Toronto 7 [Gamble]*

18 Toronto 4 at Boston 2

20 North Stars 1 at Toronto 5

21 Toronto 2 at Detroit 0 [Gamble]

24 Philadelphia 2 at Toronto 1

27 Chicago 4 at Toronto 1

28 Toronto 3 at Chicago 1 (Pulford 19:47—EN)

30 Toronto 0 at Montreal 3 [Vachon]

* Afternoon game.

FEBRUARY

3   Toronto 3 at Pittsburgh 3

4   Toronto 1 at Philadelphia 4

7   Toronto 2 at Chicago 3

11 Toronto 3 at Oakland 4

12 Toronto 0 at Los Angeles 2 [Rutledge]

14 Montreal 4 at Toronto 2 (Béliveau 19:46—EN)

17 Rangers 3 at Toronto 2

21 St. Louis 5 at Toronto 1

24 Boston 0 at Toronto 1 [Gamble]

25 Toronto 1 at Rangers 3 (Goyette 19:59—EN)*

28 Chicago 1 at Toronto 0 [DeJordy]

29 Toronto 1 at Boston 4

* Afternoon game.

MARCH

On March 7, 1968, Boston and Philadelphia played a game at Maple Leaf Gardens as the Spectrum roof had been badly damaged and the arena rendered unusable.

2   Los Angeles 2 at Toronto 5

6   Philadelphia 2 at Toronto 7

9   Detroit 5 at Toronto 7

10 Toronto 0 at Chicago 4 [Norris] (Martin 18:28—EN)*

13 Toronto 3 at St. Louis 3

16 Boston 0 at Toronto 3 [Gamble]

17 Toronto 4 at Philadelphia 7 (Sutherland 19:08—EN/Gauthier 19:41—EN)*

20 Toronto 2 at Montreal 3

21 Toronto 5 at Detroit 2

23 Rangers 1 at Toronto 3

24 Toronto 2 at Rangers 4

27 Montreal 0 at Toronto 6 [Bower]

30 Chicago 0 at Toronto 3 [Bower]

31 Toronto 4 at Boston 1

* Afternoon games.

1968–69

OCTOBER

13 Toronto 2 at Detroit 1

16 Pittsburgh 2 at Toronto 2*

19 Chicago 3 at Toronto 1

23 St. Louis 4 at Toronto 6

26 Boston 0 at Toronto 2 [Bower]

27 Toronto 5 at Rangers 3

30 Montreal 5 at Toronto 0 [Vachon]

* William Davis, Ontario minister of education, was present for the opening ceremony.

NOVEMBER

2   Philadelphia 3 at Toronto 2

6   Toronto 1 at North Stars 0 [Gamble]

9   Toronto 1 at Los Angeles 3 (Irvine 19:29—EN)

10 Toronto 3 at Oakland 1

13 Boston 1 at Toronto 1

14 Toronto 5 at Montreal 3

16 Chicago 1 at Toronto 3

17 Toronto 1 at Chicago 1

20 Pittsburgh 2 at Toronto 5 (Keon 19:38—EN)

23 Detroit 5 at Toronto 2

24 Toronto 4 at Boston 7

27 Toronto 3 at Pittsburgh 3

30 North Stars 3 at Toronto 3

DECEMBER

1	Toronto 1 at Rangers 3
4	Toronto 4 at North Stars 2
7	Rangers 2 at Toronto 5
8	Toronto 4 at Pittsburgh 1
11	Montreal 4 at Toronto 4
12	Toronto 1 at Philadelphia 0 [Bower]
14	St. Louis 2 at Toronto 3
18	Oakland 2 at Toronto 5
21	Detroit 3 at Toronto 8
22	Toronto 2 at Detroit 3
25	Toronto 4 at Chicago 3
26	Toronto 2 at Montreal 4
28	Los Angeles 4 at Toronto 1

JANUARY

1	Oakland 3 at Toronto 7
4	Rangers 3 at Toronto 5
5	Toronto 2 at Philadelphia 2
8	Philadelphia 4 at Toronto 4
9	Toronto 2 at Boston 3
11	Los Angeles 2 at Toronto 4
15	Boston 5 at Toronto 5
18	Detroit 1 at Toronto 1
19	Toronto 3 at Boston 5*
23	Toronto 3 at St. Louis 2
25	Toronto 2 at Pittsburgh 0 [Gamble]
26	Toronto 2 at Detroit 3
29	Toronto 1 at Los Angeles 3
31	Toronto 4 at Oakland 5

* Afternoon game. Johnny Bower, who replaced Bruce Gamble in the third, wore a mask for the first time.

FEBRUARY

2	Toronto 3 at St. Louis 5
5	North Stars 5 at Toronto 5
8	Oakland 4 at Toronto 1
9	Toronto 5 at Chicago 3
12	North Stars 1 at Toronto 7
15	Rangers 2 at Toronto 6
16	Toronto 2 at Rangers 4 (Balon 19:31—EN)
19	Montreal 1 at Toronto 5
20	Toronto 1 at Montreal 2
22	Chicago 4 at Toronto 2
23	Toronto 2 at North Stars 7*
26	St. Louis 2 at Toronto 3
27	Toronto 1 at Philadelphia 1

* Afternoon game.

MARCH

1	Pittsburgh 3 at Toronto 3
2	Chicago 1 at Toronto 2*

5	Los Angeles 4 at Toronto 6
6	Toronto 3 at Montreal 5
8	Philadelphia 2 at Toronto 2
12	Toronto 4 at Los Angeles 0 [Gamble]
13	Toronto 3 at Oakland 1
15	Boston 4 at Toronto 7
16	Toronto 3 at Boston 11
19	Toronto 1 at St. Louis 1
22	Detroit 1 at Toronto 3
23	Toronto 1 at Chicago 4
26	Montreal 4 at Toronto 6
27	Toronto 4 at Detroit 2
29·	Rangers 4 at Toronto 2 (Stewart 16:35—EN)
30	Toronto 0 at Rangers 4 [Giacomin]

* Afternoon game. Bruce Gamble and Johnny Bower alternated in goal all game.

1969–70

OCTOBER

11	Toronto 2 at Detroit 3
15	Montreal 2 at Toronto 2*
18	Chicago 1 at Toronto 4
19	Toronto 0 at Rangers 1 [Giacomin]
22	Philadelphia 4 at Toronto 3
25	St. Louis 2 at Toronto 4
29	Boston 2 at Toronto 4

* Foster Hewitt dropped the first puck.

NOVEMBER

1	Rangers 3 at Toronto 2
2	Toronto 4 at Boston 4
4	Toronto 5 at Oakland 2
5	Toronto 2 at Los Angeles 6
8	Toronto 3 at Montreal 6
9	Toronto 0 at Chicago 9 [Esposito]
12	Pittsburgh 3 at Toronto 0 [Binkley] (McCreary 19:41—EN)
15	Philadelphia 2 at Toronto 4 (Pulford 19:21—EN)
19	Los Angeles 4 at Toronto 4
22	Detroit 0 at Toronto 4 [Gamble]
23	Toronto 3 at Philadelphia 2
26	Montreal 3 at Toronto 1
29	North Stars 2 at Toronto 5
30	Toronto 1 at Boston 4

DECEMBER

3	Toronto 5 at North Stars 5
6	Pittsburgh 0 at Toronto 5 [Gamble]
7	Toronto 2 at Pittsburgh 3
10	Toronto 3 at Montreal 6 (Provost 19:54—EN)
11	Toronto 3 at Philadelphia 6
13	Detroit 3 at Toronto 1

14 Toronto 3 at Rangers 1

20 Rangers 5 at Toronto 2

21 Toronto 3 at Detroit 0 [Gamble]

24 Los Angeles 1 at Toronto 8

26 Toronto 1 at St. Louis 3

27 St. Louis 1 at Toronto 4

31 Oakland 1 at Toronto 1

JANUARY

3   Chicago 2 at Toronto 6

4   Toronto 4 at Pittsburgh 4

7   North Stars 3 at Toronto 3

10 Boston 3 at Toronto 4

14 Rangers 7 at Toronto 1

15 Toronto 0 at St. Louis 2 [Wakely]

17 Pittsburgh 0 at Toronto 4 [Gamble]

22 Toronto 3 at Los Angeles 2

23 Toronto 3 at Oakland 6

25 Toronto 3 at Chicago 2

28 Toronto 4 at Pittsburgh 4

31 Toronto 4 at North Stars 2

FEBRUARY

1   Toronto 6 at Boston 7*

4   St. Louis 0 at Toronto 1 [Gamble]

5   Toronto 1 at Detroit 4

7   Oakland 1 at Toronto 5

11 Toronto 3 at Montreal 3

12 Toronto 3 at Philadelphia 3

14 Philadelphia 3 at Toronto 4

15 Toronto 4 at Chicago 6

18 Montreal 3 at Toronto 5

21 Detroit 7 at Toronto 5

22 Toronto 3 at Rangers 5

25 Oakland 1 at Toronto 4

28 Los Angeles 3 at Toronto 3
* Afternoon game.

MARCH

1   Toronto 0 at North Stars 8 [Maniago]*

3   Toronto 4 at Oakland 1

5   Toronto 5 at Los Angeles 3

7   North Stars 8 at Toronto 3

11 Detroit 3 at Toronto 1

14 Boston 1 at Toronto 2

15 Montreal 3 at Toronto 3*

18 Chicago 7 at Toronto 4

21 Toronto 2 at St. Louis 0 [Edwards]

22 Toronto 5 at Rangers 2*

25 Toronto 2 at Montreal 5

28 Chicago 1 at Toronto 1

29 Toronto 0 at Chicago 4 [Esposito]
* Afternoon games.

APRIL

1   Rangers 2 at Toronto 1

2   Toronto 2 at Detroit 4

4   Boston 4 at Toronto 2

5   Toronto 1 at Boston 3

1970–71

OCTOBER

11 Toronto 3 at Vancouver 5*

14 St. Louis 3 at Toronto 7**

17 Rangers 6 at Toronto 2

18 Toronto 2 at Philadelphia 4

21 Toronto 2 at Rangers 3

24 Chicago 1 at Toronto 0 [Esposito]

28 Montreal 2 at Toronto 6

31 North Stars 3 at Toronto 1 (Burns 19:42—EN)
* Afternoon game.
** Clarence Campbell, NHL president, dropped the first puck.

NOVEMBER

1   Toronto 5 at Detroit 4

4   Toronto 2 at Los Angeles 3

6   Toronto 4 at California 8

7   Toronto 2 at Vancouver 3

11 Vancouver 4 at Toronto 2

14 Boston 2 at Toronto 3

15 Toronto 2 at Rangers 4 (Irvine 19:47—EN)

18 Buffalo 7 at Toronto 2

19 Toronto 1 at Montreal 5

21 California 3 at Toronto 5 (Henderson 19:16—EN)

24 Pittsburgh 4 at Toronto 4

26 Toronto 0 at St. Louis 1 [Wakely]

28 Detroit 4 at Toronto 9

29 Toronto 2 at Boston 4 (Orr 19:54—EN)

DECEMBER

2   Los Angeles 0 at Toronto 7 [Plante]

5   Rangers 1 at Toronto 0

6   Toronto 2 at Chicago 6

8   Toronto 0 at Pittsburgh 4 [Smith]

9   Montreal 0 at Toronto 4 [Gamble]

12 Chicago 1 at Toronto 2

13 Toronto 4 at Buffalo 0 [Gamble]

16 Toronto 4 at Pittsburgh 2

19 Buffalo 0 at Toronto 2 [Plante]

20 Toronto 4 at Buffalo 2 (Ullman 19:46—EN)

23   Vancouver 2 at Toronto 7

25   Toronto 3 at North Stars 6

26   Philadelphia 1 at Toronto 9

30   California 1 at Toronto 3

JANUARY

2   Detroit 0 at Toronto 13 [Plante/Gamble]*

5   Toronto 2 at North Stars 0 [Plante]

6   North Stars 4 at Toronto 4

9   Pittsburgh 2 at Toronto 5

10   Toronto 3 at Detroit 2

13   California 1 at Toronto 1

14   Toronto 0 at Philadelphia 3 [Favell]

16   Los Angeles 1 at Toronto 8

17   Toronto 1 at Boston 9

20   Toronto 5 at Vancouver 1

22   Toronto 2 at California 5

23   Toronto 2 at Los Angeles 3

27   Toronto 1 at Pittsburgh 3 (Pronovost 19:53—EN)

30   Toronto 5 at Montreal 4
* Bruce Gamble replaced Jacques Plante to begin the third period. They shared the shutout.

FEBRUARY

3   St. Louis 2 at Toronto 6

6   Philadelphia 2 at Toronto 4

7   Toronto 4 at Buffalo 3

9   Toronto 3 at St. Louis 3

10   Toronto 3 at Chicago 2

13   Los Angeles 1 at Toronto 8

14   Boston 5 at Toronto 1*

17   Pittsburgh 3 at Toronto 4

20   St. Louis 1 at Toronto 3 (Keon 19:55—EN)

21   Toronto 4 at North Stars 1

25   North Stars 1 at Toronto 1

27   Buffalo 0 at Toronto 2 [Plante]

28   Toronto 3 at Boston 4*
* Afternoon games.

MARCH

3   Vancouver 1 at Toronto 3 (Armstrong 19:46—EN)

5   Toronto 1 at St. Louis 3

6   Chicago 2 at Toronto 2

10   Montreal 1 at Toronto 2

13   Philadelphia 3 at Toronto 2

14   Toronto 0 at Rangers 1 [Giacomin]

18   Toronto 1 at Montreal 4

20   Rangers 1 at Toronto 3

21   Toronto 1 at Philadelphia 1

24   Toronto 6 at California 0 [Plante/Parent]

25   Toronto 3 at Los Angeles 5 (Howell 19:24—EN)

28   Toronto 1 at Detroit 2*

31   Detroit 2 at Toronto 2**
* Afternoon game.
** Gordie Howe Night.

APRIL

3   Boston 8 at Toronto 3

4   Toronto 3 at Chicago 2

1971–72

OCTOBER

8   Toronto 3 at Vancouver 2

10   Toronto 3 at California 3

13   Detroit at Toronto*

16   Rangers 5 at Toronto 3

17   Toronto 2 at Boston 2

20   Buffalo 7 at Toronto 2

22   Toronto 2 at Detroit 5

23   Philadelphia 3 at Toronto 5

27   Vancouver 0 at Toronto 0 [Wilson (V)/Parent (T)]

30   North Stars 1 at Toronto 1

31   Toronto 3 at Rangers 3
* Postponed to November 1 due to the death of Stafford Smythe.

NOVEMBER

1   Detroit 1 at Toronto 6*

3   Toronto 1 at North Stars 2

6   Toronto 3 at Los Angeles 2

7   Toronto 1 at California 8

10   Montreal 5 at Toronto 2

13   Vancouver 2 at Toronto 2

14   Toronto 3 at Philadelphia 3

17   Los Angeles 1 at Toronto 5

20   California 1 at Toronto 5

21   Toronto 4 at Buffalo 3

24   Toronto 2 at Pittsburgh 1

27   Chicago 3 at Toronto 3

28   Toronto 1 at Chicago 4
* Game rescheduled from October 13.

DECEMBER

1   St. Louis 2 at Toronto 4

4   Boston 5 at Toronto 3

8   North Stars 1 at Toronto 3

11   Chicago 3 at Toronto 1

12   Toronto 4 at Buffalo 2

14   Toronto 4 at St. Louis 2

15   Pittsburgh 2 at Toronto 3

18   Buffalo 1 at Toronto 8

19   Toronto 4 at Philadelphia 0 [Plante]

22 Toronto 2 at Montreal 4

25 Detroit 3 at Toronto 5

26 Toronto 1 at Boston 3 (Hodge 19:37—EN)

28 Toronto 4 at Pittsburgh 2 (Ullman 19:42—EN)

29 St. Louis 6 at Toronto 3

JANUARY

1   Montreal 2 at Toronto 5

5   Boston 2 at Toronto 0 [Johnston]

8   Philadelphia 2 at Toronto 2

9   Toronto 2 at Buffalo 1

12 Los Angeles 1 at Toronto 1

15 Rangers 3 at Toronto 4

16 St. Louis 4 at Toronto 3

19 Toronto 0 at Montreal 1 [Dryden]

22 Toronto 1 at North Stars 4

23 Toronto 0 at Chicago 4 [Esposito]

26 Toronto 3 at Los Angeles 5 (Widing 19:12—EN)

28 Toronto 0 at California 3 [Meloche]

29 Toronto 2 at Vancouver 5

FEBRUARY

1   Toronto 0 at Detroit 4 [Al Smith] (Berenson 19:43—EN)

2   North Stars 2 at Toronto 3

5   Philadelphia 3 at Toronto 1

6   Toronto 2 at Rangers 2

8   Toronto 2 at St. Louis 1

9   Pittsburgh 4 at Toronto 1

12 California 0 at Toronto 3 [Plante]

13 Toronto 1 at Chicago 3

16 Toronto 2 at Pittsburgh 4 (Pronovost 19:56—EN)

19 Buffalo 1 at Toronto 4

20 Toronto 1 at Philadelphia 3

22 Toronto 4 at Detroit 5

23 Pittsburgh 0 at Toronto 2 [Parent]

26 Vancouver 1 at Toronto 7

MARCH

1   Toronto 3 at St. Louis 1

4   Los Angeles 2 at Toronto 3

8   Detroit 1 at Toronto 5

11 California 1 at Toronto 2

12 Toronto 2 at North Stars 2*

15 Montreal 5 at Toronto 2

18 Chicago 2 at Toronto 2

19 Toronto 3 at Rangers 5

22 Toronto 3 at Montreal 3

24 Toronto 3 at Vancouver 5 (Schmautz 19:26—EN)

25 Toronto 4 at Los Angeles 0 [Parent]

29 Boston 1 at Toronto 4

* Afternoon game.

APRIL

1   Rangers 1 at Toronto 2

2   Toronto 4 at Boston 6 (Bailey 19:25—EN)

1972–73

OCTOBER

7   Chicago 3 at Toronto 1*

11 Montreal 2 at Toronto 2

14 Los Angeles 4 at Toronto 6

15 Toronto 2 at Buffalo 3

18 Pittsburgh 3 at Toronto 4

21 Detroit 3 at Toronto 1

22 Toronto 2 at Detroit 6

25 Toronto 4 at North Stars 3

28 Boston 3 at Toronto 2

29 Toronto 2 at Philadelphia 5

* King Clancy dropped the first puck.

NOVEMBER

1   Buffalo 1 at Toronto 7

4   St. Louis 2 at Toronto 4

5   Toronto 2 at Atlanta 2

8   Toronto 2 at Montreal 5 (P. Mahovlich 19:12—EN)

11 Toronto 0 at St. Louis 1 [Stephenson]

15 Atlanta 1 at Toronto 2

18 North Stars 4 at Toronto 4

19 Toronto 5 at Boston 6

22 Toronto 1 at North Stars 3

25 California 0 at Toronto 11 [Plante/Low]*

26 Toronto 4 at Rangers 7

28 Toronto 2 at St. Louis 4

29 Toronto 4 at Pittsburgh 7

* Ron Low replaced Jacques Plantes at 2:59 of the third period.

DECEMBER

2   Philadelphia 2 at Toronto 2

3   Toronto 3 at Detroit 0 [Plante]

5   Toronto 5 at Vancouver 2

9   Vancouver 5 at Toronto 5

10 Toronto 2 at Philadelphia 5

13 Rangers 4 at Toronto 3

16 Detroit 4 at Toronto 1

17 Toronto 0 at Buffalo 4 [D. Dryden]

20 Toronto 3 at Atlanta 5

23 Chicago 3 at Toronto 5

24 Toronto 1 at Chicago 5*

27 Pittsburgh 3 at Toronto 3

29 Toronto 4 at Pittsburgh 0 [Plante/Low]**

30 St. Louis 4 at Toronto 5

* Afternoon game.

** Plante played only 24 seconds, briefly replacing Low after he was stunned by a hard shot.

JANUARY

3   Montreal 8 at Toronto 4

6   Los Angeles 2 at Toronto 4 (Keon 19:54—EN)

7   California 0 at Toronto 4 [Low]

10   Islanders 2 at Toronto 4

12   Toronto 0 at Atlanta 1 [Bouchard]

13   Boston 4 at Toronto 1

16   Toronto 4 at Vancouver 6

17   Toronto 3 at California 3

20   Toronto 6 at Los Angeles 2

24   Toronto 2 at Pittsburgh 5

27   Toronto 2 at Montreal 4

28   Toronto 2 at Rangers 5

31   Islanders 3 at Toronto 5

FEBRUARY

1   Toronto 2 at Boston 5

3   Vancouver 2 at Toronto 1

6   Toronto 2 at Islanders 4

7   California 3 at Toronto 5 (Ellis 19:00—EN)

10   Los Angeles 4 at Toronto 2

14   Buffalo 3 at Toronto 2

17   Islanders 2 at Toronto 6

18   Montreal 2 at Toronto 1*

21   Atlanta 2 at Toronto 2

24   St. Louis 2 at Toronto 4

28   Vancouver 2 at Toronto 7

* Afternoon game.

MARCH

3   Chicago 3 at Toronto 3

4   Toronto 0 at Philadelphia 10 [Favell]

7   Toronto 1 at Montreal 4

8   Toronto 4 at Islanders 1

10   North Stars 3 at Toronto 4

11   Toronto 2 at Rangers 4*

14   Philadelphia 1 at Toronto 5

15   Toronto 2 at North Stars 5

17   Rangers 5 at Toronto 7

18   Toronto 1 at Buffalo 5

21   Toronto 1 at Los Angeles 5

23   Toronto 4 at California 7

25   Toronto 4 at Vancouver 7*

27   Detroit 8 at Toronto 1

29   Toronto 6 at Detroit 4

31   Boston 3 at Toronto 7

* Afternoon games.

APRIL

1   Toronto 4 at Chicago 4

1973–74

OCTOBER

10   Buffalo 4 at Toronto 7*

11   Toronto 0 at Philadelphia 2 [Parent]

13   Los Angeles 3 at Toronto 6

17   Toronto 5 at Montreal 3 (Jarry 19:55—EN)

20   Rangers 2 at Toronto 3

21   Toronto 3 at Buffalo 4

23   North Stars 2 at Toronto 2

27   Boston 3 at Toronto 2

28   Toronto 1 at Chicago 1

30   Detroit 0 at Toronto 7 [Johnston]

* To acknowledge the first Swedes to play for the Leafs—Borje Salming and Inge Hammarstrom—the Swedish ambassador to Canada, Ake Malmaeus, dropped the first puck.

NOVEMBER

1   Toronto 2 at Islanders 2

3   Pittsburgh 0 at Toronto 6 [Wilson]

7   Montreal 4 at Toronto 1

10   Islanders 3 at Toronto 3

11   Toronto 4 at Detroit 5

14   Toronto 4 at California 1

16   Toronto 3 at Vancouver 3

17   Toronto 4 at Los Angeles 3

20   Toronto 4 at Islanders 2 (Keon 19:55—EN)

22   Pittsburgh 4 at Toronto 2 (Pronovost 19:42—EN)

24   Chicago 3 at Toronto 1

28   Toronto 4 at Pittsburgh 3

29   St. Louis 1 at Toronto 5

DECEMBER

1   California 2 at Toronto 3

2   Toronto 4 at Rangers 6

6   Toronto 4 at North Stars 1

8   Philadelphia 3 at Toronto 1

9   Toronto 2 at Buffalo 5

11   Toronto 3 at St. Louis 7

13   Toronto 6 at Atlanta 1

15   Rangers 2 at Toronto 2

19   California 3 at Toronto 5

22   Vancouver 6 at Toronto 4 (Lever 19:27—EN)

23   Toronto 3 at Boston 4

26   Montreal 2 at Toronto 9

29   Atlanta 3 at Toronto 3

30   Toronto 4 at Chicago 3

JANUARY

2   Detroit 3 at Toronto 4

5   Toronto 3 at Los Angeles 5 (Goring 19:46—EN)

7   Atlanta 2 at Toronto 6

9   Toronto 6 at Pittsburgh 4

12   St. Louis 2 at Toronto 4

15   Toronto 2 at Vancouver 4

16   Toronto 5 at California 5

19   Toronto 3 at North Stars 5

23   Toronto 3 at Montreal 4

26   Toronto 3 at St. Louis 3

27   Toronto 5 at Atlanta 2

31   North Stars 1 at Toronto 3

FEBRUARY

2   Boston 2 at Toronto 6

3   Toronto 3 at Buffalo 3

6   Detroit 2 at Toronto 2

9   North Stars 1 at Toronto 4

13   Philadelphia 3 at Toronto 1

16   Atlanta 2 at Toronto 7

17   Toronto 1 at Chicago 4

20   Buffalo 2 at Toronto 4

23   Vancouver 4 at Toronto 3

24   Los Angeles 3 at Toronto 3

26   Toronto 3 at Detroit 7

28   Toronto 6 at Islanders 4 (Henderson 19:31—EN)

MARCH

2   Islanders 2 at Toronto 5

3   Toronto 6 at Boston 4

7   Pittsburgh 2 at Toronto 2

9   Philadelphia 2 at Toronto 1

12   Toronto 1 at St. Louis 2

14   Islanders 1 at Toronto 2

16   Boston 5 at Toronto 2*

17   Toronto 2 at Philadelphia 2

19   Toronto 1 at Los Angeles 1

22   Toronto 3 at California 2

24   Toronto 2 at Vancouver 3*

27   Chicago 5 at Toronto 3 (Pappin 19:49—EN)

30   Rangers 3 at Toronto 7

31   Toronto 3 at Rangers 3*
* Afternoon games.

APRIL

3   Toronto 5 at Montreal 3

6   Buffalo 1 at Toronto 3 (Sittler 18:38—EN)

7   Toronto 4 at Boston 6 (Cashman 19:33—EN)*
* Keon fought with Gregg Sheppard; it was the only fight of Keon's career.

1974–75

OCTOBER

9   Kansas City 2 at Toronto 6*

12   Rangers 3 at Toronto 7

13   Toronto 2 at Boston 2

16   Los Angeles 1 at Toronto 1

19   Vancouver 5 at Toronto 4

20   Toronto 5 at Buffalo 5

23   Montreal 3 at Toronto 2

26   Chicago 9 at Toronto 3

27   Toronto 4 at Washington 3

29   St. Louis at Toronto**
* Gordon Sinclair dropped the first puck.
** Game postponed until November 25.

NOVEMBER

1   Toronto 2 at Atlanta 5

2   Buffalo 6 at Toronto 3

6   North Stars 4 at Toronto 7

9   Toronto 5 at North Stars 7

13   Toronto 0 at Los Angeles 4 [Vachon]

15   Toronto 5 at California 3

16   Toronto 2 at Vancouver 5

20   Pittsburgh 8 at Toronto 5

22   Toronto 0 at Islanders 6 [B. Smith]

23   Philadelphia 6 at Toronto 3

25   St. Louis 2 at Toronto 2*

27   Toronto 1 at Rangers 4

30   Washington 1 at Toronto 7
* Game rescheduled from October 29.

DECEMBER

1   Toronto at Detroit*

4   Toronto 2 at Pittsburgh 4 (Arnason 19:57—EN)

5   Toronto 3 at Islanders 3

7   Detroit 3 at Toronto 3

8   Toronto 4 at Chicago 1 (Stoughton 19:21—EN)

11   Los Angeles 4 at Toronto 1

14   Atlanta 2 at Toronto 4

15   Toronto 1 at Washington 3

18   Pittsburgh 4 at Toronto 6

19   Toronto 1 at Philadelphia 5

21   Boston 4 at Toronto 8

22   Toronto 0 at Chicago 3 [Esposito]

28   Islanders 1 at Toronto 3

30   Toronto 5 at Pittsburgh 7
* Game postponed until February 9 because of a snowstorm.

JANUARY

1   California 3 at Toronto 3

4   Chicago 3 at Toronto 6 (Thompson 19:18—EN)

5   Toronto 1 at Detroit 0 [Favell]

7   Toronto 3 at Islanders 5

8   Vancouver 4 at Toronto 6

11   Los Angeles 7 at Toronto 5 (St. Marseille 19:59—EN)

12   Islanders 3 at Toronto 4

15 Toronto 4 at St. Louis 1 (McDonald 19:52—EN)

18 Toronto 5 at Montreal 3 (Flett 19:28—EN)

19 Toronto 3 at Boston 6

23 Toronto 0 at Los Angeles 8 [Vachon]

24 Toronto 1 at California 6

26 Toronto 4 at Vancouver 6*

29 California 2 at Toronto 4

30 Toronto 1 at Philadelphia 3

* Afternoon game.

FEBRUARY

1   Boston 2 at Toronto 3

4   Toronto 5 at St. Louis 3

6   Toronto 2 at Kansas City 3

8   St. Louis 3 at Toronto 3

9   Toronto 3 at Detroit 5*

12 Montreal 2 at Toronto 2

15 Pittsburgh 8 at Toronto 3

16 Toronto 5 at Rangers 5

19 Toronto 3 at California 3

22 Rangers 2 at Toronto 5

23 Toronto 1 at Buffalo 4

25 Toronto 9 at North Stars 2

26 Kansas City 2 at Toronto 4

* Game rescheduled from December 1.

MARCH

1   Washington 4 at Toronto 5

2   Toronto 5 at Detroit 4

5   Detroit 3 at Toronto 4

8   North Stars 3 at Toronto 5

9   Toronto 4 at Washington 2

12 Montreal 3 at Toronto 3

15 Philadelphia 4 at Toronto 4

16 Buffalo 11 at Toronto 3

19 Toronto 7 at Atlanta 8 (Ecclestone 19:09—EN; Salming [T] 19:40 with goalie out)

22 Toronto 6 at Montreal 4

24 California 3 at Toronto 5 (Keon 19:57—EN)

26 Toronto 2 at Kansas City 2

29 Boston 1 at Toronto 1

30 Toronto 5 at Buffalo 4

APRIL

2   Atlanta 3 at Toronto 0 [Bouchard]

5   Buffalo 4 at Toronto 2

6   Boston 4 at Toronto 4

1975–76

OCTOBER

11 Chicago 1 at Toronto 2*

12 Toronto 3 at Buffalo 8

15 Pittsburgh 8 at Toronto 4

18 Rangers 1 at Toronto 4

19 Toronto 0 at Boston 3 [Gilbert]

22 Vancouver 2 at Toronto 3

24 Toronto 6 at Washington 3 (Ashby 19:58—EN)

25 California 2 at Toronto 2

29 Buffalo 2 at Toronto 3

30 Toronto 2 at Philadelphia 6

* Pauline McGibbon, lieutenant governor of Ontario, was present at the opening ceremony.

NOVEMBER

1   Kansas City 0 at Toronto 3 [Thomas]

5   Detroit 3 at Toronto 7

7   Toronto 3 at Kansas City 3

8   Toronto 3 at St. Louis 3

11 Toronto 2 at Vancouver 3

14 Toronto 4 at California 2 (Neely 19:06—EN)

15 Toronto 1 at Los Angeles 1

18 Washington 2 at Toronto 4

22 Montreal 4 at Toronto 2 (Wilson 19:49—EN)

23 Toronto 3 at Boston 3

26 Toronto 4 at Chicago 4

28 Toronto 3 at Atlanta 6

29 Philadelphia 1 at Toronto 1

DECEMBER

3   Toronto 1 at North Stars 3

6   Boston 4 at Toronto 2

7   Toronto 3 at Pittsburgh 6

10 Toronto 3 at Montreal 3

13 Islanders 5 at Toronto 3

14 Toronto 6 at Rangers 1

17 St. Louis 2 at Toronto 6

18 Toronto 2 at Islanders 4

20 Kansas City 1 at Toronto 5

22 Los Angeles 3 at Toronto 4

27 Chicago 4 at Toronto 1

29 Atlanta 2 at Toronto 6

31 California at Toronto*

* Postponed to January 1.

JANUARY

1   California 1 at Toronto 5*

3   Detroit 1 at Toronto 0 [Rutherford]

4   Toronto 8 at Rangers 6

7   Philadelphia 7 at Toronto 3

8   Toronto 5 at Islanders 3

10 Los Angeles 3 at Toronto 4

11 Toronto 0 at Montreal 2 [Dryden]

14 Toronto 6 at North Stars 5

15 Toronto 6 at Kansas City 4

17 Toronto 4 at Detroit 4

22 Toronto 3 at Los Angeles 6 (Murphy 19:35—EN)

24 Toronto 5 at Vancouver 5

25 Toronto 3 at California 5

28 Islanders 3 at Toronto 2

31 Rangers 4 at Toronto 6
* Afternoon game; rescheduled from previous day.

FEBRUARY

1 Toronto 1 at Pittsburgh 7*

4 Washington 4 at Toronto 4

7 Boston 4 at Toronto 11

8 North Stars 1 at Toronto 4

11 Toronto 2 at Atlanta 5 (Bennett 19:17—EN/Ecclestone 19:47—EN)

14 Vancouver 4 at Toronto 3

16 Toronto 5 at Washington 1

18 Montreal 7 at Toronto 5

19 Toronto 5 at Pittsburgh 7

21 Buffalo 4 at Toronto 6 (Thompson 19:40—EN)

23 Atlanta 1 at Toronto 7

25 Detroit 0 at Toronto 8 [Thomas]

26 Toronto 2 at Buffalo 5

28 California 2 at Toronto 4
* Afternoon game.

MARCH

1 North Stars 2 at Toronto 4

3 Toronto 4 at St. Louis 1

6 Toronto 4 at Los Angeles 1

7 Toronto 7 at California 7

10 St. Louis 2 at Toronto 2

11 Toronto 2 at Boston 6

13 Islanders 2 at Toronto 2

17 Toronto 5 at Chicago 6

20 Washington 3 at Toronto 7

21 Toronto 2 at Philadelphia 4 (Barber 19:59—EN)

24 Toronto 2 at Montreal 1

27 Buffalo 4 at Toronto 2 (Martin 19:36—EN)

29 Pittsburgh 4 at Toronto 5

31 Toronto 4 at Detroit 4

APRIL

3 Boston 4 at Toronto 2

4 Toronto 2 at Buffalo 5

1976–77

OCTOBER

5 Toronto 2 at Colorado 4

9 Boston 5 at Toronto 7 (McDonald 18:54—EN)*

13 Los Angeles 4 at Toronto 4

15 Toronto 3 at Boston 5

16 Philadelphia 5 at Toronto 5

20 Pittsburgh 4 at Toronto 4

21 Toronto 3 at Montreal 5 (Lemaire 19:36—EN)

23 Islanders 5 at Toronto 2

27 North Stars 5 at Toronto 3

28 Toronto 3 at Detroit 1

30 Toronto 5 at North Stars 1
* Joe Primeau dropped the first puck.

NOVEMBER

1 Toronto 6 at Cleveland 3

3 St. Louis 6 at Toronto 2

5 Toronto 4 at Atlanta 2

6 Toronto 2 at St. Louis 3

10 Toronto 2 at Los Angeles 2

13 Toronto 3 at Vancouver 0 [Palmateer]

17 Montreal 0 at Toronto 1 [Palmateer]

20 North Stars 3 at Toronto 8

21 Toronto 5 at Montreal 9

24 Toronto 3 at Detroit 4

27 Boston 2 at Toronto 4

28 Cleveland 1 at Toronto 5

30 Toronto 4 at Islanders 2

DECEMBER

1 Los Angeles 3 at Toronto 6

4 Chicago 2 at Toronto 2

5 Toronto 5 at Rangers 5

8 Vancouver 4 at Toronto 3

11 Rangers 1 at Toronto 4

12 Toronto 4 at Philadelphia 7

15 St. Louis 1 at Toronto 4

17 Toronto 2 at Washington 3

18 Colorado 2 at Toronto 4

20 Atlanta 2 at Toronto 6

22 Pittsburgh 5 at Toronto 2

23 Toronto 2 at Buffalo 4 (Ramsay 19:04—EN)

26 Toronto 2 at Pittsburgh 4

29 Toronto 6 at Cleveland 2

JANUARY

1 Washington 1 at Toronto 3

2 Toronto 4 at Chicago 6

5 Colorado 4 at Toronto 6 (McDonald 19:51—EN)

8 Buffalo 4 at Toronto 2 (Martin 19:29—EN)

11 Toronto 2 at Pittsburgh 0 [Thomas]

12 Los Angeles 2 at Toronto 3

15 Chicago 4 at Toronto 1

18   Toronto 3 at Los Angeles 6

21   Toronto 3 at Vancouver 1

23   Toronto 5 at North Stars 2*

27   Toronto 2 at Islanders 1

29   Toronto 3 at Boston 3*

31   Toronto 3 at Atlanta 7
* Afternoon games.

FEBRUARY

2   Detroit 1 at Toronto 9

5   Philadelphia 7 at Toronto 5

7   Toronto at Buffalo*

9   Atlanta 1 at Toronto 5

12   Washington 0 at Toronto 10 [Palmateer]

13   Toronto 3 at Rangers 8

14   Toronto 2 at Buffalo 7**

16   Toronto 5 at Cleveland 3

17   Toronto 2 at Detroit 2

19   Pittsburgh 6 at Toronto 6

20   Toronto 10 at Chicago 8

23   Rangers 5 at Toronto 4

25   Toronto 2 at Washington 4

26   Buffalo 6 at Toronto 5
* Game postponed to February 14 due to snowstorm.
** Game rescheduled from February 7.

MARCH

2   Cleveland 4 at Toronto 1

5   Vancouver 4 at Toronto 4

7   Toronto 4 at Philadelphia 2 (Turnbull 19:55—EN)

9   Montreal 2 at Toronto 2

12   Detroit 0 at Toronto 6 [Palmateer]

13   Toronto 1 at Buffalo 6

15   Toronto 4 at St. Louis 1

16   Toronto 4 at Colorado 4

19   Atlanta 4 at Toronto 5

21   Cleveland 7 at Toronto 2

23   Islanders 1 at Toronto 1

26   Boston 7 at Toronto 5 (Smith 19:29—EN)

27   Toronto 4 at Washington 7

30   Toronto 3 at Montreal 3

APRIL

2   Buffalo 1 at Toronto 1

3   Toronto 4 at Boston 7 (Sheppard 19:21—EN/Marcotte 19:55—EN)*
* Jean Ratelle of Boston recorded his 1,000th point.

1977–78

OCTOBER

13   Toronto 3 at Detroit 3

15   Buffalo 5 at Toronto 2 (Ramsay 19:56—EN)*

19   Colorado 4 at Toronto 5

22   Philadelphia 1 at Toronto 6

23   Toronto 6 at Philadelphia 3

26   Montreal 2 at Toronto 2

29   Detroit 4 at Toronto 7
* Clarence Campbell, NHL president, dropped the first puck.

NOVEMBER

2   Toronto 5 at Vancouver 1

3   Toronto 2 at Los Angeles 4 (Murphy 19:45—EN)

5   Toronto 5 at Colorado 2

9   Toronto 4 at Atlanta 0 [Palmateer]

11   Toronto 3 at Washington 1

12   Toronto 0 at Montreal 5 [Dryden]

16   Washington 2 at Toronto 5

17   Toronto 2 at Buffalo 1

19   Boston 3 at Toronto 1

23   Toronto 3 at St. Louis 2

26   Washington 4 at Toronto 4

29   Cleveland 2 at Toronto 3

30   Toronto 3 at Cleveland 5

DECEMBER

3   Detroit 2 at Toronto 4

4   Toronto 1 at Boston 3

7   North Stars 3 at Toronto 6

9   Toronto 3 at Colorado 2

10   Toronto 3 at Los Angeles 0 [Palmateer]

14   Islanders 2 at Toronto 3

16   Toronto 8 at North Stars 5

17   Chicago 1 at Toronto 7

19   St. Louis 4 at Toronto 4

21   Montreal 3 at Toronto 2

23   Toronto 6 at Pittsburgh 2

26   Pittsburgh 5 at Toronto 4 (McDonald [T] tied game at 19:06 with goalie
      out; Chapman [P] scored winner at 19:34)

28   Toronto 0 at Chicago 4 [Veisor]

30   Toronto 5 at Cleveland 0 [Palmateer]

31   Atlanta 3 at Toronto 0 [Bélanger]

JANUARY

4   Colorado 0 at Toronto 5 [Palmateer]

5   Toronto 1 at Detroit 2

7   Vancouver 4 at Toronto 6

9   Atlanta 5 at Toronto 2 (MacMillan 18:43—EN)

11   Toronto 4 at North Stars 3

13   Toronto 2 at Cleveland 5 (MacAdam 19:45—EN)

14   Chicago 3 at Toronto 3

17   Toronto 2 at St. Louis 2

19   Toronto 3 at Vancouver 3

21   Toronto 1 at Los Angeles 2

25   Toronto 4 at Rangers 3

26   Toronto 2 at Islanders 4

28   Toronto 7 at Atlanta 5 (Ellis 19:03—EN)

FEBRUARY

1   Buffalo 2 at Toronto 2

4   Detroit 2 at Toronto 2

5   Toronto 3 at Boston 3

8   St. Louis 4 at Toronto 5

11   Rangers 2 at Toronto 3

13   Toronto 4 at Buffalo 2 (Thompson 19:46—EN)

15   Boston 4 at Toronto 2

18   North Stars 4 at Toronto 5

22   Cleveland 3 at Toronto 5

25   Washington 0 at Toronto 4 [McRae]

26   Toronto 5 at Chicago 3 (Sittler 19:17—EN)*

28   Toronto 3 at Islanders 4

* The Leafs wore their names on the backs of their sweaters for the first time, but
  the lettering was the same colour as the blue sweater, thus making the names
  indistinguishable.

MARCH

1   Philadelphia 2 at Toronto 3

4   Vancouver 3 at Toronto 4

5   Toronto 4 at Rangers 1

8   Los Angeles 5 at Toronto 1

9   Toronto 1 at Montreal 4

11   Cleveland 2 at Toronto 5

12   Toronto 7 at Pittsburgh 1

15   Toronto 5 at Washington 2

18   Pittsburgh 3 at Toronto 2

19   Toronto 4 at Boston 6

22   Islanders 6 at Toronto 2

23   Toronto 1 at Philadelphia 4

25   Rangers 5 at Toronto 2

27   Los Angeles 0 at Toronto 3 [Palmateer]

29   Toronto 4 at Atlanta 7

APRIL

1   Buffalo 2 at Toronto 3

2   Toronto 3 at Pittsburgh 6

5   Montreal 6 at Toronto 3

8   Boston 3 at Toronto 1 (Miller 19:54—EN)

9   Toronto 1 at Buffalo 2

1978–79

OCTOBER

11   Toronto 3 at Pittsburgh 2

14   Islanders 7 at Toronto 10*

15   Toronto 2 at Boston 4

18   Buffalo 0 at Toronto 2 [Palmateer]

19   Toronto 0 at Buffalo 1 [Edwards]

21   Philadelphia 0 at Toronto 2 [Palmateer]

22   Toronto 2 at Rangers 5

25   Montreal 4 at Toronto 4

26   Toronto 0 at Philadelphia 5 [Parent]

28   Boston 5 at Toronto 3

* Whipper Billy Watson was present at the opening ceremony.

NOVEMBER

1   Toronto 4 at Los Angeles 2

3   Toronto 3 at Vancouver 1

4   Toronto 4 at Colorado 4

7   Toronto 5 at St. Louis 0 [Harrison]

8   Toronto 1 at Chicago 2

11   Toronto 2 at Montreal 3

15   Buffalo 2 at Toronto 2

16   Toronto 6 at Boston 4 (Maloney 18:50—EN)

18   St. Louis 1 at Toronto 3

21   Toronto 4 at Atlanta 3

22   Toronto 3 at Rangers 3

25   Colorado 6 at Toronto 3 (Pierce 19:41—EN)

26   Pittsburgh 2 at Toronto 8

29   Toronto 5 at North Stars 3

DECEMBER

2   Rangers 2 at Toronto 5

3   Toronto 2 at Philadelphia 7

5   Boston 5 at Toronto 1

6   Toronto 4 at Pittsburgh 6

9   Islanders 3 at Toronto 2

10   Toronto 3 at Buffalo 5

13   Vancouver 1 at Toronto 5

16   Detroit 2 at Toronto 4

17   Toronto 6 at Washington 7

20   North Stars 2 at Toronto 4

22   Toronto 1 at Atlanta 3

23   Toronto 6 at St. Louis 1

26   Toronto 1 at Islanders 5

27   Boston 1 at Toronto 1

30   Washington 5 at Toronto 5

JANUARY

3   Atlanta 4 at Toronto 1

6   Chicago 5 at Toronto 3 (Mikita 19:57—EN)

8   Vancouver 5 at Toronto 1

10   North Stars 2 at Toronto 2

13   Colorado 2 at Toronto 4

14   Toronto at Chicago*

16   Toronto 3 at Colorado 2

19   Toronto 3 at Vancouver 3

20   Toronto 3 at Los Angeles 2

24 Toronto 2 at North Stars 2

26 Toronto 2 at Atlanta 4

28 Toronto 2 at Washington 2

31 St. Louis 1 at Toronto 5
* Postponed until February 12 due to snowstorm.

FEBRUARY

2   Montreal 6 at Toronto 3

4   Toronto 4 at North Stars 6

12 Toronto 5 at Chicago 2*

14 Philadelphia 2 at Toronto 2

17 Los Angeles 2 at Toronto 5 (McKechnie 19:27—EN)

19 Toronto 6 at Detroit 2

21 Toronto 1 at North Stars 5

24 Rangers 4 at Toronto 2

26 Toronto 1 at Buffalo 3

28 Atlanta 6 at Toronto 4
* Game rescheduled from January 14.

MARCH

1   Toronto 1 at Montreal 2

3   Philadelphia 3 at Toronto 4

4   Toronto 4 at Rangers 2 (Boutette 19:49—EN)

7   Vancouver 0 at Toronto 2 [Palmateer]

10 Los Angeles 4 at Toronto 9

11 Pittsburgh 0 at Toronto 4 [Palmateer]

14 Buffalo 4 at Toronto 1

15 Toronto 2 at Islanders 6 (Potvin 19:46—EN)

17 North Stars 4 at Toronto 6 (Williams 19:39—EN)

19 Toronto 3 at Boston 4

21 Detroit 4 at Toronto 2

24 Chicago 3 at Toronto 3

25 Toronto 1 at Detroit 2*

28 Washington 2 at Toronto 6

31 North Stars 2 at Toronto 6
* Afternoon game.

APRIL

1   Toronto 6 at Buffalo 3

4   Boston 3 at Toronto 3

7   Buffalo 2 at Toronto 6

8   Toronto 3 at Boston 6

1979–80

OCTOBER

10 Rangers 6 at Toronto 3 (Nilsson 19:39—EN)*

13 Colorado 1 at Toronto 2

14 Toronto 3 at Philadelphia 4

17 North Stars 2 at Toronto 6

19 Toronto 5 at Washington 3 (Sittler 19:08—EN)

20 Vancouver 0 at Toronto 2 [Palmateer]

24 Toronto 1 at Vancouver 5

26 Toronto 2 at Colorado 2

27 Toronto 5 at Los Angeles 7 (Simmer 19:48—EN)

31 Hartford 4 at Toronto 2
* Season opened by Gerald Emmett Cardinal Carter.

NOVEMBER

2   Toronto 3 at Hartford 5

3   Buffalo 4 at Toronto 3

7   Toronto 7 at St. Louis 4 (Williams 19:32—EN)

10 Toronto 8 at Winnipeg 4

11 Toronto 6 at Edmonton 3 (Butler 19:26—EN)*

14 St. Louis 2 at Toronto 7

17 Boston 2 at Toronto 0 [Cheevers] (Marcotte 19:30—EN)

18 Toronto 2 at Quebec 4

21 Edmonton 4 at Toronto 4

24 Chicago 2 at Toronto 1

25 Toronto 4 at Rangers 3

27 Toronto 5 at Atlanta 3

28 Toronto 4 at Washington 2
* Afternoon game.

DECEMBER

1   Philadelphia 4 at Toronto 4

5   Montreal 2 at Toronto 3

7   Islanders 6 at Toronto 1

12 Colorado 3 at Toronto 5

15 Atlanta 1 at Toronto 8

17 Toronto 1 at North Stars 5

19 Los Angeles 4 at Toronto 4

20 Toronto 0 at Boston 10 [Cheevers]

22 Detroit 1 at Toronto 2

23 Toronto 4 at Montreal 8

26 Washington 8 at Toronto 2

27 Toronto 3 at Buffalo 5 (Gare 19:12—EN)

29 Winnipeg 1 at Toronto 6

JANUARY

2   Islanders 3 at Toronto 1

5   Quebec 7 at Toronto 3

7   Pittsburgh 5 at Toronto 9

9   Montreal 5 at Toronto 3

12 Vancouver 4 at Toronto 6

16 Toronto 1 at Pittsburgh 6 (Lonsberry 19:20—EN)

17 Toronto 6 at Islanders 9

19 Toronto 2 at Montreal 7

22 Toronto 4 at Atlanta 2

24 Toronto 4 at Los Angeles 5

26 Toronto 3 at Edmonton 8

27 Toronto 5 at Vancouver 2

30 Detroit 4 at Toronto 6

FEBRUARY

2 Chicago 5 at Toronto 4

3 Toronto 2 at Chicago 4*

7 Toronto 6 at Boston 8 (Redmond 19:50—EN)

9 Los Angeles 7 at Toronto 2

10 Toronto 4 at Detroit 1

13 Pittsburgh 4 at Toronto 2

16 Hartford 3 at Toronto 5 (Butler 19:58—EN)

17 Toronto 6 at Rangers 4 (Williams 19:57—EN)

19 Toronto 6 at Islanders 4

20 Toronto 2 at Chicago 4

23 Toronto 9 at Winnipeg 3

26 Toronto 2 at St. Louis 5

27 Toronto 4 at Colorado 3

* Afternoon game.

MARCH

1 Philadelphia 3 at Toronto 3

2 Toronto 6 at Detroit 3 (Sittler 19:42—EN)

5 Toronto 5 at Pittsburgh 3 (Sittler 19:37—EN)

7 Quebec 2 at Toronto 3

9 Toronto 4 at Quebec 5

12 St. Louis 3 at Toronto 2*

15 Rangers 8 at Toronto 4

17 Atlanta 5 at Toronto 1

19 Winnipeg 1 at Toronto 9

20 Toronto 3 at Philadelphia 0 [Palmateer]

22 Buffalo 5 at Toronto 1

24 Washington 1 at Toronto 6

25 Toronto 2 at North Stars 7

29 Edmonton 8 at Toronto 5**

* A streaker interrupted play, the first and only such occurrence at Maple Leaf Gardens.

** The game was interrupted when three mice were thrown onto the ice.

APRIL

1 Toronto 5 at Hartford 4

2 Boston 5 at Toronto 2

5 North Stars 1 at Toronto 2

6 Toronto 3 at Buffalo 7

1980–81

OCTOBER

11 Rangers 8 at Toronto 3*

12 Toronto 4 at Philadelphia 2 (Paiement 19:46—EN)**

15 Detroit 4 at Toronto 6

18 Philadelphia 2 at Toronto 6

19 Toronto 4 at Buffalo 2

21 Pittsburgh 5 at Toronto 8

23 Toronto 5 at Calgary 4

25 Toronto 4 at Los Angeles 5

26 Toronto 5 at Vancouver 8

29 Toronto 4 at Edmonton 4

* Harold Adamson, former police chief, dropped the first puck.

** Wilf Paiement's goal was the 100,000th scored in NHL history.

NOVEMBER

1 Colorado 5 at Toronto 4

5 Toronto 2 at Pittsburgh 1

8 Toronto 3 at Colorado 3

9 Toronto 7 at Winnipeg 4

12 Islanders 4 at Toronto 2 (Bourne 19:20—EN)

15 Edmonton 2 at Toronto 4

19 Montreal 5 at Toronto 4

22 Los Angeles 5 at Toronto 2 (Simmer 18:22—EN)

23 Toronto 5 at Boston 5

26 St. Louis 6 at Toronto 4 (Patey 19:52—EN)

28 Toronto 2 at Washington 6

29 Washington 7 at Toronto 3

DECEMBER

3 Pittsburgh 4 at Toronto 4

6 Quebec 2 at Toronto 5

7 Toronto 4 at Quebec 4

10 Vancouver 8 at Toronto 5 (Rota 19:11—EN)

11 Toronto 2 at Montreal 5

13 Buffalo 5 at Toronto 4

15 Toronto 6 at North Stars 3 (Vaive 19:37—EN)

17 North Stars 2 at Toronto 4 (Ellis 19:10—EN)

18 Toronto 3 at Detroit 5 (Foligno 19:48—EN)

20 Chicago 5 at Toronto 2

23 Hartford 7 at Toronto 2

27 Boston 6 at Toronto 3

28 Toronto 6 at Chicago 3

30 Toronto 3 at St. Louis 5

JANUARY

3 Toronto 1 at Edmonton 4

4 Toronto 5 at Calgary 8

6 Toronto 3 at Islanders 6 (Tonelli 19:18—EN)

7 Winnipeg 8 at Toronto 2

10 Philadelphia 4 at Toronto 4

11 Toronto 5 at Rangers 3

14 Edmonton 7 at Toronto 4

17 Montreal 5 at Toronto 6

18 Toronto 5 at Winnipeg 4

20 Toronto 2 at Vancouver 2

22 Toronto 3 at Los Angeles 3

24 Hartford 4 at Toronto 7

26 Detroit 4 at Toronto 2

28 Islanders 6 at Toronto 4

30 Toronto 5 at Hartford 5

31 Winnipeg 2 at Toronto 0 [Mattsson]

FEBRUARY

3 Toronto 3 at Detroit 5

5 Toronto 4 at St. Louis 8

8 Toronto 6 at Colorado 6*

12 Toronto 4 at North Stars 3

14 Rangers 3 at Toronto 6

17 Toronto 8 at Islanders 5 (Saganiuk 19:52—EN)

18 Toronto 3 at Rangers 8

21 North Stars 3 at Toronto 5 (Paiement 19:23—EN)

22 Toronto 7 at Chicago 4 (T. Martin 19:41—EN)

25 Colorado 5 at Toronto 9

28 Toronto 3 at Montreal 5

* Afternoon game.

MARCH

2 Los Angeles 1 at Toronto 0 [Lessard]

4 Vancouver 5 at Toronto 2

7 Calgary 6 at Toronto 4

8 Toronto 3 at Washington 7

11 Boston 4 at Toronto 4

14 Washington 3 at Toronto 5 (Sittler 19:48—EN)

15 Toronto 4 at Philadelphia 4

18 St. Louis 2 at Toronto 6

19 Toronto 4 at Buffalo 14

21 Buffalo 6 at Toronto 2

22 Toronto 3 at Hartford 3

25 Toronto 2 at Pittsburgh 5

26 Toronto 3 at Boston 2

28 Calgary 5 at Toronto 9

APRIL

1 Chicago 2 at Toronto 2

4 Quebec 5 at Toronto 5

5 Toronto 4 at Quebec 2 (Derlago 19:11—EN)

1981–82

OCTOBER

6 Toronto 6 at Winnipeg 1

8 Toronto 3 at North Stars 3

10 Chicago 8 at Toronto 9

14 North Stars 2 at Toronto 1

17 Toronto 4 at Quebec 6

21 Colorado 4 at Toronto 4

23 Toronto 2 at Buffalo 6

24 Rangers 5 at Toronto 3

27 Toronto 5 at St. Louis 7

28 Toronto 5 at Pittsburgh 3

31 Winnipeg 6 at Toronto 5

NOVEMBER

1 Toronto 4 at Chicago 9

4 Toronto 4 at Edmonton 6 (Gretzky 19:56—EN)

6 Toronto 4 at Colorado 4

7 Toronto 9 at Los Angeles 4

11 Islanders 4 at Toronto 3

14 Philadelphia 0 at Toronto 4 [Tremblay]

18 Toronto 5 at Hartford 8

20 Toronto 3 at Pittsburgh 3

21 Boston 5 at Toronto 3

24 Toronto 3 at Philadelphia 6

25 Toronto 3 at Rangers 3

28 Buffalo 4 at Toronto 4

29 Toronto 6 at Detroit 3

DECEMBER

2 Hartford 5 at Toronto 3

5 Washington 4 at Toronto 9

6 Toronto at Boston*

9 Winnipeg 3 at Toronto 3

11 Toronto 2 at Washington 11

12 Montreal 6 at Toronto 2

16 Toronto 6 at Vancouver 6

19 Toronto 8 at Winnipeg 4

20 Toronto 3 at Chicago 1

23 Pittsburgh 4 at Toronto 4

26 Detroit 3 at Toronto 8

27 Toronto 3 at Hartford 7

30 St. Louis 6 at Toronto 4

31 Toronto 5 at Detroit 2

* Game postponed until January 21 due to snowstorm.

JANUARY

2 North Stars 6 at Toronto 2

6 Toronto 3 at North Stars 3

7 Toronto 4 at Calgary 4

9 Los Angeles 3 at Toronto 5 (Vaive 19:55—EN)

11 Toronto 2 at Boston 5

13 Colorado 1 at Toronto 2

15 Toronto 2 at Buffalo 8

16 Edmonton 1 at Toronto 7

18 Rangers 2 at Toronto 6

20 Calgary 4 at Toronto 4

21 Toronto 2 at Boston 4*

23 Toronto 2 at St. Louis 6

25 North Stars 9 at Toronto 2

27   Winnipeg 4 at Toronto 3

30   Quebec 2 at Toronto 2

31   Toronto 5 at Chicago 2 (Vaive 19:04—EN)

* Game rescheduled from December 6.

FEBRUARY

3   Toronto 1 at Vancouver 3 (Williams 19:55—EN)

6   Toronto 1 at Edmonton 5

7   Toronto 2 at Calgary 8

10   Vancouver 4 at Toronto 1

13   Chicago 6 at Toronto 4 (Secord 19:35—EN)

15   North Stars 3 at Toronto 3

17   Detroit 3 at Toronto 3

18   Toronto 3 at Detroit 4

20   St. Louis 5 at Toronto 8

23   Toronto 2 at St. Louis 3

24   Toronto 5 at North Stars 7

27   Toronto 3 at Montreal 3

MARCH

1   Islanders 9 at Toronto 5

3   Los Angeles 4 at Toronto 1 (Kelly 19:53—EN)

4   Toronto 1 at Islanders 10

6   Montreal 6 at Toronto 1

10   Chicago 7 at Toronto 6

13   Winnipeg 10 at Toronto 2

17   Quebec 3 at Toronto 6

20   Toronto 0 at Winnipeg 7 [Staniowski]

22   Chicago 5 at Toronto 8 (Vaive 18:59—EN)

24   St. Louis 3 at Toronto 4

27   Detroit 2 at Toronto 1

28   Toronto 4 at Detroit 6

30   Toronto 3 at St. Louis 5

APRIL

3   Washington 6 at Toronto 4

4   Toronto 1 at Philadelphia 7

1982–83

OCTOBER

6   Toronto 3 at Chicago 3

7   Toronto 2 at St. Louis 3

9   New Jersey 5 at Toronto 5

13   Washington 5 at Toronto 3

14   Toronto 2 at North Stars 6

16   Chicago 3 at Toronto 2

20   North Stars 2 at Toronto 5

23   Calgary 5 at Toronto 5

26   Toronto 4 at Quebec 9

27   Boston 1 at Toronto 4 (Korn 19:15—EN)

30   Buffalo 3 at Toronto 3

NOVEMBER

3   Toronto 2 at Los Angeles 6

6   Toronto 3 at St. Louis 3

7   Toronto 3 at Chicago 7

10   Detroit 2 at Toronto 8

13   North Stars 3 at Toronto 4

17   Toronto 1 at Rangers 6

20   Rangers 6 at Toronto 3

24   Toronto 3 at Pittsburgh 4

26   Toronto 3 at Washington 5

27   Winnipeg 6 at Toronto 3 (DeBlois 19:32—EN)

DECEMBER

1   Toronto 3 at New Jersey 7

4   Islanders 1 at Toronto 4

5   Toronto 5 at Rangers 6

7   Toronto 3 at Islanders 6

8   Vancouver 7 at Toronto 3

11   Detroit 6 at Toronto 2

14   Toronto 4 at Quebec 4

15   St. Louis 4 at Toronto 2

18   Chicago 8 at Toronto 5

22   Toronto 3 at Chicago 4

23   Toronto 3 at St. Louis 7

28   Toronto 4 at Montreal 4

29   Montreal 5 at Toronto 6

JANUARY

1   Hartford 5 at Toronto 7 (Poddubny 19:15—EN)

2   Detroit 3 at Toronto 6

5   Toronto 4 at New Jersey 4

6   Toronto 3 at Washington 1

8   Los Angeles 5 at Toronto 7

12   Boston 6 at Toronto 4 (Pederson 19:47—EN)

13   Toronto 1 at North Stars 2

15   Toronto 3 at Detroit 4

17   St. Louis 4 at Toronto 4

19   Toronto 3 at Winnipeg 6

22   Chicago 3 at Toronto 2

24   Pittsburgh 2 at Toronto 8

26   Toronto 6 at Edmonton 6

27   Toronto 1 at Calgary 3

29   Buffalo 3 at Toronto 5 (T. Martin 19:59—EN)

31   North Stars 4 at Toronto 2

FEBRUARY

2   Hartford 1 at Toronto 7

5   Vancouver 4 at Toronto 6

6   Toronto 0 at Detroit 3 [Micalef]

13   Toronto 3 at Hartford 5

16   St. Louis 3 at Toronto 6

17   Toronto 6 at St. Louis 3 (Harris 18:39—EN)

19   Calgary 3 at Toronto 5 (Vaive 19:13—EN)

21   Pittsburgh 2 at Toronto 4

23   Toronto 3 at North Stars 2

25   Toronto 4 at Vancouver 1 (Terrion 18:47—EN)

26   Toronto 2 at Los Angeles 6

28   Toronto 3 at Boston 6

MARCH

2   Philadelphia 2 at Toronto 2

3   Toronto 1 at Islanders 5

5   Edmonton 6 at Toronto 3

8   Toronto 3 at Montreal 3

9   St. Louis 2 at Toronto 5 (Salming 19:01—EN)

12   Chicago 2 at Toronto 4

13   Toronto 5 at Detroit 2

16   Detroit 4 at Toronto 3

18   Toronto 3 at Winnipeg 7

20   Toronto 3 at Chicago 7

21   Edmonton 4 at Toronto 1 (Messier 19:28—EN)

23   North Stars 3 at Toronto 6

24   Toronto 4 at Philadelphia 7

26   Quebec 1 at Toronto 2

29   Toronto 4 at North Stars 2 (T. Martin 19:42—EN)

30   Toronto 4 at Detroit 2

APRIL

2   Philadelphia 6 at Toronto 3

3   Toronto 4 at Buffalo 3

1983–84

OCTOBER

5   Toronto 4 at Edmonton 5

8   Toronto 6 at Los Angeles 3 (Terrion 19:10—EN/Vaive 19:50—EN)

9   Toronto 4 at Vancouver 7

12   Buffalo 4 at Toronto 4

15   Chicago 8 at Toronto 10

16   Toronto 4 at New Jersey 1

19   Quebec 8 at Toronto 1

22   Montreal 3 at Toronto 5

23   Toronto 5 at Philadelphia 8

26   Edmonton 3 at Toronto 8

28   Toronto 5 at Rangers 3 (Gavin 19:37—EN)

29   Los Angeles 5 at Toronto 5

NOVEMBER

2   Toronto 5 at North Stars 8

4   Toronto 2 at Winnipeg 8

5   Toronto 3 at Calgary 5 (Hindmarch 19:48—EN)

9   New Jersey 1 at Toronto 2

11   Toronto 1 at Buffalo 3

12   Philadelphia 5 at Toronto 3

16   Toronto 3 at Pittsburgh 2

17   Toronto 1 at Boston 4

19   Detroit 4 at Toronto 5

22   Toronto 4 at St. Louis 7 (Hickey 19:50—EN)

23   Toronto 6 at North Stars 4

26   North Stars 7 at Toronto 6 (Broten 1:42 OT)

30   Toronto 5 at Detroit 3

DECEMBER

3   Vancouver 5 at Toronto 5

7   St. Louis 4 at Toronto 3

8   Toronto 8 at Hartford 6

10   Calgary 3 at Toronto 3

14   Winnipeg 8 at Toronto 4

17   Washington 3 at Toronto 1 (Gustafson 19:32—EN)

18   Pittsburgh 3 at Toronto 3

21   St. Louis 4 at Toronto 5

23   Toronto 2 at Detroit 9

26   Detroit 2 at Toronto 6

28   Toronto 6 at North Stars 8

29   Toronto 1 at St. Louis 3

31   Los Angeles 3 at Toronto 5 (T. Martin 19:17—EN)

JANUARY

3   Toronto 3 at St. Louis 8

4   Toronto 1 at Chicago 5

7   Toronto 2 at Quebec 4 (Paiement 19:03—EN)

8   St. Louis 5 at Toronto 2

11   Montreal 6 at Toronto 4 (Carbonneau 19:53—EN)

12   Toronto 4 at North Stars 5 (McCarthy 0:35 OT)

14   Chicago 2 at Toronto 2

18   North Stars 4 at Toronto 9

21   Rangers 6 at Toronto 3

23   Chicago 6 at Toronto 2

24   Toronto 3 at St. Louis 6

27   Toronto 1 at Washington 6

28   Washington 8 at Toronto 0 [Riggin]

FEBRUARY

1   Toronto 2 at Chicago 7

4   Toronto 6 at Detroit 3 (Derlago 19:09—EN/Derlago 19:52—EN)

5   Toronto 0 at Philadelphia 7 [Froese]

8	Boston 4 at Toronto 6		11	North Stars 7 at Toronto 6
9	Toronto 6 at Boston 3		14	Los Angeles 4 at Toronto 3
11	Quebec 2 at Toronto 5		17	Winnipeg 5 at Toronto 3 (Picard 18:59—EN)
13	Islanders 1 at Toronto 3		19	Toronto 6 at Montreal 4 (Derlago 18:51—EN)
15	North Stars 3 at Toronto 1		21	Toronto 1 at North Stars 7
18	Hartford 8 at Toronto 2		23	Toronto 5 at Detroit 6
19	Detroit 6 at Toronto 2		24	North Stars 4 at Toronto 2
21	Toronto 2 at Calgary 2		27	Edmonton 7 at Toronto 1
25	Toronto 3 at Edmonton 8		30	Toronto 3 at Rangers 3
26	Toronto 4 at Vancouver 4			
29	Rangers 1 at Toronto 3 (Derlago 19:34—EN)			

DECEMBER

1	Rangers 4 at Toronto 1
4	Toronto 6 at Detroit 7
5	Detroit 4 at Toronto 2
8	Toronto 3 at St. Louis 3
9	Toronto 2 at Chicago 7
12	Philadelphia 3 at Toronto 6
14	Toronto 4 at Winnipeg 6
15	Pittsburgh 5 at Toronto 2
17	St. Louis 3 at Toronto 2
21	Toronto 3 at Chicago 4
22	Boston 4 at Toronto 6
26	Toronto 0 at Buffalo 6 [Barrasso]
27	Toronto 1 at New Jersey 4
29	Chicago 5 at Toronto 4

MARCH

3	Islanders 11 at Toronto 6
4	Toronto 4 at Chicago 5
7	New Jersey 4 at Toronto 8
8	Toronto 5 at Islanders 9
10	Detroit 3 at Toronto 4 (Gavin 0:29 OT)
12	Winnipeg 8 at Toronto 7 (MacLean 3:12 OT)
14	North Stars 3 at Toronto 3
15	Toronto 3 at Hartford 5
17	Toronto 1 at Montreal 6
21	Toronto 1 at Pittsburgh 3
24	Chicago 3 at Toronto 7
25	Toronto 4 at Chicago 5
28	Toronto 2 at Detroit 4 (Gare 19:14—EN)
31	St. Louis 4 at Toronto 6

JANUARY

2	Pittsburgh 2 at Toronto 1
5	Vancouver 4 at Toronto 1
7	Hartford 7 at Toronto 4
9	Boston 5 at Toronto 3
13	Toronto 5 at Vancouver 3
16	Toronto 4 at Los Angeles 3
19	St. Louis 1 at Toronto 6
22	Toronto 2 at Quebec 2
24	Toronto 1 at Islanders 4 (Diduck 19:13—EN)
26	Chicago 5 at Toronto 2
27	Toronto 6 at Chicago 2
30	Toronto 6 at Pittsburgh 5

APRIL

1	Toronto 2 at Buffalo 4

1984–85

OCTOBER

11	Toronto 1 at North Stars 0 [Bester] (Frycer 2:51 OT)
13	Buffalo 3 at Toronto 4 (Benning 2:41 OT)
14	Toronto 2 at Winnipeg 5 (Arniel 19:22—EN)
17	Hartford 5 at Toronto 3
19	Toronto 1 at New Jersey 4
20	Quebec 12 at Toronto 3
24	Detroit 1 at Toronto 6
26	Toronto 2 at Quebec 2
27	Calgary 5 at Toronto 3
31	Toronto 5 at St. Louis 6 (Sutter 1:08 OT)

NOVEMBER

3	Toronto 0 at Los Angeles 7 [Janecyk]
5	Toronto 3 at North Stars 5 (Payne 19:43—EN)
7	Vancouver 4 at Toronto 4
10	Chicago 4 at Toronto 4

FEBRUARY

1	Toronto 3 at Washington 3
2	North Stars 5 at Toronto 2
5	Washington 4 at Toronto 1 (Langway 19:58—EN)
6	Toronto 2 at Chicago 3
9	Toronto 6 at Montreal 2
10	Montreal 2 at Toronto 3 (Vaive 3:38 OT)
14	Toronto 3 at St. Louis 5
16	New Jersey 6 at Toronto 3

17 Toronto 5 at Hartford 4 (Daoust 1:30 OT)*

19 Edmonton 9 at Toronto 4

21 Toronto 1 at Philadelphia 4

23 Toronto 4 at Detroit 2*

25 Chicago 4 at Toronto 3 (D. Wilson 3:46 OT)

27 North Stars 1 at Toronto 6

* Afternoon games.

MARCH

2 Islanders 2 at Toronto 4 (Terrion 19:07—EN)

5 Toronto 2 at St. Louis 7

6 Detroit 5 at Toronto 3 (Foster 19:14—EN)

9 Toronto 2 at Islanders 4 (Tonelli 18:46—EN)

13 Calgary 5 at Toronto 3 (Risebrough 19:49—EN)

14 Toronto 0 at Washington 4 [Jensen]

16 Philadelphia 6 at Toronto 1

18 St. Louis 3 at Toronto 4 (J. Anderson 1:45 OT)

20 Toronto 4 at Calgary 7

22 Toronto 3 at Edmonton 3

24 Toronto 5 at Detroit 3

27 St. Louis 2 at Toronto 4 (Derlago 18:50—EN)

30 Detroit 9 at Toronto 3

31 Toronto 5 at Rangers 7

APRIL

3 Toronto 7 at North Stars 9

6 Buffalo 5 at Toronto 2 (Perreault 19:39—EN)

7 Toronto 1 at Boston 5

1985–86

OCTOBER

10 Toronto 1 at Boston 3

12 Quebec 4 at Toronto 0 [Gosselin]

13 Toronto 5 at Chicago 1

16 Washington 6 at Toronto 5 (Duchesne 0:47 OT)

19 Winnipeg 4 at Toronto 3

23 Pittsburgh 5 at Toronto 4

24 Toronto 4 at Pittsburgh 6

26 North Stars 7 at Toronto 5

30 Toronto 3 at Vancouver 5

NOVEMBER

2 Toronto 2 at Calgary 4

3 Toronto 1 at Edmonton 7

6 Islanders 5 at Toronto 4

8 Toronto 3 at Detroit 3

9 St. Louis 2 at Toronto 2

12 Toronto 3 at St. Louis 4 (Mullen 2:57 OT)

14 Boston 6 at Toronto 6

16 Chicago 4 at Toronto 6

17 Toronto 5 at Buffalo 3

20 Toronto 3 at Rangers 7

23 Detroit 3 at Toronto 9

26 Toronto 1 at St. Louis 5

27 Toronto 1 at Pittsburgh 7

30 Buffalo 2 at Toronto 3 (Thomas 0:26 OT)

DECEMBER

4 New Jersey 7 at Toronto 10

5 Toronto 6 at Philadelphia 3

7 Montreal 6 at Toronto 3

10 Toronto 2 at Washington 3

11 St. Louis 4 at Toronto 6

14 Toronto 6 at North Stars 6*

15 Toronto 3 at Winnipeg 3

18 Toronto 3 at Los Angeles 4

20 Toronto 3 at Vancouver 5 (Smyl 18:44—EN)

26 Toronto 5 at Detroit 4

28 Hartford 6 at Toronto 3

* Afternoon game.

JANUARY

1 Montreal 2 at Toronto 3

4 Los Angeles 6 at Toronto 4

5 Detroit 6 at Toronto 5

8 Edmonton 9 at Toronto 11

10 Toronto 7 at Buffalo 9

11 Quebec 5 at Toronto 1

13 Detroit 4 at Toronto 7

15 Toronto 1 at St. Louis 10

18 North Stars 5 at Toronto 2

19 Calgary 9 at Toronto 5

22 Rangers 4 at Toronto 2

23 Toronto 1 at Hartford 4

25 Toronto 2 at Montreal 3 (B. Smith 3:38 OT)

28 Toronto 2 at Islanders 9

29 Washington 2 at Toronto 5

FEBRUARY

1 Chicago 7 at Toronto 4

2 Toronto 4 at Chicago 3*

6 Toronto 7 at North Stars 8 (Rouse 4:15 OT)

8 St. Louis 2 at Toronto 3 (Courtnall 3.32 OT)

11 North Stars 4 at Toronto 2 (Acton 19:23—EN)

13 Toronto 4 at Chicago 5 (Fraser 3:29 OT)

15 Chicago 3 at Toronto 4

16 Vancouver 4 at Toronto 4

19 Toronto 5 at Edmonton 9

20 Toronto 7 at Calgary 6 (Fergus 1:41 OT)

23   Toronto 3 at North Stars 4*

25   Rangers 3 at Toronto 7

28   Toronto 7 at Detroit 3

* Afternoon games.

MARCH

1   Detroit 6 at Toronto 4

3   Winnipeg 1 at Toronto 6

5   Toronto 3 at North Stars 5

6   Toronto 4 at Philadelphia 7 (Sinisalo 19:14—EN)

8   Chicago 3 at Toronto 4

13   Toronto 7 at New Jersey 4

15   Philadelphia 6 at Toronto 5 (Crossman 2:43 OT)

17   Los Angeles 6 at Toronto 7

19   Toronto 2 at Quebec 5 (Gillis 19:52—EN)

20   Islanders 7 at Toronto 1

22   New Jersey 6 at Toronto 3

26   North Stars 6 at Toronto 1

29   St. Louis 1 at Toronto 4

30   Toronto 5 at Chicago 4 (Frycer 2:02 OT)

APRIL

1   Toronto 2 at St. Louis 2

3   Toronto 2 at Boston 4

5   Toronto 1 at Hartford 7

6   Toronto 2 at Detroit 4

1986–87

OCTOBER

9   Montreal 4 at Toronto 7 (Fergus 19:41—EN)

11   Buffalo 5 at Toronto 5

14   St. Louis 1 at Toronto 1

17   Toronto 3 at New Jersey 2

18   Chicago 2 at Toronto 3

22   Quebec 7 at Toronto 1

25   Toronto 3 at Quebec 4

26   Toronto 3 at Rangers 3

28   Chicago 1 at Toronto 2

30   Hartford 2 at Toronto 6

NOVEMBER

1   Detroit 0 at Toronto 2 [Bester]

5   St. Louis 4 at Toronto 6 (Kotsopoulos 19:31—EN)

6   Toronto 1 at North Stars 4 (Bellows 19:36—EN)

8   Vancouver 5 at Toronto 3 (Skriko 19:56—EN)

12   Toronto 2 at St. Louis 4

15   Detroit 0 at Toronto 6 [Bester]

16   Toronto 7 at Chicago 3

19   Philadelphia 2 at Toronto 2

20   Toronto 4 at Islanders 6 (Brent Sutter 19:22—EN)

22   Toronto 1 at Philadelphia 6

24   Boston 3 at Toronto 2

26   Toronto 3 at Detroit 1

28   Toronto 3 at North Stars 6

29   North Stars 7 at Toronto 2

DECEMBER

4   Toronto 3 at Los Angeles 4

7   Toronto 3 at St. Louis 5

10   Washington 2 at Toronto 8

12   Toronto 3 at Pittsburgh 8

13   Pittsburgh 2 at Toronto 3 (Thomas 4:36 OT)

17   Toronto 2 at New Jersey 3 (Sulliman 0:35 OT)

18   North Stars 6 at Toronto 5 (Broten 2:10 OT)

20   Buffalo 4 at Toronto 5 (Thomas 4:55 OT)

23   Toronto 4 at North Stars 3 (Vaive 4:02 OT)

26   Toronto 2 at Detroit 4

27   Detroit 5 at Toronto 5

31   Winnipeg 1 at Toronto 6

JANUARY

3   New Jersey 2 at Toronto 7

4   Toronto 3 at Hartford 8

6   Toronto 3 at Detroit 1 (M. Ihnacak 19:48—EN)

7   Toronto 4 at Chicago 6 (Savard 19:22—EN)

10   Toronto 2 at Islanders 3

12   Toronto 1 at Montreal 2

14   North Stars 3 at Toronto 2

15   Toronto 3 at Detroit 1 (Frycer 19:35—EN)

17   Edmonton 7 at Toronto 4 (Gretzky 18:43—EN)

21   St. Louis 2 at Toronto 4 (P. Ihnacak 19:54—EN)

23   Toronto 5 at Winnipeg 7 (Hamel 19:59—EN)

24   Hartford 3 at Toronto 0 [Weeks]

26   Calgary 6 at Toronto 5 (Patterson 1:30 OT)

28   Toronto 0 at Chicago 5 [Sauvé]

29   Toronto 2 at St. Louis 4

31   Detroit 4 at Toronto 2

FEBRUARY

2   Philadelphia 4 at Toronto 8

4   Los Angeles 4 at Toronto 5

7   Toronto 5 at Boston 8

8   Toronto 5 at Rangers 4

14   Boston 5 at Toronto 4

16   Toronto 1 at Los Angeles 1

18   Toronto 2 at Edmonton 9

20   Toronto 2 at Calgary 7

22   Toronto 2 at Vancouver 3

25   Rangers 4 at Toronto 2

28   Vancouver 6 at Toronto 8

MARCH

3 St. Louis 4 at Toronto 3

5 Pittsburgh 2 at Toronto 7

7 Islanders 2 at Toronto 7

9 Toronto 2 at St. Louis 3 (Paslawski 4:01 OT)

11 Toronto 4 at North Stars 2

13 Toronto 2 at Washington 10

14 Calgary 4 at Toronto 6

18 Chicago 6 at Toronto 3

20 Toronto 4 at Quebec 5

21 Toronto 4 at Montreal 9

24 Toronto 6 at Buffalo 5

25 North Stars 6 at Toronto 2

28 Edmonton 2 at Toronto 4

29 Toronto 6 at Winnipeg 2

31 Toronto 2 at Washington 4

APRIL

4 Chicago 1 at Toronto 3

5 Toronto 2 at Chicago 5

1987–88

OCTOBER

8 Toronto 7 at Chicago 5

10 New Jersey 2 at Toronto 5

14 Toronto 3 at North Stars 4

16 Toronto 2 at Detroit 3

17 Detroit 4 at Toronto 7

21 Montreal 10 at Toronto 3

24 North Stars 7 at Toronto 4

28 Islanders 2 at Toronto 5

29 Toronto 4 at Pittsburgh 0 [Bester]

31 Chicago 5 at Toronto 6

NOVEMBER

4 Winnipeg 3 at Toronto 7

5 Toronto 7 at Boston 6

7 St. Louis 4 at Toronto 3

9 Toronto 1 at Montreal 3

11 Boston 3 at Toronto 2

14 Toronto 6 at Philadelphia 0 [Wregget]

15 Toronto 4 at Buffalo 5

18 St. Louis 6 at Toronto 3

19 Toronto 3 at St. Louis 3

21 Los Angeles 6 at Toronto 6

24 Toronto 4 at Islanders 3

25 Toronto 3 at Rangers 5

28 Hartford 4 at Toronto 2

DECEMBER

1 Toronto 2 at North Stars 3 (Bellows 1:20 OT)

3 Toronto 3 at Calgary 5

5 Toronto 2 at Edmonton 5

7 Detroit 4 at Toronto 5 (Courtnall 2:21 OT)

12 Rangers 3 at Toronto 4

13 Toronto 1 at Chicago 5

15 Washington 3 at Toronto 5 (Olczyk 19:51—EN)

18 Toronto 2 at Washington 4 (Christian 18:33—EN)

19 Chicago 6 at Toronto 2

21 North Stars 0 at Toronto 0 [Takko (M)/Bester (T)]

23 Toronto 5 at St. Louis 1

26 Montreal 4 at Toronto 2

28 Washington 4 at Toronto 4

30 Toronto 1 at Hartford 3

JANUARY

2 Buffalo 6 at Toronto 4

4 Vancouver 7 at Toronto 7

6 North Stars 5 at Toronto 5

8 Toronto 3 at Chicago 7

10 Toronto 3 at Winnipeg 4

13 Toronto 3 at North Stars 3

15 Toronto 3 at New Jersey 7

16 Pittsburgh 4 at Toronto 3

18 Toronto 3 at Detroit 4

21 Quebec 5 at Toronto 4

23 Chicago 3 at Toronto 2

25 Calgary 11 at Toronto 3

27 Los Angeles 2 at Toronto 5 (Osborne 19:04—EN/Leeman 19:44—EN)

29 Toronto 3 at Detroit 3

30 Detroit 5 at Toronto 5

FEBRUARY

1 St. Louis 5 at Toronto 4

4 Toronto 1 at Philadelphia 6

5 Toronto 2 at Buffalo 5 (Ruuttu 19:12—EN)

7 Toronto 2 at Hartford 4

11 Islanders 3 at Toronto 4

13 Philadelphia 4 at Toronto 7 (Olczyk 19:19—EN)

14 New Jersey 7 at Toronto 2

17 Toronto 4 at Edmonton 4

19 Toronto 5 at Vancouver 0 [Wregget]

20 Toronto 0 at Los Angeles 3 [Melanson]

22 Toronto 2 at North Stars 4

24 North Stars 2 at Toronto 4

27 St. Louis 6 at Toronto 2*

* Borje Salming Night.

MARCH

2	Quebec 4 at Toronto 3
3	Toronto 3 at Boston 5 (Neely 19:54—EN)
5	Winnipeg 10 at Toronto 1
8	Toronto 2 at St. Louis 3
9	Toronto 3 at Chicago 4
12	Chicago 4 at Toronto 6
15	Toronto 2 at Quebec 3
16	Toronto 2 at Pittsburgh 5
19	Rangers 4 at Toronto 3
22	Toronto 3 at Vancouver 5
24	Toronto 1 at Calgary 7
26	Toronto 2 at St. Louis 3 (Paslawski 2:07 OT)
28	Edmonton 6 at Toronto 4 (Gretzky 19:44—EN)

APRIL

1	Toronto 3 at Detroit 7
2	Detroit 3 at Toronto 5

1988–89

OCTOBER

6	Toronto 1 at Boston 2
8	Chicago 4 at Toronto 7*
9	Toronto 8 at Chicago 4
12	St. Louis 4 at Toronto 2
14	Toronto 3 at Washington 1
15	Detroit 5 at Toronto 3 (Yzerman 19:37—EN)
17	Toronto 6 at Montreal 2
19	Buffalo 2 at Toronto 4 (Olczyk 19:52—EN)
21	Toronto 4 at Detroit 2
22	Calgary 3 at Toronto 3
25	Toronto 4 at Islanders 3
26	Toronto 3 at North Stars 2
29	Toronto 2 at St. Louis 3

* Hap Day dropped the first puck.

NOVEMBER

2	Boston 7 at Toronto 2
5	Los Angeles 6 at Toronto 4 (Nicholls 19:46—EN)
10	Toronto 1 at Pittsburgh 5
12	Edmonton 6 at Toronto 2
14	North Stars 5 at Toronto 4
16	Pittsburgh 5 at Toronto 8 (Laxdal 19:37—EN)
18	Toronto 0 at Winnipeg [Chevrier]
19	Toronto 1 at Edmonton 9
21	St. Louis 0 at Toronto 4 [Bester]
23	Chicago 3 at Toronto 4
25	Toronto 3 at North Stars 5
26	North Stars 6 at Toronto 3

DECEMBER

1	Toronto 3 at Los Angeles 9
3	Toronto 0 at St. Louis 3 [Millen] (Tuttle 19:11—EN)
9	Toronto 3 at Detroit 4
10	Detroit 8 at Toronto 2
12	Calgary 4 at Toronto 4
14	Edmonton 8 at Toronto 2
15	Toronto 3 at New Jersey 6
17	Philadelphia 7 at Toronto 1
19	St. Louis 3 at Toronto 4
21	Pittsburgh 6 at Toronto 1
23	Toronto 2 at Buffalo 5
26	Islanders 4 at Toronto 3
29	Toronto 6 at Quebec 5
31	Quebec 1 at Toronto 6

JANUARY

1	Toronto 3 at Chicago 3
6	Toronto 0 at Washington 3 [Peeters]
7	Buffalo 6 at Toronto 1
9	Vancouver 0 at Toronto 3 [Bester] (Fergus 19:54—EN)
11	Washington 3 at Toronto 2
14	Montreal 5 at Toronto 3 (Walter 19:51—EN)
16	Hartford 3 at Toronto 5
19	North Stars 3 at Toronto 3
21	Toronto 3 at Montreal 4
25	Boston 2 at Toronto 1 (Brickley 1:57 OT)
27	Toronto 1 at Detroit 8
28	Rangers 1 at Toronto 1
30	Toronto 1 at Chicago 7

FEBRUARY

2	Toronto 4 at Islanders 1 (Laughlin 19:24—EN)
4	Chicago 3 at Toronto 1
11	Philadelphia 3 at Toronto 4
13	Toronto 1 at New Jersey 8
15	Hartford 4 at Toronto 2 (Tippett 19:42—EN)
17	Toronto 10 at Rangers 6
18	New Jersey 3 at Toronto 5
20	Toronto 4 at Los Angeles 5
22	Toronto 4 at Calgary 3 (Leeman 4:11 OT)
23	Toronto 1 at Vancouver 2 (Sandlak 4:42 OT)
25	Toronto 4 at North Stars 2
27	St. Louis 7 at Toronto 5 (Vesey 19:26—EN)

MARCH

1	Toronto 4 at Rangers 7
4	Chicago 3 at Toronto 3
5	Toronto 0 at Hartford 3 [Sidorkiewicz]
7	Toronto 6 at Quebec 4

9 Toronto 1 at St. Louis 4

11 Detroit 3 at Toronto 5 (Osborne 19:43—EN)

12 Toronto 7 at Winnipeg 9

14 Toronto 5 at North Stars 3

18 Winnipeg 10 at Toronto 2

19 Toronto 6 at Philadelphia 8

22 Vancouver 3 at Toronto 5

24 Toronto 2 at Detroit 6

25 Detroit 5 at Toronto 6 (Olczyk [T] 19:19—EN/Kocur [D] 19:55 with goalie out)

29 North Stars 1 at Toronto 3

APRIL

1 Toronto 3 at St. Louis 4 (G. Cavallini 4:10 OT—EN)*

2 Toronto 3 at Chicago 4 (T. Murray 0:48 OT)

* In an effort to catch Chicago in the standings for the final playoff spot, the Leafs pulled goalie Allan Bester during the five-on-five overtime, resulting in the first-ever empty-net goal in overtime.

1989–90

OCTOBER

5 Toronto 2 at Los Angeles 4

7 Toronto 8 at St. Louis 5

11 Buffalo 7 at Toronto 1

12 Toronto 6 at Chicago 9

14 Winnipeg 5 at Toronto 1

17 Toronto 5 at Pittsburgh 7 (Lemieux 19:17—EN/Iafrate 19:27 with goalie out/Lemieux 19:47—EN)

18 Vancouver 3 at Toronto 4

21 Washington 4 at Toronto 8

23 New Jersey 5 at Toronto 4

25 Toronto 8 at Pittsburgh 6 (Franceschetti 19:34—EN)

27 Toronto 5 at Buffalo 6 (P. Turgeon 2:30 OT)

28 Detroit 4 at Toronto 6

31 Toronto 6 at North Stars 4

NOVEMBER

3 Toronto 1 at Washington 2

4 Philadelphia 7 at Toronto 4

6 North Stars 1 at Toronto 2

9 Toronto 4 at Philadelphia 1

11 Detroit 2 at Toronto 4

12 Toronto 3 at North Stars 6

15 St. Louis 2 at Toronto 5

16 Toronto 2 at Islanders 6

18 Toronto 3 at Montreal 4 (Naslund 3:25 OT)

22 Toronto 3 at North Stars 6 (Gavin 19:35—EN)

23 Toronto 0 at Boston 6 [Moog]

25 Rangers 4 at Toronto 7

29 Toronto 3 at Vancouver 2 (Damphousse 3:48 OT)

DECEMBER

2 Toronto 4 at Calgary 7

3 Toronto 3 at Edmonton 5

6 Toronto 4 at Chicago 6 (Wilson 19:32—EN)

7 Toronto 5 at St. Louis 2 (Franceschetti 19:47—EN)

9 Montreal 4 at Toronto 7

11 St. Louis 1 at Toronto 3 (Leeman 19:06—EN)

13 Toronto 4 at Detroit 2

16 North Stars 4 at Toronto 3

18 St. Louis 3 at Toronto 6

20 Toronto 2 at Detroit 4

22 Toronto 5 at Chicago 3 (Leeman 19:37—EN)

23 Chicago 7 at Toronto 5

26 Toronto 4 at Boston 6

27 Detroit 7 at Toronto 7

30 Boston 6 at Toronto 7 (Clark 3:19 OT)

JANUARY

3 Quebec 4 at Toronto 5

6 Los Angeles 4 at Toronto 7 (Franceschetti 18:28—EN)

8 Washington 6 at Toronto 8

10 Islanders 3 at Toronto 1

13 Calgary 5 at Toronto 6

15 Chicago 6 at Toronto 7

18 Toronto 4 at St. Louis 1

24 North Stars 3 at Toronto 7

26 Toronto 5 at New Jersey 1

27 Montreal 5 at Toronto 3

31 Toronto 5 at Winnipeg 5

FEBRUARY

2 Toronto 2 at Detroit 5 (Yzerman 19:33—EN)

3 Pittsburgh 4 at Toronto 8

6 Toronto 4 at St. Louis 6

7 St. Louis 1 at Toronto 7

10 Toronto 2 at Hartford 6

12 Los Angeles 3 at Toronto 5 (Leeman 19:15—EN)

14 Hartford 6 at Toronto 6

15 Toronto 0 at Philadelphia 3 [Peeters] (Tocchet 19:32—EN)

17 New Jersey 4 at Toronto 5

22 Toronto 2 at Calgary 12

23 Toronto 6 at Edmonton 5

26 Toronto 2 at Vancouver 5

28 Quebec 4 at Toronto 5

MARCH

2 Toronto 2 at Detroit 3 (Yzerman 3:44 OT)

3 Detroit 5 at Toronto 2

8 Toronto 7 at Hartford 6

10 Edmonton 2 at Toronto 3

12	North Stars 4 at Toronto 1
14	Rangers 8 at Toronto 2
16	Toronto 4 at Buffalo 3
17	Winnipeg 5 at Toronto 4 (Taglianetti 4:52 OT)
19	Chicago 3 at Toronto 2
21	Toronto 5 at Rangers 5
24	Toronto 4 at Quebec 3 (Osborne 0:49 OT)
26	Toronto 4 at North Stars 5
28	Islanders 6 at Toronto 3 (Don Maloney 18:52—EN)
29	Toronto 2 at Chicago 4
31	Chicago 4 at Toronto 6

1990–91

OCTOBER

4	Toronto 1 at Winnipeg 7
6	Toronto 1 at Calgary 4
7	Toronto 2 at Edmonton 3
10	Quebec 8 at Toronto 5 (Sakic 19:18—EN)
13	Detroit 3 at Toronto 3
17	Hartford 3 at Toronto 1 (Cyr 19:18—EN)
18	Toronto 0 at Chicago 3 [Belfour]
20	Chicago 2 at Toronto 6
22	Toronto 1 at Rangers 5
24	St. Louis 8 at Toronto 3
25	Toronto 5 at St. Louis 8 (Bassen 19:24—EN)
27	Buffalo 3 at Toronto 1
30	North Stars 4 at Toronto 5

NOVEMBER

1	Toronto 4 at Detroit 5
3	Calgary 7 at Toronto 3
4	Philadelphia 7 at Toronto 1
6	Toronto 3 at Islanders 4
8	Vancouver 5 at Toronto 3
10	Chicago 5 at Toronto 1
12	Winnipeg 2 at Toronto 5 (Reid 19:24—EN)
14	Washington 3 at Toronto 5
17	Detroit 8 at Toronto 4
19	Boston 5 at Toronto 2
21	Toronto 3 at Washington 5
23	Toronto 1 at Philadelphia 4*
24	Edmonton 4 at Toronto 1 (Simpson 19:40—EN)
27	Toronto 4 at St. Louis 3 (Clark 3:58 OT)
29	Toronto 1 at Vancouver 2
* Afternoon game.

DECEMBER

| 1 | Toronto 4 at Los Angeles 3 |
| 5 | North Stars 3 at Toronto 2 |

6	Toronto 2 at North Stars 1
8	Chicago 2 at Toronto 1
12	Montreal 1 at Toronto 4
15	St. Louis 4 at Toronto 2
18	Toronto 2 at Islanders 2
19	Toronto 4 at Rangers 1 (DeBlois 19:52—EN)
22	Toronto 5 at Washington 2*
23	Toronto 2 at New Jersey 4
27	St. Louis 4 at Toronto 6
29	Pittsburgh 3 at Toronto 6
* Afternoon game.

JANUARY

3	Toronto 3 at North Stars 3
5	Los Angeles 4 at Toronto 2
8	Calgary 5 at Toronto 3
10	Toronto 2 at Chicago 7
12	Hartford 2 at Toronto 2
14	Buffalo 9 at Toronto 3
17	Pittsburgh 6 at Toronto 5 (Young 3:31 OT)
22	Toronto 4 at Quebec 4
23	Toronto 3 at Montreal 7
26	Toronto 1 at Chicago 5
28	North Stars 0 at Toronto 4 [Ing]

FEBRUARY

1	Toronto 1 at Detroit 4 (Ysebaert 19:55—EN)
2	Detroit 5 at Toronto 2
4	St. Louis 5 at Toronto 6 (Hannan 3:58 OT)
6	Toronto 5 at Winnipeg 5
7	Toronto 2 at North Stars 4
9	Islanders 2 at Toronto 3
13	Philadelphia 6 at Toronto 3
16	Edmonton 2 at Toronto 3
17	Toronto 3 at Buffalo 0 [Reese]
19	Toronto 2 at St. Louis 3
21	Toronto 4 at Pittsburgh 11
23	Toronto 3 at Montreal 3
25	Toronto 4 at Detroit 5 (Racine 1:26 OT)
27	New Jersey 3 at Toronto 7

MARCH

2	Rangers 5 at Toronto 2
3	Toronto 4 at Hartford 4
5	Boston 3 at Toronto 6
7	Vancouver 3 at Toronto 3
9	Toronto 0 at Boston 2 [Moog]*
12	Toronto 4 at Quebec 3
13	Toronto 2 at New Jersey 3
16	North Stars 3 at Toronto 4 (Petit 2:44 OT)

17 Toronto 3 at North Stars 4

20 Toronto 4 at Los Angeles 4

22 Toronto 3 at Detroit 1 (Damphousse 19:33—EN)

23 Detroit 1 at Toronto 4 (Gill 19:47—EN)**

26 Chicago 2 at Toronto 2

28 Toronto 3 at Chicago 5 (Goulet 19:52—EN)

30 Toronto 2 at St. Louis 5 (Tilley 19:54—EN)

* Afternoon game.

** The Leafs honoured Gulf War veterans Master Corporal Don Andrea, Leading Seaman
    Gerry Ross, and Master Corporal Louise Williams.

1991—92

OCTOBER

3 Toronto 3 at Montreal 4

5 Detroit 5 at Toronto 8

7 St. Louis 0 at Toronto 3 [Fuhr] (Loiselle 19:16—EN)

9 Washington 5 at Toronto 4

12 Vancouver 2 at Toronto 1

15 Toronto 1 at St. Louis 5

17 Toronto 4 at Calgary 6

19 Toronto 2 at Winnipeg 4

21 Toronto 1 at Vancouver 4 (Valk 19:52—EN)

25 Toronto 0 at Detroit 4 [Cheveldae]

26 Detroit 1 at Toronto 6

28 St. Louis 1 at Toronto 1

NOVEMBER

1 Toronto 0 at Washington 4 [Liut]

2 Los Angeles 5 at Toronto 2

4 San Jose 1 at Toronto 4

6 North Stars 3 at Toronto 4

8 Toronto 3 at Rangers 3

9 Calgary 6 at Toronto 1

12 Toronto 0 at North Stars 7 [Casey]

14 Toronto 0 at Chicago 3 [Belfour] (Roenick 19:57—EN)

16 Chicago 2 at Toronto 2

17 Hartford 3 at Toronto 1

20 Toronto 2 at St. Louis 5

22 Toronto 3 at San Jose 1

26 Toronto 4 at Los Angeles 4

29 Toronto 3 at North Stars 2

30 North Stars 4 at Toronto 3

DECEMBER

4 Toronto 3 at Hartford 0 [Reese] (Zezel 19:58—EN)

7 Vancouver 3 at Toronto 6

9 Montreal 4 at Toronto 1 (Corson 19:37—EN)

11 Islanders 5 at Toronto 4

12 Toronto 1 at Philadelphia 1

14 Toronto 3 at Boston 4

18 Edmonton 7 at Toronto 5

20 Toronto 3 at Washington 4

21 Buffalo 4 at Toronto 1

23 Winnipeg 1 at Toronto 3

26 Toronto 1 at Pittsburgh 12

28 Detroit 5 at Toronto 4

30 Toronto 2 at Quebec 5 (Paslawski 19:56—EN)

JANUARY

3 Toronto 4 at Detroit 6 (Ysebaert 19:24—EN)

4 Chicago 4 at Toronto 2

6 St. Louis 2 at Toronto 3 (Ellett 4:51 OT)

9 Toronto 0 at Chicago 2 [Hasek]

11 Toronto 4 at New Jersey 3

16 Toronto 0 at Chicago 4 [Belfour]

22 Boston 5 at Toronto 2 (Neely 18:26—EN)

23 Toronto 4 at Islanders 3

25 Philadelphia 4 at Toronto 6 (Zezel 19:52—EN)

29 Quebec 2 at Toronto 5

FEBRUARY

1 New Jersey 4 at Toronto 6 (Clark 18:58—EN)

3 Toronto 2 at North Stars 4 (Johnson 19:29—EN)

5 North Stars 2 at Toronto 3 (Clark 0:18 OT)

7 Toronto 4 at Detroit 3

8 Montreal 4 at Toronto 6

11 Detroit 3 at Toronto 4 (Bradley won game at 19:58)

15 Winnipeg 3 at Toronto 1

16 Edmonton 5 at Toronto 7 (Gilmour 18:45—EN)

18 Toronto 1 at Pittsburgh 7

20 Toronto 2 at Detroit 3

22 Toronto 3 at St. Louis 4

25 New Jersey 5 at Toronto 5

27 Toronto 2 at Boston 4

29 Chicago 5 at Toronto 6 (Clark 1:02 OT)

MARCH

1 North Stars 2 at Toronto 6

4 Toronto 5 at Edmonton 2

5 Toronto 5 at Calgary 5

8 Toronto 1 at San Jose 4*

9 Toronto 1 at Los Angeles 4

11 Toronto 3 at North Stars 0 [Fuhr]

14 Pittsburgh 3 at Toronto 6 (G. Anderson 19:18—EN)

17 Quebec 3 at Toronto 4 (G. Anderson 2:08 OT)

21 Chicago 3 at Toronto 1 (Goulet 19:52—EN)

23 St. Louis 2 at Toronto 3

25 Toronto 2 at Buffalo 5 (Mogilny 19:53—EN)

28 Toronto 3 at St. Louis 2

29 Toronto 1 at Chicago 5

* Afternoon game.

APRIL

1 Islanders at Toronto*

4 Rangers at Toronto*

5 Toronto at Philadelphia*

12 Islanders 6 at Toronto 2**

13 Rangers 2 at Toronto 4**

15 Toronto 2 at Philadelphia 6**

* Games cancelled due to players' strike.

** Make-up games for those cancelled.

1992–93

To celebrate the NHL's 75th anniversary, all Original Six teams wore their dark sweaters at home in games against each other.

OCTOBER

6 Washington 6 at Toronto 5

10 Toronto 2 at Calgary 3

11 Toronto 3 at Edmonton 3

15 Tampa Bay 3 at Toronto 5

17 Chicago 3 at Toronto 4

18 North Stars 5 at Toronto 1

20 Ottawa 3 at Toronto 5 (Gilmour 19:39—EN)*

22 Toronto 5 at Tampa Bay 2

24 San Jose 1 at Toronto 5

28 Buffalo 4 at Toronto 4

30 Toronto 1 at Detroit 7

31 Detroit 1 at Toronto 3

* Game played at Copps Coliseum, Hamilton.

NOVEMBER

5 Toronto 0 at Chicago 1 [Belfour]

7 Pittsburgh 2 at Toronto 4 (Clark 19:16—EN)

9 Toronto 3 at Ottawa 1

14 Toronto 4 at Boston 1

16 St. Louis 2 at Toronto 2

17 Toronto 1 at Quebec 3*

19 Toronto 2 at San Jose 0 [Fuhr]

21 Toronto 4 at Los Angeles 6 (Granato 19:50—EN)

24 Tampa Bay 3 at Toronto 2

26 Quebec 5 at Toronto 4 (Nolan 0:23 OT)

28 Los Angeles 2 at Toronto 3

* Game played at Copps Coliseum, Hamilton.

DECEMBER

1 Toronto 3 at New Jersey 8

3 Toronto 3 at Chicago 4

5 Chicago 2 at Toronto 2

6 Toronto 0 at Rangers 6 [Vanbiesbrouck]

9 Detroit 3 at Toronto 5

11 Calgary 6 at Toronto 3

15 Toronto 5 at North Stars 6

19 Ottawa 1 at Toronto 5

20 Toronto 4 at Buffalo 5

22 Toronto 4 at Detroit 4

26 Detroit 5 at Toronto 1

27 Toronto 6 at St. Louis 3 (Ellett 18:33—EN)

29 Toronto 3 at Islanders 2

31 Toronto 3 at Pittsburgh 3

JANUARY

2 St. Louis 2 at Toronto 2

4 Toronto 4 at Detroit 2 (Osborne 19:57—EN)

6 Vancouver 5 at Toronto 2

8 San Jose 1 at Toronto 5

9 Toronto 5 at Montreal 4

11 Tampa Bay 2 at Toronto 4

13 St. Louis 3 at Toronto 4

16 Chicago 5 at Toronto 3 (Larmer 19:41—EN)

17 Toronto 3 at Chicago 5

19 Toronto 5 at St. Louis 1

21 Toronto 6 at Tampa Bay 1

23 Montreal 0 at Toronto 4 [Potvin]

26 North Stars 2 at Toronto 1

30 Rangers 1 at Toronto 3

FEBRUARY

1 Toronto 1 at St. Louis 1

3 Islanders 3 at Toronto 2

9 Toronto 1 at Tampa Bay 3 (Zamuner 19:31—EN)

11 Vancouver 2 at Toronto 5

13 North Stars 1 at Toronto 6

14 Toronto 6 at North Stars 5

17 Calgary 2 at Toronto 4

19 Tampa Bay 1 at Toronto 4

20 Boston 4 at Toronto 4

22 Toronto 8 at Vancouver 1

25 Toronto 5 at San Jose 0 [Puppa]

27 Toronto 5 at Los Angeles 2

MARCH

3 North Stars 1 at Toronto 3

5 Toronto 1 at Detroit 5

6 Winnipeg 2 at Toronto 4

9 Toronto 1 at Washington 3 (Hatcher 19:58—EN)

10 Hartford 3 at Toronto 5

12 Tampa Bay 2 at Toronto 8

15 Toronto 2 at Quebec 4 (Cavallini 19:14—EN)

18 Toronto 4 at Tampa Bay 2

20   Edmonton 2 at Toronto 4

23   Toronto 5 at Winnipeg 4

25   Toronto 3 at North Stars 3

27   Toronto 6 at Edmonton 2

28   Toronto 4 at Calgary 0 [Puppa]

31   Los Angeles 5 at Toronto 5

APRIL

1   Toronto at Philadelphia*

3   New Jersey 0 at Toronto 1 [Potvin]

4   Toronto 0 at Philadelphia 4 [Soderstrom]**

8   Toronto 3 at Winnipeg 5

10   Philadelphia 4 at Toronto 0 [Soderstrom]

11   Toronto 4 at Hartford 2

13   St. Louis 1 at Toronto 2 (Zezel 1:46 OT)

15   Toronto 2 at Chicago 3

* Game postponed until April 4.
** Game rescheduled from April 1.

1993–94

OCTOBER

7   Dallas 3 at Toronto 6 (Clark 19:09—EN)

9   Chicago 1 at Toronto 2

10   Toronto 5 at Philadelphia 4

13   Washington 1 at Toronto 7

15   Detroit 3 at Toronto 6 (Gilmour 18:18—EN)

16   Toronto 2 at Detroit 1

19   Hartford 2 at Toronto 7

21   Toronto 4 at Florida 3 (Pearson 2:17 OT)

23   Toronto 2 at Tampa Bay 0 [Potvin]

28   Toronto 4 at Chicago 2

30   Toronto 2 at Montreal 5

NOVEMBER

1   Toronto 3 at Dallas 3

3   Florida 3 at Toronto 6

4   Toronto 3 at Detroit 3

6   Philadelphia 3 at Toronto 5

9   Toronto 2 at San Jose 2

11   Toronto 2 at St. Louis 3

13   Chicago 3 at Toronto 2

15   Edmonton 5 at Toronto 5

17   Toronto 4 at Anaheim 3

18   Toronto 3 at Los Angeles 2

20   Toronto 3 at Edmonton 2

22   Toronto 5 at Vancouver 2 (Osborne 19:11—EN)

24   Toronto 3 at Calgary 5 (Kisio 19:32—EN)

27   Boston 2 at Toronto 4

29   Buffalo 3 at Toronto 0 [Hasek]

DECEMBER

1   St. Louis 2 at Toronto 4

2   Toronto 5 at St. Louis 4

4   Rangers 4 at Toronto 3

8   Winnipeg 5 at Toronto 4

11   Calgary 1 at Toronto 3 (Andreychuk 19:25—EN)

12   Toronto 3 at Winnipeg 3

15   Anaheim 1 at Toronto 0 [Hebert]

17   Toronto 2 at Islanders 6

18   Los Angeles 1 at Toronto 4

22   San Jose 2 at Toronto 2

23   Toronto 2 at New Jersey 3

27   Toronto 2 at Chicago 5

29   Toronto 0 at Dallas 4 [Wakaluk]

JANUARY

1   Los Angeles 7 at Toronto 4

2   Toronto 3 at Buffalo 3

4   Tampa Bay 1 at Toronto 0 [Puppa]*

6   Ottawa 3 at Toronto 6

8   Vancouver 3 at Toronto 5

10   Toronto 3 at Boston 0 [Potvin]

11   Toronto 2 at Washington 1

13   Dallas 3 at Toronto 4 (G. Anderson 4:46 OT)

15   Toronto 5 at Winnipeg 1

18   Anaheim 3 at Toronto 3

19   Toronto 3 at Hartford 3

26   Islanders 3 at Toronto 4

29   Pittsburgh 4 at Toronto 4

* Game played at Copps Coliseum, Hamilton.

FEBRUARY

1   Toronto 4 at St. Louis 4

5   Detroit 4 at Toronto 3

7   Tampa Bay 2 at Toronto 1

11   Toronto 3 at Winnipeg 1

12   Toronto 2 at Calgary 3

15   Detroit 4 at Toronto 5 (Clark 2:55 OT)

17   New Jersey 1 at Toronto 2

19   Edmonton 2 at Toronto 3

21   Toronto 6 at Los Angeles 4 (Berg 19:54—EN)

23   Toronto 3 at Edmonton 6

26   Montreal 3 at Toronto 0 [Roy]

28   Toronto 4 at Ottawa 1

MARCH

4   Toronto 6 at Detroit 5 (Clark 0:53 OT)

5   Toronto 1 at Quebec 4

7   St. Louis 3 at Toronto 2

9   Dallas 2 at Toronto 4

10	Toronto 4 at Pittsburgh 2
12	Winnipeg 1 at Toronto 3
16	Vancouver 4 at Toronto 1 (Bure 19:24—EN)
18	St. Louis 2 at Toronto 4
20	Calgary 6 at Toronto 3 (Roberts 19:37—EN)
23	Toronto 1 at Florida 1*
24	San Jose 2 at Toronto 1
26	Quebec 3 at Toronto 6 (Gartner 17:18—EN)
28	Toronto 2 at Vancouver 3 (Clark tied game at 19:33 with goalie out; Craven 3:57 OT)
31	Toronto 3 at San Jose 5

* Game played at Copps Coliseum, Hamilton.

APRIL

2	Toronto 1 at Anaheim 3
5	Toronto 6 at Dallas 4 (Osborne 18:54—EN)
8	Toronto 3 at Rangers 5
10	Winnipeg 0 at Toronto 7 [Potvin]
12	Chicago 4 at Toronto 3
14	Toronto 6 at Chicago 4

1994–95

Season was revised to a 48-game schedule.

JANUARY

20	Toronto 3 at Los Angeles 3
21	Toronto 2 at San Jose 3
25	Vancouver 2 at Toronto 6
27	Toronto 1 at Chicago 4
28	Calgary 1 at Toronto 2
30	Toronto 2 at Dallas 1

FEBRUARY

1	Toronto 4 at Vancouver 4
3	Toronto 3 at Edmonton 5 (Corson 19:46—EN)
4	Toronto 1 at Calgary 4 (Titov 19:55—EN)
6	San Jose 3 at Toronto 7
8	Dallas 3 at Toronto 3 (Sundin [T] tied game at 19:58 with goalie out)
10	Toronto 2 at Detroit 1
11	Los Angeles 5 at Toronto 2 (Granato 19:29—EN)
13	Chicago 2 at Toronto 4
15	Edmonton 4 at Toronto 1
18	St. Louis 1 at Toronto 3
20	Detroit 4 at Toronto 2 (Ciccarelli 19:23—EN)
22	Toronto 1 at Detroit 4 (Johnson 19:38—EN)
23	Anaheim 1 at Toronto 3
25	Winnipeg 2 at Toronto 5 (Eastwood 18:39—EN)
27	Toronto 2 at St. Louis 3

MARCH

2	San Jose 4 at Toronto 3

4	Calgary 2 at Toronto 3
8	Dallas 2 at Toronto 3
11	Chicago 2 at Toronto 2
13	Los Angeles 4 at Toronto 1 (Gretzky 19:33—EN)
15	Toronto 2 at San Jose 1
17	Toronto 3 at Anaheim 3
18	Toronto 5 at Los Angeles 3 (Sundin 19:26—EN)
21	Toronto 1 at Vancouver 3 (Ruuttu 19:59—EN)
24	Winnipeg 2 at Toronto 3
25	Toronto 3 at Winnipeg 3
27	Edmonton 3 at Toronto 4
31	Toronto 3 at Chicago 3

APRIL

3	Toronto 2 at St. Louis 5 (Laperrière 19:14—EN)
5	St. Louis 6 at Toronto 4
7	Detroit 4 at Toronto 2
8	Winnipeg 3 at Toronto 4
14	Dallas 1 at Toronto 2
15	Toronto 1 at Winnipeg 5
17	Toronto 3 at Chicago 1 (Gartner 19:39—EN)
19	Anaheim 2 at Toronto 3
21	St. Louis 3 at Toronto 1
22	Toronto 4 at Dallas 6
26	Vancouver 2 at Toronto 5
29	Toronto 2 at Calgary 2

MAY

1	Toronto 6 at Edmonton 5
3	Toronto 1 at Anaheim 6

1995–96

OCTOBER

7	Toronto 3 at Pittsburgh 8
10	Islanders 3 at Toronto 7
14	Rangers 2 at Toronto 0 [Richter]
17	San Jose 2 at Toronto 7
20	Calgary 3 at Toronto 4 (Craig 1:31 OT)
21	Toronto 3 at Montreal 4 (Turgeon scored winner at 19:59)
24	Florida 6 at Toronto 1*
26	Toronto 2 at Chicago 1
28	Los Angeles 2 at Toronto 2
29	Toronto 2 at Rangers 3

* Bob Davidson was presented with the Bickell Cup.

NOVEMBER

1	Toronto 4 at Winnipeg 2
3	Toronto 4 at Vancouver 4
4	Toronto 3 at Edmonton 3
7	Anaheim 3 at Toronto 6 (Gilmour 19:42—EN)

10 Washington 1 at Toronto 6

11 Toronto 3 at Boston 1 (Gartner 19:41—EN)

14 Toronto 2 at Florida 5

16 Toronto 5 at Tampa Bay 4 (Hogue [T] tied game at 19:05 with goalie out; Hogue 0:32 OT)

18 Winnipeg 1 at Toronto 2

21 St. Louis 2 at Toronto 5*

24 Hartford 4 at Toronto 0 [Reese]

25 Toronto 2 at St. Louis 2

28 Toronto 3 at Winnipeg 4

30 Toronto 2 at Philadelphia 3

* Leafs honour King Clancy's and Tim Horton's number 7.

DECEMBER

2 Anaheim 4 at Toronto 4

5 Ottawa 1 at Toronto 4

7 Toronto 2 at New Jersey 1

9 Dallas 1 at Toronto 3

11 Colorado 5 at Toronto 1

14 Toronto 4 at San Jose 1

16 Toronto 6 at Los Angeles 3 (Wood 19:11—EN)

17 Toronto 3 at Anaheim 2 (Andreychuk 2:05 OT)

20 Chicago 4 at Toronto 2

21 Toronto 3 at Chicago 3 (Murphy tied game at 19:10 with goalie out)

23 Edmonton 1 at Toronto 6*

27 Toronto 0 at Calgary 4 [Kidd]

29 Toronto 2 at Colorado 3**

30 Toronto 4 at St. Louis 3 (Sundin 0:06 OT)

* Doug Gilmour of Toronto scored his 1,000th point on a goal, but the video goal judge ruled that the net was off before the puck crossed the line. Minutes later, Gilmour assisted on a Mats Sundin goal to officially register the milestone point.

** Coach Pat Burns missed the third period because of the flu.

JANUARY

1 Toronto 1 at Dallas 0 [Potvin]*

3 Boston 4 at Toronto 4**

5 Toronto 1 at Buffalo 3

6 Colorado 2 at Toronto 5***

10 Los Angeles 4 at Toronto 5

11 Toronto 3 at Islanders 4

13 Vancouver 5 at Toronto 2

17 Winnipeg 4 at Toronto 2

24 Chicago 2 at Toronto 2

27 Toronto 2 at Ottawa 2 (Alfredsson [O] tied game at 19:50 with goalie out)

30 Toronto 2 at Detroit 4 (Yzerman 18:59 EN)

31 St. Louis 4 at Toronto 0 [Fuhr] (MacInnis 19:06—EN)

* Afternoon game.

** Doug Gilmour was honoured for recording his 1,000th point the previous month.

*** The first 6:50 was played without a whistle.

FEBRUARY

3 Montreal 4 at Toronto 1 (Rucinsky 19:31—EN)

5 Toronto 4 at San Jose 6

7 Toronto 2 at Anaheim 1

8 Toronto 3 at Los Angeles 4

10 Buffalo 2 at Toronto 2

12 Pittsburgh 1 at Toronto 4

14 San Jose 3 at Toronto 4

16 Toronto 3 at Washington 4

18 Detroit 3 at Toronto 2*

21 Tampa Bay 3 at Toronto 2 (Bellows 1:42 OT)

22 Toronto 3 at Detroit 5

24 Dallas 3 at Toronto 2

28 Toronto 3 at Winnipeg 4

* Afternoon game.

MARCH

2 Toronto 1 at Dallas 5

3 Toronto 0 at Colorado 4 [Roy]

6 New Jersey 2 at Toronto 2

8 Toronto 4 at Hartford 7

9 Calgary 3 at Toronto 4

13 Winnipeg 3 at Toronto 3

15 Dallas 0 at Toronto 3 [Potvin] (Gilmour 19:01—EN)

17 Vancouver 2 at Toronto 4*

19 Toronto 5 at Detroit 6

20 Detroit 4 at Toronto 3 (McCarty 2:41 OT)

23 Philadelphia 4 at Toronto 0 [Hextall]

25 Toronto 4 at Calgary 2

27 Toronto 6 at Vancouver 2**

30 Toronto 4 at Edmonton 3

* Afternoon game.

** Toronto's Larry Murphy registered his 1,000th point.

APRIL

3 Chicago 5 at Toronto 2 (Probert 18:53—EN)

4 Toronto 3 at St. Louis 1

6 St. Louis 1 at Toronto 5

11 Toronto 2 at Chicago 5

13 Edmonton 3 at Toronto 6 (Gagner 19:51—EN)*

* Larry Murphy was honoured for recording his 1,000th point the previous month, and received the Horton Trophy.

1996–97

OCTOBER

5 Anaheim 1 at Toronto 4*

8 Edmonton 4 at Toronto 2 (Smyth 19:52 EN)

12 Tampa Bay 7 at Toronto 4 (Gratton 19:59—EN)

15 Chicago 3 at Toronto 1 (Amonte 19:17—EN)

17 Toronto 1 at St. Louis 6

19 Toronto 0 at Dallas 2 [Moog]

22 San Jose 3 at Toronto 4

24 Toronto 2 at Boston 1

26 Phoenix 2 at Toronto 5 (Craig 19:53—EN)

29   Los Angeles 5 at Toronto 2 (Perreault 19:45—EN)

31   Toronto 5 at Islanders 3

* Opening ceremony was attended by 28 members of Canada's team from the 1996 Summer Olympics.

NOVEMBER

2   Detroit 2 at Toronto 6*

5   St. Louis 3 at Toronto 6

7   Toronto 2 at Ottawa 6

9   Edmonton 3 at Toronto 7

10   Toronto 1 at Philadelphia 3**

13   Toronto 2 at Anaheim 3

14   Toronto 1 at Los Angeles 4

16   Toronto 2 at Phoenix 3

19   Buffalo 3 at Toronto 4

21   Toronto 3 at Buffalo 6 (Barnaby 19:58—EN)

23   Montreal 4 at Toronto 3***

26   Vancouver 2 at Toronto 3 (Roberts [V] 19:14 with goalie out)

27   Toronto 2 at Detroit 5

30   Toronto 2 at Dallas 5

* Sixty-fifth anniversary of Maple Leaf Gardens; Red Horner and Mush March were in attendance, and both teams wore old-style sweaters.
** Goalies Félix Potvin and Ron Hextall fought as part of an end-of-game melee.
*** Borje Salming Night.

DECEMBER

3   St. Louis 0 at Toronto 2 [Cousineau/Potvin]*

6   Toronto 5 at Rangers 6 (Berg won game at 19:33)

7   Rangers 4 at Toronto 0 [Healy]

9   Toronto 3 at Chicago 1 (Warriner 19:48—EN)

10   New Jersey 5 at Toronto 2

14   Phoenix 5 at Toronto 3 (Tkachuk 19:59—EN)

15   Toronto 1 at Detroit 3

17   Toronto 6 at San Jose 3 (Sundin 19:15—EN)

20   Toronto 2 at Phoenix 5

21   Toronto 6 at Colorado 2

23   Pittsburgh 6 at Toronto 5 (Modin [T] 19:32 with goalie out)

27   Toronto 3 at St. Louis 2**

28   Chicago 4 at Toronto 5

30   Islanders 0 at Toronto 2 [Cousineau]

* Félix Potvin replaced Marcel Cousineau at 14:06 of the second period.
** During the pre-game ceremony, Brett Hull was honoured for having scored his 500th goal.

JANUARY

3   Toronto 3 at Edmonton 4*

4   Toronto 3 at Vancouver 7*

7   Toronto 3 at Calgary 4 (Fleury (C) tied game at 19:29 with goalie out; Gagner 4:00 OT)**

11   Colorado 3 at Toronto 2

13   Toronto 3 at Washington 6

15   Los Angeles 3 at Toronto 2***

20   Toronto 1 at Hartford 3 (Cassels 19:53—EN)

22   Calgary 3 at Toronto 5 (Sundin 19:59—EN)

24   Toronto 2 at Chicago 1 (Muller 2:07 OT)*

25   Dallas 5 at Toronto 1

27   Colorado 5 at Toronto 2

29   St. Louis 4 at Toronto 0 [Fuhr]

31   Toronto 3 at New Jersey 3

* The Leafs wore white sweaters for these three games.
** The clock stopped at 9:54 of the third for 21 seconds of play, but was never corrected.
*** Six Ontario Hockey League players from the World Junior Championship team dropped the puck.

FEBRUARY

1   Ottawa 2 at Toronto 1

5   Anaheim 2 at Toronto 4

8   Vancouver 2 at Toronto 4

12   Toronto 2 at Anaheim 5

13   Toronto 4 at Los Angeles 4

15   Toronto 0 at Calgary 3 [Kidd]

18   Toronto 6 at Vancouver 5

19   Toronto 5 at Edmonton 6

22   Toronto 5 at Montreal 1*

26   Washington 3 at Toronto 1

* The Leafs wore their 65th-anniversary sweaters.

MARCH

1   San Jose 2 at Toronto 3

3   Boston 2 at Toronto 4

5   Detroit 4 at Toronto 4

8   Hartford 1 at Toronto 1

10   Dallas 3 at Toronto 3 (Hendrickson [T] tied game at 19:18 with goalie out)

12   Chicago 3 at Toronto 2

15   Toronto 3 at Florida 3

16   Toronto 3 at Tampa Bay 1

19   Philadelphia 6 at Toronto 3 (Lindros 19:12—EN)

20   Toronto 3 at Pittsburgh 6

22   Phoenix 3 at Toronto 0 [Khabibulin]

26   Toronto 2 at San Jose 1

27   Toronto 1 at Phoenix 1

29   Toronto 3 at Colorado 2

APRIL

2   Florida 1 at Toronto 3

3   Toronto 2 at Detroit 2

5   Detroit 4 at Toronto 2

9   Toronto 2 at Dallas 3

10   Toronto 1 at St. Louis 5

12   Calgary 1 at Toronto 4 (Clark 19:05—EN)*

* Opening ceremony honoured Canada's Women's World Championship team. The puck never went in the net for Clark's goal. Albelin of Calgary jumped off the bench to stop the puck, thus the goal was automatically awarded.

1997–98

OCTOBER

1   Washington 4 at Toronto 1*

4   Toronto 0 at Islanders 3 [Salo]

7   Toronto 2 at Calgary 1

9   Toronto 2 at Vancouver 2

11   Toronto 1 at Edmonton 2

14   Detroit 3 at Toronto 2

15   Toronto 4 at Detroit 3

18   Dallas 5 at Toronto 4

22   Ottawa 6 at Toronto 2

25   Calgary 3 at Toronto 4

28   Anaheim 2 at Toronto 2

* Don Cherry and Ken Dryden faced off the opening puck.

NOVEMBER

1   Toronto 1 at Montreal 5

4   Toronto 0 at San Jose 0 [Healy (T)/Cousineau (T)/Vernon (S)]

5   Toronto 4 at Calgary 3

8   Phoenix 3 at Toronto 0 [Khabibulin] (Tkachuk 18:49—EN)*

11   Chicago 2 at Toronto 5 (Hendrickson 19:42—EN)**

13   Toronto 2 at Chicago 1 (all goals in 1st)

15   Pittsburgh 5 at Toronto 0 [Barrasso]***

17   St. Louis 3 at Toronto 2 (MacInnis scores winner at 19:58 of 3rd from centre ice)

19   Philadelphia 1 at Toronto 3****

21   Toronto 1 at Colorado 3 (Sakic 19:35—EN)

22   Toronto 0 at Phoenix 2 (Khabibulin) (Roenick 19:37—EN)

25   San Jose 1 at Toronto 3 (McCauley 19:44—EN)

29   Vancouver 4 at Toronto 2

* Jamie Macoun was honoured for playing his 1,000th game.
** "O Canada" was played with bagpipes for Remembrance Day.
*** Mario Lemieux, Bryan Trottier, and Glen Sather, newest inductees to the Hockey Hall of Fame, faced off the opening puck.
**** Pinball Clemons, Paul Masotti, and Doug Flutie of the Grey Cup champion Toronto Argonauts faced off the opening puck.

DECEMBER

2   Anaheim 3 at Toronto 3

4   Toronto 3 at St. Louis 4 (D. King scored at 19:34 with goalie out)

6   Los Angeles 2 at Toronto 7

8   Dallas 0 at Toronto 3 [Potvin] (Sundin 18:49—EN)*

10   Colorado 2 at Toronto 2

13   New Jersey 3 at Toronto 0 [Brodeur]

15   Toronto 2 at Colorado 3

17   Toronto 6 at Anaheim 2

18   Toronto 2 at Los Angeles 5

20   Toronto 3 at Phoenix 2

23   Edmonton 4 at Toronto 5

26   Toronto 1 at Detroit 4

27   Detroit 8 at Toronto 1

31   Boston 2 at Toronto 2

* Toronto's 5,000th NHL game.

JANUARY

1   Toronto 3 at Chicago 3

3   Toronto 2 at New Jersey 4

6   Toronto 3 at Washington 5

7   Toronto 5 at Tampa Bay 2

10   Chicago 4 at Toronto 3

12   Toronto 2 at Rangers 3

14   Buffalo 4 at Toronto 1

21   Toronto 3 at Detroit 0 [Potvin] (Smith 19:59—EN)

22   Toronto 3 at Chicago 0 [Potvin] (Schneider 18:38—EN)

24   Tampa Bay 2 at Toronto 5

26   Toronto 1 at Dallas 5

29   Toronto 0 at St. Louis 2 [Fuhr]

31   Phoenix 5 at Toronto 2

FEBRUARY

2   Dallas 5 at Toronto 1

4   St. Louis 2 at Toronto 3

5   Toronto 2 at Ottawa 3

7   Florida 2 at Toronto 3*

8–24   *Olympic Break*

25   Toronto 2 at Buffalo 2 (Sundin tied game at 19:55 with goalie out)

26   Rangers 5 at Toronto 2**

28   Montreal 0 at Toronto 4 [Potvin]***

* Afternoon game; four players—Mathieu Schneider and Mats Sundin (Toronto) and Robert Svehla and John Vanbiesbrouck (Florida)—were honoured prior to the game in recognition of their participation in the Nagano Olympics.
** Medallists from Nagano were again honoured in a ceremony.
*** Banners to honour George Armstrong and Charlie Conacher were raised to the rafters of Maple Leaf Gardens.

MARCH

2   Toronto 1 at Pittsburgh 3 (all goals in 1st)

4   Colorado 5 at Toronto 3 (Deadmarsh 19:50—EN)

7   Edmonton 1 at Toronto 4

9   Toronto 2 at San Jose 3 (all goals in 3rd) (Gill 19:23—EN)

11   Toronto 3 at Anaheim 1 (Sundin 19:54—EN)

12   Toronto 2 at Los Angeles 1

14   Calgary 1 at Toronto 2

16   Toronto 1 at Philadelphia 4

18   Detroit 5 at Toronto 2 (Draper 19:09—EN)

19   Toronto 0 at Boston 4 [Dafoe]

21   Vancouver 1 at Toronto 1

24   Toronto 2 at Phoenix 4 (all goals in 3rd) (Tocchet 19:44—EN)

26   Toronto 1 at Dallas 0 [Potvin]

28   Islanders 3 at Toronto 4 (D. King [T] tied game at 19:09 with goalie out; Côté won game at 4:56 OT)

30   Los Angeles 3 at Toronto 2 (Clark scored at 19:45 with goalie out)

APRIL

1   St. Louis 6 at Toronto 4

4   San Jose 5 at Toronto 3

6   Toronto 2 at Dallas 4

7   Toronto 3 at Florida 1

9   Toronto 2 at Carolina 5 (Roberts 19:33—EN)

11   Carolina 1 at Toronto 5 (Schneider 17:37—EN)

15   Chicago 2 at Toronto 3

18   Toronto 3 at Edmonton 4

19   Toronto 2 at Vancouver 1

1998–99

OCTOBER

10   Detroit 1 at Toronto 2*

13   Toronto 3 at Edmonton 2

16   Toronto 7 at Calgary 3

17   Toronto 1 at Vancouver 4

23   Toronto 5 at Detroit 3

24   Toronto 6 at Pittsburgh 4 (K. King 19:33—EN)

26   Pittsburgh 2 at Toronto 0 [Skudra]

30   Toronto 1 at Buffalo 4

31   Buffalo 6 at Toronto 3

* Final home opener at Maple Leaf Gardens. The Leafs wore their Original Six sweaters, as
  they would for games against Original Six opponents this season.

NOVEMBER

4   Colorado 0 at Toronto 3 [Joseph] (all goals in 2nd)

5   Toronto 1 at Boston 4

7   Rangers 6 at Toronto 6

9   Islanders 3 at Toronto 1 (all goals in 3rd)

11   Edmonton 2 at Toronto 3

12   Toronto 10 at Chicago 3

14   Ottawa 1 at Toronto 2

18   Toronto 1 at Washington 4

20   Toronto 1 at Buffalo 4

21   Buffalo 1 at Toronto 2

23   Calgary 2 at Toronto 3

25   Vancouver 1 at Toronto 5 (Yushkevich 10:58—EN—PP)

27   Toronto 3 at Philadelphia 4

28   Ottawa 2 at Toronto 3 (D. King 0:42 OT)

DECEMBER

2   Los Angeles 1 at Toronto 3

5   Toronto 4 at Montreal 3 (Kaberle 0:34 OT)

7   Toronto 2 at Rangers 6

11   Toronto 3 at Chicago 2

12   Philadelphia 3 at Toronto 0 [Vanbiesbrouck]

16   Phoenix 2 at Toronto 5

19   Rangers 4 at Toronto 7*

21   Pittsburgh 1 at Toronto 7

---

23   Dallas 5 at Toronto 1

26   Montreal 2 at Toronto 1**

30   Anaheim 1 at Toronto 4

31   Toronto 4 at Detroit 2

* Last game Wayne Gretzky played at Maple Leaf Gardens.

** A moment of silence was held to remember the passing of Syl Apps.

JANUARY

2   Washington 5 at Toronto 2 (Johansson 19:37—EN)

4   Tampa Bay 4 at Toronto 5 (Modin 1:54 OT)

7   Toronto 1 at Boston 2

9   Boston 3 at Toronto 6*

12   Toronto 4 at Tampa Bay 3

13   Toronto 3 at Florida 3

16   Toronto 4 at Philadelphia 3

18   Toronto 2 at Carolina 4

20   Toronto 6 at Dallas 4

21   Toronto 4 at St. Louis 2

28   Toronto 0 at Pittsburgh 6 [Skudra]

30   Washington 3 at Toronto 5 (Sundin 19:53—EN)

* Bobby Orr and George Armstrong faced off the opening puck.

FEBRUARY

2   Toronto 3 at Tampa Bay 0 [Joseph]

3   Toronto 2 at Florida 5 (Niedermayer 19:35—EN)

6   Toronto 3 at New Jersey 2

10   Carolina 6 at Toronto 5

13   Chicago 6 at Toronto 2*

15   Toronto 3 at New Jersey 3

17   Toronto 3 at Buffalo 2 (Sundin 4:04 OT)

20   Montreal 2 at Toronto 3 (Thomas 3:48 OT)**

22   Toronto 3 at Washington 4

24   Carolina 2 at Toronto 2

25   Toronto 4 at Islanders 1

27   Florida 1 at Toronto 4

* Last game at Maple Leaf Gardens—the final goal was scored by Bob Probert of
  Chicago at 11:05 of the third period. The last Toronto goal was scored by Derek King
  at 8:15 of the second.

** First game at Air Canada Centre.

MARCH

3   New Jersey 5 at Toronto 2 (Elias 19:16—EN)

4   Toronto 4 at St. Louis 0 [Joseph]*

6   Toronto 1 at Ottawa 3

8   Toronto 2 at Rangers 3 (Nedved 4:46 OT)

9   Tampa Bay 1 at Toronto 6

11   Toronto 2 at Islanders 1

13   Toronto 1 at Montreal 2 (all goals in 2nd)

17   Boston 4 at Toronto 1 (Carter 19:54—EN)

20   New Jersey 1 at Toronto 3

22   Philadelphia 3 at Toronto 1

24   San Jose 8 at Toronto 5 (Murphy 19:57—EN)

26 Toronto 7 at Carolina 2

27 Boston 2 at Toronto 2

31 Toronto 6 at Vancouver 5

* Leafs recorded just nine shots on goal, the lowest total for a winning team in NHL history.

APRIL

1 Toronto 5 at Edmonton 1

3 Toronto 5 at Calgary 1

5 St. Louis 2 at Toronto 2

7 Ottawa 2 at Toronto 4

8 Toronto 1 at Ottawa 3

10 Florida 1 at Toronto 9

14 Islanders 2 at Toronto 3 (Berard 0:42 OT)

17 Toronto 2 at Montreal 3

1999–2000

OCTOBER

2 Toronto 4 at Montreal 1*

4 Boston 0 at Toronto 4 [Joseph]

6 Colorado 1 at Toronto 2

9 Toronto 3 at Ottawa 4

11 Nashville 4 at Toronto 2

13 Florida 2 at Toronto 3

15 Toronto 2 at Chicago 1

16 Toronto 2 at St. Louis 4

20 Carolina 3 at Toronto 3

23 Montreal 2 at Toronto 3

25 Dallas 0 at Toronto 4 [Joseph]

27 Atlanta 0 at Toronto 4 [Healy]

30 Calgary 1 at Toronto 2

* Sprinter Bruny Surin faced off the opening puck.

NOVEMBER

3 Toronto 6 at Carolina 0 [Joseph]

5 Toronto 3 at Washington 5

6 Toronto 3 at New Jersey 3

9 Anaheim 2 at Toronto 0 [Hebert] (Kariya 19:47—EN)

11 Toronto 3 at Boston 4 (Axelsson 3:58 OT)

13 Detroit 1 at Toronto 1

15 San Jose 2 at Toronto 4

17 St. Louis 3 at Toronto 2

20 Rangers 3 at Toronto 4 (Korolev 1:16 OT)*

23 Toronto 1 at Pittsburgh 3 (Titov 19:38—EN)

26 Toronto 2 at Philadelphia 3 (Berezin (T) tied game at 19:48 with goalie out; Recchi 4:08 OT)

27 Edmonton 2 at Toronto 5

29 Washington 1 at Toronto 3 (Thomas 19:40—EN)

* The Hockey Hall of Fame Game—new inductees Scotty Morrison, Andy Van Hellemond, and Wayne Gretzky dropped the opening puck, accompanied by many previous Hall of Famers. Players of the game replaced the Three-Star selection on the night: Adam Graves for the Rangers and Yanic Perreault for Toronto.

DECEMBER

2 Toronto 2 at Carolina 2

4 Pittsburgh 2 at Toronto 3 (Sundin 0:27 OT)

6 Buffalo 2 at Toronto 3 (Thomas 1:05 OT)

9 Toronto 2 at Philadelphia 4

11 Philadelphia 4 at Toronto 6 (Hoglund 19:48—EN)

13 Ottawa 3 at Toronto 1

15 Islanders 1 at Toronto 5

18 Montreal 1 at Toronto 2*

20 Toronto 6 at Florida 4

21 Toronto 4 at Tampa Bay 2

23 New Jersey 1 at Toronto 4

29 Toronto 2 at Islanders 1 (Hoglund 19:11—EN)

* Canada Post unveiled the *Hockey Night in Canada* stamps, with Foster Hewitt's daughter attending the ceremony.

JANUARY

1 Toronto 1 at Buffalo 8

3 Buffalo 2 at Toronto 6

5 Toronto 2 at Rangers 3 (Graves 4:26 OT)

7 Toronto 2 at Pittsburgh 5 (Straka 18:56—EN)

8 Rangers 5 at Toronto 3

11 Toronto 3 at Boston 2

14 Toronto 3 at Edmonton 2 (Sundin 2:59 OT)

15 Toronto 0 at Calgary 4 [Brathwaite]

17 Toronto 5 at Vancouver 4 (Thomas 4:55 OT)

22 Washington 5 at Toronto 5

24 Ottawa 3 at Toronto 3

26 Toronto 2 at Detroit 4

27 Toronto 4 at Rangers 3

29 Los Angeles 2 at Toronto 3

FEBRUARY

1 Toronto 5 at Tampa Bay 3 (Korolev 19:21—EN)

3 Toronto 2 at Boston 4

9 Philadelphia 4 at Toronto 2

12 Vancouver 4 at Toronto 1 (Bertuzzi 18:41—EN)

14 Carolina 5 at Toronto 2

16 Boston 3 at Toronto 3

19 Toronto 1 at Montreal 2

23 Phoenix 3 at Toronto 5 (Perreault 19:07—EN)

25 Toronto 3 at New Jersey 1

26 Buffalo 2 at Toronto 5

29 Toronto 4 at Atlanta 0 [Healy]*

* Assistant coach Rick Ley assumed head coaching duties while Pat Quinn attended GM meetings.

MARCH

1 Toronto 1 at Florida 3

4 Montreal 3 at Toronto 4

6 Toronto 6 at Vancouver 5 (Sundin 3:13 OT)

7	Toronto 2 at Edmonton 0 [Joseph] (both goals in 1st)
9	Toronto 6 at Calgary 2
11	Toronto 4 at Ottawa 2
15	Chicago 5 at Toronto 2
16	Toronto 4 at Detroit 3 (Sundin 1:38 OT)
18	Atlanta 4 at Toronto 1
22	Islanders 5 at Toronto 2
23	Toronto 2 at Ottawa 3
25	New Jersey 3 at Toronto 5
29	Toronto 3 at St. Louis 2
30	Toronto 0 at Chicago 4 [Thibault]

APRIL

1	Toronto 4 at Washington 3
3	Toronto 2 at Buffalo 3 (all goals in 1st)
5	Pittsburgh 4 at Toronto 2
7	Toronto 2 at Islanders 1
8	Tampa Bay 2 at Toronto 4

2000–01

OCTOBER

7	Montreal 0 at Toronto 2 [Joseph]
9	Dallas 3 at Toronto 1
11	Islanders 2 at Toronto 3
14	Ottawa 4 at Toronto 0 [Lalime]
16	Toronto 2 at Vancouver 5 (Naslund 18:52—EN)
19	Toronto 4 at Edmonton 1
21	Toronto 2 at Calgary 1
25	Minnesota 1 at Toronto 6
27	Toronto 1 at Buffalo 2
28	Toronto 2 at Boston 1 (Sundin 3:36 OT)
31	Toronto 3 at Ottawa 4

NOVEMBER

2	New Jersey 3 at Toronto 5
4	Toronto 0 at St. Louis 0 [Joseph (T)/Turek (S)]
5	Boston 1 at Toronto 7
8	Carolina 0 at Toronto 5 [Joseph]
10	Toronto 1 at Carolina 3
11	Chicago 3 at Toronto 3*
15	Philadelphia 2 at Toronto 1 (Recchi 3:26 OT)
17	Tampa Bay 2 at Toronto 2
18	Toronto 6 at Montreal 1
21	Toronto 3 at Rangers 1
22	Edmonton 3 at Toronto 4
25	Ottawa 4 at Toronto 2
29	St. Louis 6 at Toronto 5 (Hecht 0:18 OT)
30	Toronto 6 at Islanders 4 (Tucker 19:45—EN)

* Hockey Hall of Fame game.

DECEMBER

2	Rangers 2 at Toronto 8
4	Florida 4 at Toronto 4
6	Toronto 3 at Detroit 0 [Joseph]
9	Pittsburgh 1 at Toronto 5
13	Toronto 7 at Pittsburgh 4 (Perreault 19:01—EN)
15	Toronto 2 at Islanders 3
16	Calgary 6 at Toronto 5 (V. Bure 0:34 OT)
20	Nashville 3 at Toronto 1 (Walker 19:48—EN)
21	Toronto 0 at Boston 4 [Dafoe]
23	Toronto 5 at Montreal 2
26	Toronto 3 at Thrashers 5 (Audette 19:54—EN)
27	Toronto 0 at Pittsburgh 5 [Snow]
30	Toronto 4 at Florida 1
31	Toronto 3 at Tampa Bay 2

JANUARY

3	Buffalo 1 at Toronto 1
5	Toronto 3 at Buffalo 3
6	Washington 3 at Toronto 2
10	Tampa Bay 3 at Toronto 1 (Modin 19:58—EN)
12	Phoenix 2 at Toronto 3
13	Toronto 4 at New Jersey 4
17	Los Angeles 2 at Toronto 1
18	Toronto 1 at Rangers 2 (Leetch 4:33 OT)
20	Buffalo 0 at Toronto 2 [Joseph]
24	Boston 2 at Toronto 1
25	Toronto 2 at Thrashers 1 (McCabe 0:39 OT)
27	Rangers 1 at Toronto 3
29	Toronto 1 at St. Louis 2
31	Toronto 4 at Carolina 3

FEBRUARY

1	Toronto 4 at Washington 5
7	Thrashers 1 at Toronto 7
8	Toronto 1 at Detroit 2
10	Detroit 3 at Toronto 3
14	Columbus 2 at Toronto 2
15	Toronto 2 at Philadelphia 5
17	Colorado 5 at Toronto 5
19	New Jersey 2 at Toronto 0 [Brodeur]
22	Vancouver 1 at Toronto 4
24	Montreal 1 at Toronto 5
25	Toronto 4 at Chicago 6 (Sullivan 19:52—EN)
28	San Jose 1 at Toronto 2

MARCH

1	Toronto 3 at Washington 2 (Roberts 1:21 OT)
3	Ottawa 3 at Toronto 2 (Yashin 0:42 OT)

6   Toronto 3 at Calgary 1 (Thomas 19:38—EN)

7   Toronto 0 at Edmonton 4 [Salo]

10 Toronto 3 at Vancouver 3

14 Anaheim 2 at Toronto 3

15 Toronto 2 at Tampa Bay 3

17 Toronto 5 at Florida 3 (Sundin 19:52—EN)

20 Toronto 0 at Buffalo 3 [Hasek]

21 Florida 3 at Toronto 1

24 Philadelphia 3 at Toronto 5 (Tucker 19:59—EN)

28 Boston 3 at Toronto 0 [Dafoe]

29 Toronto 2 at Philadelphia 1

31 Toronto 1 at Montreal 4

APRIL

4   Islanders 2 at Toronto 4

6   Toronto 1 at Chicago 0 [Joseph]

7   Toronto 3 at Ottawa 5

2001–02

OCTOBER

3   Ottawa 5 at Toronto 4

6   Toronto 2 at Montreal 2

8   Anaheim 1 at Toronto 6

11 Toronto 3 at Carolina 2

13 St. Louis 5 at Toronto 2

16 Toronto 4 at Edmonton 1

18 Toronto 6 at Vancouver 5

20 Toronto 1 at Calgary 4

23 Boston 0 at Toronto 2 [Joseph] (Green 19:52—EN)

25 Toronto 1 at Boston 2 (Thornton 0:12 OT)

27 Pittsburgh 0 at Toronto 4 [Joseph]

30 Tampa Bay 2 at Toronto 3

NOVEMBER

1   Toronto 1 at Pittsburgh 3

3   Colorado 1 at Toronto 4 (Tucker 19:24—EN)

6   Washington 2 at Toronto 4

9   Toronto 2 at New Jersey 3 (Elias 3:26 OT)

10 New Jersey 1 at Toronto 1

14 Toronto 3 at Florida 2

15 Toronto 3 at Tampa Bay 2

17 Toronto 1 at Ottawa 2 (Rachunek 4:55 OT)

19 Florida 1 at Toronto 5*

21 Toronto 2 at Buffalo 4

23 Toronto 1 at Islanders 3

24 Boston 0 at Toronto 2 [Joseph]

27 Carolina 5 at Toronto 2 (Kapanen 18:48—EN)

30 Toronto 2 at Chicago 1

* Hockey Hall of Fame game.

DECEMBER

1   Chicago 1 at Toronto 4

4   Pittsburgh 1 at Toronto 0 [Hedberg]

6   Toronto 6 at Rangers 3

8   Rangers 3 at Toronto 4

11 Phoenix 3 at Toronto 6

13 Toronto 4 at St. Louis 3 (Sundin 0:43 OT)

15 Montreal 4 at Toronto 6

18 Los Angeles 3 at Toronto 1

21 Toronto 3 at Buffalo 3

22 Buffalo 2 at Toronto 3

26 Toronto 3 at Carolina 4

28 Toronto 4 at Thrashers 5

29 Toronto 2 at Florida 4

31 Toronto 4 at Tampa Bay 1

JANUARY

3   Toronto 2 at Boston 1

5   Ottawa 1 at Toronto 3

7   Toronto 3 at Ottawa 4

8   Nashville 3 at Toronto 4

11 Toronto 3 at Washington 3

12 Montreal 1 at Toronto 1

15 Thrashers 3 at Toronto 2

17 Toronto 2 at Nashville 3 (G. Johnson 0:47 OT)

19 Philadelphia 3 at Toronto 0 [Cechmanek] (Fedoruk 19:22—EN)

22 Toronto 6 at Calgary 1

25 Toronto 1 at Vancouver 6

26 Toronto 1 at Edmonton 4 (Marchant 19:07—EN)

29 San Jose 3 at Toronto 4

30 Toronto 6 at Thrashers 0 [Joseph]

FEBRUARY

5   Minnesota 1 at Toronto 3

7   Toronto 1 at Islanders 4

9   Montreal 1 at Toronto 4 (Lumme 18:49—EN)

11 Thrashers 4 at Toronto 5

14–25 *Olympic Break*

26 Carolina 1 at Toronto 4 (Roberts 19:53—EN)

MARCH

1   Toronto 2 at New Jersey 4

2   Buffalo 3 at Toronto 3*

4   Toronto 3 at Washington 2

6   Toronto 2 at Detroit 6

9   Toronto 1 at Montreal 1

10 Toronto 3 at Philadelphia 1 (Roberts 19:45—EN)

12 Philadelphia 1 at Toronto 1

14 Toronto 2 at Boston 1

16   Dallas 5 at Toronto 5

19   Islanders 2 at Toronto 3

21   Washington 4 at Toronto 3

23   Buffalo 0 at Toronto 2 [Schwab]

25   Toronto 1 at Philadelphia 4 (McGillis 19:54—EN)

26   Tampa Bay 2 at Toronto 7

28   Islanders 5 at Toronto 4

30   New Jersey 3 at Toronto 1
* The Leafs played in green St. Pats sweaters and brown pants.

APRIL

1   Toronto 5 at Detroit 4 (Sundin 3:34 OT)

4   Rangers 4 at Toronto 2

6   Florida 2 at Toronto 2

8   Columbus 1 at Toronto 4

10   Toronto 7 at Rangers 2

12   Toronto 5 at Pittsburgh 2

13   Toronto 5 at Ottawa 2

2002–03

OCTOBER

10   Toronto 6 at Pittsburgh 0 [Belfour]

12   Ottawa 2 at Toronto 1

14   Pittsburgh 5 at Toronto 4

15   Toronto 4 at Rangers 5

17   Phoenix 3 at Toronto 5

19   Toronto 2 at Montreal 2

21   Boston 4 at Toronto 1 (Huml 19:47—EN)

23   Florida 4 at Toronto 1 (Jokinen 19:29—EN)

26   Rangers 4 at Toronto 3

28   Anaheim 2 at Toronto 5

31   Thrashers 3 at Toronto 3

NOVEMBER

2   Montreal 5 at Toronto 2 (Markov 19:40—EN)*

5   Tampa Bay 3 at Toronto 4

8   Toronto 1 at Dallas 2

9   Toronto 3 at St. Louis 6

12   Los Angeles 3 at Toronto 4 (Sundin 3:20 OT)

15   Toronto 3 at Buffalo 2

16   Detroit 2 at Toronto 1

19   Boston 0 at Toronto 2 [Belfour]

23   Philadelphia 0 at Toronto 6 [Belfour]

25   Toronto 0 at Ottawa 2 [Lalime]

26   Washington 4 at Toronto 5

29   Toronto 3 at Philadelphia 0 [Esche] (Renberg 18:24—EN)

30   Buffalo 1 at Toronto 3
* Hockey Hall of Fame game.

DECEMBER

3   Tampa Bay 3 at Toronto 4 (Pilar 3:48 OT)

6   Toronto 2 at Islanders 4

7   New Jersey 0 at Toronto 1 [Belfour]

10   Pittsburgh 2 at Toronto 4 (Healey 19:25—EN)

12   Toronto 1 at Philadelphia 2

14   Rangers 1 at Toronto 4

16   Toronto 0 at Thrashers 1 [Nurminen]

18   Toronto 2 at Florida 2

19   Toronto 2 at Tampa Bay 1

21   San Jose 3 at Toronto 3

23   Thrashers 1 at Toronto 5

27   Toronto 4 at Calgary 3

28   Toronto 2 at Edmonton 3 (Marchant 4:35 OT)

31   Toronto 5 at Vancouver 3 (Reichel 19:58—EN)

JANUARY

3   Toronto 0 at New Jersey 2 [Schwab]

4   New Jersey 1 at Toronto 2

7   Boston 2 at Toronto 5

9   Toronto 4 at Pittsburgh 2 (Mogilny 19:05—EN)

11   Toronto 2 at Boston 6

13   Toronto 1 at Rangers 5

14   Calgary 2 at Toronto 3

17   Toronto 4 at Washington 1 (Sundin 19:30—EN)

18   Toronto 3 at Montreal 2 (Antropov 0:56 OT)

21   Philadelphia 3 at Toronto 1

24   Toronto 0 at Buffalo 4 [Biron]

25   Colorado 3 at Toronto 0 [Roy]

29   Toronto 3 at Carolina 2

30   Toronto 5 at Thrashers 2

FEBRUARY

5   Toronto 6 at Florida 0 [Belfour]

6   Toronto 3 at Tampa Bay 2 (Antropov 3:49 OT)

8   Montreal 1 at Toronto 3*

11   Edmonton 5 at Toronto 4

12   Toronto 3 at Chicago 1

15   Ottawa 1 at Toronto 2

18   Carolina 3 at Toronto 4

20   Toronto 6 at Washington 2

22   Toronto 5 at Montreal 3 (Roberts 19:36—EN)

23   Nashville 5 at Toronto 2

25   Islanders 2 at Toronto 5

27   Toronto 2 at Detroit 7
* The Leafs honoured Darryl Sittler's number 27.

MARCH

1   Carolina 1 at Toronto 4

3   Florida 2 at Toronto 1

4   Toronto 1 at Ottawa 4

6   Toronto 2 at Buffalo 4 (C. Brown 19:50—EN)

8   Vancouver 3 at Toronto 3

10   Toronto 3 at Edmonton 2

13   Toronto 3 at Calgary 4 (Clark 4:30 OT)

15   Toronto 1 at Vancouver 0 [Belfour]

18   Islanders 3 at Toronto 3

20   Toronto 3 at Columbus 4 (Wright 4:16 OT)

22   Buffalo 2 at Toronto 3 (McCabe 0:36 OT)

24   Toronto 2 at Boston 3

25   Toronto 3 at Carolina 3

28   Toronto 5 at Islanders 2

29   Washington 3 at Toronto 4 (Sundin 2:56 OT)

APRIL

1   Toronto 3 at New Jersey 2 (Kaberle 2:44 OT)

3   Minnesota 1 at Toronto 2

5   Ottawa 3 at Toronto 1

2003–04

OCTOBER

11   Montreal 4 at Toronto 0 [Theodore]

13   Washington 2 at Toronto 2

16   Toronto 2 at New Jersey 2

18   Toronto 1 at Montreal 0 [Belfour]

20   Toronto 2 at Islanders 5

22   Toronto 3 at Dallas 1 (Reichel 19:37—EN)

23   Toronto 5 at Phoenix 4

25   Washington 1 at Toronto 4 (Tucker 19:30—EN)

27   Thrashers 3 at Toronto 2 (Savard 4:45 OT)

30   Toronto 3 at Buffalo 5 (Pyatt 19:33—EN)

NOVEMBER

1   Philadelphia 7 at Toronto 1*

2   Toronto 2 at Carolina 1

4   Pittsburgh 2 at Toronto 4

7   Toronto 1 at New Jersey 1

8   Edmonton 1 at Toronto 4 (Mogilny 19:10—EN)

12   Toronto 1 at Anaheim 5

13   Toronto 4 at Los Angeles 4

15   Toronto 2 at San Jose 2

18   Toronto 2 at Calgary 3 (Lydman 1:24 OT)

20   Toronto 2 at Edmonton 3

22   Toronto 5 at Vancouver 3 (Sundin 19:22—EN)

24   Vancouver 1 at Toronto 2

27   Toronto 3 at Thrashers 1 (Nolan 19:00—EN)

29   Toronto 2 at Ottawa 1

30   Toronto 4 at Rangers 2

* Hockey Hall of Fame game.

DECEMBER

2   Rangers 4 at Toronto 5

4   Toronto 6 at Boston 0 [Belfour]

6   Detroit 2 at Toronto 5

9   St. Louis 3 at Toronto 2 (Pronger 0:30 OT)

11   Toronto 1 at Minnesota 0 [Belfour]

13   Rangers 1 at Toronto 3

16   Tampa Bay 0 at Toronto 3 [Belfour] (Tucker 18:53—EN)

19   Toronto 2 at Washington 2

20   Montreal 2 at Toronto 4

23   Florida 2 at Toronto 5

26   Toronto 6 at Rangers 5 (Sundin 3:35 OT)

27   Toronto 1 at Islanders 3 (Parrish 19:53—EN)

29   Toronto 4 at Florida 4

JANUARY

1   Toronto 2 at Boston 3

3   Buffalo 3 at Toronto 3

5   Toronto 5 at Pittsburgh 0 [Kidd]

6   Nashville 1 at Toronto 2

8   Ottawa 7 at Toronto 1

10   New Jersey 1 at Toronto 0 [Brodeur]

13   Calgary 1 at Toronto 4

16   Toronto 1 at Philadelphia 4

17   Philadelphia 4 at Toronto 0 [Esche]

20   Islanders 0 at Toronto 2 [Belfour]

21   Toronto 3 at Washington 2

24   Toronto 4 at Montreal 1

27   Carolina 2 at Toronto 0 [Weekes]

30   Toronto 4 at Thrashers 1

31   Ottawa 1 at Toronto 5

FEBRUARY

3   Chicago 4 at Toronto 1

5   Toronto 5 at Ottawa 4 (Nolan 4:29 OT)

10   Toronto 4 at Tampa Bay 4

12   Columbus 1 at Toronto 4 (Renberg 19:37—EN)

14   Buffalo 6 at Toronto 4 (Noronen 19:17—EN)

16   Toronto 8 at Pittsburgh 4

17   Boston 5 at Toronto 2

19   Toronto 2 at Carolina 1 (Tucker 2:18 OT)

21   Montreal 4 at Toronto 5

23   Carolina 2 at Toronto 1

25   Toronto 0 at Florida 4 [Luongo]

26   Toronto 3 at Tampa Bay 4

28   New Jersey 0 at Toronto 3 [Belfour]

MARCH

2   Boston 2 at Toronto 3

4   Islanders 2 at Toronto 6

6   Buffalo 5 at Toronto 1

9   Florida 0 at Toronto 5 [Belfour]

11   Pittsburgh 3 at Toronto 2

13   Toronto 3 at Montreal 4

15   Toronto 6 at Buffalo 5 (Kaberle 3:45 OT)

16   Boston 2 at Toronto 1

18   Toronto 3 at Philadelphia 2

20   Colorado 2 at Toronto 5

23   Tampa Bay 7 at Toronto 2

25   Toronto 3 at Boston 0 [Belfour] (Antropov 18:17—EN)

27   Ottawa 2 at Toronto 2

29   Thrashers 2 at Toronto 4

APRIL

2   Toronto 2 at Buffalo 0 [Belfour] (Nieuwendyk 19:42—EN)

3   Toronto 6 at Ottawa 0 [Belfour]

2004–05

No season.

2005–06

OCTOBER

5   Ottawa 3 at Toronto 2 (SO)*

8   Montreal 5 at Toronto 4

10   Toronto 5 at Ottawa 6 (SO)

11   Philadelphia 2 at Toronto 4

14   Toronto 9 at Thrashers 1

15   Toronto 3 at Montreal 2

20   Carolina 4 at Toronto 5 (Klee 4:44 OT)

22   Philadelphia 5 at Toronto 2

24   Boston 4 at Toronto 5 (SO)

27   Toronto 1 at Boston 2

29   Ottawa 8 at Toronto 0 [Hasek]

31   Florida 1 at Toronto 2

* First shootout in NHL history.

NOVEMBER

3   Toronto 3 at Carolina 4

5   Tampa Bay 3 at Toronto 5 (Kilger 19:57—EN)*

6   Toronto 4 at Washington 5

8   Washington 4 at Toronto 6

11   Toronto 2 at Buffalo 5 (Vanek 19:48—EN)

12   Toronto 5 at Montreal 4 (O'Neill 4:13 OT)

15   Rangers 1 at Toronto 2

17   Toronto 4 at Boston 1

19   Thrashers 1 at Toronto 5

23   Boston 5 at Toronto 1

25   Toronto 3 at Carolina 4

26   Montreal 3 at Toronto 4 (Sundin 1:29 OT)

28   Toronto 2 at Florida 1

30   Toronto 1 at Tampa Bay 2

* Hockey Hall of Fame game.

DECEMBER

1   Toronto 4 at Thrashers 0 [Tellqvist]

3   San Jose 5 at Toronto 4

6   Los Angeles 2 at Toronto 1

10   Dallas 2 at Toronto 1

12   Anaheim 2 at Toronto 3

17   Toronto 2 at Ottawa 8

19   Islanders 6 at Toronto 9

22   Toronto 1 at Boston 4

23   Boston 1 at Toronto 2

26   New Jersey 1 at Toronto 2

27   Toronto 3 at Pittsburgh 2 (Kaberle 2:26 OT)

29   Buffalo 3 at Toronto 4

31   Toronto 6 at New Jersey 3

JANUARY

2   Pittsburgh 2 at Toronto 3 (McCabe 1:02 OT)

6   Toronto 0 at Calgary 1 [Kiprusoff]

7   Toronto 3 at Edmonton 2

10   Toronto 3 at Vancouver 4

14   Phoenix 4 at Toronto 3

17   Toronto 3 at Colorado 5

18   Toronto 3 at Minnesota 5 (Chouinard 19:38—EN)

21   Toronto 0 at Ottawa 7 [Hasek]

23   Toronto 3 at Ottawa 4

26   Buffalo 8 at Toronto 4

28   Montreal 4 at Toronto 3 (S. Koivu 1:04 OT)

30   Toronto 4 at Florida 2

31   Toronto 2 at Tampa Bay 3 (SO)

FEBRUARY

3   Toronto 1 at Washington 4

4   New Jersey 2 at Toronto 4 (Kilger 19:15—EN)

7   Thrashers 1 at Toronto 4

10   Toronto 2 at Rangers 4

11   Rangers 4 at Toronto 2

13–27   Olympic Break

28   Washington 5 at Toronto 3

MARCH

3   Toronto 2 at Buffalo 6

4   Ottawa 4 at Toronto 2 (Chara 19:48—EN)

7   Montreal 3 at Toronto 5

10   Toronto 1 at Islanders 2 (SO)

11   Tampa Bay 1 at Toronto 5

14   Boston 4 at Toronto 5 (SO)

16 Toronto 1 at Buffalo 3 (Drury 19:01—EN)

18 Toronto 2 at Rangers 5 (Sykora 19:23—EN)

19 Toronto 1 at Pittsburgh 0 [Tellqvist]

21 Carolina 2 at Toronto 3

23 Toronto 1 at Montreal 5

25 Toronto 2 at Montreal 6

26 Toronto 4 at New Jersey 3

28 Toronto 3 at Philadelphia 2

APRIL

1 Buffalo 0 at Toronto 7 [Aubin]

3 Buffalo 3 at Toronto 2 (SO)

5 Islanders 2 at Toronto 3

6 Toronto 2 at Boston 3 (SO)

8 Toronto 5 at Philadelphia 2 (Kilger 19:54—EN)

11 Florida 5 at Toronto 6 (Kaberle 4:49 OT)

13 Toronto 4 at Islanders 3 (Stajan 3:52 OT)

15 Ottawa 1 at Toronto 5

16 Toronto 0 at Buffalo 6 [Miller]

18 Pittsburgh 3 at Toronto 5

2006–07

OCTOBER

4 Ottawa 4 at Toronto 1 (Alfredsson 19:37—EN)*

5 Toronto 6 at Ottawa 0 [Raycroft]

7 Montreal 3 at Toronto 2 (SO)

9 Florida 1 at Toronto 2 (SO)

12 Toronto 6 at New Jersey 7 (SO)

14 Calgary 4 at Toronto 5 (Sundin 0:50 OT)

18 Colorado 4 at Toronto 1

20 Toronto 4 at Columbus 2

21 Rangers 5 at Toronto 4 (SO)

24 Ottawa 6 at Toronto 2

26 Toronto 2 at Ottawa 7

28 Toronto 5 at Montreal 4 (SO)

30 Thrashers 2 at Toronto 4
* The Leafs honoured Borje Salming's number 21, Hap Day's number 4, and Red Kelly's number 4.

NOVEMBER

1 Toronto 4 at Tampa Bay 2 (Ponikarovsky 18:40—EN)

2 Toronto 2 at Florida 4 (Gratton 19:23—EN)

4 Toronto 4 at Buffalo 1

6 Philadelphia 1 at Toronto 4 (Kaberle 18:47—EN)

9 Toronto 6 at Boston 4 (Antropov 19:49—EN)

11 Montreal 1 at Toronto 5*

16 Toronto 1 at Boston 2 (Bergeron 0:34 OT)

18 New Jersey 2 at Toronto 1

20 Islanders 2 at Toronto 4

22 Toronto 4 at Buffalo 7 (Drury 19:12—EN)

24 Toronto 7 at Washington 1

25 Boston 3 at Toronto 1

28 Boston 4 at Toronto 1 (Boyes 19:36—EN)

30 Toronto 0 at Thrashers 5 [Lehtonen]
* Hockey Hall of Fame game.

DECEMBER

2 Toronto 3 at Montreal 4 (SO)

5 Thrashers 5 at Toronto 2 (Kovalchuk 19:03—EN)

7 Toronto 1 at Boston 3

9 Toronto 1 at Detroit 5

12 Tampa Bay 4 at Toronto 5

15 Toronto 4 at Carolina 3

16 Rangers 2 at Toronto 9

19 Florida 7 at Toronto 3

22 Toronto 1 at Chicago 3

23 Washington 3 at Toronto 2

26 Minnesota 3 at Toronto 4

29 Toronto 1 at Pittsburgh 4

30 Ottawa 3 at Toronto 2 (Phillips 2:39 OT)

JANUARY

1 Boston 1 at Toronto 5

4 Toronto 10 at Boston 2

6 Buffalo 4 at Toronto 3

9 Carolina 4 at Toronto 1 (Williams 19:44—EN)

11 Toronto 4 at Buffalo 2

13 Vancouver 6 at Toronto 1

16 Toronto 4 at Tampa Bay 2 (Ponikarovsky 19:05—EN)

18 Toronto 3 at Florida 2

20 Toronto 2 at Pittsburgh 8

27 Montreal 1 at Toronto 4

30 Toronto 4 at Carolina 1 (Kaberle 19:40—EN)

31 Toronto 2 at Rangers 1

FEBRUARY

3 Toronto 3 at Ottawa 2 (SO)

6 Toronto 2 at St. Louis 1

8 Toronto 2 at Nashville 4 (Fiddler 19:28—EN)

10 Pittsburgh 6 at Toronto 5 (J. Staal 3:54 OT)

13 Islanders 3 at Toronto 2 (SO)

15 Toronto 4 at Philadelphia 2

17 Edmonton 3 at Toronto 4

20 Boston 3 at Toronto 0 [Thomas]

22 Toronto 2 at Islanders 3 (SO)

24 Toronto 5 at Philadelphia 2

26 Toronto 4 at Montreal 5

27 Buffalo 6 at Toronto 1

MARCH

2 Toronto 4 at New Jersey 3 (SO)

3 Buffalo 3 at Toronto 1

6 Washington 0 at Toronto 3 [Raycroft]

8 Toronto 1 at Ottawa 5

10 Ottawa 3 at Toronto 4 (Tucker 3:11 OT)

13 Tampa Bay 2 at Toronto 3

16 Toronto 1 at Washington 5

17 Toronto 2 at Montreal 3 (SO)

20 New Jersey 1 at Toronto 2

23 Toronto 4 at Buffalo 5

24 Buffalo 1 at Toronto 4

27 Carolina 1 at Toronto 6

29 Toronto 2 at Thrashers 3 (Kozlov 4:13 OT)

31 Pittsburgh 4 at Toronto 5 (Kaberle 3:55 OT)

APRIL

1 Toronto 2 at Rangers 7

3 Philadelphia 2 at Toronto 3 (McCabe 2:18 OT)

5 Toronto 2 at Islanders 5 (Satan 18:05—EN)

7 Montreal 5 at Toronto 6

2007–08

OCTOBER

3 Ottawa 4 at Toronto 3 (Heatley 2:57 OT)

4 Toronto 2 at Ottawa 3

6 Montreal 3 at Toronto 4 (Kaberle 3:26 OT)

9 Carolina 7 at Toronto 1

1 Islanders 1 at Toronto 8

13 Pittsburgh 6 at Toronto 4 (Talbot 19:10—EN)

15 Toronto 4 at Buffalo 5 (Gaustad 4:56 OT)

18 Florida 2 at Toronto 3

20 Chicago 6 at Toronto 4 (Ruutu 19:35—EN)

23 Thrashers 5 at Toronto 4 (SO)

25 Toronto 5 at Pittsburgh 2

27 Toronto 4 at Rangers 1 (Kilger 19:44—EN)

29 Washington 7 at Toronto 1

NOVEMBER

2 Toronto 2 at New Jersey 3

3 Toronto 3 at Montreal 2

6 Toronto 1 at Ottawa 5

9 Toronto 3 at Buffalo 0 [Raycroft]*

13 Montreal 4 at Toronto 3 (Komisarek 0:35 OT)

15 Toronto 2 at Boston 5

17 Ottawa 0 at Toronto 3 [Toskala]

20 Boston 4 at Toronto 2 (Kobasew 19:33—EN)

23 Toronto 1 at Dallas 3 (Halpern 19:20—EN)

24 Toronto 1 at Phoenix 5

27 Montreal 4 at Toronto 3 (SO)

29 Toronto 4 at Thrashers 2

* Hockey Hall of Fame game.

DECEMBER

1 Pittsburgh 2 at Toronto 4 (Ponikarovsky 19:02—EN)

4 Nashville 1 at Toronto 3

6 Toronto 6 at Rangers 2

7 Boston 2 at Toronto 1

10 Tampa Bay 1 at Toronto 6

14 Toronto 4 at Thrashers 0 [Toskala]

15 Toronto 1 at Montreal 4

18 Toronto 2 at Carolina 3 (Walker 4:27 OT)

20 Toronto 1 at Tampa Bay 2

22 Toronto 2 at Florida 1 (Kubina 0:34 OT)

26 Toronto 3 at Islanders 4 (Comrie 4:50 OT)

27 Toronto 1 at Philadelphia 4

29 Rangers 6 at Toronto 1

JANUARY

1 Tampa Bay 3 at Toronto 4 (SO)

3 Toronto 2 at Pittsburgh 6

5 Philadelphia 3 at Toronto 2

9 Toronto 0 at Anaheim 5 [Giguère]

10 Toronto 2 at Los Angeles 5

12 Toronto 2 at San Jose 3

15 Carolina 4 at Toronto 5

17 Toronto 3 at Boston 2 (SO)

19 Buffalo 2 at Toronto 4

20 Toronto 2 at New Jersey 3

23 Washington 2 at Toronto 3

24 Toronto 1 at Washington 2

29 St. Louis 3 at Toronto 2

31 Toronto 2 at Carolina 3 (Brind'Amour 3:20 OT)

FEBRUARY

2 Ottawa 2 at Toronto 4

5 Florida 8 at Toronto 0 [Vokoun]

7 Toronto 4 at Montreal 2 (Tucker 19:31—EN)

9 Detroit 2 at Toronto 3 (Antropov 1:02 OT)

13 Toronto 0 at Buffalo 1 [Miller]

14 Islanders 5 at Toronto 4

16 Boston 3 at Toronto 4 (Tucker 3:39 OT)

19 Columbus 1 at Toronto 3

21 Buffalo 5 at Toronto 1

23 Thrashers 1 at Toronto 3

25 Toronto 5 at Ottawa 0 [Toskala]

27 Toronto 4 at Florida 3 (SO)

29 Toronto 2 at Tampa Bay 3 (Boyle 2:02 OT)

MARCH

1   Toronto 3 at Washington 2

4   New Jersey 4 at Toronto 1

6   Toronto 8 at Boston 2

8   New Jersey 2 at Toronto 1

11 Philadelphia 3 at Toronto 4 (Kubina 4:04 OT)

12 Toronto 3 at Philadelphia 2

15 Buffalo 6 at Toronto 2

18 Toronto 3 at Islanders 1 (Ponikarovsky 19:32—EN)

21 Toronto 4 at Buffalo 1

22 Toronto 5 at Ottawa 4

25 Boston 6 at Toronto 2

27 Toronto 2 at Boston 4

29 Montreal 2 at Toronto 4

APRIL

1   Buffalo 4 at Toronto 3 (SO)

3   Ottawa 8 at Toronto 2

5   Toronto 1 at Montreal 3

2008–09

OCTOBER

9   Toronto 3 at Detroit 2

11 Montreal 6 at Toronto 1

13 St. Louis 5 at Toronto 4 (SO)

17 Toronto 0 at Rangers 1 (SO) [Toskala (T)/Valiquette (R)]

18 Toronto 1 at Pittsburgh 4

21 Anaheim 3 at Toronto 2 (SO)

23 Toronto 4 at Boston 2 (Hagman 19:57—EN)

25 Ottawa 2 at Toronto 3

28 Tampa Bay 3 at Toronto 2

29 Toronto 6 at New Jersey 5 (SO)

NOVEMBER

1   Rangers 2 at Toronto 5

2   Toronto 4 at Carolina 6 (E. Staal 19:38—EN)

4   Carolina 5 at Toronto 4 (Wallin 1:52 OT)

6   Toronto 2 at Boston 5 (Wheeler 19:07—EN)

8   Montreal 3 at Toronto 6*

11 Toronto 3 at Calgary 4

13 Toronto 5 at Edmonton 2

15 Toronto 2 at Vancouver 4

17 Boston 3 at Toronto 2

22 Chicago 5 at Toronto 4 (Bolland 0:49 OT)**

25 Thrashers 6 at Toronto 3

27 Toronto 1 at Ottawa 2 (SO)

29 Philadelphia 2 at Toronto 4

* Hockey Hall of Fame game.

** Leafs honoured Wendel Clark's number 17.

DECEMBER

1   Toronto 3 at Los Angeles 1 (Finger 19:49—EN)

2   Toronto 2 at San Jose 5

4   Toronto 3 at Phoenix 6

6   Washington 2 at Toronto 1

8   Islanders 2 at Toronto 4

12 Toronto 2 at Buffalo 1

16 New Jersey 2 at Toronto 3 (SO)

18 Toronto 5 at Boston 8

20 Toronto 7 at Pittsburgh 3

22 Toronto 6 at Thrashers 2

23 Dallas 8 at Toronto 2

26 Toronto 1 at Islanders 4

28 Toronto 1 at Washington 4 (Ovechkin 19:26—EN)

30 Thrashers 3 at Toronto 4 (Kubina 0:33 OT)

JANUARY

1   Buffalo 4 at Toronto 1

3   Ottawa 1 at Toronto 3

6   Florida 4 at Toronto 2

8   Toronto 2 at Montreal 6

10 Toronto 1 at Philadelphia 4 (Carter 18:12—EN)

13 Nashville 2 at Toronto 0 [Rinne]

15 Toronto 6 at Carolina 4 (Blake 19:49—EN)

16 Toronto 3 at Thrashers 4 (Peverley 3:51 OT)

19 Carolina 2 at Toronto 0 [Ward]

21 Boston 4 at Toronto 3 (SO)

27 Toronto 1 at Minnesota 6

29 Toronto 7 at Colorado 4

31 Pittsburgh 4 at Toronto 5*

* Leafs honoured Doug Gilmour's number 93.

FEBRUARY

3   Florida 4 at Toronto 3 (McCabe 3:30 OT)

4   Toronto 0 at Buffalo 5 [Miller]

7   Toronto 5 at Montreal 2

10 Toronto 4 at Florida 5 (Zednik 1:08 OT)

12 Toronto 4 at Tampa Bay 6

14 Pittsburgh 2 at Toronto 6

17 Buffalo 4 at Toronto 1

19 Columbus 4 at Toronto 3 (SO)

21 Vancouver 3 at Toronto 2 (SO)

22 Toronto 3 at Rangers 2 (Hagman 3:00 OT)

25 Rangers 1 at Toronto 2 (SO)

26 Toronto 5 at Islanders 4 (SO)

28 Toronto 4 at Ottawa 3 (Kubina 0:33 OT)

MARCH

3   New Jersey 3 at Toronto 2 (Oduya 4:48 OT)

5   Toronto 2 at Washington 1

| 7 | Edmonton 4 at Toronto 1 (Brodziak 19:32—EN) |

7   Edmonton 4 at Toronto 1 (Brodziak 19:32—EN)

9   Toronto 1 at Ottawa 2

10   Islanders 2 at Toronto 3 (Grabovski 0:50 OT)

12   Tampa Bay 4 at Toronto 1

14   Calgary 6 at Toronto 8 (Grabovski 19:01—EN)

17   Toronto 4 at Tampa Bay 3 (SO)

19   Toronto 1 at Florida 3

21   Toronto 5 at Montreal 2

24   Washington 2 at Toronto 3 (SO)

27   Toronto 3 at Buffalo 5

28   Boston 7 at Toronto 5

APRIL

1   Philadelphia 2 at Toronto 3

3   Toronto 5 at Philadelphia 8

4   Montreal 6 at Toronto 2

7   Toronto 4 at New Jersey 1

8   Buffalo 3 at Toronto 1

11   Ottawa 2 at Toronto 5 (Hagman 19:16—EN)

2009–10

OCTOBER

1   Montreal 4 at Toronto 3 (Gorges 4:47 OT)

3   Toronto 4 at Washington 6

6   Ottawa 2 at Toronto 1

10   Pittsburgh 5 at Toronto 2

12   Toronto 2 at Rangers 7

13   Colorado 4 at Toronto 1

17   Rangers 4 at Toronto 1

24   Toronto 1 at Vancouver 3 (Raymond 19:52—EN)

26   Toronto 6 at Anaheim 3

28   Toronto 3 at Dallas 4 (Neal 2:57 OT)

30   Toronto 2 at Buffalo 3 (Connolly 1:04 OT)

31   Toronto 4 at Montreal 5 (SO)

NOVEMBER

3   Tampa Bay 2 at Toronto 1 (Malone 2:21 OT)

6   Toronto 3 at Carolina 2

7   Detroit 1 at Toronto 5*

10   Minnesota 5 at Toronto 2 (Nolan 19:57—EN)

13   Toronto 2 at Chicago 3

14   Calgary 5 at Toronto 2

17   Toronto 2 at Ottawa 3

19   Toronto 5 at Carolina 6 (SO)

21   Washington 1 at Toronto 2 (SO)

23   Islanders 4 at Toronto 3 (Bailey 4:17 OT)

25   Toronto 4 at Tampa Bay 3

27   Toronto 6 at Florida 4 (Stajan 19:56—EN)

30   Buffalo 3 at Toronto 0 [Miller]

* Hockey Hall of Fame game.

DECEMBER

1   Toronto 3 at Montreal 0 [MacDonald/Gustavsson]

3   Toronto 6 at Columbus 3

5   Toronto 2 at Boston 7

7   Atlanta 2 at Toronto 5

9   Islanders 2 at Toronto 3

10   Toronto 2 at Boston 5 (Recchi 19:48—EN)

12   Washington 3 at Toronto 6

14   Ottawa 2 at Toronto 3

16   Phoenix 6 at Toronto 3 (Vrbata 19:48—EN)

18   Toronto 2 at Buffalo 5

19   Boston 0 at Toronto 2 [Gustavsson]

21   Buffalo 3 at Toronto 2 (Roy 3:35 OT)

23   Toronto 1 at Islanders 3 (Comeau 19:25—EN)

26   Montreal 3 at Toronto 2 (A. Kostitsyn 0:34 OT)

27   Toronto 4 at Pittsburgh 3

30   Toronto 1 at Edmonton 3

JANUARY

2   Toronto 1 at Calgary 3 (Glencross 19:09—EN)

5   Florida 2 at Toronto 3

6   Toronto 2 at Philadelphia 6

8   Toronto 2 at Buffalo 3

9   Pittsburgh 4 at Toronto 1

12   Carolina 4 at Toronto 2 (Whitney 19:16—EN)

14   Philadelphia 0 at Toronto 4 [Toskala]

15   Toronto 1 at Washington 6

18   Toronto 4 at Nashville 3

19   Toronto 3 at Atlanta 4

21   Toronto 2 at Tampa Bay 3 (St. Louis 4:50 OT)

23   Toronto 0 at Florida 2 [Vokoun]

26   Los Angeles 5 at Toronto 3 (Frolov 19:50—EN)

29   Toronto 4 at New Jersey 5 (Zajac 4:14 OT)

30   Vancouver 5 at Toronto 3 (Burrows 19:22—EN)

FEBRUARY

2   New Jersey 0 at Toronto 3 [Giguère]

5   Toronto 3 at New Jersey 4

6   Ottawa 0 at Toronto 5 [Giguère]

8   San Jose 3 at Toronto 2

12   Toronto 0 at St. Louis 4 [Mason]

13–03/1   *Olympic Break*

MARCH

2   Carolina 5 at Toronto 1

4   Toronto 2 at Boston 3 (SO)

6   Toronto 2 at Ottawa 1 (SO)

7   Toronto 1 at Philadelphia 3

9   Boston 3 at Toronto 4 (Kulemin 4:10 OT)

11   Tampa Bay 3 at Toronto 4 (Kessel 3:33 OT)

13	Edmonton 4 at Toronto 6
14	Toronto 1 at Islanders 4
16	Toronto 4 at Ottawa 1 (Wallin 19:10—EN)
18	New Jersey 1 at Toronto 2 (SO)
20	Montreal 2 at Toronto 3 (SO)
23	Florida 4 at Toronto 1 (Garrison 18:29—EN)
25	Toronto 2 at Atlanta 1 (Grabovski 0:39 OT)
27	Rangers 2 at Toronto 3 (Kulemin 0:39 OT)
28	Toronto 4 at Pittsburgh 5 (SO)
30	Atlanta 3 at Toronto 2

APRIL

1	Buffalo 2 at Toronto 4 (Sjostrom 19:23—EN)
3	Boston 2 at Toronto 1 (Satan 3:25 OT)
6	Philadelphia 2 at Toronto 0 [Boucher] (Richards 18:44—EN)
7	Toronto 1 at Rangers 5
10	Toronto 4 at Montreal 3 (Phaneuf 2:06 OT)

2010–11

OCTOBER

7	Montreal 2 at Toronto 3
9	Ottawa 1 at Toronto 5
13	Toronto 4 at Pittsburgh 3
15	Toronto 4 at Rangers 3 (Kessel 3:08 OT)
18	Islanders 2 at Toronto 1 (Tavares 3:26 OT)
21	Rangers 2 at Toronto 1
23	Toronto 2 at Philadelphia 5
26	Florida 1 at Toronto 3
28	Toronto 0 at Boston 2 [Thomas]
30	Rangers 2 at Toronto 0 [Lundqvist]

NOVEMBER

2	Ottawa 3 at Toronto 2
3	Toronto 4 at Washington 5 (SO)
6	Buffalo 3 at Toronto 2 (SO)*
9	Toronto 0 at Tampa Bay 4 [Ellis]
10	Toronto 1 at Florida 4
13	Vancouver 5 at Toronto 3 (Hamhuis 19:10—EN)
16	Nashville 4 at Toronto 5
18	New Jersey 1 at Toronto 3
20	Toronto 0 at Montreal 2 [Price]
22	Dallas 1 at Toronto 4 (Versteeg 19:49—EN)
26	Toronto 1 at Buffalo 3
27	Toronto 0 at Ottawa 3 [Elliott]
30	Tampa Bay 4 at Toronto 3 (Gagne 1:15 OT)

* Hockey Hall of Fame game.

DECEMBER

2	Edmonton 5 at Toronto 0 [Khabibulin]
4	Boston 2 at Toronto 3 (SO)
6	Toronto 5 at Washington 4 (SO)
8	Toronto 2 at Pittsburgh 5
9	Philadelphia 4 at Toronto 1
11	Montreal 1 at Toronto 3 (Versteeg 19:22—EN)
14	Toronto 4 at Edmonton 1
16	Toronto 2 at Calgary 5
18	Toronto 1 at Vancouver 4 (H. Sedin 19:29—EN)
20	Thrashers 6 at Toronto 3 (Ladd 19:35—EN)
26	Toronto 4 at New Jersey 1
28	Carolina 4 at Toronto 3
30	Columbus 3 at Toronto 2

JANUARY

1	Toronto 5 at Ottawa 1
3	Boston 2 at Toronto 1
6	St. Louis 5 at Toronto 6 (SO)
7	Toronto 9 at Thrashers 3
10	Toronto 3 at Los Angeles 2
11	Toronto 4 at San Jose 2 (MacArthur 19:21—EN)
13	Toronto 1 at Phoenix 5
15	Calgary 2 at Toronto 1 (SO)
19	Toronto 0 at Rangers 7 [Lundqvist]
20	Anaheim 2 at Toronto 5
22	Washington 4 at Toronto 1 (Ovechkin 19:36—EN)
24	Toronto 4 at Carolina 6 (Cole 19:13—EN)
25	Toronto 0 at Tampa Bay 2 [Roloson]

FEBRUARY

1	Florida 3 at Toronto 4 (SO)
3	Carolina 0 at Toronto 3 [Ward]
5	Toronto 2 at Buffalo 6
7	Thrashers 4 at Toronto 5
8	Toronto 5 at Islanders 3
10	New Jersey 2 at Toronto 1 (Kovalchuk 4:36 OT)
12	Toronto 0 at Montreal 3 [Price]
15	Toronto 4 at Boston 3
16	Toronto 2 at Buffalo 1
19	Ottawa 1 at Toronto 0 (SO) [Anderson (O)/Reimer (T)]
22	Islanders 1 at Toronto 2
24	Toronto 5 at Montreal 4
26	Pittsburgh 6 at Toronto 5 (SO)
27	Toronto 2 at Thrashers 3 (Hainsey 2:31 OT)

MARCH

2	Pittsburgh 2 at Toronto 3 (Grabovski 0:42 OT)
3	Toronto 3 at Philadelphia 2
5	Chicago 5 at Toronto 3
8	Toronto 3 at Islanders 4 (Comeau 4:02 OT)
10	Philadelphia 3 at Toronto 2
12	Buffalo 3 at Toronto 4

14	Tampa Bay 6 at Toronto 2
16	Toronto 3 at Carolina 1
17	Toronto 0 at Florida 4 [Clemmensen]
19	Boston 2 at Toronto 5
22	Toronto 3 at Minnesota 0 [Reimer]
24	Toronto 4 at Colorado 3
26	Toronto 2 at Detroit 4 (Bertuzzi 19:08—EN)
29	Buffalo 3 at Toronto 4
31	Toronto 4 at Boston 3 (SO)

APRIL

2	Toronto 4 at Ottawa 2
5	Washington 3 at Toronto 2 (SO)
6	Toronto 2 at New Jersey 4 (Elias 19:50—EN)
9	Montreal 4 at Toronto 1

2011–12

OCTOBER

6	Montreal 0 at Toronto 2 [Reimer]
8	Ottawa 5 at Toronto 6
15	Calgary 2 at Toronto 3
17	Colorado 3 at Toronto 2 (D. Jones 1:11 OT)
19	Winnipeg 3 at Toronto 4 (SO)
20	Toronto 2 at Boston 6
22	Toronto 5 at Montreal 4 (Grabovski 1:23 OT)
24	Toronto 2 at Philadelphia 4
27	Toronto 4 at Rangers 2
29	Pittsburgh 3 at Toronto 4
30	Toronto 2 at Ottawa 3

NOVEMBER

2	Toronto 5 at New Jersey 3
3	Toronto 4 at Columbus 1
5	Boston 7 at Toronto 0 [Thomas]
8	Florida 5 at Toronto 1
10	Toronto 3 at St. Louis 2 (SO)
12	Ottawa 5 at Toronto 2 (M. Michalek 19:17—EN)*
15	Phoenix 3 at Toronto 2 (SO)
17	Toronto 1 at Nashville 4 (Halischuk 19:37—EN)
19	Washington 1 at Toronto 7
20	Toronto 2 at Carolina 3
22	Toronto 7 at Tampa Bay 1
25	Toronto 4 at Dallas 3 (SO)
27	Toronto 5 at Anaheim 2 (Schenn 19:48—EN)
30	Boston 6 at Toronto 3 (Marchand 19:08—EN)

* Hockey Hall of Fame game.

DECEMBER

3	Toronto 1 at Boston 4
5	Toronto 4 at Rangers 2 (Steckel 19:55—EN)

6	New Jersey 3 at Toronto 2 (Clarkson 2:40 OT)
9	Toronto 2 at Washington 4
13	Carolina 1 at Toronto 2 (Connolly 0:44 OT)
16	Toronto 4 at Buffalo 5
17	Vancouver 5 at Toronto 3
19	Los Angeles 3 at Toronto 2 (SO)
22	Buffalo 2 at Toronto 3
23	Toronto 5 at Islanders 3 (Lupul 19:51—EN)
27	Toronto 3 at Florida 5
29	Toronto 3 at Carolina 4 (E. Staal 3:09 OT)
31	Toronto 2 at Winnipeg 3

JANUARY

3	Tampa Bay 3 at Toronto 7
5	Winnipeg 0 at Toronto 4 [Gustavsson]
7	Detroit 3 at Toronto 4
10	Buffalo 0 at Toronto 2 [Gustavsson]
13	Toronto 2 at Buffalo 3
14	Rangers 3 at Toronto 0 [Biron]
17	Ottawa 3 at Toronto 2
19	Minnesota 1 at Toronto 4
21	Montreal 3 at Toronto 1
23	Islanders 0 at Toronto 3 [Gustavsson]
24	Toronto 4 at Islanders 3 (MacArthur 2:06 OT)
31	Toronto 4 at Pittsburgh 5 (SO)

FEBRUARY

1	Pittsburgh 0 at Toronto 1 [Reimer]
4	Toronto 5 at Ottawa 0 [Reimer]
6	Edmonton 3 at Toronto 6 (Kessel 18:55—EN)
7	Toronto 1 at Winnipeg 2
9	Toronto 3 at Philadelphia 4
11	Montreal 5 at Toronto 0 [Price]*
14	Toronto 1 at Calgary 5
15	Toronto 4 at Edmonton 3 (Connolly 1:39 OT)
18	Toronto 2 at Vancouver 6
21	New Jersey 4 at Toronto 3 (Fayne 1:18 OT)
23	San Jose 2 at Toronto 1
25	Washington 4 at Toronto 2
28	Florida 5 at Toronto 3
29	Toronto 4 at Chicago 5

* Leafs honoured Mats Sundin's number 13.

MARCH

3	Toronto 3 at Montreal 1
6	Boston 5 at Toronto 4
7	Toronto 2 at Pittsburgh 3
10	Philadelphia 1 at Toronto 0 (SO)
11	Toronto 0 at Washington 2 [Neuvirth]
13	Toronto 2 at Florida 5 (Bergenheim 18:40—EN)

15   Toronto 3 at Tampa Bay 1

17   Toronto 3 at Ottawa 1

19   Toronto 0 at Boston 8 [Thomas]

20   Islanders 5 at Toronto 2 (Moulson 18:25—EN)

23   Toronto 4 at New Jersey 3 (SO)

24   Rangers 4 at Toronto 3 (SO)

27   Carolina 3 at Toronto 0 [Ward]

29   Philadelphia 7 at Toronto 1

31   Buffalo 3 at Toronto 4

APRIL

3   Toronto 5 at Buffalo 6 (D. Roy 3:29 OT)

5   Tampa Bay 2 at Toronto 3 (Phaneuf 4:01 OT)

7   Toronto 1 at Montreal 4 (Staubitz 18:02—EN)

2012–13

Season was revised to a 48-game schedule.

JANUARY

21   Buffalo 2 at Toronto 1

23   Toronto 5 at Pittsburgh 2

24   Islanders 7 at Toronto 4 (Grabner 18:50—EN)

26   Toronto 2 at Rangers 5 (Gaborik 18:45—EN)

29   Toronto 4 at Buffalo 3 (Frattin 4:58 OT)

31   Washington 2 at Toronto 3

FEBRUARY

2   Boston 1 at Toronto 0 [Rask]

4   Carolina 4 at Toronto 1

5   Toronto 3 at Washington 2

7   Toronto 3 at Winnipeg 2

9   Toronto 6 at Montreal 0 [Reimer]

11   Philadelphia 2 at Toronto 5

14   Toronto 1 at Carolina 3

16   Ottawa 0 at Toronto 3 [Scrivens] (Liles 19:22—EN)

18   Toronto 3 at Florida 0 [Scrivens]

19   Toronto 2 at Tampa Bay 4

21   Buffalo 1 at Toronto 3

23   Toronto 2 at Ottawa 3

25   Philadelphia 2 at Toronto 4 (McClement 19:47—EN)

27   Montreal 5 at Toronto 2

28   Toronto 5 at Islanders 4 (Phaneuf 1:11 OT)

MARCH

4   New Jersey 2 at Toronto 4

6   Ottawa 4 at Toronto 5

7   Toronto 2 at Boston 4 (Seguin 19:45—EN)

9   Pittsburgh 5 at Toronto 4 (SO)

12   Toronto 2 at Winnipeg 5

14   Pittsburgh 3 at Toronto 1 (C. Adams 19:50—EN)

16   Winnipeg 5 at Toronto 4 (SO)

20   Tampa Bay 2 at Toronto 4

21   Toronto 4 at Buffalo 5 (SO)

23   Boston 2 at Toronto 3

25   Toronto 2 at Boston 3 (SO)

26   Florida 2 at Toronto 3

28   Carolina 3 at Toronto 6 (McClement 19:15—EN/Kulemin 19:57—EN)

30   Toronto 4 at Ottawa 0 [Reimer]

APRIL

4   Philadelphia 5 at Toronto 3 (Schenn 19:43—EN)

6   Toronto 2 at New Jersey 1

8   Rangers 3 at Toronto 4

10   Toronto 2 at Rangers 3 (SO)

13   Montreal 1 at Toronto 5

15   New Jersey 0 at Toronto 2 [Reimer] (McClement 19:23—EN)

16   Toronto 1 at Washington 5

18   Islanders 5 at Toronto 3

20   Toronto 4 at Ottawa 1

24   Toronto 2 at Tampa Bay 5 (St. Louis 17:11—EN)

25   Toronto 4 at Florida 0 [Reimer]

27   Montreal 4 at Toronto 1

2013–14

OCTOBER

1   Toronto 4 at Montreal 3

2   Toronto 3 at Philadelphia 1

5   Ottawa 4 at Toronto 5 (SO)

8   Colorado 2 at Toronto 1

10   Toronto 4 at Nashville 0 [Bernier]

12   Edmonton 5 at Toronto 6 (Bolland 2:09 OT)

15   Minnesota 1 at Toronto 4 (Raymond 19:01—EN)

17   Carolina 3 at Toronto 2

19   Toronto 1 at Chicago 3

22   Anaheim 2 at Toronto 4

25   Toronto 2 at Columbus 5 (Johansen 19:33—EN)

26   Pittsburgh 1 at Toronto 4 (Bolland 19:18—EN)

29   Toronto 4 at Edmonton 0 [Reimer]

30   Toronto 4 at Calgary 2 (Ranger 18:38—EN)

NOVEMBER

2   Toronto 0 at Vancouver 4 [Luongo]

8   New Jersey 1 at Toronto 2 (SO)

9   Toronto 1 at Boston 3 (Bergeron 19:38—EN)

13   Toronto 1 at Minnesota 2 (SO)

15   Toronto 1 at Buffalo 3 (Ehrhoff 19:32—EN)

16   Buffalo 2 at Toronto 4

19   Islanders 2 at Toronto 5

21   Nashville 4 at Toronto 2

23 Washington 1 at Toronto 2 (SO)

25 Columbus 6 at Toronto 0 [Bobrovsky]

27 Toronto 5 at Pittsburgh 6 (SO)

29 Toronto 2 at Buffalo 3 (Ehrhoff 0:38 OT)

30 Toronto 2 at Montreal 4

DECEMBER

3   San Jose 4 at Toronto 2 (Couture 18:36—EN)

5   Dallas 2 at Toronto 3 (T. Smith 4:18 OT)

7   Toronto 4 at Ottawa 3 (SO)

8   Boston 5 at Toronto 2 (Bergeron 19:49—EN)

11 Los Angeles 3 at Toronto 1

12 Toronto 3 at St. Louis 6 (Backes 19:30—EN)

14 Chicago 3 at Toronto 7

16 Toronto 1 at Pittsburgh 3 (B. Sutter 19:56—EN)

17 Florida 3 at Toronto 1

19 Phoenix 1 at Toronto 2 (SO)

21 Detroit 5 at Toronto 4 (SO)

23 Toronto 1 at Rangers 2 (SO)

27 Buffalo 3 at Toronto 4 (SO)

29 Carolina 2 at Toronto 5 (Phaneuf 19:52—EN)

JANUARY

1   Detroit 3 at Toronto 2 (SO)*

4   Rangers 7 at Toronto 1

7   Islanders 5 at Toronto 3 (Clutterbuck 19:51—EN)

9   Toronto 1 at Carolina 6

10 Toronto 2 at Washington 3

12 New Jersey 2 at Toronto 3 (SO)

14 Toronto 4 at Boston 3

15 Buffalo 3 at Toronto 4 (SO)

18 Montreal 3 at Toronto 5 (Lupul 19:56—EN)

20 Toronto 4 at Phoenix 2

21 Toronto 5 at Colorado 2 (McClement 17:47—EN)

23 Toronto 1 at Dallas 7

25 Toronto 4 at Winnipeg 5 (Byfuglien 2:44 OT)

28 Tampa Bay 2 at Toronto 3

30 Florida 3 at Toronto 6

* Winter Classic, played at Michigan Stadium in front of a world-record crowd of 105,491.

FEBRUARY

1   Ottawa 3 at Toronto 6 (Kadri 19:31—EN)

4   Toronto 1 at Florida 4 (Goc 17:30—EN)

6   Toronto 4 at Tampa Bay 1 (Bozak 17:08—EN)

8   Vancouver 1 at Toronto 3

9–25 *Olympic Break*

27 Toronto 4 at Islanders 5 (Visnovsky 1:55 OT)

MARCH

1   Toronto 3 at Montreal 4 (Pacioretty 3:28 OT)

3   Columbus 2 at Toronto 1

5   Toronto 3 at Rangers 2 (Bozak 1:51 OT)

8   Philadelphia 3 at Toronto 4 (Lupul 2:21 OT)

10 Toronto 3 at Anaheim 1

11 Toronto 2 at San Jose 6

13 Toronto 3 at Los Angeles 2

16 Toronto 2 at Washington 4 (Brouwer 19:56—EN)

18 Toronto 2 at Detroit 3

19 Tampa Bay 5 at Toronto 3

22 Montreal 4 at Toronto 3

23 Toronto 2 at New Jersey 3

25 St. Louis 5 at Toronto 3 (Backes 18:53—EN)

28 Toronto 2 at Philadelphia 4

29 Detroit 4 at Toronto 2

APRIL

1   Calgary 2 at Toronto 3

3   Boston 3 at Toronto 4 (Kadri 2:51 OT)

5   Winnipeg 4 at Toronto 2

8   Toronto 0 at Tampa Bay 3 [Bishop/Lindback] (Hedman 19:47—EN)

10 Toronto 2 at Florida 4

12 Toronto 0 at Ottawa 1 [Anderson]

2014–15

OCTOBER

8   Montreal 4 at Toronto 3

11 Pittsburgh 5 at Toronto 2

12 Toronto 6 at NY Rangers 3*

14 Colorado 2 at Toronto 3 (Kessel 0:34 OT)

17 Detroit 4 at Toronto 1

18 Toronto 0 at Detroit 1 (Zetterberg 4:50 OT) [Bernier(T)/Gustavsson(D)]

21 Toronto 5 at NY Islanders 2

22 Toronto at Ottawa**

25 Boston 4 at Toronto 1

28 Buffalo 0 at Toronto 4 [Bernier]***

31 Toronto 4 at Columbus 1

* This was the 600th all-time game between the two teams.

** Postponed until November 9 after Parliament Hill shooting.

*** Leafs tie team record by allowing only 10 shots.

NOVEMBER

1   Chicago 2 at Toronto 3

4   Toronto 2 at Arizona 3

6   Toronto 3 at Colorado 4 (SO)

8   NY Rangers 4 at Toronto 5

9   Toronto at Ottawa*

12 Boston 1 at Toronto 6

14 Pittsburgh 2 at Toronto 1**

15 Toronto 2 at Buffalo 6

18 Nashville 9 at Toronto 2

20 Tampa Bay 2 at Toronto 5

22   Detroit 1 at Toronto 4

26   Toronto 3 at Pittsburgh 4 (Comeau 2:53 OT)

29   Washington 2 at Toronto 6***
* Rescheduled from October 22.
** Hockey Hall of Fame game.
*** Leafs pay tribute to the late Pat Quinn.

DECEMBER

2   Dallas 3 at Toronto 5

4   New Jersey 5 at Toronto 3

6   Vancouver 2 at Toronto 5

9   Calgary 1 at Toronto 4

10   Toronto 2 at Detroit 1 (SO)

13   Detroit 1 at Toronto 4

14   Los Angeles 3 at Toronto 4 (SO)

16   Anaheim 2 at Toronto 6

18   Toronto 1 at Carolina 4

20   Philadelphia 7 at Toronto 4

21   Toronto 0 at Chicago 4 [Raanta]

23   Toronto 4 at Dallas 0 [Bernier]

28   Toronto 4 at Florida 6

29   Toronto 2 at Tampa Bay 3

31   Toronto 4 at Boston 3 (SO)

JANUARY

2   Toronto 1 at Minnesota 3

3   Toronto 1 at Winnipeg 5

7   Washington 6 at Toronto 2

9   Columbus 2 at Toronto 5

12   Toronto 0 at Los Angeles 2 [Jones]

14   Toronto 0 at Anaheim 4 [Andersen]

15   Toronto 1 at San Jose 3

17   Toronto 0 at St. Louis 3 [Elliott]

19   Carolina 4 at Toronto 1

21   Toronto 3 at Ottawa 4

28   Toronto 1 at New Jersey 2 (SO)

29   Arizona 3 at Toronto 1

31   Toronto 0 at Philadelphia 1 [Mason]

FEBRUARY

3   Toronto 3 at Nashville 4

6   Toronto 1 at New Jersey 4

7   Edmonton 1 at Toronto 5

10   NY Rangers 5 at Toronto 4

12   Toronto 2 at NY Islanders 3

14   Toronto 1 at Montreal 2 (SO)

17   Florida 3 at Toronto 2

20   Toronto 1 at Carolina 2

21   Winnipeg 3 at Toronto 4 (van Riemsdyk 3:47 OT)

26   Philadelphia 2 at Toronto 3

28   Toronto 0 at Montreal 4 [Price]

MARCH

1   Toronto 0 at Washington 4 [Holtby]

3   Toronto 3 at Florida 2

5   Toronto 2 at Tampa Bay 4

7   St. Louis 6 at Toronto 1

9   NY Islanders 4 at Toronto 3 (Tavares 4:38 OT)

11   Buffalo 3 at Toronto 4 (SO)

13   Toronto 3 at Calgary 6

14   Toronto 1 at Vancouver 4

16   Toronto 1 at Edmonton 4

19   San Jose 4 at Toronto 1

21   Toronto 3 at Ottawa 5

23   Minnesota 2 at Toronto 1

26   Florida 4 at Toronto 1

28   Ottawa 3 at Toronto 4 (Brewer 3:17 OT)

31   Tampa Bay 1 at Toronto 3

APRIL

1   Toronto 3 at Buffalo 4

4   Toronto 1 at Boston 2 (SO)

5   Ottawa 2 at Toronto 3 (SO)

8   Toronto 0 at Columbus 5 [Bobrovsky]

11   Montreal 4 at Toronto 3 (SO)

ALL-TIME DRAFT CHOICES

1963 **Montreal, June 5** (6th choice overall)

Round 1	6	Walt McKechnie	London Nationals (WOJBHL)
Round 2	12	Neil Clairmont	Parry Sound Midgets (OAAAMHL)
Round 3	17	Jim McKenny	Neil McNeil Maroons (MJAHL)
Round 4	21	Gerry Meehan	Neil McNeil Maroons (MJAHL)

1964 **Montreal, June 11** (5th choice overall)

Round 1	5	Tom Martin	Toronto Marlboro Midgets (OAAAMHL)
Round 2	11	Dave Cotey	Aurora Tigers (SJCHL)
Round 3	17	Mike Pelyk	Toronto Marlboro Midgets (OAAAMHL)
Round 4	23	Jim Dorey	Stamford Bruins (NDJBHL)

1965 **Montreal, April 27** (3rd choice overall)

No players selected (Leafs passed on all rounds)

1966 **Montreal, April 25** (4th choice overall)

Round 1	4	John Wright	Westclair York Steel (MJBHL)
Round 2	10	Cam Crosby	Toronto Marlboros (OHA)
Round 3	16	Rick Ley	Niagara Falls Flyers (OHA)
Round 4	22	Dale MacLeish	Peterborough Petes (OHA)

1967 **Montreal, June 7** (9th choice overall)

| Round 2 | 16 | Bob Kelly | Port Arthur Marrs (TBJHL) |

1968 **Montreal, June 13** (8th choice overall)

| Round 1 | 10 | Brad Selwood | Niagara Falls Flyers (OHA) |

1969 **Montreal, June 12** (7th choice overall)

Round 1	9	Ernie Moser	Estevan Bruins (WCHL)
Round 2	20	Doug Brindley	Niagara Falls Flyers (OHA)
Round 3	31	Larry McIntyre	Moose Jaw Canucks (SJHL)
Round 4	43	Frank Hughes	Edmonton Oil Kings (WCHL)
Round 5	55	Brian Spencer	Swift Current Broncos (SJHL)
Round 6	67	Bob Neufeld	Dauphin Kings (MJHL)

1970 **Montreal, June 11** (8th choice overall)

Round 1	8	Darryl Sittler	London Knights (OHA)
Round 2	22	Errol Thompson	Charlottetown Royals (NBSHL)
Round 3	36	Gerry O'Flaherty	Kitchener Rangers (OHA)
Round 4	50	Bob Gryp	Boston University Terriers (ECAC)
Round 5	64	Luc Simard	Trois-Rivières Dukes (QMJHL)
Round 6	78	Calvin Booth	Weyburn Red Wings (SJHL)

| Round 7 | 91 | Paul Larose | Quebec Remparts (QMJHL) |
| Round 8 | 103 | Ron Low | Dauphin Kings (MJHL) |

1971 **Montreal, June 10** (9th choice overall)

Round 1	9	Traded to Philadelphia (Pierre Plante) with Bruce Gamble on February 1, 1971, for Bernie Parent and a second-round draft choice in 1971 (Rick Kehoe).
Round 2a	22	Rick Kehoe	Hamilton Red Wings (OHA)
Round 2	23	Dave Fortier	St. Catharines Black Hawks (OHA)
Round 3	37	Gavin Kirk	Toronto Marlboros (OHA)
Round 4	51	Rick Cunningham	Peterborough Petes (OHA)
Round 5	65	Bob Sykes	Sudbury Wolves (OHA)
Round 6	79	Mike Ruest	Cornwall Royals (QMJHL)
Round 7	93	Dale Smedsmo	Bemidji State University Beavers (NAIA)
Round 7b	98	Steve Johnson	Verdun Maple Leafs (QMJHL)
Round 8	107	Bob Burns	Canadian Armed Forces (Greenwood, N.S.)

a. Acquired from Philadelphia with Bernie Parent on February 1, 1971, for Bruce Gamble and a first-round draft choice in 1971 (Pierre Plante).
b. Acquired from Boston for cash on June 10, 1971.

1972 **Montreal, June 8** (11th choice overall)

Round 1	11	George Ferguson	Toronto Marlboros (OHA)
Round 2	27	Randy Osburn	London Knights (OHA)
Round 3	43	Denis Deslauriers	Shawinigan Bruins (QMJHL)
Round 4	59	Brian Bowles	Cornwall Royals (QMJHL)
Round 5	75	Michel Plante	Drummondville Rangers (QMJHL)
Round 6	91	Dave Shardlow	Flin Flon Bombers (WCHL)
Round 7	107	Monte Miron	Clarkson University Golden Knights (ECAC)
Round 8	123	Peter Williams	University of P.E.I. Panthers (CIAU)
Round 9	139	Pat Boutette	University of Minnesota Golden Gophers (WCHA)
Round 9a	143	Gary Schofield	Clarkson University Golden Knights (ECAC)

a. Acquired from Boston for cash on June 8, 1972.

1973 **Montreal, May 15** (4th choice overall)

Round 1	4	Lanny McDonald	Medicine Hat Tigers (WCHL)
Round 1a	10	Bob Neely	Peterborough Petes (OHA)
Round 1b	15	Ian Turnbull	Ottawa 67's (OHA)
Round 2	20	Traded to Philadelphia (Larry Goodenough) and the rights to Bernie Parent on May 15, 1973, for Doug Favell and a first-round draft choice in 1973 (Bob Neely).
Round 3	36	Traded to Boston (Doug Gibson) with Jacques Plante on March 3, 1973, for a first-round draft choice in 1973 (Ian Turnbull) and future considerations (Ed Johnston).
Round 4	52	François Rochon	Sherbrooke Beavers (QMJHL)

Round 5	68	Gord Titcomb	St. Catharines Black Hawks (OHA)
Round 6	84	Doug Marit	Regina Pats (WCHL)
Round 7	100	Dan Follet	Downsview Bombers (OPJHL)
Round 8	116	Les Burgess	Kitchener Rangers (OHA)
Round 9	132	Dave Pay	University of Wisconsin Badgers (WCHA)
Round 9c	144	Lee Palmer	Clarkson University Golden Knights (ECAC)
Round 10	147	Bob Peace	Cornell University Big Red (ECAC)
Round 10d	159	Norm McLeod	Ottawa M&W Rangers (CJHL)

a. Acquired from Philadelphia with Doug Favell on May 15, 1973, for the rights to Bernie Parent and a second-round draft choice in 1973 (Larry Goodenough).
b. Acquired from Boston with future considerations (Ed Johnston) on March 3, 1973, for Jacques Plante and a third-round draft choice in 1973 (Doug Gibson).
c. Acquired from the Islanders with an 11th-round draft choice in 1973 (Norm McLeod) for cash on May 15, 1973.
d. Acquired from the Islanders with a 10th-round draft choice in 1973 (Lee Palmer) for cash on May 15, 1973.

1974   **Montreal, May 28**   (13th choice overall)

Round 1	13	Jack Valiquette	Sault Ste. Marie Greyhounds (OHA)
Round 2	31	Dave Williams	Swift Current Broncos (WCHL)
Round 3	49	Per-Arne Alexandersson	Leksands IF (Sweden)
Round 4	67	Peter Driscoll	Kingston Canadians (OHA)
Round 5	85	Mike Palmateer	Toronto Marlboros (OHA)
Round 6	103	Bill Hassard	Wexford Raiders (OPJHL)
Round 7	121	Kevin Devine	Toronto Marlboros (OHA)
Round 8	139	Kevin Kemp	Ottawa 67's (OHA)
Round 9	155	Dave Syvret	St. Catharines Black Hawks (OHA)
Round 10	170	Andy Stoesz	Selkirk Steelers (MJHL)
Round 11	185	Martin Feschuk	Saskatoon Blades (WCHL)

1975   **Montreal, June 3**   (6th choice overall)

Round 1	6	Don Ashby	Calgary Centennials (WCHL)
Round 2	24	Doug Jarvis	Peterborough Petes (OMJHL)
Round 3	42	Bruce Boudreau	Toronto Marlboros (OMJHL)
Round 4	60	Traded to Boston (Rick Adduono) on June 3, 1975, for a third-round draft choice in 1976 (Gary McFayden).	
Round 5	78	Ted Long	Hamilton Fincups (OMJHL)
Round 6	96	Kevin Campbell	St. Lawrence University Skating Saints (ECAC)
Round 7	114	Mario Rouillard	Trois-Rivières Draveurs (QMJHL)
Round 8	132	Ron Wilson	Providence College Friars (HE)
Round 9	149	Paul Evans	Peterborough Petes (OMJHL)
Round 10	165	Jean Latendresse	Shawinigan Falls Dynamos (QMJHL)
Round 10a	166	Paul Crowley	Sudbury Wolves (OMJHL)
Round 10	179	Dan D'Alvise	Royal York Rangers (OPJHL)
Round 10	180	Jack Laine	Bowling Green State University Falcons (CCHA)
Round 11	188	Ken Holland	Medicine Hat Tigers (WCHL)

Round 11	189	Bob Barnes	Hamilton Fincups (OMJHL)
Round 11	191	Gary Burns	University of New Hampshire Wildcats (ECAC)
Round 11	193	Jim Montgomery	Hull Olympics (QMJHL)
Round 12	199	Rick Martin	London Knights (OMJHL)

a. Acquired from Chicago for cash on June 3, 1975.

1976   **Montreal, June 1**   (12th choice overall)

Round 1	12	Traded to Montreal (Peter Lee) on June 17, 1975, for Wayne Thomas.	
Round 2	30	Randy Carlyle	Sudbury Wolves (OMJHL)
Round 3	48	Alain Bélanger	Sherbrooke Castors (QMJHL)
Round 3a	52	Gary McFayden	Hull Festivals (QMJHL)
Round 4	66	Tim Williams	Victoria Cougars (WCHL)
Round 5	84	Greg Hotham	Kingston Canadians (OMJHL)
Round 6	102	Dan Djakalovic	Kingston Canadians (OMJHL)
Round 7	116	Chuck Skjodt	Windsor Spitfires (OMJHL)

a. Acquired from Boston on June 3, 1975, for a fourth-round draft choice in 1975 (Rick Adduono).

1977   **Montreal, June 14**   (11th choice overall)

Round 1	11	John Anderson	Toronto Marlboros (OMJHL)
Round 1a	12	Trevor Johansen	Toronto Marlboros (OMJHL)
Round 2b	24	Bob Gladney	Oshawa Generals (OMJHL)
Round 2	29	Rocky Saganiuk	Medicine Hat Tigers (WCHL)
Round 3	47	Traded to Colorado (Randy Pierce) on March 8, 1977, for Tracy Pratt.	
Round 4	65	Dan Eastman	London Knights (OMJHL)
Round 5	83	John Wilson	Windsor Spitfires (OMJHL)
Round 6	101	Roy Sommer	Calgary Centennials (WCHL)
Round 7	119	Lynn Jorgensen	Toronto Marlboros (OMJHL)
Round 8	134	Kevin Howe	Sault Ste. Marie Greyhounds (OMJHL)
Round 9	149	Ray Robertson	St. Lawrence University Skating Saints (ECAC)

a. Acquired from Pittsburgh with Blaine Stoughton on September 13, 1974, for Rick Kehoe.
b. Acquired from Chicago on September 28, 1976, for the rights to Jim Harrison.

1978   **Montreal, June 15**   (12th choice overall)

Round 1	12	Traded to Detroit (Brent Peterson) with Errol Thompson, a second-round draft choice in 1978 (Al Jensen), and a first-round draft choice in 1980 (Mike Blaisdell) on March 13, 1978, for Dan Maloney and a second-round draft choice in 1980 (Craig Muni).	
Round 2a	21	Joel Quenneville	Windsor Spitfires (QMJHL)
Round 2	31	Traded to Detroit (Al Jensen) with Errol Thompson, a first-round draft choice in 1978 (Brent Peterson), and a first-round draft choice in 1980 (Mike Blaisdell) on March 13, 1978, for Dan Maloney and a second-round draft choice in 1980 (Craig Muni).	
Round 3	48	Mark Kirton	Peterborough Petes (OMJHL)
Round 4	65	Bob Parent	Kitchener Rangers (OMJHL)
Round 5	81	Jordy Douglas	Flin Flon Bombers (WCHL)

Round 6b	92	Mel Hewitt	Calgary Centennials (WCHL)
Round 6	98	Norman Lefebvre	Trois-Rivières Draveurs (QMJHL)
Round 7	115	John Scammell	Lethbridge Broncos (WCHL)
Round 8	132	Kevin Reinhart	Kitchener Rangers (OMJHL)
Round 9	149	Mike Waghorne	University of New Hampshire Wildcats (HE)
Round 10	166	Laurie Cuvelier	St. Francis Xavier University (CIAU)
Round 11	181	Traded to St. Louis (Jean-François Boutin) for cash on June 15, 1978.	
Round 12	197	Traded to St. Louis (Paul Stasiuk) for cash on June 15, 1978.	
Round 13	210	Traded to St. Louis (Brian Crombeen) for cash on June 15, 1978.	
Round 14	221	Traded to St. Louis (Blair Wheeler) for cash on June 15, 1978.	

a. Acquired from St. Louis with cash as compensation for the signing of Rod Seiling on September 9, 1976.
b. Acquired from Pittsburgh with Dave Burrows on June 14, 1978, for Randy Carlyle and George Ferguson.

1979   Montreal, August 9   (9th choice overall)

Round 1	9	Laurie Boschman	Brandon Wheat Kings (WHL)
Round 2	30	Traded to Los Angeles (Mark Hardy) with Brian Glennie, Kurt Walker, and Scott Garland on June 14, 1978, for Dave Hutchison and Lorne Stamler.	
Round 3	51	Normand Aubin	Verdun Black Hawks (QMJHL)
Round 4	72	Vincent Tremblay	Quebec Remparts (QMJHL)
Round 5	93	Frank Nigro	London Knights (OMJHL)
Round 6	114	Bill McCreary	Colgate University Red Raiders (ECAC)

1980   Montreal, June 11   (11th choice overall)

Round 1	11	Traded to Detroit (Mike Blaisdell) with Errol Thompson, a first-round draft choice in 1978 (Brent Peterson), and a second-round draft choice in 1978 (Al Jensen) on March 13, 1978, for Dan Maloney and a second-round draft choice in 1980 (Craig Muni).	
Round 2a	25	Craig Muni	Kingston Canadians (OMJHL)
Round 2	32	Traded to Calgary (Kevin Lavallee) for Dave Shand and a third-round draft choice in 1980 (Torrie Robertson) on June 10, 1980.	
Round 2b	26	Bob McGill	Victoria Cougars (WHL)
Round 3c	43	Fred Boimistruck	Cornwall Royals (QMJHL)
Round 3	53	Traded to Minnesota (Randy Velischek) on October 5, 1978, for Walt McKechnie.	
Round 3	55	Acquired from Calgary, then traded to Washington (Torrie Robertson) with Mike Palmateer on June 11, 1980, for Robert Picard, Tim Coulis, and a second-round draft choice in 1980 (Bob McGill). Originally acquired with Dave Shand on June 10, 1980, for a second-round draft choice in 1980 (Kevin Lavallee).	
Round 4	74	Stewart Gavin	Toronto Marlboros (OMJHL)
Round 5	95	Hugh Larkin	Sault Ste. Marie Greyhounds (OMJHL)
Round 6	116	Ron Dennis	Princeton University Tigers (ECAC)
Round 7	137	Russ Adam	Kitchener Rangers (OMJHL)

Round 8	158	Fred Perlini	Toronto Marlboros (OMJHL)
Round 9	179	Darwin McCutcheon	Toronto Marlboros (OMJHL)
Round 10	200	Paul Higgins	Henry Carr Catholic Secondary School (Toronto)

a. Acquired from Detroit with Dan Maloney on March 13, 1978, for Errol Thompson, a first-round draft choice in 1978 (Brent Peterson), a second-round draft choice in 1978 (Al Jensen), and a first-round draft choice in 1980 (Mike Blaisdell).
b. Acquired from Washington with Robert Picard and Tim Coulis on June 11, 1980, for Mike Palmateer and a third-round draft choice in 1980 (Torrie Robertson).
c. Acquired from Colorado on March 3, 1980, for Walt McKechnie.

1981   Montreal, June 10   (6th choice overall)

Round 1	6	Jim Benning	Portland Winter Hawks (WHL)
Round 2a	24	Gary Yaremchuk	Portland Winter Hawks (WHL)
Round 2	27	Traded to Minnesota (Dave Donnelly) on March 10, 1981, for Ron Zanussi and a third-round draft choice in 1981 (Ernie Godden).	
Round 3	48	Traded to Colorado (Ulrich Heimer) on January 30, 1981, for René Robert.	
Round 3b	55	Ernie Godden	Windsor Spitfires (OHL)
Round 4	69	Traded to Minnesota (Terry Tait) on June 14, 1978, for Paul Harrison.	
Round 5	90	Normand Lefrançois	Trois-Rivières Draveurs (QMJHL)
Round 5c	102	Barry Brigley	Calgary Wranglers (WHL)
Round 6	111	Traded to Edmonton (Steve Smith) on August 22, 1979, for Reg Thomas.	
Round 7	132	Andrew Wright	Peterborough Petes (OHL)
Round 8	153	Richard Turmel	Shawinigan Cataractes (QMJHL)
Round 9	174	Greg Barber	Victoria Cougars (WHL)
Round 10	195	Marc Magnan	Lethbridge Broncos (WHL)

a. Acquired from Colorado on October 19, 1978, for Jack Valiquette.
b. Acquired from Minnesota on March 10, 1981, with Ron Zanussi for a second-round draft choice in 1981 (Dave Donnelly).
c. Acquired from Los Angeles on March 10, 1981, for Jim Rutherford.

1982   Montreal, June 9   (3rd choice overall)

Round 1	3	Gary Nylund	Portland Winter Hawks (WHL)
Round 2	24	Gary Leeman	Regina Pats (WHL)
Round 2a	25	Peter Ihnacak	Sparta Praha (Czechoslovakia)
Round 3	45	Ken Wregget	Lethbridge Broncos (WHL)
Round 4	66	Traded to Detroit (Craig Coxe) with a fifth-round draft choice in 1983 (Joey Kocur) on March 8, 1982, for Jim Korn.	
Round 4b	73	Vladimir Ruzicka	CHZ Litvinov (Czechoslovakia)
Round 5	87	Eduard Uvira	Dukla Jihlava (Czechoslovakia)
Round 5c	99	Sylvain Charland	Shawinigan Cataractes (QMJHL)
Round 6	108	Ron Dreger	Saskatoon Blades (WHL)
Round 6d	115	Craig Kales	Niagara Falls Flyers (OHL)
Round 7	129	Dom Campedelli	Cohasset High School (Massachusetts)
Round 7e	139	Jeff Triano	Toronto Marlboros (OHL)
Round 8	150	Traded to Montreal (Steve Smith) with Robert Picard on March 10, 1981, for Michel Larocque.	
Round 9	171	Miroslav Ihnacak	TJ VSZ Kosice (Czechoslovakia)

Round 10	192	Leigh Verstraete	Calgary Wranglers (WHL)
Round 11	213	Tim Loven	Red River High School (North Dakota)
Round 12	234	Jim Appleby	Winnipeg Warriors (WHL)

a. Acquired from Philadelphia via Hartford with Rick Costello and future considerations (Ken Strong) on January 20, 1982, for Darryl Sittler.
b. Acquired from Pittsburgh on September 11, 1981, for Paul Harrison.
c. Acquired from the Rangers on October 16, 1981, for Pat Hickey.
d. Acquired from Pittsburgh on February 3, 1982, for Greg Hotham.
e. Acquired from Quebec with Miroslav Frycer on March 9, 1982, for Wilf Paiement.

1983   **Montreal, June 8**   (7th choice overall)

Round 1	7	Russ Courtnall	Victoria Cougars (WHL)
Round 2	28	Jeff Jackson	Brantford Alexanders (OHL)
Round 3	49	Allan Bester	Brantford Alexanders (OHL)
Round 4	70	Traded to Los Angeles (later traded to Detroit—David Korol) on October 19, 1982, for Greg Terrion.
Round 5a	83	Dan Hodgson	Prince Albert Raiders (WHL)
Round 5	91	Traded to Detroit (Joey Kocur) with a fourth-round draft choice in 1982 (Craig Coxe) on March 8, 1982, for Jim Korn.
Round 6	112	Traded to Los Angeles (Kevin Stevens) with Bob Gladney on August 10, 1981, for Don Luce.
Round 7	133	Cam Plante	Brandon Wheat Kings (WHL)
Round 8	154	Paul Bifano	Burnaby Bluehawks (BCJHL)
Round 9	175	Cliff Albrecht	Princeton University Tigers (ECAC)
Round 10b	191	Greg Rolston	Power High School (Michigan)
Round 10	196	Brian Ross	Kitchener Rangers (OHL)
Round 11	217	Mike Tomlak	Cornwall Royals (OHL)
Round 12	238	Ron Choules	Trois-Rivières Draveurs (QMJHL)

a. Acquired from Pittsburgh with a sixth-round draft choice in 1982 (Craig Kales) on February 3, 1982, for Greg Hotham.
b. Acquired from Hartford on October 5, 1982, for Paul Marshall.

1984   **Montreal, June 9**   (4th choice overall)

Round 1	4	Al Iafrate	Belleville Bulls (OHL)
Round 2	25	Todd Gill	Windsor Spitfires (OHL)
Round 3	46	Traded to Montreal (later traded to Minnesota—Ken Hodge Jr.) on December 17, 1982, for Dan Daoust.
Round 4	67	Jeff Reese	London Knights (OHL)
Round 5	88	Jack Capuano	Kent High School (Massachusetts)
Round 6	109	Fabian Joseph	Victoria Cougars (WHL)
Round 7	130	Joe MacInnis	Watertown High School (Massachusetts)
Round 8	151	Derek Laxdal	Brandon Wheat Kings (WHL)
Round 9	172	Dan Turner	Medicine Hat Tigers (WHL)
Round 10	192	David Buckley	Trinity-Pawling High School
Round 11	213	Mikael Wurst	Ohio State University Buckeyes (CCHA)
Round 12	233	Peter Slanina	TJ VSZ Kosice (Czechoslovakia)

1985   **Toronto, June 15**   (1st choice overall)

Round 1	1	Wendel Clark	Saskatoon Blades (WHL)
Round 2	22	Ken Spangler	Calgary Wranglers (WHL)

Round 3	43	Dave Tomlinson	Brandon Wheat Kings (WHL)
Round 4	64	Greg Vey	Peterborough Petes (OHL)
Round 5	85	Jeff Serowik	Lawrence Academy (New Hampshire)
Round 6	106	Jiri Latal	Sparta Praha (Czechoslovakia)
Round 7	127	Tim Bean	North Bay Centennials (OHL)
Round 8	148	Andy Donahue	Belmont Hill High School (Massachusetts)
Round 9	169	Todd Whittemore	Kent High School (Massachusetts)
Round 10	190	Bob Reynolds	St. Clair Shores (Michigan)
Round 11	211	Tim Armstrong	Toronto Marlboros (OHL)
Round 12	232	Mitch Murphy	St. Paul's High School (Minnesota)

1986   **Montreal, June 21**   (6th choice overall)

Round 1	6	Vincent Damphousse	Laval Titans (QMJHL)
Round 2	27	Traded to Montreal (Benoît Brunet) on December 17, 1982, for Gaston Gingras.
Round 2a	36	Darryl Shannon	Windsor Spitfires (OHL)
Round 3	48	Sean Boland	Toronto Marlboros (OHL)
Round 4	69	Kent Hulst	Windsor Spitfires (OHL)
Round 5	90	Scott Taylor	Kitchener Rangers (OHL)
Round 6	111	Stéphane Giguère	St. Jean Castors (QMJHL)
Round 7	132	Danny Hie	Ottawa 67's (OHL)
Round 8	153	Steve Brennan	New Prep High School (Massachusetts)
Round 9	174	Brian Bellefeuille	Canterbury High School (Massachusetts)
Round 10	195	Sean Davidson	Toronto Marlboros (OHL)
Round 11	216	Mark Holick	Saskatoon Blades (WHL)
Round 12	237	Brian Hoard	Hamilton Steelhawks (OHL)

a. Acquired from Montreal on September 18, 1985, for Dom Campedelli.

1987   **Detroit, June 13**   (7th choice overall)

Round 1	7	Luke Richardson	Peterborough Petes (OHL)
Round 2	28	Daniel Marois	Chicoutimi Saguenéens (QMJHL)
Round 3	49	John McIntyre	Guelph Platers (OHL)
Round 4	70	Traded to Calgary (Tim Harris) on May 29, 1985, for Don Edwards.
Round 4a	71	Joe Sacco	Medford High School (Massachusetts)
Round 5	91	Mike Eastwood	Western Michigan University Broncos (CCHA)
Round 6	112	Damian Rhodes	Richfield High School (Minnesota)
Round 7	133	Trevor Jobe	Moose Jaw Warriors (WHL)
Round 8	154	Chris Jensen	Northwood School (New York)
Round 9	175	Brian Blad	Belleville Bulls (OHL)
Round 10	196	Ron Bernacci	Hamilton Steelhawks (OHL)
Round 11	217	Ken Alexander	Hamilton Steelhawks (OHL)
Round 12	238	Alex Weinrich	North Yarmouth Academy (Maine)

a. Acquired from Chicago with Jerome Dupont and Ken Yaremchuk on September 6, 1986, as compensation for the Hawks' signing of Gary Nylund.

1988 **Montreal, June 11** (6th choice overall)

Round 1	6	Scott Pearson	Kingston Canadians (OHL)
Round 2	27	Tie Domi	Peterborough Petes (OHL)
Round 3	48	Peter Ing	Windsor Spitfires (OHL)
Round 4	69	Ted Crowley	Lawrence Academy (New Hampshire)
Round 5a	86	Len Esau	Humboldt Broncos (SJHL)
Round 5	90	Traded to Calgary (Scott Matusovich) on September 17, 1987, for Dale DeGray.	
Round 6	111	Traded to the Islanders (Pavel Gross) on March 8, 1988, for Brian Curran.	
Round 7	132	Matt Mallgrave	St. Paul's High School (Minnesota)
Round 8	153	Roger Elvenes	Rogle BK Angelholm (Sweden)
Round 9	174	Mike Delay	Canterbury High School (Massachusetts)
Round 10	195	David Sacco	Medford High School (Massachusetts)
Round 11	216	Mike Gregorio	Cushing Academy (Massachusetts)
Round 12	237	Peter DeBoer	Windsor Spitfires (OHL)

a. Acquired from Vancouver on October 3, 1986, for Brad Maxwell.

1989 **Minnesota, June 17** (3rd choice overall)

Round 1	3	Scott Thornton	Belleville Bulls (OHL)
Round 1a	12	Rob Pearson	Belleville Bulls (OHL)
Round 1b	21	Steve Bancroft	Belleville Bulls (OHL)
Round 2	24	Traded to Calgary (Kent Manderville) on June 16, 1989, for Rob Ramage.	
Round 3	45	Traded to the Rangers (Rob Zamuner) with Jeff Jackson on March 5, 1987, for Mark Osborne.	
Round 4	66	Matt Martin	Avon Old Farms School (Connecticut)
Round 5	87	Traded to Philadelphia (later traded to Minnesota—Pat McLeod) on December 4, 1987, for Mike Stothers.	
Round 5c	96	Keith Carney	Mount St. Charles High School (Minnesota)
Round 6	108	David Burke	Cornell University Big Red (ECAC)
Round 6d	125	Michael Doers	Northwood School (New York)
Round 7	129	Keith Merkler	Portledge School (New York)
Round 8	150	Derek Langille	North Bay Centennials (OHL)
Round 9	171	Jeffrey St. Laurent	Berwick Academy (Maine)
Round 10	192	Justin Tomberlin	Greenway High School (Minnesota)
Round 11	213	Mike Jackson	Toronto Marlboros (OHL)
Round 12	234	Steve Chartrand	Drummondville Voltigeurs (QMJHL)

a. Acquired from Philadelphia via Calgary on March 6, 1989, for Ken Wregget.
b. Acquired from Philadelphia via Calgary on March 6, 1989, for Ken Wregget.
c. Acquired from Philadelphia on February 7, 1989, for Al Secord.
d. Acquired from Montreal with John Kordic on November 7, 1988, for Russ Courtnall.

1990 **Vancouver, June 16** (10th choice overall)

Round 1	10	Drake Berehowsky	Kingston Canadians (OHL)
Round 2	31	Félix Potvin	Chicoutimi Sagueneens (QMJHL)
Round 3	52	Traded to Philadelphia (Al Kinisky) on June 16, 1990, for Kevin Maguire and an eighth-round draft choice in 1991 (Dmitri Mironov).	

Round 4	73	Darby Hendrickson	Richfield High School (Minnesota)
Round 4a	80	Greg Walters	Ottawa 67's (OHL)
Round 5	94	Traded to Washington (Mark Ouimet) on June 29, 1989, for Lou Franceschetti.	
Round 6	115	Alexander Godynyuk	Sokol Kiev (USSR)
Round 7	136	Éric Lacroix	Governor Dummer Academy (Massachusetts)
Round 8	157	Dan Stiver	University of Michigan Wolverines (CCHA)
Round 9	178	Robert Horyna	Dukla Jihlava (Czechoslovakia)
Round 10	199	Rob Chebator	Arlington Catholic High School (Massachusetts)
Round 11	220	Scott Malone	Northfield Mount Hermon School (Massachusetts)
Round 12	241	Nick Vachon	Governor Dummer Academy (Massachusetts)

a. Acquired from Edmonton on December 21, 1989, for Vladimir Ruzicka.

1991 **Buffalo, June 9** (3rd choice overall)

Round 1	3	Traded to New Jersey (Scott Niedermayer) on October 16, 1989, for Tom Kurvers.	
Round 2	25	Traded to Quebec (later traded to Washington—Éric Lavigne) with Scott Pearson and a second-round draft choice in 1992 (Tuomas Gronman) on November 17, 1990, for Aaron Broten, Michel Petit, and Lucien DeBlois	
Round 3	47	Yanic Perreault	Trois-Rivières Draveurs (QMJHL)
Round 4	69	Terry Chitaroni	Sudbury Wolves (OHL)
Round 5	91	Traded to Philadelphia (later traded to Winnipeg—Juha Ylonen) with a seventh-round draft choice in 1991 (Andrei Lomakin) on September 8, 1989, for Mark LaForest.	
Round 5a	102	Alexei Kudashov	Krylya Sovetov (USSR)
Round 6	113	Jeff Perry	Owen Sound Platers (OHL)
Round 6b	120	Alexander Kuzminsky	Sokol Kiev (USSR)
Round 7	132	Traded to Philadelphia (Andrei Lomakin) with a fifth-round draft choice in 1991 (later traded to Winnipeg—Juha Ylonen) on September 8, 1989, for Mark LaForest.	
Round 7	135	Martin Prochazka	Poldi Kladno (Czechoslovakia)
Round 8	157	Traded to Quebec (Aaron Asp) as compensation for the Leafs' signing of Doug Carpenter as coach on August 16, 1989.	
Round 8c	160	Dmitri Mironov	Krylya Sovetov (USSR)
Round 8d	164	Robb McIntyre	Dubuque Fighting Saints (USHL)
Round 8e	167	Tomas Kucharcik	Dukla Jihlava (Czechoslovakia)
Round 9	179	Guy Lehoux	Drummondville Voltigeurs (QMJHL)
Round 10	201	Gary Miller	North Bay Centennials (OHL)
Round 11	223	Jonathan Kelley	Arlington Catholic High School (Massachusetts)
Round 12	245	Chris O'Rourke	University of Alaska Fairbanks Nanooks (WCHA)

a. Acquired from Washington on January 24, 1991, for Paul Fenton and John Kordic.
b. Acquired from Detroit on March 5, 1991, for Allan Bester.
c. Acquired from Philadelphia with Kevin Maguire on June 16, 1990, for a third-round draft choice in 1990 (Al Kinisky).

d. Acquired from Detroit on February 5, 1991, for Brad Marsh.
e. Acquired from Buffalo with Mike Foligno on December 17, 1990, for Brian Curran and Lou Franceschetti.

1992   **Montreal, June 20**   (5th choice overall)

Round 1	5	Traded to the Islanders (Darius Kasparaitis) on June 20, 1992, for a first-round draft choice in 1992 (Brandon Convery) and a second-round draft choice in 1992 (later traded to Washington).	
Round 1a	8	Brandon Convery	Sudbury Wolves (OHL)
Round 1b	23	Grant Marshall	Ottawa 67's (OHL)
Round 2	29	Traded to Quebec (Tuomas Gronman) with Scott Pearson and a second-round draft choice in 1991 (later traded to Washington—Éric Lavigne) on November 17, 1990, for Aaron Broten, Michel Petit, and Lucien DeBlois.	
Round 2c	32	Traded to Washington (Jim Carey) with a third-round draft choice in 1992 (Stefan Ustorf), and a fourth-round draft choice in 1993 (later traded to Winnipeg and then Detroit—John Jakopin) on June 20, 1992, for a first-round draft choice in 1992 (Grant Marshall) and a fourth-round draft choice in 1992 (Mark Raiter).	
Round 3	53	Traded to Washington (Stefan Ustorf) with a second-round draft choice in 1992 (Jim Carey) and a fourth-round draft choice in 1993 (later traded to Winnipeg and then Detroit—John Jakopin) on June 20, 1992, for a first-round draft choice in 1992 (Grant Marshall) and a fourth-round draft choice in 1992 (Mark Raiter).	
Round 4	77	Nikolai Borschevsky	Spartak Moscow (Russia)
Round 4d	95	Mark Raiter	Saskatoon Blades (WHL)
Round 5	101	Janne Gronvall	Lukko Rauma (Finland)
Round 5e	106	Chris deRuiter	Kingston Canadians (OHL)
Round 6	125	Mikael Hakansson	Nacka (Sweden)
Round 7	149	Patrik Augusta	Dukla Jihlava (Czechoslovakia)
Round 8	173	Ryan VandenBussche	Cornwall Royals (OHL)
Round 9	197	Wayne Clarke	Rensselaer Polytechnic Institute Engineers (ECAC)
Round 10	221	Sergei Simonov	Kristall Saratov (Russia)
Round 11	245	Nathan Dempsey	Regina Pats (WHL)

a. Acquired from the Islanders with a second-round draft choice in 1992 (later traded to Washington) on June 20, 1992, for a first-round draft choice in 1992 (Darius Kasparaitis).
b. Acquired from Washington with a fourth-round draft choice in 1992 (Mark Raiter) on June 20, 1992, for a second-round draft choice in 1992 (Jim Carey), a third-round draft choice in 1992 (Stefan Ustorf), and a fourth-round draft choice in 1993 (later traded to Winnipeg and then Detroit—John Jakopin).
c. Acquired from Islanders with a first-round draft choice in 1992 (Brandon Convery) on June 20, 1992, for a first-round draft choice in 1992 (Darius Kasparaitis) before being traded to Washington (Jim Carey).
d. Acquired from Washington with a fourth-round draft choice in 1992 (Mark Raiter) on June 20, 1992, for a second-round draft choice in 1992 (Jim Carey) and a third-round draft choice in 1992 (Stefan Ustorf).
e. Acquired from Minnesota via Buffalo on March 10, 1992, for Dave Hannan.

1993   **Quebec City, June 26–27**   (19th choice overall)

Round 1a	12	Kenny Jonsson	Rogle Angelholm (Sweden)
Round 1	19	Landon Wilson	Dubuque Fighting Saints (USHL)
Round 2	45	Traded to Hartford (later traded to San Jose—Vlastimil Kroupa) on November 24, 1992, for John Cullen.	
Round 3	71	Traded to Philadelphia (Vaclav Prospal) on July 26, 1991, for Mike Bullard.	
Round 4	97	Traded to Washington (later traded to Winnipeg, then to Detroit—John Jakopin) with a second-round pick in 1992 (Jim Carey) and a third-round pick in 1992 (Stefan Ustorf) on June 20, 1992, for a first-round pick in 1992 (Grant Marshall) and a fourth-round pick in 1992 (Mark Raiter).	
Round 5	123	Zdenek Nedved	Sudbury Wolves (OHL)
Round 6	149	Paul Vincent	Cushing Academy (Massachusetts)
Round 7	175	Jeff Andrews	North Bay Centennials (OHL)
Round 8	201	David Brumby	Tri-City Americans (WHL)
Round 9	227	Traded to Ottawa (Paval Demitra) on February 25, 1993, for Brad Miller.	
Round 10	253	Kyle Ferguson	Michigan Tech University Huskies (WCHA)
Round 11	279	Mikhail Lapin	Western Michigan University Broncos (CCHA)

a. Acquired from Buffalo with Dave Andreychuk and Daren Puppa on February 2, 1993, for Grant Fuhr and a sixth-round draft choice in 1995 (later traded to Chicago—Marc Magliarditi).

1994   **Hartford, June 28–29**   (22nd choice overall)

Round 1	10	Acquired from Quebec via Philadelphia and then traded to Washington (Nolan Baumgartner) with Rob Pearson on June 28, 1994, for Mike Ridley and a first-round draft choice in 1994 (Éric Fichaud).	
Round 1a	16	Éric Fichaud	Chicoutimi Saguenéens (QMJHL)
Round 1	22	Traded to Quebec (Jeffrey Kealty) on June 28, 1994, with Wendel Clark, Sylvain Lefebvre, and Landon Wilson for Mats Sundin, Garth Butcher, Todd Warriner, and a first-round draft choice in 1994 (traded to Washington later in the day—Nolan Baumgartner—with Rob Pearson for Mike Ridley).	
Round 2	48	Sean Haggerty	Detroit Jr. Red Wings (OHL)
Round 3b	64	Fredrik Modin	Sundsvall (Sweden)
Round 3	74	Traded to Montreal (Martin Bélanger) on August 20, 1992, for Sylvain Lefebvre.	
Round 4	100	Traded to the Rangers (Alexander Korobolin) with Scott Malone on March 21, 1994, for Mike Gartner.	
Round 5	126	Mark Deyell	Saskatoon Blades (WHL)
Round 6	135	Acquired from Hartford (later traded to the Rangers—Yuri Litvinov) on January 25, 1994, with Mark Greig for Ted Crowley.	
Round 6	152	Kam White	Newmarket Royals (OHL)
Round 7	178	Tommi Rajamaki	Assat Pori Juniors (Finland)
Round 8	204	Rob Butler	Niagara Scenic (NAHL)
Round 9	230	Traded to Hartford (Matt Ball) on March 18, 1994, for Ken Belanger.	

Round 10 256 Sergei Berezin   Khimik Voskresensk (Russia)
Round 11 282 Doug Nolan   Catholic Memorial School
                                 (Massachusetts)
a. Acquired from Washington via St. Louis with Mike Ridley on June 28, 1994, for Rob
Pearson and a first-round draft choice in 1994 (Nolan Baumgartner).
b. Acquired from the Islanders June 28, 1994, for a second-round draft choice in 1995
(D.J. Smith).

1995   Edmonton, July 8   (15th choice overall)

Round 1   15   Jeff Ware   Oshawa Generals (OHL)
Round 2   41   Traded to the Islanders (D.J. Smith) on June 28, 1994, for a
                 third-round draft choice in 1994 (Fredrik Modin).
Round 3a   54   Ryan Pepperall   Kitchener Rangers (OHL)
Round 3   67   Traded to Winnipeg Jets (Brad Isbister) with Mike Eastwood
                 on April 7, 1995, for Tie Domi.
Round 4   93   Traded to Washington (Sébastien Charpentier) on February
                 10, 1995, for Warren Rychel
Round 5   119   Traded to Buffalo (Kevin Popp) with Grant Fuhr for Dave
                 Andreychuk, Daren Puppa, and a first-round draft choice in
                 1993 (Kenny Jonsson) on February 9, 1993.
Round 6b   139   Doug Bonner   Seattle Thunderbirds (WHL)
Round 6   145   Yanick Tremblay   Beauport Harfangs (QMJHL)
Round 6   146   Traded to Buffalo (later sent to Chicago—Marc Magliarditi)
                 with Grant Fuhr on February 2, 1993, for Dave Andreychuk,
                 Daren Puppa, and a first-round draft choice in 1993 (Kenny
                 Jonsson).
Round 7   171   Marek Melenovsky   Dukla Jihlava (Czech Republic)
Round 8   197   Mark Murphy   Stratford Cullitons (Midwestern Jr. B)
Round 9   223   Daniil Markov   Spartak Moscow (Russia)
a. Acquired from the Islanders with Benoît Hogue and a fifth-round draft choice in 1996
(Brandon Sugden) on April 6, 1995, for Éric Fichaud.
b. Acquired from Hartford with Mark Greig on January 25, 1994, for Ted Crowley.

1996   St. Louis, June 22   (15th choice overall)

Round 1   15   Traded to Philadelphia (Dainius Zubrus) with a second-round
                 draft choice in 1997 (Jean-Marc Pelletier) on August 30, 1995,
                 for Dmitry Yushkevich and a second-round draft choice in
                 1996 (Francis Larivée).
Round 2a   36   Marek Posmyk   Dukla Jihlava (Czech Republic)
Round 2   41   Traded to Pittsburgh (later sent to New Jersey—Joshua
                 Dewolf) with Dmitri Mironov on July 8, 1995, for Larry
                 Murphy.
Round 2b   50   Francis Larivée   Laval Titans (QMJHL)
Round 3c   66   Mike Lankshear   Guelph Storm (OHL)
Round 3   68   Konstantin Kalmikov Detroit Falcons (Colonial Hockey
                                     League)
Round 4   84   Acquired from Los Angeles on July 14, 1994, for Yanic
                 Perreault, then traded to Philadelphia with a first-round draft
                 choice in 1996 (Dainius Zubrus) and a second-round
                 choice in 1997 (Jean-Marc Pelletier) on August 30, 1995, for
                 Dmitri Yushkevich and a second-round draft choice in 1996
                 (Francis Larivée). Philadelphia later traded the selection back
                 to Los Angeles (Mikael Simons).

Round 4d   86   Jason Sessa   Lake Superior State University Lakers
                                     (CCHA)
Round 4   92   Acquired from Anaheim (later traded to Montreal—Kim
                 Staal) on March 20, 1996, for Ken Baumgartner.
Round 4   96   Traded to Los Angeles (Éric Bélanger) with Éric Lacroix and
                 Chris Snell on October 3, 1994, for Kelly Fairchild, Dixon
                 Ward, Guy Leveque, and Shayne Toporowski.
Round 4e   103   Vladimir Antipov   Torpedo Yaroslavl (Russia)
Round 5f   110   Peter Cava   Sault Ste. Marie Greyhounds (OHL)
Round 5g   111   Brandon Sugden   London Knights (OHL)
Round 5   124   Traded to Philadelphia (Per-Ragna Bergkvist) on July 8, 1995,
                 for Rob Zettler.
Round 6h   140   Dmitri Yakushin   Pembroke Lumber Kings (CJAHL)
Round 6i   148   Chris Bogas   Michigan State University Spartans
                                     (CCHA)
Round 6   151   Lucio DeMartinis   Shawinigan Cataractes (QMJHL)
Round 7   178   Reggie Berg   University of Minnesota Golden
                                     Gophers (WCHA)
Round 8   204   Tomas Kaberle   Poldi Kladno (Czech Republic)
Round 9   230   Jared Hope   Spokane Chiefs (WHL)
a. Acquired from New Jersey with either a fourth-round draft choice in 1998 or a third-round
draft choice in 1999 on March 13, 1996, for Dave Andreychuk (Toronto opted for the third-round
draft choice in 1999 and later traded the selection back to New Jersey, with Doug Gilmour and
Dave Ellett, on February 25, 1997, for Alyn McCauley, Steve Sullivan, and Jason Smith).
b. Acquired from Philadelphia with Dmitry Yushkevich on August 30, 1995, for a first-round
draft choice in 1996 (Dainius Zubrus), a fourth-round draft choice in 1996 (later traded to Los
Angeles—Mikael Simons), and a second-round draft choice in 1997 (Jean-Marc Pelletier).
c. Acquired from Calgary June 22, 1996, for Dave Gagner.
d. Acquired from Edmonton with Peter White on December 4, 1995, for Kent Manderville.
e. Acquired from Phoenix June 22, 1996, for Mike Gartner.
f. Acquired from San Jose with Jamie Baker on June 14, 1996, for Todd Gill.
g. Acquired from Islanders with Benoît Hogue and a third-round draft choice in 1995 (Ryan
Pepperall) on April 6, 1995, for Éric Fichaud.
h. Acquired from Dallas with Dave Gagner on January 26, 1996, for Benoît Hogue and
Randy Wood.
i. Acquired from Calgary on April 6, 1995, for Nikolai Borschevsky.

1997   Pittsburgh, June 24   (4th choice overall)

Round 1   4   Traded to Islanders (Roberto Luongo) with Kenny Jonsson,
                 Darby Hendrickson, and Sean Haggerty on March 13, 1996,
                 for Wendel Clark, Mathieu Schneider, and D.J. Smith.
Round 2   30   Traded to Philadelphia (Jean-Marc Pelletier) with a first-round
                 draft choice in 1996 (Dainius Zubrus) and a fourth-round
                 draft choice in 1996 (later traded to Los Angeles—Mikael
                 Simmons) on August 30, 1995, for Dmitry Yushkevich and a
                 second-round draft choice in 1996 (Francis Larivée)
Round 3   57   Jeff Farkas   Boston College Eagles (HE)
Round 4   84   Adam Mair   Owen Sound Platers (OHL)
Round 5   111   Frantisek Mrazek   Ceske Budejovice (Czech Republic)
Round 6   138   Eric Gooldy   Detroit Jr. Red Wings (OHL)
Round 7   165   Hugo Marchand   Victoriaville Tigres (QMJHL)
Round 8   194   Russ Bartlett   Phillips Exeter Academy (New
                                     Hampshire)
Round 9   221   Jonathan Hedstrom   Skelleftea (Sweden)

1998   Buffalo, June 27   (8th choice overall)

Round 1a 10   Nikolai Antropov   Torpedo Ust-Kamenogorsk (Kazakhstan)

Round 2   35   Petr Svoboda   Havlickuv Brod (Czech Republic)

Round 3   67   Traded to Tampa Bay (later sent to Edmonton—Alex Henry) for Craig Wolanin on January 31, 1997.

Round 3b 69   Jamie Hodson   Brandon Wheat Kings (WHL)

Round 4c 87   Alexei Ponikarovsky Dynamo-2 Moscow (Russia)

Round 4   94   Traded to Chicago (Matthias Trattnig) with a first-round draft choice in 1998 (Mark Bell) on June 27, 1998, for a first-round draft choice in 1998 (Nikolai Antropov), a third-round draft choice in 1998 (Jamie Hodson), and a fifth-round draft choice in 1998 (Morgan Warren).

Round 4   113 Acquired from New Jersey (later sent to Edmonton—Kristian Antila) with a second-round draft choice in 1996 (Marek Posmyk) on March 13, 1996, for Dave Andreychuk.

Round 5   123 Traded to Islanders (Jiri Dopita) on October 11, 1996, for Darby Henrickson.

Round 5d 126 Morgan Warren   Moncton Wildcats (QMJHL)

Round 6   154 Allan Rourke   Kitchener Rangers (OHL)

Round 7   181 Jonathan Gagnon   Cape Breton Screaming Eagles (QMJHL)

Round 8   208 Traded to Carolina (Jaroslav Svoboda) on March 18, 1997, for Kelly Chase.

Round 8e 215 Dwight Wolfe   Halifax Mooseheads (QMJHL)

Round 8f 228 Michal Travnicek   Chemopetrol Litvinov Juniors (Czech Republic)

Round 9   236 Sergei Rostov   Dynamo-2 Moscow (Russia)

a. Acquired from Chicago with a third-round draft choice in 1998 (Jamie Hodson) and a fifth-round draft choice in 1998 (Morgan Warren) on June 27, 1998, for a first-round draft choice in 1998 (Mark Bell) and a fourth-round draft choice in 1998 (Matthias Trattnig).
b. Acquired from Chicago with a first-round draft choice in 1998 (Nikolai Antropov) and a fifth-round draft choice in 1998 (Morgan Warren) on June 27, 1998, for a first-round draft choice in 1998 (Mark Bell) and a fourth-round draft choice in 1998 (Matthias Trattnig).
c. Acquired from Detroit via Tampa Bay on March 24, 1998, for Jamie Macoun.
d. Acquired from Chicago via Carolina with a first-round draft choice in 1998 (Nikolai Antropov) and a third-round draft choice in 1998 (Jamie Hodson) on June 27, 1998, for a first-round draft choice in 1998 (Mark Bell) and a fourth-round draft choice in 1998 (Matthias Trattnig).
e. Acquired from Ottawa on March 17, 1998, for Per Gustafsson.
f. Acquired from Dallas on March 24, 1998, for Mike Kennedy.

1999   Boston, June 26   (24th choice overall)

Round 1   24   Luca Cereda   Ambri-Piotta (Switzerland)

Round 2   60   Peter Reynolds   London Knights (OHL)

Round 3   92   Traded to Los Angeles (Cory Campbell) with Jason Podollan on March 23, 1999, for Yanic Perreault.

Round 3   95   Acquired from New Jersey with a second-round draft choice in 1996 (Marek Posmyk) on March 13, 1996, for Dave Andreychuk. Traded back to New Jersey (Andre Lakos) with Doug Gilmour and Dave Ellett for Jason Smith, Steve Sullivan, and Alyn McCauley on February 25, 1997.

Round 4a 108 Mirko Murovic   Moncton Wildcats (QMJHL)

Round 4b 110 Jonathan Zion   Ottawa 67's (OHL)

Round 4   121 Traded to Carolina (later sent to Nashville—Yevgeny Pavlov) on January 2, 1998, for Jeff Brown.

Round 5   151 Vaclav Zavoral   Chemopetrol Litvinov Juniors (Czech Republic)

Round 6c 161 Jan Sochar   Slavia Praha (Czech Republic)

Round 6   182 Traded to Islanders (later sent to Tampa Bay—Fedor Fedorov) with Félix Potvin on January 9, 1999, for Bryan Berard and a sixth-round draft choice in 1999 (Jan Sochar).

Round 7   211 Vladimir Kulikov   CSKA Moscow Juniors (Russia)

Round 8   239 Pierre Hedin   MODO Ornskoldvik (Sweden)

Round 9   267 Peter Metcalf   University of Maine Black Bears (HE)

a. Acquired from Rangers with Alexander Karpovtsev on October 14, 1998, for Mathieu Schneider.
b. Acquired from Edmonton with a second-round draft choice in 2000 (Kris Vernarsky) on March 23, 1999, for Jason Smith.
c. Acquired from Islanders with Bryan Berard on January 9, 1999, for Félix Potvin and a sixth-round draft choice in 1999 (Jan Sochar).

2000   Calgary, June 24–25   (24th choice overall)

Round 1   24   Brad Boyes   Erie Otters (OHL)

Round 2   59   Traded to Boston on October 21, 1999, for the rights to match arbitration award to Dmitri Khristich of Boston.

Round 2a 51   Kris Vernarsky   Plymouth Whalers (OHL)

Round 3b 70   Mikael Tellqvist   Djurgardens (Sweden)

Round 3   90   Jean-François Racine   Drummondville Voltigeurs (QMJHL)

Round 4c 100 Miguel Delisle   Ottawa 67's (OHL)

Round 4   121 Leafs' selection awarded to Anaheim because of tampering charges in their hiring of Thommie Bergman. Toronto also fined $100,000. (Anaheim later traded selection to Chicago, then to Washington—Ryan Vanbuskirk)

Round 5   161 Traded to Tampa Bay (Pavel Sedov) with Mike Johnson and a sixth-round draft choice in 2000 (Aaron Gionet) on February 9, 2000, for Darcy Tucker and a fourth-round draft choice in 2000 (Miguel Delisle).

Round 6   191 Traded to Tampa Bay with Mike Johnson and a fifth-round draft choice in 2000 (Pavel Sedov) on February 9, 2000, for Darcy Tucker and a fourth-round draft choice in 2000 (Miguel Delisle).

Round 6d 179 Vadim Sozinov   Metallurg Novokuznetsk (Russia)

Round 7e 209 Markus Seikola   TPS Turku Juniors (Finland)

Round 7   223 Lubos Velebny   Zvolen Juniors (Slovakia)

Round 8   254 Alexander Shinkar   Severstal Cherepovets (Russia)

Round 9f 265 Jean-Philippe Côté Cape Breton Screaming Eagles (QMJHL)

a. Acquired from Edmonton with a fourth-round draft choice in 1999 (Jonathan Zion) on March 23, 1999, for Jason Smith.
b. Acquired from Tampa Bay on November 29, 1999, for Todd Warriner.
c. Acquired from Tampa Bay with Darcy Tucker on February 9, 2000, for Mike Johnson, Marek Posmyk, a fifth-round draft choice in 2000 (Pavel Sedov), and a sixth-round draft choice in 2000 (Aaron Gionet).
d. Acquired from Anaheim with a seventh-round draft choice in 2000 (Markus Seikola) on June 25, 2000, for the rights to Jonathan Hedstrom.
e. Acquired from Anaheim with a sixth-round draft choice in 2000 (Vadim Sozinov) on June 25, 2000, for the rights to Jonathan Hedstrom.
f. Toronto and Tampa Bay exchanged ninth-round draft choices after the Lightning hired St. John's goalie Jeff Reese as a goaltending consultant on August 6, 1999 (Toronto selected Côté; Tampa Bay traded their selection to Philadelphia—Milan Kopecky).

2001   **Florida, June 23–24**   (17th choice overall)

Round 1	17	Carlo Colaiacovo	Erie Otters (OHL)
Round 2a	39	Karel Pilar	Chemopetrol Litvinov (Czech Republic)
Round 2	49	Traded to Los Angeles (Mike Cammalleri) with Adam Mair on March 13, 2001, for Aki-Petteri Berg.	
Round 3b	65	Brendan Bell	Ottawa 67's (OHL)
Round 3	82	Jay Harrison	Brampton Battalion (OHL)
Round 3c	88	Nicolas Corbeil	Sherbrooke Castors (QMJHL)
Round 4	115	Traded to Chicago (Vladimir Gusev) with Alexander Karpovtsev on October 2, 2000, for Bryan McCabe.	
Round 5d	134	Kyle Wellwood	Belleville Bulls (OHL)
Round 5	152	Traded to Tampa Bay (later traded to Los Angeles—Terry Denike) with Mike Johnson, Marek Posmyk, and a sixth-round draft choice in 2000 (Aaron Gionet) on February 9, 2000, for Darcy Tucker, a fourth-round draft choice in 2000 (Miguel Delisle), and a fifth-round draft choice in 2001 (Kyle Wellwood).	
Round 6e	168	Maxim Kondratiev	Lada Togliatti Juniors (Russia)
Round 6	183	Jaroslav Sklenar	Kometa Brno Juniors (Czech Republic)
Round 7f	198	Ivan Kolozvary	Dukla Trencin Juniors (Slovakia)
Round 7	213	Jan Chovan	Belleville Bulls (OHL)
Round 8	246	Tomas Mojzis	Moose Jaw Warriors (WHL)
Round 9	276	Mike Knoepfli	Georgetown Raiders (OPJHL)

a. Acquired from Chicago on October 8, 1999, for Sylvain Côté.
b. Acquired from Washington on December 11, 2000, for Dmitri Khristich.
c. Acquired from Chicago on June 23, 2001, for Igor Korolev.
d. Acquired from Tampa Bay with Darcy Tucker and a fourth-round draft choice in 2000 (Miguel Delisle) on February 9, 2000, for Mike Johnson, Marek Posmyk, a sixth-round draft choice in 2000 (Aaron Gionet), and a fifth-round draft choice in 2001 (Terry Denike).
e. Acquired from Atlanta on July 15, 1999, for the rights to Martin Prochazka.
f. Acquired from Tampa Bay with Cory Cross on October 1, 1999, for Fredrik Modin.

2002   **Toronto, June 21–23**   (24th choice overall)

Round 1	24	Alexander Steen	Vastra Frolunda Juniors (Sweden)
Round 2	57	Matt Stajan	Belleville Bulls (OHL)
Round 3a	74	Todd Ford	Swift Current Broncos (WHL)
Round 3b	88	Dominic D'Amour	Hull Olympiques (QMJHL)
Round 3	90	Traded to Calgary (Matt Lombardi) with a fifth-round draft choice in 2002 (Kristofer Persson) on June 22, 2002, for a third-round draft choice in 2002 (Todd Ford).	
Round 4	122	David Turon	Femax Havirov (Czech Republic)
Round 5	159	Traded to Calgary (Kristofer Persson) with a third-round draft choice in 2002 (Matt Lombardi) on June 22, 2002, for a third-round draft choice in 2002 (Todd Ford).	
Round 6	191	Ian White	Swift Current Broncos (WHL)
Round 7	222	Scott May	Ohio State University Buckeyes (CCHA)
Round 8	254	Jarkko Immonen	Assat Pori (Finland)
Round 9	285	Staffan Kronwall	Huddinge Juniors (Sweden)

a. Acquired from Calgary on June 22, 2002, for a third-round draft choice in 2002 (Matt Lombardi) and a fifth-round draft choice in 2002 (Kristofer Persson).
b. Acquired from Nashville via Buffalo on June 22, 2002, for a third-round draft choice in 2003 (Alexander Sulzer).

2003   **Nashville, June 21–22**   (21st choice overall)

Round 1	21	Traded to San Jose (later traded to Boston—Mark Stuart) with Alyn McCauley and Brad Boyes on March 5, 2003, for Owen Nolan.	
Round 2	57	John Doherty	Phillips Academy Andover (Massachusetts)
Round 3	78	Acquired from Calgary (later traded to Minnesota—Danny Irmen) with future considerations on June 30, 2002, for Curtis Joseph.	
Round 3a	91	Martin Sagat	Dukla Trencin Juniors (Slovakia)
Round 3	92	Traded to Nashville on June 22, 2002, for a third-round draft choice in 2002 (Dominic D'Amour).	
Round 4b	125	Konstantin Volkov	Dynamo-2 Moscow (Russia)
Round 4	126	Traded to Carolina (Kevin Nastiuk) on March 15, 2002, for Tom Barrasso.	
Round 5	158	John Mitchell	Plymouth Whalers (OHL)
Round 6	188	Traded to Montreal (Mark Flood) on March 11, 2003, for Doug Gilmour.	
Round 7	220	Jeremy Williams	Swift Current Broncos (WHL)
Round 8c	237	Shaun Landolt	Calgary Hitmen (WHL)
Round 8	252	Traded to Vancouver (Sergei Topol) on June 25, 2002, for Ryan Bonni.	
Round 9	282	Traded to Chicago (Chris Porter) with a fourth-round draft choice in 2004 (Karel Hromas) on March 11, 2003, for Phil Housley.	

a. Acquired from Minnesota with a fourth-round draft choice in 2003 (Konstantin Volkov) on June 21, 2003, for a third-round draft choice in 2003 (Danny Irmen).
b. Acquired from Minnesota with a third-round draft choice in 2003 (Martin Sagat) on June 21, 2003, for a third-round draft choice in 2003 (Danny Irmen).
c. Acquired from Nashville on June 30, 2002, for Tie Domi.

2004   **Carolina, June 26–27**   (24th choice overall)

Round 1	24	Traded to the Rangers (later traded to Calgary—Kris Chucko) with Maxim Kondratiev, Jarkko Immonen, and a second-round draft choice in 2005 (Michael Sauer) on March 3, 2004, for Brian Leetch.	
Round 2	59	Traded to Carolina (later traded to Columbus—Kyle Wharton) on March 9, 2003, for Glen Wesley.	
Round 3	90	Justin Pogge	Prince George Cougars (WHL)
Round 4a	113	Roman Kukumberg	Dukla Trencin (Slovakia)
Round 4	123	Traded to Chicago (Karek Hromas) with a ninth-round draft choice in 2003 (Chris Porter) on March 11, 2003, for Phil Housley.	
Round 5	157	Dmitri Vorobiev	Lada Togliatti (Russia)
Round 6	187	Robbie Earl	University of Wisconsin Badgers (WCHA)
Round 7	220	Maxim Semenov	Lada Togliatti (Russia)
Round 8	252	Jan Steber	Halifax Mooseheads (QMJHL)
Round 9	285	Pierce Norton	Thayer Academy (Massachusetts)

a. Acquired from the Rangers via Edmonton with Brian Leetch on March 3, 2004, for Maxim Kondratiev, Jarkko Immonen, a first-round draft choice in 2004 (Kris Chucko), and a second-round draft choice in 2005 (Michael Sauer).

2005   **Ottawa, July 30**   (21st choice overall)

Round 1   21   Tuukka Rask   Ilves Tampere Juniors (Finland)

Round 2   40   Traded to the Rangers (Michael Sauer) with Maxim Kondrative, Jarkko Immonen, and a first-round draft choice in 2004 (Kris Chucko) on March 3, 2004, for Brian Leetch and a fourth-round draft choice in 2004 (Roman Kukumberg).

Round 3   82   Phil Oreskovic   Brampton Battalion (OHL)

Round 4   101   Traded to Carolina (later traded to Columbus—Jared Boll) on March 9, 2004, for Ron Francis.

Round 5   153   Alex Berry   Boston Junior Bruins (EJHL)

Round 6   173   Johan Dahlberg   MODO Ornskoldsvik Juniors (Sweden)

Round 7   216   Anton Stralman   Skovde (Sweden)

Round 7a   228   Chad Rau   Des Moines Buccaneers (USHL)

a. Received compensatory pick from NHL for Group III free-agent signing of Tom Fitzgerald by Boston.

2006   **Vancouver, June 24**   (13th choice overall)

Round 1   13   Jiri Tlusty   Kladno (Czech Republic)

Round 2   44   Nikolai Kulemin   Metallurg Magnitogorsk (Russia)

Round 3   76   Traded to Chicago (Tony Lagerstrom) on June 24, 2006, for two fourth-round draft choices in 2006 (James Reimer and Korbinian Holzer).

Round 4a   99   James Reimer   Red Deer Rebels (WHL)

Round 4   106   Traded to Carolina (later traded to St. Louis—Reto Berra) on July 30, 2005, for Jeff O'Neill.

Round 4b   111   Korbinian Holzer   Bad Tolz (Germany)

Round 5   136   Traded to Columbus (Nick Sucharski) on March 8, 2006, for Luke Richardson.

Round 6c   161   Viktor Stalberg   Frolunda Juniors (Sweden)

Round 6   166   Tyler Ruegsegger   Shattuck-St. Mary's School (Minnesota)

Round 6d   180   Leo Komarov   Assat Pori (Finland)

Round 7e   188   Traded to Phoenix (Chris Frank) with a seventh-round draft choice in 2006 (Chris Frank) on June 24, 2006, for a sixth-round draft choice in 2006 (Viktor Stalberg).

Round 7   196   Traded to Phoenix (Benn Ferreiro) with a seventh-round draft choice in 2006 (Chris Frank) on June 24, 2006, for a sixth-round draft choice in 2006 (Viktor Stalberg).

a. Acquired from Chicago via Carolina and Columbus with a fourth-round draft choice in 2006 (Korbinian Holzer) on June 24, 2006, for a third-round draft choice in 2006 (Tony Lagerstrom).
b Acquired from Chicago via Colorado with a fourth-round draft choice in 2006 (James Reimer) on June 24, 2006, for a third-round draft choice in 2006 (Tony Lagerstrom).
c. Acquired from Phoenix on June 24, 2006, for two seventh-round draft choices in 2006 (Chris Frank and Benn Ferreiro).
d. Acquired from Dallas on November 6, 2005, for Nathan Perrott.
e. Acquired from Boston on June 15, 2006, for Petr Tenkrat.

2007   **Columbus, June 22–23**   (13th choice overall)

Round 1   13   Traded to San Jose (later traded to St. Louis—Lars Eller) with a second-round draft choice in 2007 (Aaron Palushaj) and a fourth-round draft choice in 2009 (Craig Smith) on June 22, 2007, for Vesa Toskala and Mark Bell.

Round 2   44   Traded to San Jose (later St. Louis—Aaron Palushaj) with a first-round draft choice in 2007 (Lars Eller) and a fourth-round draft choice in 2009 (Craig Smith) on June 22, 2007, for Vesa Toskala and Mark Bell.

Round 3   74   Dale Mitchell   Oshawa Generals (OHL)

Round 4a   99   Matt Frattin   Fort Saskatchewan Traders (AJHL)

Round 4   104   Ben Winnett   Salmon Arm Silverbacks (BCHL)

Round 5   134   Juraj Mikus   Dukla Trencin Juniors (Slovakia)

Round 6   164   Chris DiDomenico   Saint John Sea Dogs (QMJHL)

Round 7   194   Carl Gunnarsson   Linkopings (Sweden)

a. Acquired from Phoenix via Boston with Nick Boynton on June 26, 2006, for Paul Mara and a third-round draft choice in 2007 (Maxime Macenauer).

2008   **Ottawa, June 20–21**   (5th choice overall)

Round 1a   5   Luke Schenn   Kelowna Rockets (WHL)

Round 1   7   Traded to the Islanders (later traded to Nashville—Colin Wilson) with a third-round draft choice in 2008 (Shawn Lalonde) and a second-round draft choice in 2009 (Mat Clark) on June 20, 2008, for a first-round draft choice in 2008 (Luke Schenn).

Round 2   38   Traded to Phoenix (later traded to Nashville—Roman Josi) with Brendan Bell on February 27, 2007, for Yanic Perreault and a fifth-round draft choice in 2008 (Joel Champagne).

Round 2b   60   Jimmy Hayes   Lincoln Stars (USHL)

Round 3   68   Traded to the Islanders (later traded to Chicago—Shawn Lalonde) with a first-round draft choice in 2008 (later traded to Nashville—Colin Wilson) and a second-round draft choice in 2009 (later traded to Anaheim—Mat Clark) on June 20, 2008, for a first-round draft choice in 2008 (Luke Schenn).

Round 3c   70   Traded to St. Louis (James Livingston) on June 19, 2008, for Jamal Mayers.

Round 4   98   Mikhail Stefanovich   Quebec Remparts (QMJHL)

Round 5d   129   Joel Champagne   Chicoutimi Saguenéens (QMJHL)

Round 5e   130   Jerome Flaake   Kolner Haie Juniors (Germany)

Round 6   158   Grant Rollheiser   Trail Smoke Eaters (BCHL)

Round 7   188   Andrew MacWilliam   Camrose Kodiaks (AJHL)

a. Acquired from the Islanders on June 20, 2008, for a first-round draft choice in 2008 (later traded to Nashville—Colin Wilson), a third-round draft choice in 2008 (later traded to Chicago—Shawn Lalonde), and a second-round draft choice in 2009 (later traded to Anaheim—Mat Clark).
b. Acquired from Pittsburgh with a fifth-round draft choice in 2009 on February 26, 2008, for Hal Gill.
c. Acquired from Florida on February 26, 2008, for Chad Kilger.
d. Acquired from Phoenix with Yanic Perreault on February 27, 2007, for Brendan Bell and a second-round draft choice in 2008 (later traded to Nashville—Roman Josi).
e. Acquired from Florida on February 26, 2008, for Wade Belak.

2009   **Montreal, June 26–27**   (7th choice overall)

Round 1   7   Nazem Kadri   London Knights (OHL)

Round 2   37   Traded to the Islanders (later traded to Chicago—Shawn Lalonde) with a first-round draft choice in 2008 (later traded to Nashville—Colin Wilson) and a second-round draft choice in 2009 (later traded to Anaheim—Mat Clark) on June 20, 2008, for a first-round draft choice in 2008 (Luke Schenn).

Round 2a   50   Kenny Ryan   U.S. National Team Development Program

Round 2b 58 Jesse Blacker   Windsor Spitfires (OHL)

Round 3 68 Jamie Devane   Plymouth Whalers (OHL)

Round 4 98 Traded to San Jose (later traded to Nashville—Craig Smith) with a first-round draft choice in 2007 (Lars Eller) and a second-round draft choice in 2007 (Aaron Palushaj) on June 22, 2007, for Vesa Toskala and Mark Bell.

Round 4 117 Toronto forfeited draft choice for illegal signing of Jonas Frogren.

Round 5 127 Eric Knodel   Philadelphia Junior Flyers (AYHL)

Round 5c 150 Traded to the Rangers (later traded to Pittsburgh—Andy Bathgate) on July 14, 2008, for Ryan Hollweg.

Round 6 157 Jerry D'Amigo   U.S. National Team Development Program

Round 7 187 Barron Smith   Peterborough Petes (OHL)

a. Acquired from the Rangers on March 4, 2009, for Nikolai Antropov.
b. Acquired from Buffalo (via Edmonton and Calgary) on March 4, 2009, for Dominic Moore.
c. Acquired from Pittsburgh with a second-round draft choice in 2008 (Jimmy Hayes) on February 26, 2008, for Hal Gill.

2010   Los Angeles, June 25–26   (2nd choice overall)

Round 1 2 Traded to Boston (Tyler Seguin) with a second-round draft choice in 2010 (Jared Knight) and a first-round draft choice in 2011 (Dougie Hamilton) on September 18, 2009, for Phil Kessel.

Round 2 32 Traded to Montreal (later traded to Chicago, back to Toronto, then to Boston—Jared Knight) with Greg Pateryn on July 3, 2008, for Mikhail Grabovski; reacquired from Chicago for a second-round draft choice in 2011 (Brandon Saad) and a third-round draft choice in 2011 (Michael Paliotta) on September 5, 2009; traded to Boston with a first-round draft choice in 2010 (Tyler Seguin) and a first-round draft choice in 2011 (Dougie Hamilton) on September 18, 2009, for Phil Kessel.

Round 2a 43 Brad Ross   Portland Winterhawks (WHL)

Round 3 62 Greg McKegg   Erie Otters (OHL)

Round 3b 79 Sondre Olden   MODO Ornskoldsvik Juniors (Sweden)

Round 4 92 Traded to Florida (Sam Brittain) with Bryan McCabe on September 2, 2008, for Mike Van Ryn.

Round 4c 112 Traded to Washington (Philipp Grubauer) on June 26, 2010, for a fourth-round draft choice in 2010 (Petter Granberg) and a fifth-round draft choice in 2010 (Daniel Brodin).

Round 4d 116 Petter Granberg   Skelleftea Juniors (Sweden)

Round 5 122 Traded to Anaheim (Chris Wagner) on June 26, 2010, for Mike Brown.

Round 5e 144 Sam Carrick   Brampton Battalion (OHL)

Round 5f 146 Daniel Brodin   Djurgardens (Sweden)

Round 6 152 Traded to Pittsburgh (Joe Rogalski) on March 3, 2010, for Chris Peluso.

Round 7 182 Josh Nicholls   Saskatoon Blades (WHL)

Round 7g 202 Traded to Edmonton (Kellen Jones) on June 26, 2010, for a sixth-round draft choice in 2011 (David Broll).

a. Acquired from Chicago on June 26, 2010, for Jimmy Hayes.
b. Acquired from Los Angeles on June 26, 2010, for a third-round draft choice in 2012 (Jimmy Vesey).
c. Acquired from Phoenix with Matt Jones and a seventh-round draft choice in 2010 (Kellen Jones) on March 3, 2010, for Lee Stempniak.

d. Acquired from Washington with a fifth-round draft choice in 2010 (Daniel Brodin) on June 26, 2010, for a fourth-round draft choice in 2010 (Philipp Grubauer).
e. Acquired from New Jersey on March 3, 2010, for Martin Skoula.
f. Acquired from Washington with a fourth-round draft choice in 2010 (Petter Granberg) on June 26, 2010, for a fourth-round draft choice in 2010 (Philipp Grubauer).
g. Acquired from Phoenix with Matt Jones and a fourth-round draft choice in 2010 (Philipp Grubauer) on March 3, 2010, for Lee Stempniak.

2011   Minnesota, June 24–25   (9th choice overall)

Round 1 9 Traded to Boston (Dougie Hamilton) with a first-round draft choice in 2010 (Tyler Seguin) and a second-round draft choice in 2010 (Jared Knight) on September 18, 2009, for Phil Kessel.

Round 1a 22 Tyler Biggs   U.S. National Team Development Program

Round 1b 25 Stuart Percy   Mississauga St. Michael's Majors (OHL)

Round 1c 30 Traded to Anaheim (Rickard Rackell) with a second-round draft choice in 2011 (John Gibson) on June 24, 2011, for a first-round draft choice in 2011 (Tyler Biggs).

Round 2 39 Traded to Anaheim (John Gibson) with a first-round draft choice in 2011 (Rickard Rackell) on June 24, 2011, for a first-round draft choice in 2011 (Tyler Biggs).

Round 2d 43 Traded to Chicago (Brandon Saad) with a third-round draft choice in 2011 (Michael Paliotta) on September 5, 2009, for a second-round draft choice in 2010 (Jared Knight).

Round 3 69 Traded to Chicago (Michael Paliotta) with a second-round draft choice in 2011 (Brandon Saad) on September 5, 2009, for a second-round draft choice in 2010 (Jared Knight).

Round 3e 85 Josh Leivo   Sudbury Wolves (OHL)

Round 4 99 Tom Nilsson   Mora Juniors (Sweden)

Round 5 129 Tom Cameranesi   Wayzata High School (Minnesota)

Round 6f 151 David Broll   Sault Ste. Marie Greyhounds (OHL)

Round 6 159 Traded to Anaheim (Josh Manson) on June 25, 2011, for a sixth-round draft choice in 2012 (Ryan Rupert).

Round 6g 172 Dennis Robertson   Brown University Bears (ECAC)

Round 7 189 Garret Sparks   Guelph Storm (OHL)

Round 7h 202 Max Everson   Edina High School (Minnesota)

a. Acquired from Anaheim on June 24, 2011, for a first-round draft choice in 2011 (Rickard Rackell) and a second-round draft choice in 2011 (John Gibson).
b. Acquired from Philadelphia with a third-round draft choice in 2011 (Josh Leivo) on February 14, 2011, for Kris Versteeg.
c. Acquired from Boston with Joe Colborne and a second-round draft choice in 2012 (Mike Winther) on February 18, 2011, for Tomas Kaberle.
d. Acquired from Calgary with Wayne Primeau on July 27, 2009, for Colin Stuart, Anton Stralman, and a seventh-round draft choice in 2012 (Matthew De Blouw).
e. Acquired from Philadelphia with a first-round draft choice in 2011 (Stuart Percy) on February 14, 2011, for Kris Versteeg.
f. Acquired from Edmonton on June 26, 2010, for a seventh-round draft choice in 2010 (Kellen Jones).
g. Acquired from Anaheim on August 10, 2009, for Justin Pogge.
h. Acquired from Anaheim on March 3, 2010, for Joey MacDonald.

2012   Pittsburgh, June 22–23   (5th choice overall)

Round 1 5 Morgan Rielly   Moose Jaw Warriors (WHL)

Round 2 35 Matthew Finn   Guelph Storm (OHL)

Round 2a 54 Traded to Colorado (later traded to Washington and then Dallas—Mike Winther) on June 24, 2011, for John-Michael Liles.

Round 3 66 Traded to Los Angeles (later traded to Nashville—Jimmy Vesey) on June 26, 2010, for a third-round draft choice in 2010 (Sondre Olden).

Round 4 96 Traded to New Jersey (Ben Thomson) on October 4, 2011, for David Steckel.

Round 5 126 Dominic Toninato   Duluth East High School (Minnesota)

Round 6 156 Connor Brown   Erie Otters (OHL)

Round 6b 157 Ryan Rupert   London Knights (OHL)

Round 7 186 Traded to Calgary (Matthew DeBlouw) with Colin Stuart and Anton Stralman on July 27, 2009, for Wayne Primeau and a second-round draft choice in 2011 (Brandon Saad).

Round 7c 209 Viktor Loov   Sodertalje Juniors (Sweden)

a. Acquired from Boston with Joe Colborne and a first-round draft choice in 2011 (Rickard Rakell) on February 18, 2011, for Tomas Kaberle.
b. Acquired from Anaheim on June 25, 2011, for a sixth-round draft choice in 2011 (Josh Manson).
c. Acquired from the Rangers on February 28, 2011, for John Mitchell.

2013   **New Jersey, June 30**   (21st choice overall)

Round 1 21 Frederik Gauthier   Rimouski Océanic (QMJHL)

Round 2 51 Traded to Chicago (Carl Dahlstrom) with a fourth-round draft choice in 2013 (Fredrik Bergvik) and a fourth-round draft choice in 2014 (Fredrik Olofsson) on June 30, 2013, for Dave Bolland.

Round 3 82 Carter Verhaeghe   Niagara IceDogs (OHL)

Round 4 112 Traded to Nashville (later traded to St. Louis—Zachary Pochiro) with Brett Lebda and Robert Slaney on July 3, 2011, for Matthew Lombardi and Cody Franson.

Round 4a 117 Traded to Chicago (later traded to San Jose—Fredrik Bergvik) with a second-round draft choice in 2013 (Carl Dahlstrom) and a fourth-round draft choice in 2014 (Fredrik Olofsson) on June 30, 2013, for Dave Bolland.

Round 5 142 Fabrice Herzog   Zug Juniors (Switzerland)

Round 6 172 Antoine Bibeau   P.E.I. Rocket (QMJHL)

Round 7 202 Andreas Johnson   Frolunda Juniors (Sweden)

a. Acquired from Anaheim with Joffrey Lupul and Jake Gardiner on February 9, 2011, for François Beauchemin.

2014   **Philadelphia, June 27–28**   (8th choice overall)

Round 1 8 William Nylander   MODO Ornskoldsvik (Sweden)

Round 2 38 Traded to Anaheim (Marcus Pettersson) with Jesse Blacker and a seventh-round draft choice in 2014 (Ondrej Kase) on November 16, 2013, for Peter Holland and Brad Staubitz.

Round 3 68 Rinat Valiev   Kootenay Ice (WHL)

Round 4a 93 Traded to Colorado (Nicholas Magyar) on April 3, 2013, for Ryan O'Byrne.

Round 4b 94 Traded to St. Louis (Ville Husso) with Carl Gunnarsson on June 28, 2014, for Roman Polak.

Round 4 98 Traded to Chicago (Fredrik Olofsson) with a second-round draft choice in 2013 (Carl Dahlstrom) and a fourth-round draft choice in 2013 (Fredrik Bergvik) on June 30, 2013, for Dave Bolland.

Round 4c 103 John Piccinich   Youngstown Phantoms (USHL)

Round 5 128 Dakota Joshua   Sioux Falls Stampede (USHL)

Round 6 158 Nolan Vesey   South Shore Kings (USPHL)

Round 7 188 Pierre Engvall   Frolunda Juniors (Sweden)

Round 7d 205 Traded to Anaheim (Ondrej Kase) with Jesse Blacker and a second-round draft choice in 2013 (Marcus Pettersson) on November 16, 2013, for Peter Holland and Brad Staubitz.

a. Acquired from Edmonton on April 4, 2013, for Mike Brown.
b. Acquired from Calgary on September 28, 2013, for Joe Colborne.
c. Acquired from Phoenix on January 16, 2013, for Matthew Lombardi.
d. Acquired from Anaheim with Ryan Lasch on March 15, 2013, for David Steckel.

2015   **Florida, June 26–27**   (4th choice overall)

Round 1 4 Mitch Marner   London Knights (OHL)

Round 1a 24 Traded to Philadelphia (Travis Konecny) on June 26, 2015, for a first-round draft choice in 2015 (later traded to Columbus—Gabriel Carlsson) and a second-round draft choice in 2015 (Jeremy Bracco).

Round 1b 29 Traded to Columbus (Gabriel Carlsson) on June 26, 2015, for a second-round draft choice in 2015 (Travis Dermott) and a third-round draft choice in 2015 (Martins Dzierkals).

Round 2c 34 Travis Dermott   Erie Otters (OHL)

Round 2d 61 Jeremy Bracco   USA U18 (USHL)

Round 3 65 Andrew Nielsen   Lethbridge Hurricanes (WHL)

Round 3e 68 Martins Dzierkals   HK Riga (Latvia)

Round 4 95 Jesper Lindgren   MODO Ornskoldsvik Juniors (Sweden)

Round 4f 107 Traded to Edmonton (later traded to Ottawa—Christian Wolanin) with Brad Ross on June 27, 2015, for Martin Marincin.

Round 5 125 Dmytro Timashov   Quebec Remparts (QMJHL)

Round 6 155 Stephen Desrocher   Oshawa Generals (OHL)

Round 7 185 Nikita Korostelev   Sarnia Sting (OHL)

a. Acquired from Nashville with Olli Jokinen and Brendan Leipsic on February 15, 2015, for Cody Franson and Mike Santorelli.
b. Acquired from Philadelphia (later traded to Columbus—Gabriel Carlsson) with a second-round draft choice in 2015 (Jeremy Bracco) on June 26, 2015, for a first-round draft choice in 2015 (Travis Konecny).
c. Traded to Los Angeles with Ben Scrivens and Matt Frattin on June 23, 2013, for Jonathan Bernier. Re-acquired from Columbus with a third-round draft choice in 2015 (Martins Dzierkals) on June 26, 2015, for a first-round draft choice in 2015 (Gabriel Carlsson).
d. Acquired from Philadelphia with a first-round draft choice in 2015 (later traded to Columbus—Gabriel Carlsson) on June 26, 2015, for a first-round draft choice in 2015 (Travis Konecny)
e. Acquired from Columbus with a second-round draft choice in 2015 (Travis Dermott) on June 26, 2015, for a first-round draft choice in 2015 (Gabriel Carlsson).
f. Acquired from Pittsburgh with Zach Sill on February 25, 2015, for Daniel Winnik.

ALL-TIME COACHING REGISTER

Stats for each entry pre-2005 read:
Season G   W   L   T

From the 2005–06 season on (when ties were no longer allowed):
Season G   W   L   OTL

Stats refer to the regular season only.

JACK ADAMS
b. Fort William, Ontario, June 14, 1895
d. Detroit, Michigan, May 1, 1968
Hockey Hall of Fame 1959 (as a player)
Replaced Charlie Querrie on January 6, 1923.
Replaced by Eddie Powers for 1923–24.

Season	G	W	L	T
1922–23	18	10	7	1

GEORGE ARMSTRONG ("The Chief")
b. Borlands Bay, Ontario, July 6, 1930
Hockey Hall of Fame 1975 (as a player)
Hired December 19, 1988.
Fired August 15, 1989.

Season	G	W	L	T
1988–89	47	17	26	4

MIKE BABCOCK
b. Manitouwadge, Ontario, April 29, 1963
Hired May 20, 2015.

NICK BEVERLEY
b. Toronto, Ontario, April 21, 1947
Hired March 5, 1996.
Resigned April 27, 1996.

Season	G	W	L	T
1995–96	17	9	6	2

JOHN BROPHY ("The Grey Ghost")
b. Halifax, Nova Scotia, January 20, 1933
Hired July 2, 1986.
Fired December 19, 1988.

Season	G	W	L	T
1986–87	80	32	42	6
1987–88	80	21	49	10
1988–89	33	11	20	2
Totals	193	64	111	18

PAT BURNS ("Burnsie")
b. St. Henri, Quebec, April 4, 1952
d. Sherbrooke, Quebec, November 19, 2010
Hired May 29, 1992.
Fired March 4, 1996.

Season	G	W	L	T
1992–93	84	44	29	11
1993–94	84	43	29	12
1994–95	48	21	19	8
1995–96	65	25	30	10
Totals	281	133	107	41

RANDY CARLYLE
b. Sudbury, Ontario, April 19, 1956
Hired March 2, 2012.
Fired January 6, 2015.

Season	G	W	L	OTL
2011–12	18	6	9	3
2012–13	82	26	17	5
2013–14	82	38	36	8
2014–15	40	21	16	3
Totals	222	91	78	19

DOUG CARPENTER
b. Cornwall, Ontario, July 1, 1942
Hired August 24, 1989.
Fired October 26, 1990.

Season	G	W	L	T
1989–90	80	38	38	4
1990–91	11	1	9	1
Totals	91	39	47	5

DICK CARROLL
b. Guelph, Ontario, April 28, 1885
d. Guelph, Ontario, January 20, 1952
Became Arenas' first coach in NHL.
Replaced by Eddie Powers for 1921–22.

Season	G	W	L	T
1917–18	22	13	9	0
1918–19	18	5	13	0
1920–21	24	15	9	0
Totals	64	33	31	0

FRANCIS "KING" CLANCY
b. Ottawa, February 25, 1903
d. Toronto, November 8, 1986
Hockey Hall of Fame 1958 (as a player)
Hired March 24, 1953.
Reassigned to position of assistant general manager April 2, 1956.*

Season	G	W	L	T
1953–54	70	32	24	14
1954–55	70	24	24	22
1955–56	70	24	33	13
1966–67	10	7	1	2
1971–72	15	9	3	3
Totals	235	96	85	54

*Also coached: February 23, 1961, vs. Canadiens, though decision was credited to Imlach's record; game of April 9, 1966, when Imlach had the flu, but Clancy was not given official credit for the loss; February 18–March 11, 1967, while Punch Imlach was suffering from exhaustion; February 23–March 22 & March 25–April 2, 1972, while John McLellan was ill with ulcer problems.

JOE CROZIER ("Crow")
b. Winnipeg, Manitoba, February 19, 1929
Took over behind the bench March 19, 1980, although did not officially become coach until start of 1980–81 season.
Fired January 8, 1981.

Season	G	W	L	T
1980–81	40	13	22	5

CLARENCE "HAPPY"/"HAP" DAY
b. Owen Sound, Ontario, June 1, 1901
d. St. Thomas, Ontario, February 17, 1990
Hockey Hall of Fame 1961 (as a player)
Hired as coach April 17, 1940.
Resigned to become assistant general manager, and replaced by Primeau.

Season	G	W	L	T
1940–41	48	28	14	6
1941–42	48	27	18	3
1942–43	50	22	19	9
1943–44	50	23	23	4
1944–45	50	24	22	4
1945–46	50	19	24	7
1946–47	60	31	19	10
1947–48	60	32	15	13
1948–49	60	22	25	13
1949–50	70	31	27	12
Totals	546	259	206	81

DICK DUFF
b. Kirkland Lake, Ontario, February 18, 1936
Coached two games (March 15 & 17) after Floyd Smith was injured in a car crash.

Season	G	W	L	T
1979–80	2	0	2	0

ART DUNCAN ("Dunc")
b. Sault Ste. Marie, Ontario, July 4, 1891
d. Aurora, Ontario, April 13, 1975
Hired October 13, 1930.
Fired November 27, 1931.

Season	G	W	L	T
1930–31	44	22	13	9
1931–32	5	0	3	2
Totals	49	22	16	11

FRANK HEFFERNAN ("Moose")
b. Peterborough, Ontario, January 12, 1892
d. New York, New York, December 21, 1938
Coached first half of season; resigned February 4, 1920, to concentrate on playing and was replaced by team secretary Harry Sproule.

Season	G	W	L	T
1919–20	12	5	7	0

PETER HORACHEK
b. Stoney Creek, Ontario, January 26, 1960
Hired January 7, 2015.
Replaced by Mike Babcock, May 20, 2015.

Season	G	W	L	OTL
2014–15	42	9	28	5

GEORGE "PUNCH" IMLACH
b. Toronto, Ontario, March 15, 1918
d. Toronto, Ontario, December 1, 1987
Hockey Hall of Fame 1984 (as a builder)
Hired July 10, 1958, as assistant general manager; took over as coach November 28, 1958.
Fired April 6, 1969.

Season	G	W	L	T
1958–59	50	22	20	8
1959–60	70	35	26	9
1960–61	70	39	19	12
1961–62	70	37	22	11
1962–63	70	35	23	12
1963–64	70	33	25	12
1964–65	70	30	26	14
1965–66*	70	34	25	11
1966–67	60	25	26	9
1967–68	74	33	31	10
1968–69	76	35	26	15
1979–80**	10	5	5	0
Totals	760	363	274	123

* King Clancy coached for Imlach on April 9, 1966, though Imlach got official credit for the loss; Clancy also coached for the period February 18–March 11, 1967, while Imlach was ill.
** While officially coach in 1979–80, Imlach had Joe Crozier behind the bench for the final 10 games of the season; Crozier was later made coach for 1980–81.

DICK IRVIN
b. Limestone Ridge, Ontario, July 19, 1892
d. Montreal, Quebec, May 16, 1957
Hockey Hall of Fame 1958 (as a player)
Hired November 28, 1931.
Resigned April 16, 1940.

Season	G	W	L	T
1931–32	43	23	15	5
1932–33	48	24	18	6
1933–34	48	26	13	9
1934–35	48	30	14	4
1935–36	48	23	19	6
1936–37	48	22	21	5
1937–38	48	24	15	9
1938–39	48	19	20	9
1939–40	48	25	17	6
Totals	427	216	152	59

LEONARD "RED" KELLY

b. Simcoe, Ontario, July 9, 1927
Hockey Hall of Fame 1969 (as a player)
Hired August 20, 1973.
Fired June 17, 1977.

1973–74	78	35	27	16
1974–75	80	31	33	16
1975–76	80	34	31	15
1976–77	80	33	32	15
Totals	318	133	123	62

DAN MALONEY ("Harley")

b. Barrie, Ontario, September 24, 1950
Hired May 26, 1984.
Resigned June 18, 1986.

1984–85	80	20	52	8
1985–86	80	25	48	7
Totals	160	45	100	15

PAUL MAURICE

b. Sault Ste. Marie, Ontario,
January 30, 1967
Hired May 12, 2006.
Fired May 7, 2008.

2006–07	82	40	31	11
2007–08	82	36	35	11
Totals	164	76	66	22

JOHN McLELLAN

b. South Porcupine, Ontario, August 6, 1928
d. Toronto, Ontario, October 27, 1979
Hired April 6, 1969.
Resigned April 17, 1973.

1969–70	76	29	34	13
1970–71	78	37	33	8
1971–72*	63	24	28	11
1972–73	78	27	41	10
Totals	295	117	136	42

*Missed February 23–March 22 & March 25–April 2, 1972 (15 games), due to ulcers; replaced by King Clancy.

HOWIE MEEKER

b. Kitchener, Ontario, November 4, 1924
Hired April 11, 1956.
Promoted to general manager May 13, 1957, and replaced behind the bench by Billy Reay.

1956–57	70	21	34	15

MIKE MURPHY ("Murph")

b. Toronto, Ontario, September 12, 1950
Hired July 3, 1996.
Fired June 23, 1997.

1996–97	82	30	44	8

ROGER NEILSON ("Captain Video")

b. Toronto, Ontario, June 16, 1934
d. Peterborough, Ontario, June 21, 2003
Hired July 25, 1977; fired March 1, 1979; rehired March 3, 1979; fired permanently April 22, 1979.

1977–78	80	41	29	10
1978–79	80	34	33	13
Totals	160	75	62	23

MIKE NYKOLUK

b. Toronto, Ontario, December 11, 1934
Hired January 10, 1981.
Fired April 2, 1984.

1980–81	40	15	15	10
1981–82	80	20	44	16
1982–83	80	28	40	12
1983–84	80	26	45	9
Totals	280	89	144	47

EDDIE POWERS

b. Elora, Ontario, 1888
d. Stouffville, Ontario, January 17, 1943
Replaced Dick Carroll to start 1921–22; replaced by Charlie Querrie to start 1922–23; then took over from Adams, who resigned; was finally replaced by Conn Smythe to start 1926–27.

1921–22	24	13	10	1
1923–24	24	10	14	0
1924–25	30	19	11	0
1925–26	36	12	21	3
Totals	114	54	56	4

JOE PRIMEAU ("Gentleman Joe")

b. Lindsay, Ontario, January 24, 1906
d. Toronto, Ontario, May 15, 1989
Hockey Hall of Fame 1963 (as a player)
Hired May 26, 1950.
Resigned March 24, 1953.

1950–51	70	41	16	13
1951–52	70	29	25	16
1952–53	70	27	30	13
Totals	210	97	71	42

CHARLIE QUERRIE ("The Indian Chief")

b. Markham, Ontario, July 25, 1877
d. Toronto, Ontario, April 5, 1950
Coached the first six games of 1922–23; replaced by Jack Adams on January 6, 1923

1922–23	6	3	3	0

PAT QUINN

b. Hamilton, Ontario, January 29, 1943
d. Vancouver, British Columbia, November 23, 2014
Hired June 26, 1998.
Fired April 20, 2006.

1998–99	82	45	30	7	—
1999–00	82	45	27	7	3
2000–01	82	37	29	11	5
2001–02	82	43	25	10	4
2002–03	82	44	28	7	3
2003–04	82	45	24	10	3
2005–06	82	41	33	—	8
Totals	574	300	196	52	26

BILLY REAY

b. Winnipeg, Manitoba, August 21, 1918
d. Madison, Wisconsin, September 23, 2004
Hired May 13, 1957.
Fired November 28, 1958.

1957–58	70	21	38	11
1958–59	20	5	12	3
Totals	90	26	50	14

FLOYD SMITH ("Smitty")

b. Perth, May 16, 1935
Hired July 20, 1979; injured in a car crash on March 14, 1980, and was replaced by Duff, then Imlach (Crozier), and never coached again.

1979–80	68	33	30	5

CONN SMYTHE ("The Hollerin' Major")

b. Toronto, Ontario, February 1, 1895
d. Toronto, Ontario, November 18, 1980
Became coach just prior to buying the team; resigned October 13, 1930, and hired Art Duncan as his replacement.

1926–27	44	15	24	5
1927–28*	44	18	18	8
1928–29	44	21	18	5
1929–30	44	17	21	6
Totals	176	71	81	24

*Also coached the University of Toronto Grads team that won gold at the 1928 Olympics.

HARRY SPROULE

b. Unknown
d. Unknown
Replaced Frank Heffernan as coach February 4, 1920.
Replaced by Carroll for 1920–21

1919–20	12	7	5	0

TOM WATT

b. Toronto, Ontario, June 17, 1935
Hired October 27, 1990.
Reassigned to the position of director of professional development on May 29, 1992.

1990–91	69	22	37	10
1991–92	80	30	43	7
Totals	149	52	80	17

RON WILSON

b. Windsor, Ontario, May 28, 1955
Hired June 10, 2008.
Fired March 2, 2012.

2008–09	82	34	35	13
2009–10	82	30	38	14
2010–11	82	37	34	11
2011–12	64	29	28	7
Totals	310	130	135	45

ALL-TIME COACHING RECORDS (REGULAR SEASON)

MOST SEASONS

Hap Day	10
Punch Imlach	10
Dick Irvin	9

MOST GAMES

Punch Imlach	760
Pat Quinn	574
Hap Day	546

MOST WINS

Punch Imlach	363
Pat Quinn	300
Hap Day	259

MOST LOSSES

Punch Imlach	274
Pat Quinn	222
Hap Day	206

ALL–TIME COACHING RECORD BY SEASON

YEAR	COACH	REGULAR SEASON				PLAYOFFS			
		G	W	L	T	G	W	L	SERIES RECORD
1917–18	Dick Carroll	22	13	9	0	7	4	3	2–0
1918–19	Dick Carroll	18	5	13	0	DNQ			
1919–20	Frank Heffernan	12	5	7	0	—	—	—	
	Harry Sproule	12	7	5	0	DNQ			
1920–21	Dick Carroll	24	15	9	0	2	0	2	0–1
1921–22	Eddie Powers	24	13	10	1	7*	4	2	2–0
1922–23	Charlie Querrie	6	3	3	0	—	—	—	
	Jack Adams	18	10	7	1	DNQ			
1923–24	Eddie Powers	24	10	14	0	DNQ			
1924–25	Eddie Powers	30	19	11	0	2	0	2	0–1
1925–26	Eddie Powers	36	12	21	3	DNQ			
1926–27	Conn Smythe	44	15	24	5	DNQ			
1927–28	Conn Smythe	44	18	18	8	DNQ			
1928–29	Conn Smythe	44	21	18	5	4	2	2	1–1
1929–30	Conn Smythe	44	17	21	6	DNQ			
1930–31	Art Duncan	44	22	13	9	2*	0	1	0–1
1931–32	Art Duncan	5	0	3	2	—	—	—	
	Dick Irvin	43	23	15	5	7*	5	1	3–0
1932–33	Dick Irvin	48	24	18	6	9	4	5	1–1
1933–34	Dick Irvin	48	26	13	9	5	2	3	0–1
1934–35	Dick Irvin	48	30	14	4	7	3	4	1–1
1935–36	Dick Irvin	48	23	19	6	9	4	5	2–1
1936–37	Dick Irvin	48	22	21	5	2	0	2	0–1
1937–38	Dick Irvin	48	24	15	9	7	4	3	1–1
1938–39	Dick Irvin	48	19	20	9	10	5	5	2–1
1939–40	Dick Irvin	48	25	17	6	10	6	4	2–1
1940–41	Hap Day	48	28	14	6	7	3	4	0–1
1941–42	Hap Day	48	27	18	3	13	8	5	2–0
1942–43	Hap Day	50	22	19	9	6	2	4	0–1
1943–44	Hap Day	50	23	23	4	5	1	4	0–1
1944–45	Hap Day	50	24	22	4	13	8	5	2–0
1945–46	Hap Day	50	19	24	7	DNQ			
1946–47	Hap Day	60	31	19	10	11	8	3	2–0
1947–48	Hap Day	60	32	15	13	9	8	1	2–0
1948–49	Hap Day	60	22	25	13	9	8	1	2–0

*one tie

YEAR	COACH	REGULAR SEASON				PLAYOFFS			
		G	W	L	T	G	W	L	SERIES RECORD
1949–50	Hap Day	70	31	27	12	7	3	4	0–1
1950–51	Joe Primeau	70	41	16	13	11*	8	2	2–0
1951–52	Joe Primeau	70	29	25	16	4	0	4	0–1
1952–53	Joe Primeau	70	27	30	13	DNQ			
1953–54	King Clancy	70	32	24	14	5	12	4	0–1
1954–55	King Clancy	70	24	24	22	4	0	4	0–1
1955–56	King Clancy	70	24	33	13	5	1	4	0–1
1956–57	Howie Meeker	70	21	34	15	DNQ			
1957–58	Billy Reay	70	21	38	11	DNQ			
1958–59	Billy Reay	20	5	12	3	—	—	—	
	Punch Imlach	50	22	20	8	12	8	4	1–1
1959–60	Punch Imlach	70	35	26	9	10	4	6	1–1
1960–61	Punch Imlach	70	39	19	12	5	1	4	0–1
1961–62	Punch Imlach	70	37	22	11	12	8	4	2–0
1962–63	Punch Imlach	70	35	23	12	10	8	2	2–0
1963–64	Punch Imlach	70	33	25	12	14	8	6	2–0
1964–65	Punch Imlach	70	30	26	14	6	2	4	0–1
1965–66	Punch Imlach	70	34	25	11	4	0	4	0–1
1966–67	Punch Imlach	60	25	26	9	12	8	4	2–0
	King Clancy	10	7	1	2	—	—	—	
1967–68	Punch Imlach	74	33	31	10	DNQ			
1968–69	Punch Imlach	76	35	26	15	4	0	4	0–1
1969–70	John McLellan	76	29	34	13	DNQ			
1970–71	John McLellan	78	37	33	8	6	2	4	0–1
1971–72	John McLellan	63	24	28	11	5	1	4	0–1
	King Clancy	15	9	3	3	—	—	—	
1972–73	John McLellan	78	27	41	10	DNQ			
1973–74	Red Kelly	78	35	27	16	4	0	4	0–1
1974–75	Red Kelly	80	31	33	16	7	2	5	1–1
1975–76	Red Kelly	80	34	31	15	10	5	5	1–1
1976–77	Red Kelly	80	33	32	15	10	5	5	1–1
1977–78	Roger Neilson	80	41	29	10	13	6	7	2–1
1978–79	Roger Neilson	80	34	33	13	6	2	4	1–1
1979–80	Floyd Smith	68	30	33	5	—	—	—	
	Dick Duff	2	0	2	0	—	—	—	
	Punch Imlach	10	5	5	0	3	0	3	0–1
1980–81	Joe Crozier	40	13	22	5	—	—	—	
	Mike Nykoluk	40	15	15	10	3	0	3	0–1
1981–82	Mike Nykoluk	80	20	44	16	DNQ			

*one tie

YEAR	COACH	REGULAR SEASON				PLAYOFFS			
		G	W	L	T	G	W	L	SERIES RECORD
1982–83	Mike Nykoluk	80	28	40	12	4	1	3	0–1
1983–84	Mike Nykoluk	80	26	45	9	DNQ			
1984–85	Dan Maloney	80	20	52	8	DNQ			
1985–86	Dan Maloney	80	25	48	7	10	6	4	1–1
1986–87	John Brophy	80	32	42	6	13	7	6	1–1
1987–88	John Brophy	80	21	49	10	6	2	4	0–1
1988–89	John Brophy	33	11	20	2	—	—	—	
	George Armstrong	47	17	26	4	DNQ			
1989–90	Doug Carpenter	80	38	38	4	5	1	4	0–1
1990–91	Doug Carpenter	11	1	9	1	—	—	—	
	Tom Watt	69	22	37	10	DNQ			
1991–92	Tom Watt	80	30	43	7	DNQ			
1992–93	Pat Burns	84	44	29	11	21	11	10	2–1
1993–94	Pat Burns	84	43	29	12	18	9	9	2–1
1994–95	Pat Burns	48	21	19	8	7	3	4	0–1
1995–96	Pat Burns	65	25	30	10	—	—	—	
	Nick Beverley	17	9	6	2	6	2	4	0–1
1996–97	Mike Murphy	82	30	44	8	DNQ			
1997–98	Mike Murphy	82	30	43	9	DNQ			
1998–99	Pat Quinn	82	45	30	7	17	9	8	2–1
1999–2000	Pat Quinn	82	45	30	7	12	6	6	1–1
2000–01	Pat Quinn	82	37	34	11	11	7	4	1–1
2001–02	Pat Quinn	82	43	29	10	20	10	10	2–1
2002–03	Pat Quinn	82	44	31	7	7	3	4	0–1
2003–04	Pat Quinn	82	45	27	10	13	6	7	1–1
2004–05					NO SEASON				
		G	W	L	OTL	G	W	L	SERIES RECORD
2005–06	Pat Quinn	82	41	33	8	DNQ			
2006–07	Paul Maurice	82	40	31	11	DNQ			
2007–08	Paul Maurice	82	36	35	11	DNQ			
2008–09	Ron Wilson	82	34	35	13	DNQ			
2009–10	Ron Wilson	82	30	38	14	DNQ			
2010–11	Ron Wilson	82	37	34	11	DNQ			
2011–12	Ron Wilson	64	29	28	7				
	Randy Carlyle	18	6	9	3	DNQ			
2012–13	Randy Carlyle	82	26	17	5	7	3	3	0–1
2013–14	Randy Carlyle	82	38	36	8	DNQ			
2014-15	Randy Carlyle	40	21	16	3				
	Peter Horachek	42	9	28	5	DNQ			

ALL-TIME REGULAR-SEASON PLAYER REGISTER

For skaters, stats in columns read:

Season GP G A P PIM

For goaltenders:

Season GP W-L-T/OTL MIN GA SO GAA

• 1917–19 indicates Toronto Arenas; 1919–27 indicates Toronto St. Pats; 1927–present indicates Toronto Maple Leafs.

• For players' records during the 1917–18 season, dashes appear in the assist column because the NHL did not record assists.

• An F after the season indicates the player was a rookie and played his first NHL game in a Leaf uniform; the dates of all rookies' first games are also listed. An L after the year indicates the player's last year in the NHL; the date of the last game of each player's NHL career is also listed. The L or R that appears after a player's weight indicates which way a skater shoots or with which hand a goalie catches.

• From 1917–21, ties were not allowed in the NHL. Thus, for goalies' records during those years, only wins and losses are listed.

SPENCER ABBOTT #13

left wing 5'9" 170 R
b. Hamilton, Ontario, April 30, 1988
Signed as a free agent, March 28, 2012.
Traded to Chicago for T.J. Brennan, February 26, 2015.

2013–14 F	1	0	0	0	0

F October 5, 2013

DOUG ACOMB #22

centre 5'10" 165 L
b. Toronto, Ontario, May 15, 1949
Rights acquired from Portland (WHL) during 1968–69 season.

1969–70 F/L	2	0	1	1	0

F March 7, 1970 **L** March 11, 1970

RUSS ADAM #16

centre 5'10" 185 L
b. Windsor, Ontario, May 5, 1961
Selected 137th overall in 1980 Entry Draft.

1982–83 F/L	8	1	2	3	11

F October 6, 1982 **L** November 3, 1982

JACK ADAMS #5/#9

centre 5'9" 175 R
b. Fort William, Ontario, June 14, 1895
d. Detroit, Michigan, May 1, 1968
Signed as a free agent, February 7, 1918, arriving from Sarnia (OHA Senior) after the team folded; signed as a free agent by Vancouver (PCHA), December 1919. Acquired from Vancouver (PCHA) for Corb Dennenay, December 1922; sold to Ottawa before the 1926–27 season.

1917–18 F	8	0	—	0	31
1918–19	17	3	3	6	35
1922–23	23	19	9	28	64
1923–24	22	14	4	18	51
1924–25	27	21	10	31	67
1925–26	36	21	5	26	52
Totals	133	78	31	109	300

F February 11, 1918
• Hockey Hall of Fame 1959
• Became coach and GM of Detroit Cougars (later Falcons and Red Wings) in 1927.

KEVYN ADAMS ("Ads") #42

centre 6'1" 195 R
b. Washington, D.C., October 8, 1974
Signed as a free agent, August 7, 1997.
Selected by Columbus in Expansion Draft, June 23, 2000.

1997–98 F	5	0	0	0	7
1998–99	1	0	0	0	0
1999–2000	52	5	8	13	39
Totals	58	5	8	13	46

F October 1, 1997

STEWART ADAMS #12/#17/#9

left wing 5'10" 165 L
b. Calgary, Alberta, October 16, 1904
d. Calgary, Alberta, May 18, 1978
Purchased from Chicago, November 3, 1932.

1932–33 L	9	0	2	2	0

L February 16, 1933

GARY ALDCORN #21/#22/#26

forward 5'11" 180 L
b. Shaunavon, Saskatchewan, March 7, 1935
Claimed from Pittsburgh (AHL) in Inter-League Draft, June 5, 1956.
Claimed by Detroit in Intra-League Draft, June 10, 1959.

1956–57 F	22	5	1	6	4
1957–58	59	10	14	24	12
1958–59	5	0	3	3	2
Totals	86	15	18	33	18

F October 11, 1956

• Became a sculptor of hockey players and teams, commemorating Original Six hockey in particular.

CLAIRE ALEXANDER ("The Milkman") #20

defence 6'1" 175 R
b. Collingwood, Ontario, June 16, 1945
Signed as a free agent.
Sold to Vancouver, January 29, 1978.

1974–75 F	42	7	11	18	12
1975–76	33	2	6	8	6
1976–77	48	1	12	13	12
Totals	123	10	29	39	30

F November 30, 1974
• Daughter, Buffy, won bronze at Sydney Olympics in women's eight (rowing).

JASON ALLISON #41

centre 6'3" 215 R
b. Toronto, Ontario, May 29, 1975
Signed as a free agent, August 5, 2005.
Retired at end of season.

2005–06 L	66	17	43	60	76

L March 25, 2006

MIKE ALLISON ("Red") #8

left wing 6'0" 200 R
b. Fort Frances, Ontario, March 28, 1961
Acquired from New York Rangers for Walt Poddubny, August 18, 1986.
Traded to Los Angeles for Sean McKenna, December 14, 1987.

1986–87	71	7	16	23	66
1987–88	15	0	3	3	10
Totals	86	7	19	26	76

GLENN ANDERSON ("Andy") #10/#9

right wing 5'11" 175 L
b. Vancouver, British Columbia, October 2, 1960
Acquired with Grant Fuhr and Craig Berube from Edmonton for Vincent Damphousse, Peter Ing, Scott Thornton, and Luke Richardson, September 19, 1991.
Traded with Scott Malone and a fourth-round draft choice in 1994 (Alexander Korobolin) to New York Rangers for Mike Gartner, March 21, 1994.

1991–92	72	24	33	57	100
1992–93	76	22	43	65	117
1993–94	73	17	18	35	50
Totals	221	63	94	157	267

• Hockey Hall of Fame 2008

JOHN ANDERSON #10/#28

right wing 5'11" 190 R
b. Toronto, Ontario, March 28, 1957
Selected 11th overall in 1977 Amateur Draft.
Traded to Quebec for Brad Maxwell, August 21, 1985.

1977–78 F	17	1	2	3	2
1978–79	71	15	11	26	10
1979–80	74	25	28	53	22
1980–81	75	17	26	43	31
1981–82	69	31	26	57	30
1982–83	80	31	49	80	24
1983–84	73	37	31	68	22
1984–85	75	32	31	63	27
Totals	534	189	204	393	168

F December 4, 1977

LLOYD "ANDY" ANDREWS ("Shrimp") #9

forward
b. Tillsonburg, Ontario, November 4, 1894
d. Detroit, Michigan, November 17, 1974
Signed as a free agent, January 23, 1922.

1921–22 F	11	0	0	0	0
1922–23	23	5	4	9	10
1923–24	12	2	1	3	0
1924–25 L	7	1	0	1	0
Totals	53	8	5	13	10

F January 25, 1922 **L** January 5, 1925

DAVE ANDREYCHUK ("Chuckie") #14

left wing 6'3" 195 R
b. Hamilton, Ontario, September 29, 1963
Acquired with Daren Puppa and a first-round draft choice in 1993 (Kenny Jonsson) from Buffalo for Grant Fuhr and a fifth-round draft choice in 1995 (Kevin Popp), February 2, 1993. Traded to New Jersey for a second-round draft choice in 1996 (Marek Posmyk) and a third-round draft choice in 1999 (later traded back to New Jersey, with Doug Gilmour and Dave Ellett for Steve Sullivan, Jason Smith, and Alyn McCauley, February 25, 1997), March 13, 1996.

1992–93	31	25	13	38	8
1993–94	83	53	46	99	98
1994–95	48	22	16	38	34
1995–96	61	20	24	44	54
Totals	223	120	99	219	194

GREG ANDRUSAK #25

defence 6'1" 195 R

b. Cranbrook, British Columbia, November 14, 1969

Signed as a free agent, July 19, 1999.

Signed as a free agent by San Jose, August 14, 2000.

1999–2000		9	0	1	1	4

NIKOLAI ("NIK") ANTROPOV #9/#11/#80

centre 6'5" 203 L

b. Vost, Soviet Union (Russia), February 18, 1980

Selected 10th overall in 1998 Entry Draft.

Traded to New York Rangers for a second-round draft choice in 2009 (Kenny Ryan), March 4, 2009.

1999–2000	F	66	12	18	30	41
2000–01		52	6	11	17	30
2001–02		11	1	1	2	4
2002–03		72	16	29	45	124
2003–04		62	13	18	31	62
2005–06		57	12	19	31	56
2006–07		54	18	15	33	44
2007–08		72	26	30	56	92
2008–09		63	21	25	46	24
Totals		509	125	166	291	477

F October 13, 1999

SYL APPS ("Slippery Syl") #10/#16

centre 6'0" 173 R

b. Paris, Ontario, January 18, 1915

d. Kingston, Ontario, December 24, 1998

Signed as a free agent, September 2, 1936.

1936–37	F	48	16	29	45	10
1937–38		47	21	29	50	9
1938–39		44	15	25	40	4
1939–40		27	13	17	30	5
1940–41		41	20	24	44	6
1941–42		38	18	23	41	0
1942–43		29	23	17	40	2
1945–46		40	24	16	40	2
1946–47		54	25	24	49	6
1947–48	L	55	26	27	53	12
Totals		423	201	231	432	56

F November 5, 1936 **L** March 21, 1948

• Missed 1943–45 while serving in the Canadian Army.

• Later became an MPP and the Ontario Athletic Commissioner.

• Hockey Hall of Fame 1961

ALGER "AL" ARBOUR ("Radar") #3/#18

defence 6'1" 180 L

b. Sudbury, Ontario, November 1, 1932

Claimed from Chicago in Intra-League Draft, June 3, 1958.

Claimed by St. Louis in Expansion Draft, June 6, 1967.

1961–62	52	1	5	6	68
1962–63	4	1	0	1	4
1963–64	6	0	1	1	0
1965–66	4	0	1	1	2
Totals	66	2	7	9	74

• Coached New York Islanders to four Stanley Cups in the 1980s.

• Hockey Hall of Fame 1996 (Builder)

AMOS ARBOUR ("Butch") #7

forward 5'8" 160 L

b. Waubaushene, Ontario, January 26, 1895

d. Orillia, Ontario, November 2, 1943

Acquired from Hamilton with Bert Corbeau and George Carey for Corb Dennenay and Ken Randall, December 14, 1923.

1923–24	L	21	1	3	4	4

L March 5, 1924

JACK ARBOUR #2

forward 5'8" 170 L

b. Waubaushene, Ontario, March 7, 1899

d. Calgary, Alberta, September 24, 1973

Acquired from Detroit Cougars with $12,500 for Jimmy Herbert, April 9, 1928.

Sold to London (Can Pro), December 1928.

1928–29	L	10	1	0	1	10

L December 11, 1928

COLBY ARMSTRONG #9

right wing 6'2" 195 R

b. Lloydminster, Saskatchewan, November 23, 1982

Signed as a free agent, July 1, 2010.

Signed as a free agent by Montreal, July 1, 2012.

2010–11	50	8	15	23	38
2011–12	29	1	2	3	9
Totals	79	9	17	26	47

GEORGE ARMSTRONG

("The Chief"/"Army") #10/#15/#20

right wing 6'1" 194 R

b. Borlands Bay, Ontario, July 6, 1930

Retired after 1969–70, but returned November 21, 1970.

1949–50	F	2	0	0	0	0
1951–52		20	3	3	6	30
1952–53		52	14	11	25	54
1953–54		63	17	15	32	60
1954–55		66	10	18	28	80
1955–56		67	16	32	48	97
1956–57		54	18	26	44	37
1957–58		59	17	25	42	93
1958–59		59	20	16	36	37
1959–60		70	23	28	51	60
1960–61		47	14	19	33	21
1961–62		70	21	32	53	27
1962–63		70	19	24	43	27
1963–64		66	20	17	37	14
1964–65		59	15	22	37	14
1965–66		70	16	35	51	12
1966–67		70	9	24	33	26
1967–68		62	13	21	34	4
1968–69		53	11	16	27	10
1969–70		49	13	15	28	12
1970–71	L	59	7	18	25	6
Totals		1,187	296	417	713	721

F December 3, 1949 **L** April 4, 1971

• Coached Toronto Marlies and Leafs and continues to scout for the team.

• Hockey Hall of Fame 1975

MURRAY ARMSTRONG #17

centre 5'10" 170 L

b. Manor, Saskatchewan, January 1, 1916

d. St. Augustine, Florida, December 8, 2010

Claimed from Philadelphia (Can-Am) in Inter-League Draft, May 7, 1936.

Traded with Buzz Boll, Busher Jackson, and Doc Romnes to New York Americans for Sweeney Schriner, May 18, 1939.

1937–38	F	9	0	0	0	0
1938–39		3	0	1	1	0
Totals		12	0	1	1	0

F December 26, 1937

NORM "RED" ARMSTRONG #18

defence 5'11" 205 L

b. Owen Sound, Ontario, October 17, 1938

d. Sault Ste. Marie, Ontario, July 23, 1974

Traded to Springfield (AHL) for Don Westbrooke, February 20, 1971.

1962–63	F/L	7	1	1	2	2

F December 15, 1962 **L** January 17, 1963

• Career minor leaguer with Rochester, 1963–71.

• Killed in an industrial accident.

TIM ARMSTRONG #8

centre 5'11" 170 R

b. Toronto, Ontario, May 12, 1967

Selected 211th overall in 1985 Entry Draft.

1988–89	F/L	11	1	0	1	6

F December 29, 1988 **L** January 30, 1989

JOHN ARUNDEL #25

defence 5'11" 181 L

b. Winnipeg, Manitoba, November 4, 1927

d. Kemptville, Ontario, September 19, 2002

1949–50	F/L	3	0	0	0	9

F December 31, 1949 **L** January 4, 1950

DON ASHBY ("Ash") #9/#20/#8

centre 6'1" 185 L

b. Kamloops, British Columbia, March 8, 1955

d. Summerland, British Columbia, May 30, 1981

Selected 6th overall in 1975 Amateur Draft.

Traded with Trevor Johansen to Colorado Rockies for Paul Gardner, March 13, 1979.

1975–76	F	50	6	15	21	10
1976–77		76	19	23	42	24
1977–78		12	1	2	3	0
1978–79		3	0	0	0	0
Totals		141	26	40	66	34

F October 11, 1975

CARTER ASHTON #37

right wing 6'3" 215 L

b. Winnipeg, Manitoba, April 1, 1991

Acquired from Tampa Bay for Keith Aulie, February 27, 2012.

Traded with David Broll to Tampa Bay for a conditional seventh-round draft pick in 2016, February 6, 2015.

2011–12	F	15	0	0	0	13
2013–14		32	0	3	3	19
2014–15		7	0	0	0	0
Totals		54	0	3	3	32

F March 7, 2012

JEAN-SÉBASTIEN (J-S) AUBIN #30

goalie 5'11" 180 R

b. Montreal, Quebec, July 19, 1977

Signed as a free agent, August 18, 2005.

Signed as a free agent by Los Angeles, August 28, 2007.

2005–06	11	9–0–0–2	677	25	1	2.22
2006–07	20	3–5–0–2	804	46	0	3.43
Totals	31	12–5–0–4	1,481	71	1	2.88

NORM AUBIN #24/#35

centre 6'0" 185 L

b. St. Léonard, Quebec, July 26, 1960

Selected 51st overall in 1979 Entry Draft.

1981–82	F	43	14	12	26	22
1982–83	L	26	4	1	5	8
Totals		69	18	13	31	30

F December 31, 1981 **L** December 11, 1982

PATRIK AUGUSTA #24

right wing 5'10" 180 L

b. Jihlava, Czechoslovakia (Czech Republic), November 13, 1969

Selected 149th overall in 1992 Entry Draft.

Released June 27, 1995.

1993–94	F	2	0	0	0	0

F January 1, 1994

KEITH AULIE #59

defence 6'6" 228 L

b. Rouleau, Saskatchewan, June 11, 1989

Acquired from Calgary with Dion Phaneuf and Fredrik Sjostrom for Matt Stajan, Nicklas Hagman, Jamal Mayers, and Ian White, January 31, 2010.

Traded to Tampa Bay for Carter Ashton, February 27, 2012.

2010–11	F	40	2	0	2	32
2011–12		17	0	2	2	16
Totals		57	2	2	4	48

F November 13, 2010

PETE BACKOR #14

defence 6'0" 185 L

b. Fort William (Thunder Bay), Ontario, April 29, 1919

d. Thunder Bay, Ontario, June 30, 1988

Assigned to Pittsburgh (AHL) for 1945–46 season.

1944–45	F/L	36	4	5	9	6

F October 28, 1944 **L** February 18, 1945

BOB BAILEY ("Bashin' Bob")
#17/#18/#20/#21/#23

right wing 6'0" 197 R
b. Kenora, Ontario, May 29, 1931
d. Cleveland, Ohio, October 24, 2003
Acquired with Gerry Foley from Cleveland (AHL) for Chuck Blair and $30,000, May 20, 1953.
Sold with Bob Sabourin to Springfield (AHL) for $22,000, May 28, 1956.

1953–54	F	48	2	7	9	70
1954–55		32	4	2	6	52
1955–56		6	0	0	0	6
Totals		86	6	9	15	128

F October 10, 1953

CASEY BAILEY #37

centre 6'3" 195 R
b. Anchorage, Alaska, October 27, 1991
Signed as a free agent, March 21, 2015.

2014–15	F	6	1	0	1	2

F April 1, 2015

IRVINE "ACE" BAILEY #6/#12/#8

right wing 5'11" 160 L
b. Bracebridge, Ontario, July 3, 1903
d. Toronto, Ontario, April 7, 1992
Signed as a free agent, November 3, 1926

1926–27	F	42	15	13	28	82
1927–28		43	9	3	12	72
1928–29		44	22	10	32	78
1929–30		43	22	21	43	69
1930–31		40	23	19	42	46
1931–32		41	8	5	13	64
1932–33		47	10	8	18	52
1933–34	L	13	2	3	5	11
Totals		313	111	82	193	472

F November 17, 1926 L December 12, 1933
• Career ended after an Eddie Shore hit on December 12, 1933.
• Worked in the penalty box at Maple Leaf Gardens virtually up until his death.
• Hockey Hall of Fame 1975

REID BAILEY #4

defence 6'2" 200 L
b. Toronto, Ontario, May 28, 1956
Acquired from Edmonton for Serge Boisvert, January 15, 1983.
Signed as a free agent by Hartford, December 9, 1983.

1982–83		1	0	0	0	2

• Only Leaf game March 24, 1983.

JAMIE BAKER ("Bakes") #16

centre 6'0" 190 L
b. Ottawa, Ontario, August 31, 1966
Acquired with a fifth-round draft choice in 1996 (Peter Cava) from San Jose for Todd Gill, June 14, 1996.
Released at end of 1997–98 season.

1996–97		58	8	8	16	28
1997–98		13	0	5	5	10
Totals		71	8	13	21	38

DOUG BALDWIN #19

defence 6'0" 175 L
b. Winnipeg, Manitoba, November 2, 1922
d. July 10, 2007
Traded with Billy Taylor and Ray Powell to Detroit for Harry Watson and Gerry Brown, September 21, 1946.

1945–46	F	15	0	1	1	6

F January 19, 1946
• Underwent appendectomy after 15 games with the Leafs.

EARL BALFOUR ("Spider")
#16/#22/#24/#25/#23

left wing 6'1" 180 L
b. Toronto, Ontario, January 4, 1933
Marlboros graduate
Claimed by Chicago in Intra-League Draft, June 4, 1958.

1951–52	F	3	0	0	0	2
1953–54		17	0	1	1	6
1955–56		59	14	5	19	40
1957–58		1	0	0	0	0
Totals		80	14	6	20	48

F March 5, 1952

ANDY BARBE #14

right wing 6'0" 175 R
b. Coniston, Ontario, July 27, 1923
d. January 15, 2004

1950–51	F/L	1	0	0	0	2

F/L January 18, 1951

BILL BARILKO
("Bashing Bill"/"Billy The Kid")
#5/#19/#21

defence 5'11" 184 L
b. Timmins, Ontario, March 25, 1927
d. Cochrane, Ontario, August 26, 1951

1946–47	F	18	3	7	10	33
1947–48		57	5	9	14	147
1948–49		60	5	4	9	95
1949–50		59	7	10	17	85
1950–51	L	58	6	6	12	96
Totals		252	26	36	62	456

F February 6, 1947 L March 25, 1951
• Killed in a plane crash 50 miles north of Cochrane on August 26, 1951; wreckage found June 6, 1962.

TOM BARRASSO #30

goalie 6'3" 210 R
b. Boston, Massachusetts, March 31, 1965
Acquired from Carolina for a fourth-round draft choice in 2003 (Kevin Nastiuk), March 15, 2002.
Signed as a free agent by St. Louis, October 24, 2002.

2001–02		4	2–2–0	219	10	0	2.74

ALDEGE "BAZ" BASTIEN #1

goalie 5'7" 160 L
b. Timmins, Ontario, August 29, 1920
d. Pittsburgh, Pennsylvania, March 15, 1983
Signed as a free agent, October 30, 1940.
Sold to Pittsburgh (AHL), December 26, 1945.

1945–46	F	55	0–4–1	300	20	0	4.00

F October 27, 1945 L November 7, 1945
• Missed 1942–45 while serving in the Canadian Army.
• Played while regular goaltender Frank McCool held out over a contract dispute.
• Forced to retire when struck in the eye by a puck at training camp on September 19, 1949.

ANDY BATHGATE
("Handy Andy"/"Tubby") #9

right wing 6'0" 180 R
b. Winnipeg, Manitoba, August 28, 1932
Acquired with Don McKenney from New York Rangers for Arnie Brown, Bill Collins, Dick Duff, Bob Nevin, and Rod Seiling, February 22, 1964.
Traded with Billy Harris and Gary Jarrett to Detroit for Marcel Pronovost, Lowell MacDonald, Ed Joyal, Larry Jeffrey, and Aut Erickson, May 20, 1965.

1963–64		15	3	15	18	8
1964–65		55	16	29	45	34
Totals		70	19	44	63	42

• Ran a golf driving range west of Toronto.
• Hockey Hall of Fame 1978

JON "BATES" BATTAGLIA #33

left wing 6'2" 205 L
b. Chicago, Illinois, December 13, 1975
Signed as a free agent, July 11, 2006.
Retired at end of 2007–08 season.

2006–07		82	12	19	31	45
2007–08	L	13	0	0	0	7
Totals		95	12	19	31	52

L November 24, 2007

KEN BAUMGARTNER ("Bomber")
#8/#22

forward 6'1" 200 L
b. Flin Flon, Manitoba, March 11, 1966
Acquired with Dave McLlwain from New York Islanders for Daniel Marois and Claude Loiselle, March 10, 1992.
Traded to Anaheim for a fourth-round draft choice in 1996 (traded to Montreal—Kim Staal), March 20, 1996.

1991–92		11	0	0	0	23
1992–93		63	1	0	1	155
1993–94		64	4	4	8	185
1994–95		2	0	0	0	5
1995–96		60	2	3	5	152
Totals		200	7	7	14	520

• Missed most of 1994–95 with separated shoulder.
• Later admitted to Harvard School of Business.

BOB BAUN ("Boomer") #21/#26

defence 5'9" 182 R
b. Lanigan, Saskatchewan, September 9, 1936
Marlboros graduate
Claimed by Oakland in Expansion Draft, June 6, 1967.
Acquired from St. Louis for Brit Selby, November 13, 1970; retired December 1972.

1956–57	F	20	0	5	5	37
1957–58		67	1	9	10	91
1958–59		51	1	8	9	87
1959–60		61	8	9	17	59
1960–61		70	1	14	15	70
1961–62		65	4	11	15	94
1962–63		48	4	8	12	65
1963–64		52	4	14	18	113
1964–65		70	0	18	18	160
1965–66		44	0	6	6	68
1966–67		54	2	8	10	83
1970–71		58	1	17	18	123
1971–72		74	2	12	14	101
1972–73	L	5	1	1	2	4
Totals		739	29	140	169	1,155

F November 29, 1956 L October 21, 1972
• Owned Tim Hortons franchises and a golf course in southern Ontario.

FRANÇOIS BEAUCHEMIN #22

defence 6'1" 207 L
b. Sorel, Quebec, June 4, 1980
Signed as a free agent, July 6, 2009.
Traded to Anaheim for Joffrey Lupul, Jake Gardiner, and a fourth-round draft choice in 2013 (later traded to San Jose—Fredrik Bergvik), February 9, 2011.

2009–10		82	5	21	26	33
2010–11		54	2	10	12	16
Totals		136	7	31	38	49

DON BEAUPRE #33

goalie 5'10" 172 L
b. Waterloo, Ontario, September 19, 1961
Acquired from New York Islanders in a three-way trade, January 23, 1996. Leafs sent Damian Rhodes and Ken Belanger to Islanders; Ottawa sent Beaupre, Bryan Berard, and Martin Straka to Islanders; Islanders sent Rhodes and Wade Redden to Ottawa and Beaupre and Kirk Muller to Leafs.
Demoted to St. John's (AHL), November 19, 1996.

1995–96		8	0–5–0	336	26	0	4.64
1996–97		3	0–3–0	110	10	0	5.45
Totals		11	0–8–0	446	36	0	4.84

WADE BELAK #3/#2/#33

right wing 6'5" 222 R
b. Saskatoon, Saskatchewan, July 3, 1976
d. Toronto, Ontario, August 31, 2011
Claimed off waivers from Calgary, February 16, 2001.
Traded to Florida for a fifth-round draft choice in 2008 (Jerome Flaake), February 26, 2008.

2000–01	16	1	1	2	31
2001–02	63	1	3	4	142
2002–03	55	3	6	9	196
2003–04	34	1	1	2	109
2005–06	55	0	3	3	109
2006–07	65	0	3	3	110
2007–08	30	1	0	1	66
Totals	318	7	17	24	763

ALAIN "BAM BAM" BÉLANGER #18

right wing 6'1" 190 R
b. St. Janvier, Quebec, January 18, 1956
Selected 48th overall in 1976 Amateur Draft.

1977–78 F/L	9	0	1	1	6

F February 1, 1978 **L** February 25, 1978

KEN BELANGER #43

left wing 6'4" 225 L
b. Sault Ste. Marie, Ontario, May 14, 1974
Acquired from Hartford for a ninth-round draft choice in 1994 (Matt Ball), March 18, 1994.
Traded to New York Islanders in a three-way deal, January 23, 1996. Leafs sent Damian Rhodes and Belanger to Islanders; Ottawa sent Don Beaupre, Bryan Berard, and Martin Straka to Islanders; Islanders sent Rhodes and Wade Redden to Ottawa and Beaupre and Kirk Muller to Leafs.

1994–95 F	3	0	0	0	9

F March 4, 1995

ED BELFOUR ("Eddie the Eagle") #20

goalie 6'0" 214 L
b. Carman, Manitoba, April 21, 1965
Signed as a free agent, July 2, 2002.
Signed as a free agent by Florida, July 25, 2006.

2002–03	62	37–20–5	3,738	141	7	2.26
2003–04	59	34–19–6	3,444	122	10	2.13
2005–06	49	22–22–0–4	2,897	159	0	3.29
Totals	170	93–61–11–4	10,079	422	17	2.51

• Hockey Hall of Fame 2011

BRENDAN BELL #36

defence 6'2" 205 L
b. Ottawa, Ontario, March 31, 1983
Selected 65th overall in 2001 Entry Draft.
Traded with a second-round draft choice in 2008 (later traded to Nashville—Roman Josi) to Phoenix for Yanic Perreault and a fifth-round draft choice in 2008 (Joel Champagne), February 27, 2007.

2005–06	1	0	0	0	0
2006–07	31	1	4	5	19
Totals	32	1	4	5	19

GORDIE BELL #1/#24

goalie 5'10" 164 L
b. Portage la Prairie, Manitoba, March 13, 1925
d. Belleville, Ontario, November 3, 1980
Acquired with Dudley "Red" Garrett and first postwar call on Charlie Rayner from New York Rangers for Bucko McDonald, November 25, 1943.
Traded to Springfield (AHL) with Armand Lemieux, Leo Curik, and Rod Roy for Eldred Kobussen, April 26, 1948.

1945–46 F	8	3–5–0	480	31	0	3.87

F November 8, 1945
• Played eight games while regular goaltender Frank McCool held out over a contract dispute.
• Missed 1943–45 while serving in the Canadian Armed Forces.
• Later won a gold medal with Belleville McFarlands at the 1959 World Championship.

MARK BELL #9

left wing 6'4" 220 L
b. St. Pauls, Ontario, August 5, 1980
Acquired with Vesa Toskala from San Jose for a first-round draft choice in 2007 (later traded to St. Louis—Lars Eller) and second-round draft choice in 2007 (Aaron Palushaj) and a fourth-round draft choice in 2009 (later traded to Nashville—Craig Smith), June 22, 2007.
Claimed off waivers by New York Rangers on February 25, 2009.

2007–08	35	4	6	10	60

PETE BELLEFEUILLE ("Fleeting Frenchman"/"French Pete") #1

right wing 5'8" 155 R
b. Trois-Rivières, Quebec, October 19, 1901
d. Trois-Rivières, Quebec, July 14, 1970
Signed as a free agent after playing with Quebec and Iroquois Falls, 1925; loaned to London (Can Pro) for Butch Keeling, December 27, 1926.
Traded to Detroit Cougars for Slim Halderson, January 10, 1927.

1925–26 F	36	14	2	16	22
1926–27	13	0	0	0	12
Totals	49	14	2	16	34

F November 28, 1925

JIM BENNING ("Benji") #3/#15

defence 6'0" 183 L
b. Edmonton, Alberta, April 29, 1963
Selected 6th overall in 1981 Entry Draft.
Traded with Dan Hodgson to Vancouver for Rick Lanz, December 2, 1986.

1981–82 F	74	7	24	31	46
1982–83	74	5	17	22	47
1983–84	79	12	39	51	66
1984–85	80	9	35	44	55
1985–86	52	4	21	25	71
1986–87	5	0	0	0	4
Totals	364	37	136	173	289

F October 6, 1981

MAX "THE HAT" BENTLEY ("The Dipsy-Doodle Dandy from Delisle") #7

centre 5'8" 158 L
b. Delisle, Saskatchewan, March 1, 1920
d. Saskatoon, Saskatchewan, January 19, 1984
Acquired with Cy Thomas from Chicago for Gus Bodnar, Ernie Dickens, Bob Goldham, Bud Poile, and Gaye Stewart, November 2, 1947.
Sold to New York Rangers for cash, August 11, 1953.

1947–48	53	23	25	48	14
1948–49	60	19	22	41	18
1949–50	69	23	18	41	14
1950–51	67	21	41	62	34
1951–52	69	24	17	41	40
1952–53	36	12	11	23	16
Totals	354	122	134	256	136

• Left the team between November 28, 1952, and January 17, 1953, because he felt his performance was weak.
• Hockey Hall of Fame 1966

BRYAN BERARD ("Bee") #34

defence 6'1" 190 L
b. Woonsocket, Rhode Island, March 5, 1977
Acquired with a sixth-round draft choice in 1999 (Jan Socher) from New York Islanders for Félix Potvin and a sixth-round draft choice in 1999 (later traded to Tampa Bay—Fedor Fedorov), January 9, 1999.
Signed as a free agent by New York Rangers, September 29, 2001.

1998–99	38	5	14	19	22
1999–2000	64	3	27	30	42
Totals	102	8	41	49	64

• Suffered serious eye injury vs. Ottawa, March 11, 2000.

DRAKE BEREHOWSKY ("Bear") #29/#24/#55

defence 6'1" 210 R
b. Toronto, Ontario, January 3, 1972
Selected 10th overall in 1990 Entry Draft.
Traded to Pittsburgh for Grant Jennings, April 7, 1995.

1990–91 F	8	0	1	1	25
1991–92	1	0	0	0	0
1992–93	41	4	15	19	61
1993–94	49	2	8	10	63
1994–95	25	0	2	2	15
2003–04	9	1	2	3	17
Totals	133	7	28	35	181

F October 4, 1990

SERGEI BEREZIN #94

forward 5'10" 172 R
b. Voskresensk, Soviet Union (Russia), November 5, 1971
Selected 256th overall in 1994 Entry Draft.
Traded to Phoenix for Mikael Renberg, June 22, 2001.

1996–97 F	73	25	16	41	2
1997–98	68	16	15	31	10
1998–99	76	37	22	59	12
1999–2000	61	26	13	39	2
2000–01	79	22	28	50	8
Totals	357	126	94	220	34

F October 5, 1996

AKI-PETTERI BERG #8

defence 6'3" 213 L
b. Turku, Finland, July 28, 1977
Acquired from Los Angeles for Adam Mair and a second-round draft choice in 2001 (Mike Cammalleri), March 13, 2001.
Returned to play in Finland after 2005–06 season.

2000–01	12	3	0	3	2
2001–02	81	1	10	11	46
2002–03	78	4	7	11	28
2003–04	79	2	7	9	40
2005–06	75	0	8	8	56
Totals	325	10	32	42	172

BILL BERG #10

centre 6'1" 190 L
b. St. Catharines, Ontario, October 21, 1967
Claimed off waivers from New York Islanders, December 3, 1992.
Traded to New York Rangers with Sergio Momesso for Nick Kypreos and Wayne Presley, February 29, 1996.

1992–93	58	7	8	15	54
1993–94	83	8	11	19	93
1994–95	32	5	1	6	26
1995–96	23	1	1	2	33
Totals	196	21	21	42	206

TIM BERNHARDT ("Timber") #1

goalie 5'9" 160 L
b. Sarnia, Ontario, January 17, 1958
Signed as a free agent, December 5, 1984.

1984–85	37	13–19–4	2,182	136	0	3.74
1985–86	23	4–12–3	1,266	107	0	5.07
1986–87 L	1	0–0–0	20	3	0	9.00
Totals	61	17–31–7	3,468	246	0	4.26

L October 22, 1986

JONATHAN BERNIER #45

goalie 6'0" 185 L
b. Laval, Quebec, August 7, 1988
Acquired from Los Angeles for Matt Frattin, Ben Scrivens, and a second-round draft choice in 2015, June 23, 2013.

2013–14	55	26–19–7	3,084	138	1	2.68
2014–15	58	21–28–7	3,177	152	2	2.87
Totals	113	17–47–14	6,261	290	3	2.78

CRAIG BERUBE #16

left wing 6'2" 205 L

b. Calihoo, Alberta, December 17, 1965
Acquired with Grant Fuhr and Glenn Anderson from Edmonton for Vincent Damphousse, Peter Ing, Scott Thornton, and Luke Richardson, September 19, 1991.
Traded with Gary Leeman, Michel Petit, Jeff Reese, and Alexander Godynyuk to Calgary for Doug Gilmour, Jamie Macoun, Ric Nattress, Rick Wamsley, and Kent Manderville, September 19, 1991.

1991–92	40	5	7	12	109

ALLAN BESTER
("Ernie"/"Beast"/"Worm") #31/#30

goalie 5'7" 150 L

b. Hamilton, Ontario, March 26, 1964
Selected 49th overall in 1983 Entry Draft.
Traded to Detroit for a sixth-round draft choice in 1991 (Alexander Kuzminsky), September 19, 1991.

1983–84 F	32	11–16–4	1,848	134	0	4.35
1984–85	15	3–9–1	767	54	1	4.22
1985–86	1	0–0–0	20	2	0	6.00
1986–87	36	10–14–3	1,808	110	2	3.65
1987–88	30	8–12–5	1,607	102	2	3.81
1988–89	43	17–20–3	2,460	156	2	3.80
1989–90	42	20–16–0	2,206	165	0	4.49
1990–91	6	0–4–0	247	18	0	4.37
Totals	205	69–91–16	10,963	741	7	4.06

F January 8, 1984

FRANK BIALOWAS ("The Animal") #36

left wing 5'11" 225 L

b. Winnipeg, Manitoba, September 25, 1970
Signed as a free agent, March 20, 1994.
Released June 28, 1995.

1993–94 F	3	0	0	0	12

F March 26, 1994

PAUL BIBEAULT #1

goalie 5'9" 160 L

b. Montreal, Quebec, April 13, 1919
d. Rigaud, Quebec, August 2, 1970
Signed for $3,000, after being discharged from the army, with permission from Montreal and on the condition the Habs could reclaim him for $1 at year's end, January 24, 1944.
Reclaimed by Habs on September 13, 1944.

1943–44	29	13–14–2	1740	87	5	3.00

• Married Frank Selke's daughter.

JACK BIONDA #22

defence 6'0" 175 L

b. Huntsville, Ontario, September 18, 1933
d. London, Ontario, November 3, 1999
Sold to Boston for $30,000, April 23, 1956.

1955–56 F	13	0	1	1	18

F October 16, 1955
• Member of Canada's Sports Hall of Fame as one of Canada's greatest lacrosse players.

ANDY BLAIR #5/#12/#11

centre/defence 6'2" 176 L

b. Winnipeg, Manitoba, February 27, 1908
d. Seattle, Washington, December 27, 1977
Signed as a free agent, October 28, 1928.
Sold to Chicago for $7,500, May 8, 1936.

1928–29 F	44	12	15	27	41
1929–30	42	11	10	21	27
1930–31	44	11	8	19	32
1931–32	48	9	14	23	35
1932–33	43	6	9	15	38
1933–34	47	14	9	23	35
1934–35	45	6	14	20	22
1935–36	45	5	4	9	60
Totals	358	74	83	157	290

F November 15, 1928
• Won Allan Cup with University of Manitoba, 1928.

CHUCK BLAIR #22

right wing 5'10" 175 R

b. Edinburgh, Scotland, July 23, 1928
d. December 14, 2006
Marlboros graduate
Traded to Cleveland (AHL) with $30,000 for Bob Bailey and Jerry Foley, summer 1953.

1948–49 F/L	1	0	0	0	0

F/L December 4, 1948

GEORGE "DUSTY" BLAIR #14

centre 5'8" 160 R

b. South Porcupine, September 15, 1929
Acquired from Detroit for Johnny Wilson, 1949
Traded to Buffalo (AHL) with Frank Sullivan and Jackie LeClair for Brian Cullen, April 1954.

1950–51 F/L	2	0	0	0	0

F December 30, 1950 **L** January 6, 1951

MIKE BLAISDELL ("Blazer") #22

right wing 6'1" 195 R

b. Moose Jaw, Saskatchewan, January 18, 1960
Signed as a free agent, July 10, 1987.

1987–88	18	3	2	5	2
1988–89 L	9	1	0	1	4
Totals	27	4	2	6	6

L January 28, 1989
• Joined Canadian National Team in 1989.
• Later played and coached in England.

FRANK "MICKEY" BLAKE #3/#20

defence 5'10" 186 L

b. Barriefield, Ontario, October 31, 1912
d. June 23, 2000
Claimed for $1,000 in dispersal draft of St. Louis Eagles players, October 15, 1935.
Traded to Cleveland (AHL) for Bill Cunningham, summer 1936.

1935–36 L	8	0	0	0	2

L February 29, 1936

JASON BLAKE #55

left wing 5'10" 190 L

b. Moorhead, Minnesota, September 2, 1973
Signed as a free agent, July 1, 2007.
Traded to Anaheim with Vesa Toskala for J-S Giguère, January 31, 2010.

2007–08	82	15	37	52	28
2008–09	78	25	38	63	40
2009–10	56	10	16	26	26
Totals	216	50	91	141	94

TROY BODIE #40

left wing 6'4" 220 R

b. Portage la Prairie, Manitoba, January 25, 1985
Signed as a free agent, July 10, 2013.

2013–14	47	3	7	10	26
2014–15	5	0	0	0	5
Totals	52	3	7	10	31

AUGUST "GUS" BODNAR #8/#21

centre 5'10" 160 R

b. Fort William, August 24, 1925
d. Oshawa, Ontario, July 1, 2005
Fort William Juniors graduate
Signed as a free agent, October 29, 1943.
Traded with Ernie Dickens, Bob Goldham, Bud Poile, and Gaye Stewart to Chicago for Max Bentley and Cy Thomas, November 2, 1947.

1943–44 F	50	22	40	62	18
1944–45	49	8	36	44	18
1945–46	49	14	23	37	14
1946–47	39	4	6	10	10
Totals	187	48	105	153	60

F October 30, 1943
• Later coached in OHL and was one of three coaches of Canada's WJC team in 1978 (winning bronze).

GARTH BOESCH #5/#18

defence 6' 180 R

b. Milestone, Saskatchewan, October 7, 1920
d. California, May 14, 1998
Signed in 1945.

1946–47 F	35	4	5	9	47
1947–48	45	2	7	9	52
1948–49	59	1	10	11	43
1949–50 L	58	2	6	8	63
Totals	197	9	28	37	205

F October 16, 1946 **L** March 26, 1950
• Only moustachioed player of his era.

LONNY BOHONOS ("Bo") #16

right wing 5'11" 190 R

b. Winnipeg, Manitoba, May 20, 1973
Acquired from Vancouver for Brandon Convery, March 7, 1998.
Called up from AHL before leaving NHL for Switzerland (also played in 1999 playoffs).

1997–98	6	3	3	6	4
1998–99	7	3	0	3	4
Totals	13	6	3	9	8

FRED BOIMISTRUCK #11

defence 5'11" 191 R

b. Sudbury, Ontario, November 4, 1962
Selected 43rd overall in 1980 Entry Draft.
Released summer 1983.

1981–82 F	57	2	11	13	32
1982–83 L	26	2	3	5	13
Totals	83	4	14	18	45

F October 6, 1981 **L** December 11, 1982

SERGE BOISVERT #12

right wing 5'9" 172 R

b. Drummondville, Quebec, June 1, 1959
Signed as a free agent, October 9, 1980; played 1981–82 with Yukijirushi (Japan).
Traded to Edmonton for Reid Bailey, January 15, 1983.

1982–83 F	17	0	2	2	4

F October 6, 1982
• Played for Canada at 1988 Olympics (fourth place).

LÉO BOIVIN ("Billy") #16/#18/#19/#21

defence 5'7" 190 L

b. Prescott, Ontario, August 2, 1932
Acquired with Fern Flaman, Phil Maloney, and Ken Smith from Boston for Bill Ezinicki and Vic Lynn, November 15, 1950.
Traded to Boston for Joe Klukay, November 9, 1954.

1951–52 F	2	0	1	1	0
1952–53	70	2	13	15	97
1953–54	58	1	6	7	81
1954–55	7	0	0	0	8
Totals	137	3	20	23	186

F March 8, 1952
• After retiring as a player, became a coach with St. Louis and a scout.
• Hockey Hall of Fame 1986

FRANK "BUZZ" BOLL #8/#17

left wing 5'10" 166 L

b. Fillmore, Saskatchewan, March 6, 1911
d. Regina, Saskatchewan, January 23, 1990
Marlboros graduate
Traded with Murray Armstrong, Busher Jackson, and Doc Romnes to New York Americans for Sweeney Schriner, May 18, 1939.

1933–34 F	42	12	8	20	21
1934–35	47	14	4	18	4
1935–36	44	15	13	28	14
1936–37	25	6	3	9	12
1937–38	44	14	11	25	18
1938–39	11	0	0	0	0
Totals	213	61	39	100	69

F November 9, 1933

DAVE BOLLAND #63

centre 6' 184 R

b. Mimico, Ontario, June 5, 1986
Acquired from Chicago for a second-round draft choice in 2013 (Carl Dahlstrom), a fourth-round draft choice in 2013 (Fredrik Bergvik), and a fourth-round draft choice in 2014 (Frederik Olofsson), June 30, 2013.
Signed as a free agent by Florida, July 1, 2014.

| 2013–14 | 23 | 8 | 4 | 12 | 24 |

HUGH BOLTON ("Yug") #4/#19/#23/#20

defence 6'3" 190 R

b. Toronto, Ontario, April 15, 1929
d. Toronto, Ontario, October 17, 1999
Marlboros graduate

1949–50 F	2	0	0	0	2
1950–51	13	1	3	4	4
1951–52	60	3	13	16	73
1952–53	9	0	0	0	10
1953–54	9	0	0	0	10
1954–55	69	2	19	21	55
1955–56	67	4	16	20	65
1956–57 L	6	0	0	0	2
Totals	235	10	51	61	221

F December 1, 1949 **L** October 25, 1956
• Missed many games in 1952–53 with mono-nucleosis, and in 1953–54 with a broken jaw.
• Taught physics in Toronto high schools.

DAVID BOOTH #20

left wing 6' 212 L

b. Detroit, Michigan, November 24, 1984
Signed as a free agent, July 22, 2014.

| 2014–15 | 59 | 7 | 6 | 13 | 25 |

GEORGE BOOTHMAN ("Pruneface") #14/#16

defence 6'2" 175 R

b. Calgary, Alberta, September 25, 1916
d. September 13, 2003
Signed as a free agent, October 23, 1942; loaned with Bucko McDonald and Jack Forsey, for the rest of the season only, to Providence (AHL) for Ab DeMarco and Buck Jones, February 2, 1943.
Traded with Don Webster to Buffalo (AHL) for Bill Ezinicki, October 13, 1944.

1942–43 F	9	1	1	2	4
1943–44 L	49	16	18	34	14
Totals	58	17	19	36	18

F December 17, 1942 **L** March 18, 1944

NIKOLAI BORSCHEVSKY ("Nick the Stick") #16

right wing 5'9" 170 L

b. Tomsk, Soviet Union (Russia), January 12, 1965
Selected 77th overall in 1992 Entry Draft.
Traded to Calgary for a sixth-round draft choice in 1996 (Chris Bogas), April 6, 1995.

1992–93 F	78	34	40	74	28
1993–94	45	14	20	34	10
1994–95	19	0	5	5	0
Totals	142	48	65	113	38

F October 6, 1992
• Later ran popular hockey schools in Toronto and southern Ontario.

LAURIE BOSCHMAN #12

centre 6' 185 L

b. Major, Saskatchewan, June 4, 1960
Selected 9th overall in 1979 Entry Draft.
Traded to Edmonton for Walt Poddubny and Phil Drouilliard, March 8, 1982.

1979–80 F	80	16	32	48	78
1980–81	53	14	19	33	178
1981–82	54	9	19	28	150
Totals	187	39	70	109	406

F October 10, 1979
• A born-again Christian, he later became the Ottawa and eastern Ontario director for Hockey Ministries International, combining belief and hockey programs.

BRUCE BOUDREAU ("Gabby") #12/#19/#35/#11/#17/#28

centre 5'9" 175 L

b. Toronto, Ontario, January 9, 1955
Selected 42nd overall in 1975 Amateur Draft.
Signed as a free agent by Chicago, October 10, 1985.

1976–77 F	15	2	5	7	4
1977–78	40	11	18	29	12
1978–79	26	4	3	7	2
1979–80	2	0	0	0	2
1980–81	39	10	14	24	18
1981–82	12	0	2	2	6
Totals	134	27	42	69	44

F February 5, 1977
• Later coached in minors for nearly two decades before getting a chance to coach in NHL.

LÉO BOURGAULT #8/#16

defence 5'6" 165 L

b. Sturgeon Falls, Ontario, January 17, 1903
d. July 14, 1978
Purchased from Saskatoon (WHL) with Corb Dennenay and Laurie Scott, 1926.
Sold to New York Rangers, January 25, 1927.

| 1926–27 F | 22 | 0 | 0 | 0 | 44 |

F November 17, 1926

PAT BOUTETTE ("Booter") #15

right wing 5'8" 175 L

b. Windsor, Ontario, March 1, 1952
Selected 139th overall in 1972 Amateur Draft.
Traded to Hartford for Bob Stephenson, December 24, 1979.

1975–76 F	77	10	22	32	140
1976–77	80	18	18	36	107
1977–78	80	17	19	36	120
1978–79	80	14	19	33	136
1979–80	32	0	4	4	17
Totals	349	59	82	141	520

F October 11, 1975

JOHNNY BOWER ("China Wall") #1

goalie 5'11" 182 L

b. Prince Albert, Saskatchewan, November 8, 1924
Claimed from New York Rangers in Intra-League Draft, June 3, 1958.

1958–59	39	15–17–7	2,340	107	3	2.74
1959–60	66	34–24–8	3,960	177	5	2.68
1960–61	58	33–15–10	3,480	145	2	2.50
1961–62	59	31–18–10	3,540	151	2	2.56
1962–63	42	20–15–7	2,520	109	1	2.60
1963–64	51	24–16–11	3,009	106	5	2.11
1964–65	34	13–13–8	2,040	81	3	2.38
1965–66	35	18–10–5	1,998	75	3	2.25
1966–67	24	12–9–3	1,431	63	2	2.64
1967–68	43	14–18–7	2,239	84	4	2.25
1968–69	20	5–4–3	779	37	2	2.85
1969–70 L	1	0–1–0	60	5	0	5.00
Totals	475	219–160–79	27,396	1139	32	2.49

L December 10, 1969
• Became Leafs' goalie coach upon retirement, a position he held until well into the 1980s.
• Hockey Hall of Fame 1976

DARRYL BOYCE #47/#50

left wing 6' 200 L

b. Summerside, Prince Edward Island, July 7, 1984
Signed as a free agent, January 1, 2008.
Claimed off waivers by Columbus, February 25, 2012.

2007–08	1	0	0	0	0
2010–11	46	5	8	13	33
2011–12	17	1	1	2	16
Totals	64	6	9	15	49

F January 24, 2008

WALLY BOYER #15

centre 5'8" 165 L

b. Cowan, Manitoba, September 27, 1937
Marlboros graduate
Claimed by Montreal in Intra-League Draft, June 15, 1966.

| 1965–66 F | 46 | 4 | 17 | 21 | 23 |

F December 11, 1965

TYLER BOZAK #42

centre 6'1" 195 R

b. Regina, Saskatchewan, March 19, 1986
Signed as a free agent, April 3, 2009.

2009–10 F	37	8	19	27	6
2010–11	82	15	17	32	14
2011–12	73	18	29	47	22
2012–13	46	12	16	28	6
2013–14	58	19	30	49	14
2014–15	82	23	26	49	44
Totals	378	95	137	232	106

F October 13, 2009

BRIAN BRADLEY #44

centre 5'9" 160 R

b. Kitchener, Ontario, January 21, 1965
Acquired from Vancouver for Tom Kurvers, January 12, 1991.
Claimed by Tampa Bay in Expansion Draft, June 18, 1992.

1990–91	26	0	11	11	20
1991–92	59	10	21	31	48
Totals	85	10	32	42	68

T.J. BRENNAN #25

defence 6'1" 216 L

b. Willingboro, New Jersey, April 3, 1989
Acquired from Chicago for Spencer Abbott, February 26, 2015.

| 2014–15 | 6 | 0 | 1 | 1 | 9 |

JOHN BRENNEMAN #24

left wing 5'10" 175 L

b. Fort Erie, January 5, 1943
Claimed from New York Rangers in Intra-League Draft, June 15, 1966.
Claimed by St. Louis in Expansion Draft, June 6, 1967.

| 1966–67 | 41 | 6 | 4 | 10 | 4 |

• Started 1966–67 with Leafs; sent to minors February 22, 1967.

TIM BRENT #37

centre 6' 188 R

b. Cambridge, Ontario, March 10, 1984
Signed as a free agent, July 4, 2009.
Signed as a free agent by Carolina, July 1, 2011.

2009–10	1	0	0	0	0
2010–11	79	8	12	20	33
Totals	80	8	12	20	33

CARL BREWER #2/#18/#28

defence 5'10" 180 L

b. Toronto, Ontario, October 21, 1938
d. Toronto, Ontario, August 25, 2001
Marlboros graduate
Traded with Frank Mahovlich, Pete Stemkowski, and Garry Unger to Detroit for Paul Henderson, Norm Ullman, and Floyd Smith, March 3, 1968.
Signed as a free agent, January 2, 1980; retired after 1979–80 season.

1957–58 F	2	0	0	0	0
1958–59	69	3	21	24	125
1959–60	67	4	19	23	150
1960–61	51	1	14	15	92
1961–62	67	1	22	23	89
1962–63	70	2	23	25	168
1963–64	57	4	9	13	114
1964–65	70	4	23	27	177
1979–80 L	20	0	5	5	2
Totals	473	19	136	155	917

F February 16, 1958 **L** March 25, 1980

ERIC BREWER #2

defence 6'4" 216 L
b. Vernon, British Columbia, April 7, 1979
Acquired from Anaheim with a fifth-round draft choice in 2016 for Korbinian Holzer, March 2, 2015.

2014–15		18	2	3	5	12

DOUG BRINDLEY #17

centre 6'1" 175 L
b. Walkerton, Ontario, June 8, 1949
Selected 20th overall in 1969 Amateur Draft. Traded to Vancouver for André Hinse, fall 1971.

1970–71 F/L	3	0	0	0	0

F December 6, 1970 **L** December 9, 1970

GREG BRITZ #16/#32

right wing 6' 190 R
b. Buffalo, New York, January 3, 1961
Signed as a free agent, November 2, 1983.
Signed as a free agent by Hartford, October 1986.

1983–84 F	6	0	0	0	2
1984–85	1	0	0	0	2
Totals	7	0	0	0	4

F November 2, 1983

WALTER "TURK" BRODA
("The Fabulous Fat Man"/"Turkey Face") #1/#19/#23

goalie 5'9" 180 L
b. Brandon, Manitoba, May 15, 1914
d. Toronto, Ontario, October 17, 1972
Purchased from Windsor (IHL) for $7,500, May 8, 1936.

1936–37 F	45	22–19–4	2,770	106	3	2.30
1937–38	48	24–15–9	2,980	127	6	2.56
1938–39	48	19–20–9	2,990	107	8	2.15
1939–40	47	25–17–5	2,900	108	4	2.23
1940–41	48	28–14–6	2,970	99	5	2.00
1941–42	48	27–18–3	2,960	136	6	2.76
1942–43	50	22–19–9	3,000	159	1	3.18
1945–46	15	6–6–3	900	53	0	3.53
1946–47	60	31–19–10	3,600	172	4	2.87
1947–48	60	32–15–13	3,600	143	5	2.38
1948–49	60	22–25–13	3,600	161	5	2.68
1949–50	68	30–25–12	4,040	167	9	2.48
1950–51	31	14–11–5	1,827	68	6	2.24
1951–52 L	1	0–1–0	30	3	0	5.81
Totals	629	302–224–101	38,168	1,609	62	2.53

F November 5, 1936 **L** March 23, 1952
• Missed 1943–45 while serving in the Canadian Army.
• Later coached Marlboros.
• Hockey Hall of Fame 1967

DAVID BROLL #46

left wing 6'2" 216 L
b. Mississauga, Ontario, January 4, 1993
Selected 152nd overall in 2011 Entry Draft.

2013–14 F	5	0	1	1	5

F October 10, 2013

ART BROOKS #1

goalie
b. Guelph, Ontario, March 29, 1887
d. Unknown
Signed as a free agent, December 15, 1917.
Released January 6, 1918, after Harry Holmes signed.

1917–18 L	4	2–1–0	220	23	0	5.75

L December 29, 1917

WILLIE BROSSART #25

defence 6' 190 L
b. Allan, Saskatchewan, May 29, 1949
Purchased from Philadelphia, May 23, 1973.
Traded with Tim Ecclestone to Washington for Rod Seiling, November 2, 1974.

1973–74	17	0	1	1	20
1974–75	4	0	0	0	2
Totals	21	0	1	1	22

AARON BROTEN #21

left wing 5'10" 175 L
b. Roseau, Minnesota, November 14, 1960
Acquired with Michel Petit and Lucien DeBlois from Quebec for Scott Pearson and a second-round draft choice in 1991 (later traded to Washington—Eric Lavigne) and 1992 (Tuomas Gronman), November 17, 1990.
Signed as a free agent by Winnipeg, January 21, 1992.

1990–91	27	6	4	10	32

ARNIE BROWN ("Brownie") #16/#22

defence 5'11" 185 L
b. Apsley, Ontario, January 28, 1942
St. Mike's graduate
Traded with Bill Collins, Dick Duff, Bob Nevin, and Rod Seiling to New York Rangers for Andy Bathgate and Don McKenney, February 22, 1964.

1961–62 F	2	0	0	0	0
1963–64	4	0	0	0	6
Totals	6	0	0	0	6

F October 28, 1961
• Became a sales manager for Monsanto Corporation.

JEFF BROWN #33

defence 6'1" 204 R
b. Ottawa, Ontario, April 30, 1966
Acquired from Carolina for future considerations, January 2, 1998.
Traded to Washington for Sylvain Côté, March 24, 1998.

1997–98	19	1	8	9	10

MIKE BROWN #18

right wing 5'11" 200 R
b. Chicago, Illinois, June 24, 1985
Acquired from Anaheim for a fifth-round draft choice in 2010 (Chris Wagner), June 26, 2010.
Traded to Edmonton for a fourth-round draft choice in 2014 (later traded to Colorado—Nicholas Magyar), March 4, 2013.

2010–11	50	3	5	8	69
2011–12	50	2	2	4	74
2012–13	12	0	1	1	70
Totals	112	5	8	13	213

JEFF BRUBAKER ("Bru") #23

left wing 6'2" 210 L
b. Hagerstown, Maryland, February 24, 1958
Claimed from Edmonton in Waiver Draft, October 9, 1984.
Claimed off waivers by Edmonton, December 5, 1985.

1984–85	68	8	4	12	209
1985–86	21	0	0	0	67
Totals	89	8	4	12	276

BILL BRYDGE #3

defence 5'9" 180 R
b. Renfrew, Ontario, October 22, 1901
d. Kirkland Lake, Ontario, November 3, 1949
Signed after winning Allan Cup with Port Arthur Bearcats, 1926.
Traded to Detroit Cougars for Art Duncan, 1927.

1926–27 F	41	6	3	9	76

F November 17, 1926
• Later coached the Lakeshore Blue Devils to the Canadian senior amateur title.

GORD BRYDSON #14

forward 5'7" 150 R
b. Toronto, Ontario, January 3, 1907
d. Mississauga, Ontario, February 4, 2001
Acquired from Buffalo (IHL) for future considerations (Wes King and the loan of Carl Voss), November 14, 1929.
Sold to London (IHL) after Toronto signed Harvey Jackson, December 6, 1929.

1929–30 F/L	9	2	0	2	8

F November 14, 1929 **L** December 5, 1929
• Worked as a golf pro in Mississauga almost to the day he died.

AL BUCHANAN #24/#25

left wing 5'8" 160 L
b. Winnipeg, Manitoba, May 17, 1927
d. January 17, 1994

1948–49 F	3	0	1	1	2
1949–50 L	1	0	0	0	0
Totals	4	0	1	1	2

F January 2, 1949 **L** January 14, 1950

MIKE BULLARD #22

centre 5'10" 185 L
b. Ottawa, Ontario, March 10, 1961
Acquired from Philadelphia for a third-round draft choice in 1993 (Vaclav Prospal), July 29, 1991.
Released summer 1992 and signed with Rapperswil (Switzerland).

1991–92 L	65	14	14	28	42

L March 25, 1992

BILL BUREGA ("Boogie") #20

defence 6'1" 200 L
b. Winnipeg, Manitoba, March 13, 1932

1955–56 F/L	4	0	1	1	4

F January 14, 1956 **L** January 19, 1956

DAVE BURROWS ("Bone Rack") #26

defence 6'1" 190 L
b. Toronto, Ontario, January 11, 1949
Acquired from Pittsburgh for Randy Carlyle and George Ferguson, June 14, 1978.
Traded with Paul Gardner to Pittsburgh for Kim Davis and Paul Marshall, November 18, 1980.

1978–79	65	2	11	13	28
1979–80	80	3	16	19	42
1980–81	6	0	0	0	2
Totals	151	5	27	32	72

• Became director of hockey operations for Teen Ranch, a Christian sports camp in Caledon, Ontario.

GARTH BUTCHER #2

defence 6' 194 R
b. Regina, Saskatchewan, January 8, 1963
Acquired with Mats Sundin, Todd Warriner, and a first-round draft choice in 1994 (traded to Washington—Nolan Baumgartner—with Rob Pearson for Mike Ridley and a first-round draft choice in 1994—Éric Fichaud) from Quebec for Wendel Clark, Sylvain Lefebvre, Landon Wilson, and a first-round draft choice in 1994 (Jeffrey Kealty), June 28, 1994.
Released October 16, 1995.

1994–95 L	45	1	7	8	59

L May 3, 1995
• Opened a restaurant called The Pump near Toronto after retiring.

JERRY BUTLER ("Bugsy") #17

right wing 6' 180 R
b. Sarnia, Ontario, February 27, 1951
Acquired from St. Louis for Inge Hammarstrom, November 1, 1977.
Traded with Tiger Williams to Vancouver for Bill Derlago and Rick Vaive, February 18, 1980.

1977–78	73	9	7	16	49
1978–79	76	8	7	15	52
1979–80	55	7	8	15	29
Totals	204	24	22	46	130

MIKE BYERS #24

right wing 5'10" 185 R
b. Toronto, Ontario, September 11, 1946
Marlboros graduate
Traded with Gerry Meehan and Bill Sutherland to Philadelphia for Brit Selby and Forbes Kennedy, March 2, 1969.

1967–68 F	10	2	2	4	0
1968–69	5	0	0	0	2
Totals	15	2	2	4	2

F December 30, 1967

JACK CAFFERY #25

centre 6' 175 R
b. Kingston, Ontario, June 30, 1934
d. Toronto, Ontario, December 2, 1992
St. Mike's graduate
Recalled from Pittsburgh (AHL), December 9, 1954.
Sold to Boston for cash, May 7, 1956.

1954–55 F	3	0	0	0	0

F December 11, 1954

LARRY CAHAN ("Hank") #20

defence 6' 195 R
b. Fort William (Thunder Bay), Ontario, December 25, 1933
d. Thunder Bay, Ontario, June 25, 1992
Signed and assigned to Pittsburgh (AHL), 1953.
Sold to New York Rangers for $15,000, June 6, 1956.

1954–55 F	58	0	6	6	64
1955–56	21	0	2	2	46
Totals	79	0	8	8	110

F October 7, 1954

JIM "DUTCH" CAIN #9

defence 5'11" 180 L
b. Newmarket, Ontario, February 1, 1902
d. January 13, 1962
Acquired from Montreal Maroons for Toots Holway, January 11, 1926.

1925–26 L	23	0	0	0	8

L March 17, 1926

HARRY CAMERON ("Cammie") #10/#2

defence 5'10" 154 R
b. Pembroke, Ontario, February 6, 1890
d. Vancouver, British Columbia, October 20, 1953
Signed by Arenas from Blue Shirts; loaned to Ottawa for the balance of the season, January 18, 1918; traded to Montreal for Goldie Prodger (after game on January 14, 1920). Returned from Montreal for 1921–22 season; claimed off waivers by Saskatoon (WCHL), summer 1923.

1917–18	21	17	—	17	28
1918–19	7	6	2	8	9
1919–20	7	3	0	3	6
1920–21	24	18	9	27	35
1921–22	24	18	17	35	22
1922–23 L	22	9	7	16	27
Totals	105	71	35	106	127

L March 5, 1923

• Missed game of February 2, 1918, after breaking training rules (also fined $100); suspended January 13, 1919, along with Reg Noble, for breaking training rules.
• Hockey Hall of Fame 1962

JACK CAPUANO #26

defence 6'2" 210 L
b. Cranston, Rhode Island, July 7, 1966
Selected 88th overall in 1984 Entry Draft.
Traded with Paul Gagné and Derek Laxdal to New York Islanders for Gilles Thibaudeau and Mike Stevens, December 20, 1989.

1989–90 F	1	0	0	0	0

F October 11, 1989

LUCA CAPUTI #33

left wing 6'3" 200 L
b. Toronto, Ontario, October 1, 1988
Acquired from Pittsburgh with Martin Skoula for Alexei Ponikarovsky, March 2, 2010.
Traded to Anaheim for Nicolas Deschamps, January 3, 2012.

2009–10	19	1	5	6	10
2010–11	7	0	0	0	4
Totals	26	1	5	6	14

GEORGE CAREY #6

right wing 5'6" 140 R
b. Montreal, Quebec, November 4, 1892
d. Toronto, Ontario, December 31, 1974
Signed in 1923.

1923–24 L	4	0	0	0	0

L December 26, 1923

WAYNE CARLETON ("Swoop") #25/#12

left wing 6'2" 215 L
b. Sudbury, Ontario, August 4, 1946
Traded to Boston for Jim Harrison, December 10, 1969.

1965–66 F	2	0	1	1	0
1966–67	5	1	0	1	14
1967–68	65	8	11	19	34
1968–69	12	1	3	4	6
1969–70	7	0	1	1	6
Totals	91	10	16	26	60

F January 1, 1966

• Spent most of time in minors because of injuries and poor relations with Punch Imlach.
• Became a car salesman in Collingwood, Ontario.

RANDY CARLYLE #23/#28

defence 5'10" 200 L
b. Sudbury, Ontario, April 19, 1956
Selected 30th overall in 1976 Amateur Draft.
Traded with George Ferguson to Pittsburgh for Dave Burrows, June 14, 1978.

1976–77 F	45	0	5	5	51
1977–78	49	2	11	13	31
Totals	94	2	16	18	82

F October 5, 1976
• Later coached the Leafs.

AL "RED" CARR #14

left wing 5'8" 178 L
b. Winnipeg, Manitoba, December 29, 1916
d. May 16, 1990

1943–44 F/L	5	0	1	1	4

F October 30, 1943 L November 21, 1943

LORNE CARR #9

right wing 5'8" 161 R
b. Stoughton, Saskatchewan, July 2, 1910
d. Calgary, Alberta, June 9, 2007
Acquired from New York Americans for Red Heron, Nick Knott, Gus Marker, and Peanuts O'Flaherty on a one-year lease, all subject to recall, October 30, 1941; officially became Toronto property February 2, 1942, when Leafs sent Jack Church and cash to Americans.

1941–42	47	16	17	33	4
1942–43	50	27	33	60	15
1943–44	50	36	38	74	9
1944–45	47	21	25	46	7
1945–46 L	42	5	8	13	2
Totals	236	105	121	226	37

L March 17, 1946
• Began the 1945–46 season as a coach in Schumacher; rejoined Leafs on November 22, 1945.

SAM CARRICK #53

centre 6' 188 R
b. Markham, Ontario, February 4, 1992
Selected 144th overall in 2010 Entry Draft.

2014–15 F	16	1	1	2	9

F November 1, 2014

LARRY CARRIÈRE #3

defence 6'1" 190 L
b. Montreal, Quebec, January 30, 1952
Signed as a free agent, August 5, 1979.

1979–80 L	2	0	1	1	0

L April 6, 1980

DR. BILL CARSON ("Doc") #15/#5

centre 5'8" 158 L
b. Bracebridge, Ontario, November 25, 1900
d. Parry Sound, Ontario, May 29, 1967
Signed as a free agent by St. Pats, April 17, 1926.
Sold to Boston for $20,000, January 24, 1928.

1926–27 F	40	16	6	22	41
1927–28	32	20	6	26	36
1928–29	24	7	6	13	45
Totals	96	43	18	61	122

F November 17, 1926
• Initially signed from Grimsby (OHA Intermediate), January 13, 1924, but changed his mind and refused to come to Toronto, even though the St. Pats had bought him a pair of skates as a "signing bonus."
• Graduated in 1926 from the dentistry program at University of Toronto and practised after retiring from hockey.

SEBASTIEN CENTOMO #30

goalie 6'1" 200 L
b. Montreal, Quebec, March 26, 1981
Signed as a free agent, September 10, 1999.
Signed as a free agent by Calgary, September 7, 2004.

2001–02	1	0–0–0	40	3	0	4.50

• Only Leaf game March 6, 2002

RAY CERESINO #16

right wing 5'8" 160 R
b. Port Arthur, Ontario, April 24, 1929
Marlboros graduate
Signed with Leafs September 15, 1948; recalled from Pittsburgh (AHL), January 13, 1924.
Traded with Tod Sloan and Harry Taylor to Cleveland (AHL) for Bob Solinger, summer 1949.

1948–49 F/L	12	1	1	2	2

F December 1, 1948 L January 2, 1949

LORNE CHABOT ("Chabotsky"/"Sad Eyes"/"Old Bulwarks") #1

goalie 6'1" 185 L
b. Montreal, Quebec, October 5, 1900
d. Montreal, Quebec, October 10, 1946
Acquired with Alex Gray from New York Rangers for Butch Keeling and John Ross Roach, October 17, 1928.
Traded to Montreal for George Hainsworth, summer 1933, but retired, thus nullifying the deal. Chabot agreed to join the Habs on October 1, 1933, finalizing the trade.

1928–29	43	20–18–5	2,458	67	12	1.64
1929–30	42	16–20–6	2,620	113	6	2.59
1930–31	37	21–8–8	2,300	80	6	2.09
1931–32	44	22–16–6	2,698	106	4	2.36
1932–33	48	24–18–6	2,948	111	5	2.26
Totals	214	103–80–31	13,024	477	33	2.20

ED CHADWICK ("Chad") #1/#20

goalie 5'11" 184 L
b. Fergus, Ontario, May 8, 1933
Recalled from Winnipeg (WHL), February 6, 1956.
Traded to Boston for Don Simmons, January 31, 1961.

1955–56 F	5	2–0–3	300	3	2	0.60
1956–57	70	21–34–15	4,200	192	5	2.74
1957–58	70	21–38–11	4,200	226	4	3.23
1958–59	31	12–15–4	1,860	93	3	3.10
1959–60	4	1–2–1	240	15	0	3.75
Totals	180	57–89–34	10,740	529	14	2.96

F February 8, 1956
• Recalled from Rochester (AHL), January 31, 1961.
• Longtime scout for Edmonton Oilers and has his name on the Cup three times from wins during the 1980s.

ERWIN "MURPH" CHAMBERLAIN ("Old Hardrock") #8/#14

centre 5'11" 172 L
b. Shawville, Quebec, February 14, 1915
d. Beachville, Ontario, May 8, 1986
Signed as a free agent after winning the Allan Cup with Sudbury Frood Mines, September 28, 1937.
Sold to Montreal for $7,500, May 11, 1940.

1937–38 F	43	4	12	16	51
1938–39	48	10	16	26	32
1939–40	40	5	17	22	63
Totals	131	19	45	64	146

F November 4, 1937

ANDRE CHAMPAGNE #18

left wing 6' 190 L
b. Eastview, Ontario, September 19, 1943
St. Mike's graduate

1962–63 F/L	2	0	0	0	0

F February 23, 1963 L February 27. 1963

KELLY CHASE ("Chaser") #39

right wing 5'11" 193 R
b. Porcupine Plain, Saskatchewan, October 25, 1967
Acquired from Hartford for an eighth-round draft choice in 1998, March 18, 1997.
Traded to St. Louis for future considerations, September 30, 1997.

1996–97	2	0	0	0	27

• Only games for the Leafs March 26 & 27, 1997

GERRY CHEEVERS ("Cheesey") #1

goalie 5'11" 175 L
b. St. Catharines, Ontario, December 7, 1940
St. Mike's graduate
Signed with Leafs July 3, 1961.
Claimed by Boston in Intra-League Draft, June 9, 1965.

1961–62 F	2	1–1–0	120	7	0	3.50

F December 2, 1961
• Later worked at Rockingham Park racetrack in Salem, New Hampshire, while managing his own stable of horses.
• Hockey Hall of Fame 1985

LEX CHISHOLM #9/#22

centre 5'11" 175 R
b. Galt, Ontario, April 1, 1915
d. August 6, 1981
Signed as a free agent, March 15, 1939.
Retired September 12, 1941.

1939–40 F	28	6	8	14	22
1940–41 L	26	4	0	4	8
Totals	54	10	8	18	30

F November 18, 1939 L March 16, 1941

JACK CHURCH #16/#19/#20

defence 5'11" 180 R
b. Kamsack, Saskatchewan, May 24, 1915
d. Toronto, Ontario, January 5, 1996
Sent, with cash, to Brooklyn on February 3, 1942, to complete acquisition of Lorne Carr, who had come to Leafs on loan but was now Toronto property.

1938–39 F	3	0	2	2	2
1939–40	31	1	4	5	62
1940–41	11	0	1	1	22
1941–42	27	0	4	4	28
Totals	72	1	11	12	114

F December 10, 1938
• Recalled from Syracuse (IAHL) for playoffs, March 27, 1939; missed 29 games in 1940–41 with a knee injury; demoted to minors and replaced by Bob Goldham, January 27, 1942.

ROB CIMETTA #34/#14

left wing 6' 190 L
b. Toronto, Ontario, February 15, 1970
Acquired from Boston for Steve Bancroft, November 9, 1990.
Signed as a free agent by Chicago, September 8, 1993.

1990–91	25	2	4	6	21
1991–92 L	24	4	3	7	12
Totals	49	6	7	13	33

L January 25, 1992

FRANCIS "KING" CLANCY #7/#5

defence 5'9 184 L
b. Ottawa, Ontario, February 25, 1903
d. Toronto, Ontario, November 8, 1986
Acquired from Ottawa Senators for Art Smith, Eric Pettinger, and $35,000, October 11, 1930.
Retired November 23, 1936, after first six games of season.

1930–31	44	7	14	21	63
1931–32	48	10	9	19	61
1932–33	48	13	12	25	79
1933–34	46	11	17	28	62
1934–35	47	5	16	21	53
1935–36	47	5	10	15	61
1936–37 L	6	1	0	1	4
Totals	286	52	78	130	383

L November 23, 1936
• Coached the Leafs, refereed in the NHL, and was employed by Toronto until his death.
• On March 15, 1932, Clancy, Red Horner, and Alex Levinsky all took turns in goal (and each let in a goal) while Lorne Chabot served a penalty.

TERRY CLANCY #7/#21

right wing 6'1" 195 L
b. Ottawa, Ontario, April 2, 1943
Signed as a free agent; claimed by Oakland in Expansion Draft, June 6, 1967.
Purchased from Oakland, May 14, 1968; sold to Montreal, December 23, 1970.
Purchased from Montreal August 30, 1971,
and rejoined Leafs for 1972–73; sold to Detroit, October 17, 1973.

1968–69	2	0	0	0	0
1969–70	52	6	5	11	31
1972–73 L	32	0	1	1	6
Totals	86	6	6	12	37

L April 1, 1973
• Played for Canada at 1964 Olympics (fourth place).

WENDEL CLARK #17

left wing 5'11" 194 L
b. Kelvington, Saskatchewan, October 25, 1966
Selected 1st overall in 1985 Entry Draft; traded with Sylvain Lefebvre, Landon Wilson, and a first-round draft choice in 1994 (Jeffrey Kealty) to Quebec for Mats Sundin, Garth Butcher, Todd Warriner, and a first-round draft choice in 1994 (later traded to Washington—Nolan Baumgartner), June 28, 1994.
Acquired with Mathieu Schneider and Denis Smith from New York Islanders for Kenny Jonsson, Darby Hendrickson, Sean Haggerty, and a first-round draft choice in 1997 (Roberto Luongo), March 13, 1996.
Signed as a free agent, January 14, 2000; retired June 29, 2000, and accepted a job in public relations with the Leafs.

1985–86	66	34	11	45	227
1986–87	80	37	23	60	271
1987–88	28	12	11	23	80
1988–89	15	7	4	11	66
1989–90	38	18	8	26	116
1990–91	63	18	16	34	152
1991–92	43	19	21	40	123
1992–93	66	17	22	39	193
1993–94	64	46	30	76	115
1995–96	13	8	7	15	16
1996–97	65	30	19	49	75
1997–98	47	12	7	19	80
1999–2000 L	20	2	2	4	21
Totals	608	260	181	441	1,535

L May 3, 2000
• Missed much of 1987–90 with recurring back injury.

DAVID CLARKSON #71

right wing 6'1" 200 R
b. Toronto, Ontario, March 31, 1984
Signed as a free agent, July 5, 2013.
Traded to Columbus for Nathan Horton, February 26, 2015.

2013–14	60	5	6	11	93
2014–15	58	10	5	15	92
Totals	118	15	11	26	185

SPRAGUE CLEGHORN ("Peg") #unknown

defence 5'10" 190 L
b. Montreal, Quebec, March 11, 1890
d. Montreal, Quebec, July 11, 1956
Acquired from Ottawa, January 24, 1921, after first half of 1920–21 season.
Released by St. Pats, March 13, 1921,
between the first and second games of the playoffs vs. Ottawa; rejoined Ottawa after the Senators eliminated the St. Pats from the 1921 playoffs.

1920–21 F	13	3	4	7	26

F January 26, 1921
• Hockey Hall of Fame 1958

SCOTT CLEMMENSEN #30

goalie 6'2" 200 L
b. Des Moines, Iowa, July 23, 1977
Signed as a free agent, July 6, 2007.
Signed as a free agent by New Jersey, July 10, 2008.

2007–08	3		1–1–0	154	10	0	3.90

CARLO COLAIACOVO #8/#45

defence 6'1" 200 L
b. Toronto, Ontario, January 27, 1983
Selected 17th overall in 2001 Entry Draft.
Traded to St. Louis with Alexander Steen for Lee Stempniak, November 24, 2008.

2002–03	2	0	1	1	0
2003–04	2	0	1	1	2
2005–06	21	2	5	7	17
2006–07	48	8	9	17	22
2007–08	28	2	4	6	10
2008–09	10	0	1	1	6
Totals	111	12	21	33	57

JOE COLBORNE #32

centre 6'5" 215 L
b. Calgary, Alberta, January 30, 1990
Acquired from Boston with a first-round draft choice in 2011 (traded to Anaheim—Rickard Rackell) and a second-round draft choice in 2012 (later traded to Washington and Dallas—Mike Winther) for Tomas Kaberle, February 18, 2011.
Traded to Calgary for a fourth-round draft choice in 2014 (later traded to St. Louis—Ville Husso), February 18, 2011.

2010–11	1	0	1	1	0
2011–12	10	1	4	5	4
2012–13	5	0	0	0	2
Totals	16	1	5	6	6

RANLEIGH "GARY" COLLINS #24

centre 5'11" 190 L
b. Toronto, Ontario, September 27, 1935
Marlboros graduate
Acquired from Chicago, May 30, 1955, as compensation for allowing Chicago to purchase Hank Ciesla from Montreal (Leafs owned Ciesla's rights, though he played with Montreal's minor league affiliate). The Leafs then transferred Bob Duncan from the Marlies to Kitchener (OHA Junior A).
Sold to Quebec (AHL) for $12,500, November 19, 1959.
• Appeared in the NHL only in the 1959 playoffs with the Leafs.

BRIAN CONACHER #17/#22/#18

left wing 6'3" 197 L

b. Toronto, Ontario, August 31, 1941
Marlboros graduate
Recalled by the Leafs October 5, 1965;
claimed by Detroit in Intra-League Draft,
June 12, 1968.
Acquired with Terry O'Malley from Minnesota North Stars for Murray Oliver, May 22,
1970; rights sold to Detroit, August 1978.

1961–62	F	1	0	0	0	0
1965–66		2	0	0	0	2
1966–67		66	14	13	27	47
1967–68		64	11	14	25	31
Totals		133	25	27	52	80

F December 31, 1961
• Played 1962–63 for the University of Western Ontario, and 1963–65 with the Canadian National Team. Played at the 1964 Olympics (fourth) and 1965 World Championship (fourth).
• Wrote a book on the state of the game called *Hockey in Canada: The Way It Is.*
• Became vice-president of building operations for Maple Leaf Gardens during the 1990s.

CHARLES "PETE" CONACHER #16

left wing 5'10" 165 L

b. Toronto, Ontario, July 29, 1932
Claimed from New York Rangers in Intra-League Draft, June 4, 1957.

1957–58	L	5	0	1	1	5

L November 16, 1957
• Won a gold medal with Belleville McFarlands at the 1959 World Championship.
• Worked on the trading floor of the Toronto Stock Exchange.

CHARLIE CONACHER ("The Bomber") #9/#6

right wing 6'1" 195 R

b. Toronto, Ontario, December 20, 1910
d. Toronto, Ontario, December 30, 1967
Marlboros graduate
Sold to Detroit for $16,000, October 11, 1938.

1929–30	F	38	20	9	29	48
1930–31		37	31	12	43	78
1931–32		44	34	14	48	66
1932–33		40	14	19	33	64
1933–34		42	32	20	52	38
1934–35		47	36	21	57	24
1935–36		44	23	15	38	74
1936–37		15	3	5	8	13
1937–38		19	7	9	16	6
Totals		326	200	124	324	411

F November 14, 1929
• Played in goal on three occasions (with no goals against): November 20, 1932, when Lorne Chabot was serving a penalty; March 16, 1933, again when Chabot was penalized; and March 16, 1935, when George Hainsworth was badly cut.
• Hockey Hall of Fame 1961

TIM CONNOLLY #12

centre 6'1" 190 R

b. Syracuse, New York, May 7, 1981
Signed as a free agent, July 2, 2011.

2011–12	L	70	13	23	46	40

L April 7, 2012

BRANDON CONVERY #12

centre 6'1" 182 R

b. Kingston, Ontario, February 4, 1974
Selected 8th overall in 1992 Entry Draft.
Traded to Vancouver on March 7, 1998, for Lonny Bohonos.

1995–96	F	11	5	2	7	4
1996–97		39	2	8	10	20
Totals		50	7	10	17	24

F March 2, 1996

DAVID COOPER ("Coops") #42/#33

defence 6'2" 204 L

b. Ottawa, Ontario, November 2, 1973
Signed as a free agent, September 18, 1996;
traded to Calgary for Ladislav Kohn, July 2, 1998.
Signed as a free agent, summer 2000; played in Germany in 2001–02.

1996–97	F	19	3	3	6	16
1997–98		9	0	4	4	8
2000–01		2	0	0	0	0
Totals		30	3	7	10	24

F December 15, 1996

DR. BOBBY COPP #2/#14

defence 5'11" 180 L

b. Port Elgin, New Brunswick, November 15, 1918
d. December 12, 2006
Retired March 8, 1942, after a fight with Hap Day just before going off to war.

1942–43	F	38	3	9	12	24
1950–51	L	2	0	0	0	2
Totals		40	3	9	12	26

F October 31, 1942 L October 22, 1950
• While practising dentistry and playing for Ottawa in the Quebec Senior Hockey League, Copp was called off the voluntary retired list to replace injured defencemen Hugh Bolton and Bill Barilko. He played two weekend games, then retired again and returned to Ottawa, where he continued his career as a dentist.

BERT "CON" CORBEAU ("Husky"/"Pig Iron") #2

defence 5'11" 196 L

b. Penetang, Ontario, February 9, 1894
d. Georgian Bay, Ontario, September 22, 1942
Acquired with Amos Arbour from Hamilton for Corb Dennenay and Ken Randall, 1923.

1923–24		24	8	6	14	55
1924–25		30	4	3	7	67
1925–26		36	5	5	10	121
1926–27	L	41	1	2	3	88
Totals		131	18	16	34	331

L March 26, 1927

HUBERT "CHUCK" CORRIGAN #19

right wing 6'1" 192 R

b. Moosomin, Saskatchewan, May 22, 1916
d. June 23, 1988
St. Mike's graduate
Sold to Springfield (AHL) January 21, 1938.

1937–38	F	3	0	0	0	0

F November 20, 1937

SHAYNE CORSON #27

centre 6'1" 202 L

b. Barrie, Ontario, August 13, 1966
Signed as a free agent, July 4, 2000.
Signed as a free agent by Dallas, February 18, 2004.

2000–01		77	8	18	26	189
2001–02		74	12	21	33	120
2002–03		46	7	8	15	49
Totals		197	27	47	74	358

FATHER LES COSTELLO ("Costie") #15

left wing 5'8" 158 L

b. South Porcupine, Ontario, February 16, 1928
d. Kincardine, Ontario, December 10, 2002
St. Mike's graduate

1948–49	F/L	15	2	3	5	11

F October 16, 1948 (regular season—recalled March 20, 1948, for playoffs)
L December 18, 1948
• Retired to attend seminary school and later played for the Flying Fathers, a hockey team of priests who travelled the world and played for charity.

RICH COSTELLO #8/#16

centre 6' 175 R

b. Farmington, Massachusetts, June 27, 1963
Acquired with a second-round draft choice in 1982 (Peter Ihnacak) and future considerations (Ken Strong) from Philadelphia for Darryl Sittler, January 20, 1982.
Contract bought out July 1987.

1983–84	F	10	2	1	3	2
1985–86	L	2	0	1	1	0
Totals		12	2	2	4	2

F January 12, 1984 L January 1, 1986

CHARLIE COTCH #unknown

left wing 5'11" 175 L

b. Sarnia, Ontario, February 21, 1900
d. Detroit, Michigan, November 14, 1932
Signed as a free agent, February 9, 1925.

1924–25	L	5	0	0	0	0

L March 7, 1925

SYLVAIN CÔTÉ ("Co-Co") #3

defence 6' 190 R

b. Quebec City, Quebec, January 19, 1966
Acquired from Washington for Jeff Brown, March 24, 1998.
Traded to Chicago for a second-round draft choice in 2001 (Karel Pilar), October 8, 1999.

1997–98		12	3	6	9	6
1998–99		79	5	24	29	28
1999–2000		3	0	1	1	0
Totals		94	8	31	39	34

HAROLD "BALDY" COTTON ("Lucky") #8/#11/#14

left wing 5'10" 159 L

b. Nanticoke, Ontario, November 5, 1902
d. Campbellford, Ontario, September 9, 1984
Acquired from Pittsburgh Pirates for Gerald Lowrey and $10,000, February 12, 1929.
Sold to New York Americans, October 9, 1935.

1928–29		12	1	2	3	8
1929–30		41	21	17	38	47
1930–31		43	12	17	29	45
1931–32		47	5	13	18	41
1932–33		48	10	11	21	29
1933–34		47	8	14	22	46
1934–35		47	11	14	25	36
Totals		285	68	88	156	252

• Became a longtime scout for the Bruins.

JACK "JERRY" COUGHLIN #8

forward 5'10" 170 R

b. Douro, Ontario, June 21, 1892
d. Peterborough, Ontario, June 21, 1969
Signed as a free agent, December 5, 1917.
Released January 6, 1918.

1917–18		6	2	—	2	0

RUSS COURTNALL ("Rusty") #9/#16/#26

centre 5'11" 183 R

b. Duncan, British Columbia, June 2, 1965
Selected 7th overall in 1983 Entry Draft.
Traded to Montreal for John Kordic, November 7, 1988.

1983–84	F	14	3	9	12	6
1984–85		69	12	10	22	44
1985–86		73	22	38	60	52
1986–87		79	29	44	73	90
1987–88		65	23	26	49	47
1988–89		9	1	1	2	4
Totals		309	90	128	218	243

F February 26, 1984

MARCEL COUSINEAU ("Couz") #31

goalie 5'9" 171 L

b. Delson, Quebec, April 30, 1973
Signed as a free agent, November 13, 1993.
Signed as a free agent by New York Islanders, July 29, 1998.

1996–97	F	13	3–5–1	566	31	1	3.29
1997–98		2	0–0–0	17	0	0	0.00
Totals		15	3–5–1	583	31	1	3.19

F November 21, 1996

DANNY COX ("Silent Danny") #6/#7

left wing 5'11" 176 L

b. Little Current, Ontario, October 12, 1903

d. August 8, 1982

Signed as a free agent, summer 1926, after winning Allan Cup with Port Arthur; loaned to Hamilton, January 12, 1927.

Traded to Ottawa, until season's end only, for Frank Nighbor, January 6, 1930, with an option to buy Cox's contract after the season. On May 4, 1930, Ottawa exercised the option, giving the Leafs cash to complete the deal.

1926–27	F	14	0	1	1	4
1927–28		41	9	6	15	27
1928–29		42	12	7	19	14
1929–30		19	1	5	6	18
Totals		116	22	19	41	63

F November 17, 1926

• Taken to hospital with a serious case of bronchitis, November 25, 1929.

JOEY CRABB #46

right wing 6'1" 190 R

b. Anchorage, Alaska, April 3, 1983

Signed as a free agent, July 1, 2010.

Signed as a free agent by Washington, July 1, 2012.

2010–11	48	3	12	15	24
2011–12	67	11	15	26	33
Totals	115	14	27	41	57

MIKE CRAIG #9

right wing 6'1" 185 R

b. St. Marys, Ontario, June 6, 1971

Signed as a free agent, July 29, 1994; Leafs lost Peter Zezel and Grant Marshall to Dallas as compensation.

Placed on waivers, July 28, 1997.

1994–95	37	5	5	10	12
1995–96	70	8	12	20	42
1996–97	65	7	13	20	62
Totals	172	20	30	50	116

JOHN CRAIGHEAD #44

forward 6' 195 R

b. Vancouver, British Columbia, November 23, 1971

Signed as a free agent July 6, 1996.

Demoted to St. John's (AHL) December 7, 1996; played in IHL and Germany for rest of his career.

1996–97	F/L	5	0	0	0	10

F November 21, 1996 L December 3, 1996

RUSSELL "RUSTY" CRAWFORD #8

left wing 5'11" 165 L

b. Cardinal, Ontario, November 7, 1885

d. Spruce Home, Saskatchewan, December 19, 1971

Purchased from Ottawa after Ottawa signed Frank Nighbor, February 6, 1918.

Retired after 1918–19 season, although he played later on the West Coast.

1917–18	F	8	1	—	1	51
1918–19	L	18	7	4	11	51
Totals		256	8	4	12	102

F February 9, 1918 L February 20, 1919

• Hockey Hall of Fame 1962

DAVE CREIGHTON #11/#22/#23

centre 6'1" 181 L

b. Port Arthur, Ontario, June 24, 1930

Acquired from Boston for Fern Flaman and cash, July 20, 1954; sold to Chicago, November 16, 1954.

Acquired from New York Rangers, summer 1958; traded to Buffalo (AHL) for Dick Gamble, June 1961.

1954–55	14	2	1	3	8
1958–59	34	3	9	12	4
1959–60	L	14	1	5	6	4
Totals	62	6	15	21	16

L February 21, 1960

• Became owner and manager of numerous golf courses throughout North America.

JIRI CRHA ("George") #31

goalie 5'11" 170 L

b. Pardubice, Czechoslovakia (Czech Republic), April 13, 1950

Signed as a free agent after defecting from Czechoslovakia, summer 1979.

Contract bought out December 3, 1982.

1979–80	F	15	8–7–0	830	50	0	3.61
1980–81	L	54	20–20–11	3,112	211	0	4.07
Totals		69	28–27–11	3,942	261	0	3.97

F February 16, 1980 L April 5, 1981

• Became an agent for NHL players.

CORY CROSS ("Red"/"Crosser") #4

defence 6'5" 220 L

b. Lloydminster, Alberta, January 3, 1971

Acquired from Tampa Bay with a seventh-round draft choice in 2001 (Ivan Kolozvary) for Fredrik Modin, October 1, 1999.

Signed as a free agent by New York Rangers, December 17, 2002.

1999–2000	71	4	11	15	64
2000–01	41	3	5	8	50
2001–02	50	3	9	12	54
Totals	162	10	25	35	168

JOE CROZIER ("Crow") #23

defence 6' 180 R

b. Winnipeg, Manitoba, February 19, 1929

1959–60	F/L	5	0	3	3	2

F March 12, 1960 L March 20, 1960

• Retired to GM and coach Charlotte Checkers (EHL); later became coach of the Leafs.

BARRY CULLEN #19

right wing 6' 175 R

b. Ottawa, Ontario, June 16, 1935

Signed as a free agent, 1955; recalled from Winnipeg (WHL), November 7, 1955, to replace injured Eric Nesterenko.

Traded to Detroit for Frank Roggeveen and Johnny Wilson, June 9, 1959.

1955–56	F	3	0	0	0	4
1956–57		51	6	10	16	30
1957–58		70	16	25	41	37
1958–59		40	6	8	14	17
Totals		164	28	43	71	88

F November 11, 1955

• Operated successful car dealerships in Guelph and Grimsby with brother Brian.

BRIAN CULLEN #14/#18/#22/#27/#16

centre 5'10" 164 L

b. Ottawa, Ontario, November 11, 1933

Acquired from Buffalo (AHL) for Dusty Blair, Frank Sullivan, and Jackie LeClair, May 4, 1954.

Claimed by New York Rangers in Intra-League Draft, June 10, 1959.

1954–55	F	27	3	5	8	6
1955–56		21	2	6	8	8
1956–57		46	8	12	20	27
1957–58		67	20	23	43	29
1958–59		59	4	14	18	10
Totals		220	37	60	97	80

F October 7, 1954

• Ran successful car dealership with his brother and owned a stable of horses.

JOHN CULLEN #19

centre 5'10" 185 R

b. Puslinch, Ontario, August 2, 1964

Acquired from Hartford for a second-round draft choice in 1993 (traded to San Jose—Vlastimil Kroupa), November 24, 1992.

Signed as a free agent by Pittsburgh, August 3, 1994.

1992–93	47	13	28	41	53
1993–94	53	13	17	30	67
Totals	100	26	45	71	120

• Battled back from cancer to resume career with Tampa Bay in 1995.

• Later ran a car dealership in Atlanta.

BRIAN CURRAN #28

defence 6'5" 215 L

b. Toronto, Ontario, November 5, 1963

Acquired from New York Islanders for sixth-round draft choice in 1988 (Pavel Gross), March 8, 1988.

Traded with Lou Franceschetti to Buffalo for Mike Foligno and an eighth-round draft choice in 1991 (Tomas Kucharcik), December 17, 1990.

1987–88	7	0	1	1	19
1988–89	47	1	4	5	185
1989–90	72	2	9	11	301
1990–91	4	0	0	0	7
Totals	130	3	14	17	512

MARIUSZ CZERKAWSKI #21

right wing 6' 200 L

b. Radomsko, Poland, April 13, 1972

Signed as a free agent, September 8, 2005.

Claimed off waivers by Boston, March 8, 2006.

2005–06	19	4	1	5	6

KEVIN DAHL #4

defence 5'11" 190 R

b. Regina, Saskatchewan, December 30, 1968

Claimed from St. Louis in Waiver Draft, October 5, 1998.

Signed as a free agent by New York Islanders, August 12, 1999.

1998–99	3	0	0	0	2

MARTY DALLMAN #35/#15

centre 5'10" 180 R

b. Niagara Falls, Ontario, February 15, 1963

Signed as a free agent, 1986.

1987–88	F	2	0	1	1	0
1988–89	L	4	0	0	0	0
Totals		6	0	1	1	0

F March 9, 1988 L November 21, 1988

JERRY D'AMIGO #29

left wing 5'11" 205 L

b. Binghamton, New York, February 19, 1991

Selected 158th overall in 2009 Entry Draft.

Traded to Columbus with a conditional draft pick for Matt Frattin, July 1, 2014.

2013–14	F	22	1	2	3	0

F December 5, 2013

VINCENT DAMPHOUSSE ("Vinny") #10

left wing 6'1" 190 L

b. Montreal, Quebec, December 17, 1967

Selected 6th overall in 1986 Entry Draft.

Traded with Peter Ing, Scott Thornton, and Luke Richardson to Edmonton for Grant Fuhr, Glenn Anderson, and Craig Berube, September 19, 1991.

1986–87	F	80	21	25	46	26
1987–88		75	12	36	48	40
1988–89		80	26	42	68	75
1989–90		80	33	61	94	56
1990–91		79	26	47	73	65
Totals		394	118	211	329	262

F October 9, 1986

DAN DAOUST ("Dangerous Dan"/"Doo") #24
centre 5'11" 170 L
b. Montreal, Quebec, February 29, 1960
Acquired from Montreal for a third-round draft choice in 1984 (Ken Hodge, Jr.), December 17, 1982.

1982–83	48	18	33	51	31
1983–84	78	18	56	74	88
1984–85	79	17	37	54	98
1985–86	80	7	13	20	88
1986–87	33	4	3	7	35
1987–88	67	9	8	17	57
1988–89	68	7	5	12	54
1989–90 L	65	7	11	18	89
Totals	518	87	166	253	540

L March 31, 1990

HARRY DARRAGH ("Howl") #16
forward 5'1" 145 R
b. Ottawa, Ontario, September 13, 1902
d. Ottawa, Ontario, October 28, 1993
Claimed off waivers for $5,000 from Boston, April 1931.
Retired at end of 1932–33 season.

1931–32	48	5	10	15	6
1932–33 L	19	1	2	3	0
Totals	67	6	12	18	6

L March 23, 1933

BOB DAVIDSON ("Rugged") #4/#5/#17/#18
forward 5'11" 185 L
b. Toronto, Ontario, February 10, 1912
d. Toronto, Ontario, September 26, 1996
Marlboros graduate
Signed October 29, 1934.
Retired after 1945–46 season.

1934–35 F	5	0	0	0	6
1935–36	35	4	4	8	32
1936–37	46	8	7	15	43
1937–38	48	3	17	20	52
1938–39	47	4	10	14	29
1939–40	48	8	18	26	56
1940–41	37	3	6	9	39
1941–42	37	6	20	26	39
1942–43	50	13	23	36	20
1943–44	47	19	28	47	21
1944–45	50	17	18	35	49
1945–46 L	41	9	9	18	12
Totals	491	94	160	254	398

F January 1, 1935 L February 27, 1946
• After retirement, became a scout for the Leafs for 40 years.

KIM DAVIS #18
centre 5'11" 170 L
b. Flin Flon, Manitoba, October 31, 1957
Acquired with Paul Marshall from Pittsburgh for Dave Burrows and Paul Gardner, November 18, 1980.

1980–81 L	2	0	0	0	4

L November 29, 1980

BOB DAWES #21/#23/#25
defence 6'1" 170 L
b. Saskatoon, Saskatchewan, November 29, 1924
d. May 26, 2003
Traded to Cleveland (AHL) with Phil Samis, Eric Pogue, the rights to Bob Shropshire, and $40,000 for Al Rollins, November 30, 1949.

1946–47 F	1	0	0	0	0
1948–49	5	1	0	1	0
1949–50	11	1	2	3	2
Totals	17	2	2	4	2

F March 23, 1947

CLARENCE "HAP"/"HAPPY" DAY #4/#3
left wing/defence 5'11 175 L
b. Owen Sound, Ontario, June 14, 1901
d. St. Thomas, Ontario, February 17, 1990
Signed by St. Pats, December 10, 1924, while at University of Toronto.
Traded to New York Americans for Wally Stanowski, September 24, 1937.

1924–25 F	26	10	12	22	33
1925–26	36	14	2	16	26
1926–27	44	11	5	16	50
1927–28	22	9	8	17	48
1928–29	44	6	6	12	84
1929–30	43	7	14	21	77
1930–31	44	1	13	14	56
1931–32	47	7	8	15	33
1932–33	47	6	14	20	46
1933–34	48	9	10	19	35
1934–35	45	2	4	6	38
1935–36	44	1	13	14	41
1936–37	48	3	4	7	20
Totals	538	86	113	199	587

F December 13, 1924
• Played left wing for 1924–25 and half of 1925–26, and missed much of 1927–28 with severe Achilles tendon cut sustained February 2, 1928, vs. Montreal.
• Became coach of the team in 1940 for 10 years, then GM until 1957.
• Retired to St. Marys, Ontario, where he became a leading maker of wooden axe handles.
• Hockey Hall of Fame 1961

LUCIEN DeBLOIS #27
left wing 5'11" 200 R
b. Joliette, Quebec, June 21, 1957
Acquired with Michel Petit and Aaron Broten from Quebec for Scott Pearson, a second-round draft choice in 1991 (later traded to Washington—Éric Lavigne), and a second-round choice in 1992 (Tuomas Gronman), November 17, 1990.
Traded to Winnipeg for Mark Osborne, March 10, 1992.

1990–91	38	10	12	22	30
1991–92	54	8	11	19	39
Totals	92	18	23	41	69

DALE DeGRAY ("Digger") #3
defence 6' 200 R
b. Oshawa, Ontario, September 1, 1963
Acquired from Calgary for a fifth-round draft choice in 1988 (Scott Matusovich), October 1987.
Claimed by Los Angeles in Waiver Draft, October 3, 1988.

1987–88	56	6	18	24	63

ALBERT "AB" DeMARCO #17
centre 6' 168 R
b. North Bay, Ontario, May 10, 1916
d. North Bay, Ontario, May 25, 1989
Acquired with Buck Jones from Providence (AHL) for Bucko McDonald, George Boothman, and Jack Forsey, February 2, 1943.
Injured shoulder after just four games and demoted.

1942–43	4	0	1	1	0

• Only Leaf games February 4, 6, 7, & 21, 1943.

NATHAN DEMPSEY ("Greyhound") #43
forward 6' 184 R
b. Spruce Grove, Alberta, July 14, 1974
Selected 245th overall in 1992 Entry Draft.
Signed as a free agent by Chicago, July 12, 2002.

1996–97 F	14	1	1	2	2
1999–2000	6	0	2	2	2
2000–01	25	1	9	10	4
2001–02	3	0	0	0	0
Totals	48	2	12	14	8

F January 31, 1997

CORB "FLASH" DENNENAY (also DENNENY) #5
left wing 5'8" 142 L
b. Cornwall, Ontario, January 25, 1894
d. Toronto, Ontario, January 16, 1963
Joined Arenas (NHA) in 1916 after Toronto Shamrocks (NHA) folded; traded to Vancouver (PCHA) for Jack Adams, December 1922.
Returned to Toronto the following year; traded to Hamilton with Ken Randall for Bert Corbeau and Amos Arbour, 1923.
Purchased in 1926 from Saskatoon (Prairie Hockey League) with Léo Bourgault and Laurie Scott. Legal problems with contract forced him back to Saskatoon during 1926–27 season.

1917–18	21	20	—	20	8
1918–19	16	7	3	10	15
1919–20	23	23	12	35	18
1920–21	20	17	6	23	27
1921–22	24	19	7	26	28
1922–23	1	1	0	1	0
1926–27	29	7	1	8	24
Totals	134	94	29	123	120

• Only game of 1922–23 season on December 16, 1922.

GERRY DENIORD #10
forward 5'10" 170 R
b. Toronto, Ontario, August 4, 1902
d. Toronto, Ontario, October 8, 1989
Signed from Aura Lee juniors.
Reinstated as an amateur, summer 1925.

1922–23 F/L	15	0	0	0	0

F December 16, 1922 L March 5, 1923

BILL DERLAGO ("Billy D") #19
centre 5'10" 195 R
b. Birtle, Manitoba, August 25, 1958
Acquired with Rick Vaive from Vancouver for Tiger Williams and Jerry Butler, February 18, 1980.
Traded to Boston for Tom Fergus, October 11, 1985.

1979–80	23	5	12	17	13
1980–81	80	35	39	74	26
1981–82	75	34	50	84	42
1982–83	58	13	24	37	27
1983–84	79	40	20	60	50
1984–85	62	31	31	62	21
1985–86	1	0	0	0	0
Totals	378	158	176	334	179

• Became a car salesman, along with Brad Selwood, at Al Palladini Motors in Toronto.

JAMIE DEVANE #59
left wing 6'5" 215 L
b. Mississauga, Ontario, February 20, 1991
Selected 65th overall in 2009 Entry Draft.

2013–14 F	2	0	0	0	0

F October 5, 2013

ANDRE DEVEAUX #56
centre 6'3" 240 R
b. Freeport, Bahamas, February 23, 1984
Signed as a free agent, August 1, 2008.
Signed as a free agent by New York Rangers, August 16, 2011.

2008–09	21	0	1	1	75
2009–10	1	0	0	0	0
Totals	22	0	1	1	75

BOYD DEVEREAUX #22
centre 6'2" 195 L
b. Seaforth, Ontario, April 16, 1978
Signed as a free agent, October 7, 2006.
Played in Switzerland in 2009–10.

2006–07	33	8	11	19	12
2007–08	62	7	11	18	24
2008–09	23	6	5	11	2
Totals	118	21	27	48	38

ERNIE DICKENS #16/#23
defence 6' 175 L
b. Winnipeg, Manitoba, June 25, 1921
d. September 27, 1985
Marlboros graduate
Signed by Leafs May 11, 1941; recalled from Pittsburgh (AHL), November 16, 1945. Traded with Bud Poile, Gaye Stewart, Bob Goldham, and Gus Bodnar to Chicago for Max Bentley and Cy Thomas, November 2, 1947.

1941–42 F	10	2	2	4	6
1945–46	15	1	3	4	6
Totals	25	3	5	8	12

F February 7, 1942
• Missed 1942–45 while serving in the Royal Canadian Air Force.

GERALD DIDUCK ("Dids") #2
defence 6'1" 215 R
b. Edmonton, Alberta, April 6, 1965
Signed as a free agent, February 3, 2000. Traded to Dallas for future considerations, October 29, 2000.

1999–2000	26	0	3	3	33

PAUL DiPIETRO ("Rocky") #25
centre 5'9" 189 R
b. Sault Ste. Marie, Ontario, September 8, 1970
Acquired from Montreal for a fourth-round draft choice in 1996 (Kim Staal), April 6, 1995. Signed as a free agent by Los Angeles, July 23, 1996.

1994–95	12	1	1	2	6
1995–96	20	4	4	8	4
Totals	32	5	5	10	10

TAHIR "TIE" DOMI ("The Albanian Assassin"/"Tugger") #40/#28/#8
right wing 5'10" 200 R
b. Windsor, Ontario, November 1, 1969
Selected 27th overall in 1988 Entry Draft; traded with Mark LaForest to New York Rangers for Greg Johnston, June 29, 1990. Acquired from Winnipeg for Mike Eastwood and a third-round draft choice in 1995 (Brad Isbister), April 7, 1995.

1989–90 F	2	0	0	0	42
1994–95	9	0	1	1	31
1995–96	72	7	6	13	297
1996–97	80	11	17	28	275
1997–98	80	4	10	14	365
1998–99	72	8	14	22	198
1999–2000	70	5	9	14	198
2000–01	82	13	7	20	214
2001–02	74	9	10	19	157
2002–03	79	15	14	29	171
2003–04	80	7	13	20	208
2005–06 L	77	5	11	16	109
Totals	777	84	112	196	2,265

F March 2, 1990 **L** April 18, 2006

KEN DORATY ("Cagey") #15
forward 5'7" 128 R
b. Stittsville, Ontario, June 23, 1906
d. Moose Jaw, Saskatchewan, May 4, 1981
Recalled from Syracuse to replace injured Ace Bailey, December 1932; loaned to Buffalo (IHL), December 4, 1933. Sold to Cleveland (AHL) for $2,000, December 1, 1935.

1932–33	38	5	11	16	16
1933–34	34	9	10	19	6
1934–35	11	1	4	5	0
Totals	83	15	25	40	22

• Lightest player ever in the NHL.

JIM DOREY ("Flipper") #8
defence 6'1" 190 L
b. Kingston, Ontario, August 17, 1947
Selected 23rd overall in 1964 Amateur Draft. Traded to New York Rangers for Pierre Jarry, February 20, 1972.

1968–69 F	61	8	22	30	200
1969–70	46	6	11	17	99
1970–71	74	7	22	29	198
1971–72	50	4	19	23	56
Totals	231	25	74	99	553

F October 13, 1968
• Worked at an insurance company in Kingston for 20 years after retiring from hockey.

KENT DOUGLAS #19
defence 5'10" 189 L
b. Cobalt, Ontario, February 6, 1936
d. Wasaga Beach, Ontario, April 12, 2007
Acquired from Springfield (AHL) for Roger Côté, Bill White, Jim Wilcox, Wally Boyer, and Dick Mattiussi, June 7, 1962. Claimed by Oakland in Expansion Draft, June 6, 1967.

1962–63 F	70	7	15	22	105
1963–64	43	0	1	1	29
1964–65	67	5	23	28	129
1965–66	64	6	14	20	97
1966–67	39	2	12	14	48
Totals	283	20	65	85	408

F October 10, 1962
• Enjoyed careers in both real estate and as a golf pro in the Baltimore area after retiring.

BRUCE DOWIE #1
goalie 5'10" 170 L
b. Oakville, Ontario, December 9, 1962
Signed as a free agent May 6, 1983

1983–84 F/L	2	0–1–0	72	4	0	3.33	

F March 17, 1984 **L** April 1, 1984

DAVE DOWNIE #17
centre 5'7" 168 R
b. Burks Falls, Ontario, March 11, 1909
d. Tacoma, Washington, March 18, 1963
Signed as a free agent February 12, 1933.

1932–33 F/L	11	0	1	1	2

F March 17, 1984 **L** April 1, 1984

BRUCE DRAPER #17
forward 5'10" 157 R
b. Toronto, Ontario, October 2, 1940
d. Ottawa, Ontario, January 26, 1968
St. Mike's graduate 1961 (won Memorial Cup)

1962–63 F/L	1	0	0	0	0

F/L March 3, 1963
• Career minor leaguer: played 1961–62 with Rochester (AHL) and most of 1962–63 with Rochester and Sudbury Wolves (EPHL), 1963–64 with Denver (WHL), 1964–67 with Hershey (AHL).
• Retired after 1966–67 season due to illness (leukemia) and passed away a short time later.

GORD DRILLON ("Lefty") #12/#21
left wing 6'2" 178 L
b. Moncton, New Brunswick, October 23, 1914
d. Saint John, New Brunswick, September 23, 1986
Signed April 13, 1936. Sold to Montreal, October 4, 1942.

1936–37 F	41	16	17	33	2
1937–38	48	26	26	52	4
1938–39	40	18	16	34	15
1939–40	43	21	19	40	13
1940–41	42	23	21	44	2
1941–42	48	23	18	41	6
Totals	262	127	117	244	42

F November 26, 1936
• Missed part of 1940–41 with shoulder injury.
• Hockey Hall of Fame 1975

HAROLD DRUKEN #18/#23
centre 6' 200 L
b. St. John's, Newfoundland, January 26, 1979
Claimed off waivers from Carolina, December 11, 2002; claimed off waivers by Carolina, January 17, 2003. Acquired from Carolina for Allan Rourke, May 29, 2003; played in the minors and Switzerland after 2004.

2002–03	5	0	2	2	2
2003–04 L	9	0	4	4	2
Totals	14	0	6	6	4

L January 31, 2004

DICK DUFF #9/#17
left wing 5'9" 166 L
b. Kirkland Lake, Ontario, February 18, 1936
St. Mike's graduate
Signed with Leafs September 23, 1955. Traded with Arnie Brown, Bill Collins, Bob Nevin, and Rod Seiling to New York Rangers for Andy Bathgate and Don McKenney, February 22, 1964.

1954–55 F	3	0	0	0	2
1955–56	69	18	19	37	74
1956–57	70	26	14	40	50
1957–58	65	26	23	49	79
1958–59	69	29	24	53	73
1959–60	67	19	22	41	51
1960–61	67	16	17	33	54
1961–62	51	17	20	37	37
1962–63	69	16	19	35	56
1963–64	52	7	10	17	59
Totals	582	174	165	342	535

F March 10, 1955

ART DUNCAN ("Dunc") #4/#11/#3
defence 5'11" 180 R
b. Sault Ste. Marie, Ontario, July 4, 1894
d. Aurora, Ontario, April 13, 1975
Acquired from Detroit Cougars for Bill Brydge, 1927.

1927–28	43	7	5	12	97
1928–29	39	4	4	8	53
1929–30	38	4	5	9	49
1930–31 L	4	0	0	0	0
Totals	124	15	14	29	199

L February 7, 1931

ROCKY DUNDAS #34
right wing 6' 195 R
b. Regina, Saskatchewan, January 30, 1967
Signed as a free agent, October 4, 1989.

1989–90 F/L	5	0	0	0	14

F October 5, 1989 **L** October 17, 1989

JUDGE FRANK DUNLAP #20
forward 6' 185 L
b. Ottawa, Ontario, August 10, 1924
d. Ottawa, Ontario, September 26, 1993
St. Mike's graduate; signed by Leafs November 5, 1943.

1943–44 F/L	5	0	1	1	2

F November 6, 1943 **L** November 20, 1943
• Played only home games while attending law school, and retired after the 1943–44 season (only year in pro hockey) to finish law school.
• Played football for Ottawa Rough Riders (IRFU) and Toronto Argonauts (IRFU), 1945–51.

DAVE DUNN #4
defence 6'2" 200 L
b. Wapella, Saskatchewan, August 19, 1948
Acquired from Vancouver for John Grisdale and Gary Monahan, October 16, 1974. Signed as a free agent by Winnipeg (WHA), June 1, 1976.

1974–75	72	3	11	14	142
1975–76 L	43	0	8	8	84
Totals	115	3	19	22	226

L April 25, 1976

DENIS DUPÉRÉ #17/#15

left wing 6'1" 200 L

b. Jonquière, Quebec, June 21, 1948
Acquired with Jacques Plante and Guy Trottier from the New York Rangers for Tim Horton, May 3, 1970.
Claimed by Washington in Expansion Draft, June 12, 1974.

1970–71 F	20	1	2	3	4
1971–72	77	7	10	17	4
1972–73	61	13	23	36	10
1973–74	34	8	9	17	8
Totals	192	29	44	73	26

F February 10, 1971
• Works for a wholesale sporting goods company based in Kitchener.

JEROME DUPONT ("Jerry"/"J.D.") #2

defence 6'3" 190 L

b. Ottawa, Ontario, February 21, 1962
Acquired with Ken Yaremchuk and a fourth-round draft choice in 1987 (Joe Sacco) from Chicago as compensation for Chicago's signing of free agent Gary Nylund, September 6, 1986.

1986–87 L	13	0	0	0	23

L February 8, 1987

PHILIPPE DUPUIS #11

centre 6' 195 R

b. Laval, Quebec, April 24, 1985
Signed as a free agent, July 6, 2011.
Signed as a free agent by Pittsburgh, July 4, 2012.

2011–12	30	0	0	0	16

VITEZSLAV "SLAVA" DURIS #23/#24

defence 6'1" 185 L

b. Plzen, Czechoslovakia (Czech Republic), January 5, 1954
Signed as a free agent September 25, 1980.

1980–81 F	57	1	12	13	50
1982–83 L	32	2	8	10	12
Totals	89	3	20	23	62

F October 11, 1980 L December 23, 1982
• Career ended after 1982–83 due to a chronic back injury.

CECIL "BABE" DYE #6/#14/#10/#2

right wing 5'8" 180 R

b. Hamilton, Ontario, May 13, 1898
d. Chicago, Illinois, January 2, 1962
Played with Aura Lee juniors in Toronto and signed with NHL St. Pats, December 15, 1919.
Sold to Chicago after the 1925–26 season for $14,000.

1919–20 F	23	11	3	14	10
1920–21	23	33	5	38	32
1921–22	24	31	7	38	39
1922–23	22	26	11	37	19
1923–24	19	16	3	19	23
1924–25	29	38	8	46	41
1925–26	31	18	5	23	26
1930–31 L	6	0	0	0	0
Totals	177	173	42	215	190

F December 23, 1919 L December 9, 1930
• Loaned to Hamilton for 1920–21, but when Corb Dennenay broke his hand in the St. Pats' first game of the year, Dye was recalled and remained with Toronto for the season.
• Came out of retirement to play six games in 1930–31 before retiring permanently.
• Hockey Hall of Fame 1970

DALLAS EAKINS ("Dally") #2

defence 6'2" 195 L

b. Dade City, Florida, February 27, 1967
Signed as a free agent, July 28, 1998.
Signed as a free agent by New York Islanders, August 12, 1999.

1998–99	18	0	2	2	24

ROBBIE EARL #52

left wing 5'11" 195 L

b. Chicago, Illinois, June 2, 1985
Selected 187th overall in 2004 Entry Draft.
Traded to Minnesota for Ryan Hamilton, January 21, 2009.

2007–08	9	0	1	1	0

MIKE EASTWOOD ("Easty") #21/#32

centre 6'3" 205 R

b. Ottawa, Ontario, July 1, 1967
Selected 91st overall in 1987 Entry Draft.
Traded to Winnipeg with a third-round draft choice in 1995 (Brad Isbister) for Tie Domi, April 7, 1995.

1991–92 F	9	0	2	2	4
1992–93	12	1	6	7	21
1993–94	54	8	10	18	28
1994–95	36	5	5	10	32
Totals	111	14	23	37	85

F November 16, 1991

TIM ECCLESTONE #16

right wing 5'10" 195 R

b. Toronto, Ontario, September 24, 1947
Acquired from Detroit for Pierre Jarry, November 29, 1973.
Traded with Willie Brossart to Washington for Rod Seiling, November 2, 1974.

1973–74	46	9	14	23	32
1974–75	5	1	1	2	0
Totals	51	10	15	25	32

• Later ran a restaurant in St. Louis called TJ's.

GARRY "DUKE" EDMUNDSON #25

left wing 6' 173 L

b. Sexsmith, Alberta, May 6, 1932
Acquired from Springfield (AHL) for Frank Roggeveen, summer 1959.

1959–60	39	4	6	10	47
1960–61 L	3	0	0	0	0
Totals	42	4	6	10	47

L December 15, 1960.

DON EDWARDS ("Dart") #30

goalie 5'9" 160 L

b. Hamilton, Ontario, September 28, 1955
Acquired from Calgary for fourth-round draft choice in 1987 (Tim Harris), May 29, 1985.
Released August 11, 1987.

1985–86 L	38	12–23–0	2,009	160	0	4.78

L April 6, 1986
• Both his parents were killed at their home in Hamilton, Ontario, in 1991, and Edwards became active in seeking harsher punishment for killers.

MARV EDWARDS #31

goalie 5'8" 155 L

b. St. Catharines, Ontario, August 15, 1935
Claimed from Pittsburgh in Intra-League Draft, June 11, 1969.
Claimed by Salt Lake (WHL—for parent club California) in Reverse Draft, June 8, 1972.

1969–70	25	10–9–4	1420	77	1	3.25

• Won a gold medal with Canada at the 1959 World Championship.

GERRY EHMAN ("Tex") #8/#17

right wing 6' 190 R

b. Cudworth, Saskatchewan, November 3, 1932
d. March 21, 2006
Claimed off waivers from Detroit, December 1959.
Traded to Oakland for Bryan Hextall and J.P. Parisé, October 3, 1967.

1958–59	36	12	13	25	12
1959–60	69	12	16	28	26
1960–61	14	1	1	2	2
1963–64	4	1	1	2	0
Totals	123	26	31	57	40

• Played October 30 and November 2, 7, & 9, 1963, then sent to minors for the year.
• Became director of scouting for New York Islanders.

DAVE ELLETT ("Roy") #4

defence 6'1" 200 L

b. Cleveland, Ohio, March 30, 1964
Acquired with Paul Fenton from Winnipeg for Ed Olczyk and Mark Osborne, November 10, 1990.
Traded with Doug Gilmour and a third-round draft choice in 1999 (previously acquired from Devils in Andreychuk trade) to New Jersey for Steve Sullivan, Jason Smith, and Alyn McCauley, February 25, 1997.

1990–91	60	8	30	38	69
1991–92	79	18	33	51	95
1992–93	70	6	34	40	46
1993–94	68	7	36	43	42
1994–95	33	5	10	15	26
1995–96	80	3	19	22	59
1996–97	56	4	10	14	34
Totals	446	51	172	223	371

RON ELLIS #6/#8/#11

right wing 5'9" 195 R

b. Lindsay, Ontario, January 8, 1945
Marlboros graduate
Retired just before 1975–76 season; returned September 1977; retired again in 1981.

1963–64 F	1	0	0	0	0
1964–65	62	23	16	39	14
1965–66	70	19	23	42	24
1966–67	67	22	23	45	14
1967–68	74	28	20	48	8
1968–69	72	25	21	46	12
1969–70	76	35	19	54	14
1970–71	78	24	29	53	10
1971–72	78	23	24	47	17
1972–73	78	22	29	51	22
1973–74	70	23	25	48	12
1974–75	79	32	29	61	25
1977–78	80	26	24	50	17
1978–79	63	16	12	28	10
1979–80	59	12	11	23	6
1980–81 L	27	2	3	5	2
Totals	1,034	332	308	640	207

F March 11, 1964 L January 14, 1981
• Won 1964 Memorial Cup with Marlies.
• Later worked for the Hockey Hall of Fame as director of public relations and assistant to the president.

AUTRY "AUT" ERICKSON #24

defence 6' 188 L

b. Lethbridge, Alberta, January 25, 1938
Acquired with Larry Jeffrey, Ed Joyal, Lowell MacDonald, and Marcel Pronovost from Detroit for Andy Bathgate, Billy Harris, and Gary Jarrett, May 20, 1965.
Claimed by Oakland in Expansion Draft, June 6, 1967.
• Appeared as a Leaf only in the 1967 playoffs.
• Became assistant GM with New York Islanders, then became cargo manager with an airline based in Los Angeles.

ANDERS ERIKSSON #44

defence 6'3" 225 L

b. Bollnas, Sweden, January 9, 1975
Signed as a free agent, July 9, 2001.
Signed as a free agent by Columbus, October 10, 2003.

2001–02	34	0	2	2	12
2002–03	4	0	0	0	0
Totals	38	0	2	2	12

TIM ERIXON #33

defence 6'2" 200 L

b. Port Chester, New York, February 24, 1991
Claimed off waivers from Chicago, March 1, 2015.

2014–15	15	1	0	1	6

LEN ESAU #36
defence 6'3" 190 R
b. Meadow Lake, Saskatchewan, June 3, 1968
Selected 86th overall in 1988 Entry Draft.
Traded to Quebec for Ken McRae, July 21, 1992.

1991–92 F	2	0	0	0	0

F November 17, 1991

CHRIS EVANS #26
defence 5'9" 180 L
b. Toronto, Ontario, September 14, 1946
Claimed by St. Louis in Intra-League Draft, June 9, 1970.

1969–70 F	2	0	0	0	0

F December 10, 1969

DARYL EVANS #3
left wing 5'8" 185 L
b. Toronto, Ontario, January 12, 1961
Signed as a free agent, summer 1986.

1986–87 L	2	1	0	1	0

L February 2, 1987

PAUL EVANS #17/#28/#29
centre 5'11" 175 L
b. Peterborough, Ontario, February 24, 1955
Selected 149th overall in 1975 Amateur Draft.

1976–77 F	7	1	1	2	19
1977–78 L	4	0	0	0	2
Totals	11	1	1	2	21

F March 5, 1977 L March 12, 1978

GARNET EXELBY #3/#7
defence 6'1" 215 L
b. Craik, Saskatchewan, August 16, 1981
Acquired from Atlanta with Colin Stuart for Pavel Kubina and Tim Stapleton, July 1, 2009.
Signed as a free agent by Chicago, November 26, 2010.

2009–10	51	1	3	4	73

BILL EZINICKI ("Wild Bill"/"Ezzie"/ "Sweet William") #12/#16/#17
right wing 5'10" 170 R
b. Winnipeg, Manitoba, March 11, 1924
d. Bolton, Massachusetts, October 11, 2012
Acquired from Buffalo (AHL) for Don Webster and George Boothman, October 13, 1944; traded with Vic Lynn to Boston for Léo Boivin, Fern Flaman, Phil Maloney, and Ken Smith, November 15, 1950.
Purchased from Boston, January 28, 1952; traded with Phil Maloney and Hugh Barlow to Vancouver (WHL) for $10,000, December 21, 1954.

1944–45 F	8	1	4	5	17
1945–46	24	4	8	12	29
1946–47	60	17	20	37	93
1947–48	60	11	20	31	97
1948–49	52	13	15	28	145
1949–50	67	10	12	22	144
Totals	271	56	79	135	525

F October 28, 1944
• Played semi-pro hockey and after retiring became club pro at a course just outside Boston.

KELLY FAIRCHILD #40/#7
centre 5'11" 180 L
b. Hibbing, Minnesota, April 9, 1973
Acquired with Dixon Ward, Guy Leveque, and Shayne Toporowski from Los Angeles for Éric Lacroix, Chris Snell, and a fourth-round draft choice in 1996 (Éric Bélanger).
Loaned to Orlando (IHL), February 10, 1997; contract turned over to Orlando, November 18, 1997.

1995–96 F	1	0	1	1	2
1996–97	22	0	2	2	2
Totals	23	0	3	3	4

F March 20, 1996

JEFF FARKAS #39/#19/#20
centre 6' 185 L
b. Amherst, Massachusetts, January 24, 1978
Selected 57th overall in 1997 Entry Draft.
Traded to Vancouver for Josh Holden, June 23, 2002.

2000–01	2	0	0	0	2
2001–02	6	0	2	2	4
Totals	8	0	2	2	6

• First game as a Leaf was a playoff game.

DAVE FARRISH #23/#28
defence 6'1" 195 L
b. Wingham, Ontario, August 1, 1956
Acquired with Terry Martin from Quebec for Reg Thomas, December 13, 1979.
Signed as a free agent by Philadelphia, October 7, 1985.

1979–80	20	1	8	9	30
1980–81	74	2	18	20	90
1982–83	56	4	24	28	38
1983–84 L	59	4	19	23	57
Totals	209	11	69	80	215

L April 1, 1984

ALEX FAULKNER #8
centre 5'8" 165 L
b. Bishop's Falls, Newfoundland, May 21, 1936
Signed as a free agent from Conception Bay Cee Bees (Newfoundland Senior), December 1960.
Claimed by Detroit in Intra-League Draft, June 6, 1962.

1961–62 F	1	0	0	0	0

F December 7, 1961
• First Newfoundlander to play in the NHL.

TED FAUSS #2/#34
defence 6'2" 205 L
b. Clark Mills, New York, June 30, 1961
Signed as a free agent, July 21, 1986.
Signed as a free agent by Hartford, December 2, 1988.

1986–87 F	15	0	1	1	11
1987–88 L	13	0	1	1	4
Totals	28	0	2	2	15

F January 15, 1987 L March 3, 1988

DOUG FAVELL #33
goalie 5'10" 172 L
b. St. Catharines, Ontario, April 5, 1945
Acquired with a first-round draft choice in 1973 (Bob Neely) from Philadelphia for the rights to Bernie Parent and a second-round draft choice in 1973 (Larry Goodenough), July 27, 1973.
Sold to Colorado Rockies, September 15, 1976.

1973–74	32	14-7-9	1,752	79	0	2.71
1974–75	39	12-17-6	2,149	145	1	4.05
1975–76	3	0-2-1	160	15	0	5.63
Totals	74	26-26-16	4,061	239	1	3.53

• Became manager of a car wholesale and importing business based in St. Catharines.

PAUL FENTON #16
left wing 5'11" 180 L
b. Springfield, Massachusetts, December 22, 1959
Acquired with Dave Ellett from Winnipeg for Ed Olczyk and Mark Osborne, November 10, 1990.
Traded with John Kordic to Washington for a fifth-round draft choice in 1991 (Alexei Kudashov), January 24, 1991.

1990–91	30	5	10	15	0

TOM FERGUS ("Fergie") #19
centre 6'3" 210 L
b. Chicago, Illinois, June 16, 1962
Acquired from Boston for Bill Derlago, October 11, 1985.
Sold to Vancouver, December 18, 1991.

1985–86	78	31	42	73	64
1986–87	57	21	28	49	57
1987–88	63	19	31	50	81
1988–89	80	22	45	67	48
1989–90	54	19	26	45	62
1990–91	14	5	4	9	8
1991–92	11	1	3	4	4
Totals	357	118	179	297	324

GEORGE FERGUSON ("Chief") #10
centre 6' 195 R
b. Trenton, Ontario, August 22, 1952
Selected 11th overall in 1972 Amateur Draft.
Traded with Randy Carlyle to Pittsburgh for Dave Burrows, June 4, 1978.

1972–73 F	72	10	13	23	34
1973–74	16	0	4	4	4
1974–75	69	19	30	49	61
1975–76	79	12	32	44	76
1976–77	50	9	15	24	24
1977–78	73	7	16	23	37
Totals	359	57	110	167	236

F October 7, 1972
• Became regional sales manager of a medical equipment manufacturer in Pittsburgh.

JEFF FINGER #4
defence 6'1" 210 R
b. Houghton, Michigan, December 18, 1979
Signed as a free agent, July 1, 2008.

2008–09	66	6	17	23	43
2009–10 L	39	2	8	10	20
Totals	105	8	25	33	63

L April 7, 2010

FRANK FINNIGAN ("Finny"/"Fearless Frank"/"The Shawville Express") #12
right wing 5'8" 178 R
b. Shawville, Quebec, July 9, 1901
d. Shawville, Quebec, December 25, 1991
Purchased from St. Louis Eagles for $8,000, February 13, 1935.
Retired March 28, 1937.

1931–32	47	8	13	21	45
1934–35	11	2	0	2	2
1935–36	48	2	6	8	10
1936–37 L	48	2	7	9	4
Totals	154	14	26	40	61

L March 20, 1937
• Loaned to Leafs by Ottawa for 1931–32 when Ottawa did not ice a team. Returned to Ottawa for 1932–33. His number with Ottawa, 8, was retired when the franchise was revived in the 1990s.

ALVIN FISHER #11
forward 6' 170 R
b. Sault Ste. Marie, Ontario, January 5, 1893
d. Ranger Lake, Ontario, March 1, 1937

1924–25 F/L	9	1	0	1	4

F December 5, 1924 L January 10, 1925

TOM FITZGERALD #12
right wing 6' 190 R
b. Billerica, Massachusetts, August 28, 1968
Signed as a free agent, July 17, 2002.
Signed as a free agent by Boston, July 28, 2004.

2002–03	66	4	13	17	57
2003–04	69	7	10	17	52
Totals	135	11	23	34	109

FERDINAND "FERN" FLAMAN #3/#12
defence 5'10" 190 R
b. Dysart, Saskatchewan, January 25, 1927
d. Westwood, Massachusetts, June 22, 2012
Acquired with Léo Boivin, Phil Maloney, and Ken Smith from Boston for Bill Ezinicki and Vic Lynn, November 15, 1950.
Traded to Boston for Dave Creighton and cash, July 20, 1954.

1950–51	39	2	6	8	64
1951–52	61	0	7	7	110
1952–53	66	2	6	8	110
1953–54	62	0	8	8	84
Totals	228	4	27	31	368

• Coached Northeastern University's hockey team for 20 years.
• Hockey Hall of Fame 1990

BILL "COWBOY" FLETT #19

right wing 6'1" 205 R
b. Vermillion, Alberta, July 21, 1943
d. Edmonton, Alberta, July 12, 1999
Acquired from Philadelphia for Dave Fortier and Randy Osburn, May 27, 1974.
Claimed on waivers by Atlanta, May 20, 1975.

1974–75	77	15	25	40	38

GERRY FOLEY #11

right wing 6' 172 R
b. Ware, Massachusetts, September 22, 1932
Acquired with Bob Bailey from Cleveland (AHL) for Chuck Blair and $30,000, summer 1953.
Claimed with Parker MacDonald by New York Rangers in Intra-League Draft for $30,000, June 5, 1956.

1954–55 F	4	0	0	0	8

F February 26, 1955

MIKE FOLIGNO #15/#71

right wing 6'2" 195 R
b. Sudbury, Ontario, January 29, 1959
Acquired with an eighth-round draft choice in 1991 (Tomas Kucharcik) from Buffalo for Lou Franceschetti and Brian Curran, December 17, 1990.
Traded to Florida for cash, November 5, 1993.

1990–91	37	8	7	15	65
1991–92	33	6	8	14	50
1992–93	55	13	5	18	84
1993–94	4	0	0	0	4
Totals	129	27	20	47	203

• Missed much of 1991–92 with a broken leg.

VERNON "JAKE" FORBES ("Jumping Jakie") #unknown

goalie 5'6" 140 L
b. Toronto, Ontario, July 4, 1897
d. Burlington, Ontario, December 30, 1985
Signed just before game time, February 28, 1920.
Released after 1920–21 season.

1919–20 F	5	1–4–0	300	21	0	4.20
1920–21	20	13–7–0	1,221	78	0	3.83
Totals	25	14–11–0	1,521	99	0	3.91

F February 28, 1920
• Sat out first four games of 1920–21 in contract dispute; signed January 5, 1921.

JACK FORSEY #17

forward 5'11" 175 R
b. Swift Current, Saskatchewan, November 7, 1914
d. Salmon Arm, British Columbia, January 1, 1998
Began 1942–43 with Providence (AHL); recalled December 21, 1942.
Traded with Bucko McDonald and George Boothman to Providence (AHL) for Ab DeMarco and Buck Jones, February 17, 1943.

1942–43 F/L	19	7	9	16	10

F December 22, 1942 L March 14, 1943

DAVE FORTIER #22

defence 5'11" 190 L
b. Sudbury, Ontario, June 17, 1951
Selected 23rd overall in 1971 Amateur Draft.
Traded with Randy Osburn to Philadelphia for Bill Flett, May 27, 1974.

1972–73 F	23	1	4	5	63

F February 14, 1973

ALEX FOSTER #32

centre 6' 200 L
b. Canton, Michigan, August 26, 1984
Signed as a free agent, March 8, 2006.

2007–08 F/L	3	0	0	0	0

F March 18, 2008 L March 22, 2008

JIMMY FOWLER ("The Blonde Bouncer") #3

defence 5'11" 168 L
b. Toronto, Ontario, April 6, 1915
d. Toronto, Ontario, October 17, 1985
Signed October 22, 1935.

1936–37 F	48	7	11	18	22
1937–38	48	10	12	22	8
1938–39 L	39	1	6	7	9
Totals	135	18	29	47	39

F November 5, 1936 L March 19, 1939
• Loaned to New York Americans for 1939–40 season, May 18, 1939. Americans also received option to purchase his contract for $7,500 after that season. Fowler retired, so Conn Smythe sent Murray Armstrong, Chuck Shannon, and Bummer Doran to Americans on the same terms.

LOU FRANCESCHETTI #15

left wing 6' 190 L
b. Toronto, Ontario, March 28, 1958
Acquired from Washington for fifth-round draft choice in 1990 (Mark Ouimet), June 29, 1989.
Traded with Brian Curran to Buffalo for Mike Foligno and an eighth-round draft choice in 1991 (Tomas Kucharcik), December 17, 1990.

1989–90	80	21	15	36	127
1990–91	16	1	1	2	30
Totals	96	22	16	38	157

RON FRANCIS #10

centre 6'3" 200 L
b. Sault Ste. Marie, Ontario, March 1, 1963
Acquired from Carolina for a fourth-round draft choice in 2005 (later traded to Columbus—Jared Boll), March 9, 2004.

2003–04 L	12	3	7	10	0

L May 2, 2004
• Hockey Hall of Fame 2007

CODY FRANSON #4

defence 6'5" 215 R
b. Sicamous, British Columbia, August 8, 1987
Acquired from Nashville with Matt Lombardi for Brett Lebda and Robert Slaney, July 3, 2011.
Traded to Nashville with Mike Santorelli for Brendan Leipsic, Olli Jokinen, and a first-round draft choice in 2015, February 15, 2015.

2011–12	57	5	16	21	22
2012–13	45	4	25	29	8
2013–14	79	5	28	33	30
2014–15	55	6	26	32	26
Totals	236	20	95	115	86

MARK FRASER #45

defence 6'4" 220 L
b. Ottawa, Ontario, September 29, 1986
Acquired from Anaheim for Dale Mitchell, February 27, 2012.
Traded to Edmonton for Teemu Hartikainen and Cameron Abney, January 31, 2014.

2012–13	45	0	8	8	85
2013–14	19	0	1	1	33
Totals	64	0	9	9	118

MATT FRATTIN #39

right wing 6' 205 R
b. Edmonton, Alberta, January 3, 1988
Selected 99th overall in 2007 Entry Draft.
Traded to Los Angeles with Ben Scrivens and a second-round draft choice in 2015 for Jonathan Bernier, June 23, 2013.
Acquired from Columbus for Jerry D'Amigo and a conditional draft pick, July 1, 2014.

2010–11	1	0	0	0	0
2011–12	56	8	7	15	25
2012–13	25	7	6	13	4
2014–15	9	0	0	0	4
Totals	91	15	13	28	33

JONAS FROGREN #24

defence 6'1" 190 L
b. Falun, Sweden, August 28, 1980
Signed as a free agent, July 4, 2008.

2008–09 L	41	1	6	7	28

L March 7, 2009
• Later played in Europe.

MIROSLAV FRYCER ("Mirko") #14

right wing 6' 200 R
b. Ostrava, Czechoslovakia (Czech Republic), September 27, 1959
Acquired with a seventh-round draft choice in 1982 (Jeff Triano) from Quebec for Wilf Paiement, March 9, 1982.
Traded to Detroit for Darren Veitch, June 10, 1988.

1981–82	10	4	6	10	31
1982–83	67	25	30	55	90
1983–84	47	10	16	26	55
1984–85	65	25	30	55	55
1985–86	73	32	43	75	74
1986–87	29	7	8	15	28
1987–88	38	12	20	32	41
Totals	329	115	153	268	374

GRANT FUHR ("Fuhrsie") #31

goalie 5'10" 186 R
b. Spruce Grove, Alberta, September 28, 1962
Acquired with Glenn Anderson and Craig Berube from Edmonton for Vincent Damphousse, Peter Ing, Scott Thornton, and Luke Richardson, September 19, 1991.
Traded with a fifth-round draft choice in 1995 (Kevin Popp) to Buffalo for Dave Andreychuk, Daren Puppa, and a first-round draft choice in 1993 (Kenny Jonsson), February 2, 1993.

1991–92	66	25–33–5	3,774	230	2	3.66
1992–93	29	13–9–4	1,665	87	1	3.14
Totals	95	38–42–9	5,439	317	3	3.50

• Hockey Hall of Fame 2003

PAUL GAGNÉ #18/#41

left wing 5'10" 180 L
b. Iroquois Falls, Ontario, February 6, 1962
Signed as a free agent July 28, 1988.
Traded with Jack Capuano and Derek Laxdal to New York Islanders for Gilles Thibaudeau and Mike Stevens, December 20, 1989.

1988–89	16	3	2	5	6

DAVE GAGNER #15

centre 5'10" 180 L
b. Chatham, Ontario, December 11, 1964
Acquired with a sixth-round draft choice in 1996 (Dmitri Yakushin) from Dallas for Benoît Hogue and Randy Wood, January 28, 1996.
Traded to Calgary for a third-round draft choice in 1996 (Mike Lankshear), June 22, 1996.

1995–96	28	7	15	22	59

• Later entered a business venture with an artificial ice company.

SIMON GAMACHE #39

left wing 5'10" 185 L
b. Thetford Mines, Quebec, January 3, 1981
Signed as a free agent, June 25, 2007.

2007–08 L	11	2	2	4	6

L November 3, 2007
• Later played in Europe.

BRUCE GAMBLE ("Paladin"/"Smiley Bates"/"Smiley") #1/#30

goalie 5'9" 200 L
b. Port Arthur, Ontario, May 24, 1938
d. Niagara Falls, Ontario, December 30, 1982
Acquired from Springfield (AHL) for Larry Johnston and Bill Smith, September 1965.
Traded with Mike Walton and the Leafs' first-round choice in 1971 (Pierre Plante) to Philadelphia for Bernie Parent and Philadelphia's second-round choice in 1971 (Rick Kehoe), February 1, 1971.

1965–66	10	5–2–3	501	21	4	2.51
1966–67	23	5–10–4	1,185	67	0	3.39
1967–68	41	19–13–3	2,201	85	5	2.32
1968–69	61	28–20–11	3,446	161	3	2.80
1969–70	52	19–24–9	3,057	156	5	3.06
1970–71	23	6–14–1	1,286	83	2	3.87
Totals	210	82–83–31	11,676	573	19	2.94

DICK GAMBLE #9

left wing 6' 178 L

b. Moncton, New Brunswick, November 16, 1928

Acquired from Buffalo (AHL) for Dave Creighton, June 1961.

1965–66 F	2	1	0	1	0
1966–67 L	1	0	0	0	0
Totals	3	1	0	1	0

F March 5, 1966 L February 1, 1967

• Played most of 1961–69 with Rochester, becoming player/coach in 1968–69; retired as a player the next year.

JAKE GARDINER #51

defence 6'2" 185 L

b. Minnetonka, Minnesota, July 4, 1990

Acquired from Anaheim with Joffrey Lupul and a fourth-round draft choice in 2013 (later traded to Chicago and San Jose—Fredrik Bergvik) for François Beauchemin, February 9, 2011.

2011–12	75	7	23	30	18
2012–13	12	0	4	4	0
2013–14	80	10	21	31	19
2014–15	79	4	20	24	24
Totals	246	21	68	89	61

CAL GARDNER ("Ginger"/"Red"/ "Torchy"/"Pearly") #17

centre 6'1" 175 L

b. Transcona, Manitoba, October 30, 1924

d. Toronto, Ontario, October 10, 2001

Acquired with Bill Juzda, René Trudell, Frankie Mathers, and the rights to Ray McMurray from the New York Rangers for Wally Stanowski, Moe Morris, and the rights to Orval Lavell, April 26, 1948.

Traded with Ray Hannigan, Gus Mortson, and Al Rollins to Chicago for Harry Lumley, September 11, 1952.

1948–49	53	13	22	35	35
1949–50	30	7	19	26	12
1950–51	66	23	28	51	42
1951–52	70	15	26	41	40
Totals	219	58	95	153	129

• Worked in radio in Toronto, first as an analyst, then as an ad salesman.

PAUL GARDNER #18

centre 6' 195 L

b. Fort Erie, Ontario, March 5, 1956

Acquired from Colorado Rockies for Don Ashby and Trevor Johansen, March 13, 1979. Traded with Dave Burrows to Pittsburgh for Kim Davis and Paul Marshall, November 18, 1980.

1978–79	11	7	2	9	0
1979–80	45	11	13	24	10
Totals	56	18	15	33	10

RAY GARIEPY ("Rockabye Ray") #2

defence 5'8" 180 L

b. Toronto, Ontario, September 4, 1928

d. Barrie, Ontario, March 16, 2012

Acquired from Boston for Syracuse goalie John Henderson, September 28, 1954. Purchased by Hershey (AHL) with Gil Mayer, Jack Price, Willie Marshall, Bob Hassard, and Bob Solinger when Pittsburgh (AHL) folded, June 7, 1956.

1955–56 L	1	0	0	0	4

L January 29, 1956

SCOTT GARLAND #25

centre 6'1" 185 R

b. Regina, Saskatchewan, May 16, 1952

d. Montreal, Quebec, June 9, 1979

Signed as a free agent, autumn 1973. Traded with Brian Glennie, Kurt Walker, and the Leafs' second-round choice in 1979 (Mark Hardy) to Los Angeles for Dave Hutchison and Lorne Stamler, June 14, 1978.

1975–76 F	16	4	3	7	8
1976–77	69	9	20	29	83
Totals	85	13	23	36	91

F January 11, 1976

MIKE GARTNER ("Garts") #11

right wing 6' 190 R

b. Ottawa, Ontario, October 29, 1959

Acquired from the New York Rangers for Glenn Anderson, Scott Malone, and a fourth-round draft choice in 1994 (Alexander Korobolin), March 21, 1994.

Traded to Phoenix for a fourth-round draft choice in 1996 (Vladimir Antipov), June 22, 1996.

1993–94	10	6	6	12	4
1994–95	38	12	8	20	6
1995–96	82	35	19	54	52
Totals	130	53	33	86	62

• Later became active in the NHLPA with programs aimed at helping kids around the world receive hockey equipment.

• Hockey Hall of Fame 2001

AARON GAVEY #10

centre 6'2" 190L

b. Sudbury, Ontario, February 22, 1974

Signed as a free agent, July 24, 2002. Signed as a free agent by Anaheim, September 12, 2005.

2002–03	5	0	1	1	0

STEWART "STU" GAVIN #9/#17

forward 6' 190 L

b. Ottawa, Ontario, March 15, 1960

Selected 74th overall in 1980 Entry Draft. Traded to Hartford for Chris Kotsopoulos, October 7, 1985.

1980–81 F	14	1	2	3	13
1981–82	38	5	6	11	29
1982–83	63	6	5	11	44
1983–84	80	10	22	32	90
1984–85	73	12	13	25	38
Totals	268	34	48	82	214

F October 11, 1980

• Worked for a financial services company in Toronto.

EDDIE GERARD #unknown

forward 5'9" 168 L

b. Ottawa, Ontario, February 22, 1890

d. Ottawa, Ontario, August 7, 1937

• Appeared for St. Pats only in the 1922 playoffs.

• Played NHL finals with Ottawa, then joined St. Pats after elimination, playing March 25, 1922, vs. Vancouver (PCHA) to replace injured Harry Cameron.

• Hockey Hall of Fame 1945

MARTIN GERBER #29

goalie 5'11" 200 L

b. Burgdorf, Switzerland, September 3, 1974

Claimed off waivers from Ottawa, March 4, 2009.

Signed as a free agent by Edmonton, August 6, 2010.

2008–09	12	6–5–0	706	38	0	3.23

JOHN GIBSON #23

defence 6'3" 210 L

b. St. Catharines, Ontario, June 2, 1959

Acquired with Billy Harris from Los Angeles for Ian Turnbull, November 11, 1981. Signed as a free agent by Winnipeg, September 19, 1983.

1981–82	27	0	2	2	67

JEAN-SÉBASTIEN (J-S) GIGUÈRE #35

goalie 6'1" 200 L

b. Montreal, Quebec, May 16, 1977

Acquired from Anaheim for Vesa Toskala and Jason Blake, January 31, 2010. Signed as a free agent by Colorado, July 1, 2011.

2009–10	15	6–7–2	915	38	2	2.49
2010–11	33	11–11–4	1,633	78	0	2.87
Totals	48	17–18–6	2,548	116	2	2.73

HAL GILL #25

defence 6'7" 245 L

b. Concord, Massachusetts, April 6, 1975

Signed as a free agent, July 1, 2006. Traded to Pittsburgh for a second-round draft choice in 2008 (Jimmy Hayes) and a fifth-round draft choice in 2009 (later traded to New York Rangers and then back to Pittsburgh—Andy Bathgate), February 26, 2008.

2006–07	82	6	14	20	91
2007–08	63	2	18	20	52
Totals	145	8	32	40	143

TODD GILL ("Giller") #23/#29/#11/#3

defence 6' 185 L

b. Brockville, Ontario, November 9, 1965

Selected 25th overall in 1984 Entry Draft. Traded to San Jose for Jamie Baker and a fifth-round draft choice in 1996 (Peter Cava), June 14, 1996.

1984–85 F	10	1	0	1	13
1985–86	15	1	2	3	28
1986–87	61	4	27	31	92
1987–88	65	8	17	25	131
1988–89	59	11	14	25	72
1989–90	48	1	14	15	92
1990–91	72	2	22	24	113
1991–92	74	2	15	17	91
1992–93	69	11	32	43	66
1993–94	45	4	24	28	44
1994–95	47	7	25	32	64
1995–96	74	7	18	25	116
Totals	639	59	210	269	922

F February 9, 1985

• Played left wing for 39 games in 1988–89.

DOUG GILMOUR ("Killer") #93

centre 5'11" 170 L

b. Kingston, Ontario, June 25, 1963

Acquired with Jamie Macoun, Ric Nattress, Rick Wamsley, and Kent Manderville from Calgary for Gary Leeman, Michel Petit, Jeff Reese, Craig Berube, and Alexander Godynyuk, January 2, 1992; traded with Dave Ellett and a third-round draft choice in 1999 (previously acquired from New Jersey in Andreychuk trade) to New Jersey for Steve Sullivan, Jason Smith, and Alyn McCauley, February 25, 1997.

Acquired from Montreal, for a sixth-round draft choice in 2003 (Mark Flood), March 11, 2003.

1991–92	40	15	34	49	32
1992–93	83	32	95	127	100
1993–94	83	27	84	111	105
1994–95	44	10	23	33	26
1995–96	81	32	40	72	77
1996–97	61	15	45	60	46
2002–03 L	1	0	0	0	0
Totals	393	131	321	452	386

L March 13, 2003 (suffered career-ending knee injury in first game after trade to Toronto)

• Hockey Hall of Fame 2011

GASTON GINGRAS #11

defence 6' 190 L

b. Temiscamingue, Quebec, February 13, 1959

Acquired from Montreal for second-round draft choice in 1985 or 1986 (Montreal chose 1986—Benoit Brunet)

Traded to Montreal for Larry Landon, February 14, 1985.

1982–83	45	10	18	28	10
1983–84	59	7	20	27	16
1984–85	5	0	2	2	0
Totals	109	17	40	57	26

KEN GIRARD #27

right wing 6' 184 R
b. Toronto, Ontario, December 8, 1936
Marlboros graduate

1956–57 F	3	0	1	1	2
1957–58	3	0	0	0	0
1959–60 L	1	0	0	0	0
Totals	7	0	1	1	2

F November 29, 1956 L January 14, 1960

TIM GLEASON #8

defence 6' 215 L
b. Clawson, Michigan, January 29, 1983
Acquired from Carolina for John-Michael Liles and Dennis Robertson, January 1, 2014. Signed as a free agent by Carolina, July 3, 2014.

2013–14	39	1	4	5	55

BRIAN GLENNIE ("Blunt") #24

defence 6'1" 200 L
b. Toronto, Ontario, August 29, 1946
Marlboros graduate, 1967
Traded with Scott Garland, Kurt Walker, and the Leafs' second-round choice in 1979 (Mark Hardy) to Los Angeles for Dave Hutchison and Lorne Stamler, June 14, 1978.

1969–70 F	52	1	14	15	50
1970–71	54	0	8	8	31
1971–72	61	2	8	10	44
1972–73	44	1	10	11	54
1973–74	65	4	18	22	100
1974–75	63	1	7	8	110
1975–76	69	0	8	8	75
1976–77	69	1	10	11	73
1977–78	77	2	15	17	62
Totals	554	12	98	110	599

F October 11, 1969
• Played 1967–68 with the Canadian National Team, winning a bronze medal at the 1968 Olympics.

ERNIE GODDEN #18

centre 5'7" 154 L
b. Keswick, Ontario, March 13, 1961
Selected 55th overall in 1981 Entry Draft.

1981–82 F/L	5	1	1	2	6

F November 28, 1981 L December 12, 1981

ALEXANDER GODYNYUK #93

defence 6' 207 L
b. Kiev, Soviet Union (Russia), January 27, 1970
Selected 115th overall in 1990 Entry Draft. Traded with Gary Leeman, Michel Petit, Jeff Reese, and Craig Berube to Calgary for Doug Gilmour, Jamie Macoun, Ric Nattress, Rick Wamsley, and Kent Manderville, January 2, 1992.

1990–91 F	18	0	3	3	16
1991–92	39	3	6	9	59
Totals	57	3	9	12	75

F February 6, 1991

BOB GOLDHAM ("Golden Boy," "Mark I") #2/#14/#17

defence 6'1" 195 R
b. Georgetown, Ontario, May 12, 1922
d. Toronto, Ontario, September 6, 1991
Marlboros graduate
Traded with Bud Poile, Gaye Stewart, Gus Bodnar, and Ernie Dickens to Chicago for Max Bentley and Cy Thomas, November 2, 1947.

1941–42 F	19	4	7	11	25
1945–46	49	7	14	21	44
1946–47	11	1	1	2	10
Totals	79	12	22	34	79

F January 27, 1942
• Missed 1942–45 while serving in the Royal Canadian Navy; also missed most of 1946–47 with broken arm.
• Became popular intermission analyst with *Hockey Night in Canada* throughout the 1970s.

HANK GOLDUP #20/#23

left wing 5'11" 175 L
b. Kingston, Ontario, October 29, 1918
d. Mississauga, Ontario, December 14, 2008
Played 1938–39 with Toronto Goodyears; signed as a free agent, April 20, 1939. Traded with Dudley "Red" Garrett to New York Rangers for Babe Pratt, November 27, 1942.

1940–41 F	26	10	5	15	9
1941–42	44	12	18	30	13
1942–43	8	1	7	8	4
Totals	78	23	30	53	26

F November 2, 1940 (regular season—played in 1940 playoffs)

ED GORMAN #3

defence 6' 180 L
b. Buckingham, Quebec, September 25, 1892
d. Ottawa, Ontario, March 10, 1963
Purchased from Ottawa Senators, summer 1927.
Demoted to Toronto Ravinas (Can Pro), but refused to go; suspended, then signed with Kitchener (Can Pro), February 13, 1928.

1927–28 F/L	19	0	1	1	30

F November 15, 1927 L January 12, 1928

CHRIS GOVEDARIS #8

left wing 6' 200 L
b. Toronto, Ontario, February 2, 1970
Signed as a free agent from Hartford, September 7, 1993.
Traded to Detroit for Gord Kruppke, February 17, 1995.

1993–94	12	2	2	4	14

MIKHAIL GRABOVSKI #84

centre 5'11" 185 L
b. Potsdam, Germany (East Germany), January 31, 1984
Acquired from Montreal for Greg Pateryn and a second-round draft choice in 2010 (later traded to Montreal, Chicago, back to Toronto, then Boston—Jared Knight), on July 3, 2008.
Signed as a free agent with Washington, August 22, 2013.

2008–09	78	20	28	48	92
2009–10	59	10	25	35	10
2010–11	81	29	29	58	60
2011–12	74	23	28	51	51
2012–13	48	9	7	16	24
Totals	340	91	117	208	237

BOB GRACIE #14

left wing 5'8" 155 L
b. North Bay, Ontario, November 8, 1910
d. Houston, Texas, August 3, 1963
Marlboros graduate
Signed with the Leafs March 2, 1931.
Traded to Ottawa with $12,000 for Hec Kilrea, March 14, 1933.

1930–31 F	7	4	2	6	4
1931–32	48	13	8	21	29
1932–33	48	9	13	22	27
Totals	103	26	23	49	60

F March 3, 1931

PAT GRAHAM #23

left wing 6'1" 190 L
b. Toronto, Ontario, May 25, 1961
Acquired with Nick Ricci from Pittsburgh for Rocky Saganiuk and Vincent Tremblay, August 15, 1983.
Played 1984–85 in West Germany, then signed as a free agent by Adirondack (AHL).

1983–84 L	41	4	4	8	65

L March 28, 1984

PETTER GRANBERG #26

defence 6'3" 200 R
b. Gallivare, Sweden, August 27, 1992
Selected 116th overall in 2010 Entry Draft.

2013–14 F	1	0	0	0	0
2013–14	7	0	0	0	6
Totals	8	0	0	0	6

F April 12, 2014

BENNY GRANT #1/#15/#17/#16

goalie 5'11" 160 L
b. Owen Sound, Ontario, July 14, 1908
d. Owen Sound, Ontario, July 30, 1991
Purchased from London (Can Pro), November 2, 1928.
Signed as a free agent, October 7, 1943.

1928–29 F	3	1–0–0	110	4	0	2.18	
1929–30	2	1–1–0	130	11	0	5.08	
1930–31	7	1–5–1	430	19	2	2.65	
1931–32	5	1–2–1	320	18	1	3.38	
1943–44	20	9–9–2	1,200	83	0	4.15	
Totals	36	13–17–4	2,190	135	3	3.70	

F January 10, 1929
• Loaned to New York Americans for one game, December 19, 1929; to Minneapolis (AHA) for rest of season, January 24, 1930; to Boston (Can-Am) for the season, subject to instant recall, December 27, 1930. Recalled from Syracuse (IHL) because of suspension to Lorne Chabot, February 12, 1932, then loaned to Americans for rest of season while Roy Worters recovered from injury, December 6, 1933.

ALEX GRAY #9

right wing 5'10" 170 R
b. Glasgow, Scotland, June 21, 1899
d. April 10, 1986
Acquired with Lorne Chabot from New York Rangers for Butch Keeling and John Ross Roach, October 17, 1928.
Sold to Toronto Millionaires (Can Pro), November 28, 1928.

1928–29 L	6	0	0	0	2

L November 27, 1928

TRAVIS GREEN #39

centre 6'1" 205 R
b. Castlegar, British Columbia, December 20, 1970
Acquired from Phoenix with Robert Reichel and Craig Mills for Daniil Markov, June 12, 2001; signed as a free agent by Anaheim, August 10, 2006.
Claimed off waivers from Anaheim, January 10, 2007. Later played in Switzerland.

2001–02	82	11	23	34	61
2002–03	75	12	12	24	67
2006–07 L	24	0	0	0	21
Totals	181	23	35	58	149

L March 8, 2007

MARK GREIG #11

right wing 5'11" 190 R
b. High River, Alberta, January 25, 1970
Acquired with a sixth-round draft choice in 1994 (later traded to New York Rangers—Yuri Litvinov) from Hartford for Ted Crowley, January 25, 1994.
Signed as a free agent by Calgary, August 9, 1994.

1993–94	13	2	2	4	10

JOHN GRISDALE ("Gris") #3

defence 6' 195 R
b. Geraldton, Ontario, August 23, 1948
Signed by Leafs at 1971 training camp.
Traded with Gary Monahan to Vancouver for Dave Dunn, October 16, 1974.

1972–73 F	49	1	7	8	76
1974–75	2	0	0	0	4
Totals	51	1	7	8	80

F October 21, 1972
• Played four games with Tulsa in 1970–71 on a tryout contract.

LLOYD GROSS #11

left wing 5'8" 175 L
b. Kitchener, Ontario, October 15, 1907
d. December 11, 1990
Signed March 7, 1927, after playing with Kitchener (OHA Junior) in 1925–26.

1926–27 F	16	1	1	2	0

F March 10, 1927
• Didn't play in NHL again until 1933–34, with New York Americans.

CARL GUNNARSSON #36

defence 6'2" 195 L
b. Orebro, Sweden, November 9, 1986
Selected 194th overall in 2007 Entry Draft.
Traded to St. Louis for Roman Polak and a fourth-round draft choice in 2014 (Ville Husso), June 28, 2014.

2009–10 F	43	3	12	15	10
2010–11	68	4	16	20	14
2011–12	76	4	15	19	20
2012–13	37	1	14	15	14
2013–14	80	3	14	17	34
Totals	304	15	71	86	92

F November 14, 2009

PER GUSTAFSSON ("Gus") #24

defence 6'2" 190 L
b. Osterham, Sweden, June 6, 1970
Acquired from Florida for Mike Lankshear, June 13, 1997.
Traded to Ottawa for an eighth-round draft choice in 1998 (Dwight Wolfe), March 17, 1998.

1997–98	22	1	4	5	10

JONAS GUSTAVSSON #50

goalie 6'3" 190 L
b. Danderyd, Sweden, October 24, 1984
Signed as a free agent, July 7, 2009.
Traded to Winnipeg for future considerations, June 23, 2012.

2009–10 F	42	16–15–9	2,340	112	1	2.87
2010–11	23	6–13–2	1,242	68	0	3.29
2011–12	42	17–17–4	2,301	112	4	2.92
Totals	107	39–45–15	5,883	292	5	2.98

F October 3, 2009

SEAN HAGGERTY #52

left wing 6'1" 186 L
b. Rye, New York, February 11, 1976
Selected 48th overall in 1994 Entry Draft.
Traded with Kenny Jonsson, Darby Hendrickson, and a first-round draft choice in 1997 (Roberto Luongo) to New York Islanders for Wendel Clark, Mathieu Schneider, and Denis Smith, March 13, 1996.

1995–96 F	1	0	0	0	0

F February 22, 1996

NICKLAS HAGMAN #9

left wing 5'10" 205 L
b. Espoo, Finland, December 5, 1979
Signed as a free agent, July 1, 2008
Traded to Calgary with Matt Stajan, Ian White, and Jamal Mayers for Dion Phaneuf, Keith Aulie, and Fredrik Sjostrom, January 31, 2010.

2008–09	65	22	20	42	4
2009–10	55	20	13	33	23
Totals	120	42	33	75	27

GEORGE HAINSWORTH #1

goalie 5'6" 150 L
b. Toronto, Ontario, June 26, 1895
d. Gravenhurst, Ontario, October 9, 1950
Acquired from Montreal for Lorne Chabot, summer 1933, but Chabot retired, nullifying the deal. On October 1, 1933, Chabot agreed to join Montreal, finalizing the trade. Released November 24, 1936.

1933–34	48	26–13–9	3,010	119	3	2.37
1934–35	48	30–14–4	2,957	111	8	2.25
1935–36	48	23–19–6	3,000	106	8	2.12
1936–37	3	0–2–1	190	9	0	2.84
Totals	147	79–48–20	9,157	345	19	2.26

• Hockey Hall of Fame 1961

HALDOR "SLIM" HALDERSON #14

defence 6'3" 200 R
b. Winnipeg, Manitoba, January 6, 1900
d. Winnipeg, Manitoba, August 1, 1965
Acquired from Detroit Cougars for Pete Bellefeuille, January 7, 1927.

1926–27 L	26	1	2	3	36

L March 26, 1927
• Won gold medal with Canada at 1920 Olympics.

BOB HALKIDIS ("Hawk") #33

defence 5'11" 200 L
b. Toronto, Ontario, March 5, 1966
Signed as a free agent July 24, 1991.

1991–92 L	46	3	3	6	145

L March 9, 1992

HERB "HAP" HAMEL #14

forward 5'11" 155 R
b. New Hamburg, Ontario, June 8, 1904
d. Kitchener, Ontario, April 20, 2001
Signed as a free agent, December 8, 1930.

1930–31 F/L	4	0	0	0	4

F December 9, 1930 L December 20, 1930

PIERRE HAMEL #31/#32

goalie 5'9" 170 L
b. Montreal, Quebec, September 16, 1952
Signed as a free agent at 1974 training camp.
Claimed by Winnipeg in Expansion Draft, June 13, 1979.

1974–75 F	4	1–2–0	195	18	0	5.54
1978–79	1	0–0–0	1	0	0	0.00
Totals	5	1–2–0	196	18	0	5.51

F November 15, 1974

JACK HAMILTON ("Gabby") #15/#19/#22/#17

centre 5'7 170 L
b. Trenton, Ontario, June 2, 1925
d. Toronto, Ontario, March 23, 1994
Traded with cash to Providence (AHL) to conclude trade for rights to Dan Lewicki (acquired by Leafs on August 12, 1948), September 10, 1948.

1942–43 F	13	1	6	7	4
1943–44	49	20	17	37	0
1945–46 L	40	7	9	16	12
Totals	102	28	32	60	16

F October 31, 1942 L March 17, 1946
• Missed 1944–45 while serving in the Canadian Armed Forces.

JEFF HAMILTON #51

centre 5'10" 185 R
b. Englewood, Ohio, September 4, 1977
Signed as a free agent, March 5, 2009.
Played in Europe after 2008–09.

2008–09 L	15	3	3	6	4

L April 7, 2009

REG HAMILTON #3/#5/#20/#22

defence 5'11" 180 L
b. Toronto, Ontario, April 29, 1914
d. Mississauga, Ontario, June 12, 1991
St. Mike's graduate, 1934
Traded to Chicago for future considerations, July 9, 1945.

1935–36 F	7	0	0	0	0
1936–37	39	3	7	10	32
1937–38	45	1	4	5	43
1938–39	48	0	7	7	54
1939–40	23	2	2	4	23
1940–41	45	3	12	15	59
1941–42	22	0	4	4	27
1942–43	48	4	17	21	68
1943–44	39	4	12	16	32
1944–45	50	3	12	15	41
Totals	366	20	77	97	379

F December 10, 1935
• Missed much of 1941–42 with serious knee injury.

RYAN HAMILTON #48

left wing 6'2" 220 L
b. Oshawa, Ontario, April 15, 1985
Acquired from Minnesota for Robbie Earl, January 21, 2009.
Signed as a free agent by Edmonton, July 5, 2013.

2011–12 F	2	0	1	1	2
2012–13	10	0	2	2	0
Totals	12	0	3	3	2

F March 23, 2012

INGE HAMMARSTROM #11

left wing 6' 180 L
b. Sundsvall, Sweden, January 20, 1948
Signed as a free agent, May 12, 1973.
Traded to St. Louis for Jerry Butler, November 1, 1977.

1973–74 F	66	20	23	43	14
1974–75	69	21	20	41	23
1975–76	76	19	21	40	21
1976–77	78	24	17	41	16
1977–78	3	1	1	2	0
Totals	292	85	82	167	74

F October 10, 1973

KEN HAMMOND #29

defence 6'1" 190 L
b. Port Credit, Ontario, August 22, 1963
Acquired from Denver (IHL) for loan of Chris McRae, January 30, 1989.
Sold to Boston, August 20, 1990.

1988–89	14	0	2	2	12

EDWARD "TED" HAMPSON #14

centre 5'8" 173 L
b. Togo, Saskatchewan, December 11, 1936
Claimed off waivers from New York Rangers for $20,000, September 18, 1959.
Claimed by New York Rangers in Intra-League Draft, June 7, 1960.

1959–60 F	41	2	8	10	17

F October 10, 1959

DAVE HANNAN #9

centre 5'10" 185 L
b. Sudbury, Ontario, November 26, 1961
Claimed from Pittsburgh in Waiver Draft, October 2, 1989.
Traded to Buffalo for a fifth-round draft choice in 1992 (Chris deRuiter), March 10, 1992.

1989–90	39	6	9	15	55
1990–91	74	11	23	34	82
1991–92	35	2	2	4	16
Totals	148	19	34	53	153

GORD HANNIGAN ("Hopalong")
#17/#22/#23
centre 5'7" 163 L
b. Schumacher, Ontario, January 19, 1929
d. Edmonton, Alberta, November 16, 1966
St. Mike's graduate
Acquired by Edmonton (WHL) for 1957–58
season.

1952–53 F	65	17	18	35	51
1953–54	35	4	4	8	18
1954–55	13	0	2	2	8
1955–56 L	48	8	7	15	40
Totals	161	29	31	60	117

F October 11, 1952 **L** March 18, 1956

PAT HANNIGAN #23
right wing 5'10" 190 R
b. Timmins, Ontario, March 5, 1936
St. Mike's graduate
Recalled from Rochester (AHL), December
15, 1959.
Traded with Johnny Wilson to New York
Rangers for Eddie Shack, November 7, 1960.

1959–60 F	1	0	0	0	0

F December 17, 1959
• Later became popular broadcaster of
Buffalo Sabres games.

RAY HANNIGAN #16
forward 5'8" 155 R
b. Schumacher, Ontario, July 14, 1927
St. Mike's graduate
Traded with Cal Gardner, Gus Mortson,
and Al Rollins to Chicago for Harry Lumley,
September 11, 1952.

1948–49 F/L	3	0	0	0	2

F February 26, 1949 **L** March 13, 1949

CHRISTIAN HANSON #20
centre 6'4" 230 R
b. Glens Falls, New York, March 10, 1986
Signed as a free agent, March 31, 2009.
Signed as a free agent by Boston, July 9,
2012.

2008–09 F	5	1	1	2	2
2009–10	31	2	5	7	16
2010–11	6	0	0	0	4
Totals	42	3	6	9	22

F April 3, 2009

DAVID HARLOCK #28/#38
defence 6'2" 205 L
b. Toronto, Ontario, March 16, 1971
Signed as a free agent August 20, 1993.

1993–94 F	6	0	0	0	0
1994–95	1	0	0	0	0
1995–96	1	0	0	0	0
Totals	8	0	0	0	0

F March 9, 1994

BILLY HARRIS ("Hinky") #15
centre 6' 165 L
b. Toronto, Ontario, July 29, 1935
d. Toronto, Ontario, September 20, 2001
Marlboros graduate, 1955 (Memorial Cup
winner)
Signed with Leafs, May 10, 1955.
Traded with Andy Bathgate and Gary Jarrett
to Detroit for Marcel Pronovost, Lowell
MacDonald, Aut Erickson, Larry Jeffrey, and
Ed Joyal, May 20, 1965.

1955–56 F	70	9	13	22	8
1956–57	23	4	6	10	6
1957–58	68	16	28	44	32
1958–59	70	22	30	52	29
1959–60	70	13	25	38	29
1960–61	66	12	27	39	30
1961–62	67	15	10	25	14
1962–63	65	8	24	32	22
1963–64	63	6	12	18	17
1964–65	48	1	6	7	0
Totals	610	106	181	287	187

F October 6, 1955
• An avid photographer, he wrote a book
on the Leafs of the 1960s illustrated with his
own pictures.

BILL HARRIS #16
right wing 6'2" 195 L
b. Toronto, Ontario, January 29, 1952
Acquired with John Gibson from Los Angeles for Ian Turnbull, November 11, 1981.
Rights sold to Los Angeles, February 15, 1984.

1981–82	20	2	0	2	4
1982–83	76	11	19	30	26
1983–84	50	7	10	17	14
Totals	146	20	29	49	44

• Later worked for a marina, first in Toronto,
then on Georgian Bay.

GEORGE "DUKE" HARRIS
("The Duker") #17
right wing 6' 204 R
b. Sarnia, Ontario, February 25, 1942
Purchased from Minnesota North Stars,
December 23, 1967.
Signed with Houston Aeros, summer 1972.

1967–68 L	4	0	0	0	0

L February 14, 1968

JAY HARRISON #43
defence 6'4" 220 L
b. Oshawa, Ontario, November 3, 1982
Selected 82nd overall in 2001 Entry Draft.
Signed as a free agent by Carolina, July 9,
2009.

2005–06 F	8	0	1	1	2
2006–07	5	0	0	0	6
2008–09	7	0	1	1	10
Totals	20	0	2	2	18

F January 28, 2006

JIM HARRISON ("Max") #7/#12
centre 5'11" 185 R
b. Bonnyville, Alberta, July 9, 1947
Acquired from Boston for Wayne Carleton,
December 10, 1969.
Signed with Alberta (WHA), June 21,
1972; NHL rights traded to Chicago for a
second-round draft choice in 1977 (Bob
Gladney), September 28, 1976.

1969–70	31	7	10	17	36
1970–71	78	13	20	33	108
1971–72	66	19	17	36	104
Totals	175	39	47	86	248

PAUL HARRISON #30
goalie 6'1" 175 L
b. Timmins, Ontario, February 11, 1955
Acquired from Minnesota North Stars for a
fourth-round draft choice in 1981 (Terry Tait),
June 14, 1978.
Traded to Pittsburgh for future considerations, September 1981.

1978–79	25	8–12–3	1,403	82	1	3.51
1979–80	30	9–17–2	1,492	110	0	4.42
Totals	55	17–29–5	2,895	192	1	3.98

BOB HASSARD #17/#20/#25
centre 6' 165 R
b. Lloydminster, Saskatchewan, March 26, 1929
d. Stouffville, Ontario, December 30, 2010
Marlboros graduate, 1951
Sold to Chicago for $20000, April 4, 1954.

1949–50 F	1	0	0	0	0
1950–51	12	0	1	1	0
1952–53	70	8	23	31	14
1953–54	26	1	4	5	4
Totals	109	9	28	37	18

F November 19, 1949

TODD HAWKINS #8
forward 6'1" 195 R
b. Kingston, Ontario, August 2, 1966
Acquired from Vancouver for Brian Blad,
January 22, 1991.
Signed as a free agent by Pittsburgh, August
20, 1993.

1991–92	2	0	0	0	0

GLENN HEALY ("Heals") #30
goalie 5'10" 185 L
b. Pickering, Ontario, August 23, 1962
Signed as a free agent, August 8, 1997.
Retired at end of 2000–01 season.

1997–98	21	4–10–2	1,068	53	0	2.98
1998–99	9	6–3–0	546	27	0	2.97
1999–2000	20	9–10–0	1,164	59	2	3.04
2000–01 L	15	4–7–3	871	38	0	2.62
Totals	65	23–30–5	3,649	177	2	2.91

L March 21, 2001

PAUL HEALEY #26
right wing 6'2" 200 R
b. Edmonton, Alberta, March 20, 1975
Signed as a free agent, July 24, 2001.
Signed as a free agent by New York Rangers,
July 28, 2003.

2001–02	21	3	7	10	2
2002–03	44	3	7	10	16
Totals	65	6	14	20	18

SAMMY HEBERT #9
goalie 5'10" 145 R
b. Ottawa, Ontario, March 31, 1894
d. Ottawa, Ontario, July 23, 1965
Signed as a free agent, December 5, 1917.
Loaned to Ottawa, February 17, 1918.

1917–18	2	1–1–0	80	10	0	7.50

• Only Arenas games December 19, 1917, &
January 2, 1918.

PIERRE HEDIN #3
defence 6'2" 200 L
b. Ornskoldsvik, Sweden, February 19, 1978
Selected 239th overall in 1999 Entry Draft.
Returned to Europe at end of season.

2003–04 F/L	3	0	1	1	0

F January 13, 2004 **L** January 17, 2004

FRANK HEFFERNAN ("Moose") #6
forward 6' 200 L
b. Peterborough, Ontario, January 12, 1892
d. New York, New York, December 21, 1938
Signed December 8, 1919.

1919–20 F/L	17	0	0	0	0

F December 23, 1919 **L** March 6, 1920

PAUL HENDERSON #19
left wing 5'11" 180 R
b. Kincardine, Ontario, January 28, 1943
Acquired with Norm Ullman and Floyd
Smith from Detroit for Frank Mahovlich, Pete
Stemkowski, Garry Unger, and the rights to
Carl Brewer, March 3, 1968.
Signed as a free agent by Toronto Toros
(WHA), July 1974.

1967–68	13	5	6	11	8
1968–69	74	27	32	59	16
1969–70	67	20	22	42	18
1970–71	72	30	30	60	34
1971–72	73	38	19	57	32
1972–73	40	18	16	34	18
1973–74	69	24	31	55	40
Totals	408	162	156	318	166

• Scored winning goal in games 6, 7, & 8
of Summit Series, culminating September
28, 1972.
• IIHF Hall of Fame 2013

DARBY HENDRICKSON #37/#16/#14

centre 6' 185 L

b. Richfield, Minnesota, August 28, 1972
Selected 73rd overall in 1990 Entry Draft; traded with Kenny Jonsson, Sean Haggerty, and a first-round draft choice in 1997 (Roberto Luongo) to New York Islanders for Wendel Clark, Mathieu Schneider, and Denis Smith, March 13, 1996.
Acquired from New York Islanders for fifth-round draft choice in 1998 (Jiri Dopita), October 11, 1996; sent immediately to St. John's (AHL) for conditioning; traded to Vancouver for Chris McAllister, February 16, 1999.

1994–95 F	8	0	1	1	4
1995–96	46	6	6	12	47
1996–97	64	11	6	17	47
1997–98	80	8	4	12	67
1998–99	35	2	3	5	30
Totals	233	27	20	47	195

F February 10, 1995 (regular season—also appeared in 1995 playoffs)

JIMMY HERBERT ("Sailor") #7

forward 5'10" 185 R

b. Collingwood, Ontario, October 31, 1897
d. Buffalo, New York, December 5, 1968
Acquired from Boston for $17,500 and the rights to Eric Pettinger, December 22, 1927. Traded to Detroit Cougars for Jack Arbour and $12,500, April 9, 1928.

1927–28	43	15	4	19	64

BOB "RED" HERON #16/#17/#18

centre 5'11" 170 L

b. Toronto, Ontario, December 31, 1917
d. Toronto, Ontario, December 14, 1990
Joined Syracuse (IAHL), March 1938; recalled from Syracuse for playoffs, March 27, 1939. Traded to New York Americans with Nick Knott, Gus Marker, and Peanuts O'Flaherty on a one-year lease, all subject to recall, for Lorne Carr, October 30, 1941.

1938–39 F	6	0	0	0	0
1939–40	42	11	12	23	12
1940–41	35	9	5	14	12
Totals	83	20	17	37	24

F December 24, 1938

JAMIE HEWARD #36/#26

defence 6'2" 207 R

b. Regina, Saskatchewan, March 30, 1971
Signed as a free agent, May 4, 1995.
Signed as a free agent by Philadelphia, July 10, 1997.

1995–96 F	5	0	0	0	0
1996–97	20	1	4	5	6
Totals	25	1	4	5	6

F February 3, 1996

PAT HICKEY ("Hitch") #15/#16

left wing 6'1" 190 L

b. Brantford, Ontario, May 15, 1953
Acquired with Wilf Paiement from Colorado Rockies for Lanny McDonald and Joel Quenneville, December 29, 1979.
Traded to New York Rangers for a fifth-round draft choice in 1982 (Sylvain Charland), October 16, 1981.

1979–80	45	22	16	38	16
1980–81	72	16	33	49	49
1981–82	1	0	0	0	0
Totals	118	38	49	87	65

• Became a GM in the AHL, though had previously and has since been involved in business.

PAUL HIGGINS #17/#29

right wing 6'1" 195 R

b. Saint John, New Brunswick, January 13, 1962
Selected 200th overall in 1980 Entry Draft. Released September 1983.

1981–82 F	3	0	0	0	17
1982–83 L	23	0	0	0	135
Totals	26	0	0	0	152

F February 23, 1982 **L** March 30, 1983
• First player ever drafted into NHL directly from high school.

MEL HILL ("Sudden Death") #8

right wing 5'10" 175 R

b. Glenboro, Manitoba, February 15, 1914
d. Fort Qu'Appelle, Saskatchewan, April 11, 1996
Purchased when Brooklyn Americans folded.

1942–43	49	17	27	44	47
1943–44	17	9	10	19	6
1944–45	45	18	17	35	14
1945–46 L	35	5	7	12	10
Totals	146	49	61	110	77

L February 6, 1946
• Missed most of 1943–44 with broken ankle.

LARRY HILLMAN #2/#16/#22

defence 6' 181 R

b. Kirkland Lake, Ontario, February 5, 1937
Claimed from Boston in Intra-League Draft, June 7, 1960.
Claimed by Minnesota via New York Rangers in Intra-League Draft, June 12, 1968.

1960–61	62	3	10	13	59
1961–62	5	0	0	0	4
1962–63	5	0	0	0	2
1963–64	33	0	4	4	31
1964–65	2	0	0	0	2
1965–66	48	3	25	28	34
1966–67	55	4	19	23	40
1967–68	55	3	17	20	13
Totals	265	13	75	88	185

• Missed most of 1961–62 with serious shoulder injury; played part of year with Rochester (AHL).
• Ran a tourist camp in Englehart, Ontario, and sold real estate.

ANDRÉ HINSE #23

left wing 5'9" 172 L

b. Trois-Rivières, Quebec, April 19, 1945
Signed as a free agent at training camp, 1966; sent to Phoenix (WHL), summer 1969. Acquired from Vancouver for Doug Brindley, fall 1971; signed by Houston (WHA), summer 1973.

1967–68 F/L	4	0	0	0	0

F February 7, 1968 **L** February 14, 1968

DAN HODGSON #16

centre 5'10" 165 R

b. Fort Vermillion, Alberta, August 29, 1965
Selected 85th overall in 1983 Entry Draft.
Traded with Jim Benning to Vancouver for Rick Lanz, December 2, 1986.

1985–86 F	40	13	12	25	12

F October 16, 1985

JONAS HOGLUND ("Hogie") #14

right wing 6'3" 215 R

b. Hamaro, Sweden, August 29, 1972
Signed as a free agent, July 13, 1999.
Signed as a free agent by Florida, September 4, 2003.

1999–2000	82	29	27	56	10
2000–01	82	23	26	49	14
2001–02	82	13	34	47	26
2002–03	79	13	19	32	12
Totals	325	78	106	184	62

BENOÎT HOGUE ("Benny") #28/#32/#33

centre 5'10" 190 L

b. Repentigny, Quebec, October 28, 1966
Acquired with a third-round draft choice in 1995 (Ryan Pepperall) and a fifth-round draft choice in 1996 (Brandon Sugden) from New York Islanders for Éric Fichaud, April 6, 1995. Traded with Randy Wood to Dallas for Dave Gagner and a sixth-round draft choice in 1996 (Dmitri Yakushin), January 28, 1996.

1994–95	12	3	3	6	0
1995–96	44	12	25	37	68
Totals	56	15	28	43	68

JOSH HOLDEN #9

centre 6' 190 L

b. Calgary, Alberta, January 18, 1978
Acquired from Vancouver for Jeff Farkas, June 23, 2002.
Played in Europe after 2003–04 season.

2002–03	5	1	0	1	2
2003–04	1	0	0	0	0
Totals	6	1	0	1	2

PETER HOLLAND #24

centre 6'2" 195 L

b. Toronto, Ontario, January 14, 1991
Acquired from Anaheim with Brad Staubitz for Jesse Blacker, a second-round draft choice in 2014 (Marcus Pettersson), and a seventh-round draft choice in 2014 (Ondrej Kase), November 16, 2013.

2013–14	39	5	5	10	16
2014–15	62	11	14	25	31
Totals	101	16	19	35	47

WILLIAM "FLASH" HOLLETT ("Headline") #15/#3

defence 6' 184 L

b. North Sydney, Nova Scotia, April 13, 1912
d. Mississauga, Ontario, April 20, 1999
Signed from the Toronto Maple Leaf lacrosse team, 1933; recalled from Buffalo (IHL) to replace Red Horner (suspended after Ace Bailey incident), December 20, 1933; loaned to Ottawa Senators for rest of season, January 2, 1934. Sold to Boston for $16,500, January 15, 1936.

1933–34 F	5	0	0	0	4
1934–35	48	10	16	26	38
1935–36	11	1	4	5	8
Totals	64	11	20	31	50

F December 23, 1933

RYAN HOLLWEG #44

left wing 5'10" 210 L

b. Downey, California, April 23, 1983
Acquired from New York Rangers for a fifth-round draft choice in 2009 (later traded to Pittsburgh—Andy Bathgate), July 14, 2008. Signed as a free agent by Phoenix, September 28, 2009.

2008–09	25	0	2	2	38

HARRY HOLMES ("Hap"/"Happy") #1

goalie 5'10" 170 L

b. Aurora, Ontario, April 15, 1889
d. Ft. Lauderdale, Florida, June 28, 1941
Signed by Montreal Wanderers from Seattle (PCHA), December 1917. When the Wanderers' arena burned down, became Arenas property via dispersal of Wanderers players' rights on January 5, 1918.
Signed from Seattle, fall 1918, under an agreement whereby he could be reclaimed at any time; played December 23 and 26, 1918, then was recalled by Seattle.

1917–18	16	10–6–0	965	76	0	4.73
1918–19	2	0–2–0	120	9	0	4.50
Totals	18	10–8–0	1,085	85	0	4.70

F January 9, 1918
• Hockey Hall of Fame 1972

ALBERT "TOOTS" HOLWAY (sometimes HOLLOWAY) #3

defence 6'1" 190 L

b. Toronto, Ontario, September 24, 1902
d. Belleville, Ontario, November 20, 1968
Signed as a free agent from Belleville, February 13, 1924.
Traded to Montreal Maroons for Dutch Cain, January 11, 1926.

1923–24 F	6	1	0	1	0
1924–25	25	2	2	4	20
1925–26	12	0	0	0	0
Totals	43	3	2	5	20

F February 16, 1924

KORBINIAN HOLZER #55

defence 6'3" 205 R

b. Munich, West Germany (Germany), February 16, 1988
Selected 111th overall in 2006 Entry Draft.
Traded to Anaheim for Eric Brewer and a fifth-round draft choice in 2016, March 2, 2015.

2010–11 F	2	0	0	0	2
2012–13	22	2	1	3	28
2014–15	34	0	6	6	25
Totals	58	2	7	9	55

F November 6, 2010

LARRY HOPKINS #12

left wing 6'1" 215 L

b. Oshawa, Ontario, March 17, 1954
Signed as a free agent by Winnipeg, August 15, 1979.

1977–78 F	2	0	0	0	0

F March 8, 1978 (as an amateur)

GEORGE "SHORTY" HORNE #8

forward 5'6" 170 R

b. Sudbury, Ontario, June 27, 1904
d. Gogama, Ontario, August 1, 1929
Acquired from Stratford (Can Pro) for Freddy Elliott and $2,500, April 16, 1928.

1928–29 L	39	9	3	12	32

L March 16, 1929

REG "RED" HORNER #2/#15/#11

defence 6' 190 R

b. Lynden, Ontario, May 28, 1909
d. Toronto, Ontario, April 27, 2005
Turned pro December 22, 1928, while still with Marlboros.
Retired April 18, 1940.

1928–29 F	22	0	0	0	30
1929–30	33	2	7	9	96
1930–31	42	1	11	12	71
1931–32	42	7	9	16	97
1932–33	48	3	8	11	144
1933–34	40	11	10	21	146
1934–35	46	4	8	12	125
1935–36	43	2	9	11	167
1936–37	48	3	9	12	124
1937–38	47	4	20	24	82
1938–39	48	4	10	14	85
1939–40 L	31	1	9	10	87
Totals	490	42	110	152	1,254

F December 22, 1928 L March 17, 1940

• Played in goal twice while Lorne Chabot was serving penalties: January 29, 1929, and March 15, 1932 (along with Alex Levinsky and King Clancy—each of the three players allowed a goal).
• Later became a linesman.
• Hockey Hall of Fame 1965

MILES "TIM" HORTON ("Superman") #7/#16/#20

defence 5'10" 180 R

b. Cochrane, Ontario, January 12, 1930
d. St. Catharines, Ontario, February 21, 1974
St. Mike's graduate
Traded to New York Rangers for Jacques Plante, Denis Dupéré, and Guy Trottier, March 3, 1970.

1949–50 F	1	0	0	0	2
1951–52	4	0	0	0	8
1952–53	70	2	14	16	85
1953–54	70	7	24	31	94
1954–55	67	5	9	14	84
1955–56	35	0	5	5	36
1956–57	66	6	19	25	72
1957–58	53	6	20	26	39
1958–59	70	5	21	26	76
1959–60	70	3	29	32	69
1960–61	57	6	15	21	75
1961–62	70	10	28	38	88
1962–63	70	6	19	25	69
1963–64	70	9	20	29	71
1964–65	70	12	16	28	95
1965–66	70	6	22	28	76
1966–67	70	8	17	25	70
1967–68	69	4	23	27	82
1968–69	74	11	29	40	107
1969–70	59	3	19	22	91
Totals	1,185	109	349	458	1,389

F March 26, 1950

• Missed much of 1955–56 with a broken leg and jaw, still recovering from a check by Bill Gadsby on March 12, 1955; played part of 1964–65 at right wing.
• Opened first Tim Hortons doughnut stores in 1960s while with the Leafs.
• Died in car accident driving to Buffalo after a game in Toronto.

JOE "BRONCO" HORVATH #17

centre 5'10" 185 L

b. Port Colborne, Ontario, March 12, 1930
Claimed from New York Rangers on waivers, January 1963.
Claimed by Minnesota North Stars in Expansion Draft, June 6, 1967.

1962–63		9	0	4	4	12

GREG HOTHAM #4/#2/#8

defence 5'11" 185 R

b. London, Ontario, March 7, 1956
Selected 84th overall in 1976 Amateur Draft.
Traded to Pittsburgh for a sixth-round draft choice in 1982 (Craig Kales), February 3, 1982.

1979–80 F	46	3	10	13	10
1980–81	11	1	1	2	11
1981–82	3	0	0	0	0
Totals	60	4	11	15	21

F October 10, 1979

PHIL HOUSLEY #96

defence 5'10" 185 L

b. St. Paul, Minnesota, March 9, 1964
Acquired from Chicago for a ninth-round draft choice in 2003 (Chris Porter) and a fourth-round draft choice in 2004 (Karel Hromas), on March 11, 2003.
Retired at season's end.

2002–03 L	1	0	0	0	2

L April 5, 2003 (regular season—also played in 2003 playoffs)
• IIHF Hall of Fame 2012

JACK HOWARD #17/#21

defence 6' 170 L

b. London, Ontario, October 15, 1915
d. Cambridge, Ontario, September 14, 1983
Signed as a free agent, October 22, 1935.

1936–37 F/L	2	0	0	0	0

F November 26, 1936 L November 28, 1936

SYD HOWE #15/#3

centre 5'9" 165 L

b. Ottawa, Ontario, September 18, 1911
d. Ottawa, Ontario, May 26, 1976
Loaned to Leafs for 1931–32 season when Ottawa didn't ice a team, but played most of the season with Syracuse (IHL—demoted November 19, 1931); returned to Ottawa in 1932.

1931–32 F	3	0	0	0	0

F November 12, 1931
• Hockey Hall of Fame 1965

ROLLY HUARD #9

forward 5'10" 170 L

b. Ottawa, Ontario, September 6, 1902
d. Maniwaki, Quebec, September 16, 1979
Loaned from Buffalo (IHL)

1930–31 F/L	1	1	0	1	0

F/L December 13, 1930
• Scored a goal in his only NHL game, one of only two players to do so.

GREG HUBICK #19

defence 5'11" 183 L

b. Strasbourg, Saskatchewan, November 12, 1951
Acquired from Montreal for Doug Jarvis, June 26, 1975.
Signed as a free agent by Vancouver, September 7, 1979.

1975–76 F	72	6	8	14	10

F October 11, 1975

MIKE HUDSON ("Huddy") #15

forward 6'1" 205 L

b. Guelph, Ontario, February 6, 1967
Signed as a free agent, August 28, 1995.
Claimed off waivers by St. Louis, January 4, 1996.

1995–96	28	2	0	2	29

RON HURST #21/#22

right wing 5'9" 175 R

b. Toronto, Ontario, May 18, 1931
Signed with Leafs in 1955.
Traded with Wally Boyer and Mike Nykoluk to Hershey (AHL) for Willie Marshall, summer 1958.

1955–56 F	50	7	5	12	62
1956–57 L	14	2	2	4	8
Totals	64	9	7	16	70

F November 13, 1955 L January 5, 1957

DAVE HUTCHISON #23/#33

defence 6'3" 205 R

b. London, Ontario, May 2, 1952
Acquired with Lorne Stamler from Los Angeles for Brian Glennie, Scott Garland, Kurt Walker, and a second-round draft choice in 1979 (Mark Hardy), June 14, 1978; traded to Chicago for Pat Ribble, January 10, 1980.
Signed as a free agent, November 15, 1983.

1978–79	79	4	15	19	235
1979–80	31	1	6	7	28
1983–84 L	47	0	3	3	137
Totals	157	5	24	29	400

L April 1, 1984

AL IAFRATE ("Skis") #33

defence 6'3" 220 L

b. Dearborn, Michigan, March 21, 1966
Selected 4th overall in 1984 Entry Draft.
Traded to Washington for Peter Zezel and Bob Rouse, January 16, 1991.

1984–85 F	68	5	16	21	51
1985–86	65	8	25	33	40
1986–87	80	9	21	30	55
1987–88	77	22	30	52	80
1988–89	65	13	20	33	72
1989–90	75	21	42	63	135
1990–91	42	3	15	18	113
Totals	472	81	169	250	546

F October 11, 1984
• Self-proclaimed "Human Highlight Film"; retired because of recurring injuries.

MIROSLAV IHNACAK #27

left wing 5'11" 175 L

b. Poprad, Czechoslovakia (Czech Republic), November 19, 1962
Selected 171st in 1982 Entry Draft.
Signed as a free agent by Detroit, November 18, 1988.

1985–86 F	21	2	4	6	27
1986–87	34	6	5	11	12
Totals	55	8	9	17	39

F January 10, 1986

PETER IHNACAK #18/#15

centre 5'11" 180 R

b. Poprad, Czechoslovakia (Czech Republic), May 3, 1957

Selected 25th overall in 1982 Entry Draft. Signed by Freiburg (Germany) for 1990–91 season.

1982–83	F	80	28	38	66	44
1983–84		47	10	13	23	24
1984–85		70	22	22	44	24
1985–86		63	18	27	45	16
1986–87		58	12	27	39	16
1987–88		68	10	20	30	41
1988–89		26	2	16	18	10
1989–90	L	5	0	2	2	0
Totals		417	102	165	267	175

F October 6, 1982 L March 19, 1990

• Coached extensively after retiring, primarily in Nuremberg.

BRENT IMLACH #9/#24

forward 5'9" 165 R

b. Toronto, Ontario, November 16, 1946

Sold to Buffalo with Floyd Smith, August 31, 1970.

1965–66	F	2	0	0	0	0
1966–67	L	1	0	0	0	0
Totals		3	0	0	0	0

F January 16, 1966 L December 25, 1966

• Became vice-president and GM of Vancouver Canadians baseball team.

PETER ING #31/#1

goalie 6'2" 165 L

b. Toronto, Ontario, April 28, 1969

Selected 48th overall in 1988 Entry Draft. Traded with Vincent Damphousse, Luke Richardson, and Scott Thornton to Edmonton for Grant Fuhr, Glenn Anderson, and Craig Berube, September 19, 1991.

1989–90	F	3	0–2–1	182	18	0	5.93
1990–91		56	16–29–8	3,162	200	1	3.80
Totals		59	16–31–9	3,344	218	1	3.91

F November 16, 1989

JOHNNY INGOLDSBY ("Ding") #11/#20

right wing 6'2" 210 R

b. Toronto, Ontario, June 21, 1924

d. August 10, 1982

Signed while still with the Marlboros, November 17, 1942.

Left to join the Canadian Army, February 7, 1944.

1942–43	F	8	0	1	1	0
1943–44	L	21	5	0	5	15
Totals		29	5	1	6	15

F November 26, 1942 L January 29, 1944

RALPH INTRANUOVO #20

centre 5'8" 185 L

b. East York (Toronto), Ontario, December 11, 1973

Claimed from Edmonton for $60,000 in Waiver Draft, September 30, 1996.

Lost on waivers to Edmonton, October 25, 1996.

1996–97		3	0	1	1	0

• Only Leaf games October 5, 8, & 12, 1996.

JOE IRONSTONE ("Kelly") #1

goalie 5'6" 180 R

b. Sudbury, Ontario, June 28, 1898

d. Sudbury, Ontario, December 12, 1972

1927–28	L	1	0–0–1	70	0	1	0.00

L March 3, 1928

• Recorded shutout in only appearance in a Leaf uniform (0–0 overtime tie with Boston at Arena Gardens); replaced John Ross Roach, who had kidney stones.

• Also played with Niagara Falls (Can Pro) and Toronto Ravinas (Can Pro—1927–28).

BRAYDEN IRWIN #44

centre 6'5" 215 R

b. Toronto, Ontario, March 24, 1987

Signed as a free agent, March 29, 2010

2009–10	F/L	2	0	0	0	2

F April 1, 2010 L April 3, 2010

• Career minor leaguer.

RICHARD "RIC" JACKMAN #55

defence 6'2" 215 R

b. Toronto, Ontario, June 28, 1978

Acquired from Boston for Kris Vernarsky, May 13, 2002.

Traded to Pittsburgh for Drake Berehowsky, February 11, 2004.

2002–03		42	0	2	2	41
2003–04		29	2	4	6	13
Totals		71	2	6	8	54

ART JACKSON #16/#17/#18/#20/#15

centre 5'8" 155 L

b. Toronto, Ontario, December 15, 1915

d. St. Catharines, Ontario, May 14, 1971

St. Mike's graduate, 1934

Sold to Boston for cash, September 24, 1937.

Purchased from Boston for $7,500, December 23, 1944.

1934–35	F	20	1	3	4	4
1935–36		48	5	15	20	14
1936–37		14	2	0	2	2
1944–45	L	31	9	13	22	6
Totals		113	17	31	48	26

F November 8, 1934 L March 18, 1945

HARVEY "BUSHER" JACKSON #11/#9

forward 5'11" 195 L

b. Toronto, Ontario, January 19, 1911

d. Toronto, Ontario, June 25, 1966

Marlboros graduate, 1928; signed with Toronto, December 6, 1929.

Traded with Murray Armstrong, Buzz Boll, and Doc Romnes to New York Americans for Sweeney Schriner, May 18, 1939.

1929–30	F	31	12	6	18	29
1930–31		43	18	13	31	81
1931–32		48	28	25	53	63
1932–33		48	27	17	44	43
1933–34		38	20	18	38	38
1934–35		42	22	22	44	27
1935–36		47	11	11	22	19
1936–37		46	21	19	40	12
1937–38		48	17	17	34	18
1938–39		41	10	17	27	12
Totals		432	186	165	351	342

F December 7, 1929

• Missed first game of 1935–36 in contract dispute.

JEFF JACKSON ("Jax"/"Jesse") #12/#25

left wing 6'1" 195 L

b. Dresden, Ontario, April 24, 1965

Selected 28th overall in 1983 Entry Draft. Traded with third-round draft choice in 1989 (Rob Zamuner) to New York Rangers for Mark Osborne, March 5, 1987.

1984–85	F	17	0	1	1	24
1985–86		5	1	2	3	2
1986–87		55	8	7	15	64
Totals		77	9	10	19	90

F October 11, 1984

• Won gold medal with Canada at 1985 World Junior Championship.

STANTON "STAN" JACKSON #10

left wing 6' 180 L

b. Amherst, Nova Scotia, August 27, 1898

d. Ridgeway, Ontario, November 28, 1955

Signed by St. Pats from Amherst (Maritime Independent League), 1921.

Released December 15, 1924; signed as a free agent with Boston, December 17, 1924.

1921–22	F	1	0	0	0	0
1923–24		21	1	1	2	6
1924–25		4	0	0	0	0
Totals		26	1	1	2	6

F December 24, 1921

PAUL JACOBS #12

forward 5'8" 160 L

b. Montreal, Quebec, March 9, 1894

d. Kahnawake, Quebec, May 1, 1973

1918–19	F/L	5	0	0	0	0

F January 7, 1919 L February 4, 1919

• A First Nations athlete who played lacrosse with the Leasides in 1917–18.

EDWIN "GERRY" JAMES #11/#16/#19

right wing 5'11" 191 R

b. Regina, Saskatchewan, October 22, 1934

Marlboros graduate, 1955

Signed with Leafs, November 22, 1955.

Released in 1960.

1954–55	F	1	0	0	0	0
1955–56		46	3	3	6	50
1956–57		53	4	12	16	90
1957–58		15	3	2	5	61
1959–60	L	34	4	9	13	56
Totals		149	14	26	40	257

F February 24, 1955 L March 20, 1960

• Missed one month in 1956–57 with torn shoulder ligaments; missed all of 1958–59 with injury (broken left leg).

• Played football for Winnipeg Blue Bombers (WIFU, CFL) 1952–63.

VALMORE "VAL" JAMES #28

left wing 6'2" 205 L

b. Ocala, Florida, February 14, 1957

Signed as a free agent from Buffalo, October 3, 1985.

1986–87	L	4	0	0	0	14

L November 29, 1986.

GARY JARRETT #24

left wing 5'8" 170 L

b. Toronto, Ontario, September 3, 1942

Traded with Andy Bathgate and Billy Harris to Detroit for Marcel Pronovost, Aut Erickson, Larry Jeffrey, Ed Joyal, and Lowell MacDonald, May 20, 1965.

1960–61	F	1	0	0	0	0

F November 26, 1960

PIERRE JARRY ("Pete") #8

left wing 5'11" 182 R

b. Montreal, Quebec, March 30, 1949

Acquired from the New York Rangers for Jim Dorey, February 20, 1972.

Traded to Detroit for Tim Ecclestone, November 29, 1973.

1971–72		18	3	4	7	13
1972–73		74	19	18	37	42
1973–74		12	2	8	10	10
Totals		104	24	30	54	65

JIM "BUD" JARVIS #17

left wing 5'6" 165 L

b. Fort William, Ontario, December 7, 1907

d. Thunder Bay, Ontario, May 7, 1983

Acquired from Buffalo (IAHL) when team folded, December 18, 1936.

Sold by Syracuse (IAHL) to Providence (IAHL) for cash, November 7, 1937.

1936–37	L	24	1	0	1	0

L February 21, 1937

WES JARVIS #12/#11/#32/#16

centre 5'11" 185 L

b. Toronto, Ontario, May 30, 1958

Signed as a free agent, October 2, 1984.

1984–85		26	0	1	1	2
1985–86		2	1	0	1	2
1987–88	L	1	0	0	0	0
Totals		29	1	1	2	4

L March 26, 1988

• Played all of 1986–87 and most of 1987–90 with Newmarket (AHL).

• Later ran mini-hockey rink in Newmarket designed for children and three-on-three adult play.

LARRY JEFFREY #15/#22
left wing 5'11" 189 L
b. Zurich, Ontario, October 12, 1940
Acquired with Marcel Pronovost, Lowell MacDonald, Ed Joyal, and Aut Erickson from Detroit for Andy Bathgate, Billy Harris, and Gary Jarrett, May 20, 1965.
Claimed by Pittsburgh in Expansion Draft, June 6, 1967.

1965–66	20	1	1	2	22
1966–67	56	11	17	28	27
Totals	76	12	18	30	49

• Settled in Goderich, Ontario, and ran a sporting goods store, ad agency, and farming business.

ROGER "BROADWAY" JENKINS #12
defence 5'11" 173 R
b. Appleton, Wisconsin, November 18, 1911
d. May 4, 1994
Acquired on loan from Chicago via London (IHL) because of injury to Charlie Conacher, December 4, 1930.
Recalled by Chicago, February 4, 1931.

1930–31 F	21	0	0	0	12

F December 6, 1930

GRANT JENNINGS #3
defence 6'3" 210 L
b. Hudson Bay, Saskatchewan, May 5, 1965
Acquired from Pittsburgh for Drake Berehowsky, April 7, 1995.
Released June 27, 1995.

1994–95	10	0	2	2	7

TREVOR JOHANSEN #2/#4
defence 5'9" 200 R
b. Thunder Bay, Ontario, March 30, 1957
Selected 12th overall in 1977 Amateur Draft; traded with Don Ashby to Colorado Rockies for Paul Gardner, March 13, 1979.
Claimed off waivers from Los Angeles, February 19, 1982.

1977–78 F	79	2	14	16	82
1978–79	40	1	4	5	48
1981–82 L	13	1	3	4	4
Totals	132	4	21	25	134

F October 13, 1977   L March 24, 1982

CALLE JOHANSSON #9
defence 5'11" 205 L
b. Gothenburg, Sweden, February 14, 1967
Signed as a free agent, March 9, 2004.
Retired at season's end.

2003–04 L	8	0	6	6	0

L April 3, 2004 (regular season—also played in 2004 playoffs)

BILL "RED" JOHNSON #21
centre 6' 163 R
b. Oslo Norway, July 27, 1928
d. Thunder Bay, Ontario, March 21, 2001
Sold to Providence (AHL), December 21, 1954.

1949–50 F/L	1	0	0	0	0

F/L November 26, 1949

• Changed name from Johansen to sound more "Canadian" (son Trevor later played for Leafs with traditional family spelling).

CRAIG JOHNSON #33
left wing 6'2" 200 L
b. St. Paul, Minnesota, March 18, 1972
Claimed off waivers from Anaheim, January 10, 2004.
Claimed off waivers by Washington, March 5, 2004.

2003–04	10	1	1	2	6

DANNY JOHNSON #22
centre 5'11" 170 L
b. Winnipegosis, Manitoba, October 1, 1944
d. March 6, 1993
Claimed by Vancouver in Expansion Draft, June 10, 1970.

1969–70 F	1	0	0	0	0

F March 5, 1970

MIKE JOHNSON #20
right wing 6'2" 190 R
b. Scarborough (Toronto), October 3, 1974
Signed as a free agent March 15, 1997.
Traded to Tampa Bay with Marek Posmyk, a fifth-round draft choice in 2000 (Pavel Sedov), a sixth-round draft choice in 2000 (Aaron Gionet), and future considerations for Darcy Tucker, a fourth-round draft choice in 2000 (Miguel Delisle), and future considerations, February 9, 2000.

1996–97 F	13	2	2	4	4
1997–98	82	15	32	47	24
1998–99	79	20	24	44	35
1999–2000	52	11	14	25	23
Totals	226	48	72	120	86

F March 16, 1997
• Later became a commentator on TSN.

TERRY JOHNSON #20/#34
defence 6'3" 210 L
b. Calgary, Alberta, November 28, 1958
Acquired from Calgary for Jim Korn, October 3, 1986.

1986–87 L	48	0	1	1	104

L February 8, 1987

EDDIE JOHNSTON ("E.J.") #1
goalie 6' 190 L
b. Montreal, Quebec, November 23, 1935
Acquired with a first-round draft choice in 1973 (Ian Turnbull) from Boston for Jacques Plante and a third-round draft choice in 1973 (Doug Gibson), May 22, 1973.
Traded to St. Louis for Gary Sabourin, May 27, 1974.

1973–74	26	12–9–4	1,516	78	1	3.09

GREG JOHNSTON #16
right wing 6'1" 205 R
b. Barrie, Ontario, January 14, 1965
Acquired June 29, 1990, from the New York Rangers for Tie Domi and Mark LaForest.

1990–91	1	0	0	0	0
1991–92 L	3	0	1	1	5
Totals	4	0	1	1	5

L February 15, 1992

ROSS JOHNSTONE ("Blondie") #12
defence 6' 185 L
b. Montreal, Quebec, April 7, 1926
d. Toronto, Ontario, December 31, 2009
Signed after graduating from the Oshawa Generals, October 24, 1943.

1943–44 F	18	2	0	2	6
1944–45 L	24	3	4	7	8
Totals	42	5	4	9	14

F October 30, 1943   L February 27, 1945
• Suspended at 1946 training camp after refusing to go to Tulsa; reinstated January 1, 1947, and sent on loan to Springfield (AHL).

OLLI JOKINEN #11
centre 6'2" 210 L
b. Kuopio, Finland, December 5, 1978
Acquired February 15, 2015, with Brendan Leipsic and a first-round draft choice in 2015 from Nashville for Cody Franson and Mike Santorelli.
Traded to St. Louis for Joakim Lindstrom and a conditional sixth-round draft choice in 2016, March 2, 2015.

2014–15	6	0	1	1	2

ALVIN "BUCK" JONES #14
defence 6' 180 R
b. Owen Sound, Ontario, August 17, 1918
d. August 23, 2007
Acquired from Providence (AHL) with Ab DeMarco on February 3, 1943 for loan of George Boothman and Jack Forsey.
Sold to Tulsa (USHL), May 14, 1947.

1942–43 L	16	0	0	0	22

L March 14, 1943
• Missed 1943–46 serving in the Royal Canadian Electrical and Mechanical Engineers.

JIMMY JONES #16
centre 5'9" 177 R
b. Woodbridge, Ontario, January 2, 1953
Signed as a free agent, October 25, 1977.
Released prior to 1980–81 season.

1977–78	78	4	9	13	23
1978–79	69	9	9	18	45
1979–80 L	1	0	0	0	0
Totals	148	13	18	31	68

L October 14, 1979

KENNY JONSSON #19
defence 6'3" 195 L
b. Angelholm, Sweden, October 6, 1974
Selected 12th overall in 1993 Entry Draft.

Traded with Darby Hendrickson, Sean Haggerty, and a first-round draft choice in 1997 (Roberto Luongo) to New York Islanders for Wendel Clark, Mathieu Schneider, and Denis Smith, March 13, 1996.

1994–95 F	39	2	7	9	16
1995–96	50	4	22	26	22
Totals	89	6	29	35	38

F January 20, 1995

CURTIS JOSEPH ("CUJO") #31
goalie 5'11" 190 L
b. Keswick, Ontario, April 29, 1967
Signed as a free agent, July 15, 1998; rights traded to Calgary for a third-round draft choice in 2003 (later traded to Minnesota—Danny Irmen) and future considerations, June 30, 2002.
Signed as a free agent, July 1, 2008.

1998–99	67	35–24–7	4,001	171	3	2.56
1999–2000	63	36–20–7	3,801	158	4	2.49
2000–01	68	33–27–8	4,100	163	6	2.39
2001–02	51	29–17–5	3,065	114	4	2.23
2008–09 L	21	5–9–0–1	841	50	0	3.57
Totals	270	138–97–27–1	15,808	656	17	2.49

L April 8, 2009

EDDIE JOYAL #24
centre 6' 180 L
b. Edmonton, Alberta, May 8, 1940
Acquired with Marcel Pronovost, Lowell MacDonald, Aut Erickson, and Larry Jeffrey from Detroit for Andy Bathgate, Billy Harris, and Gary Jarrett, May 20, 1965.
Claimed by Los Angeles in Expansion Draft, June 6, 1967.

1965–66	14	0	2	2

• Recalled from Rochester (AHL), October 5, 1965, then demoted November 24 and played the rest of the season with Tulsa (CPHL) and Rochester.
• Established a real estate business with his wife in San Diego.

BILL JUZDA ("Fireman"/"Beast") #18
defence 5'8" 203 R
b. Winnipeg, Manitoba, October 29, 1920
d. Winnipeg, Manitoba, February 17, 2008
Acquired with Cal Gardner, René Trudel, Frankie Mathers, and the rights to Ray McMurray from the New York Rangers for Wally Stanowski, Moe Morris, and the rights to Orval Lavell, April 26, 1948.
Released, September 2, 1952.

1948–49	38	1	2	3	23
1949–50	62	1	14	15	68
1950–51	65	0	9	9	64
1951–52 L	46	1	4	5	65
Totals	211	3	29	32	220

L March 19, 1952
• Moved from his summer job to a full-time job after retiring, becoming an engineer for CPR in Manitoba.

TOMAS KABERLE ("Kaba"/"Kabby") #15
defence 6'2" 200 L
b. Rakovnik, Czechoslovakia (Czech Republic), March 2, 1978
Selected 204th overall in 1996 Entry Draft
Traded to Boston on for Joe Colborne, a first-round draft choice in 2011 (traded to Anaheim—Rickard Rackell), and a second-round draft choice in 2012 (traded to Colorado, later Washington and Dallas—Mike Winther), February 18, 2011.

1998–99 F	57	4	18	22	12
1999–2000	82	7	33	40	24
2000–01	82	6	39	45	24
2001–02	69	10	29	39	2
2002–03	82	11	36	47	30
2003–04	71	3	28	31	18
2005–06	82	9	58	67	46
2006–07	74	11	47	58	20
2007–08	82	8	45	53	22
2008–09	57	4	27	31	8
2009–10	82	7	42	49	24
2010–11	58	3	35	38	16
Totals	878	83	437	520	246

F October 10, 1998

NAZEM KADRI #43
centre 6' 188 L
b. London, Ontario, October 6, 1990
Selected 7th overall in 2009 Entry Draft.

2009–10 F	1	0	0	0	0
2010–11	29	3	9	12	8
2011–12	21	5	2	7	8
2012–13	48	18	26	44	23
2013–14	78	20	30	50	67
2014–15	73	18	21	39	28
Totals	250	64	88	152	134

F February 8, 2010

RUDOLPH "BINGO" KAMPMAN ("Samson") #7/#17/#20
defence 5'9" 187 R
b. Kitchener, Ontario, March 12, 1914
d. Kitchener, Ontario, December 23, 1987
Sent to Boston to complete deal that sent Art Jackson to Toronto, October 28, 1945.

1937–38 F	32	1	2	3	56
1938–39	41	2	8	10	52
1939–40	39	6	9	15	59
1940–41	39	1	4	5	53
1941–42 L	38	4	7	11	67
Totals	189	14	30	44	287

F December 25, 1937 **L** February 22, 1942 (regular season—played in 1942 playoffs)
• Won Allan Cup with Sudbury Tigers 1936–37.
• Joined the Canadian Armed Services after 1941–42.

ALEXANDER KARPOVTSEV ("Potsie") #52
defence 6'1" 205 R
b. Moscow, Soviet Union (Russia), April 7, 1970
Acquired from New York Rangers with a fourth-round draft choice in 1999 (Mirko

Murovic) for Mathieu Schneider, October 14, 1998.
Traded to Chicago with a fourth-round draft choice in 2001 (Vladimir Gusev) for Bryan McCabe, October 2, 2000.

1998–99	56	2	25	27	52
1999–2000	69	3	14	17	54
Totals	125	5	39	44	106

MIKE KASZYCKI #14/#16/#20
centre 5'9" 190 L
b. Milton, Ontario, February 27, 1956
Acquired from Washington for Pat Ribble, February 16, 1980.

1979–80	25	4	4	8	10
1980–81	6	0	2	2	2
1982–83 L	22	1	13	14	10
Totals	53	5	19	24	22

L January 12, 1983

MEL "BUTCH" KEELING #10/#18
left wing 6' 180 L
b. Owen Sound, Ontario, August 10, 1905
d. Toronto, Ontario, November 13, 1984
Acquired from London (Can Pro) for Pete Bellefeuille, December 27, 1926.
Traded with John Ross Roach to New York Rangers for Lorne Chabot and Alex Gray, October 17, 1928.

1926–27 F	30	11	2	13	29
1927–28	43	10	6	16	52
Totals	73	21	8	29	81

F December 30, 1926

LARRY KEENAN #8
left wing 5'10" 177 L
b. North Bay, Ontario, October 1, 1940
St. Mike's graduate
Signed by Leafs, June 21, 1961.
Claimed by St. Louis in Expansion Draft, June 6, 1967.

1961–62 F	2	0	0	0	0

F February 18, 1962
• Established a successful coffee supply business in North Bay.

RICK KEHOE #16/#17
right wing 5'11" 180 R
b. Windsor, Ontario, July 15, 1951
Selected 22nd overall in 1971 Entry Draft.
Traded to Pittsburgh for Blaine Stoughton and a first-round draft choice in 1977 (Trevor Johansen), September 13, 1974.

1971–72 F	38	8	8	16	4
1972–73	77	33	42	75	20
1973–74	69	18	22	40	8
Totals	184	59	72	131	32

F January 1, 1972

LEONARD "RED" KELLY #4
centre 6' 195 L
b. Simcoe, Ontario, July 9, 1927
Acquired from Detroit for Marc Reaume, February 10, 1960.

Traded to Los Angeles for Ken Block and immediately named team's first head coach, June 8, 1967.

1959–60	18	6	5	11	8
1960–61	64	20	50	70	12
1961–62	58	22	27	49	6
1962–63	66	20	40	60	8
1963–64	70	11	34	45	16
1964–65	70	18	28	46	8
1965–66	63	8	24	32	12
1966–67 L	61	14	24	38	4
Totals	470	119	232	351	74

L March 26, 1967
• On February 5, 1960, Kelly and Detroit teammate Billy McNeill were traded to New York Rangers for Bill Gadsby and Eddie Shack. However, both Kelly and McNeill refused to go.
• Acted as a member of Parliament while an active player; later ran an international aircraft maintenance company.
• Hockey Hall of Fame 1969 (five-year waiting period waived)

REGIS "PEP" KELLY ("Pepper") #9/#15/#16/#5
forward 5'6" 152 R
b. North Bay, Ontario, January 17, 1914
d. North Bay, Ontario, August 22, 1990
St. Mike's graduate, 1934
Signed October 3, 1934.
Traded to Chicago for Bill Kendall, but only for the balance of the season, December 29, 1936; sold to Chicago, May 10, 1940.

1934–35 F	47	11	8	19	14
1935–36	42	11	8	19	24
1936–37	16	2	0	2	8
1937–38	43	9	10	19	25
1938–39	48	11	11	22	12
1939–40	34	11	9	20	15
Totals	230	55	46	101	98

F November 8, 1934

STAN KEMP #16
defence 5'9" 165 R
b. Hamilton, Ontario, March 2, 1924
d. August 15, 1999
Acquired by Pittsburgh (AHL) from Providence (AHL) in 1946 for $7,000.

1948–49 F/L	1	0	0	0	2

F/L January 23, 1949

BILL "COWBOY" KENDALL #24
forward 5'8" 168 R
b. Winnipeg, Manitoba, April 1, 1910
d. Chillicothe, Missouri, April 10, 1976
Acquired from Chicago for Pep Kelly, December 29, 1936, but only for the balance of the season.

1936–37	15	2	4	6	4

FORBES KENNEDY ("Spud") #22
centre 5'8" 185 L
b. Dorchester, New Brunswick, August 18, 1935
Acquired with Brit Selby from Philadelphia for Mike Byers, Bill Sutherland, and Gerry Meehan, March 2, 1969.
Sold to Pittsburgh, May 30, 1969.

1968–69 L	13	0	3	3	24

L March 30, 1969
• Coached in minor pros for decades.

MIKE KENNEDY #39
centre 6'1" 195 R
b. Vancouver, British Columbia, April 13, 1972
Signed as a free agent, July 2, 1997.
Traded to Dallas for an eighth-round draft choice in 1998 (Mikhail Travnicek), on March 24, 1998.

1997–98	13	0	1	1	14

TED "TEEDER" KENNEDY #9/#10/#12/#20
centre 5'11" 180 R
b. Humberstone, Ontario, December 12, 1925
d. Port Colborne, Ontario, August 14, 2009
Acquired February 28, 1943, from Montreal for postwar rights to Frankie Eddolls.
Retired April 4, 1954; came out of retirement July 20, 1954; returned again on January 6, 1957, to help team until season's end.

1942–43 F	2	0	1	1	0
1943–44	49	26	23	49	2
1944–45	49	29	25	54	14
1945–46	21	3	2	5	4
1946–47	60	28	32	60	27
1947–48	60	25	21	46	32
1948–49	59	18	21	39	25
1949–50	43	20	24	44	34
1950–51	63	18	43	61	32
1951–52	70	19	33	52	33
1952–53	43	14	23	37	42
1953–54	67	15	23	38	78
1954–55	70	10	42	52	74
1956–57 L	30	6	16	22	35
Totals	686	231	329	560	432

F March 7, 1943 **L** March 17, 1957
• Later ran a racetrack in southern Ontario.
• Hockey Hall of Fame 1966

DAVE KEON #14

centre 5'9" 167 L
b. Noranda, Quebec, March 22, 1940
St. Mike's graduate, 1960
Signed as a free agent with Minnesota (WHA) after 1974–75 season.

1960–61	F	70	20	25	45	6
1961–62		64	26	35	61	2
1962–63		68	28	28	56	2
1963–64		70	23	37	60	6
1964–65		65	21	29	50	10
1965–66		69	24	30	54	4
1966–67		66	19	33	52	2
1967–68		67	11	37	48	4
1968–69		75	27	34	61	12
1969–70		72	32	30	62	6
1970–71		76	38	38	76	4
1971–72		72	18	30	48	4
1972–73		76	37	36	73	2
1973–74		74	25	28	53	7
1974–75		78	16	43	59	4
Totals		1,062	365	493	858	75

F October 6, 1960
• Moved to Florida to sell real estate in Palm Beach Gardens.
• Hockey Hall of Fame 1986

PHIL KESSEL #81

right wing 6' 200 R
b. Madison, Wisconsin, October 2, 1987
Acquired from Boston for a first-round draft choice in 2010 (Tyler Seguin), a second-round draft choice in 2010 (Jared Knight), and a first-round draft choice in 2011 (Dougie Hamilton), September 18, 2009.

2009–10	70	30	25	55	21
2010–11	82	32	32	64	24
2011–12	82	37	45	82	20
2012–13	48	20	32	52	18
2013–14	82	37	43	80	27
2014–15	82	25	36	61	30
Totals	446	181	213	394	140

ALEXANDER KHAVANOV #25

defence 6'2" 205 L
b. Moscow, Soviet Union (Russia), January 30, 1972
Signed as a free agent, August 10, 2005.
Later played in Switzerland.

2005–06	L	64	6	6	12	60

L March 25, 2006

DMITRI KHRISTICH ("Deem") #8/#19

left wing 6'2" 195 R
b. Kiev, Soviet Union (Russia), July 23, 1969
Acquired from Boston for a second-round draft choice in 2000 (Ivan Huml), on October 20, 1999.
Traded to Washington for a third-round draft choice in 2001 (Brendan Bell), on December 11, 2000.

1999–2000	53	12	18	30	24
2000–01	27	3	6	9	8
Totals	80	15	24	39	32

TREVOR KIDD #37

goalie 6'2" 215 L
b. Dugald, Manitoba, March 26, 1972
Signed as a free agent, August 26, 2002.
Later played in Europe.

2002–03	19	6–10–2	1,143	59	0	3.10
2003–04 L	15	6–5–2–1	883	48	1	3.26
Totals	34	12–15–4	2,026	107	1	3.17

L March 15, 2004 (also played May 2, 2004, in playoffs)

CHAD KILGER #18

left wing 6'4" 225 L
b. Cornwall, Ontario, November 27, 1976
Claimed off waivers from Montreal, March 9, 2004.
Traded to Florida on for a third-round draft choice in 2008 (later traded to St. Louis—James Livingston), February 26, 2008.

2003–04	5	1	1	2	2
2005–06	79	17	11	28	63
2006–07	82	14	14	28	58
2007–08 L	53	10	7	17	18
Totals	219	42	33	75	141

L February 25, 2008

HEC KILREA ("Hurricane Hec") #12

left wing 5'7 175 L
b. Blackburn, Ontario, June 11, 1907
d. Detroit, Michigan, December 6, 1969
Acquired from Ottawa for Bob Gracie and $12,500, March 14, 1933.
Traded to Detroit for Norm Schultz and $7,500, fall 1935.

1933–34	43	10	13	23	15
1934–35	46	11	13	24	16
Totals	89	21	26	47	31

DEREK KING ("Yoda"/"Kinger") #7

left wing 6' 212 L
b. Hamilton, Ontario, February 11, 1967
Signed as a free agent, July 4, 1997.
Traded to St. Louis for Tyler Harlton and future considerations, October 20, 1999.

1997–98	77	21	25	46	43
1998–99	81	24	28	52	20
1999–2000	3	0	0	0	2
Totals	161	45	53	98	65

KRIS KING ("Kinger") #12

left wing 5'11" 208 L
b. Bracebridge, Ontario, February 18, 1966
Signed as a free agent, July 23, 1997.
Released summer 2000.

1997–98	82	3	3	6	199
1998–99	67	2	2	4	105
1999–2000	39	2	4	6	55
Totals	188	7	9	16	359

MARK KIRTON ("Kirt") #20

centre 5'10" 170 L
b. Regina, Saskatchewan, February 3, 1958
Selected 48th overall in 1987 Entry Draft.
Traded to Detroit for Jim Rutherford, December 4, 1980.

1979–80	F	2	1	0	1	2
1980–81		11	0	0	0	0
Totals		13	1	0	1	2

F October 10, 1979

BILL KITCHEN #26

defence 6'1" 200 L
b. Schomburg, Ontario, October 2, 1960
d. Ottawa, Ontario, July 30, 2012
Signed as a free agent, August 16, 1984.

1984–85	L	29	1	4	5	27

L February 21, 1985

KEN KLEE #22

defence 6'1" 210 R
b. Indianapolis, Indiana, April 24, 1971
Signed as a free agent, September 27, 2003.
Traded to New Jersey for Aleksander Suglobov, March 8, 2006.

2003–04	66	4	25	29	36
2005–06	56	3	12	15	66
Totals	122	7	37	44	102

JOE KLUKAY ("Duke of Paducah"/ "Kluke") #8/#17/#19

left wing 6' 175 L
b. Sault Ste. Marie, Ontario, November 6, 1922
d. Sault Ste. Marie, Ontario, February 3, 2006
Signed by Leafs, March 15, 1943; sold to Boston, September 16, 1952.
Acquired from Boston for Léo Boivin, November 9, 1954.

1946–47	F	55	9	20	29	12
1947–48		59	15	15	30	28
1948–49		45	11	10	21	11
1949–50		70	15	16	31	19
1950–51		70	14	16	30	16
1951–52		43	4	8	12	6
1954–55		56	8	8	16	44
1955–56	L	18	0	1	1	2
Totals		416	76	94	170	138

F October 16, 1946 (played one game in 1943 playoffs—March 28) L November 20, 1955
• Missed 1943–45 while serving in the Royal Canadian Navy.
• Operated a machine at a tool-and-die company for 45 years.

PAUL "BILL" KNOX #11

right wing 5'10" 160 R
b. Toronto, Ontario, November 23, 1933
St. Mike's graduate
Recalled from University of Toronto Blues, March 11, 1955.

1954–55	F/L	1	0	0	0	0

F/L March 12, 1955
• Won bronze medal with Canada at the 1956 Olympics.

LADISLAV KOHN #39

right wing 5'11" 194 L
b. Uherske Hradiste, Czechoslovakia (Czech Republic), March 4, 1975
Acquired from Calgary for David Cooper, July 2, 1998.
Claimed by Atlanta in Waiver Draft, September 27, 1999.

1998–99	16	1	3	4	4

MARK KOLESAR #37

left wing 6'1" 188 R
b. Neepawa, Manitoba, January 23, 1973
Signed as a free agent, May 24, 1994.
Played remainder of career in minors and Europe.

1995–96	F	21	2	2	4	14
1996–97	L	7	0	0	0	0
Totals		28	2	2	4	14

F October 28, 1995 L February 1, 1997

LEO KOMAROV #47

centre 5'10" 187 L
b. Narva, Soviet Union (Estonia), January 23, 1987
Selected 180th overall in 2006 Entry Draft.

2012–13	F	42	4	5	9	18
2014–15		62	8	18	26	18
Totals		104	12	23	35	36

F January 19, 2013

MIKE KOMISAREK #8

defence 6'4" 235 R
b. West Islip, New York, January 19, 1982
Signed as a free agent, July 1, 2009.
Signed as a free agent by Carolina, July 5, 2013.

2009–10	34	0	4	4	40
2010–11	75	1	9	10	86
2011–12	45	1	4	5	41
2012–13	4	0	0	0	2
Totals	158	2	17	19	169

MAXIM KONDRATIEV #34

defence 6'1" 195 L
b. Togliatti, Soviet Union (Russia), January 20, 1983
Selected 168th overall in 2001 Entry Draft.
Traded to New York Rangers with Jarkko Immonen, a first-round draft choice in 2004 (later traded to Calgary—Kris Chucko), and a second-round draft choice in 2005 (Michael Sauer) for Brian Leetch, March 3, 2004.

2003–04	F	7	0	0	0	2

F October 11, 2003

JOHN KORDIC #27

right wing 6'2" 210 R

b. Edmonton, Alberta, March 22, 1965

d. L'Ancienne Lorette, Quebec, August 8, 1992

Acquired with a sixth-round draft choice in 1989 (Michael Doers) from Montreal for Russ Courtnall, November 7, 1988.

Traded with Paul Fenton to Washington for a fifth-round draft choice in 1991 (Alexei Kudashov), January 24, 1991.

1988–89	46	1	2	3	185
1989–90	55	9	4	13	252
1990–91	3	0	0	0	9
Totals	104	10	6	16	446

JIM KORN #20

forward 6'3" 210 L

b. Hopkins, Minnesota, July 28, 1957

Acquired from Detroit for a fourth-round draft choice in 1982 (Craig Coxe) and a fifth-round draft choice in 1983 (Joey Kocur), March 8, 1982.

Traded to Calgary for Terry Johnson, October 3, 1986.

1981–82	11	1	3	4	44
1982–83	80	8	21	29	236
1983–84	65	12	14	26	257
1984–85	41	5	5	10	171
Totals	197	26	43	69	708

IGOR KOROLEV ("Iggy") #22

right wing 6'1" 187 L

b. Moscow, Soviet Union (Russia), September 6, 1970

d. Yaroslavl, Russia, September 7, 2011

Signed as a free agent, September 29, 1997.

Traded to Chicago for a third-round draft choice in 2001 (Nicolas Corbeil), on June 23, 2001.

1997–98	78	17	22	39	22
1998–99	66	13	34	47	46
1999–2000	80	20	26	46	22
2000–01	73	10	19	29	28
Totals	297	60	101	161	118

• Perished in a plane crash along with the entire Yaroslavl (KHL) hockey team.

MIKE KOSTKA #53

defence 6'1" 210 R

b. Etobicoke (Toronto), Ontario, November 28, 1985

Signed as a free agent, July 1, 2012.

Signed as a free agent by Chicago on July 19, 2013.

2012–13	35	0	8	8	27

CHRIS KOTSOPOULOS ("Kotsy") #26

defence 6'3" 215 R

b. Toronto, Ontario, November 27, 1958

Acquired from Hartford for Stewart Gavin, October 7, 1985.

Signed as a free agent by Detroit, June 23, 1989.

1985–86	61	6	11	17	83
1986–87	43	2	10	12	75

1987–88	21	2	2	4	19
1988–89	57	1	14	15	44
Totals	182	11	37	48	221

LES KOZAK #8

forward 6' 185 L

b. Yorkton, Saskatchewan, October 28, 1940

St. Mike's graduate

Signed by Leafs, June 28, 1961.

1961–62 F/L	12	1	0	1	2

F January 13, 1962   L February 7, 1962

BRANDON KOZUN #67

right wing 5'8" 167 R

b. Los Angeles, California, March 8, 1990

Acquired from Los Angeles for Andrew Crescenzi, January 22, 2014.

2014–15 F	20	2	2	4	6

F October 8, 2014

STEVE KRAFTCHECK #4

defence 5'10" 185 R

b. Tinturn, Ontario, March 3, 1929

d. Providence, Rhode Island, August 10, 1997

Signed after being acquired from Cleveland (AHL) for cash and the rights to Ian Anderson, August 21, 1958.

Demoted to Rochester (AHL) to become player/coach, October 31, 1958.

1958–59 L	8	1	0	1	0

L October 29, 1958

STAFFAN KRONWALL #44

defence 6'5" 225 L

b. Jarfalla, Sweden, September 10, 1982

Selected 285th overall at 2002 Entry Draft

Claimed off waivers by Washington on February 6, 2009.

2005–06	34	0	1	1	14
2007–08	18	0	0	0	7
Totals	52	0	1	1	21

MIKE KRUSHELNYSKI ("Kruiser") #26

centre 6'2" 200 L

b. Montreal, Quebec, April 27, 1960

Acquired from Los Angeles for John McIntyre, November 9, 1990.

Signed as a free agent by Detroit, August 1, 1994.

1990–91	59	17	22	39	48
1991–92	72	9	15	24	72
1992–93	84	19	20	39	62
1993–94	54	5	6	11	28
Totals	269	50	63	113	210

PAVEL KUBINA #31

defence 6'4" 255 R

b. Celadna, Czechoslovakia (Czech Republic), April 15, 1977

Signed as a free agent, July 1, 2006.

Traded to Atlanta with Tim Stapleton for Garnet Exelby and Colin Stuart, July 1, 2009.

2006–07	61	7	14	21	48
2007–08	72	11	29	40	116

2008–09	82	14	26	40	94
Totals	215	32	69	101	258

ALEXEI KUDASHOV #20

centre 6' 190 R

b. Moscow, Soviet Union (Russia), July 21, 1971

Selected 102nd overall in 1991 Entry Draft.

Released June 27, 1995.

1993–94 F	25	1	0	1	4

F October 15, 1993

NIKOLAI KULEMIN #41

left wing 6'1" 225 L

b. Magnitogorsk, Soviet Union (Russia), July 14, 1986

Selected 44th overall in 2006 Entry Draft.

Signed as a free agent by New York Islanders, July 2, 2014.

2008–09 F	73	15	16	31	18
2009–10	78	16	20	36	16
2010–11	82	30	27	57	26
2011–12	70	7	21	28	6
2012–13	48	7	16	23	22
2013–14	70	9	11	20	24
Totals	421	84	111	195	112

F October 9, 2008

ORLAND KURTENBACH #25

centre 6'2" 195 L

b. Cudworth, Saskatchewan, September 7, 1936

Acquired with Pat Stapleton and Andy Hebenton from Boston for Ron Stewart, June 8, 1965.

Claimed by New York Rangers in Intra-League Draft, June 15, 1966.

1965–66	70	9	6	15	54

• Became an insurance broker in British Columbia after retiring.

TOM KURVERS #25

defence 6'2" 195 L

b. Minneapolis, Minnesota, September 14, 1962

Acquired from New Jersey for a first-round draft choice in 1991 (Scott Niedermayer), October 16, 1989.

Traded to Vancouver for Brian Bradley, January 12, 1991.

1989–90	70	15	37	52	29
1990–91	19	0	3	3	8
Totals	89	15	40	55	37

NICK KYPREOS ("Kipper") #32

left wing 6' 205 L

b. Toronto, Ontario, June 4, 1966

Acquired with Wayne Presley from New York Rangers for Sergio Momesso and Bill Berg, February 29, 1996.

1995–96	19	1	1	2	30
1996–97 L	35	3	2	5	62
Totals	54	4	3	7	92

L September 15, 1997

• Became hockey analyst for Sportsnet.

ÉRIC LACROIX #41

left wing 6'1" 205 L

b. Montreal, Quebec, July 15, 1971

Selected 136th overall in 1990 Entry Draft.

Traded with Chris Snell and a fourth-round draft choice in 1996 (Éric Bélanger) to Los Angeles for Dixon Ward, Guy Leveque, Shayne Toporowski, and Kelly Fairchild, October 3, 1994.

1993–94 F	3	0	0	0	2

F November 27, 1993

MARK LaFOREST ("Trees") #1

goalie 5'11" 190 L

b. Welland, Ontario, July 10, 1962

Acquired from Philadelphia for a fifth-round draft choice in 1991 (later traded to Winnipeg—Juha Ylonen) and a seventh-round draft choice in 1991 (Andrei Lomakin), September 8, 1989.

Traded with Tie Domi to New York Rangers for Greg Johnston, June 29, 1990.

1989–90 L	27	9–14–0	1,343	87	0	3.89

L March 28, 1990

LARRY LANDON #11

right wing 6' 191 R

b. Niagara Falls, Ontario, May 4, 1958

Acquired from Montreal for Gaston Gingras, February 14, 1985.

Released after 1984–85 season.

1984–85 L	7	0	0	0	2

L March 24, 1985

PETE LANGELLE ("Snake Hips") #8/#21

centre 5'10" 170 L

b. Winnipeg, Manitoba, November 4, 1917

d. Winnipeg, Manitoba, November 29, 2010

Winnipeg Monarchs graduate; signed October 27, 1937; recalled March 15, 1939 from Syracuse.

1938–39 F	2	1	0	1	0
1939–40	39	7	14	21	2
1940–41	47	4	15	19	0
1941–42 L	48	10	22	32	9
Totals	136	22	51	73	11

F March 18, 1939   L March 19, 1942

• Served in Royal Canadian Air Force, 1942–46.

• Worked for a brewery in Manitoba for 30 years.

RICK LANZ ("Rico"/"Lanzer") #4

defence 6'2" 203 R

b. Karlouy Vary, Czechoslovakia (Czech Republic), September 16, 1961

Acquired from Vancouver for Jim Benning and Dan Hodgson, December 2, 1986.

Signed as a free agent by Chicago, August 13, 1990.

1986–87	44	2	19	21	32
1987–88	75	6	22	28	65
1988–89	32	1	9	10	18
Totals	151	9	50	59	115

MICHEL "BUNNY" LAROCQUE #1

goalie 5'10" 185 L
b. Hull, Quebec, April 16, 1952
d. Hull, Quebec, July 29, 1992
Acquired from Montreal for Robert Picard and an eighth-round draft choice in 1982 (Steve Smith), March 10, 1981.
Traded to Philadelphia for Rick St. Croix, January 11, 1983.

1980–81	8	3–3–2	460	40	0	5.22
1981–82	50	10–24–8	2,647	207	0	4.69
1982–83	16	3–8–3	835	68	0	4.89
Totals	74	16–35–13	3,942	315	0	4.79

GUY LAROSE ("Rosie") #11

centre 5'9" 175 L
b. Hull, Quebec, August 31, 1967
Acquired from the New York Rangers for Mike Stevens, December 26, 1991.
Claimed off waivers by Calgary, January 1, 1994.

1991–92	34	9	5	14	27
1992–93	9	0	0	0	8
1993–94 L	10	1	2	3	10
Totals	53	10	7	17	45

L December 29, 1993

MATT LASHOFF #29

defence 6'2" 205 L
b. East Greenbush, New York, September 29, 1986
Acquired from Tampa Bay for Alex Berry and Stefano Giliati, August 27, 2010.
Later played in Europe.

2010–11 L	11	0	1	1	6

L April 9, 2011

CRAIG LAUGHLIN #14/#18

right wing 6' 190 R
b. Toronto, Ontario, September 19, 1957
Signed as a free agent from Los Angeles, June 10, 1988.
Released after 1988–89 season.

1988–89 L	66	10	13	23	41

L March 14, 1988

PAUL LAWLESS #20

left wing 5'11" 185 L
b. Toronto, Ontario, July 2, 1964
Acquired from Vancouver for Peter DeBoer, February 25, 1989.

1988–89	7	0	0	0	0
1989–90 L	6	0	1	1	0
Totals	13	0	1	1	0

L October 17, 1989

DEREK LAXDAL #34/#28/#3/#15

right wing 6'1" 175 R
b. St. Boniface, Manitoba, February 21, 1966
Selected 151st overall in 1984 Entry Draft.
Traded with Paul Gagné and Jack Capuano to New York Islanders for Gilles Thibaudeau and Mike Stevens, December 20, 1989.

1984–85 F	3	0	0	0	6
1986–87	2	0	0	0	7
1987–88	5	0	0	0	6
1988–89	41	9	6	15	65
Totals	51	9	6	15	84

F April 3, 1985

BRETT LEBDA #23

defence 5'9" 195 L
b. Buffalo Grove, Illinois, January 15, 1982
Signed as a free agent, July 7, 2010.
Traded to Nashville on with Robert Slaney for Cody Franson and Matt Lombardi, July 3, 2011.

2010–11	41	1	3	4	14

BRAD LEEB #38

right wing 5'11" 185 R
b. Red Deer, Alberta, August 27, 1979
Acquired from Vancouver for Tomas Mojzis, September 4, 2002.
Later played in Germany.

2003–04 L	1	0	0	0	0

L January 8, 2004

GARY LEEMAN #4/#11/#16

right wing 5'11" 175 R
b. Toronto, Ontario, February 19, 1964
Selected 24th overall in 1982 Entry Draft.
Traded with Michel Petit, Craig Berube, Alexander Godynyuk, and Jeff Reese to Calgary for Doug Gilmour, Jamie Macoun, Ric Nattress, Rick Wamsley, and Kent Manderville, January 2, 1992.

1983–84 F	52	4	8	12	31
1984–85	53	5	26	31	72
1985–86	53	9	23	32	20
1986–87	80	21	31	52	66
1987–88	80	30	31	61	62
1988–89	61	32	43	75	66
1989–90	80	51	44	95	63
1990–91	52	17	12	29	39
1991–92	34	7	13	20	44
Totals	545	176	231	407	463

F October 8, 1983

BRIAN LEETCH #2

defence 6' 185 L
b. Corpus Christi, Texas, March 3, 1968
Acquired from New York Rangers for Maxim Kondratiev, Jarkko Immonen, a first-round draft choice in 2004 (later traded to Calgary—Kris Chucko), and a second-round draft choice in 2005 (Michael Sauer), March 3, 2004.
Signed as a free agent by Boston, August 3, 2005.

2003–04	15	2	13	15	10

• Hockey Hall of Fame 2009

SYLVAIN LEFEBVRE #2

defence 6'2" 204 L
b. Richmond, Quebec, October 14, 1967
Acquired from Montreal for a third-round draft choice in 1994 (Martin Belanger), August 20, 1992.
Traded with Wendel Clark, Landon Wilson, and a first-round draft choice in 1994 (Jeffrey Kealty) to Quebec for Mats Sundin, Garth Butcher, Todd Warriner, and a first-round draft choice in 1994 (later traded to Washington—Nolan Baumgartner), June 28, 1994.

1992–93	81	2	12	14	90
1993–94	84	2	9	11	79
Totals	165	4	21	25	169

JOSH LEIVO #32

left wing 6'1" 175 R
b. Innisfil, Ontario, May 26, 1993
Selected 86th overall in 2011 Entry Draft.

2013–14 F	7	1	1	2	0
2014–15	9	1	0	1	4
Totals	16	2	1	3	4

F October 25, 2013

ALEX LEVINSKY ("Mine Boy") #3/#16

defence 5'10" 184 R
b. Syracuse, New York, February 2, 1910
d. Toronto, Ontario, September 1, 1990
Marlboros graduate, 1930
Signed March 2, 1931.
Sold to New York Rangers for $10,000, April 12, 1934.

1930–31 F	8	0	1	1	2
1931–32	47	5	5	10	29
1932–33	48	1	4	5	61
1933–34	47	5	11	16	38
Totals	150	11	21	32	130

F March 3, 1931
• Played in goal, as did Red Horner and King Clancy, while Lorne Chabot served a penalty on March 15, 1932. Each of the three players allowed a goal.

DANNY LEWICKI ("Dashin' Danny") #21/#23

left wing 5'9" 152 L
b. Fort William, Ontario, March 12, 1931
Acquired August 12, 1948, from Providence (AHL) for cash and a player to be named later (Jack Hamilton—September 10, 1948).
Sold to New York Rangers, July 20, 1954.

1950–51 F	61	16	18	34	26
1951–52	51	4	9	13	26
1952–53	4	1	3	4	2
1953–54	7	0	1	1	12
Totals	123	21	31	52	66

F October 14, 1950
• Played February 1, 5, 7, & 8, 1953, after being recalled due to injuries to Max Bentley and Rudy Migay.

RICK LEY #2/#26

defence 5'9" 185 L
b. Orillia, Ontario, November 2, 1948
Selected 16th overall in 1966 Amateur Draft; signed by New England (WHA), July 1972.
Selected in WHA Reclamation Draft, June 1979; claimed June 1979 by Hartford in Expansion Draft.

1968–69 F	38	1	11	12	39
1969–70	48	2	13	15	102
1970–71	76	4	16	20	151
1971–72	67	1	14	15	124
Totals	229	8	54	62	416

F October 13, 1968

BOB LIDDINGTON #26

left wing 6' 175 L
b. Calgary, Alberta, September 15, 1948
Signed as a free agent, October 1969.

1970–71 F/L	11	0	1	1	2

F October 11, 1970 L November 7, 1970
• Played all of 1969–70 and most of 1970–71 with Tulsa (CHL).

JOHN-MICHAEL LILES #24

defence 5'10" 185 L
b. Indianapolis, Indiana, November 25, 1980
Acquired from Colorado for a second-round draft choice in 2012 (later traded to Washington and Dallas—Mike Winther), June 24, 2011.
Traded to Carolina with Dennis Robertson for Tim Gleason, January 1, 2014.

2011–12	66	7	20	27	20
2012–13	32	2	9	11	4
2013–14	6	0	0	0	0
Totals	104	9	29	38	24

ERIC LINDROS #88

centre 6'4" 240 R
b. London, Ontario, February 28, 1973
Signed as a free agent, August 11, 2005.
Signed as a free agent by Dallas, July 17, 2006.

2005–06	33	11	11	22	43

BERT LINDSAY #1

goalie 5'7" 160 R
b. Guelph, Ontario, July 23, 1881
d. Sarnia, Ontario, November 11, 1960

1918–19 F/L	16	5–11–0	979	83	0	5.09

F December 28, 1918 L February 20, 1919
• Replaced Harry Holmes in goal after Holmes was recalled by Seattle (PCHA), December 26, 1918.
• Father of Ted Lindsay.

JOAKIM LINDSTROM #15

centre 6' 187 L
b. Skelleftea, Sweden, December 5, 1983
Acquired from St. Louis with a conditional sixth-round draft choice in 2016 for Olli Jokinen, March 2, 2015.

2014–15	19	1	3	4	4

KEN LINSEMAN ("The Rat") #13

centre 5'11" 180 L

b. Kingston, Ontario, August 11, 1958
Purchased from Edmonton October 7, 1991.
Released near start of 1991–92 season.

1991–92 L	2	0	0	0	2

L October 21, 1991

ED LITZENBERGER ("Litz") #25

right wing 6'3" 194 R

b. Neudorf, Saskatchewan, July 15, 1932
d. Toronto, Ontario, November 1, 2010
Claimed on waivers from Detroit, December 29, 1961.
Demoted to Rochester (AHL), December 4, 1963.

1961–62	37	10	10	20	14
1962–63	58	5	13	18	10
1963–64 L	19	2	0	2	0
Totals	114	17	23	40	24

L December 1, 1963
• Involved in NHL alumni activities in the Toronto area.

HOWIE LOCKHART ("Holes") #1

goalie 5'8" 180 L

b. North Bay, Ontario, March 21, 1895
d. Haliburton, Ontario, August 2, 1956
Signed December 15, 1919; sold to Hamilton December 16, 1920
Signed December 18, 1923; sold to Boston December 24, 1924

1919–20 F	7	4–2–0	310	25	0	4.84
1923–24	1	0–1–0	60	5	0	5.00
Totals	6	4–2–0	328	25	0	3.67

F January 31, 1920
• Played with Quebec Bulldogs, March 6, 1920.
• Played with St. Pats December 19, 1923, after John Ross Roach suffered a finger injury.

CLAUDE LOISELLE #15

centre 5'11" 195 L

b. Ottawa, Ontario, May 29, 1963
Claimed on waivers from Quebec, March 5, 1991.
Traded with Daniel Marois to New York Islanders for Ken Baumgartner and Dave McLlwain, March 10, 1992.

1990–91	7	1	1	2	2
1991–92	64	6	9	15	102
Totals	71	7	10	17	104

MATT LOMBARDI #15

centre 5'11" 195 L

b. Montreal, Quebec, March 18, 1982
Acquired from Nashville with Cody Franson for Brett Lebda and Robert Slaney, July 3, 2011.
Traded to Phoenix for a fourth-round draft choice in 2014 (John Piccinich), January 16, 2013.

2011–12	62	8	10	18	10

WILF LOUGHLIN #8

forward 6'2" 200 L

b. Carroll, Manitoba, February 28, 1896
d. June 25, 1966
Purchased from Victoria (PCHA) in 1923.

1923–24 F/L	14	0	0	0	2

F December 15, 1923 **L** February 13, 1924

RON LOW #30

goalie 6'1" 205 L

b. Birtle, Manitoba, June 21, 1950
Selected 103rd overall in 1970 Amateur Draft.
Claimed by Washington in Expansion Draft, June 12, 1974.

1972–73 L	42	12–24–4	2343	152	1	3.89

L April 1, 1973
• Later became only former goalie to coach two teams (Edmonton, New York Rangers) and also became the winningest former goalie to coach.

GERRY LOWREY #9/#14

left wing 5'8" 150 L

b. Ottawa, Ontario, February 14, 1906
d. Ottawa, Ontario, October 17, 1979
Drafted from Toronto Ravinas (Can Pro), January 11, 1928.
Traded with $10,000 to Pittsburgh Pirates for Baldy Cotton, February 12, 1929.

1927–28 F	25	6	5	11	29
1928–29	28	3	9	12	24
Totals	53	9	14	23	53

F January 12, 1928

DON LUCE #20

centre 6'2" 185 L

b. London, Ontario, October 2, 1948
Acquired from Los Angeles for Bob Gladney and a sixth-round draft choice in 1983 (Kevin Stevens), August 10, 1981.

1981–82 L	39	4	4	8	32

L February 18, 1982

HARRY LUMLEY ("Apple Cheeks") #1

goalie 6' 195 L

b. Owen Sound, Ontario, November 11, 1926
d. London, Ontario, September 13, 1998
Acquired from Chicago for Cal Gardner, Ray Hannigan, Gus Mortson, and Al Rollins, September 11, 1952.
Sold with Eric Nesterenko to Chicago for $40,000, May 21, 1956.

1952–53	70	27–30–13	4,200	167	10	2.39
1953–54	69	32–24–13	4,140	128	13	1.86
1954–55	69	23–24–22	4,140	134	8	1.94
1955–56	59	21–28–10	3,527	157	3	2.67
Totals	267	103–106–58	16,007	588	34	2.20

• Hockey Hall of Fame 1980

JYRKKI LUMME #25

defence 6'1" 210 L

b. Tampere, Finland, July 16, 1966
Acquired from Dallas for Dave Manson, November 21, 2001.
Later returned to Europe to play.

2001–02	51	4	8	12	18
2002–03 L	73	6	11	17	46
Totals	124	10	19	29	64

L April 5, 2003 (also appeared in 2003 playoffs)

JAMIE LUNDMARK #16

centre 6' 195 R

b. Edmonton, Alberta, January 16, 1981
Claimed off waivers from Calgary, February 13, 2010.
Later played in Europe.

2009–10 L	15	1	2	3	16

L April 7, 2010

JOE LUNDRIGAN #2

defence 5'11" 180 L

b. Corner Brook, Newfoundland, September 12, 1948
Signed as a free agent, 1971.
Claimed by Washington in Expansion Draft, June 12, 1974.

1972–73 F	49	2	8	10	20

F October 29, 1972

JOFFREY LUPUL #19

right wing 6'1" 205 R

b. Fort Saskatchewan, Alberta, September 23, 1983
Acquired from Anaheim with Jake Gardiner and a fourth-round draft choice in 2013 (later traded to Chicago and San Jose—Fredrik Bergvik) for François Beauchemin, on February 9, 2011.

2010–11	28	9	9	18	19
2011–12	66	25	42	67	48
2012–13	16	11	7	18	12
2013–14	69	22	22	44	44
2014–15	55	10	11	21	26
Totals	234	77	91	169	149

VIC LYNN #14

defence 5'9" 185 L

b. Saskatoon, Saskatchewan, January 26, 1925
d. Saskatoon, Saskatchewan, December 6, 2010
Acquired from Buffalo (AHL) for Gerry Brown, September 21, 1946.
Traded with Bill Ezinicki to Boston for Léo Boivin, Fern Flaman, Phil Maloney, and Ken Smith, November 15, 1950.

1946–47	31	6	14	20	44
1947–48	60	12	22	34	53
1948–49	52	7	9	16	36
1949–50	70	7	13	20	39
Totals	213	32	58	90	172

CLARKE MacARTHUR #16

left wing 6' 195 L

b. Lloydminster, Alberta, April 6, 1985
Signed as a free agent, August 28, 2010.
Signed as a free agent by Ottawa, July 5, 2013.

2010–11	82	21	41	62	37
2011–12	73	20	23	43	37
2012–13	40	8	12	20	26
Totals	195	49	76	125	100

JOEY MacDONALD #29

goalie 6' 197 L

b. Pictou, Nova Scotia, February 7, 1980
Signed as a free agent, August 10, 2009.
Traded to Anaheim for a seventh-round draft choice in 2011 (Max Everson), March 3, 2010.

2009–10	6	1–4–0	319	17	0	3.20

PARKER MacDONALD #21

left wing 5'11" 184 L

b. Sydney, Nova Scotia, June 14, 1933
Marlboros graduate, 1952
Claimed with Jerry Foley by New York Rangers for $30,000 in Intra-League Draft, June 5, 1956.

1952–53 F	1	0	0	0	0
1954–55	62	8	3	11	36
Totals	63	8	3	11	36

F February 28, 1953

DREW MacINTYRE #35

goalie 6'1" 190 L

b. Charlottetown, Prince Edward Island, June 24, 1983
Signed as a free agent, April 2, 2013.
Signed as a free agent by Carolina, July 1, 2014.

2013–14	2	0–1–0	95	4	0	2.54

• Only Leaf games March 23 & April 10, 2014.

BLAIR MacKASEY #16

defence 6'2" 200 R

b. Hamilton, Ontario, December 13, 1955
Rights acquired from Washington for Grant Cole, September 27, 1976.

1976–77 F/L	1	0	0	0	2

F/L October 5, 1976

FLEMING MacKELL ("Mac"/"Sukey"/ "Flame") #16/#22

centre 5'7" 167 L

b. Montreal, Quebec, April 30, 1929
St. Mike's graduate, 1947
Signed by Leafs, September 25, 1947.
Traded to Boston for Jim Morrison, January 9, 1952.

1947–48 F	3	0	0	0	2
1948–49	11	1	1	2	6
1949–50	36	7	13	20	24
1950–51	70	12	13	25	40
1951–52	32	2	8	10	16
Totals	152	22	35	57	88

F October 18, 1947
• After retiring, worked as a car salesman in Montreal for 27 years.

DON MacLEAN ("Mac") #37

centre 6'2" 199 L
b. Sydney, Nova Scotia, January 14, 1977
Acquired from Los Angeles for Craig Charron, February 23, 2000.
Signed as a free agent by Columbus, July 17, 2002.

2000–01	3	0	1	1	2

• Only Leaf games October 14, 16, & 25, 2000

BILLY MacMILLAN #12/#23

right wing 5'10" 180 L
b. Charlottetown, Prince Edward Island, March 7, 1943
Claimed by Atlanta in Expansion Draft, June 6, 1972.

1970–71 F	76	22	19	41	42
1971–72	61	10	7	17	39
Totals	137	32	26	58	81

F October 11, 1970
• Won bronze medal with Canada at the 1966 World Championship and 1968 Olympics.
• Stayed in the NHL as coach and GM after retiring.

JOHN MacMILLAN #8/#24/#25

right wing 5'9" 185 L
b. Milk River, Alberta, October 25, 1935
Denver University graduate, 1960
Signed as a free agent, October 1960.
Claimed off waivers by Detroit for $20,000, December 3, 1963.

1960–61 F	31	3	5	8	8
1961–62	31	1	0	1	8
1962–63	6	1	1	2	6
1963–64	13	0	0	0	10
Totals	81	5	6	11	32

F December 3, 1960

AL MacNEIL #11/#22/#24

defence 5'10" 180 L
b. Sydney, Nova Scotia, September 27, 1935
Called up from Marlboros, January 27, 1956.
Traded to Montreal for Stan Smrke, June 1960.

1955–56 F	1	0	0	0	2
1956–57	53	4	8	12	84
1957–58	13	0	0	0	9
1959–60	4	0	0	0	2
Totals	71	4	8	12	97

F January 28, 1956
• Later coached Montreal to Stanley Cup.

ANDREW MacWILLIAM # 57

defence 6'2" 214 L
b. Calgary, Alberta, March 25, 1990
Selected 188th overall in the 2008 NHL Entry Draft.

2014–15 F	12	0	2	2	12

F March 11, 2015

JAMIE MACOUN ("Cooner") #34

defence 6'2" 197 L
b. Newmarket, Ontario, August 17, 1961
Acquired with Doug Gilmour, Ric Nattress, Rick Wamsley, and Kent Manderville from Calgary for Gary Leeman, Michel Petit, Craig Berube, Jeff Reese, and Alexander Godynyuk, January 2, 1992.
Traded to Detroit for a fourth-round draft choice in 1998 (previously acquired from Tampa Bay—Alexei Ponikarovsky), March 24, 1998.

1991–92	39	3	13	16	18
1992–93	77	4	15	19	55
1993–94	82	3	27	30	115
1994–95	46	2	8	10	75
1995–96	82	0	8	8	87
1996–97	73	1	10	11	93
1997–98	67	0	7	7	63
Totals	466	13	88	101	506

• One of only a few undrafted players to play 1,000 NHL games.

DARYL MAGGS #24

defence 6'2" 195 R
b. Victoria, British Columbia, April 6, 1949
Signed as a free agent after returning from German league, December 1979.

1979–80 L	5	0	0	0	0

L January 5, 1980

MARC MAGNAN #35

left wing 5'11" 195 L
b. Beaumont, Alberta, February 17, 1962
Selected 195th overall in 1981 Entry Draft.

1982–83 F/L	4	0	1	1	5

F December 14, 1982 L December 29, 1982

KEVIN MAGUIRE #28/#18

right wing 6'2" 200 R
b. Toronto, Ontario, January 5, 1963
Signed as a free agent, October 10, 1984; claimed by Buffalo in Waiver Draft, October 5, 1987.
Acquired with an eighth-round draft choice in 1991 (Dmitri Mironov) from Philadelphia for a third-round draft choice in 1990 (Al Kinisky), June 16, 1990.

1986–87 F	17	0	0	0	74
1990–91	63	9	5	14	180
1991–92L	8	1	0	1	4
Totals	88	10	5	15	258

F December 26, 1986 L January 4, 1992
• Retired after 1991–92 season and became an NHL referee.

FRANK MAHOVLICH ("The Big M"/ "Gutch") #22/#27

left wing 6' 205 L
b. Timmins, Ontario, January 10, 1938
St. Mike's graduate
Signed with Leafs, May 13, 1957.
Traded with Pete Stemkowski, Garry Unger, and the rights to Carl Brewer to Detroit for Paul Henderson, Norm Ullman, and Floyd Smith, March 3, 1968.

1956–57 F	3	1	0	1	2
1957–58	67	20	16	36	67
1958–59	63	22	27	49	94
1959–60	70	18	21	39	61
1960–61	70	48	36	84	131
1961–62	70	33	38	71	87
1962–63	67	36	37	73	56
1963–64	70	26	29	55	66
1964–65	59	23	28	51	76
1965–66	68	32	24	56	68
1966–67	63	18	28	46	44
1967–68	50	19	17	36	30
Totals	720	296	301	597	782

F March 20, 1957
• Ran successful travel agency after retiring.
• Named to Canada's Senate by Prime Minister Jean Chrétien.
• Hockey Hall of Fame 1981

ADAM MAIR ("Bomber") #21

centre 6'2" 195 R
b. Hamilton, Ontario, February 15, 1979
Selected 84th overall in 1997 Entry Draft.
Traded to Los Angeles with a second-round draft choice in 2001 (Mike Cammalleri) for Aki-Petteri Berg, March 13, 2001.

1999–2000 F	8	1	0	1	6
2000–01	16	0	2	2	14
Totals	24	1	2	3	20

F December 18, 1999

DAN MALONEY ("Harley") #9

left wing 6'2" 195 L
b. Barrie, Ontario, September 24, 1950
Acquired with a second-round draft choice in 1980 (Craig Muni) from Detroit for Errol Thompson, a first-round draft choice in 1977 (Brent Peterson), a second-round draft choice in 1978 (Al Jensen), and a first-round draft choice in 1980 (Mike Blaisdell), March 13, 1978.

1977–78	13	3	4	7	25
1978–79	77	17	36	53	157
1979–80	71	17	16	33	102
1980–81	65	20	21	41	183
1981–82 L	44	8	7	15	71
Totals	270	65	84	149	538

L March 30, 1982
• Retired after 1981–82 season to become Leafs' assistant coach, later becoming head coach.

PHIL MALONEY #25–23

centre 5'9" 170 L
b. Ottawa, Ontario, October 6, 1927
Acquired with Léo Boivin, Fern Flaman, and Ken Smith from Boston for Vic Lynn and Bill Ezinicki, November 15, 1950.
Sold with Bill Ezinicki and Hugh Barlow to Vancouver (WHL) for $10,000, December 21, 1954.

1950–51	1	1	0	1	0
1952–53	29	2	6	8	2
Totals	30	3	6	9	2

KENT MANDERVILLE ("Mandy") #18

left wing 6'3" 207 L
b. Edmonton, Alberta, April 12, 1971
Acquired with Doug Gilmour, Jamie Macoun, Ric Nattress, and Rick Wamsley from Calgary for Gary Leeman, Michel Petit, Jeff Reese, Craig Berube and Alexander Godynyuk, January 2, 1992.
Traded to Edmonton for Peter White and a fourth-round draft choice in 1996 (Jason Sessa), December 4, 1995.

1991–92 F	15	0	4	4	0
1992–93	18	1	1	2	17
1993–94	67	7	9	16	63
1994–95	36	0	1	1	22
Totals	136	8	15	23	102

F March 4, 1992
• Won gold medals with Canada at 1990 and 1991 World Junior Championships and silver at the 1992 Olympics.

CESARE MANIAGO ("Hail Caesar") #1

goalie 6'3" 195 L
b. Trail, British Columbia, January 13, 1939
St. Mike's graduate
Claimed by Montreal in Intra-League draft, June 13, 1961.

1960–61 F	7	4–2–1	420	18	0	2.57

F March 18, 1961
• Ran a sporting goods business after retiring.

NORM MANN #8/#21/#19

right wing 5'10" 155 R
b. Bradford, England, March 3, 1914
d. Mattawa, Ontario, February 9, 1994
Signed October 7, 1935; lost to New York Rangers in Inter-League Draft, May 10, 1937.
Purchased from New York Rangers for $4,000, November 7, 1938; kept with Leafs on four-game trial to replace injured Gord Drillon; sold to Pittsburgh (AHL), October 30, 1941.

1938–39 F	16	0	0	0	2
1940–41 L	15	0	3	3	2
Totals	31	0	3	3	4

F November 10, 1938 L March 11, 1941
• Joined Royal Canadian Navy in 1941— never played in NHL again.

BOB MANNO #3/#18

defence 6' 185 L

b. Niagara Falls, Ontario, October 31, 1956
Signed as a free agent, September 30, 1981.
Signed as a free agent by Detroit, August 2, 1983.

1981–82	72	9	41	50	67

• Played in Merano (Italian League) in 1982–83.

DAVE MANSON ("Charlie") #3

defence 6'2" 200 L

b. Prince Albert, Saskatchewan, January 27, 1967
Signed as a free agent, August 16, 2000.
Traded to Dallas for Jyrkki Lumme, November 21, 2001.

2000–01	74	4	7	11	93
2001–02	13	0	1	1	10
Totals	87	4	8	12	103

MILAN MARCETTA ("Millie") #25

centre 6'1" 195 L

b. Cadomin, Alberta, September 19, 1936
Acquired from defunct Calgary team (WHL), August 8, 1963.
Sold to Minnesota North Stars, December 27, 1967.

• Appeared as a Leaf only in the 1967 playoffs.
• Managed a condominium building in Coquitlam, B.C., after retiring.

BRIAN MARCHINKO #22

centre 6' 180 R

b. Weyburn, Saskatchewan, August 2, 1948
Signed as a free agent, October 1, 1969.
Claimed by New York Islanders at Expansion Draft, June 6, 1972.

1970–71 F	2	0	0	0	0
1971–72	3	0	0	0	0
Totals	5	0	0	0	0

F October 11, 1970

BRYAN MARCHMENT #27

defence 6'1" 200 L

b. Scarborough (Toronto), Ontario, May 1, 1969
Signed as a free agent, July 11, 2003.
Signed as a free agent by Calgary, October 11, 2005.

2003–04	75	1	3	4	106

GUS MARKER ("Senator") #14/#18

forward 5'9" 162 R

b. Wetaskewin, Saskatchewan, August 1, 1907
d. Kingston, Ontario, October 7, 1997
Purchased from Montreal Maroons, November 3, 1938.
Traded to New York Americans with Red Heron, Nick Knott, and Peanuts O'Flaherty on a one-year lease, all subject to recall, for Lorne Carr, October 30, 1941.

1938–39	29	9	6	15	11
1939–40	42	10	9	19	15
1940–41	27	4	5	9	10
Totals	98	23	20	43	36

JACK MARKLE #21

forward 5'9" 155 R

b. Thessalon, Ontario, May 15, 1907
d. Pulaski, New York, June 25, 1956
Recalled from Syracuse (IHL) to replace injured Charlie Conacher, January 19, 1936.

1935–36 F/L	8	0	1	1	0

F January 23, 1936 L February 8, 1936

DANIIL "DANNY" MARKOV ("Elvis"/"Sputnik") #55

defence 6'1" 196 L

b. Moscow, Soviet Union (Russia), July 11, 1976
Selected 223rd overall in 1995 Entry Draft
Traded to Phoenix for Robert Reichel, Travis Green, and Craig Mills, June 12, 2001.

1997–98 F	25	2	5	7	28
1998–99	57	4	8	12	47
1999–2000	59	0	10	10	28
2000–01	59	3	13	16	34
Totals	200	9	36	45	137

F February 2, 1998

JOHN "JACK" MARKS #unknown

right wing 6' 180 L

b. Brantford, Ontario, February 8, 1882
d. August 20, 1945
Signed as a free agent after Montreal Wanderers' arena burned down and Wanderers players released, January 5, 1918.

1917–18	5	0	—	0	0

• Played January 26 & 28 and February 2, 4, & 9, 1918.

DANIEL MAROIS #32

right wing 6' 190 R

b. Montreal, Quebec, October 3, 1968
Selected 28th overall at 1987 Entry Draft
Traded with Claude Loiselle to New York Islanders for Ken Baumgartner and Dave McLlwain, March 10, 1992.

1988–89 F	76	31	23	54	76
1989–90	68	39	37	76	82
1990–91	78	21	9	30	112
1991–92	63	15	11	26	76
Totals	285	106	80	186	346

F October 6, 1988 (regular season—also appeared in 1988 playoffs)

JEAN MAROIS #1

goalie 5'8" 155 L

b. Quebec City, Quebec, November 25, 1924
d. St. Antoine-de-Tilly, Quebec, January 3, 1996

1943–44 F	1	1–0–0	60	4	0	4.00

F December 18, 1943 (as an 18-year old St. Mike's student)

• Played only two other games in NHL, with Chicago in 1953–54.

BRAD MARSH #3

defence 6'3" 220 L

b. London, Ontario, March 31, 1958
Claimed in Waiver Draft, October 3, 1988; traded to Detroit for an eighth-round draft choice in 1991 (Robb McIntyre), February 5, 1991.
Purchased from Detroit, June 10, 1992; traded to Ottawa Senators for future considerations, July 20, 1992.

1988–89	80	1	15	16	79
1989–90	79	1	13	14	95
1990–91	20	0	0	0	15
Totals	179	2	28	30	189

GARY MARSH #18

left wing 5'9" 172 L

b. Toronto, Ontario, March 9, 1946
Claimed in Intra-League Draft on June 12, 1968, from Detroit.

1968–69 L	1	0	0	0	0

L October 27, 1968

DON MARSHALL #22

left wing 5'10" 166 L

b. Verdun, Quebec, March 23, 1932
Claimed from Buffalo in Intra-League Draft, June 8, 1971.
Retired after 1971–72 season.

1971–72 L	50	2	14	16	0

L April 2, 1972

• Became a sales rep for a mechanical products company in Montreal.

PAUL MARSHALL #28/#15

left wing 6'2" 180 L

b. Toronto, Ontario, September 7, 1960
Acquired with Kim Davis from Pittsburgh for Dave Burrows and Paul Gardner, November 18, 1980.
Traded to Hartford for a 10th-round draft choice in 1983 (Greg Rolston), October 5, 1982.

1980–81	13	0	2	2	2
1981–82	10	2	2	4	2
Totals	23	2	4	6	4

WILLIE MARSHALL ("The Whip") #8/#21/#24

centre 5'10" 160 L

b. Kirkland Lake, Ontario, December 1, 1931
St. Mike's graduate, 1950; traded to Hershey (AHL) for Gerry Ehman, June 1956.
Acquired from Hershey (AHL) for Ron Hurst, Mike Nykoluk, and Wally Boyer (on a two-year loan) April 29, 1958; played next 20 years in minors.

1952–53 F	2	0	0	0	0
1954–55	16	1	4	5	0
1955–56	6	0	0	0	0
1958–59 L	9	0	1	1	2
Totals	33	1	5	6	2

F February 28, 1953 L December 21, 1958

JACK MARTIN #24

forward 5'11" 184 L

b. St. Catharines, Ontario, November 29, 1940
St. Mike's graduate

1960–61 F/L	1	0	0	0	0

F/L November 27, 1960

MATT MARTIN ("Marty") #33/#3

defence 6'3" 205 L

b. New Haven, Connecticut, April 30, 1971
Selected 66th overall in 1989 Entry Draft.
Signed as a free agent by Dallas, July 24, 1998.

1993–94 F	12	0	1	1	6
1994–95	15	0	0	0	13
1995–96	13	0	0	0	14
1996–97	36	0	4	4	38
Totals	76	0	5	5	71

F October 19, 1993

• Missed much of 1995–96 with a broken ankle.

TERRY MARTIN #25

left wing 5'11" 195 L

b. Barrie, Ontario, October 25, 1955
Acquired with Dave Farrish from Quebec for Reg Thomas, December 13, 1979.
Claimed by Edmonton in Waiver Draft, October 9, 1984.

1979–80	37	6	15	21	2
1980–81	69	23	14	37	32
1981–82	72	25	24	49	39
1982–83	76	14	13	27	28
1983–84	63	15	10	25	51
Totals	317	83	76	159	152

TOM MARTIN #17

right wing 5'9" 170 R

b. Toronto, Ontario, October 16, 1947
Selected 5th overall in 1964 Amateur Draft.
Claimed by Detroit in Intra-League Draft, June 9, 1970.

1967–68 F/L	3	1	0	1	0

F December 17, 1967 L March 31, 1968

PAUL MASNICK #8

centre 5'9" 165 R

b. Regina, Saskatchewan, April 14, 1931
Purchased from Montreal, September 30, 1957.

1957–58 F/L	41	2	9	11	14

F December 7, 1957 L March 23, 1958

FRANK MATHERS #20

defence 6' 182 L

b. Winnipeg, Manitoba, March 29, 1924

d. Hershey, Pennsylvania, February 9, 2005

Acquired from the New York Rangers with Cal Gardner, Bill Juzda, René Trudell, and the rights to Ray McMurray for Wally Stanowski, Moe Morris, and the rights to Orval Lavell, April 26, 1948.

Retired September 16, 1952, then accepted demotion to Pittsburgh (AHL) on October 24, 1952; contract purchased in summer 1956 by Hershey when Pittsburgh folded.

1948–49 F	15	1	2	3	2
1949–50	6	0	1	1	2
1951–52 L	2	0	0	0	0
Totals	23	1	3	4	4

F October 16, 1948 **L** December 20, 1951

JOE MATTE #unknown

defence 5'11" 180 R

b. Bourget, Ontario, March 6, 1893

d. Montreal, Quebec, June 13, 1961

Signed while on loan from Montreal for the year, January 15, 1920; loaned to Hamilton for 1920–21 season.

1919–20 F	16	8	2	10	12

F January 17, 1920

BRAD MAXWELL #4

defence 6'2" 195 R

b. Brandon, Manitoba, July 8, 1957

Acquired from Quebec for John Anderson, August 21, 1985.

Traded to Vancouver for a fifth-round draft choice in 1988 (Len Esau), October 3, 1986.

1985–86	52	8	18	26	108

WALLY MAXWELL #26

forward 5'10" 155 L

b. Ottawa, Ontario, August 24, 1933

1952–53 F/L	2	0	0	0	0

F January 10, 1953 **L** January 14, 1953

BRAD MAY #10

left wing 6'1" 215 L

b. Toronto, Ontario, November 29, 1971

Acquired from Anaheim for future considerations, on January 7, 2009.

Signed as a free agent by Detroit, October 8, 2009.

2008–09	38	1	1	2	61

**GIL MAYER ("The Needle")
#25/#21/#22/#1/#20**

goalie 5'6" 135 L

b. Ottawa, Ontario, August 24, 1930

Purchased from Buffalo (AHL), 1949.

Purchased by Hershey (AHL) when Pittsburgh (AHL) folded, June 1956.

1949–50 F	1	0–1–0	60	2	0	2.00
1953–54	1	0–0–1	60	3	0	3.00
1954–55	1	1–0–0	60	1	0	1.00
1955–56 L	6	1–5–0	360	18	0	3.00
Totals	9	2–6–1	540	24	0	2.67

F December 1, 1949 **L** February 5, 1956

EDWIN "SHEP" MAYER #18/#22

forward 5'8" 180 R

b. Sturgeon Falls, Ontario, September 11, 1923

d. February 7, 2005

Re-signed August 24, 1945, though never played in the NHL again.

1942–43 F/L	2	1	2	3	4

F October 31, 1942 **L** November 7, 1942

• Called up to the Army on November 8, 1942.

JAMAL MAYERS #21

right wing 6'1" 220 R

b. Toronto, Ontario, October 24, 1974

Acquired from St. Louis for a third-round draft choice in 2008 (later traded to St. Louis—James Livingston), June 19, 2008. Traded to Calgary with Ian White, Matt Stajan, and Nicklas Hagman for Dion Phaneuf, Keith Aulie, and Fredrik Sjostrom, January 31, 2010.

2008–09	71	7	9	16	82
2009–10	44	2	6	8	78
Totals	115	9	15	24	160

GARY McADAM #12

left wing 5'11" 175 L

b. Smiths Falls, Ontario, December 31, 1955

Signed as a free agent, July 31, 1985.

Retired after eye injury in a game against Pittsburgh

1985–86 L	15	1	6	7	0

L November 27, 1985

CHRIS McALLISTER ("Cally") #33

defence 6'7" 235 L

b. Saskatoon, Saskatchewan, June 16, 1985

Acquired from Vancouver for Darby Hendrickson, February 16, 1999.

Traded to Philadelphia for Regan Kelly, September 20, 2000.

1998–99	20	0	2	2	39
1999–2000	36	0	3	3	68
Totals	56	0	5	5	107

CLIFF McBRIDE #12

defence 5'11" 187 R

b. Toronto, Ontario, January 10, 1909

d. February 17, 1999

Acquired from Montreal Maroons, December 7, 1928, as future considerations to complete trade of November 28, 1928, that sent Dave Trottier and $15,000 to Maroons. Sent November 13, 1929, to London (Can Pro); recalled for one game only.

1929–30 L	1	0	0	0	0

L November 26, 1929

BRYAN McCABE #24

defence 6'1" 210 L

b. St. Catharines, Ontario, June 8, 1975

Acquired from Chicago for Alexander Karpovtsev and a fourth-round draft choice in 2001 (Vladimir Gusev), October 2, 2000. Traded to Florida with a fourth-round draft

choice in 2010 (Sam Brittain) for Mike Van Ryn, September 2, 2008.

2000–01	82	5	24	29	123
2001–02	82	17	26	43	129
2002–03	75	6	18	24	135
2003–04	75	16	37	53	86
2005–06	73	19	49	68	116
2006–07	82	15	42	57	115
2007–08	54	5	18	23	81
Totals	523	83	214	297	785

BERT McCAFFREY ("Mac") #7

forward 5'10" 180 R

b. Listowel, Ontario, April 12, 1893

d. Toronto, Ontario, April 15, 1955

Signed after winning Allan Cup and Olympic gold in 1924 with Toronto Granites.

Traded with cash to Pittsburgh Pirates, December 12, 1927; Ty Arbour traded from Pirates to Chicago; Eddie Rodden from Chicago to Toronto.

1924–25 F	30	9	6	15	12
1925–26	36	14	7	21	42
1926–27	43	5	5	10	43
1927–28	8	1	1	2	9
Totals	117	29	19	48	106

F November 29, 1924

ALYN McCAULEY ("Shooter"/"Mac") #18

centre 5'11" 185 L

b. Brockville, May 29, 1977

Acquired from New Jersey with Jason Smith and Steve Sullivan for Doug Gilmour, Dave Ellett, and future considerations, February 25, 1997.

Traded to San Jose with Brad Boyes and a first-round draft choice in 2003 (later traded to Boston—Mark Stuart) for Owen Nolan, March 5, 2003.

1997–98	60	6	10	16	6
1998–99	39	9	15	24	2
1999–2000	45	5	5	10	10
2000–01	14	1	0	1	0
2001–02	82	6	10	16	18
2002–03	64	6	9	15	16
Totals	304	33	49	82	52

KEVIN McCLELLAND #20

right wing 6'2" 205 R

b. Oshawa, Ontario, July 4, 1962

Signed as a free agent, September 2, 1991. Traded to Winnipeg for cash, August 12, 1993.

1991–92	18	0	1	1	33

JAY McCLEMENT #11

centre 6'1" 205 R

b. Kingston, Ontario, March 2, 1983

Signed as a free agent, July 1, 2012.

Signed as a free agent by Carolina, July 2, 2014.

2012–13	48	8	9	17	11
2013–14	81	4	6	10	32
Totals	129	12	15	27	43

FRANK McCOOL ("Ulcers") #1

goalie 6' 170 L

b. Calgary, Alberta, October 27, 1918

d. Calgary, Alberta, May 20, 1973

Signed after being discharged from Canadian Army.

Retired when Turk Broda was discharged from the army.

1944–45 F 50	24–22–4	3,000	161	4	3.22
1945–46 L 22	10–9–3	1,320	81	0	3.68
Totals 72	34–31–7	4,320	242	4	3.36

F October 28, 1944 **L** February 3, 1946

• Missed start of 1945–46 in contract dispute. Baz Bastien played the first five games (0–4–1), followed by Gordie Bell (3–5).

JOHN McCORMACK ("Goose") #20

centre 6' 185 L

b. Edmonton, Alberta, August 2, 1925

Marlboros graduate, 1948

Brought up during 1947–48 season to replace injured Syl Apps.

Demoted by Conn Smythe to Pittsburgh (AHL) during 1950–51 season because he got married during the season; sold to Montreal, September 21, 1951.

1947–48 F	3	0	1	1	0
1948–49	1	0	0	0	0
1949–50	34	6	5	11	0
1950–51	46	6	7	13	2
Totals	84	12	13	25	2

F January 31, 1948

DALE McCOURT #12

centre 5'10" 180 R

b. Falconbridge, Ontario, January 26, 1957

Signed as a free agent, October 22, 1983.

1983–84 L	72	19	24	43	10

L April 1, 1984

• In 1978 challenged NHL's compensation rules, refusing to go to Los Angeles after Detroit signed free agent Rogie Vachon. (He won his case, but was later traded.)

BILL McCREARY #28

right wing 6' 190 R

b. Springfield, Massachusetts, April 15, 1960

Selected 114th overall in 1979 Entry Draft.

1980–81 F/L	12	1	0	1	4

F December 30, 1980 **L** January 30, 1981

JOHNNY McCREEDY #14/#20

right wing 5'8" 160 R

b. Winnipeg, Manitoba, March 23, 1911

d. Toronto, Ontario, December 7, 1979

Winnipeg Monarchs graduate

Signed with Leafs, July 15, 1941.

1941–42 F	47	15	8	23	14
1944–45 L	17	2	4	6	11
Totals	64	17	12	29	25

F November 8, 1941 **L** March 18, 1945

• Replaced injured Don Metz in 1941–42

• Missed 1942–44 while serving in the Royal Canadian Air Force; returned to university after 1944–45 season.

DARWIN McCUTCHEON #2

defence 6'4" 190 L

b. Listowel, Ontario, April 19, 1962
Selected 179th overall in 1980 Entry Draft.

1981–82 F/L	1	0	0	0	2

F/L December 31, 1981

JACK McDONALD #unknown

left wing R

b. Quebec City, Quebec, February 28, 1887
d. Montreal, Quebec, January 24, 1958
Started 1920–21 with Montreal; loaned to
St. Pats, February 11, 1921, for remainder
of season.

1920–21	8	0	1	1	0

LANNY McDONALD #7

right wing 6' 194 R

b. Hanna, Alberta, February 16, 1953
Selected 4th overall in 1973 Amateur Draft.
Traded with Joel Quenneville to Colorado
Rockies for Pat Hickey and Wilf Paiement,
December 29, 1979.

1973–74 F	70	14	16	30	43
1974–75	64	17	27	44	86
1975–76	75	37	56	93	70
1976–77	80	46	44	90	77
1977–78	74	47	40	87	54
1978–79	79	43	42	85	32
1979–80	35	15	15	30	10
Totals	477	219	240	459	372

F October 10, 1973
• Joined Calgary Flames' front office after
retiring.
• Named chairman of Hockey Hall of Fame,
May 2015.
• Hockey Hall of Fame 1992

WILFRED "BUCKO" McDONALD #3/#19

defence 5'9" 205 L

b. Fergus, Ontario, October 31, 1911
d. Burks Falls, Ontario, July 19, 1991
Purchased from Detroit for Bill Thomson and
$10,000, December 19, 1938; loaned to Prov-
idence (IAHL) for the rest of the reason with
George Boothman and Jack Forsey for Ab
DeMarco and Buck Jones, February 2, 1943.
Traded to New York Rangers for Gordie Bell,
Dudley Garrett, and first postwar call on
Charlie Rayner, November 25, 1943.

1938–39	33	3	3	6	20
1939–40	34	2	5	7	13
1940–41	31	6	11	17	12
1941–42	48	2	19	21	24
1942–43	40	2	11	13	39
1943–44	9	2	4	6	8
Totals	195	17	53	70	116

• Later entered politics and became a
member of parliament.

BOB "BIG DADDY" McGILL
#4/#15/#8/#26

defence 6'1" 193 R

b. Edmonton, Alberta, April 27, 1962
Selected 26th overall in 1980 Entry Draft;
traded with Rick Vaive and Steve Thomas
to Chicago for Ed Olczyk and Al Secord,
September 4, 1987.
Claimed off waivers from Tampa Bay,
September 9, 1992; signed as a free agent
by New York Islanders, September 7, 1993.

1981–82 F	68	1	10	11	263
1982–83	30	0	0	0	146
1983–84	11	0	2	2	51
1984–85	72	0	5	5	250
1985–86	61	1	4	5	141
1986–87	56	1	4	5	103
1992–93	19	1	0	1	34
Totals	317	4	25	29	988

F October 6, 1981

JOHN McINTYRE ("Mac") #44

centre 6'1" 180 L

b. Ravenswood, Ontario, April 29, 1969
Selected 49th overall in 1987 Entry Draft.
Traded to Los Angeles for Mike Krushelnyski,
November 9, 1990.

1989–90 F	59	5	12	17	117
1990–91	13	0	3	3	25
Totals	72	5	15	20	142

F October 25, 1989

LARRY McINTYRE #25

defence 6'1" 190 L

b. Moose Jaw, Saskatchewan, July 13, 1949
Selected 31st overall in 1969 Amateur Draft.
Traded with Murray Heatley to Vancouver for
Dunc Wilson, May 29, 1973.

1969–70 F	1	0	0	0	0
1972–73 L	40	0	3	3	26
Totals	41	0	3	3	26

F January 7, 1970 **L** April 1, 1973

WALT McKECHNIE #11

centre 6'2" 200 L

b. London, Ontario, June 19, 1947
Acquired from Minnesota North Stars for
a third-round draft choice in 1980 (Randy
Velischek), October 5, 1978.
Traded to Colorado Rockies for a third-round
draft choice in 1980 (Fred Boimistruck),
March 3, 1980.

1978–79	79	25	36	61	18
1979–80	54	7	36	43	4
Totals	133	32	72	104	22

• Later opened a restaurant in southern
Ontario cottage country called McKech's.

GREG McKEGG #39

centre 6' 190 L

b. St. Thomas, Ontario, June 17, 1992
Selected 62nd overall in 2010 Entry Draft.

2013–14 F	1	0	0	0	0
2014–15	3	0	0	0	0
Totals	4	0	0	0	0

F February 1, 2014

SEAN McKENNA #8/#21

right wing 6' 190 L

b. Asbestos, Quebec, March 7, 1962
Acquired from Los Angeles for Mike Allison,
December 14, 1987.

1987–88	40	5	5	10	12
1988–89	3	0	1	1	0
1989–90 L	5	0	0	0	20
Totals	48	5	6	11	32

L November 16, 1989

DON McKENNEY ("Slip") #17

centre 6' 175 L

b. Smiths Falls, Ontario, April 30, 1934
Acquired with Andy Bathgate from the
New York Rangers for Dick Duff, Bob Nevin,
Rod Seiling, Bill Collins, and Arnie Brown,
February 22, 1964.
Claimed off waivers by Detroit, June 8, 1965.

1963–64	15	9	17	26	2
1964–65	52	6	13	19	6
Totals	67	15	30	45	8

• Assisted Fern Flaman at Northeastern
University for 19 years as coach and scout.

JIM McKENNY ("Howie") #18/#25

defence 6' 185 R

b. Ottawa, Ontario, December 1, 1946
Selected 17th overall in 1963 Amateur Draft.
Traded to Minnesota North Stars for cash
and future considerations (Owen Lloyd), May
10, 1978.

1965–66 F	2	0	0	0	2
1966–67	6	1	0	1	0
1967–68	5	1	0	1	0
1968–69	7	0	0	0	2
1969–70	73	11	33	44	34
1970–71	68	4	26	30	42
1971–72	76	5	31	36	27
1972–73	77	11	41	52	55
1973–74	77	14	28	42	36
1974–75	66	8	35	43	31
1975–76	46	10	19	29	19
1976–77	76	14	31	45	36
1977–78	15	2	2	4	8
Totals	594	81	246	327	292

F February 26, 1966
• Missed most of 1967–68 with leg injury.
• Longtime sports reporter for CITY-TV in
Toronto.

MURRAY McLACHLAN #31

goalie 6' 195 L

b. London, Ontario, October 20, 1948
Signed after graduating from University of
Minnesota.

1970–71 F/L	2	0–1–0	25	4	0	9.60

F November 18, 1970 **L** November 19, 1970

FRAZER McLAREN #38

left wing 6'5" 230 L

b. Winnipeg, Manitoba, October 29, 1987
Claimed off waivers from San Jose, January
31, 2013.

2012–13	35	3	2	5	102
2013–14	27	0	0	0	77
Totals	62	3	2	5	179

JACK McLEAN #7/#18

centre 5'8" 165 R

b. Winnipeg, Manitoba, January 31, 1923
d. October 14, 2003
Signed as a free agent, November 10, 1942.

1942–43 F	27	9	8	17	33
1943–44	32	3	15	18	30
1944–45 L	8	2	1	3	13
Totals	67	14	24	38	76

F November 12, 1942 **L** December 16, 1944
• Played only home games in 1944–45 while
attending university, missed part of the
season with a broken ankle, and retired at
the end of the season.

JOHN McLELLAN #14

centre 5'11" 150 L

b. South Porcupine, Ontario, August 6, 1928
d. Toronto, Ontario, October 27, 1979
Marlboros graduate
Traded with cash to Cleveland (AHL) for
Hugh Barlow, September 16, 1954.

1951–52 F/L	2	0	0	0	0

F December 29, 1951 **L** December 30, 1951
• Won a gold medal with Belleville McFarlands
at the 1959 World Championship.
• Later became Leafs coach.

DAVE McLLWAIN #7

forward 6' 190 L

b. Seaforth, Ontario, January 9, 1967
Acquired with Ken Baumgartner from New
York Islanders for Daniel Marois and Claude
Loiselle, March 10, 1992.
Claimed by Ottawa Senators in Waiver Draft,
October 3, 1993.

1991–92	11	1	2	3	4
1992–93	66	14	4	18	30
Totals	77	15	6	21	34

GERRY McNAMARA #1

goalie 6'2" 190 L
b. Sturgeon Falls, Ontario, September 22, 1934
St. Mike's graduate
Recalled from Sudbury Wolves in February 1961 to replace injured Johnny Bower.

1960–61	F	5	2–2–1	300	13	0	2.60
1969–70	L	2	0–0–0	23	2	0	5.22
Totals		7	2–2–1	323	15	0	2.79

F February 15, 1961 L January 23, 1970
• Later became Leafs' GM.

BASIL McRAE #26

left wing 6'2" 205 L
b. Beaverton, Ontario, January 5, 1961
Acquired from Quebec for Richard Turmel, August 12, 1983.
Signed as a free agent by Detroit, July 17, 1985.

1983–84		3	0	0	0	19
1984–85		1	0	0	0	0
Totals		4	0	0	0	19

CHRIS McRAE #32/#29

left wing 6' 200 L
b. Beaverton, Ontario, August 26, 1965
Signed as a free agent, October 16, 1985.
Traded to New York Rangers for Ken Hammond, February 21, 1989.

1987–88	F	11	0	0	0	65
1988–89		3	0	0	0	12
Totals		14	0	0	0	77

F December 18, 1987

GORD McRAE ("The Bird") #1/#31

goalie 6' 180 L
b. Sherbrooke, Quebec, April 12, 1948
Signed as a free agent, 1970.

1972–73	F	11	7–3–0	620	39	0	3.77
1974–75		20	10–3–6	1,063	57	0	3.22
1975–76		20	6–5–2	956	59	0	3.70
1976–77		2	0–1–1	120	9	0	4.50
1977–78	L	18	7–10–1	1,040	57	1	3.29
Totals		71	30–22–10	3,799	221	1	3.49

F January 31, 1973 L April 9, 1978

KEN McRAE #36/#40

centre 6'1" 195 R
b. Winchester, Ontario, April 23, 1968
Acquired from Quebec for Len Esau, July 21, 1992.
Signed as a free agent by Edmonton, September 9, 1994.

1992–93	2	0	0	0	2
1993–94	9	1	1	2	36
Totals	11	1	1	2	38

GERRY MEEHAN #26/#27

centre 6'2" 200 L
b. Toronto, Ontario, September 3, 1946
Selected 21st overall in 1963 Amateur Draft.
Traded with Mike Byers and Bill Sutherland to Philadelphia for Forbes Kennedy and Brit Selby, March 2, 1969.

1968–69	F	25	0	2	2	2

F December 1, 1968

HOWIE MEEKER ("Hurricane Howie") #11/#15

right wing 5'8" 165 R
b. Kitchener, Ontario, November 4, 1924
Signed April 12, 1946, from Stratford Indians (OHA Senior).

1946–47	F	55	27	18	45	76
1947–48		58	14	20	34	62
1948–49		30	7	7	14	56
1949–50		70	18	22	40	35
1950–51		49	6	14	20	24
1951–52		54	9	14	23	50
1952–53		25	1	7	8	26
1953–54	L	5	1	0	1	0
Totals		346	83	102	185	329

F October 16, 1946 L November 29, 1953
• Fractured collarbone in practice, December 26, 1948; missed most of the rest of the year. Missed much of 1952–53 with back injury that forced him to retire at 1953 training camp. He was allowed to coach Stratford (OHA Senior) subject to immediate recall; recalled November 20, 1953, when both George Armstrong and Bob Bailey were injured.
• Later became coach and then GM of the Leafs.
• Worked as game analyst for *Hockey Night in Canada* for many years, espousing skills for young players.

HARRY MEEKING ("Meek") #7

left wing 5'7" 160 R
b. Berlin (Kitchener), Ontario, November 4, 1894
d. Toronto, Ontario, December 13, 1971
Signed from Glace Bay (Maritime Independent League).
Released, February 18, 1919, and left to play for Glace Bay.

1917–18	20	10	—	10	19
1918–19	14	7	3	10	22
Totals	34	17	3	20	41

• Suspended by Arenas for the rest of the season, February 12, 1919. Manager Querrie wrote: "Under paragraph No. 2 in your contract you are suspended. Your play in the last three games has not been satisfactory to the club, and we feel you didn't give your best services to us or try at all in the last Ottawa fixture."

BARRY MELROSE #26

defence 6' 205 R
b. Kelvington, Saskatchewan, July 15, 1956
Claimed off waivers from Minnesota North Stars, November 30, 1980.
Signed as a free agent by Detroit, September 6, 1983.

1980–81	57	2	5	7	166
1981–82	64	1	5	6	186
1982–83	52	2	5	7	68
Totals	173	5	15	20	420

• Later became coach in Los Angeles and then colour commentator for that team.

DON METZ #11/#15/#18

right wing 5'9" 165 R
b. Wilcox, Saskatchewan, January 10, 1916
d. Regina, Saskatchewan, November 16, 2007
Joined Leafs late in 1938–39 after three years with Toronto Goodyears (OHA Senior).
Retired April 19, 1949.

1939–40	F	10	1	1	2	4
1940–41		31	4	10	14	6
1941–42		25	2	3	5	8
1945–46		7	1	0	1	0
1946–47		40	4	9	13	10
1947–48		26	4	6	10	2
1948–49	L	33	4	6	10	12
Totals		172	20	35	55	42

F November 19, 1939 L March 20, 1949
• Missed 1942–45 while serving in the Royal Canadian Air Force.
• Returned to farming in Saskatchewan with his brother.

NICK METZ ("Handy Andy"/"Red"/"Pop") #5/#15/#19/#17/#10

left wing 5'11" 160 L
b. Wilcox, Saskatchewan, February 16, 1914
d. Regina, Saskatchewan, August 25, 1990
St. Mike's graduate, 1934
Retired April 22, 1948.

1934–35	F	18	2	2	4	4
1935–36		38	14	6	20	14
1936–37		48	9	11	20	19
1937–38		48	15	7	22	12
1938–39		47	11	10	21	15
1939–40		31	6	5	11	2
1940–41		47	14	21	35	10
1941–42		30	11	9	20	20
1944–45		50	22	13	35	26
1945–46		41	11	11	22	4
1946–47		60	12	16	28	15
1947–48	L	60	4	8	12	8
Totals		518	131	119	250	149

F November 8, 1934 L March 21, 1948
• Missed many games December 1939–January 1940 with concussion; missed 1942–44 while serving in the Royal Canadian Engineers; returned to Leafs on October 19, 1944.
• After retirement from hockey, returned to Saskatchewan to farm with his brother.

LARRY MICKEY #12

right wing 5'11" 180 R
b. Lacombe, Alberta, October 21, 1943
d. Amherst, New York, July 23, 1982
Claimed from New York Rangers in Intra-League Draft, June 12, 1968.
Claimed by Montreal in Intra-League Draft, June 11, 1969.

1968–69	55	8	19	27	43

• Coached minor hockey after retiring in 1975, primarily in Northeastern Hockey League.

RUDY MIGAY ("Toy Terrier") #11/#14/#22/#21

centre 5'10" 175 L
b. Fort William, Ontario, November 18, 1928
St. Mike's graduate
Signed September 15, 1948.

1949–50	F	18	1	5	6	8
1951–52		19	2	1	3	12
1952–53		40	5	4	9	22
1953–54		70	8	15	23	60
1954–55		67	8	16	24	66
1955–56		70	12	16	28	52
1956–57		66	15	20	35	51
1957–58		48	7	14	21	18
1958–59		19	1	1	2	4
1959–60	L	1	0	0	0	0
Totals		418	59	92	151	293

F December 1, 1949 L October 10, 1959
• Missed much of 1951–52 after suffering torn knee ligaments, November 8, 1951.

JOHN "JIM" MIKOL #16

defence 6' 175 R
b. Kitchener, Ontario, June 11, 1938
Acquired from Cleveland (AHL), summer 1962.
Sold to Cleveland (AHL), August 26, 1963.

1962–63	F	4	0	1	1	2

F October 14, 1962

MIKE MILLAR #36

right wing 5'10" 170 L
b. St. Catharines, Ontario, April 28, 1965
Signed as a free agent, July 19, 1990.

1990–91	F	7	2	2	4	2

F December 12, 1990
• Played most of 1990–91 with Newmarket, then retired.

EARL MILLER #15

forward 5'11" 185 L
b. Regina, Saskatchewan, September 12, 1905
d. Regina, Saskatchewan, June 20, 1936
Purchased from Chicago, February 7, 1932.

1931–32	L	15	3	3	6	10

L March 22, 1932

DMITRI MIRONOV ("Tree") #15

defence 6'2" 191 R
b. Moscow, Soviet Union (Russia), December 25, 1965
Selected 160th overall in 1991 Entry Draft.
Traded with a second-round draft choice in 1996 (later sent to New Jersey—Joshua Dewolf) to Pittsburgh for Larry Murphy, July 8, 1995.

1991–92	F	7	1	0	1	0
1992–93		59	7	24	31	40
1993–94		76	9	27	36	78
1994–95		33	5	12	17	28
Totals		175	22	63	85	146

F March 17, 1992

JOHN MITCHELL #39

centre 6'1" 205 L

b. Oakville, Ontario, January 22, 1985
Selected 158th overall in 2003 Entry Draft.
Traded to New York Rangers for a seventh-round draft choice in 2012 (Viktor Loov), February 28, 2011.

2008–09	76	12	17	29	33
2009–10	60	6	17	23	31
2010–11	23	2	1	3	12
Totals	159	20	35	55	76

IVAN "MIKE" MITCHELL #unknown

goalie

b. Winnipeg, Manitoba, July 9, 1893
d. Winnipeg, Manitoba, May 8, 1942
Signed from PCHA; signed as a free agent by Hamilton, Decmeber 5, 1921; loaned from Hamilton when John Ross Roach injured in practice prior to 1921–22 season opener.

1919–20 F	16		6–7–0	830	60	0	4.34
1920–21	4		2–2–0	240	22	0	5.50
1921–22 L	2		2–0–0	120	6	0	3.00
Totals	21		11–9–0	1,232	93	0	4.53

F December 23, 1919 L December 21, 1921
• Played first two games of 1921–22; missed rest of season with food poisoning.

FREDRIK "FREDDY" MODIN #19

forward 6'3" 202 L

b. Sundsvall, Sweden, October 8, 1974
Selected 64th overall in 1994 Entry Draft.
Traded to Tampa Bay for Cory Cross and a seventh-round draft choice in 2001 (Ivan Kolozvary), on October 1, 1999.

1996–97 F	76	6	7	13	24
1997–98	74	16	16	32	32
1998–99	67	16	15	31	35
Totals	217	38	38	76	91

F October 5, 1996
• Member of the IIHF Triple Gold Club

LYLE MOFFAT #26

left wing 5'10" 180 L

b. Calgary, Alberta, March 19, 1948
Signed at training camp 1971.
Signed by Cleveland (WHA) as a free agent, July 1975.

1972–73 F	1	0	0	0	0
1974–75	22	2	7	9	13
Totals	23	2	7	9	13

F March 4, 1973

ALEXANDER MOGILNY #89

right wing 6' 210 L

b. Khabarovsk, Soviet Union (Russia), February 18, 1969
Signed as a free agent, July 3, 2001.
Signed as a free agent by New Jersey, August 16, 2005.

2001–02	66	24	33	57	8
2002–03	73	33	46	79	12
2003–04	37	8	22	30	12
Totals	176	65	101	166	32

SERGIO MOMESSO ("Mo") #7

left wing 6'3" 215 L

b. Montreal, Quebec, September 4, 1965
Acquired from Vancouver for Mike Ridley, July 8, 1995.
Traded to New York Rangers with Bill Berg for Nick Kypreos and Wayne Presley, February 29, 1996.

1995–96	54	7	8	15	112

GARRY MONAHAN ("Mondo") #14/#20

left wing 6' 185 L

b. Barrie, Ontario, October 20, 1946
Acquired with Brian Murphy from Los Angeles for Bob Pulford, September 3, 1970; traded with John Grisdale to Vancouver for Dave Dunn, October 16, 1974.
Purchased from Vancouver, September 13, 1978; played 1979–80 season with Seibu, Tokyo.

1970–71	78	15	22	37	79
1971–72	78	14	17	31	47
1972–73	78	13	18	31	53
1973–74	78	9	16	25	70
1974–75	1	0	0	0	0
1978–79 L	62	4	7	11	25
Totals	375	55	80	135	274

L April 7, 1979
• Became a broadcaster, stockbroker, and later real estate agent in Vancouver after retiring.

DICKIE MOORE ("Digging Dicker") #16

right wing 5'10" 185 R

b. Montreal, Quebec, January 6, 1931
Claimed from Montreal in Intra-League Draft, June 10, 1964.
Retired due to chronic back injury at end of 1964–65 season.

1964–65	38	2	4	6	68

• Runs construction equipment rental businesses in Montreal.
• Hockey Hall of Fame 1974

DOMINIC MOORE #19

centre 6' 190 L

b. Thornhill, Ontario, August 3, 1980
Claimed off waivers from Minnesota, January 11, 2008.
Traded to Buffalo for a second-round draft choice in 2009 (Jesse Blacker), March 4, 2009.

2007–08	38	4	10	14	14
2008–09	63	12	29	41	69
Totals	101	16	39	55	83

MARC MORO #33

defence 6'1" 220 L

b. Toronto, Ontario, July 17, 1977
Acquired from Nashville for Denis Smith and Marty Wilford, March 1, 2002.

2001–02	2	0	0	0	2

• Only Leaf games March 4 & 6, 2002; career minor leaguer thereafter.

ELWYN "MOE" MORRIS #5

defence 5'7" 185 L

b. Toronto, Ontario, January 3, 1921
d. Toronto, Ontario, February 6, 2000
Marlboros graduate
Signed by Leafs, June 15, 1943.
Acquired by New York Rangers with Wally Stanowski and the rights to Orval Lavell for Cal Gardner, Rene Trudell, Bill Juzda, and the rights to Ray McMurray, April 26, 1948.

1943–44 F	50	12	21	33	22
1944–45	29	0	2	2	18
1945–46	38	1	5	6	10
Totals	117	13	28	41	50

F October 30, 1943
• Also played football for the Toronto Argonauts (IRFU) in 1940 and 1946.

JIM MORRISON ("Moe") #3/#14/#21/#22/#24

defence 5'10" 183 L

b. Montreal, Quebec, October 11, 1931
Acquired from Boston for Fleming Mackell, January 9, 1952.
Traded to Boston for Allan Stanley, October 3, 1958.

1951–52	17	0	1	1	4
1952–53	56	1	8	9	36
1953–54	60	9	11	20	51
1954–55	70	5	12	17	84
1955–56	63	2	17	19	77
1956–57	63	3	17	20	44
1957–58	70	3	21	24	62
Totals	399	23	87	110	358

GERALD "GUS" MORTSON ("Old Hardrock"/"The Nugget"/"The Gold Dust Twins" with Jim Thomson) #3/#19

defence 5'11" 190 L

b. New Liskeard, Ontario, January 24, 1925
St. Mike's graduate
Traded with Al Rollins, Cal Gardner, and Ray Hannigan to Chicago for Harry Lumley, September 11, 1952.

1946–47 F	60	5	13	18	133
1947–48	58	7	11	18	118
1948–49	60	2	13	15	85
1949–50	68	3	14	17	125
1950–51	60	3	10	13	142
1951–52	65	1	10	11	106
Totals	371	21	71	92	709

F October 16, 1946
• Released from Canadian Navy in 1945.
• Later sold mining equipment.

MARCEL MUELLER #45

centre 6'3" 220 L

b. Berlin, West Germany (Germany), July 10, 1988
Signed as a free agent, July 14, 2010.
Later played in Sweden.

2010–11 F/L	3	0	0	0	2

F January 15, 2011 L January 20, 2011

RICHARD MULHERN #8

defence 6'1" 188 L

b. Edmonton, Alberta, March 1, 1955
Claimed off waivers from Los Angeles, February 10, 1980.
Sold to Winnipeg, December 2, 1980.

1979–80	26	0	10	10	11

KIRK MULLER #21

left wing 6' 205 L

b. Kingston, Ontario, February 8, 1966
Acquired from New York Islanders in a three-way trade, January 23, 1996. Leafs sent Damian Rhodes and Ken Belanger to Islanders; Ottawa sent Don Beaupre, Bryan Berard, and Martin Straka to Islanders; Islanders sent Rhodes and Wade Redden to Ottawa and Beaupre and Muller to Leafs.
Traded to Florida for Jason Podollan, March 18, 1997.

1995–96	36	9	16	25	42
1996–97	66	20	17	37	85
Totals	102	29	33	62	127

• Later coached in the NHL.

HARRY MUMMERY ("Mumm") #2/#10

defence 6' 245 L

b. Chicago, Illinois, August 25, 1889
d. Brandon, Manitoba, December 9, 1945
Acquired in the dispersal of players from Quebec (NHA), December 1917.
Signed by Quebec Bulldogs, summer 1919.

1917–18	18	3	—	3	24
1918–19	13	2	0	2	27
Totals	31	5	0	5	51

• Missed first three games of 1917–18 in contract dispute.

CRAIG MUNI #32/#33/#29/#26/#34

defence 6'3" 200 L

b. Toronto, Ontario, July 19, 1962
Selected 25th overall in 1980 Entry Draft.
Signed as a free agent by Edmonton, August 18, 1986.

1981–82 F	3	0	0	0	2
1982–83	2	0	1	1	0
1984–85	8	0	0	0	0
1985–86	6	0	1	1	4
Totals	19	0	2	2	6

F December 31, 1982

GERRY MUNRO #9

defence 5'10" 175 L

b. Sault Ste. Marie, Ontario, November 20, 1897
d. Sudbury, Ontario, January 20, 1960
Purchased from Montreal Maroons, summer 1925.

1925–26 L	7	0	0	0	8

L January 1, 1926

LARRY MURPHY #55

defence 6'2" 210 R

b. Scarborough (Toronto), Ontario, March 8, 1961

Acquired from Pittsburgh for Dmitri Mironov and a second-round draft choice in 1996 (later sent to New Jersey—Joshua Dewolf), July 8, 1995.

Traded to Detroit for future considerations, March 18, 1997.

1995–96	82	12	49	61	34
1996–97	69	7	32	39	20
Totals	151	19	81	100	54

• Hockey Hall of Fame 2004

KEN MURRAY #3/#7

defence 6' 180 R

b. Toronto, Ontario, January 22, 1948

Signed as a free agent, April 5, 1970.

Claimed by Buffalo in Intra-League Draft, June 8, 1971.

1969–70 F	1	0	1	1	2
1970–71	4	0	0	0	0
Totals	5	0	1	1	2

F April 5, 1970

RANDY MURRAY #26/#3

defence 6'1" 195 R

b. Chatham, Ontario, August 24, 1945

1969–70 F/L	4	0	0	0	2

F November 9, 1969 L April 5, 1970

ERIC "RIC" NATTRESS #2

defence 6'2" 210 R

b. Hamilton, Ontario, May 25, 1962

Acquired with Doug Gilmour, Jamie Macoun, Rick Wamsley, and Kent Manderville from Calgary for Gary Leeman, Michel Petit, Craig Berube, Alexander Godynyuk, and Jeff Reese, January 2, 1992.

Signed as a free agent by Philadelphia, August 21, 1992.

1991–92	36	2	14	16	32

ZDENEK NEDVED ("Zed") #45/#20/#10

right wing 6' 185 L

b. Kladno, Czechoslovakia (Czech Republic), March 3, 1975

Selected 123rd overall in 1993 Entry Draft. Recalled from St. John's (AHL), January 6, 1997; demoted March 19, 1997.

1994–95 F	1	0	0	0	2
1995–96	7	1	1	2	6
1996–97	23	3	5	8	6
Totals	31	4	6	10	14

F February 8, 1995

• Played all of 1993–94 and most of 1994–95 with Sudbury (OHL); missed half of 1995–96 with shoulder injury.

BOB NEELY ("Waldo") #3

left wing 6'1" 210 L

b. Sarnia, Ontario, November 9, 1953

Selected 10th overall in 1973 Amateur Draft.

Sold to Colorado Rockies, May 30, 1978.

1973–74 F	54	5	7	12	98
1974–75	57	5	16	21	61
1975–76	69	9	13	22	89
1976–77	70	17	16	33	16
1977–78	11	0	1	1	0
Totals	261	36	53	89	264

F October 10, 1973

GORD NELSON #27

defence 5'7" 180 L

b. Kinistino, Saskatchewan, May 10, 1947

Signed as a free agent, December 10, 1969.

Acquired by Phoenix (WHL), summer 1971.

1969–70 F/L	3	0	0	0	11

F December 10, 1969 L December 13, 1969

ERIC NESTERENKO ("Elbows"/ "Nester") #16/#19/#25

right wing 6'2" 197 R

b. Flin Flon, Manitoba, October 31, 1933

Sold with Harry Lumley to Chicago for $40,000, May 21, 1956.

1951–52 F	1	0	0	0	0
1952–53	35	10	6	16	27
1953–54	68	14	9	23	70
1954–55	62	15	15	30	99
1955–56	40	4	6	10	65
Totals	206	43	36	79	261

F March 5, 1952

MIKE NEVILLE #8

forward 5'9" 170 R

b. Toronto, Ontario, October 11, 1902

d. January 16, 1958

Acquired from London (OHA Senior) for 1924–25 season.

Signed with Hamilton (Can Pro) prior to 1926–27 season.

1924–25	13	1	2	3	4
1925–26	33	3	3	6	8
Totals	46	4	5	9	12

BOB NEVIN ("Nevvy") #11

right wing 6' 190 R

b. South Porcupine, Ontario, March 18, 1938

Marlboros graduate

Signed with Leafs, June 11, 1958.

Traded with Dick Duff, Rod Seiling, Arnie Brown, and Bill Collins to New York Rangers for Andy Bathgate and Don McKenney, February 22, 1964.

1957–58 F	4	0	0	0	0
1958–59	2	0	0	0	2
1960–61	68	21	37	58	13
1961–62	69	15	30	45	10
1962–63	58	12	21	33	4
1963–64	49	7	12	19	26
Totals	250	55	100	155	55

F December 8, 1957

KRIS NEWBURY #54

centre 5'11" 205 L

b. Brampton, Ontario, February 19, 1982

Signed as a free agent, October 2, 2003.

Signed as a free agent by Detroit, July 6, 2009.

2006–07	15	2	2	4	26
2007–08	28	1	1	2	32
2008–09	1	0	0	0	2
Totals	44	3	3	6	60

JOE NIEUWENDYK #25

centre 6'2" 205 L

b. Oshawa, Ontario, September 10, 1966

Signed as a free agent, September 10, 2003.

Signed as a free agent by Florida, August 1, 2005.

2003–04	64	22	28	50	26

• Hockey Hall of Fame 2011

FRANK "DUTCH" NIGHBOR ("The Pembroke Peach"/"The Pembroke Pippin"/"The Flying Dutchman") #7

centre 5'9" 160 L

b. Pembroke, Ontario, January 26, 1893

d. Pembroke, Ontario, April 13, 1966

Acquired from Ottawa for Danny Cox until season's end only, January 6, 1930, with Ottawa gaining an option to buy Cox's contract. Ottawa exercised the option, May 4, 1930, giving the Leafs cash to complete the deal.

1929–30 L	22	2	0	2	2

L March 18, 1930

• Hockey Hall of Fame 1947

FRANK NIGRO #32/#16

centre 5'9" 180 R

b. Richmond Hill, Ontario, February 11, 1960.

Selected 93rd overall in 1979 Entry Draft.

Signed with Merano (Italy), summer 1984.

1982–83 F	51	6	15	21	23
1983–84 L	17	2	3	5	16
Totals	68	8	18	26	39

F October 23, 1982 L March 28, 1984

REG NOBLE #8/#4

left wing 5'8" 180 L

b. Collingwood, Ontario, June 23, 1895

d. Alliston, Ontario, January 19, 1962

Joined Arenas after NHA disbanded.

Sold to Montreal Maroons for $6,000, December 9, 1924.

1917–18	20	30	—	30	35
1918–19	17	10	5	15	35
1919–20	24	24	9	33	52
1920–21	24	19	8	27	54
1921–22	24	17	11	28	19
1922–23	24	12	11	23	47
1923–24	23	12	5	17	79
1924–25	3	1	0	1	8
Totals	159	125	49	174	329

• Suspended for game of February 2, 1918, and fined $100 for breaking training rules; also suspended with Harry Cameron, January 13, 1919, for breaking training rules; reinstated January 18.

• Hockey Hall of Fame 1962

OWEN NOLAN #11

right wing 6'1" 215 R

b. Belfast, Ireland, February 12, 1972

Acquired from San Jose for Alyn McCauley, Brad Boyes, and a first-round draft choice in 2003 (later traded to Boston—Mark Stuart), March 5, 2003.

Signed as a free agent by Phoenix, August 16, 2006.

2002–03	14	7	5	12	16
2003–04	65	19	29	48	110
Totals	79	26	34	60	126

PAT NOLAN #unknown

forward 5'8" 170 L

b. Charlottetown, Prince Edward Island, December 1, 1897

d. New Glasgow, Nova Scotia, April 12, 1957

1921–22 F/L	

F December 24, 1921 L January 14, 1922

• Played most of 1921–22 with New Glasgow (Maritime Independent League).

MIKE NYKOLUK #24/#27

right wing 5'11" 212 R

b. Toronto, Ontario, December 11, 1934

Marlboros graduate

Traded with Ron Hurst and Wally Boyer to Hershey (AHL) for Willie Marshall, summer 1958.

1956–57 F/L	32	3	1	4	20

F October 31, 1956 L February 10, 1957

• Later became cigar-chomping coach of the Leafs.

GARY NYLUND ("Beaker") #2

defence 6'4" 210 L

b. Surrey, British Columbia, October 28, 1963

Selected 3rd overall in 1982 Entry Draft.

Signed as a free agent by Chicago, August 27, 1986.

1982–83 F	16	0	3	3	16
1983–84	47	2	14	16	103
1984–85	76	3	17	20	99
1985–86	79	2	16	18	180
Totals	218	7	50	57	398

F February 6, 1982

• Won gold medal with Canada at 1982 World Junior Championship.

RYAN O'BYRNE #23

defence 6'5" 235 R

b. Victoria, British Columbia, July 19, 1984

Acquired from Colorado for a fourth-round draft choice in 2014 (Nicholas Magyar), April 3, 2013.

Later played in KHL.

2012–13	8	1	1	2	6

GERRY O'FLAHERTY #16

left wing 5'10" 182 L

b. Pittsburgh, Pennsylvania, August 31, 1950

Selected 36th overall in 1970 Amateur Draft.

Claimed by Vancouver in Intra-League Draft, June 5, 1972.

1971–72 F	2	0	0	0	0

F December 25, 1971

ED OLCZYK ("Eddie O") #16

centre 6'1" 200 L

b. Chicago, Illinois, August 16, 1966
Acquired with Al Secord from Chicago for Rick Vaive, Steve Thomas, and Bob McGill, September 4, 1987.
Traded with Mark Osborne to Winnipeg for Dave Ellett and Paul Fenton, November 10, 1990.

1987–88	80	42	33	75	55
1988–89	80	38	52	90	75
1989–90	79	32	56	88	78
1990–91	18	4	10	14	13
Totals	257	116	151	267	221

MURRAY OLIVER #11

centre 5'9" 170 L

b. Hamilton, Ontario, November 14, 1937
d. Edina, Minnesota, November 23, 2014
Acquired with cash from Boston for Eddie Shack, May 15, 1967.
Traded to Minnesota North Stars for Brian Conacher and Terry O'Malley, May 22, 1970.

1967–68	74	16	21	37	18
1968–69	76	14	36	50	16
1969–70	76	14	33	47	16
Totals	226	44	90	134	50

• Later became a pro scout for Minnesota and Vancouver.

BERT OLMSTEAD #16

left wing 6'2" 183 L

b. Sceptre, Saskatchewan, September 4, 1926
Claimed from the Montreal in Intra-League draft, June 4, 1958.

1958–59	70	10	31	41	74
1959–60	53	15	21	36	63
1960–61	67	18	34	52	84
1961–62 L	56	13	23	36	10
Totals	246	56	109	165	231

L March 11, 1962
• Hockey Hall of Fame 1985

BEN ONDRUS #25/#26/#46

right wing 6' 195 R

b. Sherwood Park, Alberta, June 25, 1982
Signed as a free agent, May 27, 2004.
Signed as a free agent by Edmonton, July 9, 2010.

2005–06	22	0	0	0	18
2006–07	16	0	2	2	20
2007–08	3	0	0	0	5
2008–09	11	0	0	0	34
Totals	52	0	2	2	77

JEFF O'NEILL #92

centre 6'1" 195 R

b. Richmond Hill, Ontario, February 23, 1976
Acquired from Carolina for a fourth-round draft choice in 2006 (traded to St. Louis—Reto Berra), July 30, 2005.

2005–06	74	19	19	38	64
2006–07 L	74	20	22	42	54
Totals	148	39	41	80	118

L March 23, 2007

TOM "WINDY" O'NEILL #18

right wing 5'10" 155 R

b. Deseronto, Ontario, September 28, 1923
d. Toronto, Ontario, February 13, 1973
St. Mike's graduate, 1942

1943–44 F	33	8	7	15	29
1944–45 L	33	2	5	7	24
Totals	66	10	12	22	53

F November 27, 1942 L March 10, 1945

PHIL ORESKOVIC #40

defence 6'4" 215 R

b. North York (Toronto), Ontario, January 26, 1987
Selected 82nd overall in 2005 Entry Draft.

2008–09 F/L	10	1	1	2	21

F March 9, 2009 L March 28, 2009

COLTON ORR #28

right wing 6'3" 220 R

b. Winnipeg, Manitoba, March 3, 1982
Signed as a free agent, July 1, 2009.

2009–10	82	4	2	6	239
2010–11	46	2	0	2	128
2011–12	5	1	0	1	5
2012–13	44	1	3	4	155
2013–14	54	0	0	0	110
2014–15	1	0	0	0	0
Totals	232	8	5	13	637

MARK OSBORNE ("Ozzie") #12/#21

left wing 6'2" 205 L

b. Toronto, Ontario, August 13, 1961
Acquired from the New York Rangers for Jeff Jackson and a third-round draft choice in 1989 (Rob Zamuner), March 5, 1987; traded with Ed Olczyk to Winnipeg for Dave Ellett and Paul Fenton, November 10, 1990. Acquired from Winnipeg for Lucien DeBlois, March 10, 1992; signed as a free agent by New York Rangers, August 26, 1994.

1986–87	16	5	10	15	12
1987–88	79	23	37	60	102
1988–89	75	16	30	46	112
1989–90	78	23	50	73	91
1990–91	18	3	3	6	4
1991–92	11	3	1	4	8
1992–93	76	12	14	26	89
1993–94	73	9	15	24	145
Totals	426	94	160	254	563

RANDY OSBURN #16

left wing 6' 190 L

b. Collingwood, Ontario, November 26, 1952
Selected 27th overall in 1972 Amateur Draft.
Traded with Dave Fortier to Philadelphia for Bill Flett, May 27, 1974.

1972–73 F	26	0	2	2	0

F October 7, 1972

WILF PAIEMENT #99/#14

right wing 6'1" 210 R

b. Earlton, Ontario, October 16, 1955
Acquired with Pat Hickey from Colorado Rockies for Lanny McDonald and Joel Quenneville, December 29, 1979.
Traded to Quebec for Miroslav Frycer and a seventh-round draft choice in 1982 (Jeff Triano), March 9, 1982.

1979–80	41	20	28	48	72
1980–81	77	40	57	97	145
1981–82	69	18	40	58	203
Totals	187	78	125	203	420

MIKE PALMATEER ("The Popcorn Kid"/"Palmy") #29

goalie 5'9" 170 R

b. Toronto, Ontario, January 13, 1954
Selected 85th overall in 1974 Amateur Draft; traded with a third-round draft choice in 1980 (Torrie Robertson) to Washington for Robert Picard, Tim Coulis, and a second-round draft choice in 1980 (Bob McGill), June 11, 1980.
Purchased from Washington, September 9, 1982.

1976–77 F	50	23–18–8	2,877	154	4	3.21	
1977–78	63	34–19–9	3,760	172	5	2.74	
1978–79	58	26–21–10	3,396	167	4	2.95	
1979–80	38	16–14–3	2,039	125	2	3.68	
1982–83	53	21–23–7	2,965	197	0	3.99	
1983–84 L	34	9–17–4	1,831	149	0	4.88	
Totals	296	129–112–41	16,868	964	15	3.43	

F October 28, 1976 L February 5, 1984
• Later ran a hamburger fast-food restaurant just north of Toronto.

RICHARD PANIK #18

right wing 6'1" 208 L

b. Martin, Czechoslovakia (Slovakia), February 7, 1991
Claimed off waivers, October 9, 2014.

2014–15	76	11	6	17	49

JIM PAPPIN ("Pappy") #17/#18

right wing 6'1" 190 R

b. Copper Cliff, Ontario, September 10, 1939
Marlboros graduate, 1960
Traded to Chicago for Pierre Pilote, March 23, 1968.

1963–64 F	50	11	8	19	33
1964–65	44	9	9	18	33
1965–66	7	0	3	3	8
1966–67	64	21	11	32	89
1967–68	58	13	15	28	37
Totals	223	54	46	100	200

F November 23, 1963
• Played first seven games of 1965–66, then was demoted to Rochester (AHL) November 7 for the rest of the season.
• Became a scout for the St. Louis Blues.

BERNIE PARENT #30

goalie 5'10" 180 R

b. Montreal, Quebec, April 3, 1945
Acquired with a second-round draft choice in 1971 (Rick Kehoe) from Philadelphia for Bruce Gamble, Mike Walton, and a first-round draft choice in 1971 (Pierre Plante), February 1, 1971.
Rights traded with a second-round draft choice in 1973 (Larry Goodenough) to Philadelphia for Doug Favell and a first-round draft choice in 1973 (Bob Neely), July 27, 1973.

1970–71	18	7–7–3	1,040	46	0	2.65
1971–72	47	17–18–9	2,715	116	3	2.56
Totals	65	24–25–12	3,755	162	3	2.59

• Hockey Hall of Fame 1984

BOB PARENT #31

goalie 5'9" 175 R

b. Windsor, Ontario, February 19, 1958
Selected 65th overall in 1978 Amateur Draft.

1981–82 F	2	0–2–0	120	13	0	6.50
1982–83 L	1	0–0–0	40	2	0	3.00
Totals	3	0–2–0	160	15	0	5.63

F March 6, 1982 L February 26, 1983

JEAN-PAUL "J.P." PARISÉ #17

left wing 5'9" 175 L

b. Smooth Rock Falls, Ontario, December 11, 1941
d. Prior Lake, Minnesota, January 7, 2015
Acquired with Bryan Hextall from Oakland for Gerry Ehman, October 3, 1967.
Sold to Minnesota North Stars, December 27, 1967.

1967–68	1	0	1	1	0

• Only Leaf game November 15, 1967, then sent to Rochester (AHL) for the year.
• Became involved in insurance for many years until he accepted an offer to run a hockey program at a prep school in Minnesota.

GEORGE PARSONS ("Bubs"/"Cannonball") #16/#18/#25/#22

left wing 5'11" 174 L

b. Toronto, Ontario, June 28, 1914
d. Toronto, Ontario, June 30, 1998
Signed October 22, 1935.

1936–37 F	5	0	0	0	0
1937–38	30	5	6	11	6
1938–39 L	29	7	7	14	14
Totals	64	12	13	25	20

F November 28, 1936 L March 4, 1939
• Struck in the eye by Earl Robinson's stick in a game vs. Chicago, March 4, 1939—forced to retire.
• Later worked for CCM and the NHL, designing the gauge used by officials to determine the legality of a stick's curve.

GEORGE "PADDY" PATTERSON #6

right wing 6'1" 176 R

b. Kingston, Ontario, May 22, 1906

d. Kingston, Ontario, January 22, 1977

Purchased from Hamilton (Can Pro), February 6, 1927.

Traded to Montreal for Gerry Carson, February 8, 1928.

1926–27 F	17	4	2	6	17
1927–28	12	1	0	1	17
Totals	29	5	2	7	34

F February 8, 1927

• Scored first goal for Maple Leaf franchise, February 17, 1927.

ROB PEARSON #12

right wing 6'1" 185 R

b. Oshawa, Ontario, August 3, 1971

Selected 12th overall in 1989 Entry Draft.

Traded with a first-round draft choice in 1994 (Nolan Baumgartner) to Washington for Mike Ridley and a first-round draft choice in 1994 (Éric Fichaud), June 28, 1994.

1991–92 F	47	14	10	24	58
1992–93	78	23	14	37	211
1993–94	67	12	18	30	189
Totals	192	49	42	91	458

F October 3, 1991

SCOTT PEARSON #18/#22

left wing 6'1" 205 L

b. Cornwall, Ontario, December 19, 1969

Selected 6th overall in 1988 Entry Draft; traded with a second-round draft choice in 1991 (later traded to Washington—Éric Lavigne) and a second-round draft choice in 1992 (Tuomas Gronman) to Quebec for Michel Petit, Lucien DeBlois, and Aaron Broten, November 17, 1990.

Signed as a free agent July 8, 1996.

1988–89 F	9	0	1	1	2
1989–90	41	5	10	15	90
1990–91	12	0	0	0	20
1996–97	1	0	0	0	2
Totals	63	5	11	16	114

F October 6, 1988

MICHAEL PECA #27

centre 5'11" 185 R

b. Toronto, Ontario, March 26, 1974

Signed as a free agent, July 18, 2006.

Signed as a free agent by Columbus, August 22, 2007.

2006–07	35	4	11	15	60

TOM PEDERSON #24

defence 5'9" 175 R

b. Bloomington, Minnesota, January 14, 1970

Signed as a free agent, December 13, 1996.

Signed by Fort Wayne (IHL), summer 1997.

1996–97	15	1	2	3	9

• Started 1996–97 in Japan, playing for Seibu Tetsudo Bears.

MIKE PELYK ("Mike Mikita"/"Kita") #4/#21/#28/#20

defence 6'1" 188 L

b. Toronto, Ontario, September 29, 1947

Selected 17th overall in 1964 Amateur Draft; signed by Cincinnati (WHA), July 1974, but loaned to Vancouver (WHA) for the 1974–75 season.

Signed from Cincinnati, September 1976 (in exchange for Leafs agreeing to take on the balance of Pelyk's contract, Cincinnati withdrew its claim on the rights to Randy Carlyle, who had agreed to terms but had not signed with Cincinnati). Signed as a free agent by Buffalo, August 22, 1979.

1967–68 F	24	0	3	3	55
1968–69	65	3	9	12	146
1969–70	36	1	3	4	37
1970–71	73	5	21	26	54
1971–72	46	1	4	5	44
1972–73	72	3	16	19	118
1973–74	71	12	19	31	94
1976–77	13	0	2	2	4
1977–78 L	41	1	11	12	14
Totals	441	26	88	114	566

F February 7, 1968 L April 9, 1978

• Missed November 19, 1969–January 4, 1970, with a broken collarbone.

• Became involved in commercial real estate after retiring.

STUART PERCY #50

defence 6'1" 187 L

b. Oakville, Ontario, May 18, 1993

Drafted 25th overall in 2011 Entry Draft.

2014–15 F	9	0	3	3	2

F October 8, 2014

FRED PERLINI #8/#28/#29/#32/#34

centre 6'2" 175 R

b. Sault Ste. Marie, Ontario, April 12, 1962

Selected 158th overall in 1980 Entry Draft.

1981–82 F	7	2	3	5	0
1983–84 L	1	0	0	0	0
Totals	8	2	3	5	0

F December 30, 1981 L April 1, 1984

• Played afternoon game with Marlies, night game with Leafs, Saturday, February 20, 1982.

YANIC PERREAULT ("Yan") #44/#94

centre 5'11" 182 L

b. Sherbrooke, Quebec, April 4, 1971

Selected 47th overall in 1991 Entry Draft; traded to Los Angeles for a fourth-round draft choice in 1996 (later traded to Philadelphia, later traded back to Los Angeles—Mikael Simons), July 14, 1994.

Acquired from Los Angeles for Jason Podollan and a third-round draft choice in 1999 (Cory Campbell), March 23, 1999.

Signed as a free agent by Chicago on July 1, 2007

1993–94 F	13	3	3	6	0
1998–99	12	7	8	15	12
1999–2000	58	18	27	45	22

2000–01	76	24	28	52	52
2006–07	17	2	3	5	4
Totals	176	54	69	123	90

F November 6, 1993

NATHAN PERROTT #26

right wing 6' 225 R

b. Owen Sound, Ontario, December 8, 1976

Acquired from Nashville for Bob Wren, December 31, 2002.

Traded to Dallas for a sixth-round draft choice in 2006 (Leo Komarov), November 6, 2005.

2003–04	40	1	2	3	116
2005–06	3	0	0	0	2
Totals	43	1	2	3	118

• Later pursued as a career as a pro boxer.

MICHEL PETIT #22/#24

defence 6'1" 205 R

b. St. Malo, Quebec, February 12, 1964

Acquired with Lucien DeBlois and Aaron Broten from Quebec for Scott Pearson, a second-round draft choice in 1991 (later traded to Washington—Éric Lavigne), and a second-round draft choice in 1992 (Tuomas Gronman), November 17, 1990.

Traded with Gary Leeman, Craig Berube, Jeff Reese, and Alexander Godynyuk to Calgary for Doug Gilmour, Jamie Macoun, Ric Nattress, Kent Wamsley, and Kent Manderville, January 2, 1992.

1990–91	54	9	19	28	132
1991–92	34	1	13	14	85
Totals	88	10	32	42	217

• Held NHL record for playing with most teams (10).

ERIC "COWBOY" PETTINGER ("Gosh") #10

left wing 6' 175 L

b. North Bierley, England, December 14, 1904

d. Wallaceburg, Ontario, December 24, 1968

Acquired with the rights to Hugh Plaxton from Boston in return for the rights to George Owen, January 8, 1929.

Traded with Art Smith and $35,000 to Ottawa for King Clancy, October 11, 1930.

1928–29	25	3	3	6	24
1929–30	43	4	9	13	40
Totals	68	7	12	19	64

DION PHANEUF #3

defence 6'3" 215 L

b. Edmonton, Alberta, April 10, 1985

Acquired from Calgary with Keith Aulie and Fredrik Sjostrom for Ian White, Matt Stajan, Nicklas Hagman, and Jamal Mayers, January 31, 2010.

2009–10	26	2	8	10	34
2010–11	66	8	22	30	88
2011–12	82	12	32	44	92
2012–13	48	9	19	28	65
2013–14	80	8	23	31	144
2014–15	70	3	26	29	108
Totals	372	42	130	172	531

• Named captain on June 14, 2010.

ROBERT PICARD #4

defence 6'2" 207 L

b. Montreal, Quebec, May 25, 1957

Acquired with Tim Coulis and a second-round draft choice in 1980 (Bob McGill) from Washington for Mike Palmateer and a third-round draft choice in 1980 (Torrie Robertson), June 11, 1980.

Traded with an eighth-round draft choice in 1982 (Steve Smith) to Montreal for Michel Larocque, March 10, 1981.

1980–81	59	6	19	25	68

KAREL PILAR #29

defence 6'3" 210 R

b. Prague, Czechoslovakia (Czech Republic), December 23, 1977

Selected 39th overall in 2001 Entry Draft.

Signed as a free agent by Atlanta, August 8, 2007.

2001–02	23	1	3	4	8
2002–03	17	3	4	7	12
2003–04	50	2	17	19	22
Totals	90	6	24	30	42

PIERRE PILOTE ("Pete") #2

defence 5'10" 178 L

b. Kenogami, Quebec, December 11, 1931

Acquired from Chicago for Jim Pappin, May 23, 1968.

Claimed by Buffalo (AHL) in Reverse Draft, June 12, 1969.

1968–69 L	69	3	18	21	46

L March 30, 1969

• Owned a car dealership and small chain of laundromats, and became a hobby farmer after his playing days.

• Hockey Hall of Fame 1975

CAM PLANTE #11

defence 6'1" 195 L

b. Brandon, Manitoba, March 12, 1964

Selected 133rd overall in 1983 Entry Draft.

1984–85 F/L	2	0	0	0	0

F March 16, 1985 L March 18, 1985

JACQUES PLANTE ("Jake the Snake") #1
goalie 6' 175 L
b. Mont Carmel, Quebec, January 17, 1929
d. Geneva, Switzerland, February 26, 1986
Acquired with Denis Dupéré and Guy Trottier from the New York Rangers for Tim Horton, May 3, 1970.
Traded with a third-round draft choice in 1973 (Doug Gibson) to Boston for a first-round draft choice in 1973 (Ian Turnbull) and future considerations (Eddie Johnston), March 3, 1973.

1970–71	40	24–11–4	2,329		73	4	1.88
1971–72	34	16–13–5	1,965		86	2	2.63
1972–73	32	8–14–6	1,717		87	1	3.04
Totals	106	48–38–15	6,011		246	7	2.46

• Wrote the first book on goaltending and later coached goalies in the WHA.
• Hockey Hall of Fame 1978

WALT PODDUBNY ("Sarge") #8/#12
left wing 6'1" 210 L
b. Thunder Bay, Ontario, February 14, 1960
d. Thunder Bay, Ontario, March 21, 2009
Acquired with Phil Drouilliard from Edmonton for Laurie Boschman, March 8, 1982.
Traded to New York Rangers for Mike Allison, August 18, 1986.

1981–82	11	3	4	7	8
1982–83	72	28	31	59	71
1983–84	38	11	14	25	48
1984–85	32	5	15	20	26
1985–86	33	12	22	34	25
Totals	186	59	86	145	178

JASON PODOLLAN ("Pods") #7/#37
right wing 6'1" 192 R
b. Vernon, British Columbia, February 18, 1976
Acquired from Florida for Kirk Muller, March 18, 1997.
Traded to Los Angeles with a third-round draft choice in 1999 (Cory Campbell) for Yanic Perreault, March 23, 1999.

1996–97	10	0	3	3	6
1998–99	4	0	0	0	0
Totals	14	0	3	3	6

JUSTIN POGGE #29/#1
goalie 6'3" 205 L
b. Fort McMurray, Alberta, April 22, 1986
Selected 90th overall in 2004 Entry Draft.
Traded to Anaheim for a sixth-round draft choice in 2011 (Dennis Robertson), August 10, 2009.

2008–09	F/L	7	1–4–0–1	372		27	0	4.35

F December 22, 2008 **L** March 28, 2009

JOHN POHL #21/#53
centre 6'1" 195 R
b. Rochester, Minnesota, June 29, 1979
Acquired from St. Louis for future considerations, August 24, 2005.
Later played in Europe.

2005–06	7	3	1	4	4
2006–07	74	13	16	29	10
2007–08 L	33	1	4	5	10
Totals	114	17	21	38	24

L April 5, 2008

NORMAN "BUD" POILE #7/#11/#16/#25
centre 6' 185 R
b. Fort William (Thunder Bay), Ontario, February 10, 1924
d. Vancouver, British Columbia, January 4, 2005
Traded with Gus Bodnar, Gaye Stewart, Bob Goldham, and Ernie Dickens to Chicago for Max Bentley and Cy Thomas, November 2, 1947.

1942–43 F	48	16	19	35	24
1943–44	11	6	8	14	9
1945–46	9	1	8	9	0
1946–47	59	19	17	36	19
1947–48	4	2	0	2	0
Totals	131	44	52	96	52

F October 31, 1942
• Missed 1944–45 while serving in the Canadian Armed Forces; returned February 27, 1946.
• Became GM in Vancouver and Philadelphia after expansion, and later commissioner of IHL for many years.
• Hockey Hall of Fame 1990 (Builder)

ROMAN POLAK #46
defence 6' 236 R
b. Ostrava, Czechoslovakia (Czech Republic), April 28, 1986
Acquired from St. Louis for Carl Gunnarsson and a fourth-round draft choice in 2014 (Ville Husso), June 28, 2014.

2014–15	56	5	4	9	48

ALEXEI PONIKAROVSKY ("Pony") #39/#22/#23
right wing 6'4" 196 L
b. Kiev, Soviet Union (Ukraine), April 9, 1980
Selected 87th overall in 1998 Entry Draft.
Traded to Pittsburgh for Martin Skoula and Luca Caputi, on March 2, 2010.

2000–01 F	22	1	3	4	14
2001–02	8	2	0	2	0
2002–03	13	0	3	3	11
2003–04	73	9	19	28	44
2005–06	81	21	17	38	68
2006–07	71	21	24	45	63
2007–08	66	18	17	35	36
2008–09	82	23	38	61	38
2009–10	61	19	22	41	44
Totals	477	114	143	257	318

F January 10, 2001

FÉLIX POTVIN ("The Cat") #29
goalie 6' 180 L
b. Montreal, Quebec, June 23, 1971
Selected 31st overall in 1990 Entry Draft.
Traded to New York Islanders with a sixth-round draft choice in 1999 (later traded to Tampa Bay—Fedor Fedorov) for Bryan Berard and a sixth-round draft choice in 1999 (Jan Sochar), January 9, 1999.

1991–92 F	4	0–2–1	210		8	0	2.29
1992–93	48	25–15–7	2,781		116	2	2.50
1993–94	66	34–22–9	3,883		187	3	2.89
1994–95	36	15–13–7	2,144		104	0	2.91
1995–96	69	30–26–11	4,009		192	2	2.87
1996–97	74	27–36–7	4,271		224	0	3.15
1997–98	67	26–33–7	3,864		176	5	2.73
1998–99	5	3–2–0	299		19	0	3.81
Totals	369	160–149–49	21,461		1,026	12	2.87

F November 14, 1991

TRACY PRATT #4
defence 6'2" 195 L
b. New York, New York, March 8, 1943
Acquired from Colorado Rockies for a third-round draft choice in 1977 (Randy Pierce), March 8, 1977.

1976–77 L	11	0	1	1	8

L April 2, 1977

WALTER "BABE" PRATT ("The Honest Brakeman"/"The Big Pussycat") #4/#2/#12
defence 6'3" 210 L
b. Stony Mountain, Manitoba, January 7, 1916
d. Vancouver, British Columbia, December 16, 1988
Acquired from New York Rangers for Hank Goldup and Dudley Garrett, November 27, 1942.
Sold to Boston for cash and the rights to Eric Pogue, June 23, 1946.

1942–43	40	12	25	37	44
1943–44	50	17	40	57	30
1944–45	50	18	23	41	39
1945–46	41	5	20	25	36
Totals	181	52	108	160	149

• Hockey Hall of Fame 1966

ERIC PRENTICE ("Doc") #17
defence 5'11" 150 L
b. Schumacher, Ontario, August 22, 1926
d. Coleman, Alberta, December 8, 2002
Signed October 29, 1943.
Traded to Detroit for George Mara, October 11, 1945.

1943–44 F/L	5	0	0	0	4

F October 30, 1943 **L** November 18, 1943

WAYNE PRESLEY #18
right wing 5'11" 180 R
b. Dearborn, Michigan, March 23, 1965
Acquired with Nick Kypreos from New York Rangers for Sergio Momesso and Bill Berg, February 29, 1996.
Bought out mid-October 1996.

1995–96	19	2	2	4	14

NOEL PRICE #23
defence 6' 185 L
b. Brockville, Ontario, December 9, 1935
St. Mike's graduate
Traded to New York Rangers for Hank Ciesla, Earl Johnson, and the rights to Bill Kennedy, October 25, 1959.

1957–58 F	1	0	0	0	5
1958–59	28	0	0	0	4
Totals	29	0	0	0	9

F October 23, 1957

JOE PRIMEAU ("Little Joe"/"Gentleman Joe") #10/#7/#15
centre 5'11" 153 L
b. Lindsay, Ontario, January 29, 1906
d. Toronto, Ontario, May 15, 1989
St. Mike's graduate
Loaned to London, November 28, 1928, subject to immediate recall.
Retired August 21, 1936.

1927–28 F	2	0	0	0	0
1928–29	6	0	1	1	2
1929–30	43	5	21	26	22
1930–31	38	9	32	41	18
1931–32	46	13	37	50	25
1932–33	48	11	21	32	4
1933–34	45	14	32	46	8
1934–35	37	10	20	30	16
1935–36 L	45	4	13	17	10
Totals	310	66	177	243	105

F November 22, 1927 **L** March 21, 1936
• Hockey Hall of Fame 1963

WAYNE PRIMEAU #18
centre 6'4" 225 L
b. Scarborough (Toronto), Ontario, June 4, 1976
Acquired from Calgary with a second-round draft choice in 2011 (later traded to Chicago—Brandon Saad) for Anton Stralman, Colin Stuart, and a seventh-round draft choice in 2012 (Matthew de Blouw), July 27, 2009.

2009–10 L	59	3	5	8	35

L April 10, 2010

MARTIN PROCHAZKA #21
right wing 5'11" 180 R
b. Slany, Czechoslovakia (Czech Republic), March 3, 1972
Selected 135th overall in 1991 Entry Draft.
Traded to Atlanta for a sixth-round draft choice in 2001 (Maxim Kondratiev), July 15, 1999.

1997–98 F	29	2	4	6	8

F October 9, 1997

GEORGE "GOLDIE" PRODGER
forward 5'10" 180 R
b. London, Ontario, February 18, 1891
d. London, Ontario, October 25, 1935
Acquired from Montreal for Harry Cameron, January 14, 1920 (after that night's game).
Traded to Montreal with Joe Matte for Harry Cameron, November 27, 1920.

1919–20 F	16	8	6	14	2

F January 17, 1920

MARCEL PRONOVOST #3

defence 6' 190 L
b. Lac-à-la-Tortue, Quebec, June 15, 1930
d. Windsor, Ontario, April 26, 2015
Acquired with Lowell MacDonald, Larry Jeffrey, Ed Joyal, and Aut Erickson from Detroit for Andy Bathgate, Billy Harris, and Gary Jarrett, May 20, 1965.

1965–66	54	2	8	10	34
1966–67	58	2	12	14	28
1967–68	70	3	17	20	48
1968–69	34	1	2	3	20
1969–70 L	7	0	1	1	4
Totals	223	8	40	48	134

L December 27, 1969
• Played most of 1969–70 and part of 1970–71 with Tulsa (CHL) as a player/coach before retiring as a player to continue as coach.
• Part of Detroit front office for Stanley Cups in 1997 and 1998.
• Hockey Hall of Fame 1978

AL PUDAS #14

left wing L
b. Siikajoki, Finland, February 17, 1899
d. Thunder Bay, Ontario, October 28, 1976
Signed October 28, 1926, and assigned to Windsor (Can Pro), December 28, 1926; never returned to NHL.

1926–27 F/L	4	0	0	0	0

F December 30, 1926 L January 8, 1927
• Coached Canada's 1936 Olympic team (silver medal).

BOB PULFORD ("Pully") #20

left wing 5'11" 188 L
b. Newton Robinson, Ontario, March 31, 1936
Marlboros graduate (won Allan Cup 1955 and 1956)
Traded to Los Angeles for Garry Monahan and Brian Murphy, September 3, 1970.

1956–57 F	65	11	11	22	32
1957–58	70	14	17	31	48
1958–59	70	23	14	37	53
1959–60	70	24	28	52	81
1960–61	40	11	18	29	41
1961–62	70	18	21	39	98
1962–63	70	19	25	44	49
1963–64	70	18	30	48	73
1964–65	65	19	20	39	46
1965–66	70	28	28	56	51
1966–67	67	17	28	45	28
1967–68	74	20	30	50	40
1968–69	72	11	23	34	20
1969–70	74	18	19	37	31
Totals	947	251	312	563	691

F October 25, 1956
• Hockey Hall of Fame 1991

DAREN PUPPA ("Poops") #1

goalie 6'3" 205 R
b. Kirkland Lake, Ontario, March 23, 1963
Acquired with Dave Andreychuk and a first-round draft choice in 1993 (Kenny Jonsson) from Buffalo for Grant Fuhr and a fifth-round draft choice in 1995 (Kevin Popp), February 2, 1993.
Claimed by Florida in Expansion Draft, June 24, 1993.

1992–93	8	6–2–0	479	18	2	2.25

JOEL QUENNEVILLE ("Herbie") #3

defence 6'1" 200 L
b. Windsor, Ontario, September 15, 1958
Selected 21st overall in 1978 Amateur Draft.
Traded with Lanny McDonald to Colorado Rockies for Pat Hickey and Wilf Paiement, December 29, 1979.

1978–79 F	61	2	9	11	60
1979–80	32	1	4	5	24
Totals	93	3	13	16	84

F October 22, 1978
• Longtime NHL coach after he retired.

PAT QUINN #23

defence 6'3" 215 L
b. Hamilton, Ontario, January 19, 1943
d. Vancouver, British Columbia, November 23, 2014
Purchased from St. Louis, March 25, 1968.
Claimed by Vancouver in Expansion Draft, June 10, 1970.

1968–69 F	40	2	7	9	95
1969–70	59	0	5	5	88
Totals	99	2	12	14	183

F November 27, 1968
• Coached Canada to Olympic gold in 2002.

ROB RAMAGE ("Rammer") #8

defence 6'2" 200 L
b. Byron, Ontario, January 11, 1959
Acquired from Calgary for a second-round draft choice in 1989 (Kent Manderville), June 16, 1989.
Claimed by Minnesota North Stars in Expansion Draft, May 30, 1991.

1989–90	80	8	41	49	202
1990–91	80	10	25	35	173
Totals	160	18	66	84	375

BEATTIE RAMSAY #2

defence 143
b. Lumsden, Saskatchewan, December 12, 1895
d. Regina, Saskatchewan, October 1, 1952
Signed for the 1927–28 season on March 16, 1927, while coaching hockey at Princeton University.

1927–28 F/L	43	0	2	2	10

F November 15, 1927 L March 24, 1928
• Member of the University of Toronto Grads gold medal team at 1928 Olympics.

KEN RANDALL #3

right wing 5'10" 180 R
b. Kingston, Ontario, December 14, 1888
d. Toronto, Ontario, June 17, 1947
Signed as a free agent, December 9, 1917.
Traded with Corb Dennenay to Hamilton for Bert Corbeau and Amos Arbour, December 14, 1923.

1917–18	21	12	—	12	96
1918–19	14	8	6	14	27
1919–20	22	10	8	18	42
1920–21	22	6	5	11	74
1921–22	24	10	6	16	32
1922–23	24	3	5	8	58
Totals	127	49	30	79	329

• Missed first three games of 1920–21 in contract dispute.
• Coached after retiring in 1928.

PAUL RANGER #15

defence 6'3" 210 L
b. Whitby, Ontario, September 12, 1984
Signed as a free agent, July 24, 2013.
Signed as a free agent by Genève Servette (Switzerland), summer 2014.

2013–14	53	6	8	14	36

ANDREW RAYCROFT #1

goalie 6'1" 180 L
b. Belleville, Ontario, May 4, 1980
Acquired from Boston for Tuukka Rask, on June 24, 2006.
Signed as a free agent by Colorado, July 1, 2008.

2006–07	72	37–25–9	4,108	205	2	2.99
2007–08	19	2–9–5	965	63	1	3.92
Totals	91	39–34–14	5,073	268	3	3.17

MASON RAYMOND #12

left wing 6' 185 L
b. Cochrane, Alberta, September 17, 1985
Signed as a free agent, September 23, 2013.
Signed as a free agent by Calgary, July 1, 2014.

2013–14	82	19	26	45	22

MARC REAUME #2/#25

defence 6'1" 185 L
b. LaSalle, Ontario, February 7, 1934
St. Mike's graduate 1952
Traded to Detroit for Red Kelly, February 10, 1960.

1954–55 F	1	0	0	0	4
1955–56	48	0	12	12	50
1956–57	63	6	14	20	81
1957–58	68	1	7	8	49
1958–59	51	1	5	6	67
1959–60	36	0	1	1	6
Totals	267	8	39	47	257

F March 20, 1955

JEFF REESE ("Reeser") #1/#35

goalie 5'9" 170 L
b. Brantford, Ontario, March 24, 1966
Selected 67th overall in 1984 Entry Draft; traded with Gary Leeman, Michel Petit, Craig Berube and Alexander Godynyuk to Calgary for Doug Gilmour, Jamie Macoun, Ric Nattress, Rick Wamsley, and Kent Manderville, January 2, 1992.
Signed as a free agent, January 5, 1999; traded to Tampa Bay with a ninth-round draft choice in 2000 (later traded to Philadelphia—Milan Kopecky) for a ninth-round draft choice in 2000 (Jean-Philippe Côté), August 6, 1999.

1987–88 F	5	1–2–1	249	17	0	4.10
1988–89	10	2–6–1	486	40	0	4.94
1989–90	21	9–6–3	1,101	81	0	4.42
1990–91	30	6–13–3	1,430	92	1	3.86
1991–92	8	1–5–1	413	20	1	2.91
1998–99	2	1–1–0	106	8	0	4.53
Totals	76	20–33–9	3,785	258	2	4.09

F January 10, 1988
• While with Calgary, set a record for goalies by recording three assists in one game.

LARRY REGAN #8

right wing 5'9" 178 R
b. North Bay, Ontario, August 9, 1930
d. Ottawa, Ontario, March 9, 2009
Claimed off waivers from Boston, January 7, 1959.

1958–59	32	4	21	25	2
1959–60	47	4	16	20	6
1960–61 L	37	3	5	8	2
Totals	116	11	42	53	10

L March 19, 1961
• Became playing coach of Pittsburgh (AHL), June 14, 1961; later coached in Austria.

ROBERT REICHEL #21

centre 5'10" 180 L
b. Litvinov, Czechoslovakia (Czech Republic), June 25, 1971
Acquired from Phoenix with Travis Green and Craig Mills for Danny Markov, June 12, 2001.
Finished his career in Czech Republic.

2001–02	78	20	31	51	26
2002–03	81	12	30	42	26
2003–04	69	11	19	30	30
Totals	228	43	80	123	82

• IIHF Hall of Fame 2015

DAVID REID #18/#25

forward 6'2" 180 L
b. Toronto, Ontario, January 11, 1934
d. 1978

1952–53 F	2	0	0	0	0
1954–55	1	0	0	0	0
1955–56 L	4	0	0	0	0
Totals	7	0	0	0	0

F December 10, 1952

DAVE REID #34/#14

left wing 6'1" 205 L
b. Toronto, Ontario, May 15, 1964
Signed as a free agent, June 23, 1988.
Signed as a free agent by Boston, October 1991.

1988–89	77	9	21	30	22
1989–90	70	9	19	28	9
1990–91	69	15	13	28	18
Totals	216	33	53	86	49

REG "RUSTY" REID #12

forward 5'8" 138 L
b. Seaforth, Ontario, February 17, 1899
d. Stratford, Ontario, January 14, 1986
Signed from Seaforth (OHA Intermediate), November 12, 1924.

1924–25 F	28	2	0	2	2
1925–26 L	12	0	0	0	2
Totals	40	2	0	2	4

F November 29, 1924 L January 9, 1926
• Moved to Stratford, Ontario, and became a salesman after retiring.

JAMES REIMER #34

goalie 6'2" 208 L
b. Morweena, Manitoba, March 15, 1988
Selected 99th overall in 2006 Entry Draft.

2010–11 F	37	20–10–5	2,080	90	3	2.60
2011–12	34	14–14–4	1,879	97	3	3.10
2012–13	33	19–8–5	1,856	76	4	2.46
2013–14	36	12–16–1	1,785	98	1	3.29
2014–15	35	9–16–1	1,767	93	0	3.16
Totals	175	74–64–16	9,367	454	11	2.91

F December 20, 2010

MIKAEL RENBERG #19

right wing 6'2" 235 L
b. Pitea, Sweden, May 5, 1972
Acquired from Phoenix for Sergei Berezin, June 22, 2001.
Finished his career in Sweden.

2001–02	71	14	38	52	36
2002–03	67	14	21	35	36
2003–04	59	12	13	25	50
Totals	197	40	72	112	122

L April 3, 2004 (regular season—also played in 2004 playoffs)

BOBBY REYNOLDS #20

left wing 5'11" 175 L
b. Flint, Michigan, July 14, 1967
Selected 190th overall in 1985 Entry Draft.
Traded to Washington for Robert Mendel, March 5, 1991.

1989–90 F/L	7	1	1	2	0

F March 14, 1990 L March 28, 1990

DAMIAN RHODES ("Dusty") #31/#1

goalie 6' 165 L
b. St. Paul, Minnesota, May 28, 1969
Selected 112th overall in 1987 Entry Draft
Traded to New York Islanders in a three-way trade, January 23, 1996. Leafs sent Rhodes and Ken Belanger to Islanders; Ottawa sent Don Beaupre, Bryan Berard, and Martin Straka to Islanders; Islanders sent Rhodes and Wade Redden to Ottawa and Beaupre and Kirk Muller to Leafs.

1990–91 F	1	1–0–0	60	1	0	1.00
1993–94	22	9–7–3	1,213	53	0	2.62
1994–95	13	6–6–1	760	34	0	2.68
1995–96	11	4–5–1	624	29	0	2.79
Totals	47	20–18–5	2,657	117	0	2.64

F March 22, 1991

PAT RIBBLE #3

defence 6'4" 210 L
b. Leamington, Ontario, April 26, 1954
Acquired from Chicago for Dave Hutchison, January 10, 1980.
Traded to Washington for Mike Kaszycki, February 16, 1980.

1979–80	13	0	2	2	2

LUKE RICHARDSON #2/#22

defence 6'3" 215 L
b. Ottawa, Ontario, March 26, 1969
Selected 7th overall in 1987 Entry Draft; traded with Vincent Damphousse, Peter Ing, and Scott Thornton to Edmonton for Grant Fuhr, Glenn Anderson, and Craig Berube, September 19, 1991.
Acquired from Columbus for a fifth-round draft choice in 2006 (Nick Sucharski), March 8, 2006; signed as a free agent by Tampa Bay, July 11, 2006.

1987–88 F	78	4	6	10	90
1988–89	55	2	7	9	106
1989–90	67	4	14	18	122
1990–91	78	1	9	10	238
2005–06	21	0	3	3	41
Totals	299	11	39	50	597

F October 8, 1987

CURT RIDLEY #1/#33/#35

goalie 6' 190 L
b. Minnedosa, Manitoba, October 24, 1951
Purchased from Vancouver, February 10, 1980.

1979–80	3	0–1–0	110	8	0	4.36
1980–81 L	3	1–1–0	124	12	0	5.81
Totals	6	1–2–0	234	20	0	5.13

L November 28, 1980

MIKE RIDLEY #7

centre 6' 195 L
b. Winnipeg, Manitoba, July 8, 1963
Acquired with a first-round draft choice in 1994 (Éric Fichaud) from Washington for Rob Pearson and a first-round draft choice in 1994 (Nolan Baumgartner), June 28, 1994.
Traded to Vancouver for Sergio Momesso, July 9, 1995.

1994–95	48	10	27	37	14

MORGAN RIELLY #44

defence 6'1" 205 L
b. Vancouver, British Columbia, March 9, 1994
Selected 5th overall in 2012 Entry Draft.

2013–14	73	2	25	27	12
2014–15	81	8	21	29	14
Totals	154	10	46	56	26

F October 5, 2013

DAVE RITCHIE #11

forward 5'8" 180 R
b. Montreal, Quebec, October 1, 1891
d. Montreal, Quebec, March 6, 1973
Signed with Quebec Bulldogs for the 1919–20 season.

1918–19	5	0	0	0	9

• Only Arenas games January 21 & 28 and February 4, 6, & 11, 1919.

JOHN ROSS ROACH ("The Port Perry Woodpecker"/"Rossie") #1

goalie 5'5" 130 L
b. Port Perry, Ontario, June 23, 1900
d. Windsor, Ontario, July 9, 1973
Signed from Toronto Granites, December 5, 1921.
Traded with Butch Keeling to New York Rangers for Lorne Chabot, Alex Gray, and $20,000, October 17, 1928.

1921–22 F	22	11–10–1	1,340	91	0	4.07
1922–23	24	13–10–1	1,469	88	1	3.59
1923–24	23	10–13–0	1,380	80	1	3.48
1924–25	30	19–11–0	1,800	84	1	2.80
1925–26	36	12–21–3	2,231	114	2	3.10
1926–27	44	15–24–5	2,764	94	4	2.04
1927–28	43	18–18–7	2,690	88	4	1.96
Totals	222	98–107–17	13,674	639	13	2.81

F December 24, 1921

MICHAEL "MICKEY" ROACH ("Port") #8

centre 5'7" 160 R
b. Glace Bay, Nova Scotia, May 7, 1895
d. Whitby, Ontario, April 1, 1977
Signed from Hamilton (OHA Senior), December 16, 1919.
Sold to Hamilton (NHL), January 21, 1921.

1919–20 F	20	10	2	12	4
1920–21	8	1	0	1	2
Totals	28	11	2	13	6

F December 23, 1919

RENÉ ROBERT #14

right wing 5'10" 184 R
b. Trois-Rivières, Quebec, December 31, 1948
Claimed by Pittsburgh in Intra-League Draft, June 8, 1971.
Acquired from Colorado Rockies for a third-round draft choice in 1981 (Uli Hiemer); released during 1981–82 season, January 30, 1981.

1970–71 F	5	0	0	0	0
1980–81	14	6	7	13	8
1981–82 L	55	13	24	37	37
Totals	74	19	31	50	45

F March 13, 1971 L March 3, 1982
• Later became president of NHL Alumni Association.

GARY ROBERTS #7

left wing 6'1" 190 L
b. North York, May 23, 1966
Signed as a free agent, July 4, 2000.
Signed as a free agent by Florida, August 1, 2005.

2000–01	82	29	24	53	109
2001–02	69	21	27	48	63
2002–03	14	5	3	8	10
2003–04	72	28	20	48	84
Totals	237	83	74	157	266

FRED ROBERTSON #18/#17

defence 5'10" 198 L
b. Carlisle, England, October 22, 1911
d. Barrie, Ontario, September 20, 1997
Marlboros graduate, 1931
Signed as a free agent, February 24, 1932.
Sold to Detroit during 1933–34 season for $6,500.

1931–32 F	11	0	0	0	23

F March 22, 1932

STEPHANE ROBIDAS #12

defence 5'11" 190 R
b. Sherbrooke, Quebec, March 3, 1977
Signed as a free agent, July 1, 2014.

2014–15	52	1	6	7	34

EDDIE RODDEN #12

forward 5'7" 150 R
b. Toronto, Ontario, March 22, 1901
d. Toronto, Ontario, September 10, 1986
Acquired from Chicago in three-way trade, December 12, 1927 (Leafs sent Bert McCaffery and cash to Pittsburgh Pirates; Pirates sent Ty Arbour to Chicago).
Sold to Boston on June 20, 1928.

1927–28	25	3	6	9	36

ELWIN "AL" ROLLINS ("Ally") #23

goalie 6'2" 175 L

b. Vanguard, Saskatchewan, October 9, 1926

d. Calgary, Alberta, July 27, 1996

Acquired from Cleveland (AHL) for Bob Dawes, Phil Samis, Eric Pogue, the rights to Bob Shropshire and $40,000, November 30, 1949.

Traded with Gus Mortson, Cal Gardner, and Ray Hannigan to Chicago for Harry Lumley, September 11, 1952.

1949–50	F	2	1–1–0	100	4	1	2.40
1950–51		40	27–5–8	2,373	70	5	1.77
1951–52		70	29–24–16	4,170	154	5	2.22
Totals		112	57–30–24	6,643	228	11	2.06

F December 24, 1949

ELWIN "DOC" ROMNES #7

forward 5'11" 156 L

b. White Bear, Minnesota, January 1, 1907

d. Colorado Springs, Colorado, July 21, 1984

Acquired from Chicago for Bill Thoms, December 7, 1938.

Traded with Busher Jackson, Buzz Boll, and Murray Armstrong to New York Americans for Sweeney Schriner, May 18, 1939.

1938–39		36	7	16	23	0

BILL ROOT ("Rooter") #25/#28/#34

defence 6'2" 210 R

b. Toronto, Ontario, September 6, 1959

Acquired with a second-round draft choice in 1986 (Darryl Shannon) from Montreal for Dom Campedelli, August 21, 1984; traded to Hartford for Dave Semenko, September 9, 1987.

Acquired from Philadelphia for Mike Stothers, June 21, 1988.

1984–85	35	1	1	2	23
1985–86	27	0	1	1	29
1986–87	34	3	3	6	37
Totals	96	4	5	9	89

JAY ROSEHILL #38

left wing 6'3" 215 L

b. Olds, Alberta, July 16, 1985

Acquired from Tampa Bay for future considerations, March 10, 2009.

Signed as a free agent by Anaheim, January 16, 2013.

2009–10	F	15	1	1	2	67
2010–11		26	1	2	3	71
2011–12		31	0	0	0	60
Totals		72	2	3	5	198

F October 1, 2009

BOB ROUSE #28/#3

defence 6'1" 210 R

b. Surrey, British Columbia, June 18, 1964

Acquired with Peter Zezel from Washington for Al Iafrate, January 16, 1991.

Signed as a free agent by Detroit, August 5, 1994.

1990–91	13	2	4	6	10
1991–92	79	3	19	22	97
1992–93	82	3	11	14	130
1993–94	63	5	11	16	101
Totals	237	13	45	58	338

DUANE RUPP #3/#4/#17

defence 6'1" 185 L

b. MacNutt, Saskatchewan, March 29, 1938

Acquired with Ed Ehrenverth from New York Rangers for Lou Angotti and Ed Lawson, June 25, 1964.

Claimed by Minnesota in Intra-League Draft, June 12, 1968.

1964–65	2	0	0	0	0
1965–66	2	0	1	1	0
1966–67	3	0	0	0	0
1967–68	71	1	8	9	42
Totals	78	1	9	10	42

• Coached in AHL for years before becoming manager of an arena in Pittsburgh.

JIM RUTHERFORD #1

goalie 5'8" 168 L

b. Beeton, Ontario, February 17, 1949

Acquired from Detroit for Mark Kirton, December 4, 1980.

Traded to Los Angeles for a fifth-round draft choice in 1981 (Barry Brigley), March 10, 1981.

1980–81	18	4–10–2	961	82	0	5.12

• Longtime GM of Carolina Hurricanes.

WARREN RYCHEL #21

left wing 6' 190 L

b. Tecumseh, Ontario, May 12, 1967

Acquired from Washington for a fourth-round draft choice in 1995 (Sebastien Charpentier), February 10, 1995.

Traded to Colorado for future considerations, October 2, 1995.

1994–95	26	1	6	7	101

JUSSI RYNNAS #40

goalie 6'5" 212 L

b. Pori, Finland, May 22, 1987

Signed as a free agent, April 23, 2010.

Signed as a free agent by Dallas, July 7, 2014.

2011–12	F	2	0–1–0	99	7	0	4.24
2012–13		1	0–0–0	10	0	0	0.00
Totals		3	0–1–0	109	7	0	3.85

F March 27, 2012

BOB SABOURIN #16

right wing 5'9" 205 L

b. Sudbury, Ontario, March 17, 1933

St. Mike's graduate

Sold to Springfield (AHL) with Bob Bailey for $22,000, May 28, 1956.

1951–52	F/L	1	0	0	0	2

F/L March 13, 1952 (while attending St. Mike's)

GARY SABOURIN #15

right wing 5'11" 180 R

b. Parry Sound, Ontario, December 4, 1943

Acquired from St. Louis for Eddie Johnston, May 27, 1974.

Traded to California for Stan Weir, June 20, 1975.

1974–75	55	5	18	23	26

• Has run a food franchise in Chatham, Ontario, since his retirement due to knee injuries.

DAVID SACCO #7

forward 6' 180 R

b. Malden, Massachusetts, July 31, 1970

Selected 195th overall in 1988 Entry Draft.

Traded to Anaheim for Terry Yake, September 28, 1994.

1993–94	F	4	1	1	2	4

F March 4, 1994

JOE SACCO #20/#24

left wing 6'1" 180 R

b. Medford, Massachusetts, February 4, 1969

Selected 71st overall in 1987 Entry Draft.

Claimed by Anaheim in the Expansion Draft, June 24, 1993.

1990–91	F	20	0	5	5	2
1991–92		17	7	4	11	6
1992–93		23	4	4	8	8
Totals		60	11	13	24	16

F November 10, 1990

ROCKY SAGANIUK #7/#8

forward 5'8" 185 R

b. Myrnam, Alberta, October 15, 1957

Selected 29th overall in 1977 Amateur Draft.

Traded with Vincent Tremblay to Pittsburgh for Pat Graham and Nick Ricci, August 15, 1983.

1978–79	F	16	3	5	8	9
1979–80		75	24	23	47	52
1980–81		71	12	18	30	52
1981–82		65	17	16	33	49
1982–83		3	0	0	0	2
Totals		230	56	62	118	164

F December 13, 1978

RICK ST. CROIX #1

goalie 5'10" 160 L

b. Kenora, Ontario, January 3, 1955

Acquired from Philadelphia for Michel Larocque, January 11, 1983.

Released after 1984–85 season.

1982–83	17	4–9–2	920	58	0	3.78
1983–84	20	5–10–0	939	80	0	5.11
1984–85	L	11	2–9–0	628	54	0	5.16
Totals		48	11–28–2	2,487	192	0	4.63

BORJE SALMING ("King"/"B.J.") #21

defence 6'1" 193 L

b. Kiruna, Sweden, April 17, 1951

Signed as a free agent, May 12, 1973.

Signed as a free agent by Detroit, June 12, 1989.

1973–74	F	76	5	34	39	48
1974–75		60	12	25	37	34
1975–76		78	16	41	57	70
1976–77		76	12	66	78	46
1977–78		80	16	60	76	70
1978–79		78	17	56	73	76
1979–80		74	19	52	71	94
1980–81		72	5	61	66	154
1981–82		69	12	44	56	170
1982–83		69	7	38	45	104
1983–84		68	5	38	43	92
1984–85		73	6	33	39	76
1985–86		41	7	15	22	48
1986–87		56	4	16	20	42
1987–88		66	2	24	26	82
1988–89		63	3	17	20	86
Totals		1,099	148	620	768	1,292

F October 10, 1973

• Hockey Hall of Fame 1996; IIHF Hall of Fame 1998

PHIL SAMIS #23

defence 5'10" 180 R

b. Edmonton, Alberta, December 28, 1927

Signed by Leafs on September 25, 1947.

Traded to Cleveland (AHL) on November 30, 1949, with Bob Dawes, Eric Pogue, the rights to Bob Shropshire, and $40,000 for Al Rollins

1949–50	F/L	2	0	0	0	0

F November 20, 1949 (regular season—called up for 1948 playoffs)

L November 23, 1949

CHARLIE SANDS #3/#16/#17

centre 5'9" 160 R

b. Fort William, Ontario, May 23, 1911

d. Hollywood, California, April 6, 1953

Signed as a free agent, March 27, 1932; recalled to replace injured Ace Bailey, March 17, 1933.

Sold to Boston at the beginning of the 1934–35 season.

1932–33	F	3	0	3	3	0
1933–34		45	8	8	16	2
Totals		48	8	11	19	2

F March 18, 1933

MIKE SANTORELLI #25

centre 6' 189 R

b. Vancouver, British Columbia, December 14, 1985

Signed as a free agent, July 3, 2014.

Traded to Nashville with Cody Franson for Brendan Leipsic, Olli Jokinen, and a first-round draft choice, February 15, 2015.

2014–15	57	11	18	29	8

TERRY SAWCHUK ("Ukey"/"Saw") #30/#24

goalie 6' 195 L

b. Winnipeg, Manitoba, December 28, 1929

d. Long Beach, New York, May 31, 1970

Claimed from Detroit in Intra-League Draft, June 10, 1964.

Claimed by Los Angeles in Expansion Draft, June 6, 1967.

1964–65	36	17–13–6	2,160	92	1	2.56
1965–66	27	10–11–3	1,521	80	1	3.16
1966–67 L	28	15–5–4	1,409	66	2	2.81
Totals	91	42–29–13	5,090	238	4	2.81

L April 2, 1967 (regular season—also appeared in playoffs)

• During game of April 2, 1966, he and Bruce Gamble alternated every five minutes as an experiment by coach Punch Imlach.

LUKE SCHENN #2

defence 6'2" 230 R

b. Saskatoon, Saskatchewan, November 2, 1989

Selected 5th overall in 2008 Entry Draft.

Traded to Philadelphia for James van Riemsdyk, June 23, 2012.

2008–09 F	70	2	12	14	71
2009–10	79	5	12	17	50
2010–11	82	5	17	22	34
2011–12	79	2	20	22	62
Totals	310	14	61	75	217

F October 9, 2008

MATHIEU SCHNEIDER #72

defence 5'11" 189 L

b. New York, New York, June 12, 1969

Acquired with Wendel Clark and Denis Smith from New York Islanders for Kenny Jonsson, Darby Hendrickson, Sean Haggerty, and a first-round draft choice in 1997 (Roberto Luongo), March 13, 1996.

Traded to New York Rangers for Alexander Karpovtsev and a fourth-round draft choice in 1999 (Mirko Murovic), on October 14, 1998.

1995–96	13	2	5	7	10
1996–97	26	5	7	12	20
1997–98	76	11	26	37	44
Totals	115	18	38	56	74

• Missed 56 games in 1996–97 with groin injury.

DAVE "SWEENEY" SCHRINER #11

left wing 6' 185 L

b. Saratov, Russia, November 30, 1911

d. Calgary, Alberta, July 4, 1990

Acquired from New York Americans for Busher Jackson, Doc Romnes, Buzz Boll, and Murray Armstrong, May 18, 1939.

1939–40	39	11	15	26	10
1940–41	48	24	14	38	6
1941–42	47	20	16	36	21
1942–43	37	19	17	36	13
1944–45	26	22	15	37	10
1945–46 L	47	13	6	19	15
Totals	244	109	83	192	75

L March 17, 1946

• Missed 1943–44, serving in Canadian Army (returned January 9, 1945).

• Hockey Hall of Fame 1962

ROD SCHUTT #25

left wing 5'10" 185 L

b. Bancroft, Ontario, October 13, 1956

Signed as a free agent, October 3, 1985.

1985–86 L	6	0	0	0	0

L December 20, 1985

COREY SCHWAB #35

goalie 6' 180 L

b. North Battleford, Saskatchewan, November 4, 1970

Signed as a free agent, October 1, 2001.

Signed as a free agent by New Jersey, July 9, 2002.

2001–02	30	12–10–5	1,646	75	1	2.73

GANTON SCOTT #11/#12/#7

right wing 5'9" 165 R

b. Preston, Ontario, March 23, 1902

d. June 9, 1977

Signed on October 9, 1922; sold to Hamilton on January 16, 1924.

1922–23 F	17	0	0	0	0
1923–24	4	0	0	0	0
Totals	21	0	0	0	0

F December 16, 1922

BEN SCRIVENS #30

goalie 6'2" 193 L

b. Spruce Grove, Alberta, September 11, 1986

Signed as a free agent, April 28, 2010.

Traded to Los Angeles with Matt Frattin and a second-round draft choice in 2015 for Jonathan Bernier, June 23, 2013.

2011–12 F 12	4–5–0–2	672	35	0	3.13
2012–13	20	7–9–0–0	1,025	46	2	2.69
Totals	32	11–14–0–2	1,697	81	2	2.86

F November 3, 2011

AL SECORD #20

left wing 6'1" 205 L

b. Sudbury, Ontario, March 3, 1958

Acquired with Ed Olczyk from Chicago for Rick Vaive, Steve Thomas, and Bob McGill, September 4, 1987.

Traded to Philadelphia for a fifth-round draft choice in 1989 (Keith Carney), February 7, 1989.

1987–88	74	15	27	42	221
1988–89	40	5	10	15	71
Totals	114	20	37	57	292

• Later became a commercial pilot.

RON SEDLBAUER #18

left wing 6'3" 200 L

b. Burlington, Ontario, October 22, 1954

Purchased from Chicago, February 18, 1981.

1980–81 L	21	10	4	14	14

L April 5, 1981

ROD SEILING #16/#17

defence 6' 195 L

b. Elmira, Ontario, November 14, 1944

Marlboros graduate

Traded with Dick Duff, Bob Nevin, Bill Collins, and Arnie Brown to New York Rangers for Andy Bathgate and Don McKenney, February 22, 1964; acquired from Washington for Tim Ecclestone and Willie Brossart, November 2, 1974.

Signed as a free agent by St. Louis, September 9, 1976. As compensation, Leafs received a second-round draft choice in 1978 (Joel Quenneville) and cash.

1962–63 F	1	0	1	1	0
1974–75	60	5	12	17	40
1975–76	77	3	16	19	46
Totals	138	8	29	37	86

F March 2, 1963

• Later worked in tourism for Toronto and the Ontario Racing Commission.

BRITON "BRIT" SELBY ("Panda") #8/#11/#15

left wing 5'10" 175 L

b. Kingston, Ontario, March 27, 1945

Marlboros graduate

Claimed by Philadelphia in Expansion Draft, June 6, 1967.

Acquired with Forbes Kennedy from Philadelphia for Mike Byers, Gerry Meehan, and Bill Sutherland, March 2, 1969; traded to St. Louis for Bob Baun, November 13, 1970.

1964–65 F	3	2	0	2	2
1965–66	61	14	13	27	26
1966–67	6	1	1	2	0
1968–69	14	2	2	4	19
1969–70	74	10	13	23	40
1970–71	11	0	1	1	6
Totals	169	29	30	59	93

F January 2, 1965

• Later taught history and economics in the Toronto high school system.

BRAD SELWOOD #3

defence 6'1" 200 L

b. Leamington, Ontario, March 18, 1948

Selected 10th overall in 1968 Amateur Draft.

Claimed by Montreal in Intra-League Draft, June 5, 1972.

1970–71 F	28	2	10	12	13
1971–72	72	4	17	21	58
Totals	100	6	27	33	71

F October 11, 1970

• Missed much of 1970–71 with back injury.

DAVE SEMENKO ("Sammy") #27

left wing 6'3" 200 L

b. Winnipeg, Manitoba, July 12, 1957

Acquired from Hartford for Bill Root, September 9, 1987.

Left team March 22, 1988.

1987–88 L	70	2	3	5	107

L March 19, 1988

JEFF SEROWIK #34

defence 6' 190 R

b. Manchester, New Hampshire, October 1, 1967

Selected 85th overall in 1985 Entry Draft.

Signed as a free agent by Florida, July 20, 1993.

1990–91 F	1	0	0	0	0

F October 6, 1990

EDDIE SHACK ("The Entertainer"/ "Clown Prince of Hockey") #23

right wing 6'1" 200 L

b. Sudbury, Ontario, February 11, 1937

Acquired from New York Rangers for Pat Hannigan and Johnny Wilson, November 7, 1960; traded to Boston for Murray Oliver and cash, May 15, 1967.

Purchased from Pittsburgh, July 3, 1973; released after 1974–75 season.

1960–61	55	14	14	28	90
1961–62	44	7	14	21	62
1962–63	63	16	9	25	97
1963–64	64	11	10	21	128
1964–65	67	5	9	14	68
1965–66	63	26	17	43	88
1966–67	63	11	14	25	58
1973–74	59	7	8	15	74
1974–75 L	26	2	1	3	11
Totals	504	99	96	195	676

L February 23, 1975

• Became popular in Toronto for his sale of Christmas trees every December.

DAVE SHAND #3/#4

defence 6'2" 200 R

b. Cold Lake, Alberta, August 11, 1956
Acquired with a third-round draft choice in 1980 (later traded to Washington for a second-round draft choice in 1980—Torrie Robertson) from Calgary for a second-round choice in 1980 (Kevin LaVallee), June 10, 1980.
Traded October 6, 1983, to Washington for Lee Norwood

1980–81	47	0	4	4	60
1982–83	1	0	1	1	2
Totals	48	0	5	5	62

• Later graduated from University of Michigan Law School and practises employment law in Michigan. Has become a player agent for a handful of minor pros.

DARRYL SHANNON #34/#29/#28/#4

defence 6'2" 195 L

b. Barrie, Ontario, June 21, 1968
Selected 36th overall in 1986 Entry Draft.
Signed as a free agent by Winnipeg, June 30, 1993.

1988–89 F	14	1	3	4	6
1989–90	10	0	1	1	12
1990–91	10	0	1	1	0
1991–92	48	2	8	10	23
1992–93	16	0	0	0	11
Totals	98	3	13	16	52

F March 1, 1989

NORMAND SHAY #3

forward 5'9" 155 L

b. Huntsville, Ontario, February 3, 1899
d. Hamden, Connecticut, November 28, 1968
Purchased from Boston January 13, 1926.
Retired after season.

1925–26 L	22	3	1	4	18

L March 17, 1926

DOUG SHEDDEN #37/#12

centre 6' 185 R

b. Wallaceburg, Ontario, April 29, 1961
Signed as a free agent, August 4, 1988.

1988–89	1	0	0	0	2
1990–91 L	23	8	10	18	10
Totals	24	8	10	18	12

L January 12, 1991

• Played most of 1988–89 and 1990–91 and all of 1989–90 with Newmarket (AHL).

JACK SHILL ("Porky") #7/#19/#20/#18

defence 5'11" 181 L

b. Toronto, Ontario, January 12, 1913
d. Toronto, Ontario, October 25, 1976
Marlboros graduate
Signed March 1, 1934; traded to Boston, summer 1934.
Re-signed by Toronto in 1935; sold to New York Americans, September 24, 1937.

1933–34 F	7	0	1	1	0
1935–36	3	0	1	1	0
1936–37	32	4	4	8	26
Totals	42	4	6	10	26

F March 3, 1934

JAIME SIFERS #59

defence 5'11" 210 R

b. Stratford, Connecticut, January 18, 1983
Signed as a free agent, March 15, 2006.
Signed as a free agent by Minnesota, July 8, 2009.

2008–09 F	23	0	2	2	18

F December 8, 2008

ZACH SILL #22

centre 6' 202 L

b. Truro, Nova Scotia, May 24, 1988
Acquired from Pittsburgh with a second-round draft choice in 2016 and a fourth-round draft choice in 2015 for Daniel Winnik, February 25, 2015.

2014–15	21	0	1	1	24

DON SIMMONS ("Dippy") #1/#24

goalie 5'10" 150 R

b. Port Colborne, Ontario, September 13, 1931
d. September 24, 2010
Acquired from Boston for Ed Chadwick, January 31, 1961.
Claimed by New York Rangers in Intra-League Draft, June 8, 1965.

1961–62	9	5–3–1	540	21	1	2.33
1962–63	28	15–8–5	1,680	69	1	2.46
1963–64	21	9–9–1	1,191	63	3	3.17
Totals	58	29–20–7	3,411	153	5	2.69

• Began tradition of goalies going to bench on delayed penalties.

DARRYL SITTLER ("Sit") #27

centre 6' 190 L

b. Kitchener, Ontario, September 18, 1950
Selected 8th overall in 1970 Amateur Draft.
Traded to Philadelphia for Rich Costello, a second-round draft choice in 1982 (Peter Ihnacak), and future considerations (Ken Strong), January 20, 1982.

1970–71 F	49	10	8	18	37
1971–72	74	15	17	32	44
1972–73	78	29	48	77	69
1973–74	78	38	46	84	55
1974–75	72	36	44	80	47
1975–76	79	41	59	100	90
1976–77	73	38	52	90	89
1977–78	80	45	72	117	100
1978–79	70	36	51	87	69
1979–80	73	40	57	97	62
1980–81	80	43	53	96	77
1981–82	38	18	20	38	24
Totals	844	389	527	916	763

F October 11, 1970

• Missed 28 games in 1970–71 (January 17–March 21) with a broken wrist.
• In the calendar year of 1976, he scored 10 points in one game, five goals in a playoff game, and scored the winner in overtime in the Canada Cup finals.
• Currently performs public relations work for the Leafs.

FREDRIK SJOSTROM #11

left wing 6'1" 218 L

b. Fargelanda, Sweden, May 6, 1983
Acquired from Calgary with Dion Phaneuf and Keith Aulie for Nicklas Hagman, Jamal Mayers, Matt Stajan, and Ian White, January 31, 2010.
Finished his career in Sweden.

2009–10	19	2	3	5	4
2010–11 L	66	2	3	5	14
Totals	85	4	6	10	18

L April 6, 2011

ALFRED "ALFIE" SKINNER #6

right wing 5'10" 180 R

b. Toronto, Ontario, January 26, 1896
d. Toronto, Ontario, April 23, 1961
Signed with Blue Shirts after Toronto Shamrocks (NHA) folded, 1915.
Left to play for Vancouver (PCHA) after 1918–19 season.

1917–18	20	13	—	13	28
1918–19	17	12	4	16	26
Totals	37	25	4	29	54

ALOYSIUS "TOD" SLOAN ("Trigger"/ "Slinker") #11/#15/#20/#22

centre 5'10" 175 R

b. Vinton, Quebec, November 30, 1927
St. Mike's graduate
Signed April 30, 1946; traded to Cleveland (AHL) with Harry Taylor and Ray Ceresino for Bob Solinger, 1949.
Purchased from Cleveland (AHL) during training camp 1950; sold to Chicago, June 4, 1958.

1947–48 F	1	0	0	0	0
1948–49	29	3	4	7	0
1950–51	70	31	25	56	105
1951–52	68	25	23	48	89
1952–53	70	15	10	25	76
1953–54	67	11	32	43	100
1954–55	63	13	15	28	89
1955–56	70	37	29	66	100
1956–57	52	14	21	35	33
1957–58	59	13	25	38	58
Totals	549	162	184	346	650

F December 25, 1947

• Ran a resort on Jacksons Point, Ontario, until he retired.

DARRYL SLY #21

defence 5'10" 185 R

b. Collingwood, Ontario, April 3, 1939
d. Collingwood, Ontario, August 28, 2007
St. Mike's graduate, 1961

1965–66 F	2	0	0	0	0
1967–68	17	0	0	0	4
Totals	19	0	0	0	4

F December 15, 1965

DALE SMEDSMO #23

left wing 6'1" 195 L

b. Roseau, Minnesota, April 23, 1951
Selected 93rd overall in 1971 Amateur Draft.
Signed by Cincinnati (WHA), June 6, 1976.

1972–73 F/L	4	0	0	0	0

F February 14, 1973 L February 24, 1973

AL SMITH ("Fat Albert"/"The Bear") #1/#30/#31

goalie 6'1" 200 L

b. Toronto, Ontario, November 10, 1945
d. Toronto, Ontario, August 7, 2002
Marlboros graduate
Claimed by Pittsburgh in Intra-League Draft, June 11, 1969.

1965–66 F	2	2–0–0	62	2	0	1.94
1966–67	1	0–1–0	60	5	0	5.00
1968–69	7	2–2–1	335	16	0	2.87
Totals	10	4–3–1	457	23	0	3.02

F February 20, 1966

• Later became a cab driver and playwright in Toronto.

ART SMITH #2/#3/#12

forward 5'10" 190 R

b. Toronto, Ontario, November 29, 1906
d. Toronto, Ontario, May 15, 1962
Signed as a free agent, October 27, 1927.
Traded with Eric Pettinger and $35,000 to Ottawa for King Clancy, October 11, 1930.

1927–28 F	15	5	3	8	22
1928–29	43	5	0	5	91
1929–30	43	3	3	6	75
Totals	101	13	6	19	188

F February 11, 1928

• Played most of 1927–28 with Toronto Ravinas (Can Pro).

BRAD SMITH ("Motor City Smitty") #29

right wing 6'1" 195 R

b. Windsor, Ontario, April 13, 1958
Signed as a free agent from Detroit, July 2, 1985.
Retired after 1986–87 season due to chronic back condition.

1985–86	42	5	17	22	84
1986–87 L	47	5	7	12	172
Totals	89	10	24	34	256

L April 4, 1987

DENIS "D.J." SMITH #4

defence 6'1" 200 L
b. Windsor, Ontario, May 13, 1977
Acquired with Wendel Clark and Mathieu Schneider from New York Islanders for Kenny Jonsson, Darby Hendrickson, Sean Haggerty, and a first-round draft choice in 1997 (Roberto Luongo), March 13, 1996.
Traded to Nashville with Marty Wilford for Marc Moro, March 1, 2002.

1996–97 F	8	0	1	1	7
1999–2000	3	0	0	0	5
Totals	11	0	1	1	12

F March 26, 1997
• Played mostly in minors with St. John's (AHL).
• Later coached in OHL.

FLOYD SMITH ("Smitty") #17

right wing 5'10" 180 R
b. Perth, May 16, 1935
Acquired with Paul Henderson and Norm Ullman from Detroit for Frank Mahovlich, Garry Unger, Pete Stemkowski, and the rights to Carl Brewer, March 3, 1968.
Sold with Brent Imlach to Buffalo, August 31, 1970.

1967–68	6	6	1	7	0
1968–69	64	15	19	34	22
1969–70	61	4	14	18	13
Totals	131	25	34	59	35

• Later became coach of the Leafs and then a scout for the team.

GARY SMITH ("Suitcase") #1

goalie 6'4" 215 L
b. Ottawa, Ontario, February 4, 1944
Marlboros graduate.
Claimed by Oakland in Expansion Draft, June 6, 1967.

1965–66 F	3		0–2–0	118	7	0	3.56
1966–67	2		0–2–0	115	7	0	3.65
Totals	5		0–4–0	233	14	0	3.61

F February 19, 1966
• Later served court papers to citizens in Vancouver.

GLENN SMITH #unknown

forward 5'8" 180 L
b. Meaford, Ontario, April 25, 1895
d. Toronto, Ontario, October 6, 1949

1921–22 F/L	9	0	0	0	0

F December 21, 1921 L January 28, 1922

JASON SMITH #25

defence 6'3" 205 R
b. Calgary, Alberta, November 2, 1973
Acquired with Steve Sullivan and Alyn McCauley from New Jersey for Doug Gilmour, Dave Ellett, and a third-round draft choice in 1999 (previously acquired from Devils for Andreychuk trade), February 25, 1997.
Traded to Edmonton for a fourth-round draft choice in 1999 (Jonathan Zion) and a second-round draft choice in 2000 (Kris Vernarsky), March 23, 1999.

1996–97	21	0	5	5	16
1997–98	81	3	13	16	100
1998–99	60	2	11	13	8
Totals	162	5	29	34	124

SID SMITH ("Muff") #8/#16/#22/#24

left wing 5'10 177 L
b. Toronto, Ontario, July 11, 1925
d. April 29, 2004
Signed as a free agent, December 8, 1946.
Placed on waivers, November 11, 1957.

1946–47 F	14	2	1	3	0
1947–48	31	7	10	17	10
1948–49	1	0	0	0	0
1949–50	68	22	23	45	6
1950–51	70	30	21	51	10
1951–52	70	27	30	57	6
1952–53	70	20	19	39	6
1953–54	70	22	16	38	28
1954–55	70	33	21	54	14
1955–56	55	4	17	21	8
1956–57	70	17	24	41	4
1957–58 L	12	2	1	3	2
Totals	601	186	183	369	94

F February 6, 1947 L November 10, 1957
• Played half of 1946–47 and 1947–48 and most of 1948–49 with Pittsburgh (AHL) to recuperate after sustaining a serious knee injury March 27, 1948, vs. Boston.
• Became playing coach of Whitby Dunlops same day he was placed on waivers. Was reinstated as an amateur; won gold medal with Canada at 1958 World Championship.
• Sold fine paper stock for a printing company for 25 years.

TREVOR SMITH #23

centre 6'1" 195 L
b. Ottawa, Ontario, February 8, 1985
Signed as a free agent, July 5, 2013.

2013–14	28	4	5	9	4
2014–15	54	2	3	5	12
Totals	82	6	8	14	16

JERRED SMITHSON #22

centre 6'3" 210 R
b. Vernon, British Columbia, February 4, 1979
Signed as a free agent, November 6, 2013.

2013–14	18	0	0	0	9

DR. ROD SMYLIE #9/#11

left wing 5'10" 170 L
b. Toronto, Ontario, September 28, 1895
d. Toronto, Ontario, March 1985
Signed December 15, 1920; signed by Ottawa on January 2, 1924.
Signed on January 27, 1925.

1920–21 F	23	2	1	3	2
1921–22	20	0	0	0	2
1922–23	2	0	0	0	0
1924–25	11	1	0	1	0
1925–26 L	5	0	0	0	0
Totals	61	3	1	4	4

F December 22, 1920 L January 15, 1926
• Played 1920–22 while studying medicine and interning at St. Michael's Hospital; later retired to run a private practice in Toronto.

GREG SMYTH #28/#25

defence 6'3" 212 R
b. Oakville, Ontario, April 23, 1966
Purchased from Florida, December 7, 1993; claimed off waivers by Florida, January 8, 1994. Signed as a free agent, August 13, 1996; claimed off waivers by Chicago, December 1996.

1993–94 F	11	0	1	1	38
1996–97	2	0	0	0	0
Totals	13	0	1	1	38

F December 11, 1993

CHRIS SNELL #38

defence 5'10" 190 L
b. Regina, Saskatchewan, May 12, 1971
Signed as a free agent, August 3, 1993.
Traded with Éric Lacroix and a fourth-round draft choice in 1996 (Éric Bélanger) to Los Angeles for Dixon Ward, Guy Leveque, Kelly Fairchild, and Shayne Toporowski, October 5, 1994.

1993–94 F	2	0	0	0	2

F February 26, 1994

BOB SOLINGER ("Solly") #11/#21/#23/#25

left wing 5'10" 190 L
b. Star City, Saskatchewan, September 23, 1925
d. Edmonton, Alberta, December 10, 2014
Acquired from Cleveland (AHL) for Tod Sloan, Harry Taylor, and Ray Ceresino, summer 1949.
Purchased by Hershey when Pittsburgh (AHL) folded, June 7, 1956.

1951–52 F	24	5	3	8	4
1952–53	18	1	1	2	2
1953–54	39	3	2	5	2
1954–55	17	1	5	6	11
Totals	98	10	11	21	19

F November 1, 1951
• Called up from Pittsburgh (AHL) on December 27, 1954, to replace injured Ron Stewart.

GORD SPENCE #unknown

right wing 5'7" 150 L
b. Haileybury, Ontario, July 25, 1897
d. St. Catharines, Ontario, November 21, 1984
Signed as a free agent, December 31, 1925.

1925–26 F/L	3	0	0	0	0

F January 12, 1926 L January 23, 1926

BRIAN SPENCER ("Spinner") #15/#22

left wing 5'11" 185 L
b. Fort St. James, British Columbia, September 3, 1949
d. Riviera Beach, Florida, June 3, 1988
Selected 55th overall in 1969 Amateur Draft.
Claimed by New York Islanders in Expansion Draft, June 6, 1972.

1969–70 F	9	0	0	0	12
1970–71	50	9	15	24	115
1971–72	36	1	5	6	65
Totals	95	10	20	30	192

F March 14, 1970
• Murdered in 1988. Five years later, Atom Egoyan made a TV film about his life.

CHRIS SPEYER #11

defence 5'10" 170 L
b. Toronto, Ontario, February 9, 1902
d. Toronto, Ontario, December 26, 1966
Signed in 1924 from Aura Lee (OHA Senior).
Released December 15, 1924.

1923–24 F	4	0	0	0	0
1924–25	2	0	0	0	0
Totals	6	0	0	0	0

F February 23, 1924

JESSE SPRING ("Jess") #14

defence 6' 185 L
b. Alba, Pennsylvania, January 18, 1901
d. Toronto, Ontario, March 25, 1942

1926–27	5	0	0	0	0

• Played with Pittsburgh Pirates 1925–26 and New York Americans 1928–29.
• One-time middleweight boxing champion.

THEODORE "TED" STACKHOUSE #unknown

defence 6'1" 200 R
b. New Glasgow, Nova Scotia, November 2, 1894
d. Mount Holly, New Jersey, November 24, 1975

1921–22 F/L	12	0	0	0	2

F December 24, 1921 L March 4, 1922
• Played part of 1921–22 in Maritime Independent League (New Glasgow).

MATT STAJAN #14/#41

centre 6'1" 192 L

b. Mississauga, Ontario, December 19, 1983
Selected 57th overall in 2002 Entry Draft.
Traded to Calgary with Ian White, Nicklas
Hagman, and Jamal Mayers for Dion
Phaneuf, Keith Aulie, and Fredrik Sjostrom,
January 31, 2010.

2002–03 F	1	1	0	1	0
2003–04	69	14	13	27	22
2005–06	80	15	12	27	50
2006–07	82	10	29	39	44
2007–08	82	16	17	33	47
2008–09	76	15	40	55	54
2009–10	55	16	25	41	30
Totals	445	87	136	223	247

F April 5, 2003

VIKTOR STALBERG #45

left wing 6'3" 210 L

b. Gothenburg, Sweden, January 17, 1986
Selected 161st overall in 2006 Entry Draft.
Traded to Chicago with Chris DiDomenico
and Philippe Paradis for Kris Versteeg and
Bill Sweatt, June 30, 2010.

2009–10 F	40	9	5	14	30

F October 1, 2009

LORNE STAMLER #12

left wing 6' 190 L

b. Winnipeg, Manitoba, August 9, 1951
Acquired with Dave Hutchison from Los
Angeles for Brian Glennie, Kurt Walker, Scott
Garland, and a second-round draft choice in
1979 (Mark Hardy), June 14, 1978.
Claimed by Winnipeg in Expansion Draft,
June 13, 1979.

1978–79	45	4	3	7	2

**ALLAN STANLEY ("Sam"/"Snowshoes")
#26**

defence 6'2" 191 L

b. Timmins, Ontario, March 1, 1926
d. Bobcaygeon, Ontario, October 18, 2013
Acquired from Boston for Jim Morrison,
October 3, 1958.
Selected by Quebec (AHL) in Reverse Draft,
June 13, 1968.

1958–59	70	1	22	23	47
1959–60	64	10	23	33	22
1960–61	68	9	25	34	42
1961–62	60	9	26	35	24
1962–63	61	4	15	19	22
1963–64	70	6	21	27	60
1964–65	64	2	15	17	30
1965–66	59	4	14	18	35
1966–67	53	1	12	13	20
1967–68 L	64	1	13	14	16
Totals	633	47	186	233	318

L March 31, 1968
• Operated a resort in Bobcaygeon, Ontario,
after retiring from hockey.
• Hockey Hall of Fame 1981

**WALLY STANOWSKI ("Whirling
Dervish"/"The Hat") #2/#3/#20/#16**

defence 5'11" 180 L

b. Winnipeg, Manitoba, April 28, 1919
d. Toronto, Ontario, June 28, 2015
Acquired from New York Americans for Hap
Day, September 24, 1937.
Traded to New York Rangers with Moe
Morris and the rights to Orval Lavell for Cal
Gardner, Bill Juzda, René Trudell, Frank
Mathers, and the rights to Ray McMurray,
April 26, 1948.

1939–40 F	27	2	7	9	11
1940–41	47	7	14	21	35
1941–42	24	1	7	8	10
1944–45	34	2	9	11	16
1945–46	45	3	10	13	10
1946–47	51	3	16	19	12
1947–48	54	2	11	13	12
Totals	282	20	74	94	106

F November 4, 1939
• Missed 1942–44 serving in Canadian Armed
Forces; discharged November 23, 1944.
• Sold construction equipment for 20 years
after retiring.

TIM STAPLETON #42

centre 5'9" 180 R

b. Forest Park, Illinois, July 19, 1982
Signed as a free agent, June 6, 2008.
Traded to Atlanta with Pavel Kubina for Garnet
Exelby and Colin Stuart, July 1, 2009.

2008–09 F	4	1	0	1	0

F February 26, 2009

MARIAN STASTNY #10

right wing 5'10" 195 L

b. Bratislava, Czechoslovakia (Czech Republic),
January 8, 1953
Signed as a free agent, August 12, 1985.

1985–86 L	70	23	30	53	21

L April 6, 1986

DAVID STECKEL #20

centre 6'6" 215 L

b. Milwaukee, Wisconsin, March 15, 1982
Acquired from New Jersey for a fourth-
round draft choice in 2012 (Ben Thomson),
October 4, 2011.
Traded to Anaheim for Ryan Lasch and a
seventh-round draft choice in 2014 (later
traded back to Anaheim—Ondrej Kase),
March 15, 2013.

2011–12	76	8	5	13	10
2012–13	13	0	1	1	0
Totals	89	8	6	14	10

ALEXANDER STEEN #10

centre 5'11" 212 L

b. Winnipeg, Manitoba, March 1, 1984
Selected 24th overall in 2002 Entry Draft.
Traded to St. Louis on with Carlo Colaiacovo
for Lee Stempniak, November 24, 2008.

2005–06	75	18	27	45	42
2006–07	82	15	20	35	26

2007–08	76	15	27	42	32
2008–09	20	2	2	4	6
Totals	253	50	76	126	106

PHIL STEIN ("The Happy Dutchman") #1

goalie 5'10" 160 L

b. Toronto, Ontario, September 13, 1913
d. Toronto, Ontario, April 4, 1997
Signed as a free agent October 30, 1934,
and assigned to Syracuse (IHL).
Sold to New Haven (AHL), October 21, 1940.

1939–40 F	1	0–0–1	70	2	0	1.71

F/L January 18, 1940
• Recalled from Omaha (AHA) to replace
injured Turk Broda, January 15, 1940.

**PETE STEMKOWSKI ("Stemmer")
#12/#25**

centre 6'1" 210 L

b. Winnipeg, Manitoba, August 25, 1943
Traded with Frank Mahovlich, Garry Unger,
and the rights to Carl Brewer to Detroit for
Norm Ullman, Paul Henderson, and Floyd
Smith, March 3, 1968.

1963–64 F	1	0	0	0	2
1964–65	36	5	15	20	33
1965–66	56	4	12	16	55
1966–67	68	13	22	35	75
1967–68	60	7	15	22	82
Totals	221	29	64	93	247

F January 18, 1964
• Later scouted for San Jose.

LEE STEMPNIAK #12

right wing 5'11" 196 R

b. West Seneca, New York, February 4, 1983
Acquired from St. Louis for Alexander Steen
and Carlo Colaiacovo, November 24, 2008.
Traded to Phoenix for a fourth-round draft
choice in 2010 (traded to Washington—
Philipp Grubauer) and a seventh-round draft
choice in 2010 (Kellen Jones), March 3, 2010.

2008–09	61	11	20	31	31
2009–10	62	14	16	30	18
Totals	123	25	36	61	49

BOB STEPHENSON #15

defence 6'1" 187 R

b. Saskatoon, Saskatchewan, February 1, 1954
Acquired from Hartford for Pat Boutette,
December 24, 1979.

1979–80 L	14	2	2	4	4

L January 9, 1980

MIKE STEVENS #26

left wing 5'11" 195 L

b. Kitchener, Ontario, December 30, 1965
Acquired with Gilles Thibaudeau from New
York Islanders for Paul Gagné, Derek Laxdal,
and Jack Capuano, December 20, 1989.
Traded to New York Rangers for Guy Larose,
December 26, 1991.

1989–90 L	1	0	0	0	0

L January 27, 1990

BILL STEWART #17

defence 6'2" 180 R

b. Toronto, Ontario, October 6, 1957
Signed as a free agent, September 10, 1983.
Signed as a free agent by Minnesota North
Stars, September 15, 1985.

1983–84	56	2	17	19	116
1984–85	27	0	2	2	32
Totals	83	2	19	21	148

• Later coached briefly in NHL, then OHL.

**JAMES "GAYE" STEWART ("The Gaye
One") #15/#16**

left wing 5'11" 175 L

b. Fort William, Ontario, June 28, 1923
d. Burlington, Ontario, November 18, 2010
Marlboros graduate, 1942
Signed with Leafs, March 5, 1942.
Traded with Gus Bodnar, Bud Poile, Bob
Goldham, and Ernie Dickens to Chicago for
Max Bentley and Cy Thomas, November
2, 1947.

1942–43 F	48	24	23	47	20
1945–46	50	37	15	52	8
1946–47	60	19	14	33	15
1947–48	7	1	0	1	0
Totals	165	81	52	133	43

F October 31, 1942 (regular season—also
appeared in 1942 playoffs)
• Missed 1943–45 while serving in the
Canadian Army.
• Later became a brewery representative in
southern Ontario for 28 years.

RON STEWART ("Stew") #12/#19/#24

right wing 6'1" 197 R

b. Calgary, Alberta, July 11, 1932
d. Kelowna, British Columbia, March 17,
2012
Signed with Leafs, October 6, 1952.
Traded to Boston for Pat Stapleton, Andy
Hebenton, and Orland Kurtenbach, June
8, 1965.

1952–53 F	70	13	22	35	29
1953–54	70	14	11	25	72
1954–55	53	14	5	19	20
1955–56	69	13	14	27	35
1956–57	65	15	20	35	28
1957–58	70	15	24	39	51
1958–59	70	21	13	34	23
1959–60	67	14	20	34	28
1960–61	51	13	12	25	8
1961–62	60	8	9	17	14
1962–63	63	16	16	32	26
1963–64	65	14	5	19	46
1964–65	65	16	11	27	33
Totals	838	186	182	368	413

F October 11, 1952
• Won Memorial Cup in 1951–52 with
Guelph Biltmores.
• Joined Leafs in 1952–53—never played a
game in the minors.

MIKE STOTHERS #25

defence 6'4" 212 L

b. Toronto, Ontario, February 22, 1962
Acquired from Philadelphia for a fifth-round draft choice in 1989 (later traded to Minnesota—Pat MacLeod), December 4, 1987. Traded to Philadelphia for Bill Root, June 21, 1988.

1987–88 L	18	0	1	1	42

L February 22, 1988

BLAINE STOUGHTON ("Stash") #17

right wing 5'11" 185 R

b. Gilbert Plains, Manitoba, March 13, 1953
Acquired with a first-round draft choice in 1977 (Trevor Johansen) from Pittsburgh for Rick Kehoe, September 13, 1974. Claimed by Hartford in Expansion Draft, June 13, 1979.

1974–75	78	23	14	37	24
1975–76	43	6	11	17	8
Totals	121	29	25	54	32

ANTON STRALMAN #36

defence 5'11" 190 R

b. Tibro, Sweden, August 1, 1986
Selected 216th overall in 2005 Entry Draft. Traded to Calgary with Colin Stuart and a seventh-round draft choice in 2012 (Matthew De Blouw) for Wayne Primeau and a second-round draft choice in 2011 (later traded to Chicago—Brandon Saad), July 27, 2009.

2007–08 F	50	3	6	9	18
2008–09	38	1	12	13	20
Totals	88	4	18	22	38

F October 23, 2007

KEN STRONG #23/#32

left wing 5'11" 185 L

b. Toronto, Ontario, May 9, 1963
Acquired from Philadelphia to complete Darryl Sittler trade, January 20, 1982.

1982–83 F	2	0	0	0	0
1983–84	2	0	2	2	2
1984–85 L	11	2	0	2	4
Totals	15	2	2	4	6

F April 2, 1983 L February 14, 1985

BILLY "RED" STUART ("Ginger") #3

defence 5'11" 175 L

b. Sackville, New Brunswick, February 1, 1900
d. March 7, 1978
Joined St. Pats from Amherst (Maritime Independent League), January 4, 1921. Sold to Boston, December 14, 1924.

1920–21 F	19	2	1	3	4
1921–22	24	3	7	10	16
1922–23	23	7	3	10	16
1923–24	24	4	3	7	22
1924–25	4	0	1	1	2
Totals	94	16	15	31	60

F January 12, 1921

ALEKSANDER SUGLOBOV #19/#9

right wing 6' 200 L

b. Elektrostal, Soviet Union (Russia), January 15, 1982
Acquired from New Jersey for Ken Klee, March 8, 2006.
Played remainder of career in Russia.

2005–06	2	0	0	0	0
2006–07	14	0	0	0	4
Totals	16	0	0	0	4

FRANK "SULLY" SULLIVAN #25

defence 5'11" 178 R

b. Toronto, Ontario, June 16, 1929
d. April 5, 2009
Recalled from Pittsburgh (AHL), November 10, 1952.
Traded with Dusty Blair and Jackie LeClair to Buffalo (AHL) for Brian Cullen, April 1954.

1949–50 F	1	0	0	0	0
1952–53	5	0	0	0	2
Totals	6	0	0	0	2

F March 11, 1950

STEVE SULLIVAN ("Sully") #11

right wing 5'9" 155 R

b. Timmins, Ontario, July 6, 1974
Acquired with Jason Smith and Alyn McCauley from New Jersey for Doug Gilmour, Dave Ellett, and a third-round draft choice in 1999 (previously acquired in Dave Andreychuk trade), February 25, 1997.
Claimed off waivers by Chicago, October 23, 1999.

1996–97	21	5	11	16	23
1997–98	63	10	18	28	40
1998–99	63	20	20	40	28
1999–2000	7	0	1	1	4
Totals	154	35	50	85	95

MATS SUNDIN ("Weed") #13

centre 6'4" 215 R

b. Bromma, Sweden, February 13, 1971
Acquired with Garth Butcher, Todd Warriner, and a first-round draft choice in 1994 (later traded to Washington—Nolan Baumgartner) from Quebec for Wendel Clark, Sylvain Lefebvre, Landon Wilson, and a first-round draft choice in 1994 (Jeffrey Kealty), June 28, 1994.
Signed as a free agent by Vancouver, December 18, 2008.

1994–95	47	23	24	47	14
1995–96	76	33	50	83	46
1996–97	82	41	53	94	59
1997–98	82	33	41	74	49
1998–99	82	31	52	83	58
1999–2000	73	32	41	73	46
2000–01	82	28	46	74	76
2001–02	82	41	39	80	94
2002–03	75	37	35	72	58
2003–04	81	31	44	75	52
2005–06	70	31	47	78	58
2006–07	75	27	49	76	62
2007–08	74	32	46	78	76
Totals	981	420	567	987	748

• Became first non-Canadian captain of Leafs.
• Hockey Hall of Fame 2012; IIHF Hall of Fame 2013

BILL SUTHERLAND #15

centre 5'10" 176 L

b. Regina, Saskatchewan, November 10, 1934
Claimed from Minnesota North Stars in Intra-League Draft, June 12, 1968. Traded to Philadelphia with Gerry Meehan and Mike Byers for Brit Selby and Forbes Kennedy, March 2, 1969.

1968–69	44	7	5	12	14

RICH SUTTER #20

right wing 5'11" 188 R

b. Viking, Alberta, December 2, 1963
Acquired from Tampa Bay for cash, March 13, 1995.
Released June 27, 1995.

1994–95 L	18	0	3	3	10

L May 1, 1995

ROBERT SVEHLA #67

defence 6'1" 210 R

b. Martin, Czechoslovakia (Slovakia), January 2, 1969
Acquired from Florida for Dmitri Yushkevich, July 19, 2002.
Finished career in Slovakia.

2002–03 L	82	7	38	45	46

L April 5, 2003 (regular season—also played in 2003 playoffs)

PETR SVOBODA #23

defence 6'3" 200 R

b. Jihlava, Czechoslovakia (Czech Republic), June 20, 1980
Selected 35th overall in 1998 Entry Draft.

2000–01 F/L	18	1	2	3	10

F October 7, 2000 L January 6, 2001

BOB SYKES #25

left wing 6' 200 L

b. Sudbury, Ontario, September 26, 1951
Selected 65th overall in 1971 Amateur Draft.

1974–75 F/L	2	0	0	0	0

F February 12, 1974 L February 15, 1974

BILLY TAYLOR ("Billy the Kid") #19/#21/#7

centre 5'9" 150 R

b. Winnipeg, Manitoba, May 3, 1919
d. Oshawa, Ontario, June 12, 1990
Signed by Leafs, May 1, 1939.
Traded with Doug Baldwin and Ray Powell to Detroit for Harry Watson and Gerry Brown, September 21, 1946.

1939–40 F	29	4	6	10	9
1940–41	47	9	26	35	15
1941–42	48	12	26	38	20
1942–43	50	18	42	60	2
1945–46	48	23	18	41	14
Totals	222	66	118	184	60

F November 4, 1939
• Leafs' mascot when 1931–32 team won Cup and has his name on the Stanley Cup as such.
• Missed 1943–45 while serving in the Canadian Army; re-signed August 24, 1945.

HARRY TAYLOR #17/#21

centre 5'8" 165 R

b. St. James, Manitoba, March 28, 1926
d. Sidney, British Columbia, November 16, 2009
Signed as a free agent, May 1, 1946. Loaned to Providence (AHL) for 1947–48 season; traded with Tod Sloan and Ray Ceresino to Cleveland (AHL) for Bob Solinger, summer 1949.

1946–47 F	9	0	2	2	0
1948–49	42	4	7	11	30
Totals	51	4	9	13	30

F November 17, 1946

MIKAEL TELLQVIST #32

goalie 6' 189 L

b. Sundbyberg, Sweden, September 19, 1979
Selected 70th overall in 2000 Entry Draft. Traded to Phoenix for Tyson Nash and a fourth-round draft choice in 2007 (Matt Frattin), November 28, 2006.

2002–03 F	3	1–1–0–0	86	4	0	2.79
2003–04	11	5–3–2–0	647	31	0	2.87
2005–06	25	10–11–0–2	1,399	73	2	3.13
2006–07	1	0–1–0–0	59	2	0	2.03
Totals	40	16–16–2–2	2,191	110	2	3.01

F January 18, 2004

GREG TERRION ("Tubby") #7

left wing 5'11" 190 L

b. Marmora, Ontario, May 2, 1960
Acquired from Los Angeles for a fourth-round draft choice in 1983 (later transferred to Detroit—David Korol), October 19, 1982.

1982–83	74	16	16	32	59
1983–84	79	15	24	39	36
1984–85	72	14	17	31	20
1985–86	76	10	22	32	31
1986–87	67	7	8	15	6
1987–88 L	59	4	16	20	65
Totals	427	66	103	169	217

L April 2, 1988
• Later operated a gas station in Marmora, Ontario.

GILLES THIBAUDEAU ("T-Bone"/"Bud") #7

centre 5'10" 165 L
b. Montreal, Quebec, March 4, 1963
Acquired with Mike Stevens from New York Islanders for Paul Gagné, Derek Laxdal, and Jack Capuano, December 20, 1989.
Left to join Lugano (Switzerland) for 1991–92 season.

	GP	G	A	PTS	PIM
1989–90	21	7	11	18	13
1990–91 L	20	2	7	9	4
Totals	41	9	18	27	17

L November 19, 1990

CYRIL "CY" THOMAS #22

forward 5'10" 185 L
b. Dowlais, Wales, August 5, 1926
d. January 2, 2009
Acquired with Max Bentley from Chicago for Gus Bodnar, Bob Goldham, Bud Poile, Gaye Stewart, and Ernie Dickens, November 2, 1947.

	GP	G	A	PTS	PIM
1947–48 L	8	1	2	3	4

L December 25, 1947

STEVE THOMAS ("Stumpy") #12/#32/#25

left wing 5'11" 185 R
b. Stockport, England, July 15, 1963
Signed as a free agent, May 12, 1984; traded with Rick Vaive and Bob McGill to Chicago for Ed Olczyk and Al Secord, September 4, 1987.
Signed as a free agent, July 30, 1998; signed as a free agent by Chicago, July 17, 2001.

	GP	G	A	PTS	PIM
1984–85 F	18	1	1	2	2
1985–86	65	20	37	57	36
1986–87	78	35	27	62	114
1998–99	78	28	45	73	33
1999–2000	81	26	37	63	68
2000–01	57	8	26	34	46
Totals	377	118	173	291	299

F November 7, 1984

WAYNE THOMAS #30/#33

goalie 6'2" 195 L
b. Ottawa, Ontario, October 9, 1947
Acquired from Montreal for a first-round draft choice in 1976 (Peter Lee), June 17, 1975.
Claimed by New York Rangers in Waiver Draft, October 10, 1977.

	GP	W-L-T	MIN	GA	SO	GAA
1975–76	64	28–24–12	3,684	196	2	3.19
1976–77	33	10–13–6	1,803	116	1	3.86
Totals	97	38–37–18	5,487	312	3	3.41

ERROL THOMPSON ("Spud") #12/#22

left wing 5'8" 180 L
b. Summerside, Prince Edward Island, May 28, 1950
Selected 22nd overall in 1970 Amateur Draft. Traded with a first-round draft choice in 1978 (Brent Peterson), a second-round draft choice in 1978 (Al Jensen), and a first-round draft choice in 1980 (Mike Blaisdell) to Detroit

for Dan Maloney and a second-round draft choice in 1980 (Craig Muni), March 13, 1978.

	GP	G	A	PTS	PIM
1970–71 F	1	0	0	0	0
1972–73	68	13	19	32	8
1973–74	56	7	8	15	6
1974–75	65	25	17	42	12
1975–76	75	43	37	80	26
1976–77	41	21	16	37	8
1977–78	59	17	22	39	10
Totals	365	126	119	245	70

F March 28, 1971

BILL THOMS #7/#14/#16/#29

centre 5'9" 170 L
b. Newmarket, Ontario, March 5, 1910
d. Toronto, Ontario, December 26, 1964
Marlboros graduate
Traded to Chicago for Doc Romnes, December 7, 1938.

	GP	G	A	PTS	PIM
1932–33 F	29	3	9	12	15
1933–34	47	8	18	26	24
1934–35	47	9	13	22	15
1935–36	48	23	15	38	29
1936–37	48	10	9	19	14
1937–38	48	14	24	38	14
1938–39	12	1	4	5	4
Totals	279	68	92	160	115

F January 3, 1933

• Retired from hockey in 1945 after serious illness.
• Later worked for *Toronto Telegram* until his death.

JIM THOMSON ("Jeems"/"The Gold Dust Twins" with Gus Mortson) #2/#20

defence 6' 190 R
b. Winnipeg, Manitoba, February 23, 1927
d. Toronto, Ontario, May 18, 1991
St. Mike's graduate
Signed with Leafs, October 16, 1945; contract sold to Chicago for one year for $15,000, August 5, 1957.
Contract returned to Toronto after 1957–58 season, but Thomson retired August 17, 1958.

	GP	G	A	PTS	PIM
1945–46 F	5	0	1	1	4
1946–47	60	2	14	16	97
1947–48	59	0	29	29	82
1948–49	60	4	16	20	56
1949–50	70	0	13	13	76
1950–51	69	3	33	36	76
1951–52	70	0	25	25	86
1952–53	69	0	22	22	73
1953–54	61	2	24	26	86
1954–55	70	4	12	16	63
1955–56	62	0	7	7	96
1956–57	62	0	12	12	50
Totals	717	15	208	223	845

F November 10, 1945

• Heavily involved with Ted Lindsay of Detroit in trying to form a players' association.

RHYS THOMSON #17

defence 6'1" 195 L
b. Toronto, Ontario, August 9, 1918
d. Toronto, Ontario, October 12, 1993
Purchased from Buffalo (AHL) for cash, November 6, 1942.
Released December 1942.

	GP	G	A	PTS	PIM
1942–43 F/L	18	0	2	2	22

F November 12, 1942 L December 20, 1942

SCOTT THORNTON #24

centre 6'2" 200 L
b. London, Ontario, January 9, 1971
Selected 3rd overall in 1989 Entry Draft. Traded with Vincent Damphousse, Luke Richardson, and Peter Ing to Edmonton for Grant Fuhr, Glenn Anderson, and Craig Berube, September 19, 1991.

	GP	G	A	PTS	PIM
1990–91 F	33	1	3	4	30

F October 4, 1990

RAY TIMGREN ("Golden Boy," Mark II) #22

left wing 5'9" 161 L
b. Windsor, Ontario, September 29, 1928
d. Lindsay, Ontario, November 25, 1999
Marlboros graduate
Traded to Chicago for Jack Price, October 4, 1954; loaned from Chicago, November 16, 1954.

	GP	G	A	PTS	PIM
1948–49 F	36	3	12	15	9
1949–50	68	7	18	25	22
1950–51	70	1	9	10	20
1951–52	50	2	4	6	11
1952–53	12	0	0	0	4
1954–55 L	1	0	0	0	2
Totals	237	13	43	56	68

F December 18, 1948 L March 19, 1955

• Later became a schoolteacher in Toronto.

JIRI TLUSTY #11

centre 6' 210 L
b. Slany, Czechoslovakia (Czech Republic), March 16, 1988
Selected 13th overall in 2006.
Traded to Carolina for Philippe Paradis, December 3, 2009.

	GP	G	A	PTS	PIM
2007–08 F	58	10	6	16	14
2008–09	14	0	4	4	0
2009–10	2	0	0	0	0
Totals	74	10	10	20	14

F October 25, 2007

DAVE TOMLINSON #14/#37

centre 5'11" 177 L
b. North Vancouver, British Columbia, May 8, 1969
Selected 43rd overall in 1985 Entry Draft.
Sold to Florida, August 3, 1993.

	GP	G	A	PTS	PIM
1991–92 F	3	0	0	0	2
1992–93	3	0	0	0	2
Totals	6	0	0	0	4

F December 12, 1991

SHAYNE TOPOROWSKI #41

forward 6'2" 222 R
b. Paddockwood, Saskatchewan, August 6, 1975
Acquired with Dixon Ward, Guy Leveque, and Kelly Fairchild for Éric Lacroix, Chris Snell, and a fourth-round draft choice in 1996 (Éric Bélanger), October 3, 1994.
Signed as a free agent by St. Louis, September 9, 1997.

	GP	G	A	PTS	PIM
1996–97 F/L	3	0	0	0	7

F January 7, 1997

VESA TOSKALA #35

goalie 5'10" 198 L
b. Tampere, Finland, May 20, 1977
Acquired from San Jose with Mark Bell for a first-round draft choice in 2007 (later traded to St. Louis—Lars Eller), a second-round draft choice in 2007 (later traded to St. Louis—Aaron Palushaj), and a fourth-round draft choice in 2009 (later traded to Nashville—Craig Smith), June 22, 2007.
Traded to Anaheim with Jason Blake for J-S Giguère, January 31, 2010.

	GP	W-L-T	MIN	GA	SO	GAA
2007–08	66	33–25–6	3,837	175	3	2.74
2008–09	53	22–17–11	3,056	166	1	3.26
2009–10	26	7–12–3	1,393	85	1	3.66
Totals	145	62–54–20	8,286	426	5	3.08

VINCENT TREMBLAY #1/#30/#29

goalie 5'11" 185 L
b. Quebec City, Quebec, October 21, 1959
Selected 72nd overall in 1979 Entry Draft.
Traded with Rocky Saganiuk to Pittsburgh for Pat Graham and Nick Ricci, August 15, 1983.

	GP	W-L-T	MIN	GA	SO	GAA
1979–80 F	10	2–1–0	329	28	0	5.11
1980–81	3	0–3–0	143	16	0	6.71
1981–82	40	10–18–8	2,033	153	1	4.52
1982–83	1	0–0–0	40	2	0	3.00
Totals	54	12–22–8	2,545	199	1	4.69

F January 7, 1980

YANNICK TREMBLAY #38

defence 6'2" 178 R
b. Montreal, Quebec, November 15, 1975
Selected 145th overall in 1995 Entry Draft.
Claimed by Atlanta in Expansion Draft, June 25, 1999.

	GP	G	A	PTS	PIM
1996–97 F	5	0	0	0	0
1997–98	38	2	4	6	6
1998–99	35	2	7	9	16
Totals	78	4	11	15	22

F March 27, 1997

GUY TROTTIER ("The Mouse") #11

right wing 5'8" 165 L
b. Hull, Quebec, April 1, 1941
Acquired with Jacques Plante and Denis Dupéré from New York Rangers for Tim Horton, March 3, 1970.
Signed with Ottawa (WHA) for 1972–73 season.

	GP	G	A	PTS	PIM
1970–71	61	19	5	24	21
1971–72 L	52	9	12	21	16
Totals	113	28	17	45	37

L April 9, 1972

DARCY TUCKER #16

centre 5'11" 185 L

b. Castor, Alberta, March 15, 1975
Acquired from Tampa Bay with a fourth-round draft choice in 2000 (Miguel Delisle) and future considerations for Mike Johnson, Marek Posmyk, a fifth-round draft choice in 2000 (Pavel Sedov), a sixth-round draft choice in 2000 (Aaron Gionet), and future considerations, February 9, 2000.
Signed as a free agent by Colorado, July 1, 2008.

1999–2000	27	7	10	17	55
2000–01	82	16	21	37	141
2001–02	77	24	35	59	92
2002–03	77	10	26	36	119
2003–04	64	21	11	32	68
2005–06	74	28	33	61	100
2006–07	56	24	19	43	81
2007–08	74	18	16	34	100
Totals	531	148	171	319	756

• Later became a player agent.

IAN TURNBULL ("Bull"/"Hawk") #2

defence 6' 200 L

b. Montreal, Quebec, December 22, 1953
Selected 15th overall in 1973 Amateur Draft.
Traded to Los Angeles for John Gibson and Billy Harris, November 11, 1981.

1973–74	F	78	8	27	35	74
1974–75		22	6	7	13	44
1975–76		76	20	36	56	90
1976–77		80	22	57	79	84
1977–78		77	14	47	61	77
1978–79		80	12	51	63	80
1979–80		75	11	28	39	90
1980–81		80	19	47	66	104
1981–82		12	0	2	2	8
Totals		580	112	302	414	651

F October 10, 1973
• Started selling real estate in California, which in turn led him to start a company that funds mortgages for companies in that state.

NORM ULLMAN #9

centre 5'10" 185 L

b. Provost, Alberta, December 26, 1935
Acquired with Paul Henderson and Floyd Smith from Detroit for Frank Mahovlich, Pete Stemkowski, Garry Unger, and the rights to Carl Brewer, March 3, 1968.
Released after 1974–75 season.

1967–68	13	5	12	17	2
1968–69	75	35	42	77	41
1969–70	74	18	42	60	37
1970–71	73	34	51	85	24
1971–72	77	23	50	73	26
1972–73	65	20	35	55	10
1973–74	78	22	47	69	12
1974–75	L	80	9	26	35	8
Totals	535	166	305	471	160

L April 6, 1975
• Hockey Hall of Fame 1982

GARRY UNGER ("Iron Man") #15

centre 6' 185 L

b. Edmonton, Alberta, December 7, 1947
Signed fall 1966.
Traded with Frank Mahovlich, Pete Stemkowski, and the rights to Carl Brewer to Detroit for Norm Ullman, Paul Henderson, and Floyd Smith, March 3, 1968.

1967–68	F	15	1	1	2	4

F November 4, 1967
• Went on to establish Iron Man record for consecutive games played (915—later surpassed).

RICK VAIVE ("Squid") #22/#20

right wing 6' 200 R

b. Ottawa, Ontario, May 14, 1959
Acquired with Bill Derlago from Vancouver for Tiger Williams and Jerry Butler, February 18, 1980.
Traded with Steve Thomas and Bob McGill to Chicago for Ed Olczyk and Al Secord, September 4, 1987.

1979–80	22	9	7	16	77
1980–81	75	33	29	62	229
1981–82	77	54	35	89	157
1982–83	78	51	28	79	105
1983–84	76	52	41	93	114
1984–85	72	35	33	68	112
1985–86	61	33	31	64	85
1986–87	73	32	34	66	61
Totals	534	299	238	537	940

• Turned to coaching and broadcasting after retiring.

JACK VALIQUETTE #8

centre 6'2" 195 L

b. St. Thomas, Ontario, March 18, 1956
Selected 13th overall in 1974 Amateur Draft.
Traded to Colorado Rockies for a second-round draft choice in 1981 (Gary Yaremchuk), October 19, 1978.

1974–75	F	1	0	0	0	0
1975–76		45	10	23	33	30
1976–77		66	15	30	45	7
1977–78		60	8	13	21	15
Totals		172	33	66	99	52

F November 22, 1974

GARRY VALK #10

left wing 6'1" 205 L

b. Edmonton, Alberta, November 27, 1967
Signed as a free agent, October 8, 1998.
Signed as a free agent by Chicago, October 9, 2002.

1998–99	77	8	21	29	53
1999–2000	73	10	14	24	44
2000–01	74	8	18	26	46
2001–02	63	5	10	15	28
Totals	287	31	63	94	171

JAMES van RIEMSDYK #21

left wing 6'3" 200 L

b. Middletown, New Jersey, May 4, 1989
Acquired from Philadelphia for Luke Schenn, June 23, 2012.

2012–13	48	18	14	32	26
2013–14	80	30	31	61	50
2014–15	82	27	29	56	43
Totals	210	75	74	149	119

MIKE VAN RYN #26

defence 6'1" 213 R

b. London, Ontario, May 14, 1979
Acquired from Florida for Bryan McCabe and a fourth-round draft choice in 2010 (Sam Brittain), on September 2, 2008.
Retired at season's end.

2008–09	L	27	3	8	11	14

L March 7, 2009

DARREN VEITCH #25/#26

defence 5'11" 195 R

b. Saskatoon, Saskatchewan, April 24, 1960
Acquired from Detroit for Miroslav Frycer, June 10, 1988.
Traded to St. Louis for Keith Osborne, March 5, 1991.

1988–89	37	3	7	10	16
1990–91	L	2	0	1	1	0
Totals	39	3	8	11	16

L October 25, 1990

KRIS VERSTEEG #32

right wing 5'11" 176 R

b. Lethbridge, Alberta, May 13, 1986
Acquired from Chicago with Bill Sweatt for Viktor Stalberg, Chris DiDomenico, and Philippe Paradis, June 30, 2010.
Traded to Philadelphia for a first- and a third-round draft choice in 2011, February 14, 2011.

2010–11	53	14	21	35	29

LEIGH VERSTRAETE #34/#28/#25

right wing 5'11" 185 R

b. Pincher Creek, Alberta, January 6, 1962
Selected 192nd overall in 1982 Entry Draft.
Retired at end of 1987–88 season.

1982–83	F	3	0	0	0	5
1984–85		2	0	0	0	2
1987–88	L	3	0	1	1	9
Totals		8	0	1	1	16

F December 14, 1982 L October 24, 1987

CARL VOSS #6

centre 5'8" 168 L

b. Chelsea, Massachusetts, January 6, 1907
d. Lake Park, Florida, September 13, 1994
Signed as a free agent, February 16, 1927.
Loaned to Buffalo (IHL) for 1929–30 season as part of deal that brought Gord Brydson to Leafs (Toronto also received Wes King), November 14, 1929

1926–27	F	12	0	0	0	0
1928–29		2	0	0	0	0
Totals		14	0	0	0	0

F February 17, 1927
• First player to sign with Leafs under Conn Smythe's management.
• Was the NHL's referee-in-chief for many years, and was inducted into the Hockey Hall of Fame as a builder in 1974.
• Also played for the 1924 Grey Cup winners, Queen's University Golden Gaels.

KURT WALKER #26/#4

defence 6'3" 200 R

b. Weymouth, Massachusetts, June 10, 1954
Signed as a free agent.
Traded with Brian Glennie, Scott Garland, and a second-round draft choice in 1979 (Mark Hardy) to Los Angeles for Dave Hutchison and Lorne Stamler, June 14, 1978.

1975–76	F	5	0	0	0	49
1976–77		26	2	3	5	24
1977–78	L	40	2	2	4	69
Totals		71	4	5	9	142

F March 20, 1976 L March 27, 1978

RICKARD WALLIN #51

centre 6'2" 195 L

b. Stockholm, Sweden, April 9, 1980
Signed as a free agent, July 10, 2009.
Finished his career in Sweden.

2009–10	L	60	2	7	9	20

L April 7, 2010

MIKE WALTON ("Shaky") #15/#16

centre 5'10" 175 R

b. Kirkland Lake, Ontario, January 3, 1945
Traded with Bruce Gamble and a first-round draft choice in 1971 (Pierre Plante) to Philadelphia for Bernie Parent and a second-round draft choice in 1971 (Rick Kehoe), February 1, 1971.

1965–66	F	6	1	3	4	0
1966–67		31	7	10	17	13
1967–68		73	30	29	59	48
1968–69		66	22	21	43	34
1969–70		58	21	34	55	68
1970–71		23	3	10	13	21
Totals		257	84	107	191	184

F November 20, 1965,
• Later ran a restaurant in Toronto called Shakey's.

RICK WAMSLEY ("Wammer"/"Gump") #30

goalie 5'11" 185 L

b. Simcoe, Ontario, May 25, 1959
Acquired with Doug Gilmour, Jamie Macoun, Ric Nattress, and Kent Manderville from Calgary for Gary Leeman, Michel Petit, Craig Berube, Alexander Godynyuk, and Jeff Reese, January 2, 1992.
Retired during 1992–93 season to become Leafs' goaltending consultant.

1991–92	8	4–3–0	428	27	0	3.79
1992–93 L	3	0–3–0	160	15	0	5.63
Totals	11	4–6–0	588	42	0	4.29

L January 17, 1993

DIXON WARD #12

right wing 6' 200 R

b. Leduc, Alberta, September 23, 1968
Acquired with Guy Leveque, Kelly Fairchild, and Shayne Toporowski from Los Angeles for Éric Lacroix, Chris Snell, and a fourth-round draft choice in 1996 (Éric Bélanger), October 3, 1994.
Released June 28, 1995.

1994–95	22	0	3	3	31

RON WARD #25

centre 5'10" 180 R

b. Cornwall, Ontario, September 12, 1944
Turned pro with Tulsa (CHL) in 1965.
Claimed by Vancouver in Expansion Draft, June 10, 1970.

1969–70 F	18	0	1	1	2

F October 11, 1969

JEFF WARE #23

defence 6'4" 220 L

b. Toronto, Ontario, May 19, 1977
Selected 15th overall in 1995 Entry Draft.
Traded to Florida for David Nemirovsky, February 17, 1999.

1996–97 F	13	0	0	0	6
1997–98	2	0	0	0	0
Totals	15	0	0	0	6

F October 5, 1996

BOB WARNER #16

defence 5'11" 180 L

b. Grimsby, Ontario, December 13, 1950
Signed as a free agent, September 3, 1975.

1976–77 F/L	10	1	1	2	4

F February 25, 1977   L April 2, 1977

TODD WARRINER #8

left wing 6'1" 188 L

b. Blenheim, Ontario, January 3, 1974
Acquired with Mats Sundin, Garth Butcher, and first-round draft choice in 1994 (later traded to Washington—Nolan Baumgartner) from Quebec for Wendel Clark, Sylvain Lefebvre, Landon Wilson, and a first-round draft choice in 1994 (Jeffrey Kealty), June 28, 1994.
Traded to Tampa Bay for a third-round draft choice in 2000 (Mikael Tellqvist), November 29, 1999.

1994–95 F	5	0	0	0	0
1995–96	57	7	8	15	26
1996–97	75	12	21	33	41
1997–98	45	5	8	13	20
1998–99	53	9	10	19	28
1999–2000	18	3	1	4	2
Totals	253	36	48	84	117

F February 20, 1995

HARRY WATSON ("Whipper") #4

left wing 6'1" 203 L

b. Saskatoon, Saskatchewan, May 6, 1923
d. November 19, 2002
Acquired with Gerry Brown from Detroit for Doug Baldwin, Billy Taylor, and Ray Powell, September 21, 1946.
Sold to Chicago, December 10, 1954.

1946–47	44	19	15	34	10
1947–48	57	21	20	41	16
1948–49	60	26	19	45	0
1949–50	60	19	16	35	11
1950–51	68	18	19	37	18
1951–52	70	22	17	39	18
1952–53	63	16	8	24	8
1953–54	70	21	7	28	30
1954–55	8	1	1	2	0
Totals	500	163	122	285	111

• After coaching for years, worked for a small business in Markham supplying pricing machines to retail shops.
• Hockey Hall of Fame 1994

DON WEBSTER #19

left wing 5'7" 180 L

b. Toronto, Ontario, July 3, 1924
d. Fresno, California, April 12, 1978
Signed as a free agent, October 24, 1942, and assigned to Providence (AHL).
Traded with George Boothman to Buffalo (AHL) for Bill Ezinicki, October 13, 1944.

1943–44 F/L	27	7	6	13	28

F November 11, 1943   L March 18, 1944

STAN WEIR #14

centre 6'1" 180 L

b. Ponoka, Alberta, March 17, 1952
Acquired from California for Gary Sabourin, June 20, 1975; signed as a free agent by Edmonton (WHA) after the 1977–78 season. Reclaimed by Toronto prior to the 1979 Expansion Draft; claimed off waivers by Edmonton, July 4, 1979.

1975–76	64	19	32	51	22
1976–77	65	11	19	30	14
1977–78	30	12	5	17	4
Totals	159	42	56	98	40

KYLE WELLWOOD #42

centre 5'10" 180 R

b. Windsor, Ontario, May 16, 1983
Selected 134th overall in 2001 Entry Draft.
Claimed off waivers by Vancouver, June 25, 2008.

2003–04 F	1	0	0	0	0
2005–06	81	11	34	45	14
2006–07	48	12	30	42	0
2007–08	59	8	13	21	0
Totals	189	31	77	108	14

F January 8, 2004

TREVOR "BLAKE" WESLEY #28

defence 6'1" 200 L

b. Red Deer, Alberta, July 10, 1959
Signed as a free agent, July 31, 1985
Signed as a free agent by Boston, August 1987.

1985–86 L	27	0	1	1	21

L January 19, 1986

GLEN WESLEY #22

defence 6'1" 207 L

b. Red Deer, Alberta, October 2, 1968
Acquired from Carolina for a second-round draft choice in 2004 (later traded to Columbus—Kyle Wharton), on March 9, 2003.
Signed as a free agent by Carolina, July 8, 2003.

2002–03	7	0	3	3	4

ERIK WESTRUM #39

centre 6' 204 L

b. Minneapolis, Minnesota, July 26, 1979
Signed as a free agent, July 13, 2006.
Continued his career in Switzerland.

2006–07 L	2	0	0	0	0

L January 9, 2007

IAN WHITE #7

defence 5'10" 191 R

b. Steinbach, Manitoba, June 4, 1984
Selected 191st overall in 2002 Entry Draft.
Traded to Calgary on with Matt Stajan, Nicklas Hagman, and Jamal Mayers for Dion Phaneuf, Keith Aulie, and Fredrik Sjostrom, January 31, 2010.

2005–06 F	12	1	5	6	10
2006–07	76	3	23	26	40
2007–08	81	5	16	21	44
2008–09	71	10	16	26	57
2009–10	56	9	17	26	39
Totals	296	28	77	105	190

F March 26, 2006

PETER WHITE #18

centre 5'11" 200 L

b. Montreal, Quebec, March 15, 1969
Acquired with a fourth-round draft choice in 1996 (Jason Sessa) from Oilers for Kent Manderville, December 4, 1995; demoted to St. John's (AHL), December 7, 1995; loaned to Atlanta for balance of season, January 23, 1996.
Signed as a free agent by Philadelphia, August 19, 1996.

1995–96	1	0	0	0	0

• Only Leaf game December 5, 1995

ROD WILLARD #28

left wing 6' 190 L

b. New Liskeard, Ontario, May 1, 1960
Signed as a free agent, September 14, 1982.
Traded to Chicago for Dave Snopek, January 23, 1983.

1982–83 F/L	1	0	0	0	0

F/L November 17, 1982

DAVE "TIGER" WILLIAMS #22

left wing 5'11" 190 L

b. Weyburn, Saskatchewan, February 3, 1954
Selected 31st overall in 1974 Amateur Draft.
Traded with Jerry Butler to Vancouver for Rick Vaive and Bill Derlago, February 18, 1980.

1974–75 F	42	10	19	29	187
1975–76	78	21	19	40	299
1976–77	77	18	25	43	338
1977–78	78	19	31	50	351
1978–79	77	19	20	39	298
1979–80	55	22	18	40	197
Totals	407	109	132	241	1,670

F January 7, 1975
• Later played professional roller hockey.

JEREMY WILLIAMS #18/#48

right wing 6' 191 R

b. Regina, Saskatchewan, January 26, 1984
Selected 220th overall in 2003.
Signed as a free agent by Detroit, July 7, 2009.

2005–06 F	1	1	0	1	0
2006–07	1	1	0	1	0
2007–08	18	2	0	2	4
2008–09	11	5	2	7	2
Totals	31	9	2	11	6

F April 18, 2006

CLARKE WILM #39

centre 6' 202 L

b. Central Butte, Saskatchewan, October 24, 1976
Signed as a free agent, October 28, 2003.
Later played in Europe.

2003–04	10	0	0	0	7
2005–06 L	60	1	7	8	43
Totals	70	1	7	8	50

L April 18, 2006

CAROL "CULLY" WILSON #7

right wing 5'8" 180 L

b. Winnipeg, Manitoba, June 5, 1892
d. Seattle, Washington, July 7, 1962
Signed November 27, 1919; loaned to Montreal on January 21, 1921, but suspended for remainder of season on February 11, 1921, when Toronto recalled him and he refused to report.
Traded to Hamilton on November 9, 1921, for Ed Carpenter.

1919–20 F	23	21	5	26	79
1920–21	8	2	1	3	16
Totals	31	23	6	29	95

F December 23, 1919

DUNC WILSON #1/#30
goalie 5'11" 175 L
b. Toronto, Ontario, March 22, 1948
Acquired from Vancouver for Murray Heatley and Larry McIntyre, May 29, 1973.
Claimed off waivers by New York Rangers, February 15, 1975.

1973–74	24	9–11–3	1,412	68	1	2.89
1974–75	25	8–11–4	1,393	86	0	3.70
Totals	49	17–22–7	2,805	154	1	3.29

JOHNNY WILSON ("Iron Man") #19
left wing 5'10" 175 L
b. Kincardine, Ontario, June 14, 1929
Acquired with Frank Roggeveen from Detroit for Barry Cullen, June 9, 1959; traded with Pat Hannigan to New York Rangers for Eddie Shack, November 7, 1960.

1959–60	70	15	16	31	8
1960–61	3	0	1	1	0
Totals	73	15	17	32	8

ROSS "LEFTY" WILSON #1
goalie 5'11" 178 L
b. Toronto, Ontario, October 15, 1919
d. Naples, Florida, November 4, 2002

1955–56	1	0–0–0	13	0	0	0.00

• Replaced injured Harry Lumley during third period of game, January 22, 1956.
• Trainer for Detroit Red Wings for decades.

RON WILSON #11/#14
defence 5'10" 170 R
b. Windsor, Ontario, May 28, 1955
Selected 132nd overall in 1975 Amateur Draft. Played with Kloten and Davos (Switzerland), 1980–85; signed as a free agent by Minnesota North Stars, March 7, 1986.

1977–78 F	13	2	1	3	0
1978–79	46	5	12	17	4
1979–80	5	0	2	2	2
Totals	64	7	15	22	6

F March 4, 1978
• Later coached in the NHL and internationally for the USA, notably that country's win in the 1996 World Cup of Hockey.

DANIEL WINNIK #26
centre 6'2" 207 L
b. Toronto, Ontario, March 6, 1985
Signed as a free agent, July 28, 2014.
Traded to Pittsburgh for Zack Sill, a second-round draft choice in 2016, and a fourth-round draft choice in 2015, February 25, 2015.

2014–15	58	7	18	25	19

BRIAN WISEMAN #15
centre 5'6" 175 L
b. Chatham, Ontario, July 13, 1971
Signed as a free agent, August 14, 1996.

1996–97 F/L	3	0	0	0	0

F December 4, 1996 L December 21, 1996
• Career minor leaguer.

CRAIG WOLANIN ("Wooly") #26
defence 6'4" 215 L
b. Grosse Pointe, Michigan, July 27, 1967
Acquired from Tampa Bay for a third-round draft choice in 1998 (later traded to Edmonton—Alex Henry), January 31, 1997.
Signed as a free agent by Detroit (IHL), January 31, 1999.

1997–98	10	0	0	0	6

• Missed most of 1997–98 with a serious knee injury.

RANDY WOOD #24
left wing 6' 195 L
b. Princeton, New Jersey, October 12, 1963
Claimed off waivers from Buffalo, January 18, 1995.
Traded with Benoît Hogue to Dallas for Dave Gagner and a sixth-round draft choice (Dmitri Yakushin), January 28, 1996.

1994–95	48	13	11	24	34
1995–96	46	7	9	16	36
Totals	94	20	20	40	70

ANDY WOZNIEWSKI #56
defence 6'5" 225 L
b. Buffalo Grove, Illinois, May 25, 1980
Signed as a free agent, May 27, 2004.
Signed as a free agent by St. Louis, July 17, 2008.

2005–06 F	13	0	1	1	13
2006–07	15	0	2	2	14
2007–08	48	2	7	9	54
Totals	79	2	10	12	81

F October 5, 2005

KEN WREGGET #31/#30
goalie 6'1" 195 L
b. Brandon, Manitoba, March 25, 1964
Selected 45th overall in 1982 Entry Draft.
Traded to Philadelphia for two first-round draft choices in 1989 (Rob Pearson and Steve Bancroft), March 6, 1989.

1983–84 F	3	1–1–1	165	14	0	5.09
1984–85	23	2–15–3	1,278	103	0	4.84
1985–86	30	9–13–4	1,566	113	0	4.33
1986–87	56	22–28–3	3,026	200	0	3.97
1987–88	56	12–35–4	3,000	222	2	4.44
1988–89	32	9–20–2	1,888	139	0	4.42
Totals	200	55–112–17	10,923	791	2	4.34

BOB WREN #33
left wing 5'10" 190 L
b. Preston, Ontario, September 16, 1974
Signed as a free agent, July 24, 2001.
Traded to Nashville for Nathan Perrott, December 31, 2002.

2001–02 L	1	0	0	0	0

L October 8, 2001 (regular season—also appeared in playoffs, May 4, 2002)

TERRY YAKE ("Yaker") #25
right wing 5'11" 190 R
b. New Westminster, British Columbia, October 22, 1968
Acquired from Anaheim for David Sacco, September 28, 1994.
Released June 27, 1995.

1994–95	19	3	2	5	2

DMITRI YAKUSHIN #49
defence 6' 200 L
b. Kharkov, Soviet Union (Russia), January 21, 1978
Selected 140th overall in 1996 Entry Draft.
Later played in Europe.

1999–2000 F/L	2	0	0	0	2

F November 26, 1999 L December 6, 1999

GARY YAREMCHUK ("Weasel") #8/#25/#28/#32
centre 6' 185 L
b. Edmonton, Alberta, August 15, 1961
Selected 24th overall in 1981 Entry Draft.
Signed as a free agent by Detroit, August 13, 1985.

1981–82 F	18	0	3	3	10
1982–83	3	0	0	0	2
1983–84	1	0	0	0	0
1984–85 L	12	1	1	2	16
Totals	34	1	4	5	28

F October 6, 1981 L April 7, 1985

KEN YAREMCHUK ("Yammer") #16/#15/#34/#13
centre 5'11" 185 R
b. Edmonton, Alberta, January 1, 1964
Acquired with Jerome Dupont and a fourth-round draft choice in 1987 (Joe Sacco) from Chicago as compensation for the free-agent signing of Gary Nylund, September 6, 1986.

1986–87	20	3	8	11	16
1987–88	16	2	5	7	10
1988–89 L	11	1	0	1	2
Totals	47	6	13	19	28

L February 18, 1989

DMITRI YUSHKEVICH (later DMITRY) ("Tree"/"Yushkie") #26/#36
defence 5'11" 208 R
b. Yaroslavl, Soviet Union (Russia), November 19, 1971
Acquired with a second-round draft choice in 1996 (Francis Larivée) from Philadelphia for a first-round draft choice in 1996 (Dainius Zubrus), a fourth-round draft choice in 1996 (later traded to Los Angeles—Mikael Simons), and a second-round draft choice in 1997 (Jean-Marc Pelletier), August 30, 1995.
Traded to Florida for Robert Svehla, July 18, 2002.

1995–96	69	1	10	11	54
1996–97	74	4	10	14	56
1997–98	72	0	12	12	78
1998–99	78	6	22	28	88
1999–2000	77	3	24	27	55
2000–01	81	5	19	24	52
2001–02	55	6	13	19	26
Totals	506	25	110	135	409

RON ZANUSSI #39/#32
right wing 5'11" 180 R
b. Toronto, Ontario, August 31, 1956
Acquired with a third-round draft choice in 1981 (Ernie Godden) from Minnesota North Stars for a second-round draft choice in 1981 (Dave Donnelly), March 10, 1981.

1980–81	12	3	0	3	6
1981–82 L	43	0	8	8	14
Totals	55	3	8	11	20

L February 10, 1982

ROB ZETTLER ("Zets") #3/#2
defence 6'3" 195 L
b. Sept-Îles, Quebec, March 8, 1968
Acquired from Philadelphia for a fifth-round draft choice in 1996 (Per-Ragna Bergqvist), July 8, 1995.
Claimed by Nashville in Expansion Draft, June 26, 1998.

1995–96	29	0	1	1	48
1996–97	48	2	12	14	51
1997–98	59	0	7	7	108
Totals	136	2	20	22	207

• Later became assistant coach with Leafs.

PETER ZEZEL #25
centre 5'11" 200 L
b. Toronto, Ontario, April 22, 1965
d. Toronto, Ontario, May 26, 2009
Acquired with Bob Rouse from Washington for Al Iafrate, January 16, 1991.
Lost to Dallas with Grant Marshall as compensation for Leafs' free-agent signing of Mike Craig, August 10, 1994.

1990–91	32	14	14	28	4
1991–92	64	16	33	49	26
1992–93	70	12	23	35	24
1993–94	41	8	8	16	19
Totals	207	50	78	128	73

MIKE ZIGOMANIS #26
centre 6' 200 R
b. Toronto, Ontario, January 17, 1981
Signed as a free agent, July 15, 2010.

2010–11 L	8	0	1	1	4

L October 28, 2010
• Played in the AHL for the remainder of his career.

PHOTO CREDITS

HOCKEY HALL OF FAME:

iii (Imperial Oil–Turofsky); iv (Imperial Oil–Turofsky); 2 (Imperial Oil–Turofsky); 3 (Craig Campbell); 4–5 (Imperial Oil–Turofsky); 6L (Hal Roth); 6c (Imperial Oil–Turofsky); 6R (Matthew Manor); 7L (Dave Sandford); 7R (Frank Prazak); 8L (Imperial Oil–Turofsky); 8R (Phil Pritchard); 9L (Hal Roth); 9c (Doug MacLellan); 10TR (Imperial Oil–Turofsky); 10TC (Frank Prazak); 10TR (Graphic Artists); 10BL (Mecca); 10BC (Mecca); 10BR (Miles Nadal); 11TL (Paul Bereswill); 11TR (Dave Sandford); 12–13 (Imperial Oil–Turofsky); 18–19 (Frank Prazak); 20–21 (Imperial Oil–Turofsky); 22–23, 25 (HHOF); 27 (Imperial Oil–Turofsky); 28–29 (HHOF); 20 (Imperial Oil–Turofsky); 32–33 (Imperial Oil–Turofsky); 34 (Imperial Oil–Turofsky); 35 (Michael Burns Sr.); 36–37 (Graphic Artists); 40 (Dave Sandford); 66 (Imperial Oil–Turofsky); 67 (Imperial Oil–Turofsky); 69 (Imperial Oil–Turofsky); 70 (Imperial Oil–Turofsky); 73 (Imperial Oil–Turofsky); 74 (Graphic Artists); 77 (Imperial Oil–Turofsky); 78 (Imperial Oil–Turofsky); 81 (Doug MacLellan); 83 (Chris Relke); 84 (Chris Relke); 89 (Graig Abel); 90 (Dave Sandford); 91 (Dave Sandford); 95 (HHOF); 96 (Imperial Oil–Turofsky); 98 (Imperial Oil–Turofsky); 99 (Imperial Oil–Turofsky); 100 (Imperial Oil–Turofsky); 101 (Imperial Oil–Turofsky); 102 (Graphic Artists); 104 (Imperial Oil–Turofsky); 105 (Imperial Oil–Turofsky); 106 (Imperial Oil–Turofsky); 108 (Graphic Artists); 109 (Graphic Artists); 125 (Miles Nadal); 126–127 (Frank Prazak); 129 (HHOF); 130–131 (HHOF); 132–133 (Imperial Oil–Turofsky); 134 (Imperial Oil–Turofsky); 136 (Imperial Oil–Turofsky); 138–139 (Imperial Oil–Turofsky); 141 (Imperial Oil–Turofsky); 142–143 (Imperial Oil–Turofsky); 144–145 (Imperial Oil–Turofsky); 146–147 (Imperial Oil–Turofsky); 148–149 (Imperial Oil–Turofsky); 150–151 (Graphic Artists); 152–153 (Frank Prazak); 155 (Imperial Oil–Turofsky); 159 (Graphic Artists); 162 (HHOF); 163 (Frank Prazak); 165 (Dave Sandford); 188 (Frank Prazak); endpapers (Imperial Oil–Turofsky).

GRAIG ABEL:

11BL; 14–15; 38; 42; 44–45; 46–47; 82; 85; 92–93; 111; 123; 157; 186–187.

GETTY IMAGES:

9R (Graig Abel/NHL); 11BR (Graig Abel/NHL); 16–17 (Graig Abel/NHL).

Centre ice photo courtesy of the Toronto Maple Leafs.